DS-TS

(

Also by GILBERTO FREYRE

NEW WORLD IN THE TROPICS (1959)

THE MASTERS AND THE SLAVES • *A Study in the Development of Brazilian Civilization* (1946, 1956)

THE MANSIONS AND THE SHANTIES • *The Making of Modern Brazil* (1963)

MOTHER AND SON (1967)

These are BORZOI BOOKS *published in New York by* ALFRED A. KNOPF

Order and Progress

GILBERTO FREYRE

Order and Progress

Brazil from Monarchy to Republic

Edited and Translated from the Portuguese by

ROD W. HORTON

Alfred·A·Knopf / New York

1970

To the Memory of

Gilberto Amado

Lúcia Miguel-Pereira

Rodrigo M. F. de Andrade

Antônio de Barros Carvalho

My Friends

Le progrès est le développement de l'ordre.

AUGUSTE COMTE

Translator's Note

IN PREPARING the English-language version of *Ordem e Progresso*, cuts and condensations were made in the original text in the interest of readability. In making these abridgments, which were effected with the author's permission, the translator attempted to preserve the author's ideas and original emphasis and to eliminate only that material which supported a point already clearly made. The note on Brazilian monetary values, the historical note, and the glossary are the work of the translator. Footnotes included to explain points for the benefit of readers unfamiliar with Brazilian history are generally those of the translator and are so designated; unmarked footnotes are the author's, as are the preface to the English-language edition, the historical outline, the note on method, and the bibliographies.

ROD W. HORTON

CONTENTS

Preface to the English-Language Edition

THIS BOOK, ORIGINALLY PUBLISHED in Portuguese under the title *Ordem e Progresso*, is now in its third edition in that language: two in Brazil and one in Portugal. It will soon appear also in Italian and German. Now, through the initiative of Alfred A. Knopf, Inc., we have an English-language version in the excellent translation of Rod W. Horton.

Chronologically, *Order and Progress* covers the half-century of Brazilian history between the first decisive steps in the early 1870's toward the abolition of slavery and the years immediately following Brazilian participation in the First World War. At the suggestion of Mr. Knopf, this introduction is written in an attempt to show how the developments of that half-century affected subsequent decades. It seeks to point out, in a rather impressionistic way, some of the significant contemporary characteristics of Brazil as a Republic and to show how these characteristics have been the result of a series of transitions: from a purely colonial society, through stages which could be called pre-national and national, to the country's present state as a unified culture with increasingly important international interests and responsibilities. In the course of these transitions, Brazil has been a colony, a monarchy, and a democratic Republic, without having entirely lost certain cultural characteristics from each of its previous stages. As a Republic, it has never ceased to show vestiges of its monarchical period, particularly in its sporadic reactions against what some political leaders—and their more or less scholarly advisers—consider to be excessive manifestations of economic and political liberalism, of states rights in opposition to national unity, and of partisan politics in conflict with national interest.

. . .

This book is the third of a series. At the same time, it is an autonomous work. The first volume in the series, which bears the Portuguese title *Casa-Grande & Senzala* (published in English by Alfred A. Knopf, Inc., as *The Masters and the Slaves*), deals with the colonial beginnings of Brazil as a predominantly though not exclusively European patriarchal society in tropical and subtropical America. It deals also with some of the permanent historical traits of this type of society, the most characteristic and enduring elements which have marked Brazil since colonial times as an essentially Iberian-Catholic system of co-existence and as a composite European-tropical culture.

The second volume, *Sobrados e Mucambos* (published by Knopf under the title *The Mansions and the Shanties*), deals with the same subject in its development in social, rather than chronological, sequence: its varying ramifications in different regions within the general tendency toward urbanization or "rurbanization"—a combination of rural and urban patterns—seen throughout the entire nation.

The present book, the third of the series, attempts a further, deeper analysis of the decline of the patriarchal system which has been—and to some extent still is—the basis of the Brazilian social structure and one of the most characteristic expressions of its national culture. It treats that system in its first, or orthodox, phase as a predominantly rural phenomenon, when there was a close connection between social behavior and Catholic religious beliefs, and continues through its second half-urbanized, less orthodoxly patriarchal period to the third stage as an increasingly urban, industrial, secular, liberal institution incorporating both free labor and the separation of Church and State.

Although I have placed chronological limits on this third volume and have attempted to terminate it with the end of the First World War—in which Brazil very significantly participated—my awareness of time as a dynamically social rather than conventionally chronological phenomenon is such that the reader will find numerous references to past periods, as well as projections into more contemporary times. This volume, indeed, could serve as a sort of introduction to present-day Brazil, and particularly to its social situation. For the nation today is still facing problems which have their roots in the rather unpopular replacement of a half-patriarchal, paternalistic, and in some aspects undemocratic monarchical regime by an exotic, fraternalistic, federalist Republic copied from the United States. In its first stage, this new regime was radically anti-patriarchal; after a few years of such radicalism it became half-patriarchal. But it was not until Getúlio Vargas became President in 1930 that it was able to deal with any effectiveness with the difficulties that had arisen from the sudden transition from monarchy to Republic and from slavery to free labor.

Vargas may be considered a sort of bridge between two epochs in Brazilian development. Although formally republican, if not entirely legal or regular, Vargas's presidency, especially between 1937 and 1946, was somewhat monarchical in its sociological expression (more monarchical, in some respects, than preceding Brazilian Presidents had ever dared to be). He was frankly authoritarian, but being also a very astute politician he disguised his authoritarianism by assuming the additional role of a smiling populist and a champion of labor and the common people against the interests of the bourgeois. And he adopted a nationalist posture over and above the narrow, particular interests of individual states, especially such economically and po-litically powerful states as São Paulo. It was during Vargas's long, authoritarian, and, for some time, dictatorial rule that São Paulo, as a state, and coffee, as an Imperial export and the basis of a political-economic oligarchy, ceased to be the two most important forces in the Republic.

From 1889 to 1930 the most effective Presidents of the Brazilian Republic were politicians from São Paulo—Prudente de Moraes, Campos Sales, Rodrigues Alves, Washington Luís—giving weight to the frequently heard statement that São Paulo, with its powerful coffee interests and its precocious industrial progress, was the loco-motive pulling the twenty more or less empty boxcars representing the other Brazilian states. Still, despite its dominating image of dy-namism, stability, order, and security, it was in São Paulo that dis-order broke out in 1924 to continue spasmodically throughout the decade. This was an unpleasant surprise to most Brazilians who, al-though accustomed to small outbreaks of disorder in other parts of the country, did not expect these things to happen in such relatively prosperous states as São Paulo or Minas Gerais. It was at this period that a distinguished governor of the state of Minas Gerais—João Pinheiro—said, with great emphasis, that the people of his state shared a special pride in having "a deep sense of order" (*um grave senso de Ordem*). They might love progress—though not as much as the typical Paulista—but they did not value progress without order. For them, order was essential.

Order was essential also for the political group that from the early days of the 1889 Republic to 1930 dominated the state of Rio Grande do Sul—men particularly influenced by the political or social positivistic philosophy of Auguste Comte, the French sociologist. It was from this group that Getúlio Vargas rose to be a national political leader who would also distinguish himself as a believer in progress subordinated to order. He was to champion the cause of the proletariat and the laborer, whose "integration into modern society" was a principle of the pre-Marxist philosophy. But the Brazilian Positivists in general, and Getúlio Vargas—a half-Positivist—in particular, sought to develop this integration by means of a peaceful revolution, led by statesmen, governors, and the President himself as a strong, authoritarian, almost monarchical political leader supported by the common people—in direct opposition to liberals of various types in politics, journalism, and especially to intellectuals.

It is therefore interesting to note that, not only during the Empire —when Dom Pedro II was himself an intellectual, a scholar, a friend of Agassiz, an enthusiast of Victor Hugo, and an admirer of Longfellow—but also during the 1889 Republic, the Vargas presidency, and the subsequent periods of Brazilian development, intellectuals have in fact played a not insignificant role. Some were statesmen, diplomats, and politicians; others were journalists, writers, and sociologists, preoccupied in their books or articles with national problems. President Epitácio Pessoa (1918–22) was a jurist, an orator, and a scholar. President Washington Luís Pereira de Sousa (1926–30) was also a scholar: a historian. Getúlio Vargas as a young man in Rio Grande do Sul was a journalist and disciple or enthusiast not only of Comte but of Zola; and later, when President of Brazil, was made a member of the Brazilian Academy of Letters. Baron do Rio Branco, for twelve years Secretary of State in the 1889 Republic—though a monarchist and an aristocrat—was a historian and geographer, a scholar of international reputation. Pandiá Calógeras —a Brazilian of Greek origin—was a brilliant scholar and, though a civilian, was made Secretary of Defense during the "first Republic" (an unusual thing in Brazil). In this post he was responsible for the beginning of a sort of intellectualization of the Brazilian Army under certain distinguished French Army officers. Lauro Müller, a Brazilian of German origin who was Secretary of State during the Venceslau Brás presidency, was another intellectual—if not a systematic scholar. He too was elected to the Brazilian Academy of Letters.

An imitation of the famous French Academy, the Brazilian Academy was founded at the end of the nineteenth century. As a matter of policy, it has always elected representative men, not especially men of letters but, in a broad sense, intellectuals and even men of action: Baron Jaceguay, a distinguished admiral; Archbishop Dom Silvério, a dark-skinned Negro noted as a religious leader, educator, and mystic, as well as for the classically correct style of his sermons and manifestoes; Santos Dumont, the inventor; Otávio Mangabeira, a brilliant orator and politician, for some time Secretary of State and, later, governor of the state of Bahia; Osvaldo Cruz, a medical doctor, famous for his successful campaign against yellow fever in Rio de Janeiro.

Joaquim Nabuco, Ruy Barbosa, and Oliveira Lima were all intellectuals famous for their activities in political life and diplomacy from the last years of the monarchy until the first decades of the Republic. At present, or in recent years, intellectuals like Luís Viana Filho, now governor of the state of Bahia; Arthur Reis, governor of the state of Bahia; Gilberto Amado, a Senator and, later, Ambassador; Carlos Lacerda, governor of the state of Guanabara; Munhoz da Rocha, governor of the state of Paraná; Hermes Lima, Secretary of State; Lourival Fontes, the *éminence grise* of Vargas; Afonso Arinos de Mello Franco, Secretary of State—to mention only a few —are or were (Fontes is now dead) active in public life. Some of these men were noted for initiatives that mere politicians would never have taken unless inspired by intellectual *éminences grises*. Such *éminences grises* have not been entirely absent from Brazilian public life during the last half-century. But the outstanding fact is that in few other modern countries have intellectuals played such an important role as in Brazil. Even the recent rise, from the end of the Vargas regime to 1964, of demagogic methods of the most vulgar variety and of political power backed by private money has not prevented intellectuals—though on a decreasing scale—from becoming politically active in Brazil.

In addition, Brazil is a country where books written by intellectuals have had a considerable influence, not only cultural but of a concrete political kind. José de Alencar, a novelist and politician in Imperial times, along with the poet Gonçalves Dias contributed to the development of nationalism in politics as well as literature. *Canaã*, the novel by Graça Aranha, was published at the beginning of this century and aroused considerable political interest among Brazilians in the problems raised by European immigration. *Os Sertões*, the monumental semi-historical work by Euclydes da Cunha, aroused both literary admiration for its author and political awareness of the problem it treated: the segregation of rustic populations and archaic cultures of the *sertões* from the civilized populations and cultures of the Atlantic coast. More recently, another writer, Monteiro Lobato, through the literary vigor and economic and political significance of his championing a purely Brazilian petroleum industry, aroused a nationalistic movement so important that its influence is still very much alive politically and has even gained the interest of illiterate Brazilians.

This extension of literary ideas to nonliterary or even illiterate Brazilians is not rare in Brazilian history. For example, Joaquim Nabuco, as an abolitionist writer, became so popular as to be considered almost a folk hero. The same thing happened with the glorification of Amerindians by José de Alencar in some of his novels. Recently, there has been a similar projection: some of the verses written for popular music by sophisticated and scholarly poets like Manuel Bandeira, Vinicius de Moraes, and Francisco Buarque de Holanda have become extremely popular and have even reached the United States.

A contrary tendency has also become noticeable in Brazil during the past three decades. Folklore; popular rustic concepts; Negro and Indian songs, music, tales, and beliefs: all have become "Brazilianized" through the use of this lively, vital, almost virgin material by sophisticated or scholarly writers, poets, composers, painters, sculptors, and architects. The outstanding example of this sort of acculturation is the great composer the late Heitor Villa-Lobos, acclaimed in Europe as well as in the United States as one of the most original composers of our time. Though boldly modernistic, much of his inspiration was taken from Brazilian folklore or from Negro, Indian, and *mestiço* sources (the pure Indian or the pure Negro are, in modern Brazil, extremely rare both as racially segregated groups and ethnically segregated cultures). *Mestiço* ethnical types and *mestiço* cultural expressions are perhaps more abundant in modern Brazil than in any other country. They are now represented consciously in the sort of art and literature Brazilians are proud to acknowledge as an expression of their characteristically mixed European, Amerindian, and Negro national culture. This is happening not only in art and literature of the most distinguished kind but also in the minor arts: cookery, for example.

In the last four decades, their national cuisine has become a matter of open pride, not secret delight, for Brazilians. Fifty years ago most sophisticated Brazilians were ashamed of their very Brazilian *feijoada*, of such Afro-Brazilian culinary masterpieces as *caruru* and *vatapá*, of their manioc flour and their rustic and indigenous fruits, some of which are ideal—*caju, maracajá, pitanga, genipapo* or *goiaba*—for refreshing drinks, desserts, juices, syrups, wines, and preserves. Brazilian *goiaba* (guava) preserve, like the *feijoada*, was until half a century ago a purely domestic, informal dessert that most Brazilians would not dare to include in planning a "really nice dinner," especially if a distinguished foreigner had been invited. Now it is an elegant national dessert which Brazilians have ceased to be ashamed to include in formal dinners, serving it with cheese—not a common practice in Europe but standard in Brazil. Even some Brazilian Ambassadors in Europe and the United States do not now hesitate to invite distinguished Europeans or North Americans for a *feijoada* or to offer them guava paste with cheese for dessert. The one-time Ambassador to the Court of St. James, Assis Chateaubriand, even went so far as to serve a dessert of *rapadura* (a small brick of brown sugar much used by rustic Brazilians of the northeastern interior). But together with this *rapadura*, the Ambassador took special pride in including pineapple and other northeastern tropical fruits famous for their flavor and perfume, having them flown especially for the occasion. Other Ambassadors may not go as far as Chateaubriand in adopting the Brazilian cuisine for official functions; but in recent years there has been a decided move toward the inclusion of more national dishes in Brazilian entertainment abroad.

In the last half-century Brazilians, having expanded their contacts with Europe—in addition to Paris—and with the United States, Japan, Spanish America, and even parts of Africa, have simultaneously maintained and in some ways even increased their Brazilianness. An example of this is the increased pride that Brazilians are now taking in their Carnaval in Rio and Recife: a carnival that —replete with African and Amerindian orgiastic survivals in its dances, masks, decorations, and music—had been a source of shame to proper Brazilians two generations ago. They felt that such

sensual dances and barbarian ornaments could only appear disgust-
ing to puritanical North Americans, hypocritical Britons, and
pedantic Frenchmen or Germans. Now, it is this very Puritanism—
represented by the North American and European bourgeois civilization prior to the Second World War—that is in disfavor, while
the spirit of the Dionysiac Brazilian Carnaval rides high. Indeed,
anti-Puritan attitudes are so widespread—even among the British—
that such orgiastic elements in the Brazilian Carnaval are becoming,
in comparison, moderate and even Apollonean.

The Dionysiac elements in Brazilian culture, as in other contemporary national cultures, have tended in the last thirty or forty
years to become predominant, that is, to become more freely expressive. This seems to account for certain romantic and, at the
same time, naturalistic explosions in Brazilian contemporary literature, in Brazilian forms of the plastic arts, in the theatre, the
cinema, in sexual morality, and in attitudes toward religion. In recent years, religion in Brazil has become highly secularized and
rationalized. "God is dead" Christianity is finding adherents even
among certain Brazilian clergymen: ordinarily the same ones who
are revolting, not only against theology, but also against celibacy,
traditional liturgy, and clerical dress. What is happening, as a result
of this so-called "progressive" secular attitude in the most populous
Catholic country in the world, is that large numbers of the nation's
population are abandoning Catholicism in order to become evangelical Protestants, spiritualists, Afro-Brazilian animists, or a weird combination of animist-Christians. Despite these revolutionary shiftings,
Brazilians continue to be a deeply religious people, attracted by the
mysteries of spiritual faith and motivated by a mystical respect for
what they consider sacred values or traditions. If some members of
the Roman Catholic clergy deny to traditionally Catholic rustic
Brazilians the satisfaction of their religious inclinations, the reaction
of such Brazilians is not to cease being religious, but rather to cease
being Catholic.

The most lucid contemporary Catholic leaders in Brazil—Gustavo Corção among the laymen; Dom Oscar, Bishop of Mariana;
the Archbishop (now Cardinal) of Pôrto Alegre; and the Archbishop Cardinal of São Paulo—are now opposing the excesses of
"progressive" secularists. Recently, the official newspaper of the
archdiocese of Mariana admitted that so-called "folk-lore Catholicism" (considered so inferior by Catholics of the "progressive,"

"rationalist," and "secularist" type) is a legitimate form of Catholic worship. Certain radical clergymen, whose identification with the Communists is regarded by some observers as not only apparent but real, claim to strive for the "intellectualization," "modernization," even "secularization" of Catholicism. But it has been noted by critics of the Catholic crisis in Brazil that, for these "rationalists," "intellectualization" is a purely logical, strictly Cartesian, process rather than the Pascalian variety, which admits the "reasons of the Heart" that "Reason does not understand."

It seems to some analysts of the Brazilian ethos and Brazilian intellectual and social history that there exists an intellectualism flexible enough to embrace Pascal, William James, Bergson, and more recently Gabriel Marcel (who has lectured in Brazil and who probably has more admirers there than Teilhard de Chardin); and that Brazilian thought has long been flexible enough to allow for elements of the nonrational in its examination of human and cultural relationships. Indeed, the concept of a Catholicism without God and without Christ, as desired by contemporary "progressives" of the most radical type, should not be considered in any way a novelty in a country where, since the middle of the nineteenth century, Comtean Positivism has attained such great influence in intellectual circles. More than a century before present-day "progressives" engaged in the task of secularizing and rationalizing Catholicism in Brazil, a similar attempt was made by a small but systematic group of Comtean Positivists who went so far as to build, in Rio, a "Temple of Humanity," where a sort of ethical, logical imitation of religion was practiced with a minimum of religious ritual. Teixeira Mendes, a mathematician and a man noted for his bourgeois virtues, officiated in the sermons as main priest of the Temple dressed in a green gown. And Clôtilde de Vaux, the woman whom Auguste Comte considered his inspiration and for whom he is said to have felt a somewhat platonic love, occupied a place similar to that which in Catholic churches was given to the Virgin Mary. This logical, rational, ethical substitute for Catholicism, limited after a few years of activity to a small group of adherents, has now become a mere curiosity and even an object of mild pleasantry for Brazilians—whether intellectuals or no.

It may be said of Brazilian intellectuals that their predominant—though not exclusive—tendency since pre-national days has been to allow for nonlogical elements in their analysis and interpretation of social situations. This tendency was characteristic of José Bonifácio de Andrada e Silva, that remarkable scholar, poet, and scientist who sparked the move toward political independence at the beginning of the nineteenth century. If José Bonifácio had been strictly a rationalist in 1822, he would have worked for the establishment of an independent Brazilian Republic, eliminating all the illogical mythology and ritual of a monarchy. However, this man of action realized from the outset that such myths and rites had an ineradicable place in the already developed Brazilian ethos and should be allowed to continue in a free and independent Brazil.

José Bonifácio de Andrada e Silva's political and social philosophy may be considered typical of what has since his time developed into an intellectual foundation for most—if not all—of the solutions that Brazilians have found, and continue to find, for their national problems. He also seems to have been the first to connect intellectuals with political and national activities in Brazil. Later intellectuals of Ruy Barbosa's type, however, did not necessarily conform to the model of José Bonifácio. Barbosa, though brilliant and scholarly, was too rhetorical as well as too much of a jurist and a grammarian to avoid formalism in his dealing with practical problems. But José Bonifácio has been the prototype of the intellectual as man of action, as statesman or politician; and as such, he has had a succession of followers whose behavior has been in sharp contrast to Spanish-American and even Anglo-American intellectuals of the rather abstract type who, if involved in active politics, are inclined to be strictly logical or rational in their attitudes. Men like Balthazar Brum in Uruguay, the García Calderóns in Peru, Estanislau Zeballos in Argentina, José Vasconcelos in Mexico, and Woodrow Wilson and Adlai Stevenson in the United States all seem to have been too intellectual for their political positions and, consequently, to have failed in their political careers. In Brazil, of intellectuals like the Viscount do Rio Branco in the Empire, and his son, Baron do Rio Branco, in the 1889 Republic; of the two Nabucos—José Thomaz, the famous jurist and statesman of the Dom Pedro era, and Joaquim, the great abolitionist, political leader, and later Ambassador to the United States; of Baron de Penedo, Amaro Cavalcante, David Campista, Epitácio Pessoa, Pandiá Calógeras, and Barbosa Lima, it may, perhaps, be said that they were either relatively or completely successful, in their political careers. They follow the José Bonifácio model in not being overlogical or rational in handling problems that involve certain irrational or illogical considerations.

In the past half-century, Brazilians have generally adopted the Bonifácio approach in facing their national and international problems, and the results may be said to indicate a blend of reason and emotion. The "Valorization Plan" of some decades ago for supporting coffee prices is an example in point. Logical, scientific economists, like Lincoln Gordon, are right in considering this plan as economic heresy. But such heresy was for some time highly useful to Brazil; indeed, so pronounced was its value that a number of other nations adopted it for the "protection" of products other than coffee.

Other "heresies" of a similar kind, with their positive as well as negative aspects, have been perpetrated by Brazilian political intellectuals. The so-called "Estado Nôvo," a scheme fashioned for Getúlio Vargas by the scholarly jurist Francisco Campos, is another example. And in 1964 and 1968, drastic changes in the political system of the country have reduced some liberal electoral aspects in favor of more pragmatic authoritarian procedures without abolishing what has always been an essentially democratic tendency toward social and political flexibility. This style of democracy is certainly not the exact equivalent of the British, Swiss, Scandinavian, North American, or Soviet Russian types of democracy; but is there, in the modern world, a purely orthodox type of democracy? Present-day Brazil, with its great regional, economic, and social variety, is simply trying to develop a style of political democracy suited to its own needs.

This brings us to an important point about Brazilian development in the last twenty years: namely, the influence of the Brazilian War College (Escola Superior de Guerra), an inadequately named center of military graduate studies of highly intellectual objectivity. It is doubtful whether, with the possible exceptions of the Colegio de México in Mexico and the Ateneu in Argentina, there are any other intellectual centers in Latin America so effectively dedicated to the interdisciplinary study of national and international problems. For the past twenty years, such problems have been carefully studied in this college not only by military men but also by civilians: political and industrial leaders, educators, economists, sociologists, natural scientists, writers, and journalists. If Brazil, both as monarchy and Republic, has traditionally avoided any inclination toward militarism of the Caudillist type, this tendency has been further strengthened in the past twenty years by the combined civilian and military study of domestic and international problems.

For it is a fact that, during the monarchy and early Republic, practical, realistic knowledge of national and international problems by political leaders was confined to a few scholarly statesmen, such as the Viscount do Rio Branco. Most other intellectuals active in politics and the administration were excessively academic, abstract, intellectual. This was especially true of graduates of the schools of juridical and social sciences, where the teaching itself became more abstract, bookish, theoretical, and exotic, so that "constitutionalists" were far better acquainted with books in English about the Constitution of the United States as a juridical masterpiece (for the United States) or with masterful essays like Bagehot's on British political institutions adapted to specifically British conditions than they were with concrete, peculiarly Brazilian social realities.

It is precisely as a corrective to this tendency that the War College has proved so useful. With its new approach, both intellectual and practical, to specifically Brazilian problems, it avoids militaristic bias and refutes the archaic concept of military men as the natural opponents of civilians in their attitudes toward problems of human development.

However, it would be incorrect to say that the War College has been the only institution contributing to form a new type of leader in Brazil: leaders who, trained to political leadership and diplomatic action, are also particularly aware not only of natural and economic conditions but also of the attitudes and social characteristics peculiar to their country. This movement toward objective and direct study of Brazilian problems and cultural characteristics has been increasingly strengthened, since the 1920's, by the establishment of additional institutions. The University of São Paulo, with its notable group of French geographers and social scientists imported to teach in the faculty of philosophy, is one such example; or the School of Sociology and Politics, also in São Paulo, in which foreign social scientists—Americans from the United States—teach the social sciences to young Brazilians by new methods and direct their efforts toward the examination of Brazilian social problems; or the University of the Federal District, established by Professor Anísio Teixeira —a Brazilian disciple of John Dewey at Columbia—as a pioneer university, where perhaps an even greater emphasis was put on anthropological, sociological, geographical, and historical studies. It was at this university that social and cultural anthropology was first studied in Brazil, when specific Brazilian problems were considered not only in this department but also in that of sociology—a subject that was first taught in Brazil in the Normal School of the state of Pernambuco in 1928.

Can it be said that in contemporary Brazil there is a more conscious movement to adapt the institutions and forms of social and cultural expression to the essential elements of the national character? Perhaps so. The beginning of a systematic search for Brazilianness (*Brasileiridade*) is recent, dating from the modernist movement, which originated in São Paulo in 1922 and spread to Rio two years later, and from the regionalist and traditionalist (and, in its own way, modernist) movement in Recife (1924), which gave us the first modern teaching of sociology and social research (1927) and launched the First Congress for the Study of Afro-Brazilian subjects (1934). However, the less systematic predecessors of those modern developments should not be forgotten: the growth of Indian influences in literature and music during the Empire (Gonçalves Dias, José de Alencar, Carlos Gomes); the rather arbitrary search for telluric, traditional values in the *sertões*, the dry interior subregions of the country (Euclydes da Cunha, Afonso Arinos); the study of African survivals in Bahian culture (Nina Rodrigues, Arthur Ramos); the study and protection of Amerindian culture (Couto de Magalhães, Cândido Rondon, Roquette-Pinto, Heloiso Alberto Tôrres); the first attempts in the 1870's to consider non-European influences on Brazilian institutions with the Escola do Recife led by Tobias Barreto, and including such distinguished Brazilians as Sylvio Romero, Clóvis Bevilaqua, Martins Júnior, Joaquim Nabuco, Capistrano de Abreu, João Ribeiro, Oliveira Lima, Eduardo Prado; as well as Alberto Tôrres, Pontes de Miranda, Vicente Licínio Cardoso, and Oliveira Viana in the field of social analysis. Almost all these earlier, less systematic seekers of *Brasileiridade* are considered in the course of the present volume.

This preface has been intended to act as a temporary but functional bridge between the Brazil of the late monarchy and early Republic described in the present volume and the characteristic, current-day Brazil. Today, the search continues for those essential Brazilian elements that remain as constants in an ever-changing national scene. The discovery and definition of these elements gives a sense of permanence, of an enduring but evolving national culture. With these constants in mind, one may equally consider as nationally Brazilian a seventeenth-century sermon by Father Antônio Vieira and a contemporary poem by Carlos Drummond de Andrade; a colonial sculpture by Aleijadinho and an ultra-modern *chôro* by the *carioca* Villa-Lobos; the early-twentieth-century style of Euclydes da Cunha's *Os Sertões* and the very contemporary prose style of Nelson Rodrigues; the Afro-Brazilian dances performed by Brazilians in the time of Debret and the Dionysiac style of football brilliantly exemplified by Pelé (in contrast to the originally Apollonian style of this sport imparted by the British).

This preface has pursued the same method as the text of the book itself in mentioning personalities as symbols of significant social phenomena considered, hypothetically, characteristic of the development of an entire society. To a considerable extent, *Order and Progress* was conceived as a somewhat new experiment, differing in important ways from that already classic work by William J. Thomas, *The Polish Peasant in Europe and America*. I believe that from the concrete, existential, personal, sometimes even confidential material supplied by numerous eyewitnesses, it has been possible to interpret an entire body of mass phenomena.

In dealing with a phase of the Brazilian past that was neither too remote for firsthand recollection nor too immediate for objective detachment, I felt myself, as analyst and interpreter, to be in almost direct contact with some of the events and cultural tendencies mentioned in the nearly two hundred detailed testimonies I was able to collect. At the same time, not being the contemporary of the men and women who agreed to write or (when illiterate) dictate these depositions, I could feel a reasonably scientific lack of personal involvement.

This preface, however, is written from a perspective that differs from that of the main text itself. Here, a contemporary is dealing with contemporary representative personalities and with what he considers representative events and tendencies in Brazil, without feeling himself to be an impartial, impersonal analyst of the events of recent decades or of the immediate present. Of course, it is doubtful that such perfectly objective analysts of human behavior or national situations exist or have ever existed anywhere. Was Tocqueville—whose famous book remains a lively masterpiece—a purely scientific analyst of the United States of his time? Was Santayana this ideal observer of the England he analyzed in *Soliloquies in England*, another masterpiece? Or did the Beards attain this perfect scientific neutrality in their excellent study of American (United

States) civilization, or Francisco García Calderón in his equally penetrating survey and interpretation of Latin American democracies?

Human behavior differs from animal behavior. This is such a truism that it seems almost ludicrous to have to state it. Yet it must be stressed that zoologists may be perfectly scientific in their studies of animals, but that social psychologists, anthropologists, sociologists, historians, and other students of human behavior deal with subjects which are so uncertain, so complex, so multiple in their reactions and motivations that it is practically impossible for an analyst of human behavior to be totally scientific about them and, at the same time, remain human. Perhaps the best solution to this prime problem is for the analyst of human behavior to resign himself to being, at best, a scientific humanist.

Recife, 1970   G.F.

Note on Method

ORDER AND PROGRESS is the third volume of the series begun with *The Masters and the Slaves* and continued with *The Mansions and the Shanties*. The series will be completed by a fourth volume tentatively entitled *Tombs and Shallow Graves*. Together, this tetralogy will form a sociological and anthropological interpretation of the history of Brazilian patriarchal society.

"We carefully analyze the present in order better to understand the past and thus better to plan for the future," wrote Vicente Licínio Cardoso in his essay on Brazilian authors whose birth coincided with the founding of the Republic.[1] My own criterion, in the work at hand, is quite different: the analysis of a recent period of the Brazilian past in order better to comprehend that nation's present and future, and at the same time to show the forms and processes of the three periods: their similarities, their resistance to a progress often more apparent than real, and their occasional differences, resulting in the erosion of institutions once considered stable and enduring. It will also take into account the variations in patterns of living which make it impossible to consider the Brazil of the period as a single unit in a homogeneous state of development. The lives of Antônio Conselheiro and Rodrigues Alves, for example, reflected entirely different times and cultures, although they were contemporaries and each was extremely important in his way.

The patriarchal society examined in these four volumes is seen as essentially constant in form but somewhat variable in substance: variations which may be regarded as merely chronological or histori-

[1] Vicente Licínio Cardoso: *À Margem da História da República (Footnotes to the History of the Republic)* (Rio de Janeiro, 1924).

cal rather than social. What interests us more closely here are the internal changes within the social structure, which came about as a result of the predominating inequalities of regions, classes, races, and cultures. Thus, observations made in the first volume of this series are carried over into the second, and those of the second pass into the present volume. This leads to a certain amount of reiteration, perhaps undesirable from the literary or aesthetic standpoint but necessary in a study of this nature. For the same reason, there is considerable flexibility in the chapter divisions of the present volume, which attempts to cover fifty years of Brazilian society.

This sociological introduction to the history of Brazilian patriarchal society has from the outset followed the thesis that the development of Brazil has seen, not progress, but rather a series of progresses. It has also taken the view that Brazil is not one monolithic society, but rather a variety of social orders joined together into a national system, a nation both singular and plural in its life and culture. Thus while on one level progress can be discerned, on another we find disorder and lack of unity. The sense of Catholic order manifested by Dom Vital, Bishop of Olinda, at a dramatic point in Brazilian history[2] met with a sense of political order of an anti-clerical nature. The principal statesmen of the Empire were therefore aligned against the orthodox clergy in an odd antagonism involving two of the basic elements, not only of nation, but also of patriarchal society. Again, within the Church itself, we find Catholic progress furthered by the suppression of certain popular rites of indubitably African origin in an effort to regain an orthodox purity. And in the economic sector, agricultural progress is sacrificed in favor of a more rapid industrial advance.

In his classic *Human Nature and the Social Order*, Professor Charles Horton Cooley warns of the difficulties of studying a past era markedly different from our own. "We can scarcely rid ourselves of the impression that the way of life we are used to is the normal and the other ways are eccentric," he says.[3] Thus there is a tendency to consider the nineteenth century, and even the beginnings of the twentieth, as more picturesque than commonplace, bizarre in its manners, absurd in some of its customs. In contrast to these oddities, I calculate the more "normal" present as beginning, if

[2] The author is here referring to the famous "affair of the bishops" in the 1870's, when an orthodox faction in the clergy, headed by the bishops of Olinda and Pará, tried, with papal assistance, to force all members of the invested and lay clergy to resign their membership in the Masonic orders. (Translator.)

[3] Charles Horton Cooley: *Human Nature and the Social Order* (New York, 1922), p. 73.

not with the Vargas dictatorship of 1930, at least with the post-First World War revolutionary movements of 1922 and 1924[4] that eventually brought this dictatorship into being. These movements, which marked the end of the period of this study, were phenomena of an age of transition in which the military, as a responsible force in the guidance of the national destiny, was deeply concerned with the maintenance of legality in the political sector. But this same championship of legality can also be found in the regimes of Deodoro da Fonseca or Floriano Peixoto; in the confronting of later local uprisings such as those of Antônio Conselheiro in Canudos; or in the naval rebellion of João Cândido, or the military outbreaks in the northeast in 1911. The principal figure in this pseudomilitarism is General Dantas Barreto, who was the first to become more noted for his regalia as a member of the Brazilian Academy of Letters than for his military finery. It is seen too in Marshal Hermes da Fonseca, modernizer of the Armed Forces in both equipment and discipline, reforms made necessary after the excessively civilian prejudices of the "philosophical Emperor" had plunged the military into a state of decrepitude.

The conclusion which emerges from the testimony collected in preparation for this study is that the equilibrium of the Empire could have been maintained had the élite of the old order managed to come to terms with the ideological demands of the young republicans for a greater development in national progress. These demands not being met, the Imperial order was destroyed and the Republic became a necessity. But a necessity within certain limitations, within the framework indicated by the Positivist motto of "Order and Progress." After the abolition of slavery on May 13, 1888, and the coming of the Republic on November 15, 1889, Brazilians began to associate themselves less with the past and more with the world of their contemporaries—but without undergoing any radical alteration of their appearance, their manner of living, or other everyday links with their past.

This conclusion emerges from an examination of well-known documents, together with new material in the form of responses to questionnaires which I sent to Brazilians living between the period of the enactment of the Law of the Free Womb (1871) and the presidency of Venceslau Brás (1914–18), persons born between 1850 and 1900, of both sexes, of three races and various combina-

---

[4] Short-lived but dramatic uprisings of a "liberal" character, in which some military officers participated, not as the Army or the Navy, but as "liberals" or Brazilians with "liberal ideals." (Translator.)

tions of these races, and of many and diverse occupations, social and intellectual levels, and religious preferences.

The questionnaires, which were very difficult to assemble, were sent to more than 1,000 Brazilians, some close friends, others unknown to me. Some had to be proffered orally, since the persons interrogated were illiterate. Naturally, not everyone responded to the inquiry. Others offered information on a strictly confidential basis, confidences which have been scrupulously preserved. In all, nevertheless, nearly 300 usable replies were gathered and form the basis for this study.

In addition to the questionnaires, a large number of fresh material has been employed in the form of personal documents: letters, postcards, diaries, political papers, slave registers, inventories, wills, invoices for family purchases (mainly of clothing), family albums, songbooks, schoolbooks, cookbooks. The flavor of the period was also caught by examining lamps, china, glassware, fans, dolls, and children's toys. Particularly interesting were the Brito Alves collection of cigar bands and the Ricardo Brennand collection of wallets, cameos, and snuffboxes from the Imperial period.

Still further material has been gathered from the newspapers of the time, particularly the classified advertising, the obituaries, weddings, and anniversary notices, along with political, economic, and financial news. Illustrations, children's sections, and caricatures were also studied.

Some items on my questionnaire, apparently insignificant, aimed at discovering attitudes and values which applied subtly to questions of much greater moment—the use of the walking cane, for example: an object which acted as a powerful symbol of masculinity at the time, as well as of the patrician class. It also suggested membership in a superior race, as did the abundant curled mustaches affected by the same cane-carrying gentry, since neither the African nor the Amerindian race is noted for an abundance of facial hair.

As for ethnic attitudes, virtually every person responding to my questionnaire insisted that he did not foster the slightest trace of racial prejudice. But when this question was followed by one testing his attitude toward a hypothetical marriage between one of his children and a person of darker color, the responses were most interesting, both from the anthropological and the psychological viewpoints. They brought us back more than half a century to a period of Brazilian history long gone and yet still alive in the very existence of these witnesses. Perhaps some of these people, were they still alive today (the questionnaires were circulated in the 1940's and early 1950's), would find it necessary to modify their ethnocentric views in the light of the marriage of some of their children and grandchildren to persons of color, marriages occasioned either by the decadence of the one-time patrician family or, conversely, by the rise in social and economic importance on the part of the darker element.

This work is an attempt to interpret an era sociologically, anthropologically, and psychologically through a study of symbols and values current at the time as well as through the conventional assembly of historical facts. The result is therefore less a pure history than an attempt to reconstruct the essential social order existing between 1870 and 1920 through its value system, reflected in material things: houses, money, furniture, vehicles, clothing, jewelry, appliances, common household objects, as well as in such factors as political and social ideologies, notions of honor, patriotism, race, family, and religion. The combination of these values, as accepted more or less automatically by the majority, or by various significant minorities, constitutes altogether the most valid picture of a national culture.

Such values are, naturally, constantly in transition, making it necessary for the investigator to accept the idea of constant transmutation, to echo the words of Professor Earl E. Johnson,[5] as "a basic historical concept," but at the same time to preserve an awareness of the overall cultural patterns and processes within which these changes take place. To study this social fluidity more closely, it is necessary to subordinate the conventional preoccupation with fact to an empathetic study of the past as a living thing, expressing its existence through a vibrant complex of values and symbols. It is for this reason that Professor Johnson encourages his readers to "try your best to create a nostalgia for the past";[6] in other words, to cultivate the anti-sociological "sin" of which Brazilian scholars have frequently been accused—that of too close an emotional identification with the period under study. Professor Johnson recognizes the necessity for this close identification if we are to understand how, through the centuries, the past has extended into the present. Perhaps it was precisely the continuing impact of these past values and symbols which the Positivists had in mind when they stated that "The living are governed by the dead."

A study of the period of Brazilian history which followed the close of the Paraguayan War and included the passage of the Law of the Free Womb, the Republican Manifesto of 1870, the affair of

[5] Earl S. Johnson: *Theory and Practice of the Social Studies* (New York, 1956), p. 60.
[6] Ibid., p. 341.

the bishops, the coming of the Republic, the First World War, and the Versailles Peace Conference shows clearly the resistance of those social constants to crises which in other Latin-American countries have brought about a disintegration of the national culture. It is through the persistence of its basic culture that Brazil has shown itself to be better balanced than those other countries. By and large, the sense of national order which developed from this balance is attributable to the combination of authoritarian government and patriarchal family structure which obtained during the days of the Empire, a combination which, instead of hindering, actually in most aspects positively favored the development of Brazil into a modern democratic society.

G.F.

Note on Monetary Values

UNTIL 1943, the Brazilian monetary unit was the *real* (pl. *reis*). Since the intrinsic value of the *real* was microscopic, the working monetary unit was the *milreis*, or 1,000 *reis*. One thousand *milreis* constituted *um conto de reis*, generally referred to as a *conto*.

Throughout most of the nineteenth century, except during the Paraguayan War of 1865–70, the *milreis* was worth about 50 cents in American currency and the *conto* $500. During the 1890's, however, the *milreis* became drastically weak and in 1898 it reached its low point of 10 cents. From then on, it became gradually stronger, and during the early twentieth century generally hovered around 35 cents, with the *conto* consequently worth about $350.

To calculate the modern dollar equivalent of prices quoted in this work, therefore, it is necessary to determine whether such prices were current during the Empire, during the depression of the nineties, or during the prewar years of the present century. It is also necessary to take into account the fact that the American dollar for most of this era had at least five times its modern purchasing power.

R.W.H.

Historical Note

THE PERIOD OF BRAZILIAN HISTORY covered in *Order and Progress* extends from the establishment of the Republic in 1889 to the end of the First World War, with chief emphasis on the confusing and often turbulent transition from Empire to Republic. Although the proclamation of the Republic in 1889 came as a surprise to nearly everyone, it can be seen in retrospect that the event had a long background of preparation during the reign of Dom Pedro II. It is also evident that many of the institutions of the Empire were not ended with the Republic but continued to exist into the new century in a republican form. It is a prominent part of Gilberto Freyre's thesis that the new regime had deep roots in the Imperial past and that, in many of its attitudes and practices, the Empire foreshadowed the Republic.

It may be helpful to those readers unacquainted with Brazilian history to sketch in some of the background of the "Revolution" of 1889. Dom Pedro II had succeeded to the Brazilian throne upon the abdication of his father, Dom Pedro I, in 1831. Only five years old at the time, he was raised in a virtual prison of religious, academic, and moral instruction during a turbulent regency marked by constant insurrections in the provinces and palace revolts in Rio de Janeiro. Finally, in 1840, to end the constant bickering between the palace and Parliament, Dom Pedro declared himself of age and took over the government himself. Although this patently illegal action (he was more than three years short of the required age of eighteen) did not end the provincial uprisings, it did at least put a stop to the confusion in the capital, and by 1850 most of the violent opposition had been stilled and the country had gained an internal equilibrium which was to last for more than a generation.

As a man, Dom Pedro II is probably the most beloved figure in Brazilian history. Scholarly, dignified, devoted to his duties, an exemplary family man (unlike his rather rakish father), Dom Pedro loved his people and was loved by them in return. Nevertheless, as he himself was the first to realize, the times were against the continuation of a monarchical form of government in the New World. It was his hope to use his regime to effect a gradual and peaceful transition to an eventual Brazilian Republic, presumably to be established after his death.

Liberal as his foresights were, however, Dom Pedro II did not have the necessary temperament to lead this transition. Although progressive in ideas, he was aristocratic in tastes and not over-energetic in developing new programs to fit the changing social needs of his day. As a result, his regime was allowed merely to drift slowly in the general direction of the future, instead of adopting a dynamic, clearly charged course toward liberal republicanism. By the last decades of the century, the patience of numerous ardent republicans had worn thin and Dom Pedro, though liked and respected as a man, had been written off completely as a political leader and was being contemptuously referred to as "Pedro Banana," an epithet that speaks for itself.

In addition to being regarded generally as an inactive ruler, Pedro II by 1889 had to contend with the active opposition of most of the powerful special interest groups of the nation. The big agriculturalists had been hard hit by the uncompensated abolition of slavery in 1888; the Church felt victimized by the Emperor's rather casual attitude toward the rights of the established religious hierarchy; and the Army was smarting under its ruler's only thinly disguised contempt for all aspects of military life. Republicans, of course, were against the monarchy on principle and were vehement in their agitation for a change of political format. Even the former slaves, though grateful to the regime for having granted them their freedom, gave most of the credit for this accomplishment to the Princess Isabel, an ardent abolitionist who had signed the emancipation proclamation (*Lei Áurea*) in her capacity as regent during the absence of her Emperor-father, in Europe at the time to receive treatment for diabetes. This illness, by 1888 in a serious stage, had greatly undermined the Emperor's physical strength and was beginning to arouse genuine concern in all circles as to the succession, since the Princess Isabel, despite her popularity with the emancipated slaves, was not generally regarded favorably as a prospective Empress of Brazil. Nor was her lackluster French-born husband, the Conde d'Eu, likely to arouse much national enthusiasm, despite his genuine services to his adopted country during the war with Paraguay. Altogether, the time seemed ripe for a definitive move on the part of the republicans.

It was the Army that effected the change. Smarting under what they considered constant attacks on their sacred "military honor," an intangible quality they held to be even above the law itself, certain military elements, led by Marshal Floriano Peixoto, actively planned a coup. In this plot the Army was backed by many radical civilians, the most fervent of whom was the mathematician and former military officer Benjamin Constant de Magalhães. Equally republican but considerably less extreme members of this civilian contingent included Quintino Bocayuva, influential editor of the newspaper *O País*, and the brilliant Bahian political leader Ruy Barbosa. A more hesitant member of the republican group was Marshal Deodoro da Fonseca, who vacillated between his duty to the Emperor and his loyalty to the Army and only at the last minute decided in favor of the Army.

The coup was scheduled to coincide with the opening of Parliament on November 20, 1889, but with rumors flying thick and fast, as they have a way of doing in Brazil, it was impossible to hold off the event until that date. The Prime Minister, the Viscount de Ouro Prêto, well aware that something serious was in the wind, began rallying the police and National Guard to the defense of the Empire. Rumors had it that the Army was to be scattered to various remote provinces and certain important generals rusticated. Early in the morning of November 15, two cavalry regiments and a battalion of infantry stationed at the royal palace mutinied and marched through the city to the military headquarters at the Campo de Sant'Anna, where troops under Marshal Floriano Peixoto were assembled, theoretically to defend the barracks and the ministers of the Ouro Prêto government, who were gathered within at an emergency meeting. Instead of repelling the mutineers, however, Floriano's garrison joined them, probably according to preconceived plan. Shortly after 8 A.M. Marshal Deodoro da Fonseca arrived, still undecided in his loyalties, and informed Ouro Prêto and his ministers that they were deposed and that he would ask the Emperor to appoint a new government. Deodoro then returned to his home, where he was soon joined by Benjamin Constant, Quintino Bocayuva, and Ruy Barbosa. This trio finally succeeded in convincing Deodoro that if Dom Pedro did accede to his request to appoint a new ministry, it would almost certainly be headed by Deodoro's archenemy Senator Silveira Martins of Rio Grande do Sul. This information put an end to Deodoro's wavering and he agreed to join the republican cause. For his concession, he was made nominal leader of the movement and named provisional President of the new Republic, which was proclaimed formally in downtown Rio de Janeiro that afternoon. Ruy Barbosa was made Minister of Finance and Quintino Bocayuva Minister of Foreign Affairs. Benjamin Constant received the war portfolio.

In the face of this virtually bloodless but apparently successful coup, Pedro II showed considerably more spirit than had been expected from those who had been calling him "Pedro Banana." He refused to accept the Ouro Prêto resignation and, after being persuaded that such refusal was impossible under the circumstances, delayed appointing a new Prime Minister until he could explore the possibility of including the vacillating Deodoro da Fonseca in the new government. Only when he was convinced that Deodoro was irrevocably committed to the republican cause did he agree to abdicate. He was ordered to leave the country within twenty-four hours, which would have given him until the afternoon of November 17, but for fear of popular demonstrations of sympathy the grace period was subsequently shortened by some eight hours. At dawn on November 17 the royal family, accompanied by a few close friends and retainers, left for European exile. On December 28, 1889, the former Empress died in Oporto of a heart attack. Within two years the Emperor himself followed her to the grave. It was not until 1920 that the edict of banishment was revoked and the remains of the royal pair were brought back to Brazil from the Braganza royal plot in Lisbon and entombed in the old summer capital of Petrópolis.

Meanwhile, things were not going well with the new Republic. As provisional President, Deodoro da Fonseca showed himself to be quite devoid of political skill and unable to accept the attacks upon his regime as other than personal insults. Although elected first permanent President of the Constitutional Republic on February

25, 1891, his margin over the civilian candidate, Prudente de Morais, was slim, and during the ensuing nine months he was constantly in difficulties with a hostile Congress. Finally, on November 3, 1891, Deodoro lost all patience and dissolved the legislature, an arbitrary action which provoked revolts, some of them serious, in all parts of the country. Within three weeks Deodoro had lost virtually all support and consequently resigned his office in favor of his Vice-President, Marshal Floriano Peixoto.

Floriano was a different breed of military leader. Forceful, entirely sure of himself, he was given to hard-nosed decisions which earned him the sobriquet of the "Iron Marshal." Such decisions inevitably led to resistance, not only from civilians, but also from within the military itself. There were minor armed rebellions in Rio de Janeiro, Minas Gerais, Matto Grosso, São Paulo, Amazonas, and Maranhão, a serious one in Rio Grande do Sul and, in September of 1893, a naval revolt which lasted for six months and included a bombardment of the capital itself. Finally put down through the expense of purchasing a new fleet in Europe, the revolt ended by impoverishing the government but with Floriano in command of a consolidated Republic. When in 1894 he was succeeded by the first civilian President, Prudente de Morais, Floriano left a scarred but relatively ordered nation as his legacy.[1] Other crises were to take place, but from the time of Floriano there was no questioning the existence of the Brazilian Republic as a *fait accompli* and an increasingly powerful force in the political life of the Western Hemisphere.

R.W.H.

---

[1] Under the Brazilian Constitution, no President may succeed himself.

Historical Outline,
1864–1914

1841: Antônio Gonçalves Dias, born in 1823, dies in shipwreck near the shore of his native province of Maranhão after an influential life as a romantic Indianist-nationalist poet.

1865: The Empire of Brazil signs a treaty of alliance with Argentina for the prosecution of the war against Paraguay. This war has political consequences not only for the foreign relations of Brazil but also for internal social development within the Empire.

Six thousand Crown slaves win freedom by volunteering to fight against Paraguay. Pedro II emancipates the state-owned blacks on the Imperial *fazenda* of Santa Cruz and provides educational facilities for their children.

1866: Rio de Janeiro installs a modern system of sewage disposal.

1869: At the request of Pedro II, Pimenta Bueno, future Marquis of São Vicente, prepares an emancipation project providing for the emancipation of babies born to slave mothers. This "Law of the Free Womb" (*Lei do Ventre Livre*) aims at total abolition by 1899.

1870: The *Manifesto Republicano* is published by the republican newspaper *A República*.

Machado de Assis, who is to become the foremost novelist of Brazil, begins his career with a volume of tales, *Contos Fluminenses*. His first novel, *Helena*, appears two years later.

1871: The Viscount of Rio Branco introduces a bill in the Imperial Chamber of Deputies calling for immediate emancipation of all slaves belonging to the nation, as well as those employed by the Crown, those abandoned by their masters, and those to whom title of inheritance was vague. It also calls for the freedom of all children born thereafter to slave mothers. The bill, after passing the Senate, is signed by the Princess Regent.

Antônio Castro Alves, the popular abolitionist poet (b. 1847), dies in Bahia.

1872: Friar Vital Maria Gonçalves de Oliveira, a twenty-nine-year-old Capuchin born in Pernambuco and educated in Paris, assumes office as Bishop of Olinda and Recife.

1874: The bishops of Olinda and Pará are arrested. This causes a dramatic national split, with Masons on one side and orthodox Catholics on the other.

Transatlantic telegraphic communication with Europe is inaugurated in Brazil.

1877: José de Alencar, born in 1829, dies in Rio after brilliant and influential activity as politician and author of highly popular novels on Brazilian themes.

Great drought in Ceará.

1880: Joaquim Nabuco, representing the province of Pernambuco, unsuccessfully introduces in the Chamber a resolution proposing complete emancipation for 1890.

Carlos Gomes, the Brazilian composer and protégé of the Emperor, becomes a national hero after his opera *O Guarani* is produced with great success in Italy. The popularity of this opera is due as much to its abolitionist theme as to its music.

Installation of modern water supply system in Rio de Janeiro.

Luís Cruls, a Belgian scientist who becomes Brazilian, is appointed director of the Observatório in Rio de Janeiro.

Death of Luís Alves de Lima e Silva, Duke of Caxías (b. 1802), great hero of the Paraguayan War (1865–69) and outstanding statesman particularly during his term as Prime Minister (1873–75).

1881: *O Mulato*, a sociological novel by Aluísio de Azevedo, is published in Rio de Janeiro.

1883: Joaquim Nabuco's remarkable book *O Abolicionismo* is published in London.

Inauguration of electric light in the city of Campos (province of Rio de Janeiro)—the first Brazilian city to have this modern system of illumination.

1884. Slaves are emancipated in the province of Ceará.

1885: Inauguration of the Corcovado cog railroad.

1887: The Emperor becomes seriously ill and goes to Europe for treatment of a liver ailment complicated by diabetes, leaving Princess Isabel in charge of the government.

1888: Passage of abolition law (*Lei Áurea*) by the Chamber, declaring slavery extinct in Brazil. In the Senate, Baron de Cotegipe warns that such a radical abolition with no provision for compensating slaveowners could overthrow the monarchy.

The Emperor and the Empress return from Europe.

História da Literatura Brasileira, a monumental study by Sylvio Romero, is published in Rio de Janeiro.

1889: Proclamation of the Brazilian Republic by General Deodoro de Fonseca with the support of a considerable part of the Army, of the Republican Party of São Paulo, and of some intellectuals, especially those of the Positivist group. Choice of the positivistic slogan *"Ordem e Progresso"* to replace the Imperial arms on the Brazilian flag.

Deodoro da Fonseca becomes the first President of the Republic of the United States of Brazil.

Innocência, a novel by Alfredo de E. Taunay, is published in Rio de Janeiro.

Tobias Barreto (b. 1839) dies in Recife. A *mestiço* of humble origin, he had become one of the most influential and violently polemical intellectuals in Brazil. Famous for his cult of everything German, he was instrumental in making Recife the center of a powerful cultural movement (*Escola do Recife*) to liberate Brazilian jurisprudence, philosophy, and literature from French influence in favor of Germanic models.

1891: A republican Constitution, written by Ruy Barbosa and modeled after the Constitution of the United States of America, becomes effective in February.

President Deodoro da Fonseca dissolves Parliament and resigns, to be succeeded by General Floriano Peixoto.

1892: Eduardo Prado's *A Ilusão Americana*, a violent and sensational attack upon the foreign policy of the Brazilian Republic and Brazilian friendship with the United States, is published and immediately prohibited by the police.

An insurrection or revolt that is to last for three years breaks out in Rio Grande do Sul.

Inauguration, in Rio de Janeiro, of the first regular line of electric tramcars, replacing the earlier horse-drawn vehicles.

1893: The revolt in Rio Grande do Sul is supported by virtually the entire Brazilian fleet. In the ensuing crisis, the Army for the first time assumes its subsequently traditional (and indispensable) role as a national, nonpartisan, and super-regional force in the preservation of order.

1894: President Floriano Peixoto is succeeded by Prudente de Moraes, from São Paulo, who starts a work of reconstruction that is to be followed by his immediate successors. With him, the words "*Ordem e Progresso*" begin to take on a concrete meaning in spite of a period of financial depression.

1896: *Cartas de Inglaterra*, by Ruy Barbosa, is published in Rio de Janeiro.

Beginning of the peasant rebellion in Canudos led by Antônio Conselheiro, a religious mystic.

1898: Campos Sales, also from São Paulo, becomes President of the Republic and through the adoption of austere measures effectively re-establishes the national credit. One of these measures is the suspension, for some time, of specie payments; another is the withdrawal and destruction of large quantities of paper money.

The boundary between French Guiana and Pará is fixed (Treaty of Berne). Already the 100-year-old boundary dispute between Argentina and Brazil had been settled during Prudente de Moraes's administration, with the United States acting as arbitrator. The Baron do Rio Branco, soon to become Minister of Foreign Relations, is influential in reaching these solutions, inaugurating his distinguished career as diplomat and political intellectual. Perhaps Brazil's greatest statesman during the years from 1894 until his death in 1912, Rio Branco never ceased to be a monarchist at heart.

1899: The Butantan Institute, subsequently to be world famous for its work in the development of anti-snake-bite serums, is established in São Paulo under the direction of Dr. Vital Brasil.

1900: Joaquim Nabuco's autobiography, *Minha Formação*, which is to become a classic and be compared to *The Education of Henry Adams*, is published in Rio de Janeiro.

Eça de Queiroz dies in Paris. No Portuguese writer had had so much influence on Brazil as the author of *Os Maias*.

1902: Euclydes da Cunha's monumental epic *Os Sertões* (*Rebellion in the Backlands*) appears in Rio de Janeiro.

Canaã, a novel of ideas by J. P. Graça Aranha, is published in Rio de Janeiro.

Rodrigues Alves, another Paulista, becomes President of the Republic. Through the efforts of members of the Rodrigues Alves Cabinet, and with the vital collaboration of Prefect of Police Pereira Passos and Public Health Director Oswaldo Cruz, yellow fever is eradicated in Rio de Janeiro and a great part of the city is pulled down and rebuilt on what are considered to be attractive modern lines.

1904: The marble and granite Monroe Palace, in which Brazilian products were exhibited in the St. Louis (U.S.A.) Exposition, is sensationally transferred to Rio de Janeiro and reassembled to become one of the most attractive buildings of the newly rebuilt city. New gardens and promenades are built to give a new aspect to the urban center. A magnificent avenue —the Avenida Central, five miles long and 140 feet wide—is opened with new buildings. A municipal theatre and other public buildings, equally magnificent, are begun, along with the largest and most modern docking facilities in South America.

1906: The Brazilian Alberto Santos Dumont's pioneering aeronautical truimphs in France transform him into the most beloved national hero of his time.

Afonso Pena, from Minas Gerais, is elected President of the Republic.

The Baron do Rio Branco, as Foreign Minister, opens the Pan-American Conference in the Monroe Palace. Joaquim Nabuco presides and Elihu Root, United States Secretary of State, is present, along with 80 representatives of 20 American nations.

1907: Having made a tour through most of the states of Brazil before taking office, President Pena embarks upon a program of railway extension and harbor works in Bahia, Santos, Pará, Vitória, Pernambuco, and Rio Grande do Sul. He also continues the rehabilitation of the capital and calls for the revitalization of the Brazilian Navy.

Brazil's participation in The Hague Peace Conference becomes a matter of patriotic rejoicing for Brazilians as a result of the eloquent speeches of the Brazilian chief delegate, Ruy Barbosa.

Gilberto Amado begins his activity as a literary journalist in *Diário de Pernambuco*, in which field he is soon to be followed by Francisco de Assis Chateaubriand Bandeira de Melo.

1908: The National Exposition in Rio de Janeiro attracts a considerable number of Brazilians from the various states to the federal capital. The exposition is organized in commemoration of the first centenary of the opening of Brazilian ports to international commerce, and its purpose is to show Brazilian progress within national order. As an appropriate feature of the festival, many of the visitors from the provinces arrive on the ships of the newly organized merchant marine, Lloyd Brasileiro.

Death of Machado de Assis, greatest Brazilian literary figure and first president of the Brazilian Academy of Letters.

Celebrated visit of the United States Navy to Brazil. Some 10,000 American sailors happily fraternize with the *cariocas* of Rio de Janeiro.

It is announced that Brazilian railways reach a total length of 11,432 miles in comparison to 5,358 miles in 1889. The difficult construction of the Madeira-Mamoré, in the extreme north of the Republic, progresses despite the loss of many lives from malaria.

1909: Euclydes da Cunha, celebrated author of *Os Sertões*, is assassinated.

1910: Marshal Hermes da Fonseca, a distinguished soldier and a Brazilian of northeastern (Alagoas) origin, is elected President of the Republic, defeating Ruy Barbosa. His administration is one of political agitation, though improvements in sanitation and harbor works go on. A revolt of sailors on the battleship *Minas Gerais*, led by a Negro, João Cândido, breaks out against naval officers and the government.

Joaquim Nabuco dies in Washington where he is serving as the first Ambassador of Brazil to the United States.

1911: The country is agitated by revolts against the so-called "political oligarchies" in favor of their replacement, through election, by military men.

1912: The Baron do Rio Branco, distinguished Brazilian Foreign Minister, dies in Rio de Janeiro.

1914: Venceslau Brás, from Minas Gerais, is elected President of the Republic. During his administration, Brazil at first remains neutral in the European war but later takes the side of the Allies. President Brás stimulates agricultural production and industrialization. The civil code of Brazil is written by Clóvis Bevilaqua and approved by the legislature.

A Organização Nacional and *O Problema Nacional Brasileiro*, two nationalistic studies of political sociology by Alberto Tôrres (1865–1917), are published in Rio de Janeiro and exert considerable influence on Brazilian political thought.

G.F.

Order and Progress

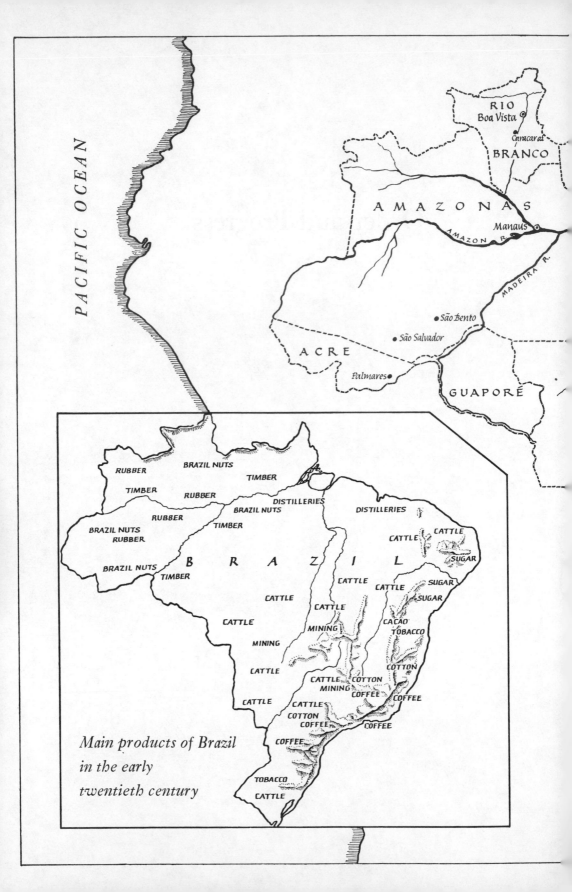

PACIFIC OCEAN

RIO
Boa Vista ○
Caracaraí •

BRANCO

A M A Z O N A S

Manaus ○

AMAZON R.

MADEIRA R.

São Bento •

São Salvador •

A C R E

Palmares •

G U A P O R É

RUBBER   BRAZIL NUTS
                        TIMBER
TIMBER   RUBBER
        RUBBER   BRAZIL NUTS   DISTILLERIES
                                DISTILLERIES
BRAZIL NUTS   TIMBER
RUBBER   CATTLE   CATTLE
                                        CATTLE
                                                    SUGAR
BRAZIL NUTS   B R A Z I L
                TIMBER   CATTLE   CATTLE   SUGAR
                        CATTLE   CATTLE   SUGAR
            CATTLE   CATTLE
                                MINING   CACAO
                                        TOBACCO
        MINING
                                            COTTON
    CATTLE
    CATTLE   CATTLE
                MINING   COTTON
                        COFFEE   COFFEE
            CATTLE
            COTTON   COFFEE
            COFFEE
                COFFEE

Main products of Brazil
in the early
twentieth century

                TOBACCO
                CATTLE

ATLANTIC OCEAN

Miles

MARACÁ I.

AMAPÁ

CAVIANA I.

MARAJÓ I.

Belém
(Pará)

Barbacena

São Luís do Maranhão

Rosario

PARÁ

MARANHÃO

Fortaleza (Ceará)

Teresina   Madalena   Aracati
                        Mossoró

CEARÁ

RIO GRANDE
DO NORTE   Natal

Sousa

PARAIBA   João Pessoa (Paraíba)

Triunfo   Monteiro   Itamaracá
PERNAMBUCO   Olinda   Recife

Bonito

ALAGOAS

Maceió
Pilar
São Cristóvão
Murut

PARNAÍBA R.

PIAUI

TOCANTINS R.

SÃO FRANCISCO R.

MATO GROSSO

Parana

BAHÍA

Rio Pardo   Cachoeira

Salvador (Bahía)
de Todos os Santos

Praia Rica

Cuiabá

Goias

Goyania

Taracatú

JEQUITINHONHA R.

Minas
Nova

Mucuri

AMAZON R.

XINGU R.

GOYAZ

MINAS

Serro Frio

Pitangui
Belo Horizonte   Sabará
Guapé   Ouro Preto

GERAIS

ESPÍRITO SANTO

Espírito Santo

PARAGUAY R.

PARANÁ R.

SÃO PAULO

São Pedro

Itu

Sorocaba   Jundiai

São Paulo

Santos
São Vicente

Paraiba do Sul

RIO DE
JANEIRO   Piratininga

Paraibuna   Rio de Janeiro

PARANÁ

Iguaçú   IGUAÇÚ R.   Curitiba

SANTA CATARINA

Florianapolis
SANTA CATARINA I.

URUGUAY R.

RIO GRANDE
DO SUL

Porto Alegre
Viamão

Mostardas

Pelotas

(URUGUAY)

Santa Lucia

RIO DE LA PLATA

BRAZIL
in the early twentieth century,
including areas considered territories.
The cities are those that flourished
in that period.

❧ [I] ❧

The Fifteenth of November

IN 1889 AN ENGLISHMAN named Edward Frederick Knight found himself in the tropical waters of the Atlantic, involved in a Robert Louis Stevensonian adventure: that of searching the Brazilian island of Trindade[1] for the vast treasure of ecclesiastical gold and silver that had reputedly been buried there by a mysterious band of men in 1821. According to the legend—which is at certain points confirmed by history—at the beginning of the nineteenth century pirates had made a practice of sacking Spanish ships that were transporting colonial treasure to Spain to avoid its falling into the hands of the republicans during the wars of independence. The burial of this treasure was thus probably pirates' doing.

Mr. Knight was no ordinary Englishman, but rather a cultivated man whose description of his Brazilian adventure is one of the more interesting narratives in the extant literature of buried treasure. His description of the event is minute: the painstaking description of a failure. But the book, although almost entirely about this deserted and mysterious island, makes occasional reference to continental Brazil.

Salvador da Bahia served as a continental beachhead for the adventurers of these overgrown and perhaps none too benevolent children bound for the island of Trindade. Seen for the first time from the bay on a moonlit night, Salvador presented a beautiful

---

[1] Trindade is a Brazilian island off the coast of Rio de Janeiro, not to be confused with the British island of Trinidad (also called Trindade in Portuguese). Mr. Knight's ship was the *Alerte*. (Translator.)

picture for the admiration of the British visitors. The churches and houses of the upper city seemed to glisten like marble; palm trees and other tropical forms of vegetation broke into the evening sky, forming a charming backdrop for the vast pattern of houses and well-lighted streets. In the lower city the buildings seemed to the men of the *Alerte* to be emerging majestically directly from the glistening moonlit waters.

But much of this supposed magnificence was drastically modified the next morning when the Englishmen saw the city by the light of day. Romantics only at night, these daytime realists of the *Alerte* saw that the old "Portuguese city," while undoubtedly picturesque, could with difficulty be considered "magnificent." [2] Filthy streets . . . A confusion of screaming colors—of people, animals, parrots, the turbans of Negro women, the strange fruits . . . An equal confusion of strange smells in great variety, the smells of poverty and disease, possibly even that of the dreaded yellow fever.

A city of noise as well: of church bells constantly tolling and fireworks continually exploding in midair in what Knight describes as the Bahian obsession with a constant celebration of holy days. The city is called the City of All Saints precisely because every day of the year is marked as the festival of one of the beatified: the patron of one of the quarters of the city, or of some street, or simply of some individual family. If the racket of these barbarous religious celebrations ever ceased, Mr. Knight felt, the inhabitants of Salvador would be terrified, certain that some great misfortune had suddenly descended upon the city: earthquake or revolution.

From Salvador, the Englishmen of the *Alerte* continued to the island of Trindade, intending to return to the capital of Bahia after a few months of persistent search for a perhaps mythical treasure.[3] This return, the first of two, took place in January, 1890, on which occasion the explorers noted that a strange flag floated over the forts and public buildings, as well as from the masts of the small Brazilian boats in the bay. This flag was unlike any banner they had seen before. What had happened in Brazil? What kind of revolu-

[2] Edward F. Knight: *The Cruise of the Alerte. The Narrative of a Search for Treasure on the Desert Island of Trinidad* (London, 1890), p. 140.

[3] It is possible that Knight's expedition on Trindade contributed to the British occupation of the island a few years later. The case was settled through the mediation of Portugal, as requested by the Brazilian Foreign Minister, Counselor Carlos de Carvalho. The incident has been treated recently by J. de Castro Nunes in *Alguns Homens do Meu Tempo* (Rio de Janeiro, 1957), p. 46.

tion could have taken place? The Englishmen were mystified until Mr. Knight, upon entering the small boat that was to take him ashore, questioned the oarsman, in bad Portuguese, as to the meaning of the change. The Negro replied with an indifferent air, "Ah, the Republic." [4] The answer was so cool, so matter-of-fact, so much like that of the Englishman in a thousand Brazilian jokes, that Mr. Knight was convinced that the Brazilians were a people "almost oriental" in their apathy: an indolent race.[5]

An Englishman resident in Bahia,[6] a ship's chandler named Wilson, later offered a more detailed explanation: there had been a Revolution that had driven "the beloved Emperor" from the throne. It had been a third-rate Revolution, to be sure, without a single casualty to lend it dignity or respectability. The people, said Mr. Wilson, seemed to be ashamed of the event and few even mentioned it in the city.

Perhaps Mr. Wilson underestimated the local apathy. Perhaps he didn't realize that the City Council of Salvador had officially taken a proud stand against the Republic, protesting its solidarity with the Emperor. Or that this attitude, in less ostensible form, had been voiced by many individual Bahians who, like most Brazilians of their time, were lukewarm adherents of republicanism and tolerated the idea of a new regime only so long as it guaranteed them the same order and unity they had enjoyed for so many years under the Empire.[7]

---

[4] Knight: op. cit., p. 140. The national flag had not yet been chosen at the time of Mr. Knight's arrival in Bahia after his first visit to the island of Trindade; the one he saw flying over the forts, public buildings, and harbor craft was merely that of the new state of Bahia.

[5] Ibid., p. 304.

[6] It is customary in Brazil to employ the state name in referring to the capital city of Bahia. Thus, the names Salvador and Bahia are used interchangeably. (Translator.)

[7] This attitude extended even to the former nobility. The Baron do Rio Branco, a member of the Paranhos family and son of a Bahian viscount, continued loyal to the old regime although condescending to the existence of the new in the interests of domestic order and economic progress. Rio Branco wrote to Ruy Barbosa (according to the historian Luís Viana) that the question was not one of choice "between monarchy and republic, but between republic and anarchy." May the new regime succeed in "maintaining order, assuring, like the former, the integrity, the propriety, and the glory of our great and beloved Brazil and at the same time in consolidating the liberties bequeathed us by our forefathers, liberties rarely found in so many so-called republics of South America." This, concluded Rio Branco, was his "most sincere desire" (José Carlos Rodrigues: *Religiões Acatólicas* [Rio de Janeiro, 1900], p. 119).

It is certain that among Brazilians in general there were many who conformed immediately and easily to the victory of the Republic over the monarchy: a monarchy which, largely through the weakness of the Emperor, had shown itself incapable of offering armed resistance to the declaration of the fifteenth of November— that surprise move before which even the barons of the Empire had momentarily been struck dumb. The almost suicidal way in which the old regime had marched toward its downfall had caused even its natural allies to feel indifferent to the fate of the Crown. How then could the simple folk—even those Negroes and *mestiços* whose gratitude to Princess Isabel should have been strong enough for them to oppose any republican movement—be expected miraculously to become suddenly united in the face of the new regime?

Still, there had been some token opposition to the new Republic on the part of the recently emancipated blacks. The newspaper *Itatiaia* in the province of Rio de Janeiro stated that ex-slaves had refused to work "on the plantations whose owners had joined the republican party,[8] alleging that they would not serve persons rebelling against the Princess Regent who had freed them. There were other manifestations of this sort as well." [9] And "the general public would dispense itself very willingly of this benefit [the Republic] that the spiteful and selfish had accorded them without consulting their wishes or considering their traditions," said the *Era Nova* in an editorial of January 27, 1902. "The freedmen saw the Princess as their redeemer and idolized her. . . . All Brazilians except a small number of republicans were overcome with astonishment when they learned that the Republic had been proclaimed in Rio de Janeiro."

There was thus among the colored people a deep-seated spirit of gratitude to the paternalistic monarchy for having given them the protection necessary for their development in a democracy that was truly social. Joaquim Nabuco remembered this when he cited these genuinely expressive statements by the first Rebouças,[1] a pure Negro, on the attitude of the Brazilian monarchy toward his people: the Portuguese court, from its earliest days, had tried "through its wise pronouncements, incorporated into law, to combat and ex-

---

[8] *A Província* (July 10, 1889).

[9] According to oral testimony given in 1941 by various persons who recalled the events of the period, among them the Baroness of Bonfim.

[1] André Rebouças (1838–1898), a close friend and adviser of Pedro II, serves as one of many examples of the fact that racial characteristics were not in themselves a bar to advancement under the Empire. (Translator.)

tinguish entirely any prejudice against the accident of race in all colonial territories." Thus, according to Rebouças, "all men of mixed blood should particularly defend the constitutional monarchy, an institution which might not be so vital to other Brazilian citizens." [2] Consequently, the so-called "Imperial Black Guard"—formed out of gratitude by humble Negroes and *mestiços*—rose to the defense of the monarchial cause which had traditionally protected such people against the wealthy.

Perhaps the reaction of Mr. Knight to the republican Revolution of 1889 had not been his alone or that of his companions in adventure, but also that of numerous Europeans in contact with Portuguese America and sympathetic to the retention of the monarchist form of government which still formed a sort of bridge to the culture of the Old World. In all other parts of Latin America, the predominating republicanism had become notorious for its turbulence, for the frequency of its revolutions, for the endless parade of its leaders, generally messianic generals who became Presidents by decree. Only aristocratic Chile and Mexico were free from this state of things, the latter because of the somewhat benevolent Positivist dictatorship of Don Porfírio. Brazil was the only nation that for years had avoided the common uproar known as Latin republicanism, which may have been the real reason for the political "apathy" that Mr. Knight regarded as a racial characteristic.[3] Other shortsighted Europeans shared Mr. Knight's attitude, and it was thus that the story has been told and repeated in the official history books. But it was not in fact so. "With the proclamation of the Brazilian Republic, blood was shed in São Luis (de Maranhão) by several Negroes who were convinced that they owed their liberty to the throne," records a Positivist and republican sympathizer, José Luso Tôrres (b. Maranhão, 1879). "The bullets which killed them were fired by a platoon of the Fifth Battalion and after that I respected Major Tavares Tôrres [commander of the platoon] more than ever." [4]

Thus Luso Tôrres's deposition was actually in favor of the re-

---

[2] Joaquim Nabuco: *O Dever dos Monarquistas—Carta ao Almirante Jaceguay* (Rio de Janeiro, 1895), pp. 8-9.

[3] Knight: op. cit., p. 305.

[4] Major Tavares Tôrres (future engineer and frequenter of the lectures of Teixeira Mendes of the Positivist Apostolate in Rio de Janeiro), when still a small boy in Maranhão had been so envious of the gold braid and the sense of importance of major military officers that he enrolled, as an adolescent, in the military college at Praia Vermelha and went from there to Rio Pardo.

publican soldier in Maranhão who had not hesitated to order the shooting of unarmed Negroes faithful to the monarchy. If in retrospect such loyalty is valued above other virtues, we also have to recognize that there was considerable confusion in the conscience of Brazilians of 1889, forced as they were to choose between the throne and the Republic. But we must also recognize those heroes and martyrs ignored by official histories, texts which, in their direct and narrow way, have a tendency to support the winning side. The Negroes who fell victim to Major Tavares in São Luis de Maranhão, former slaves who spontaneously came to the support of the throne that had given them their freedom, were among those overlooked by history. It is hard indeed to understand why the readiness of loyal Negroes and ex-slaves to fight for the monarchy should ever have been denied. In Maranhão, several fell at the hands of the cowardly soldiers of Major Tavares. And in Rio de Janeiro, others were shot down by republican youths armed like the soldiers with rifles against a so-called "Black Guard" carrying simple razors or clubs bearing the legend "Petrópolis." [5] The second story is vouched for incontestably by Medeiros e Albuquerque, who was one of the republican agitators at the time. He confesses to having left his home carrying an excellent Smith and Wesson and two cartons of bullets in open defiance of the monarchy in order to face the monarchist forces—the Black Guard. Thus armed, the bravos of the Republican Club, among whom there were certainly some *mestiços*, set out to repel what seemed to them to be "aggression" on the part of the Negroes of a Black Guard armed only, Medeiros states, with clubs and razors. It is not surprising that the volleys of the Club produced many victims among the heroic blacks, whose bodies, according to Medeiros, "were hidden by the police." [6] "The Travessa da Barreira was literally jammed with a bloody and panicky multitude," that is, of the mass of Negroes from the Black Guard, all of whom had relied only on their skill in *capoeira*[7] or upon the said clubs and razors. Medeiros adds another detail about

[5] The reference is to the city of Petrópolis, site of the Imperial summer palace. (Translator.)

[6] Medeiros e Albuquerque: *Minha Vida da Infância à Mocidade—Memórias (1867–1893)* (2nd edn., Rio de Janeiro, 1933), pp. 124, 125.

[7] *Capoeira*, once a lightning-fast method of fighting with the feet, which were often armed with knives; it has now become stylized into the extremely picturesque slow-motion combination of wrestling and acrobatics displayed for the tourist trade in the city of Salvador. See Glossary also. (Translator.)

the way the republicans confronted that mob of blacks: "We loaded our revolvers and, opening the windows a crack, extended one arm outward, discharging the five bullets in the chamber. Then we reloaded and repeated the process." It was a sort of Ku Klux Klan affair, similar to incidents in the American South, a racial war between blacks and whites. This white—or near-white—bourgeois minority organized the republican movement on the basis of the technical superiority of armed force, and employed it against colored people whose only crime was one that could never be attributed to the republicans: an excessive and active feeling of loyalty and gratitude.

The fraternization between blacks and whites achieved during the campaigns of the Paraguayan War[8] was seriously compromised as a result. As the historian Nélson Werneck Sodré has noted in his *Panorama of the Second Empire*,[9] the Paraguayan War made it necessary for many Negro soldiers to live side by side with whites and had given Negroes, and especially *mestiços*, excellent new opportunities for social advancement. But it had also created among Army officers a profound aversion to the idea of "employing their arms, destined for the defense of the country, in the repression of members of a race which, in time of crisis, had given so many of its sons to the country's Armed Forces." [1]

Another negative effect of the republican movement on the growing social intercourse between blacks and whites after the Paraguayan campaign was to promote an increasingly scornful attitude toward elements of Afro-Brazilian culture which had begun to be assimilated by Brazilian society in general. Thus, Horácio Pires Galvão states that he and other members of the élite learned aspects of the *capoeira* from Negro soldiers during the war.[2] This Afro-Brazilian art became highly prized by some upper-class whites, not only for self-defense but also as an expression of physical elegance. With the republican movement, however, *capoeira* came to be con-

[8] The Paraguayan War (1865–70)—in which Brazil, in alliance with Uruguay and Argentina, fought against the stubborn forces of the Paraguayan dictator Francisco Solano López—created a number of national heroes but no decisive military victories. The boundary differences which were one of the causes of the war were finally settled by treaty on March 27, 1872. (Translator.)

[9] Nélson Werneck Sodré: *Panorama do Secondo Império* (São Paulo, 1939).

[1] R. Magalhães Júnior: *Deodoro, a Espada contra o Império* (São Paulo, 1957), I, 310.

[2] Oral testimony given the author by descendants of Horácio Pires Galvão.

sidered shameful and degrading. Coelho Neto recalls associating with colored laborers—shortly after the Paraguayan War—in order to "learn the secrets of *capoeiragem*, so useful for those in politics, in teaching, or in the Army and Navy." Later, while a member of the federal legislature as a delegate from Maranhão, he had considered sponsoring a project to make the teaching of *capoeira* obligatory in the Armed Forces as being a truly national sport. The attempt, needless to say, was unsuccessful.[3] The Frenchman Émile Allain classified *capoeira* as "a gymnastic exercise or special dance . . ." [4]—anything but the "blot on Brazilian civilization" alleged by the republican youth, who could not bring themselves to pardon the Negroes for the skill and courage with which they had employed these arts in their last-ditch martyrdom to defend a regime that was to them, in the tenderest sense of the word, the *Pátria*. Although admitting the existence of disorders among the practitioners of *capoeira*, Allain saw no lack of safety in Imperial Rio de Janeiro; on the contrary, he claimed, there were few cities where both the center and the suburbs were equally tranquil day and night.

When the *Alerte* anchored in Bahia for the third time, it was no longer a banner of the state of Bahia which floated provisionally from the mastheads, but rather one similar to that of the now-defunct Empire.[5] Knight was moved to ask himself if there hadn't been still another Revolution in his absence, and if some "strange form of government—communist, oligarchy, or what you will" was being tried in Brazil.[6] Not, needless to say, as a result of the will of the "apathetic race which dwelt there" (so the Britisher must have thought) but forced upon inert masses by uneasy intellectuals and bookish military types who took advantage of the passivity of the people to conduct their political experiments. The new

[3] Among others, Duque Estrada Teixeira, Captain Ataliba Nogueira, Lieutenants Lapa and Leite Ribeiro, Midshipman Antônio Sampaio, and "Juca Paranhos, who gloried in the title of Rio Branco in his great work in the Itamaraty and who, in his youth, was a devotee, a fact in which he took great pride and to which he referred often in conversation." Coelho Neto: *Bazar* (Oporto, 1928), p. 310.

[4] Émile Allain: *Rio de Janeiro, Quelques Données sur la Capitale et sur l'Administration du Brésil* (2nd edn., Rio de Janeiro, 1886), p. 272. See also J. C. Alves Lima: *Recordações de Homens e Cousas do Meu Tempo* (Rio de Janeiro, 1926).

[5] The Imperial flag was the same color and general composition as that of the present Brazilian Republic, but the center diamond contained the Imperial coat of arms instead of the globe and Republican motto "*Ordem e Progresso*." (Translator.)

[6] Knight: op. cit., p. 311.

flag, of course, was that of the Republic, with its Positivist slogan: "Order and Progress." To some this motto might have been interpreted as a confession that the Revolution was essentially a conservative one—that as a prerequisite to the desired progress, they would require the maintenance of civic and social order. It seemed to indicate that the new order, however progressive, would never lose sight of the tradition of order which had been one of the country's strongest and most unique characteristics, differentiating it from the Bolivarian tendencies of Spanish America. Like the Anglo-Saxons of the New World, these republicans were progressives. But like the Anglo-Saxons of Europe over the past two centuries, they were inclined to effect their technical and social progress within the framework of a strong public order. Besides, the Brazilian Positivists suspected the violently libertarian methods of the French Revolution which, since the beginning of the nineteenth century, had been repudiated in France by the radicals themselves: by Saint-Simon and Fourier and, most emphatically, by Auguste Comte. From these radicals came new ideas which had far greater repercussions in the Brazilian Empire and in the United States than in the Spanish-American countries, where a deep and lasting commitment to the spirit of 1789 prevented receptivity to the new revolutionary ideas which superseded the mystique of the republican guillotine. Such creeds, emanating from the "goddess of reason," had been conspicuous for their violent and even macabre revolutionary methods. From the ideas of philosophers such as Comte, Brazilians understood that the desire for progress went hand in hand with that for a harmony among men, among classes, nations, races, and sexes; and that this harmony could be represented only by a true sense of order, both national and international, even to the point of admitting the existence of dictatorships as powerful as the most vigorous monarchical governments. On this subject, the notes of a French engineer, Henrique Augusto Milet, who arrived in Brazil in 1841, had recently been published in Portuguese. This man (if not truly Positivist, at least para-Positivist) was the disciple of another French engineer, Louis Léger Vauthier, who had been perhaps the first European to attempt to introduce systematically into the Brazilian Empire the socialist and, in a sense, pre-Positivist ideas of Fourier. Milet—[7] who became a Brazilian, married a Brazilian woman, and

---

[7] Among Milet's sociological works the article "O Quebra-Quilos e a Crise da Lavoura," published in the *Jornal do Recife* in 1876 and later in the same year in *A Província*, is of especial interest. Here Milet points out, in anticipation of Eu-

abandoned engineering to become a sugar planter—modified the possible excesses of (Vauthier's) Fourierist progressivism with ideas of order and down-to-earth common sense.

It is not surprising to those who have read Milet and other polemicists of the pre-revolutionary era that the republican movement was inspired by Positivist thought and was characterized by a greater sense of progressive reform and maintenance of public order than was the monarchy. However, this sense of authoritarianism must not be confused with the messianic *caudilhismo* of the uneasy Bolivarian countries of Spanish America—a principle of leadership suggested by the French revolutionary ideals of liberty and equality, but subsequently perverted by the despotism of certain military dictators who, more or less out of necessity, had to adopt such measures to stifle anarchy.

Neither in 1890 nor in the remaining years of the nineteenth century did any visitor comparable to Mr. Knight interpret the new Brazilian flag with its motto "Order and Progress" as representing a regime more authoritarian than libertarian. Almost all Europeans in contact with Brazil at the time feared the new situation and lamented the collapse of the monarchy, even while hailing the beginning of a possible new progressive economic policy which could regard European exports to Brazil more favorably than had been the case under the monarchy. But rarely was it understood that the ideas of the founders of the Republic were substantively authoritarian, in contrast to the extreme liberal beliefs of the statesmen of the Empire, many of whom were only nominally monarchists in their ideas and procedures. Dom Pedro II himself proved to be a leader who, in spite of his position as head of a monarchist state, had become too bourgeois in his ways. He failed to inspire the proper spirit of dedication in conservative circles to the cause of preserving a monarchy of the traditional authoritarian and paternalistic pattern felt by many Europeans and some Brazilians to be necessary in a nation as underdeveloped and uncertain as Brazil. The statements of several contemporaries, notably Joaquim Nabuco,[8] bear out this

---

clydes da Cunha in *Os Sertões* (*Rebellion in the Backlands*), that peasant rebellions such as that of the so-called "*Quebra-Quilos*" (Tough Guys) could not be attributed to purely political or purely religious causes.

[8] Joaquim Nabuco, who reappears a great deal in the course of this narrative, was a writer and a statesman from Recife and a leader of the abolitionist group during the final days of the monarchy. His last years until his death in 1910 were spent as Brazilian Ambassador to the United States. (Translator.)

conviction that Brazil in 1889 was not ready for a Republic that would weaken, rather than reinforce, the central or national authority of the chief of state and reduce that office to the administration of the provinces.

Evidently, only the external trappings of monarchy had become archaic to the Positivists—not the authoritarian form of government. Indeed, in rising to power this group tried, through Benjamin Constant and Demétrio Ribeiro,[9] to strengthen the authority of the executive and the effective power of the governing forces so that the cause of progress-within-order would not be lost as a result of uncoordinated and irresponsible statements or actions. At the time, none of these men seemed to have a clear, scientific, black and white idea of the distinction between substance and form in the political regime. But several disciples of Comte did participate in the republican Revolution in Brazil, not for the sake of absolute principles, but rather as revolutionaries moved by the spirit of authoritarianism and the feeling that they—rather than the deposed monarchists—represented the responsible force necessary to combat the rising tide of liberal individualism. The progress desired by Positivists like Demétrio Ribeiro falls under the heading of socially responsible authoritarianism, not that of a liberalism which, on the enticing pretext of being democratic, would only serve to encourage the rise of a government as socially irresponsible as that of the last years of the Empire.

This Empire, so deficient in both the form and substance of authority, was referred to as the "crowned Republic." The Emperor, with his often sterile liberalism and his pose of ultra-republican simplicity, gave credence to the sneer. Moreover, there was a fear of large-scale, purely material progress. This fear, though healthy to a certain point, suggests less an enlightened conservatism than an irrational or instinctive traditionalism, or even the reactionary hiding beneath the cloak of liberalism.

A Frenchman, Max Leclerc, who became known for his comments on the fall of the monarchy and the proclamation of the Brazilian Republic, wrote (in one of his articles from Rio de Janeiro between 1889 and 1890 published in the *Journal des Débats*)[1] that

---

[9] Demétrio Ribeiro was a republican Positivist from Rio Grande do Sul. He was Minister of Agriculture in the provisional government, but eventually joined the provincial opposition group headed by Júlio de Castilhos. (Translator.)

[1] Max Leclerc: *Cartas do Brasil*, translated from the French, with preface and

Dom Pedro II combined with "affability and simplicity in dress and manners a reluctance to take sides," to take actions which would make him in European eyes a "more paternal, liberal, and unprejudiced sovereign." Although he was skillful in unobtrusively imposing his will upon his ministers, "an instinctive lack of confidence in the younger element gave his policies, if not his ideas, a reactionary tinge." Thus Dom Pedro developed a "power of inertia" to oppose his ministers and advisers who called for civil marriage laws, and for a naturalization code. He had never taken a favorable view of European immigration on a large scale, fearing that "the Brazilian element would be submerged and that Brazilian customs would disappear or be altered."

From what Leclerc wrote of Pedro II and other Europeans observed at first hand, it would seem that the last Emperor of Brazil had a more liberal effect on Europe and the United States than he achieved locally or nationally. Brazil, as a Spaniard once pointed out, required a government which would conserve the punitive weight of the Luso-Catholic tradition, a government which knew how to cope with these paternalistic and burdensome attitudes and even to perform the more difficult task of turning them to advantage in effecting changes for the better. It developed, however, that it was difficult for Dom Pedro II to live the double life necessary for the role in which he cast himself, piously attending mass and making the sign of the Cross before crowds of Brazilians and, on other occasions, adopting a Voltairian pose for the Europeans. The upshot was that the European—and probably more authentic—side of his nature eventually triumphed over the anti-European and anti-progressive tendencies. Thus in the crises with the bishops and with the Army he behaved exactly like any republican liberal (even anti-clerical) politician, making no promises either to the Church, which was upholding the principle of legitimate authority over that of insubordination, or to the military, equally concerned in maintaining its dignity against the ultra-republican demagoguery of an irresponsible press tolerated by the liberals of the Empire and even by the Emperor himself.

---

notes, by Sérgio Milliet (São Paulo, 1942), p. 135. According to the Brazilian preface, this French writer reflected "the point of view of a good part of Europe, if not of the entire world," concerning the newly established Brazilian Republic. Part of this attitude showed a "lack of complete confidence in the word of Ruy Barbosa."

This Imperial conduct was political suicide, as the fifteenth of November clearly proved. Perhaps the Emperor regretted this in the final moments, but it was too late. He was already doomed by the poisons he had voluntarily consumed, not all of which were subtle and some crude in the extreme.

Years after the exile and death of Pedro II, his grandson, in a significant book, acknowledged that it was natural that the Imperial Army should have turned republican. Since his early manhood Dom Pedro had treated the Army casually. Between the Crown —the feminine element of the regime—and the Army—the masculine, protective element needed by that fragile institution—there had never developed the reciprocity necessary to constitute the political equivalent of a successful marriage. Had this rapport existed, it would perhaps have given the Brazilian Empire the psychological and sociological aspects of a monogamous association in the midst of republics nearly all promiscuous in their liaisons with military strong men, only one of whom, Porfírio Diaz of Mexico, seemed to have more inherent Imperial qualities than his contemporary Dom Pedro de Alcântara, descendant of kings and emperors.

Instead of trying to work with the military, Dom Pedro disdained the Armed Forces to the point of abandoning them to the fury of the demagogic press, which thirsted for royal blood. Not only Max Leclerc but many of his contemporaries, both national and foreign, referred to Dom Pedro's "misdirected liberalism," pointing out that the "pretext of a free press" allowed "no honor and no reputation to remain intact." And of one of the worst abuses of this unconscionable liberalism, Leclerc added: "The paid anonymous attacks accepted by the newspapers are the most certain source of political disaffection; the discipline of both Army and government officials is profoundly weakened thereby."[2]

Thus one of the most persistent criticisms of the Positivists against the Brazilian monarchy was that the Emperor, aging and ill, was lacking in "energy" and "spirit," in the Imperial spirit that Brazilian disciples of Comte wished to see replaced, not by that of parliamentary or democratic republicanism, but rather by that of a dictatorship. In its annual circular of 1888 the Brazilian Positivist Church, speaking of the so-called *"Lei Áurea,"*[3] decried the old

[2] Ibid., p. 42. Other Europeans who visited Brazil at the time were similarly scandalized by the exaggerated liberty of the press during the reign of Pedro II.

[3] The *Lei Áurea* was the act which emancipated the slaves in 1888. (Translator.)

Emperor's "political ineptitude" and his "natural lack of energy," [4] contrasting these with the firmness and purposefulness of Princess Isabel.

This was the logical attitude followed by Miguel Lemos and Raimundo Teixeira Mendes, two orthodox Positivists who spoke through the Brazilian Positivist Church. These two men were still burning from the strong reaction in Paris against Comte's successor, M. Lafitte—a sort of pope or high priest of the "Religion of Humanity." [5] While in France in 1880, Lemos had received the degree of "aspirant to the priesthood" and it was thus, duly consecrated and anointed, that he had returned to Brazil certain of being able to induce Brazilian society to accept a Positivist triumph in both politics and social customs. In his book *Resumo Histórico do Movimento Positivista no Brasil (Historical Résumé of the Positivist Movement in Brazil)*,[6] Lemos recalls that Comte himself had predicted the rapid success of his doctrines in Latin America, where there were "no powerful priests, no basic traditions, no powerful industrialism." Besides which, "the children of fervent idolators of the Virgin" should "respond with strongest sympathy" to a religion which would "establish the cult of the woman and proclaim the supremacy of love." Mariolatry was strongly evident in Brazil, where many women sought the maternal image of the Virgin as a refuge—and symbol of revolt—against the excessive paternalistic authoritarianism of the Brazilian family system. It was expressly because of this Mariology, according to the apostolic Lemos, that "Brazil, among all nations of Iberian origin, is best prepared for the triumph of the new doctrine." And there is no doubt that the republican mystique quickly assumed a messianic character through its identification with the concept of the Perfect Woman, saintly and suffering.

A good example of the sentimental vigor attained by this political

[4] *Circular Anual* (of the Brazilian Positivist Church) (Rio de Janeiro, 1888), p. 12.

[5] After the death of Auguste Comte in 1857, the Positivist movement split into two factions. The orthodox group, which upheld the so-called "Religion of Humanity," with its churches and its panoply of saints drawn from the "benefactors of mankind," was headed by Pierre Lafitte (1823–1903), whom Comte had named as his literary executor. The dissident faction, which rejected the "Religion of Humanity" as being incompatible with rational thought, was headed by Émile Littré. (Translator.)

[6] Miguel Lemos: *Resumo Histórico do Movimento Positivista no Brasil* (Rio de Janeiro, 1882), pp. 38–9.

mystique is found in the verses of the ardent propagandist and itinerant journalist Ricardo Guimarães, who collaborated in Recife with Martins Júnior, but who was assassinated before the triumph of the Republic. The verses are entitled "The Republic" and they appeared in the twentieth number (Novembr 30, 1887) of *Anti-Rebate, Semanário Abolicionista e Republicano (Counter-Alarm, an Abolitionist and Republican Seminary)*, published at that time in the Pernambucan capital of Recife under the "political collaboration" of Martins Júnior, Pardal Mallet, and Monteiro Filho.[7] The poem exalted the Republic in the image of the Blessed Virgin, "Mother-protector of peoples":

> . . . in her ruby lips
> The pure nectar of the heavens,
> Mother-protector of peoples,
> Beautiful daughter of God.
> Statue fashioned of bronze
> That repulsed Louis XI
> Embrace and kiss Saint-Just;
> Lady of seductive glance,
> In whose benevolent shadow
> Flourish the lily and the rose.

Further:

> In your maternal bosom
> Sleep those of great ideas
> The sublime Prometheus
> The immortal Briareus,
> Through your blond tresses
> The soft breezes
> Waft their grateful freshness;
> The birds sing you their threnodies
> As, smiling, you gather the peoples
> In the warmth of your comforting love.

Later, in a crescendo of mystical exaltation of the feminine image of the ideal Republic:

---

[7] Martins Júnior, Pardal Mallet, and Monteiro Filho were republican intellectuals who, during the early Republic, opposed the leadership of Floriano Peixoto. Martins Júnior was leader of a short-lived literary movement to encourage the writing of "scientific" poetry. Pardal Mallet was the publisher of the anti-Floriano newspaper *O Combate*. (Translator.)

> She—the constant victim
> Of hatred and perversion,
> Has for the sad—a smile,
> Has for the blind—a light.
> Ever grand, gracious, and good,
> She suffers, suffers but pardons
> The Judases, as did Jesus.
> She too was betrayed,
> She too was sold,
> She too has her Calvary, her Cross.

And finally, in the same tone of fervent mysticism:

> Let us in our hearts
> Build an altar to this goddess,
> With our gift of Reason
> Make secure her throne.
> When from the heights of mountains
> The guiding light sparkles
> On the pure spring water—
> May we in the public square
> Shout: Long live the Republic
> In the land of the Blessed Cross!

Verses such as these were not rare during the decade which preceeded the fifteenth of November. From them the belief of Miguel Lemos that the appeal to the Marian cult was highly effective for propaganda, both republican and Positivist, can indeed be confirmed.

In its first stage, the Positivists believed, this propaganda ought to be directed at the "liberal classes, whose conversion would necessarily attract popular acceptance of Positivism." In the liberal classes were to be found those Mariolators most likely to oppose forms of paternalism: the feudal despotism of the plantation lords, the ecclesiastical authoritarianism of the bishops and priests, the academic rigidity of the pre-Positivist doctors, all of which were so repugnant to the Positivists. In their place, they would subsitute a neo-fraternalism built around a new priesthood dedicated to "scientific" leadership and "scientific" solutions to the problem of government.

Positivist propaganda to this effect, intensified after 1880, had a considerable impact in Brazilian military circles. A good deal of this impact was intensified by the study of mathematics, as in the case of Benjamin Constant Botelho de Magalhães, a soldier who became a great devotee of the doctrine and who, as tutor and teacher, exercised a considerable influence upon the young people of his time.[8] But it is also true that the cult of the Virgin Mary—or of Woman —served some military figures as the impetus for casting themselves in the romantic role of manly protectors of a cause. The existence of such an attitude may be seen as a reaction to the Emperor's ill-concealed disdain of the military and to his policy of separating it as much as possible from the "feminine mystique" of the Crown.

Benjamin Constant, writing to his wife from Paraguay in 1867, significantly placed her "above God and country," [9] while in another letter he stated: "You are for me more, much more, than Clotilde de Vaux ever was for the wise and honored Augusto Comte." Here the cult of Woman is carried to the extreme, instilling in a wartime soldier the primary devotion one would expect him to feel for his nation's cause, for the monarchy, and the Crown. This is particularly curious when one considers that the enemy's passionate identification with the conception of "the Homeland" was also Marian in nature; for Francisco Solano López it was "the Nation";[1] and "*La Guaira*" for the intrepid Paraguayan peasants, who threw themselves against the Imperial soldiers with the same psychological incentive—a loving identification with a feminine cause in need of their masculine protection.

Years after the Paraguayan War, Benjamin Constant, in disseminating republican propaganda among his younger compatriots, attempted to transfer to this idealized Marian image—the Republic— a Positivist spirit that would outdo Comte himself in his dedication to a feminine cause. Perhaps his attempt was more suggestive of that of M. Laffitte, against whom Miguel Lemos and Raimundo Teixeira Mendes had rebelled, and who was himself rather feminine

[8] Benjamin Constant Botelho de Magalhães, generally referred to as Benjamin Constant, was a mathematician, teacher, and military engineer who eventually became Minister of War after the proclamation of the Republic. Named after the French political philosopher Benjamin Constant, Botelho de Magalhães was the leading propagandist for Positivism in his time. (Translator.)

[9] R. Teixeira Mendes: *Benjamin Constant* (Rio de Janeiro, 1892–4), pp. 19–21.

[1] Francisco Solano López was President of Paraguay from 1862 until his death at the battle of Cerro Corda on March 1, 1870. His death brought an end to the Paraguayan War, perhaps the bloodiest conflict ever fought in the New World; during its six years, the population of Paraguay was reduced by half. (Translator.)

in his complex and subtle personality. In a manner which reflected
no discredit on their moral stature, both Constant and Lafitte gave
evidence of that "feminine delicacy" which some critics have always found characteristic of the French and which Brazilian Fran-
cophobes identified, probably unjustly, with "excessive vanity, extraordinary pusillanimity, and an almost total lack of the dignity
necessary to the exercise of important functions." [2] Perhaps this attitude stemmed from Benjamin Constant's need for protection by
devoted disciples and republican co-religionaries rather than from
his own capacity to protect the changing nation by means of the
rough virility of the statesman. Or perhaps he thought of himself as
the intellectual, whose training had been more that of learned doctrinaire than practitioner of the so-called "manly science" of politics. It is even more likely that both Lafitte and Benjamin Constant
shared a breadth and depth of spirit which, while enhancing their
stature as intellectuals, prejudiced them as men of action in that it
made them averse to simplifications and to excessively sectarian
dogma. Thus we see that in the rift between the two Brazilian Positivist leaders and the supreme chief in Paris, the sympathies of Benjamin Constant were more with Lafitte than with the insurgents of
Rio, who eventually ended by repudiating the "Religion of Humanity."

The principal accusation against Lafitte on the part of Brazilian
insurgents was that he favored "a free interpretation of the work of
the master" Auguste Comte, thereby subordinating everything to
intellectual considerations and effecting a "monstrous" distortion
of Positivist doctrine. Lemos and Teixeira Mendes, for their part,
set themselves up as the propagators of the "regenerated doctrine,
without prejudice or passion . . ." [3] Almost evangelically, these
two orthodox Comtians proclaimed what they considered to be the
pure doctrine—the doctrine as left by Comte himself, in its integrity, irrevocable and not subject to revision.

It was precisely this literalism that caused the British Positivist
Harrison to criticize his two Brazilian co-religionists and to assert
that it was not justified either by the letter or the spirit of Comte;
on the contrary, it reminded him more of the biblical liberalism of
certain Protestants. To raise the writings of Auguste Comte to the
level of Holy Scripture dictated by inspiration, or to treat all the

[2] Lemos: op. cit. Also see Rodrigues: op. cit., p. 120.
[3] Lemos: op. cit., pp. 79–147. Also Rodrigues: op. cit., p. 119.

strictures and utopias of political Positivism as absolute prescriptions (Harrison claimed) is little more than rigid Protestantism. Such puerile fanaticism would reduce Positivism to "a sterile repetition of forms, a Pharasaic list of negations." [4]

Among those who had a part in the founding of the Brazilian Republic, neither Benjamin Constant, nor Martins Júnior, nor Pereira Barreto,[5] nor any of the others among the truly scientific politicians allowed themselves to fall in with this type of extremism, even though they were nearly all men handicapped by "feminine delicacy" in their intellectual approach to the making or influencing of political policy. Although their intellectualism kept them from some of the cruder aspects of political activity, it had considerable moral impact on the public life of the times. Benjamin Constant and Martins, along with Joaquim Nabuco and the Baron do Rio Branco, believed that the Army should follow the Positivist line in setting itself up as a nonpartisan, apolitical trustee of the Crown in all factional struggles; while the more sectarian Positivists wished to make the Army into an organ of party doctrine.

This was the clear-cut but difficult situation at the crucial point of Floriano Peixoto's still-infant Republic. Peixoto was of temperament exactly opposed to that of Benjamin Constant or Martins Júnior, a man more instinctive than theoretical, who had absorbed just enough Positivist doctrine to justify the rude excesses of his dictatorial actions in the almost messianic terms with which the Comtian system was then regarded by many members of the Brazilian élite. Incapable of allowing such subtleties as intellectualism or "feminine delicacy" to get in the way of direct action, this "regenerator and protector" of the Republic was the hard, rugged, strongly masculine leader the Brazilian Positivist Church considered ideal for that Republic on whose banner they had succeeded in inscribing their own orthodox motto.

Roughly suppressing all attempts to bring about a restoration of the monarchy, Floriano became the "consolidator of the Republic" in terms of a ruling Brazilian principle established by the Empire: that of national order inseparable from the Brazilian mystique of unity. In this sense the Floriano government represented a change of form rather than a change of policy, and it was thus that numer-

---

[4] Rodrigues: op. cit., p. 119.

[5] Luís Pereira Barreto, like Benjamin Constant and Martins Júnior, was a leading Positivist intellectual of the period. (Translator.)

ous supporters of the old regime were willing to accommodate the new Republic. Certainly it was the sincere desire of numerous barons, viscounts, and counselors of the old Empire—as many of them protested in letters to the newspapers—to accept the pronouncement of the fifteenth of November in the hope that the new regime would solidify and, "like the former," guarantee the virtues of the old order. The Viscount do Bom Conselho, for example, hastened to direct a letter to the Minister of the Interior of the provisional government, assuring the new government of his "maximum support and obedience" and wishing that "gentle winds" would waft the exiled royal family to its new destiny and, above all, that the federal government would be successful "in its important task of preserving internal and external order and in ever strengthening the bonds of brotherhood among all Brazilians." [6]

The Viscount do Abrantes also lost no time in expressing his sentiments in the press, declaring to his "friends and fellow citizens" that "in the face of the political events which have just brought about changes in the country's form of government without creating either victors or defeated" he considered it his duty, "after having consulted with my friends in the state of Minas Gerais," to urge everyone to "accept the consequences of those events" and to lend their "open support to the provisional government and especially to the governor designated for that state." A designation that Arantes considered a "happy one," convinced as he was that the nominee could and would of necessity perform a "very good service, guaranteeing the peace and tranquility of the state and striving for its continued progress and prosperity." [7]

Another declaration by a former member of the nobility was that of the Count of Araruama, which appeared on November 19, shortly after the proclamation of the Republic. Directed especially to his friends of the municipalities of Macaé and Barra de São João in the former province of Rio de Janeiro, the letter avowed, "with all the frankness and loyalty" with which he had always spoken, his resolution and that of his family and friends to "support the provisional government." "In fact," added the good Count, "after the notorious and grave events, following the retirement of the Imperial family, I am convinced that the greatest service I can

---

[6] M. E. de Campos Pôrto: *Apontamentos para a História da República dos Estados Unidos do Brasil* (Rio de Janeiro, 1890), p. 838.

[7] Ibid., p. 839.

do for my country is to aid the provisional government in the maintenance of public order and tranquility, the only guarantee of liberty." "The final decision as to the form of government," he continued, "will be in the hands of the Constitutional Assembly, which will soon convene in the name of the sovereign people. In the meantime, it is in the country's best interests that we refrain from hindering the government; rather, we should all come to its support with a view to establishing the general good of all." His appeal was made to "all true patriots and lovers of order, without distinction as to political affiliation."

Counselor[8] Antônio Prado—"Citizen" Antônio Prado, as he styled himself—was another who appeared promptly in the press—the *Correio Paulistano* of São Paulo—to give a clear definition of his attitude: "In all conscience and in the light of the march of events, a monarchical restoration through counterrevolution being impossible" and, on the other hand, the "existence of a public power being indispensable to the maintenance of order and of civil and political rights," it is imperative to "recognize the necessity of accepting the present state of things as they are, without questioning their origin." [9]

In addition, in reply to an inquiry from his friend Almeida Nogueira (editor of the *Correio Paulistano*) as to how Brazilians should proceed in the present political situation, the former senator Manuel Antônio Duarte de Azevedo—another illustrious figure of the Imperial period—held that "in view of the definitely accomplished changes in our basic situation, it would be seriously inappropriate to promote a restoration of the monarchy in Brazil" and Brazilians should, "in the interests of patriotism, accept the accomplished facts. . . ." He pointed out, moreover, that at the moment of bidding farewell to his loyal friends, the old and distinguished ex-Emperor Pedro II had said resolutely, but not without emotion, that "What's done is done; it is now up to the Brazilians to make every effort to draw up a good Constitution." [1]

Família Spirita, the spiritualist organization of São Paulo,[2] also

[8] The Brazilian title of *Conselheiro* was an honorific one granted for outstanding service to the country. It was not inherited. Theoretically—and often in fact—holders of this title served as members of the Emperor's advisory council. (Translator.)

[9] Ibid., p. 849.

[1] *Correio Paulistano* (Nov.–Dec., 1889).

[2] Spiritualism of the white Protestant variety has been extant in Brazil for well

pledged its allegiance to the Republic, stating its conviction that, while it was the "enlightened landscape of the empire of the spirit" that it primarily desired, it recognized the need for a "profane Republic, proceeding correctly along the paths of justice, order, and progress." [3] Acknowledging that the nation had changed its government "in order to maintain the spirit of order," it judged that it should not permit the existence of newspapers which advanced "anachronistic ideas," that is, ideas of monarchy. Nevertheless, it did not agree with the "provisional flag raised by the Republic," because this flag did not respect "the glorious traditions of the nation, with its legendary green and gold insignia, defended heroically by the Army and the Navy in sanguinary engagements in order to maintain the honor of the nation." Even the Brazilian spiritualists, then, were concerned with the preservation of order and national integrity incumbent upon a "profane Republic"; responsibility for progress of the spirits could presumably be left to the empire of the occult.

We have seen that the way in which Brazilians accepted and supported the Republic had appeared to Mr. Knight a manifestation of "oriental apathy." But in truth, the readiness with which some of the most clearheaded conservatives or dedicated imperialists adapted the idea of a new political regime to their own moral system of basic Brazilian values—namely, a systematic national order encompassing stability and integrity as well as progress—reveals on their part less "oriental apathy" than the desire and ability to be realistic; a Britannic virtue almost frighteningly developed in the American tropics by those pliant Brazilian conservatives well aware of the needs of the future. It is understandable that, to a Spaniard or a Russian, Brazilian behavior might have seemed apathetic or pusillanimous; but it should not have appeared so to an Englishman. Mr. Knight was quite untypically British in noting with disgust that the

---

over a century. Its followers have been increasing in recent years and probably now number well over 1 million, although there is considerable diversity in the types of spiritualism practiced, from séances, table rappings, and extrasensory perception to rituals involving demons and spirits closely akin to African or American Indian religions. Brazilians group these divergencies under the headings of "higher" or "lower" spiritualism. Spiritualists of all levels, however, are associated with a central federation which maintains places of worship in larger cities. For most devotees, spiritualism is a religion in itself, but some of course remain nominally Catholic on the grounds that "one can never tell." (Translator.)

[3] Campos Pôrto: op. cit., p. 876.

transformation of Brazil from a monarchy into a Republic took place without a single fatality.

To some Brazilians, however, this sense of accommodation was not sufficiently evident, even after the death of Pedro II, to make them admit that the Republic was either necessary or inevitable. Anglicized statesmen like Ruy Barbosa[4] or Joaquim Nabuco saw the Empire as eventually adapting itself to the challenge of the future and becoming a modern monarchical system—decentralized, Americanized, federal, but still a monarchy. More widely separated from the influence of the Church and the propertied than had been the monarchy of Pedro II, it could become, they hoped, more closely identified with the Armed Forces and with the civilian middle class.

In one of his memorable articles against the policies of the Viscount of Ouro Prêto,[5] Ruy Barbosa was particularly critical of the latter's anti-federalism, of his placing the Crown against the federal cause, and of isolating the Emperor from the so-called "armed classes" by replacing many former Army functions with elements from the National Guard. This was a tremendous error, said Ruy, because in a country like Brazil the Armed Forces served as a stabilizing force against "disorders, exaggeration, and utopianism." This criticism of the moderate policies of Ouro Prêto was made, not as an anti-monarchist, but rather as a simple federalist and enemy of the messianic tendencies Ruy Barbosa perceived in the more radical republicans.

In a society such as that of Brazil, where there was a lack of "points of resistance," Ruy continued, the Armed Forces were "the great palladium of peace, of liberty, and of the Constitution." How then could the apparent champions of monarchism replace this traditionally national body, these nonpartisan defenders of "institutions and order" with a "guard" entitled national but really a partisan militia whose function it was to guard the royal family "against the nation"?[6] How could this militia be given "excellent arms superior to those of the line forces"? How could one justify its being

[4] Ruy Barbosa, one of the great Brazilians of all time, was a Bahian statesman and orator who, though no radical, became a leading republican through conviction that the Empire had outlived its time. His name will reoccur frequently. (Translator.)

[5] Ouro Prêto was the last Prime Minister of the Brazilian Empire. (Translator.)

[6] Article: "O Plano contra a Pátria" from the newspaper *Diário de Notícias*, in Campos Pôrto: op. cit., p. xxv.

made into a sort of super-army? If we can't have confidence in the
Army, he went on, then we can't have confidence in the nation
itself.

In taking this stand, however, Ruy was perhaps overlooking the
fact that the situation the Viscount of Ouro Prêto was attempting
to correct by reorganizing that militia had been developing for
years and stemmed from the patent, systematic disdain of Pedro II
for the Armed Forces and the military leaders. Under the shadow
of this disdain, a considerable portion of the Armed Forces had
increasingly allowed itself to be seduced by republican-Positivist
ideologies. Consequently, it had become questionable whether the
Army and Navy were any longer willing to give the support necessary to the survival of the Crown. Were not these institutions developing into a national force superior to that of the monarchy itself? And if so, was not the Viscount of Ouro Prêto acting wisely,
from a literally conservative and monarchist point of view, in organizing the National Guard into a body which could defend the
Crown in the critical days that followed the precipitate abolition of
slavery on May 13, 1888? And since this militia was drawn from
the working class, was it not, consequently, quite as national—or
even more national—than if it had been formed solely from the
middle class?

From the viewpoint of the conservative elements, whose weakness Ruy Barbosa had lamented, the abolition of slavery was a be-
trayal of the agrarian interests. True, these interests were disorganized and without a political spokesman; the planters and sugar
barons had to some degree lost their political power to their college-
trained sons-in-law, as was the case with João Alfredo and the
Baron of Goiana.[7] But even so, they still represented a substantial
group whose direct—or indirect—support of the republican cause
could not help but represent a loss of stability on the part of the
Crown. Furthermore, this loss of stability was not merely regional
but nationwide, since at the end of the nineteenth century the
Brazilian agrarian and pastoral system extended from the north
to the south, from the coast to the interior, as a powerful civilizing,
though feudal, presence in the vast tropical landscape.

The reaction of important Brazilian newspapers, including those
connected most directly with conservative agrarian interests, to the

---

[7] João Alfredo (Correia de Oliveira) was Prime Minister during the last years
of the Republic. He was the Baron of Goiana's son-in-law. (Translator.)

Revolution of November 15 is as significant as that of the nobles already cited. The Rio de Janeiro *Gazeta da Tarde* noted in an editorial of November 16: "One could say that the new form of government was accepted almost unanimously, for in the last years of the monarchy even the most dedicated royalists clearly placed the nation above all other considerations." This acceptance was shared, let me emphasize once more, not only by military men cool to the monarchical cause and by staunch Catholics disaffected by the continued royal oppression of the bishops, but also by the great plantation lords who felt betrayed by the sudden abolition of slave labor. It was natural that, for all these solidly conservative groups, the monarchist cause had crumbled into insignificance and no longer aroused in them the slightest feeling of solidarity. Although disinclined after November 15 to go about shouting "Down with the Empire; long live the Republic!" they nevertheless concurred with the attitude of newspapers such as the *Gazeta da Tarde* in saluting the nation itself, and, along with their *vivas* for Brazil and the fatherland, included a few discreet cheers for "liberty" and "democracy." In good conservative manner, the *Gazeta da Tarde* expressed the wish that the new regime would "lead the nation toward its great destiny" and that the victors would legitimize their assumption of power with the seal of moderation, "preventing any violence whatever toward the vanquished." Disenchantment with the monarchy did not succeed in making all of the disenchanted into republicans or even into willing fellow travelers; but nearly all, if not willing to support, were at least able to accept the new order.

This was also the attitude of the newspaper *Novidades*, which on November 15 noted that the populace of the capital had been surprised that morning by "the news of events which went beyond all prediction." Attempting to speak "in the name of the nation and in the national interest," *Novidades* emphasized the necessity of "preserving this grand entity called Brazil along with all the foreign and national interests it represents." It was through the cooperation of "all living forces" that Brazil would "decide our destiny" and the nation's future. All of these forces should become, above everything, "defenders of the social order." The new political situation could have no other bases than those of "order, liberty, and national integrity." May we, above all other interests, share "the ideal of a strong, united, well-directed land," which will "maintain its stature as a great nation." The military, which had taken part in the political change, was and should remain "our principal bulwark." This institution well knew how to "resist all forms of excess and maintain the purity of the national Revolution" which, thanks to its "firmness" it had brought about "without bloodshed" and (*nota bene*) "without attacking the industrial interests." Instead of shouting "Down with the Empire; long live the Republic!" this conservative Rio journal also ended its editorial with an all-but apolitical sentiment: "Order and liberty! This is our obligation!"

Even the virtually republican *O Dia* couldn't bring itself to the point of damning the Empire and cheering the Republic. In its editorial of November 15, it merely stated that the death of the Empire would cause few regrets. This statement, however, would probably have been contested by many Brazilians, if not for the regime itself, at least for the deposed Emperor, the "Old Man" whom everyone, without the slightest degree of animosity, had for so long ridiculed as "Pedro Banana."

There had been general discontent within the country since the Paraguayan War, but not to the extent of causing hatred or rancor. As early as November 15, 1885, the Rio *Vanguarda*, in a serious editorial, had seen Brazil as "throwing itself into the abyss of revolution . . . working toward political demoralization, religious indifference and charlatanism in public education." Made precisely four years before the Revolution, this statement reflects a generalized social rather than a specifically political discontent and is certainly not directed at either the Emperor or the Empire in particular.

The story of the fifteenth of November that appeared in Ruy Barbosa's *Diário de Notícias* on the day following the coup is also noteworthy: "The Army and the Navy, invoking the rights granted them by the Imperial government, yesterday deposed the [entire] Cabinet, with the general assent of the people of the city." And, noting a not insignificant detail of this "civic movement of national character, which will establish the future of the nation on a firmly American basis": "Called yesterday afternoon by Marshal Manuel Deodoro da Fonseca and invited to collaborate with the new government as Minister of the Treasury, the editor-in-chief of this journal, Sr. Ruy Barbosa, considered himself obliged not to refuse his services in a situation where the interests of social order and the public good of his country require the support and self-sacrifice [of all true Brazilians]." Not a word of support for the Republic, merely the statement that the new government "proposes to inaugurate the federal Republic" and to endeavor at the same time to "guarantee property rights and the national credit" in the hands of those functionaries who "continue to serve the nation well" and to effect "the absolute and implacable repression of disorder."

From this, and from the reactions of other journals on November 15 and 16, one can sense the largely conservative attitude of the Brazilian press, even those papers which had most incisively attacked the Ouro Prêto government. Their tendency was to present the event in moderate terms, to soften the shock to nationals and foreigners alike of so complete and unexpected a political change. Ruy Barbosa's *Diário de Notícias* had significantly stressed the fact that the change would "establish the nation on an Amerian basis," implying that the old regime had had ties to Europe which had now been destroyed. The *Diário de Notícias* also pointed out the national aspects of the Revolution: the necessity of Brazilian progress as an American nation, the need for the maintenance of social order, including the organization of the Brazilian economy and the sustaining of the national credit. It was thus a Revolution essentially and paradoxically conservative.

Not only the *Diário de Notícias*, but also *Novidades* and other papers give the impression that it had been the arbitrary creation of the Black Guard that had broken the Brazilian rule of order; that this arbitrary action on the part of the monarchy had been directed against the regular Army which, according to the conservative *Diário de Commercio* (Rio de Janeiro) of November 16, had developed into "the sole corrective against the arbitrary use of executive power." The truth is, this article continues, that "in proportion to the weakening of civic elements in our society, the military class has increased in education, public spirit, and civic courage." It further expressed the hope that the new political situation would not be taken over by partisan politicians but rather by the nonpartisan military. "The civilian element was ineffectual and useless and emerged only after the coup had been realized, probably with the view to taking over the official positions. It is most important that the military should be considered as the only force presently able to determine the success or failure of the Revolution." The Armed Forces should take the initiative in directing themselves to competent representatives of the people, the *Diário de Commercio* concluded, in order to determine the form of government to be adopted to render the Revolution of November 15 the legal and effective means of guaranteeing the rights of all citizens.

As a commercial organ, the *Diário* of November 16 called upon the new government to calm the immensely disturbed business world. These disturbances will be studied in a subsequent chapter. Sufficient to note here that in 1889 there were Brazilians who felt that the national course to be followed assiduously by the revolutionary government should be marked out not so much in terms of Spanish-American progress as of an assured future for the financial interests.

The movement of November 15 was thus closely linked to a concept of the future, but rarely in the history of the Brazilian nation do we find so many diversified interpretations of that future, some hypothetical, some sociologically dangerous. Yet, while the sudden republican triumph confronted Brazilians with the future, it also caused them to examine the little-explored facts of their past. One problem of this two-way quest was the survival (or no) of the monarchy, a form of government republican demagogues and ideologists had scorned as being shamefully archaic. The notion that this anachronistic monarchy was placing Brazil in a bad position among the progressive nations of America was fully propagated in discourses and pamphlets favorable to the new regime. But such attacks did not pass without provoking a counterblast, which represented the first vigorous attempt to re-evaluate the specifically Brazilian characteristics of the monarchy and of the colonial days. Such writings on the Brazilian experience generally concluded on the note that the nation, temporarily republican, would eventually seek its future in a reversion to monarchy. Of these apologists for the monarchical past, none was more provocative, from the sociological point of view, than Eduardo Prado of São Paulo, whose series of articles written after the proclamation of the Republic combine the talents of an admirable sociologist-statesman with the remarkable erudition of a social historian.

In reinterpreting the Brazilian past, Eduardo Prado was one of the first to point out the importance of the Luso-Catholic influence in tropical America. In a polemic exchange with the Positivist Luís Pereira Barreto, he stated that it "redounded to the glory of our race that we were able to adapt ourselves, though not without struggle and suffering, to the natural conditions with which destiny has surrounded us. . . . Of all the civilized groups in the tropical zone, we can state without boasting that we are the most prosperous." [8] And, "this triumph was due to the efforts of an immigrant race"—the Portuguese—whom his learned Positivist opponent had characterized as "harrowed and drugged by Catholicism." [9] This triumph had come about in large part through the action of Catholic kings in collaboration with those religious elements—among others, the Jesuits—denounced by the Positivist Barreto as being sterile and insignificant.

The writings of Eduardo Prado exalting and calling for greater recognition of the work of this religious element are among the most vigorous ever written in the Portuguese language. His lecture on "Catholicism, the Company of Jesus, and the Colonization of the New World" evoked the admiration of Ruy Barbosa himself, who wrote to a mutual friend requesting that he congratulate the lecturer for a work he found notable for its "majesty, depth, breadth, and vigor." [1]

[8] Eduardo Prado: "O Dr. Barreto e a Ciência," a polemic article against Pereira Barreto published in the journal *Commercio de São Paulo* (1901). Found in *Coletâneas* (São Paulo, 1906), IV, 169–70.

[9] Ibid., p. 178.

[1] In not sending these congratulations over his own signature, it is possible that Ruy Barbosa was reacting to another series of Prado's criticisms of the Brazilian republican regime, as well as to his memorable observations on the period of the monarchy, published in the *Revista de Portugal* under the pseudonym "Frederico de S." In these articles, Prado had more than once referred unfavorably to Ruy Barbosa, calling him "the garrulous Ruy Barbosa" and accusing him of a lack of scruples in accepting presents from certain persons he favored for the post of Minister of State. The "presents" concerned were no simple bust or statue, portrait or medal, but "nothing less than a large and beautiful palace in the picturesque quarter of Laranjeiras" (Eduardo Prado: "Práticas e Teorias da Ditadura Republicana no Brasil," *Revista de Portugal* [Oporto, 1890], III, 9).

To Eduardo Prado this gift was a scandal; the memory of the passing of Ruy Barbosa into the republican camp, he stated, would be forever marked "by the stones of the palace he had gained while administering the public funds." And, in a burst of demagogic bad taste unworthy of his intelligence, Prado speculated that "perhaps some day popular indignation [would] destroy this house of ignominy."

The truth is that Ruy Barbosa had not received the house as a present. As Professor Luís Viana Filho explains in his life of Ruy Barbosa (*A Vida de Ruy Barbosa* [São Paulo, 1941], p. 174), Ruy had acquired it through two mortgage loans covering the purchase price. While Professor Viana admits that in the speed with which this deal was made Ruy was guilty of "serious imprudence"—and perhaps even worse—the transaction was not the crude open scandal denounced by Eduardo Prado and mirrored in the current sentiments of Brazilian people, who saw Ruy Barbosa as an unscrupulous man suddenly enriched through public office.

In his apologies for the monarchy and for Luso-Catholic deeds, Prado did not always unleash his political passions against the other side. His still-famous book *A Ilusão Americana* was, of course, marked by an exaggerated anti-republicanism and Yankeephobia. Still, he was not lacking in historical and sociological perspective in criticizing Brazilian Pan-Americanists who ingenuously saw the new Republic integrating itself, as if by magic, in a continental brotherhood of nations similar to those established by governments of Anglo-Saxon origin. In American relationships with the majority of these republics, which had adopted a caricature of the United States example, only the naïve failed to perceive the disdain of the strong for the weak, the scorn of an orderly people for a set of rowdies who, by mere accident, happened to be their neighbors. And only those ignorant of the psychology of the United States and of the history of its relations with Latin America could be unaware of its relative esteem for Brazil—in spite of its mixture of races—in contrast to the disdain exhibited for nearly all other Latin-American countries. This relative esteem was based upon the consideration that Imperial Brazil represented a form of government favorable to unity and stability and that the Luso-American Empire, through the involvement of its aristocracy in the public service, had managed to preserve a European sense of dignity and respectability in its political behavior. Such values were revered by Americans; their own republic was in some respects an elective monarchy created on something between an Imperial and a federal pattern. Americans were also sensitive to the mystique of aristocratic titles, even when these titles were not carried by people of Aryan origin. Thus Thomas Ewbank, visiting Rio de Janeiro in the days of Pedro II, had observed that in spite of being a tropical country, in which many of the first families had an admixture of Negro blood, the Brazilian Empire ranked next to France among the Latin nations in its achievement of progress. Understanding that the tropical situation of Brazil obliged it to develop its own particular system of civilization, he wrote ". . . it is for them to determine how far science and the arts within the tropics can compete with their progress in the temperate zones." [2] This was a tremendous task, he added, and to confront it the nation was retaining its monarchical form of government and its aristocratic society, while developing an ethnic democracy.

[2] Thomas Ewbank: *Life in Brazil or the Land of the Cocoa and the Palm* (London, 1856), p. 436.

In spite of being an Anglo-American, Ewbank significantly avoided the simplicism of Webb and others of his compatriots and was clearly able to understand the Brazilian paradox in which a democratic form of government, an aristocratic society, and an ethnic equality formed a unique combination of elements of tremendous promise and importance to the future of Brazil's modern civilization—a future which promised to attain the high cultural level found in the most civilized nations of the temperate zone.

It was precisely because of the Brazilian capacity to stand out, at least among the tropical countries of the New World, that Eduardo Prado was convinced, through his study of the Luso-American past, that "of all the tropical transplantations of European races and civilizations, that of the Portuguese in Brazil has had the most complete, comprehensive, and lasting success. We enjoy advantages over our Spanish-American neighbors who, in transforming themselves into many nations, have fragmented the common origin which led them through their territorial conquests in the American tropics." [3]

To some students of Brazilian society, this was exactly what the country had done in separating itself politically from Portugal; in continuing the monarchy it had had the clear advantage of preserving a social form with all the elements of European race and civilization and, simultaneously, under the influence of tropical America, of developing a new race and a new civilization. It was the monarchy which had prevented—and the Republic which favored—the romantic and somewhat anarchic republican experimentation that had so fragmented Spanish America. In his apologies for the monarchy, Eduardo Prado indicated that the Republic had ceased to be the sociological continuation of Imperial unity and that it had rather tended to favor an open conflict between order and progress, which had been contained during the Empire by the almost exclusive maintenance of the former at the expense of the latter. Since declaring its independence in 1822, Brazil, following the timely warnings of José Bonifácio,[4] had continued the form of govern-

[3] Eduardo Prado: "Práticas e Teorias . . . , III, 74–120.

[4] José Bonifácio de Andrada, sometimes referred to as "the Benjamin Franklin of Brazil," was a native of São Paulo and former professor at the University of Coímbra. He was perhaps the principal political brain behind Dom Pedro I's decision to declare independence, and as Dom Pedro's chief minister played a most important role in Brazilian affairs both before and after independence. Later, during the regency, José Bonifácio acted as political tutor to the young Dom Pedro II. His brothers, Antônio Carlos de Andrada and Martim Francisco de Andrada, were

ment which not only represented order but which—in a way unique in South America, except perhaps for the Paraguay of Francia and the first López—had developed a socio-political mystique of territorial unity in a land extending from the Amazon to the Río de la Plata.

It is clear from the newspaper accounts of the first years of Brazilian independence that the monarchical regime was regarded by most journalists as being the most suitable for the future of the country; but the colonial past was not despised, except by a few extreme nationalists.

On July 30, 1830, *O Cruzeiro*, a "political, literary, and mercantile journal," published a long article on the question of the best form of government. It adopted the contradictory line of viewing the current situation as "one of reform of former monarchical abuses without the necessity of destroying or impeding the privileges of royalty," and, at the same time, without denying the rights of the royal subjects. The regime had distinguished itself by its moderation, and was consequently the best available for the well-being of Brazil and for the "development of its future prosperity" within the pattern of royal order and political and social progress, a pattern no country of Spanish America had been able to realize in many years of terrible—often sanguinary—upheaval.

Such thoughts also occurred to Eduardo Prado sixty years later. In his essay "Theory and Practices of Republican Dictatorship," published in the *Revista de Portugal* in 1890, Prado expressed the fear that the Republic would bring to Brazil the dangerous *espanholismo* of the South American republics. Not without reason, he showed that the Republic of 1889 had already introduced a few of these *espanholismos* into Brazil in creating the title of "*Generalíssimo*," and in employing the technique of the *pronunciamento*, or military promotions "made by acclamation." These innovations Prado attributed to Quintino Bocayuva, "that admirer of Argentine and Guatamalan civilization." But he also suspected the hand of Benjamin Constant, who is reported to have told General Deodoro that "the Brazilian monarchy was an obstacle to the union of the American peoples," an opinion Prado shows to have been unsound by reviewing the amicable relationships of Brazil with the Spanish

also highly important political figures during the early years of Brazilian independence. (Translator.)

republics and with the United States. Furthermore, Prado cites Joaquim Nabuco's remark that, paradoxically, the Brazilian Empire was the only true "Republic" in the sense of having continued the right of the large majority of its citizens to influence the direction of government affairs. Most of the so-called "republics" were spurious; as one-man governments, they were monarchies in the worst sense of the word. For instance, wasn't Rosas, a type of despot more Asian than European, "inimical to Western civilization"? And weren't Sant'Anna, Guzmán Blanco, Daza, Melgarejo, and Pierola of the same stripe? Or the picturesque Santos of Uruguay, who had indulged in the oriental luxury of owning "a parasol encrusted with diamonds"? Alongside these, Prado continued, Pedro II made a striking contrast, in the lack of Imperial majesty in his dress and actions. It was in the spirit of this asceticism, more republican than the republicans, that he had agreed suicidally to the action of the fifteenth of November.

Various foreign observers pointed out Prado's excessive simplification of the case. However, none better stressed the importance of this Imperial suicide motif than the Portuguese writer Ramalho Ortigão, in his almost sociological analysis of "The Social Aspects of the Brazilian Revolution." [5] Ortigão was astonished at the surroundings in which the Imperial family lived, in the palace of São Cristóvão, with its sad air of a "poor little convent," its plain, undecorated staircase, its rooms "without carpets, without flowers, without statues," adorned only by furniture "uncharacteristically modern in mode." In this ascetic palace, the Emperor lived the arid life of a bureaucrat. He didn't even have a military staff; he was repelled by martial airs, and the "sound of sabers" made him uncomfortable. Even the Empress was not surrounded by well-dressed and well-coiffeured baronesses and viscountesses. There was no longer a Baroness of Estrêla to set herself up as a model for her time and social position (the Baroness was self-exiled in Paris). Pedro II was as suspicious of excessively elegant baronesses as he was of excessively progressive barons like Mauá.[6] This aversion to

[5] Ramalho Ortigão: "O Quadro Social da Revolução Brasileira," *Revista de Portugal* (Oporto, 1890), II, 79–102.

[6] Irineu Evangelista de Sousa, Baron (later Viscount) of Mauá (1813–1899), is often spoken of as the Brazilian J. P. Morgan. A native of Rio Grande do Sul, Mauá, through his powerful banking organization, was the leading force behind the development of Brazilian transportation systems. He built the Rio-Petrópolis railway and the famous Rio de Janeiro streetcar system. A public square and one

splendor and to all the trappings of monarchy naturally communicated itself to the diplomatic corps, which adopted the practice of
going to the royal receptions by streetcar, thus avoiding the trials
of riding in a carriage over bumpy roads. En route to this plain and
dismal palace, the diplomats wore prosaic linen dusters and simple
derby hats; their carriages, bearing only their diplomatic hats and
other finery, were sent on ahead, and their owners made the necessary changes of dress at the palace itself.

At Petrópolis, it was the same story. Amid "the lively colors of
the countryside," the straw hats, fans, and white parasols, His
Majesty, when he appeared at all, was an austere black blot on the
scene. Dressed in a frock coat and high hat at eight in the morning,
he carried under his arm a plain umbrella testifying to the philo-
sopher-Emperor's contempt for the military sword he had the right
to wear. With this attitude, it was only natural that Dom Pedro also
considered the annual opening of Parliament on January 2 a sort of
burlesque. Obliged to carry a scepter and to wear the crown and
the famous cape adorned with parrot feathers, the Emperor did his
duty in the manner of one forced against his will to dress for a
masquerade. It was part of the liturgy of monarchy, classical as
well as modern, but it held no interest whatever to a spirit so puri-
tanically austere and philosophically middle class as that of Pedro II.

Thus Pedro II was the very reverse of the chief of state demanded in the circumstances. What was needed, wrote Ortigão,
was "a youthful King, not in age but in temperament, a person in
whom the immaturity of judgment and impetuosity of action characteristic of the New World might have joined effectively with the
European sense of discipline and the dignity of command"; one
who could have been "a bulwark of order and an agent of progress, as well as an effective influence on future civilization." Ortigão
felt, however, that although Pedro II was not a martial ruler, his
government could have led to the order and progress of Brazil had
he only developed the support of a "disciplined, brilliant, well-
trained Army," one "capable of serving as an example to the nation
in its physical perfection, its strength, and its skill, a practical demonstration of discipline and respect." [7]

If there was any deficiency which stood out during the reign of
Pedro II, it was the lack of the type of education for which Ortigão

---

of the principal railway stations in Rio de Janeiro were named in his honor.
(Translator.)

[7] Ortigão: op. cit., p. 96.

was a spokesman in Portugal. Efforts toward the complete education of young people, with attention given to physical as well as intellectual training, and in which disciplined practical knowledge was superimposed upon the mere development of memory, of oratorical skill, and of the powers of abstraction, were almost totally lacking under the rule of Pedro II. His chief pleasure was to attend the elegant competitions for teaching positions in the Imperial high schools and universities, applauding demonstrations of erudition, of memory, and of facile oratory.

"An old and ailing emperor cannot maintain the complete cohesion of a tropical or semi-tropical country almost as vast as Europe, having only ten million inhabitants and struggling with the problems of a most deficient system of communication," said *The Times* (London), which devoted its November 21, 1889, issue to a discussion of the Brazilian situation, though it neglected to observe that the recently deposed Emperor, in his horror of the active life, of military matters, and of "morbid" physical exercise, had been old since adolescence. In further editorials the great English paper pointed out, with characteristic British honesty and a rare journalistic humility, that to evaluate the future of the new Republic with any degree of confidence, one would need a "minute knowledge of all the circumstances and conditions" behind the transformation of Brazil from monarchy to Republic, a knowledge "which no one possesses here and few possess in Brazil." The only information made available to Europe by the provisional government had been merely "the superfluous telegrams so easily expedited by the Treasury Minister," the exuberant (even in telegrams) Counselor Ruy Barbosa.

At much the same date as the *Times* editorial, another English journalist, a Mr. Cornely, wrote a sententious article on the Brazilian situation, reaching conclusions far more drastic than those of the more experienced paper. Mr. Cornely was rather cruel to Pedro II. Why, he asked, did the Emperor have to spend so much time in Europe? Wasn't he needed in Brazil? (This was unjust, for Pedro actually made very few trips to Europe.)

Mr. Cornely's criticism came into the category of those that considered the dethroned Emperor to have qualities excellent in a private citizen but unsuitable in a ruling monarch.[8] A chief of state in a monarchical regime is the ship's pilot, said Mr. Cornely, and

[8] The same point of view was expressed, more directly, by Ortigão and, indirectly, by Eça de Queiroz in "A Ultima Carta da Fra Mendes."

ought to pass his days and nights at the helm. Or, to change the metaphor, he is a soldier, and as a soldier should never abandon the crown and sword.

"His legs were not made to rest in the velvet of some institutional chair, but rather to be adjusted vigorously to the saddle of a battle steed." So far as this somewhat Carlylean Englishman was concerned, Dom Pedro II would have done better "if instead of being a sovereign of the academies, he had been a military man from head to foot, a soldier's soldier, ready to receive with bullets all discontented slave-owners, republican conspirators, and journalists low in funds"; and he would still have continued to be Emperor of the Brazilians.[9]

There were many other Europeans who reacted to the fifteenth of November by lamenting the lack of spirit of the dethroned Emperor and by regretting that Brazil had ceased to be an Empire. But there were no fewer who foresaw in the victorious Republic a continuation of the monarchy in a different context. A considerable number of European observers, many of whom were well versed in Brazilian affairs, were hopeful that the new leaders would be able to avoid the excesses of pure republicanism and to give greater emphasis to the social aspects of government.

The London correspondent for the *Jornal do Commercio* of Rio de Janeiro reported that, a few days after the fifteenth of November, the British Undersecretary of State for Foreign Affairs, Sir James Fergusson, had recommended not only prudence and firmness, but also "fidelity to the promises of the past" in the difficult task of Brazilian reconstruction. This sentiment was echoed by *The Times* of November 18, in its statement that the "new order of things" in Brazil would probably be as stable as the old. Attributing the fall of Dom Pedro II to the fact that his government had been "more liberal than the masses of its subjects," *The Times* felt that there was no reason why the Republic "should not be as honest in paying its debts as a monarchy." The *Daily News* of the same date pointed out that since "100 million pounds sterling of the British people" depended upon the order and progress of the new Brazilian regime, it was concerned over the Republic's ability to remain essentially the same type of government as the monarchy. It was necessary to determine what the future of the country would be under this more popular regime. "Is it preparing Brazil for self-govern-

---

[9] The Cornely article is cited in Campos Pôrto: op. cit., p. 819. (The original source of the article is not given. [Translator.])

ment?" Would the new Republic "maintain the unity and integrity which has been characteristic of monarchical Brazil amidst the constant turmoil and repeated dismemberments of the South American republics?"

The words of these and other noted European journals formed a sort of judgment of the future, a "contemporary future," as someone has called it, in the sense that such responsible foreign analysis is both dispassionate and well informed. Certainly, some members of the provisional government could appreciate such criticism; conscious of having to some extent broken with the national past, and pledged to continue in their course, they undoubtedly found much to salve their consciences in these journalistic previews of the future. The more lucid and intelligent members of the new regime tried to adapt their course to the predictions, at least in matters which would be visible to foreign eyes. They strove to convince outsiders that the government was concerned with the scrupulous maintenance of public order, with national unity, with territorial integrity, and with the respectful treatment of the vanquished faction. Indeed, such treatment frequently extended so far as to include members of that faction in the new government. The Baron of Lucena replaced Ruy Barbosa as political and juridical adviser to General Deodoro, and soon many other titled members of the old regime were called to the service of the Republic. The fact that such persons were allowed to retain and use their titles must have caused satisfaction in British circles.

One British pronouncement which could not fail to carry weight was that of the great Gladstone. In a speech given in Manchester a few days after the proclamation of the Republic, this most liberal of British statesmen was emphatic in his admiration for the dethroned Emperor: "No monarch has ever been more dedicated to the happiness of his people." [1] But at the same time he commended the Brazilian revolutionaries for the way in which they had replaced the monarchy with the Republic, "without the slightest attempt at violence, without disturbance, so to speak, of the social order, without interrupting the course of business for more than twenty-four to forty-eight hours, without firing a shot, without arrests, and without bloodshed—though I believe that one accidental injury is the sole exception to my statement—and all this in a distant society which could be considered a backward civilization, a society which until a few days ago struggled, if it is not still struggling, against the

[1] Ibid., p. 828.

pernicious curse of slavery, and where the morality of the entire country must have been considerably retarded in its development by the existence of that deplorable institution."

Was there not something Britannic in the way in which the Brazilians, struggling against all these disadvantages, nevertheless replaced the monarchy with the Republic in a manner so peaceful, so sober, so undisturbing to the course of business? From Gladstone's words we would conclude that there was, that Brazil had shown that it was a less backward society than the Knights and the Wilsons believed, in their confusion of sobriety with public apathy. The fifteenth of November had doubtless shown up the apathy of Brazilians toward their traditional system of government; but it had also demonstrated the civil responsibility of the revolutionaries, particularly those in the military forces.

In the United States, the first news of the proclamation of the Brazilian Republic brought joy to the hearts of those interested in Latin-American affairs; Brazil now seemed to have identified itself more closely with the continental system of government. "The United States of Brazil is now a natural ally of the United States of America," claimed the *New York Tribune*, a little rhetorically, though it explained that its confidence in the future of Brazil was based upon its respect for the former monarchy. "The Republic will make good progress, because it is prepared to do so through the free institutions already enjoyed there." [2]

For the *New York World* the Brazilians, in adopting the republican system of government, had freed themselves of the burden of "medieval and hereditary traditions"; a King, on the American continent, was "the most absurd of all anachronisms." One should nevertheless recognize that Dom Pedro had been a "good man." [3] In the opinion of the *Herald*, however, it was this fact of being merely a "good man" that "had led to his own downfall." *The New York Times* did not agree at all; Dom Pedro was dethroned by violence. In a serious editorial of November 17 the *Times*, while sympathetic toward Brazil, expressed its apprehension at a Revolution which represented the violent fall of a liberal monarchy led by a man [Dom Pedro] sincerely dedicated to prosperity of his country.[4]

2 Ibid., p. 633.
3 *New York World*, November 20, 1889.
4 *The New York Times*, November 17, 1889.

Thus from the United States too the new Brazilian leaders heard words of advice which, instead of accentuating their revolutionary radicalism or messianic tendencies, must have served to make them even more aware of their debt to the monarchical past, an awareness that (according to the best Anglo-American authorities) would constitute the strongest guarantee of the country's republican future.

It was not only the United States that felt this way; from Chile and Argentina came opinions only partly favorable to the Brazilian innovation. From the Buenos Aires correspondent of the Rio *Jornal do Commercio* on December 7 came the news that "for the masses, which knew only two things about Brazil—yellow fever and the name of Dom Pedro," the Revolution of November 15 had been "like the fall of the Eiffel Tower." [5] To neighboring Argentina, the name of the Emperor and the political state of the monarchy imparted to Brazil, despite the yellow fever, an appearance of solid, almost monumental organization confirmed by the "monetary supremacy" of the Empire. Argentine businessmen, the correspondent continued, "somewhat envious of the financial and monetary situation of monarchical Brazil," were quite pleased with the military *pronunciamento* in Rio de Janeiro, which would perhaps be "the source of disorder and internal warfare" in the new Republic and would lead to the end of Brazilian monetary supremacy. This attitude on the part of Buenos Aires businessmen must again have served to make the new Brazilian leaders aware of their responsibilities to their monarchical past: a past which could not be underrated, but must rather be continued in order to preserve those values that could go on lending prestige to the new republican order. The actions of the Army during the proclamation of the Republic had caused wonder among the Argentines, the same correspondent continued, because the soldiers had been content to cry " '*viva*' to the Republic and to Marshal Deodoro, without even thinking of the pleasures of sacking stores and warehouses." [6]

The truth is that the more the Brazilian Army removed itself from the excessively provincial Pedro II, and the more its officers, after the Paraguayan War, became republicanized (through the influence of Positivism and other "isms"), the greater the distinction grew between the Brazilian military tradition and that of the armies

[5] Campos Pôrto: op. cit., p. 682.
[6] Ibid., p. 682.

of Bolivarian America. Through a conjunction of circumstances peculiar to Brazil, the Army did not develop into a form of military aristocracy; it accepted young men of all races and from all walks of life and, unlike the Navy, became a truly democratic body. Moreover, it did this without allowing itself to be seduced by the demagogues who so often unleashed their attacks against the major political, military, and ecclesiastical figures of the period.

In his *Apontamentos para a História da República dos Estados Unidos do Brasil* (*Notes for the History of the Republic of the United States of Brazil*), M. E. de Campos Pôrto transcribes an interesting editorial from the ardently republican *Correio do Povo* of Rio de Janeiro. A few days after the proclamation of the Republic, this editorial tried to attribute the "reserve of the European press" to the fact that this press was "partial to the old institutions" and consequently incapable of understanding anything new or distinctively American. More specifically, it was ignorant of conditions in Brazil, "both of the political and social aspects of the situation and of the rare qualities of the Brazilian people." The extent of European information, the *Correio do Povo* indicated, was that the country was governed by a friend of the arts and sciences so superior to his subjects that the European mind could hardly grasp the anomaly of a ruler of 14 million Tupis and Negroes being a member of the Academy of Science.

But it was in referring to the "military characteristics of the movement" that the *Correio do Povo* got to the heart of the alleged reserve on the part of the Old World press. In its apology, more Positivist and sociological than political, the editorial made a point well worth bringing to the attention of European newspapers. Accustomed to South American military *pronunciamentos*, these papers, with the possible exception of *The Times*, had made the mistake of seeing the intervention of the Brazilian Armed Forces in the political scene as just another crude, purely military coup.

"Given the situation of a modern citizen body in which the old-line convention of an aristocratic Army in the service of the King has transformed itself into that of a popular militia in the service of the country, it is not possible to have what could truly be called a national revolution against the will of the armed forces," said the *Correio do Povo* (anticipating the revolutions of the twentieth century). "One might add that, with the perfection of the science of tactics and discipline and of weapons of modern warfare, the victory of a purely civil insurrection has become totally impossible. The support of a popular revolutionary Army is necessary, and with such support given, the victory becomes legitimate." And, focusing on the specifially Brazilian aspect of the problem: "One must note that in Brazil no class better represents the high qualities of the citizen body than the Army and the Navy. If the rare sense of loyalty and respect of the races which compose the mass of our proletariat increases in the hearts of simple soldiers and sailors, the officers, in their turn, through the excellent scientific education imparted by our military schools, represent the highest and most select qualities of the Brazilian spirit. To these we might add the fortunate moral situation of the military class in Brazil, free as it is from all thoughts of industrial selfishness, resigned to a dignified poverty, and passionately devoted to the cause of patriotism and honor."

As for the fifteenth of November itself, the *Correio do Povo*, in confronting the "reserve of the European press," asks: "Is this movement an egotistic military *pronounciamento?* . . . Absolutely no. The military leaders who, with the effective help of civilian republicans, led the Revolution of the fifteenth of November awaited the assurance of public opinion in the capital before proclaiming the deposition of the dynasty. Once this opinion was favorably expressed, they sanctioned the action." The composition of the government itself, in which representatives of both civilian and military classes were included, proves (finally) that we have, and have had from the beginning, a movement concerned with nothing else than the common welfare of the Brazilian people.

Confirming the Positivist thesis of the *Correio do Povo*, Ruy Barbosa's *Diário de Notícias* (usually of quite different policy) said: "The Army, having everything in its own hands, gave over everything to the people . . ." [7] Emphasizing the force of propaganda previously put out by politicos and intellectuals such as Benjamin Constant, it went on: "For such a desideratum [i.e., the Republic] they worked with pen and intellect in order to arouse a patriotic spirit and to put the Armed Forces on the side of the people. Once the period of persuasion was passed and the time for action arrived, swords were unsheathed and positions conquered." And, with the characteristic much-admired Barbosan rhetoric: "But the angel of victory has not yet smiled with all his radiance on the forces of

[7] Ibid., p. 128.

liberty and progress, and now those swords have modestly and tim-
idly returned to their scabbards, leaving the glory and all the credit
to the organizers of the movement." Moreover, "the cold dictatorship of the sword," in the present phase of the movement, had even
intended to withdraw "modestly" and deliver "to the people the
right to decide all matters as they saw fit." It was necessary, thus,
that "civilians, journalists, and intellectuals use the sword to defend
those points which need to be maintained by force, that they join
hands with the generals and oblige them once again to draw their
victorious weapons, that they urge this as the performance of a
duty, the duty of guarding positions previously won and of defending the Republic proclaimed [jointly] by the people and by the
Army and Navy. . . ." [8]

On November 22, the *Diário de Notícias* once again took up the
subject: "We are now in the eighth day of the Republic and it
seems to be more like eight months, so little has been the change
from Empire except in the sense of aggrandizement of the
nation." [9] But the reference to "aggrandizement" appears to have
been pure rhetoric. The early days of the Republic seemed to the
republicans themselves to be merely a psychological and social continuation of the monarchy, largely because the danger of military
dictatorship so feared by both citizens and foreigners had not mate-
rialized. "The military, after gaining the victory, demonstrated
their utter lack of political ambition by relinquishing the destiny of
the nation to the hands of the people," the article continues. It is
true that the word "people" is here used rhetorically, but more interesting is the attitude of compromise shown by the nonmilitary
Ruy in making an apology for the Army and so ensuring the pre-
eminence of civilians like himself in the organization of the Republic.

This point was reiterated by the *Diário* a few days later in recalling that, once the Republic had been proclaimed, General Deodoro
da Fonseca had made only one further conquest: that of the Rua do
Ouvidor, the gathering place of businessmen in Rio de Janeiro. The
opinion of the Rua do Ouvidor—"the legendary tribune, the
forum, the Monte Aventino, where the public meets daily to discuss current affairs"—was important in judging the events of the
fifteenth of November. And this forum had approved the conduct

[8] Ibid., p. 127.
[9] *Diário de Notícias* (Rio de Janeiro), November 22, 1889.

of the Army: "Representatives of all social classes concur in according the Army their acclamation, their approval, their applause, and their praise."

The *Jornal do Commercio* of November 24, in reminding the new leaders of their promise of November 15 to be "simple temporary agents of national sovereignty," recognized that so far they had shown themselves to be "firm in resolution and moderate in action." This classic, conservative, anti-romantic paper recognized that the new government was fulfilling its pledge to maintain order so that the nation could calmly deliberate "the new and definitive form of existence." [1] Apparently the *Jornal do Commercio* did not feel that the applause for Deodoro and the Army emanating from the Rua do Ouvidor was sufficient to consecrate the federal Republic as the "new and definitive form of existence"; other voices also needed to be heard. But the fact was that when voices from the distant plantations began to reach the provisional government, they were nearly all, if not directly laudatory to the Army, at least approving of its attitude in effecting the sudden change from monarchy without allowing the new government to become ideologically or factionally republican. They approved the intervention of the Army in political life so long as it acted as a nonpolitical age in serving the national will and the national interest under circumstances when all normal means of interparty peacemaking had failed. It was as a result of this type of responsibility that the Army had intervened on the fifteenth of November; acting thus quite differently from the factious and sectarian body envisioned by Benjamin Constant. So much so, in fact, that General Deodoro did not hesitate to solicit the collaboration of the titled noblemen of the old regime, such as the able Baron de Lucena. This was an effort condemned in advance by the Positivist *Correio do Povo* from the earliest days of the republican regime. In an article published in November, 1899, the *Correio do Povo* cautioned that there were still remnants of the monarchy in the government, remnants that the Republic could carry "without feeling the weight" but which would eventually cause it to succumb to the weight of "men who had made up the bad governments which saddled the decayed monarchy for half a century!" "All citizens should forget the past," continued the *Correio*. "The only exceptions to this should be the officers of the Second Empire who should remember the past, not

[1] *Jornal do Commercio* (Rio de Janeiro), November 24, 1889.

as a reason for seeking revenge, but rather as a simple reminder to ensure that the Republic not again be so corrupted." [2]

So ran the thought of the pure orthodox radical republicans both in the Army and among the civilians. But such ideas never occurred to the Army group represented by the majestic figure of Deodoro; the old soldier of the Paraguayan War lent his sword, not to the service of any "ism," but rather to that of his country.

The Army, in the new political order, thus took over the role of the Crown as a supra-political body, above the struggles of Positivists against non-Positivists, of republicans and monarchists, of old-line republicans and Johnny-come-latelys, in its effort to raise the national interest above petty factional strife. On this point the monarchist Joaquim Nabuco, like the monarchist Baron de Rio Branco, showed himself much more understanding than Eduardo Prado toward the participation of the Army group headed by Deodoro in the events of the fifteenth of November. Prado as a monarchist had been less than disarming, and unjust in his judgments and commentaries on this participation, too simplistic in his eagerness to consider it a type of Spanish-American militarism. Moreover, he had been blind to the traditional role of the Army in Brazilian life and to the constancy of its service in the national interest, far from the excesses of conventional reactionaries on the one hand and *arriviste* radicals on the other.

It is true that some members of the military, like some civilians, were affected by the *arrivisme* of the moment. But this does not seem to have affected the actions of the Armed Forces in the crisis, nor did it characterize their role during the period of consolidation under Deodoro or Floriano, neither of whom allowed the Army to serve the ephemeral ideologies of the moment. Once a republican government came to be desired by even the conservative agrarians, once there ceased to be a definitive number of monarchists in Brazil, once the dynastic and hereditary form of government ceased to be effective, the Army likewise became republican.

Before becoming "the consolidator of the Republic," Floriano had already attained the stature of an ideal figure; since the Paraguayan War, he had been held up to most Brazilian youths as the prototype of the military hero. His deeds as a soldier were associated in the popular imagination with a life of stern sacrifice in the nation's service. It is evident, then, that the Republic would benefit, as indeed it

2 Campos Pôrto: op. cit., p. 124.

did, from the support of a genuine and greatly admired military hero.

It is also evident that the Emperor, never having been a soldier-monarch, had suffered in the public eye by this lack of an aura of military sacrifice. Two or three generations of Brazilians who had grown up under the seduction of military heroism (having had relatives who had fought against the *caudilhismo* of López), early in life lost interest in an Emperor who appeared in public in a plain carriage or on foot, carrying an umbrella, dressed just like a bourgeois in frock coat, high hat, and black button shoes. No uniform, no sword, no high boots, not even a horse; any colonel in the National Guard would have been more Imperial in dress and bearing and any country landholder more instinctively patrician in his manner.

Ramalho Ortigão in "The Social Aspects of the Brazilian Revolution" commented that, with an Emperor who declared himself a republican, "it would have been very strange if there were anyone in the Brazilian monarchical party who could nourish the pretension of being more realistic than the King himself." And, in his *Estudos Brasileiros* (1877–85), José Veríssimo clearly places the fifteenth of November in the context of past history, particularly the uprisings of Maranhão under Beckman in 1684, of Pernambuco in 1710, 1817, and 1848, and of Minas Gerais in 1789 and 1842. "In the eyes of any serious person, the work of establishing the unity and integrity of the nation would reflect credit on the record of the Brazilian monarchy, in the light of the geography of the country, the unequal development of the provinces, and the separatist spirit which infiltrated Portuguese colonial organization." [3] But this work was one which could perhaps only be maintained by federation, and to Veríssimo federation in a monarchical system seemed impossible.[4] Although as shrewd a political thinker as Joaquim Na-

[3] Ortigão: op. cit., p. 101.
[4] The various rebellions spoken of by José Veríssimo in his *Estudos Brasileiros* (Rio de Janeiro, 1877–85) to which Ortigão refers generally fall into the category of conflict between local and remote authority. The Beckman revolt in Maranhão in 1684 stemmed largely from a conflict between Jesuit missionaries and the local civilians over the treatment of the Indians. The Jesuits, who were opposed to enslavement, were eventually persuaded to bow to the local need for forced labor, although the uprising itself was a failure and resulted in the execution of its principal civilian leaders. The risings in Pernambuco in 1710, 1817, and 1848, and in Minas Gerais in 1789 and 1842, were of a republican nature but were complicated

buco thought quite differently, and although Ruy Barbosa admitted the possibility of combining federation with monarchy, Veríssimo's point of view is still worth consideration. If the conciliation desired by Nabuco and admitted by Ruy was impossible, then Ramalho Ortigão, disagreeing with Eduardo Prado, was correct in saying that "the man who brought about the military accident of the fifteenth of November, so diversely interpreted by the European press, had merely accelerated progress in simplifying the resolution of the Brazilian social problem through the suppression of superfluous elements." [5]

---

by local resentment of alleged regional neglect on the part of the central government.

Veríssimo's point in this complicated passage seems to be that the Crown made progress in nationalizing Brazil, despite the economic differences and communication problems in a huge and highly diversified territory emerging from a colonial system that did little to provide a sense of political unity. The persistent succession of republican movements, however, testified to the continued feeling that true federation could not be achieved under a monarchical system. (Translator.)

[5] Ortigão: op. cit., p. 102.

❦ [I I] ❦

Brazilian Society in the

Late Nineteenth Century

T HE BOY TOLD THE PRINCIPAL that his name was Joaquim, Joaquim Amaral Jansen.[1] He had been born in the court of the
Emperor in 1882. The school was the Victoria Academy in the Rua
Haddock Lobo. There he learned his ABC's from the regulation
primer, while at home he continued to receive another sort of primitive learning from the oldest Negress in the slave quarters: stories
of the werewolf, the headless mule, the legends of Charles the
Great, and tales of enchanted princes, emperors, kings, and warriors. These were the stories most frequently told Brazilian children
of the time by their grandfathers or their Negro mammys. And
there were times when these storytellers acted out of character:
when the grandfathers told the tales of horror and the Negro re-
counted pretty legends of a dark-haired water sprite.

At home Joaquim, together with the boys in the neighborhood,
also amused himself by flying kites of various types and sizes.
Meanwhile, under the cloud-filled and ever-changing skies of Recife, another boy, Manuel Carneiro de Sousa Bandeira, was sending
his box kites and paper birds high into the winds from the banks of
the Capibaribe River. Both Joaquim in Rio de Janeiro and Manuel
in Recife spun their tops and modeled figures in clay, living the
happy life of boys free from the company of girls.

The girls, for their part, jumped rope or formed a ring and sang
songs. Dona Virgínia Cavalcante, born in the Pernambuco backlands village of São Bento and educated in Recife, recalls the favor-

[1] In this chapter the author begins his use of eyewitness material as described in
his Note on Method, pp. xxix–xxxiv. (Translator.)

51

ite pastimes of her childhood: the dances called *Ciranda, Ciran-dinha,* and *Senhora Viuva,* as well as blindman's buff and *boca-de-forno,*[2] games which some mammys considered too tomboyish for young ladies.

Manuel Bandeira, who went from Recife to Rio when still a child, testifies that the game of marbles was played differently there from his way in Pernambuco; "instead of being shot with the thumbnail tensed behind the index finger, it is discharged from the tip of the latter, with the thumb making a ring with the first finger." Bandeira also missed the cashews and guavas of Pernambuco, just as the youngsters who went south from the northern state of Pará were never quite consoled for the loss of the *açai* or *buriti* by the excellence of the *jabuticabas* and of the farms around Rio and São Paulo, famous also for their *cambucás,* but lacking *pitangas* to equal those of the north; lacking also *pitombas, macaíbas,* or *guaji-rus.* And the *mandacarus,*[3] from whose red flowers boys of the backlands somewhat poetically received their first vicarious lessons in the nature of the physical union between man and woman. In all parts of the country from north to south, the same lesson was being learned less poetically and vicariously by the sexually precocious, from the orifices in the trunk of the banana plant or from all sorts of animals, from the humble chicken to the cow whose flanks suggest the contours of the mulatto girls of Bahia.

Gastão Cruls (b. 1886), who passed his childhood in Rio de Janeiro during the first years of the Republic, records in his notes for his excellent study of the Carioca past, *Aparência do Rio de Janeiro* (*The Appearance of Rio de Janeiro*), that the favorite fruits of the youngsters of the court and the newly created federal capital were the *cambucá,* the *abiu,* the *grumixama,* the *cajá,* the *manga,* the *sapoti,* the *fruta-do-conde,* the *jambo-rosa,* and the *jambo-de-caroço,* almost all of them fruits found on the farms or in the back yards of middle-class city homes during the last days of the Empire and the early days of the Republic. The birds which the boys trapped were likewise virtually the same in the capital as those of the provinces. In the capital, however, the importing of fruits—and even of birds—from Europe took place earlier than in the rest of

[2] A game in which a "boss" orders each member of the group to perform a task. The first to complete his task becomes the next "boss." (Translator.)

[3] *Cereus peruvianus,* a plant of the cactus family, similar to the night-blooming cereus. Most of these names are explained in the Glossary. (Translator.)

the country, pear, apple, peach, and strawberry being among the newcomers. And it was almost tragic that, from the beginning of the modernization of the city under Mayor Passos, the English sparrow began to drive the native Brazilian birds from the Carioca yards and gardens. The children of Rio, along with those of Belém, were also the first to suffer the impact of urban electrification; streetcar wires had an inhibiting effect on the traditional pastime of kite flying, a sport which has since been in decline in all the principal cities of Brazil.[4]

Manuel Bandeira learned his alphabet in Recife in a little school in the Rua de Soledade run by the Barros Barreto sisters. Later, he transferred to another run by Virgínio Marques Carneiro Leão. He tells us that in neither of these schools was there a playground, and in the latter the *palmatória* was still in use. As a result, the children played only at home or in the streets, or in their daily walks to and from school. School was a place for study, for duty. And it was also a place of punishment and blisters from the *palmatória* for those who did not know their lessons or who committed some major devilment. For these children, it was the street that represented freedom, freedom from both the routine of home life and the dull monotony of the schoolroom.

Every blessed day except Sundays, holidays, and saints' days, Joaquim Amaral Jansen trudged through the streets of Rio de Janeiro carrying notebooks, pencils, and lunchbox, a child from a strict patriarchal household delighting in each new sight the streets had to offer. In his pre-school years, before this daily adventure—which soon became a routine—of going to school each morning, he had enjoyed himself mainly by playing in the yard or flying his kite in the fields behind the house. The street had been something he had seen only from the windows, the veranda, or the front door. It wasn't long before he discovered that that little stretch of thoroughfare wasn't the whole world. It was also the street of the milk peddler, a mustachioed Portuguese nearly always named Manuel, who sold his product, fresh and unwatered, drawn on the spot by his none-too-clean hands for a couple of pennies a glass. It was the

---

[4] Emiliano Ribeiro de Almeida Braga (b. São Luís de Maranhão, 1873) believes that the kites flown during his childhood were the best in Brazil. This most traditional Brazilian toy was not only beloved of children, but also of "doctors, college graduates, priests, lawyers, and judges." Adult kite flying apparently extended throughout the northern part of the country, from Recife to Manaus.

street of the turkey seller, carrying his birds trussed to enormous bamboo poles and shouting his traditional cry: "*Perus de boa roda!* (Choicest thoroughbred turkeys!)" In the still-numerous patriarchal families of Botafogo, São Cristóvão, and Santa Teresa, there was always a birthday or a baptism to celebrate and this could never be observed properly without a fat turkey on the table eaten in Carioca fashion with plenty of toasted manioc meal. Then there was the vegetable man, with his baskets of fresh—and sometimes odoriferous—vegetables carried in the Madeiran fashion from a long pole across his shoulders. And the fruit vendor, the fish peddler, the shrimp seller, the chicken man, each with his peculiar street cry, his own type of basket, his personal smell which penetrated to the interior of the houses. There was also the scissor-grinder; the lady who sold lace from the north; and the peddler, always called a "Turk," with his magical trunks filled with cloth, ready-made clothes, ribbons, thread, combs, mirrors, needles, perfume bottles, brushes, brilliantine for young men's hair and the beards of elegant ancients. The peddler had a slapstick made of two heavy boards fastened at one end to a leather belt studded with tacks. When the stick was clapped, young ladies and nursemaids would pass into a high state of excitement. Children too; perhaps some day shiny new toys would issue from the "Turk's" trunk, toys unparalleled. Toys from some marvelous land to satisfy the wildest dreams of infancy, toys smelling of exotic glues and paints utterly different from the crude pastes and colors used on their homemade kites, wooden dolls, and pinwheels. Children in the interior contented themselves with toys made from their natural surroundings: flutes from papaya stalks, rough-carved wooden tops or horses, bird traps, slingshots, or noisy boots made from the half-shells of coconuts fastened to the feet.

For example, João d'Albuquerque Maranhão (b. Rio Grande do Norte, 1883) states that he was the happiest of children so long as he could play with wooden horses made from the *carnaúba* tree. But he also learned early to ride bareback on flesh-and-blood horses, using only a rope bridle, a childhood sport in agrarian areas throughout Brazil and especially in Rio Grande do Sul, where Manuel Duarte, of Star Ranch near Vacaria, says he started to play at cattle wrangling at the age of five. On the other hand, Carlos Cordeiro da Rocha (b. in the interior of the state of Ceará, 1884) says that his principal pleasure as a child was bird catching. Maria Joa-

quina da Conceição, an illiterate servant born in Goiana, Pernambuco, in 1885, tells us that in her childhood, poor girls in the interior of Pernambuco amused themselves with rag dolls, which
were always considered a sign of lower-class origins. She herself, as
the illegitimate descendant of a local grandee, scorned such toys
and always played with a worn-out china doll, the castoff plaything
of some daughter of the rich. More fortunately situated young
ladies habitually played with china dolls—not even the cheaper half-
cloth, half-ceramic substitutes but real china dolls made in France
with blond locks and blue eyes, and often wearing silk dresses.
Other dolls were made of wax, according to Dona Antônia Lins
Vieira de Melo (b. São Sebastião, São Paulo, 1879), "the product
of skilled hands, with attractive features but without blue eyes or
red cheeks; almost always pale and lifeless in appearance." This aristocratic girl found the rag dolls sold in the marketplace often "well
made and in good taste, well designed to withstand the wear and
tear of infantile energies."

The cult of blond, blue-eyed dolls among the upper-class children of the Empire had the effect of contaminating some of them
with germs of Aryanism until they idealized blond children and
considered the French female the most desirable image of elegance
and beauty. Dona Isabel Henriqueta de Sousa e Oliveira (b. Bahia,
1853) confesses that when she was a girl she "wanted to be French
and know French manners at first hand." She also admits having
considered Negroes an inferior race, persons from whom one ought
to "maintain one's social distance." Dona Carlinda Custódia Nunes
(b. in the Imperial court, 1874), who prided herself on the "Divine
gift" of "notable [i.e., French] features," also played with blond
dolls and became convinced of the necessity for Brazil to "support
white supremacy" and always "was upset by the marriage of any
relative to a person of color." Dona Virgínia Cavalcante testifies
that "a trip to the City of Light was always the fondest wish of my
childhood, but I was never able to realize it." This devotion to Paris
on the part of many other Brazilian ladies of the period is attributable not only to the French dolls with which they had played as
children but also to the French fashion plates, which idealized
blond, rosy-cheeked ladies as being the most elegant in Europe—
and in the world. Dona Virgínia admits to having been well pleased
with the law which freed Negroes and mulattos, "children of God
and therefore our brothers," from the "horrors of slavery," but adds

that "I am utterly opposed to marriage between white and colored. Whites are for whites, mulattos for mulattos, colored for colored."

But Dona Henriqueta Galeno, who lived in Ceará from childhood and grew up in a paternalistic family where she played very little with dolls and early learned to recite the nativist poems of Gonçalves Dias, received very little impact from the French influence. Although evincing a certain enthusiasm for French literature, she had never been a devotee of either French dolls or French fashions, always preferring to dress "with the greatest simplicity." Perhaps it was due to this upbringing that, in her testimony written half a century after her childhood, she can claim to have been always free of racial prejudice. "I would not make the slightest objection to the marriage of any member of my family to a person of color."

But to return to the street vendors of the late Empire and early Republic. In Rio de Janeiro and other cities of Brazil, their arrival was announced sometimes by rattles and other devices and sometimes by street cries. Rarely did these merchants go about their business in silence, the lace sellers being one of the few exceptions. The others sang their street calls through all the byways of the city as though they were repeating a ritual from the distant but ever-present past. To some people these calls sounded most agreeable —the poet Manuel Bandeira recalls them in a celebrated poem— but to the more progressive Brazilians of the last decades of the Empire they seemed shamefully archaic and tasteless. In Recife, where they particularly flourished, extending even to the Negroes who carried pianos and heavy furniture, or to the stevedores who bore sugar from the barges to the warehouses, there were still some people who became indignant about such songs, just as they objected to the songs of the *maracatu* or the hurly-burly of the *samba*, or to anything else partly African or Negro in origin. "How long, O *maracatu*, wilt thou continue to abuse our ears and our nostrils?" wailed the *Diabo a Quatro*, a sophisticated progressive magazine opposed to the throne, the Church, to priests, processions, novenas, *sambas*, and *maracatus*, in its issue of February 18, 1877. The assumption of nearly all these progressives, made uncomfortable by the survival of a past which they referred to disdainfully as "colonial," was that these survivals irritated the eyes, ears, and nostrils of foreigners even more than they did the Anglicized or Gallicized nationals. And this was the period, particularly in the capital cities, when the foreigner was elevated to an extremely high position, far beyond that of Brazilians or Iberians, as a standard setter of taste, manners, and elegance. This idolatry stemmed from the beginning of the nineteenth century but it was accentuated during the last decades of the reign of Pedro II, who himself was inclined to value the opinions of progressive foreigners, such as Professor and Madame Agassiz,[5] over the more traditional views of nationals whose social backgrounds were predominantly patriarchal and agrarian.

Nothing was more characteristic of this idealization of the foreigner than the excitement caused among the middle classes by the auctions of the household goods of English, French, German, or Swiss families returning to their native land after several years of residence in Brazil. It would be no exaggeration to say that such auctions were more than business transactions; they were educational, as educational as the schools and hotels established by foreigners in Brazil during the same period, perhaps almost as educational as the "French" ladies (who weren't always French, by the way), such as the *cocottes* of the establishments on Rio's Rua do Ouvidor or of its famous brothel, the Alcázar. Actresses, singers, *modistes,* sales ladies in elegant shops, whatever they might call themselves, they also functioned at the time as instructors in civility, courtesy, and refinement to many a provincial Brazilian who, despite his money in the bank or the lawyer's or scholar's ring on his finger, was still a rustic in the ways of the world. One of these *cocottes* was Susana.

It is reasonable to suppose that Machado de Assis himself owed part of his manners and refined tastes to foreigners of Susana's type: *cocottes,* or actresses, or *modistes*—sellers of plumed headwear or lace cuffs—with whom "Machadinho" (as he was called) came into frequent contact during his days as theatre critic. The same could be said of his friend Quintino Bocayuva, who without having been educated in Europe (his travels were confined to the New World) assumed the post of Foreign Minister in the provisional government of 1889. And it certainly was true up to a point of José Maria da Silva Paranhos[6] who, despite being the son of an illustrious viscount and himself a baron from his early youth, seems to have learned from the European *cocottes* of Rio de Janeiro

[5] Louis Agassiz (1807–1873), world-famous geologist and zoologist, was professor of Natural History at Harvard University. In 1865, Agassiz and his wife made an extensive exploration of Brazil and collaborated on *A Journey in Brazil* published in 1868. (Translator.)

[6] José Maria da Silva Paranhos, Baron do Rio Branco, was Brazilian Foreign Minister from 1902 to 1912. The Foreign Ministry was then—as now—the Itama-

subtleties that would prove very useful in a diplomatic career, where the fine points of worldly behavior were cultivated rather than scorned (as they would have been by Imperial counselors of strictly patriarchal backgrounds). Thus it was that Paranhos, during his time as lord of the Itamaraty, gave so much encouragement to the schools run by French nuns, where young girls of Brazilian society enjoyed an elegant education not only in the French language, but also in some of the refinements of European civilization.

But to return to Susana. This young lady was virtually an institution in the Rio de Janeiro of her time, a pagan goddess, priestess of a forbidden cult. According to one informant,[7] a worthy Brazilian born in 1881 whom I shall simply call H.A., Susana was "the most famous madam in Rio de Janeiro." Around the turn of the century she was the queen of her profession and had her finger in every pie. So great was her prestige that even her practice of Sapphic love was pardoned by the indulgent Cariocas. She also became part of local folk song:

> On Sundays our Susana goes to mass
> But on weekdays, she's too indolent, alas.

But again according to H.A., who knows what he is talking about, "Susana was a good creature. She exploited only those who had means and could afford the loss. The youngsters were treated well and were given good advice. Instead of allowing them to buy the most expensive champagnes, she would furnish them with a wine from her own vineyards—a wine which had earned the *Mérite Agricole* no less. Students and young journalists went to her place and taught her girls to dance the *maxixe*, with the cost of instruction taken out in trade. With us, Susana was one of the gang."

For H.A. such high life, thanks to the influence of Susana and others of her sisterhood, enjoyed far greater prestige during his youth than it was to have in later years. At the turn of the century, it was a rare student who had not fraternized with French girls, to whom he taught Brazilian dance steps and from whom he learned innumerable subtleties—not only of the art of love but also of aes-

---

raty Palace in downtown Rio de Janeiro. Rio Branco was a high liver, and Freyre frequently refers to his reputation as a gourmand and connoisseur of pretty women. (Translator.)

[7] Handwritten manuscript in the author's possession.

thetic, literary, and social matters. From this our former frequenter of Susana's girls deduces that subsequent generations of Brazilian youths are becoming "less and less virile through the abuse of the cult of football. It is a fact well established by those who have studied Brazilian society that lesbianism has increased alarmingly even in the highest social circles, to say nothing of among the lower classes. Could this be an indication of this loss of virility? At one time, in making certain psychological studies . . . I decided to examine aspects of lesbianism in our society after 1900. I soon quit; the amount of material I assembled was frightening."

The higher class of Rio prostitutes during the late Empire and early Republic was to be found in the Catete section and in the Rua Senador Dantas. As a boy, H.A. remembers the celebrated Hotel Ravot, in the Rua do Ouvidor: "A two-story building which occupied half a block, with the girls in wrappers seated in the windows or leaning on the sills beckoning the passers-by." The cheaper type of prostitution was to be found in the Rua Sete de Setembro or the Rua Uruguaiana up to Rossio Square, spreading from there to Lapa and the Mangue sections.[8] In addition, there were "branches extending to the bay front, reaching into the Glória section . . ." One gets the impression that at the end of the nineteenth century there were more brothels than ordinary shops in Rio de Janeiro.

Because of the high prices brought in by coffee, São Paulo at the beginning of the twentieth century also attracted its share of high-class French girls. Its centers of operation were also hotels and "boardinghouses" similar to the famous one in Rio known as "Mère Louise," and these establishments were patronized not only by federal deputies but also by senators and Supreme Court judges. São Paulo had its Susana in the person of Mme Pommery, who was portrayed in a book published in 1919 as having exercised considerable change in Paulista customs. One such innovation which spread to polite society both in São Paulo and in Rio de Janeiro was that of the tango-tea.[9] Similar Susanas existed at the time in Salvador da Bahia, in Recife, and especially in Belém and Manaus. The last city

[8] Speaking of the prostitution of mulattos in Rio de Janeiro, Lamberg observed that "there are mulatto girls of eleven or twelve who already are mothers." He noted, however, that these native prostitutes always "preserved a certain decency—almost a certain dignity—in their calling." It was "only in the large cities, under the bad example given by European courtesans, that these native customs are spoiled" (Maurício Lamberg: *O Brasil*, translated from the German [Rio de Janeiro, 1896], p. 61).

[9] Hilário Tácito: *Madame Pommery* (São Paulo, 1919), p. 152.

had not only French girls, but also a number of Italians and Germans, all decked with feathers, laces, and silks, covered with jewels, high-priced courtesans—some virtually *femmes fatales*—competing with the near-nude dark-skinned *caboclas* or the imported Bahian girls who rivalled their French sisters in dispensing subtle amorous and gastronomic delights.

Some of these French Susanas grew old in Brazil and adopted the airs of the *grande dame*, attending mass every Sunday and becoming almost the second wives of rich industrialists, military men, lawyers, doctors, businessmen, and engineers. But there were also those who returned to their country of origin, a return which often caused rejoicing in the more sedate bourgeois families of the period, families alarmed by the spell cast over male members of the tribe by these blond sirens. Wives much preferred that their wayward husbands seek the company of native, fresh-water charmers, Negresses or mulattos of local origin, despite the latter's bad habit of attempting to retain their lovers by black magic of African origin.

Ferreira da Rosa, in his work *O Lupanar—Estudo sôbre o Caftismo e a Prostituição no Rio de Janeiro* (*The Bordello: A Study of Procuring and Prostitution in Rio de Janeiro*), confirms much of H.A.'s information about the French girls of the Brazilian capital during the late nineteenth century. Most lived in two-story houses; three, four, or more girls together with their superior. Such houses were found in the downtown streets of São Francisco de Assis, Sete de Setembro, Luís de Camões, Lavradio, Visconde do Rio Branco, and in Tiradentes Square. The sight of these prostitutes grouped in the windows (product of procurers protected by Brazilian custom) constituted a sad tableau.[1] "The streetcars, the customary means of transportation throughout the city, carry thousands of passengers daily and cause them to witness the most extreme evidences of this lawless traffic exhibited by these women in the windows, or even in the interiors of their depraved habitations. . . . Such women are in great number the rejects of the brothels of India, of the River Plate, and of the British colonies . . . women who have lost all respect for public decency . . . almost all of them Hungarians, Germans, Poles, Russians."[2] Very few were

[1] Ferreira da Rosa: *O Lupanar—Estudo sôbre o Caftismo e a Prostituição no Rio de Janeiro* (Rio de Janeiro, 1896), pp. 27, 251–2. See also Francisco Ferraz de Macedo: *Tese Apresentada à Faculdade de Medicina do Rio de Janeiro* (Rio de Janeiro, 1872) and Herculano Augusto Lassance Cunha: *A Prostituição, em Particular na Cidade do Rio de Janeiro* (Rio de Janeiro, 1845).

[2] Rosa: op. cit., p. 253.

French; the real French courtesans were the artists of their class, members of the elite.

In 1879 Tito de Matos, the court chief of police, directed his delegate Félix da Costa to conduct an investigation into prostitution. The latter acknowledged the presence in the country of an "association composed of Russian Jews, Germans, Austrians, and other nationalities" formed for the purpose of importing prostitutes. Some of these procurers operated under a front as jewel merchants. One of the most notorious was Siegmond Richer, a man whom the police wished to deport and who tried vainly to retain the brilliant Ferreira de Meneses in his defense. Another lawyer was found in his stead, a Brazilian at the start of his brilliant career, who proved that Richer was a man of probity and a Brazilian citizen by Imperial decree. "What can't one prove with a little good will?" comments Ferreira da Rosa in relating this incident.[3]

The same Siegmond Richer, upon seeing himself denounced as a procurer in the newspaper *O País*, requested Police Chief André Cavalcanti to furnish him with a written statement as to "whether or not he had ever been convicted or deported for being a procurer." The reply came in due course clearly stating that "the referred person has never been condemned or deported as a procurer," thus giving the petitioner an official document for the protection of his criminal activities. "Why didn't the official document proclaim 'the referred person never was deported because he is a naturalized Brazilian citizen, but it was proved in the formal investigations of August 26 and September 30, 1879, that he is a procurer'?" asks Ferreira da Rosa. Another procurer of the early Republic managed, through a bribe, to be appointed second lieutenant in the National Guard. One fine day the supreme commander of that military body, General Ouriques Jacques, ordered that the commander of the Ninth Infantry battalion "formally induct Lieutenant Izidoro Kappler." The induction never took place, because the commander petitioned was none other than Floriano Peixoto and "the lieutenant's commission granted Izidoro Kappler eventually was cancelled, despite the enormous efforts of its sponsor."[4]

In the boudoir of Anita, one of Izidoro's white slaves, "there were frequent and continuous meetings of federal deputies, wealthy businessmen, and top-flight lawyers, journalists, and military men." Anita was beautiful and intelligent, and her charms

[3] Ibid., pp. 46, 49.
[4] Ibid., pp. 126, 127, 129.

were effective in furthering the ambitions of Izidoro, who "even attained a degree in the Masonic order." Several other procurers, having become Masons, had to be "solemnly expelled from the Grand Orient of Brazil." The same Izidoro even succeeded in 1893 in being appointed an auxiliary of the 15th Police Precinct of Rio de Janeiro, according to a document in his favor drawn up by the federal delegate Damasco Gomes. There were always secretaries willing to grant naturalization papers and distribute documentary proof of lily-white character to any procurer with sufficient funds to support his request.[5]

It was mentioned in the previous chapter that the traveled and somewhat ascetic Ramalho Ortigão was surprised at the commonplace mahogany furniture of the São Cristóvão palace and at the lifelessness of the court during the reign of Pedro II, and particularly the absence of well-dressed and beautiful women. One reason was that the cream of the Brazilian aristocracy of the period was glittering brilliantly in Paris; certain baronesses and viscountesses of Pedro II's court were celebrated in Europe for their charm, beauty, and elegance, and some were even known for their coquetry, all qualities lacking the proper conditions for flourishing in Rio de Janeiro. The Baroness of Estrêla was a good case in point.

Toward the end of a life during which her charm and beauty had turned the head of many a European aristocrat, the Baroness of Estrêla confirmed to me Ortigão's observations on the tedium of the court of Pedro II. "Without sophistication, without art," (Ortigão describes it) "without furnishings, without uniforms, without balls, without flowers, without bibelots, the São Cristóvão palace seemed a graveyard to all lively people, especially to young men and pretty women. Many of the better educated Brazilians, some of them from the best families of the Empire, lived habitually in France, England, or Belgium." Thus, as Ortigão says, to become acquainted with "the most elegant ladies of the Brazilian nobility" —a Baroness de Estrêla, for example—"one would look not to the palace of São Cristóvão but rather to M. Carnot of Paris for the proper means of introduction." [6]

Perhaps we can conclude that Pedro II's court enjoyed a moral superiority over the other courts of the period, which might glad-

[5] Ibid., pp. 130, 137–8.
[6] Ramalho Ortigão: "O Quadro Social da Revolução Brasileira," *Revista de Portugal*, II, 99.

den the hearts of many Victorians still among us. Certainly the Emperor was a man of austere behavior and simple habits who shunned all outward manifestations of sex. But, as head of a monarchical government, had he the right to disdain all worldliness, even that most natural to his type of government? The truth is that such worldliness would probably have encouraged the development of the arts and would have aided the solution of national problems by bringing together socially various national leaders who scarcely knew one another and whose associations were limited to the course of their bureaucratic duties.

It seems that Pedro II's dismal youth lacked the influence of such foreign ladies, an influence which, as Senhora de Barral told him later in life, would have given him greater feeling for those graces and subtleties he never really learned to appreciate. His recently published love letters to that lady lamentably support this conclusion; a discreet silence on his part would have been much more elegant.[7] Granted as a private individual Pedro would have had the right to be as unworldly as he pleased, in a monarch this attitude was a grave defect, particularly at a time when a more dramatic monarchical image should have been created. If only for the psychological effect, he could have lived a somewhat more imaginative life, even in his less public moments: dinners and receptions, royally sponsored artistic events, the concerts he attended. Such a course would have made him a much more imposing figure and, through the personal contacts which would have ensued, would have given the Empire greater prestige in its relations with the countries of Europe.

And this contact with Europe would not have been limited to the academies of science, but would have extended to the more youthful aspects of that continent, to the vibrant, experimental Europe of art shows, schools of sculpture, and architecture. From such developments Pedro II lived in almost total isolation—even worse than that of Dom João VI—and this at a time when Brazil desperately needed the stimulus of European influence, not only in Rio de Janeiro but in all other sections of the country as well. Whatever contact of this sort did take place was made, not by the dilettante astronomer of the Imperial palace (his eyes turned to the heavens), but by Gallicized provincial leaders such as the Pernambucan Baron

[7] Alcindro Sodré, ed.: *Abrindo um Cofre: Cartas de Dom Pedro II à Condessa de Barral* (Rio de Janeiro, 1956).

de Boa Vista, who had eyes for French architecture that extended to the practical considerations of engineering and city planning. It is true that the Emperor took a certain interest in the French gardens of M. Glazou in Rio de Janeiro; but such an isolated interest does not make up for the lack of Imperial initiative in the improvement of the urban scene and in the social life of the country, matters which, over a long period of years, the Emperor allowed to take care of themselves.

Old at twenty, Pedro had already impressed Europeans as a brooding, tired man, in contrast to his father, whom Max Radiguet described as "adventurous, impetuous, and *galant* as a Frenchman of the good old days." [8] Radiguet saw the cities of Pedro II as "sad, mean, sordid, and completely out of key with the splendors of the landscape." The most important public buildings gave the impression of barracks or hospitals; only the churches and convents retained their true character.

And the same observations applied to the society of Rio de Janeiro. "Compared to that of Spanish-American cities, the private life of Rio de Janeiro is confined to the home." It was thus difficult to appreciate the Brazilian character, particularly that of the Brazilian woman, although Radiguet was able to respond to the qualities of the young misses, noting their "indolent grace," their "melancholy and pensive charm" as they reclined in their hammocks during the heat of the day.[9] What a pity that the higher circles of society did not possess some of that charm, however melancholy, and that the Empress Teresa Cristina, who for sheer melancholy was the equal of her husband, did not encourage the inclusion of some of this youthful beauty in developing a court atmosphere worthy of a Bragança-Hapsburg.

On the other hand, the aristocratic Brazilian ladies in Europe— who unfortunately lacked a Henry James—were worthy of a sociological and psychological study. With their titled husbands—barons, viscounts, generals—they formed a most interesting group of expatriates who made the designation "Brazilian" famous in the world of society and culture, not as social climbers or *nouveaux riches,* but as an exotic element of true aristocracy.

Triumphs of this sort attained by Brazilians like the Baroness de

    [8] Max Radiguet: *Souvenirs de l'Amérique Espagnole—Chili—Pérou—Brésil* (Paris, 1856), p. 285.
    [9] Ibid., 263.

Estrêla gave Europeans the impression that such exquisitely seductive ladies were representative of the court of Pedro II. Far from it. In fact, they were fleeing a society which did not give them the slightest opportunity or encouragement, on returning from their travels, to exercise a discreet force in convincing the sweet—nearly always plump—aristocratic ladies of Brazil, rooted like abbesses in their town houses or their plantation homes, to furnish those homes in better taste, to decorate them with paintings and statues by legitimate artists, and to surround them with flowerbeds or tropical plants and flowers instead of the eternal rose gardens bordered with oyster shells. They might also have succeeded in teaching them to speak less stridently and to wear fewer jewels when they went shopping, or to give dinners in which there was a greater degree of restraint over the number of courses. Such activity on the part of returning voyagers would have constituted the equivalent, on a higher plane, of the instruction given the sons and husbands of these ladies by the *cocottes*, the actresses, and the *modistes:* lessons of discretion in spitting, in picking one's teeth, dressing, blowing one's nose, laughing, in using pomades on the hair or brilliantine on the beard, perfuming one's handkerchief, and in wearing diamonds on the fingers, cuffs, or shirt fronts. Truly, as a civilizing force in Brazilian life, these *cocottes*, actresses, and *modistes* deserve greater recognition.

Another form of instruction was the auction, already mentioned, where less traveled Brazilians could purchase or become acquainted with the appurtenances of modern comfort from expatriate British, Swiss, German, or French households. Such acquaintance, to be sure, did not succeed in eliminating elements of the purely Brazilian version of household comfort: the opulent cuspidors or sumptuous urinals of fine china, often decorated with gold like beakers for the preservation of the finest essences emanating from persons of quality. There were also the thousand and one varieties of silver toothpicks, from classical Neptunes to patriotically romantic Indians whose warlike arrows formed the working part designed for aristocratic teeth.[1]

In a work published in French in 1889 on the Brazilian art of the late Empire, Eduardo da Silva Prado found that the Brazilian

---

[1] This unexpected combination of the heroic and prosaic, together with the ostentatious manner of picking one's teeth, made a convert of at least one Englishman, the famous traveler Richard Burton.

interior resembled the Portuguese in its barrenness and bad taste.[2]
Objets d'art were rare, partly because of the necessity of "paying
enormous customs duties on such items, as though they were common merchandise." Native artists, even those of recognized merit,
devoted themselves solely to the grand style and produced pictures
far too large for the average middle-class drawing room, for which
they charged prices even higher than those of living European masters. Thus, the only pictures on Brazilian walls were portraits by
painters who dared not attempt the monumental and devoted themselves to subjects that would sell. Landscapes, water colors, or moderately sized pictures of any type were not to be seen.

As for furniture, the situation was even worse. During the last
days of the Empire Prado lamented the tendency (which increased
during the early Republic under the impact of progressivism) to
substitute novelties of dubious value and questionable taste for the
lovely old pieces decorated with leather and Portuguese silver
which had dignified many of the better Brazilian homes. Such furniture had been fashioned from "ravishing native woods . . .
chests and other pieces carved in palisander, an art in which the
woodcarvers of Bahia and Minas excelled . . . armchairs in black
leather decorated with large copper nails, four-poster beds, beautiful Portuguese and Brazilian silverwork of the school of Valentia
da Fonseca and his contemporaries."[3] All these were scorned as
ugly and shameful archaisms by a middle class which had begun to
"Europeanize" or "Americanize" or simply "modernize" itself by
adopting the worst aspects of progressivism, and by suddenly losing
all sense of the values of its unique tradition of patriarchal
monarchy, the only such social tradition in the New World.

The traditional values of interior decoration in the better Brazilian homes stemmed from colonial times and extended through a
large part of the reign of Pedro II. They represented an order and a
harmony which, if not of highest aesthetic value, at least merited
respect for their authenticity and for their happy combination of
European with native tropical elements. One such example was the
hammocks, at times made of feathers; aside from being cool and
comfortable, these were often true works of art.[4] Another was the

---

[2] M. F. J. de Santa Ana Nery, *et al.: Le Brésil en 1889* (Paris, 1889), p. 573.

[3] Ibid., p. 537.

[4] The art of working with feathers was highly cultivated in Brazil; its value
had been noted as early as the beginning of the nineteenth century by the French
commentator Ferdinand Denis.

pottery, especially the interestingly shaped clay vessels used in patriarchal homes as water coolers. Placed under the window sills, the water in these jugs would remain fresh and cool throughout the night. These jars, vessels, and water jugs were studied carefully by the French artist Debret at the beginning of the nineteenth century. Debret sketched the forms he found most characteristic, noting their vague similarity to oriental pottery. It is possible that these forms were of Moorish origin, introduced into Brazil by the Portuguese, and influencing native forms to a degree not to be discounted in either its artistic or ecological importance. Debret also pointed out that the clay vessels of Santa Catarina, Bahia, and Pernambuco were sufficiently porous to cause evaporation through the shell itself, thus lowering the temperature of the water within but without the seepage and exterior sweating noted in the *gollehs* of Egypt or the *alcarrazas* of Andalusia. Silva Prado noted that the yellowish color of the latter was ugly compared to the lively red of Brazilian pottery, and that the beauty of these jars earned them a place of honor in the best Brazilian homes until, under the impact of progressivism, such traditional objects were replaced by slick varnished products from England.[5]

Survivors of this period, in furnishing material for this book, have testified that the taste and temperature of the water from these vessels was one of the most sensual memories of their youth. Unaccustomed at the time to the extreme temperature produced by modern refrigeration, which they consider a comfort more apparent than real, they remember this water not merely with the sentimental nostalgia of the aged, but rather with the sense of recalling an experience that most keenly evokes the spirit of an authentically Brazilian past.

There were also the cooking and serving vessels used in preparing native dishes to satisfy the most exacting palate, and other household objects made of native materials: brooms, feather dusters, palm-leaf fans, sieves of fiber, heavy wooden pestles used to grind corn or coffee. And there were the curtains and draperies, the bedspreads, pillow cases, tablecloths, and napkins made of the finest lace from Ceará, Alagoas, and Pernambuco.

Music had come to be a Brazilian art par excellence. Since colonial times it had been the form most congenial to aristocrat and plebian alike for the expression of their Luso-American spirit. At

[5] Santa Ana Nery, *et al.*: op. cit., p. 544.

the beginning of the nineteenth century de Freycinet had already noted that "of all the arts cultivated by the Brazilians, music is the most successful." [6] This musical propensity became one of the characteristics of Brazilian society most closely associated with the Bragança dynasty; the monarchy from the beginning had been consistently friendly to both music and musicians. The name of the *mestiço* composer Father José Maurício was closely linked to that of Dom João VI; that of Pedro I to the German Neukomm who, together with the Portuguese Marcos Portugal, did much to advance musical taste in Rio de Janeiro during the reign of the first Emperor. Neukomm also helped to arouse European appreciation of Brazilian popular music, particularly the sensual *modinhas* of such composers as Joaquim Manuel, author of the patriotic "Independence Hymn." And the reign of Pedro II was marked by the triumphs of Francisco Manuel da Silva, pupil of both Neukomm and Portugal, and of Antônio Carlos Gomes, composer of the world-renowned opera *Il Guarany*, which critics have cited as an admirable expression of the native Brazilian spirit.

The reign of Dom Pedro II was also notable for its vigorous support of the opera, which presented Italian companies of the highest quality whose performances in Rio de Janeiro were attended by the royal family and in the more advanced provinces by the provincial governors as a solemn social obligation. This spirit of *noblesse oblige* toward the form of music most representative of European elegance was also felt by other persons of cultivated tastes. It is impossible to imagine a baron, viscount, counselor, or commander of the court of Pedro II—or, for that matter, any doctor, university graduate, public functionary, important merchant, or even college student—in these principal cities who was not familiar with the lyric theatre either as occasional patron or real devotee. The predilection was for Italian singers, particularly those of the female sex, and not infrequently preferences among these artists led to conflict between student "republics" and shop employee "castles," [7] or between rival groups of university students.

The vogue of the piano during the Second Empire, a vogue which extended from the concert hall to the private home, must

6 Ibid., p. 554.
7 Like the student "republics," the "castles" were rooming houses for young single men but in this case run by and for shop employees instead of students. (Translator.)

also be mentioned here. The huge grand piano became a status symbol, a manifestation of taste and social prestige, whether in the aristocratic villas of the suburbs, the middle-class city homes, or the mansions of the more cultivated planters and sugar processors in the rural areas. Ruder plantation homes contented themselves with a mere guitar or *cavaquinho* (a small guitar), a fact which caused such dwellings to be dismissed rather disdainfully as "houses without pianos." In the city, as well as the country, the expression "He already has a grand piano" testified not only to the cultural, but also to the social and economic progress of a family. Thus the piano became part of the socio-cultural system of Brazil, a development regarded by some foreign observers as a curse, perhaps because the instrument all too often refused to be the docile slave of fashionable ladies who attempted to dominate its mysteries.

According to two American clergymen visiting in the year 1879, "pianos abound in every street . . .", particularly in the capital, whose patriarchal homes were well known to these visitors.[8] From such homes the sound of a piano played by the lady of the house could often be heard in the street, and from some, on Saturdays, came the sound of dancing, not to the music of an orchestra, but rather to that of a piano played by a professional who made his living by composing music and playing it on these occasions. According to Cássio Barbosa de Resende, in a personal letter to me, "Many of these professionals became famous and their compositions were whistled in the street and played everywhere." And I cannot overlook one of the most characteristic aspects of both street and country life during this period: the sound of the whistler. It went on morning and night, at work, at play, in the bath, everywhere.

Of the many sounds that enlivened the aristocratic or middle-class home during Imperial times, there were some, not always musical, that emanated from outside: the carriages which, on party-giving days, clattered noisily through the iron gate opened only on special occasions; the street calls of the fruit, fish, and poultry vendors; the peddlers' rattles; the cries of the mendicant nuns or the ordinary beggars asking for alms "for the love of God"; the band playing marches on the way to a ball or to the bandstand in the cathedral square; the guitar serenades; the *sambas* and *maracatu*

[8] James C. Fletcher and Daniel P. Kidder: *Brazil and the Brazilians* (4th edn., Boston, 1879), p. 163.

music of the slaves; or the simple beating of palms at front gates where a doorbell or knocker was not provided. At times a kind of musical dialogue ensued, though the voices were not always of the best quality, between the house and the street. In an attempt to breach the closed—almost hostile—facade of a building, the petitioner would clap hands and chant: "*Ó de casa!* (Hey, you in the house!)" and from within would come the response, also in a sort of chant: "*Ó de fora!* (Hey, you out there!)" Through this ritual, communications were established which could result in an invitation to step inside and even to sit in the place of honor in the living room. If the taste for family heirlooms had not been replaced by the new craze for French or Austrian furnishings, the living room would contain heavy pieces in jacaranda or *vinhático:* a sofa for the ladies, flanked symmetrically by armchairs and other chairs of ornate upholstery for the gentlemen. The visitor might be entertained with music, either popular or classical, played on the piano by the hostess or by one of the young ladies of the house. The sound of the piano, whether in honor of visitors or merely in instruction or practice, was one of the principal signs of communication between house and street, for during the Second Empire no polite young lady's education was considered complete without some knowledge of music.

It is not at all surprising that a society so replete with the suggestion of music in the most prosaic activities of daily life and permeated with the rich natural music of locusts and tropical birds should save its greatest admiration for persons of musical talent, for a Padre José Maurício or a Carlos Gomes. In this respect, as in no other, rich and poor were in complete agreement. Music, from that of the church to that of the street—the bands in the public square or the African-derived *sambas* and *maracatus* of Recife or Salvador or Rio de Janeiro—constituted so integral a part of the life of the Second Empire as to form the most unifying element in a society of otherwise wide variety in its origins, appearance, and ways of living and thinking. If some types of music suggested different racial or class origins, others acted as a harmonious synthesis of social antagonisms and contradictions. The street march, for example, was an important musical agent of Brazilian social unity, whether sung or played, whether issuing from the piano of a fashionable home or a guitar in the street or the doorway of a humble thatched hut. Its popularity with the average citizen extended well into the opening decades of the Republic. And if this sense of national community was not the only attraction in the more erudite music of Carlos Gomes, it was at least an important factor.

Gomes was perhaps the greatest nonmilitary idol of Brazil during the 1870's; his popularity with all ages and classes of people rivalled that of the heroes of the Paraguayan War. Among literary figures, not even Castro Alves, Gonçalves Dias, Joaquim Manoel de Macedo, or José de Alencar attained comparable acclaim. He began as the idol of the law students of São Paulo at a time when this group represented the flower of the young Brazilian intellectuals.[9] In 1859 Carlos Gomes composed an "Academic Hymn," to words by Bittencourt Sampaio, which became wildly popular among students, and he also in this period composed a large number of ballads of general appeal to young people of all classes. The "genius of Campinas" thus became an object of national pride, earning the admiration and support of the Emperor himself. This support enabled Carlos Gomes to enroll as a student in the court conservatory and later as a pupil of Lauro Rossi in Milan. By 1868 he had composed two or three operettas, and in 1870 he produced *O Guarani*, a work which, in the rhetorical and somewhat inexact words of admiring commentators of the time, brought the "spirit of the tropical forest and of tropical passions" to the Italian operatic style. The popularity of this new primitivism among French, Italian, and British critics was shared by the public, and for once Europe bowed to Brazil. It wasn't long before *O Guarani* was being whistled by even uneducated Brazilians with a certain patriotic pride: the work rivalled the marches and sentimental ballads in popularity.

The ballads and marches, in their turn, remain among the most cherished memories for humbler persons recalling the latter days of the Empire. The ballads were sung by romantic young men to their beloveds to the accompaniment of the guitar, the marches rendered with impressive vigor by bands and orchestras in the public square of cities and towns of all sizes. Sometimes these bands were of rival political parties: one Conservative, one Liberal. During the late Empire there were even competing bands of republicans and monarchists. The conflict between the Church and the Masons extended to the bands supported by these inimical organizations. Thus there

---

[9] Other student groups exercising intellectual leadership at the time were those of the law schools of Olinda (later Recife) and of the School of Medicine in Bahia. These students far exceeded the limits of their university studies and were particularly strong in the field of music.

was hardly a Brazilian of the time who was not affected in some way by music, whether classical or operatic, or the college songs, marches, sentimental ballads, *maracatus, côcos,* or *sambas* of the day. Among the songs remembered with particular pleasure by people who contributed recollections to me were "*Quero casar com a mulher do meu amor* (I want to marry the girl I love)," "*Quinze Dias de Viagem* (A Two-Week Journey)," and the tearful

> Adieu, Maria, for I am leaving you
> Though I shall remember you always.
> Perhaps some day I shall dream of you crying for me.
> I go, but fate may still bring me back.

Typical of the humble people who encouraged these songs was Dona Maria Teodora dos Santos, born in Jaboatão, Pernambuco, in 1878. Dona Maria learned her letters with a teacher named Minervina de Albuquerque and enjoyed the children's readers of Felisberto de Carvalho. As a grown woman she read the romances of José de Alencar and the poetry of Casimiro de Abreu. Unfortunate in her marriage to a garrulous alcoholic, she lived mainly through her work in dressmaking and embroidery. She enjoyed doing this, although her ambition had always been to become a teacher. As a child she remembers her pleasure in dancing and singing, with a predilection for the waltz, then considered a dance for young ladies of the upper class. Her favorite ballad was "*Acorda, abre a janela, Estela!* (Wake up and open the window, Estela!)" She was a member of the *Linda Flor* dance society, a club frequented by serious-minded young ladies. Almost white in appearance herself, and favoring the dances and songs of polite society, Dona Maria Teodora did not like Negroes, whom she thought constituted to be the servants rather than the equals of whites. They could dance their *maxixes* and sing their *côcos;* she preferred the waltzes and *modinhas* of white folks.

Another typical case is that of Cássio Barbosa de Resende, a gentleman of the upper middle class born in the state of Minas Gerais in 1879. He tells us that in the fashionable circles he frequented in his youth the usual dances were the waltz, the polka, the schottisch, and the American quadrille. There were times when the *maxixe* was also performed, but not in private homes, since this dance was considered a Negro vulgarity. The type of music most appreciated in these circles was opera, with *Cavalleria Rusticana, Carmen, La Gio-*

conda, Rigoletto, La Traviata, and *Il Trovatore* the favorite works, along with the inevitable *O Guarani.* Of the operettas, the most popular were *The Merry Widow* and *The Dollar Princess.* Sr. Barbosa de Resende also says that in the early days of the Republic there were innumerable family reunions in the new federal district, where on Saturday evenings he "had the opportunity to see many brilliantly lighted ballrooms, where professional orchestras furnished lively music for dancing until dawn." The music composed and played by these professionals was carried from the ballroom into the street and sung and whistled everywhere. Eventually, it was absorbed by the lower classes and performed, often with adulterated lyrics which transformed the more difficult words into caricatures of the original text. He also confirms the popularity of the guitar serenade, the words of many of which remain clear in his memory. One of the most popular of these began as follows:

> *Quisera amar-te mas não posso, Elvira*
> *Porque gelado trago o peito meu*
> *Não me incrimines que não sou culpado*
> *Amor no mundo para mim morreu.*

("I should like to love you, Elvira, but I cannot, for my heart is cold. Do not blame me, for it is not my fault. In this world, love for me is dead.") And another began:

> *Bem sei, mulher, bem conheço*
> *Que fui um louco in fitar-te*
> *Inda main louco em amar-te*
> *Sem consultar a razão.*

("I know, my dear, that I was mad to gaze at you and even madder to love you without listening to reason.") The madness seems to have lain in a poor boy's falling in love with a young lady of wealth for the song continues:

> *Mas não suponhas, não creias*
> *Que o teu desdém me consome*
> *Pois que um pobre e som nome*
> *Sei desprezar-te também.*

("But do not suppose that your disdain consumes me. Though poor and nameless, I know how to disdain you as well.")

Along with the songs idealizing pale, blond heroines were those celebrating brunettes and even mulattos. The tracing of social tendencies through these songs during the long period when they were the most popular form of musical expression in Brazil leads to conclusions which contribute greatly to the psychological and sociological interpretation of the age. Here I can merely point out a few of the more significant signs of the complex combination of romantic individualism and patriarchal authority which characterized the Brazilian social order. These conflicting tendencies, by-products of the double struggle to move from slavery to a free economy and from monarchy to Republic, seem to be particularly pronounced in the last decade of the century. Themes of romantic individualism— the right to love, independent of considerations of family, race, or economic status—are constantly sounded in popular songs of this period. The simple, idyllic passion of Romeo for Juliet, free from inhibiting formalities and conventions, is especially prominent in the "country" music of the backlands, celebrating the loves of the *caboclo*, the *sertanejo*, or the *gaúcho*. In this vogue for idealizing the loves of humble people in popular song, it is safe to say that both the operas of Carlos Gomes and the romances of José de Alencar had played their part.

The increasing democratization of Brazilian music was not always favored by the conservatives of the period, some of whom openly detested the so-called "regional" music. The case of the Army officer Raimundo Dias de Freitas (b. Piauí, 1874) is typical. "In my boyhood," he writes, "the dance music seems to me to have been far more romantic, distinguished, and aristocratic than that of the present." The most frequent dances in his social set were the waltz, the quadrille, the lancers, the *pas de quatre*, the schottisch, the mazurka, and the polka. "The waltz was danced in either the French or the American way." And, surprisingly enough: "The American method gave the couple an air of much greater distinction and elegance." The quadrille, "after having originally been danced in the French manner, began to assume American tendencies somewhere between 1891 and 1893. The American quadrille was lighter and very elegant. It had the advantage of being able to form a complete square with only four pairs of dancers." As for the lancers, "it was a dance which bore the mark of true aristocracy . . . and was thus favored in the more fashionable *salons* of the day."

This connoisseur of ballroom dances admits that he had never been a "troubadour or a serenader, because I never felt the slightest inclination toward this type of entertainment." He preferred to frequent the opera and was greatly moved by *O Guarani*, perhaps as much through patriotism as through the love of music.

João Fernandes de Carvalho (b. Recife, 1867) echoes the same aristocratic tastes as Sr. Dias de Freitas and adds that concerts given by famous European violinists also had great social prestige in his boyhood. He records that, in addition to the violin, the mandolin and the flute were considered socially prestigious, although none of these instruments could begin to compete with the piano in importance.

Dona Maria Vincentina de Azevedo Pereira de Queirós (b. São Paulo, 1868) tells us that as a girl she attended the most elegant balls of the era: at the court, the casino, and the club of the *Diários*, the Itamaraty, and at the Catete Palace. For these dances, her gowns were ordered from the court dressmakers. "A silk dress, with silk stockings and satin slippers with Louis XV heels, a hand-painted ivory or mother-of-pearl fan, full-length kid gloves, together with flowers for the bosom and the hair came to between 400 and 500 *milreis*." Dance orders were used, in which young ladies carefully noted their partners for the evening's program. To obtain such bookings, the young gentleman was required to bow before the lady and request of "her excellence" the honor of the next waltz or polka.[1]

Eurico de Sousa Leão (b. Pernambuco, 1887) laments that in his youth the best lyric companies no longer came to his part of the country, a fact probably attributable to a decline in government support of such companies in the early decades of the Republic. He and his generation had to content themselves with *pastoris*[2] and *modinhas* performed and sung on the Capibaribe on moonlit nights by groups of students. Some of these serenading groups became famous for their songs and for their authentic style of singing traditional melodies, a style which put them on a par with the best

---

[1] This elaborate politeness extended beyond the dance floor. On meeting a lady in a public place, the gentleman always removed his hat in a broad, sweeping gesture. Even among men, it was customary to uncover, or at least to touch the hat, when meeting in public.

[2] Folk plays in which five girls in red and five in blue repeat songs and dance for pennies thrown from the audience. The group which gets the most money wins the competition. The dances are often interspersed with dirty jokes by a male comic character. (Translator.)

pastoral groups of the interior and of the past. One of the most famous was that of Herotides which, patronized by leading citizens, performed regularly in Recife until about the turn of the century. Herotides himself, a mulatto of mincing gait and notorious homosexual prowess, was greatly applauded for his singing and even more for his dancing, which he performed with the coquetries of an established prima donna, a fact which in no way diminished his stature as a fighter in a city famous at the time for its street brawls.

During the reign of Pedro II and immediately after, many European singers, pianists, and violinists became the idols of the Brazilian public. One of these was Sigismund Thalberg, considered at the time the king of pianists, who came frequently to Brazil with the encouragement of the music-loving Emperor. Thalberg's debut in Rio de Janeiro in July, 1855 was an event of such importance that a medal was struck in commemoration, and years afterward Brazilians would recall the concert with emotion and pleasurable nostalgia. Thalberg was a romantic-looking blond with mutton-chop whiskers, an aquiline nose, and rosy complexion. His hands, as was appropriate in a king of pianists, were fine-fingered and immaculately kept. Some said they were the hands of an angel and claimed that his little finger alone could produce more music than a *sabiá* (Brazilian thrush) in August. Beside his piano, all other keyboard instruments were reduced to the status of marimbas.[3]

The passion in the capital for European music brought about the founding of a private musical organization, capitalized at 360 *contos*, with the purpose of bringing to Brazil "the world's greatest singers."[4] In it were such important figures as the Baron de Lajes, the Viscountess of Minho, the Viscounts of Estrêla, Jequitinhonha, Itaboraí, Eusébio de Queirós, and Abrantes. It is not surprising that, with this enthusiasm for European singers, pianists, and violinists, Louis Moreau Gottschalk could exercise such a powerful hold on the cultivated people of Rio de Janeiro, from the elegant nobility to the pupils of the fashionable Episcopal Academy of São Pedro de Alcântara. The appearance of this artist at the Brazilian court in 1869 culminated in a festival of international renown, the most eloquent affirmation in history of the devotion of the Brazilian mon-

[3] Marimbas, the African equivalent of the piano, were considered fashionable in some of the most exclusive circles, in contrast to the general attitude of contempt in Europeanized society for anything grossly African in origin. As we have seen, the contempt extended to African cooking and dances.

[4] Escragnolle Dória: *Coisas do Passado* (Rio de Janeiro, 1909), p. 50.

archy to the art of music—a devotion surpassing even its passion
for oratory. One historian who as a child attended the event at the
Lyric Theatre has stated that the concert attracted the best society
of Rio de Janeiro, the boxes filled with elegantly dressed ladies in
silks and satins from the most fashionable designers of the day
(Comaitá, Guignon, Gudin, Guimarães, and Ottiker, dressmakers
of princesses), their coiffures done at Gilet's or Carlos Binet's.
These resplendent figures were the focal point of hundreds of pairs
of opera glasses, which also scrutinized the array of precious jewels
from Faroni or Bouete. On the stage were the court military bands
—650 musicians in all—their uniforms brilliant. The curtain rose
and the first notes of a "Triumphal March" dedicated to the Emperor, based on themes from the National Anthem, thundered out.
The combination of patriotic music, composed and directed by
Gottschalk, and of the Brazilian Empire, symbolized by the aristocratic audience, raised the event to a level far beyond that of a mere
society concert. According to our witness, it became the topic of
the day: "In the Rua do Ouvidor, in the drawing room, in conversations among friends, nobody talked of anything except the gala at
the Lyric Theatre." [5]

Two days later Gottschalk, scheduled to direct a similar concert
at the same theater, to the enormous consternation of his admirers
suffered a collapse just before he was scheduled to make his entrance. Three weeks later, at 4 A.M. on December 18, 1869, he died
at the Hotel Bennet in Tijuca, after having gallantly kissed the
hand of the Brazilian doctor who had remained at his bedside until
the end. The record of his death in the archives of the Misericordia
Hospital is laconic: "I attest that Sr. Moureaud [sic] Gottschalk,
American, single, 40 years old, being treated at the Hotel Bennet in
Tijuca, died today of an incurable galloping pleuropneumonia. His
illness lasted 21 days and his body may be buried." [6]

The funeral of Gottschalk was another great spectacle and a further proof of the union of music with the Brazilian social order.
Many marchers, carrying lighted torches, accompanied the coffin
to the Largo da Lapa, where the hearse was waiting. Many were
crying, and many more were wearing mourning for this foreigner

[5] Ibid., p. 72. Also see Gilbert Chase: *America's Music* (New York, 1955) and
Francisco Curt Lange: *Vida y Muerte de Louis Moreau Gottschalk en Rio de
Janeiro. El Ambiente Musical en la Mitad del Segundo Imperio* (Mendoza, 1951)
for further references to Gottschalk's stay in Rio de Janeiro.
[6] Dória: op. cit., p. 73.

whom Brazilians looked upon as a beloved relative. His "Triumphal March" would continue to link his name with Brazil, and it could be said that this American came to occupy the position of official Brazilian musician, even more than José Maurício or Carlos Gomes, whose music was more vigorously Brazilian but who both lacked the advantage of conducting—and virtually hypnotizing—a vast group of musicians in a patriotic piece on an occasion which so dramatically symbolized the Brazilian Empire. Not only the aristocracy of Rio de Janeiro, but the middle class and the common folk too loved and admired this foreigner who had learned to speak Portuguese in order to identify himself more closely with the people of the country. During the reign of Pedro II, Gottschalk was the most beloved foreigner in Brazil, particularly in Rio de Janeiro and among the young intellectuals of São Paulo.

The enthusiasm for Gottschalk in São Paulo and Rio de Janeiro does not mean that these representative cities were lacking in admiration for other foreign artists in music and the theater. For example, Candiani was the center of veritable adulation there and in Recife. Ristori[7] was received by the Emperor and Empress. After the latter's performance in Rio de Janeiro, there was a public ceremony in her honor, during which the Baroness of Rio Negro, in the name of her admirers, offered her a crown fashioned, in a very Brazilian manner, from humming-bird feathers. After her benefit performance, "Hundreds of persons, carrying torches and balloons, escorted her to her home to the sound of band music, fireworks, and vibrant *vivas*." [8] And other celebrities in the world of music and the theater were similarly fêted by the élite and by the students of Rio de Janeiro, São Paulo, Recife, and Salvador, among them Patti, Sarasate, and Duse herself on her visit to Rio in 1885.

The benefit for the great tragedienne coincided with the "burning period of the abolition question, with its flux of republican ideas, some sincere and others affected." Political tension was in the air, which possibly accounted for a certain initial diffidence on the part of a public still unacquainted with this eminent artist. Nevertheless, the journalist and promoter Ferreira de Araújo was able to rouse public interest in the event, and despite the pressures of the times, the Empire preserved its reputation of enthusiasm for music and the theater. Duse ended by receiving the warm applause of the

[7] Candiani and Ristori were Italian singers famous at the time. (Translator.)
[8] Dória: op. cit., p. 80.

Brazilian public; the Emperor presented her with a magnificent bracelet.[9]

At the same time as Duse, the then equally celebrated Flávio Andó[1]—whose name was imparted to a style of beard for some time considered very elegant by Brazilian men of all classes—also came to Brazil. Enthusiasms of this type were characteristic of a period in which the mystique of hairdressing developed into a virtual cult. Among men of means, this cultism was expressed largely through the beard, which was not only carefully trimmed according to the style affected, but often as carefully perfumed. For the women, of course, major attention was given to the coiffure, while both sexes favored lockets or bracelets containing or made of hair, often obtained, in the words of one chronicler, "through amorous devices." [2] At other times, men enclosed their mother's hair or that of their deceased wife in a gold locket, and women in like manner often carried that of a dead child on their bosoms. This cult of hair extended to other arts, and the beauty shop of Hellot in the Rua do Ouvidor dealt also in plumes, gold ornaments, pearls, and stork feathers, probably because such articles were often used to adorn the hair.

This obsession with hair at the end of the Second Empire constitutes a psychosis worth the attention of a social psychiatrist. It seems clear that the mystique of the male beard and female coiffure was closely linked to that of a combination of European monarchy and provincial patriarchy, in which the qualities of male potency and female fecundity would be equally celebrated. And strangely enough, republican propaganda, instead of opposing this symbology of monarchism, adopted it for its own purposes. Thus it gave great prominence to the hair of the allegorical female figure of the Republic which began to appear in illustrated magazines and newspapers of the seventies, her exuberance and youth aggressively contrasted to the melancholy old age of an Emperor caricatured in the images of Pedro Cashew or Pedro Banana. As for the propagandists of republicanism, few lacked an abundant patriarchal beard. Saldanha Marinho, Prudente de Morais, Campos Sales, Silva Jardim, Barbosa Lima, Sampaio Ferraz, Quintino Bocayuva were all abundantly bearded from the time of their early youth, almost as if to

[9] Ibid., pp. 105, 106.
[1] Andó was a famous actor of the late nineteenth century who affected a pointed beard.
[2] Dória: op. cit., pp. 129–30.

demonstrate that persons of republican persuasion could be quite as virile, socially and politically, as the barons, *conselheiros*, and commanders of the Empire.[3] It also seemed as though some were trying to convey the impression that the Republic, although a new form of government, did not constitute a new social order in which men would cease to be the rulers and women the prim auxiliaries of the home, just as in the old regime. Deodoro, with his characteristically Imperial beard and his conservative social views, during the days of the provisional government would never attempt to alter anything outside the field of politics; his approach never remotely suggested the social revolution desired by the Positivists. The early republicans clearly accepted that the only profound social change really needed had already taken place in the abolition of slavery; for the rest, it was just as well for Brazil to continue to follow Imperial social traditions, including the traditional power relations between the sexes and classes. Long beards and abundant hair-dos continued to act as sex and status symbols during the first decades of the Republic, and it is significant that a social system which had disintegrated in some of its fundamental precepts by abolishing slavery should have continued in republican times to respect such social differentiation and symbols of racial and class superiority.

Recalling his young manhood, José Silva Pereira (b. Ceará, 1880) wrote to me: "In those days, poets sung of the beauty of woman's hair, braided or otherwise arranged. Those who didn't have an abundant growth of hair bought the well-prepared braids sold from trays in the streets . . ." The "infernal scissors," Silva Pereira goes on, had not yet made their depredations on those vast and lovely coiffures, nor on the male mustaches either, some of which were tufted, some drooping, and some clipped. Such appendages were particularly affected by leaders of all types. There may have been a reduction in Christ-like beards, in sideburns, or in neck whiskers, but there was never any disappearance of facial hair;

[3] Aside from the hair, the point in common in this group is that they were all republican political leaders. Saldanha Marinho and Quintino Bocayuva were among the signers of the Republican Manifesto of 1870; Prudente de Morais and Campos Sales were, respectively, the third and fourth Presidents of the Republic (1894–1902). Barbosa Lima was a strong-arm political figure of socialistic leanings who served in the Brazilian Parliament and as governor of Pernambuco; Sampaio Ferraz was an equally strong-armed police chief in Rio de Janeiro. Silva Jardim was one of the most outspoken radicals of the late Empire, an open advocate of revolution, in contrast to the more gradual republican attitudes of the signers of the manifesto. (Translator.)

the destruction of such a social symbol would have carried a suggestion incompatible with the rise of a new and inexperienced political order.

Thus the ministers and deputies of the Republic, for example, followed those of the Empire in their social habits, patronizing the same barbers, the same haberdashers, the same cosmeticians, the same hotels, the same tearooms, the same *cocottes*. They continued to smoke the same brands of cigars and cigarettes,[4] to make use of the same public coaches and the same donkey-drawn streetcars, to attend the same theatres where, as conservative statesmen and industrialists, they applauded and supported the same artists they had cheered as abolitionists and republicans in their youth. They came to drink the same wines as the Imperial counselors, to sit in the identical upholstered or morocco chairs that had replaced the traditional pieces in jacaranda or *vinhatico* during the later years of Pedro II, to listen to talented young ladies playing the same pieces on the same Erard grand pianos. In the *Jornal do Commercio* they read the same editorials in support of the status quo—now republican—they had read in earlier days in support of the Imperial order. Such Imperial figures as the Baron de Ramiz Galvão continued to serve as the learned element among public officials, and their spreadeagle style of extempore political oratory changed little if at all.

The high value placed on oratory or eloquence and rhetoric was a socio-cultural attitude, the extension into republican times of which should not be discounted. Such was the emphasis placed on eloquence—sacred, political, or merely social—that during this long period in Brazilian life it overflowed its conventional limits (the address, the sermon, or the toast) to disfigure and pervert other forms of expression: poems, novels, essays, editorials, letters, official documents and reports, even telegrams. Everything was touched by this florid contagion which, during the monarchy, had had so favorable an ambiance for its development and which continued to flourish in republican times through the efforts of such spellbinders as Ruy Barbosa, Barbosa Lima, Martins Júnior, Lopes Trovão, and Pinto da Rocha. In clerical eloquence, no one in the first decades of the Republic would equal Mont'Alverne, a Francis-

[4] From the middle of the Imperial period, some of these changed their names regularly in accordance with political and social events, as is shown most interestingly in the Brito Alves collection of cigar bands.

can whose sermons in monarchical times had been a series of continuing triumphs both for their dramatic impact and their theological and philosophical weight. But in the field of political oratory, it was the one-time monarchist Ruy Barbosa, the last Athenian of the parliamentary government, who employed his gifts within the chambers of the First Republic to resist the impact of new ideologies. Products of a political system which placed an inordinate value on rhetoric, such fluent orators as Ruy could often carry a point, even a senseless point, in the face of the sober but possibly sounder reasoning of less gifted speakers. The same sort of thing happened in academic competitions, where professorial chairs often went to the glib, much to the detriment of such fields as science, which are often better served by men of slow and prudent expression than by the facile and overflowing.

Alfredo Severo dos Santos Pereira (b. Forteleza, 1878) looks back on this festival of oratory with an incisively critical eye: "Instead of doing, we liked to talk, in voices charged with emotion, holding the floor as though we were reciting to sentimental music. The danger in the addiction to the drug of rhetoric, as Ramalho Ortigão says, is that it enables one to exaggerate and alter the facts out of all proportion." Santos Pereira has nothing but praise for the diplomatic service of Ruy Barbosa at The Hague, but this praise does not extend to his "kilometric discourses," in which "his platform talents scarcely concealed the vices of our romantic oratory, which should be as undesirable in a political assembly as it would be in those devoted to only the finest and most disciplined exercises of reason." And since it followed that the Comtean sociocracy and its republican overtones was "a social structure based on science and not on the romantic empiricism of politicians who try to solve every problem with ecstatic oratorical fireworks," Santos Pereira in his old age remained convinced that Brazilians would continue to be as addicted to rhetorical and oratorical excesses as they had been during the days of the Empire.

Another Positivist, Agilberto Xavier (b. Rio de Janeiro, 1869), states that he studied with Benjamin Constant and learned from that master to consider mathematics "the true logic" and astronomy "the best scientific model." In order to continue his scientific education in accordance with Positivist views, he studied biology with Georges Audiffret, "one of the most eminent of Comte's pupils" who, "after becoming a civil engineer at the Polytechnical School of Paris (where he studied mathematics with Comte), took the advice of the master himself to become a doctor at the Montpelier Medical School, there completing the cerebral theory of Comte." Trained under such preceptors, Xavier could not have been favorably impressed by the rhetoric of Ruy Barbosa. "When the Republic came into being," he says, "I was passing from adolescence to youth" (he was twenty), but having been taught by Benjamin Constant, he had already learned from this founder of the Republic that "great social changes obey natural laws" and he saw the monarchy "created by our ancestors for the occasion of our country's political independence as being a theological-military regime incompatible with the scientific-industrial forces of the future and thus outmoded and impeding the progress of our revolution." For this reason he was not deceived "by the metaphysics of democracy," unlike his contemporaries who felt that "once the Republic is established we will be settled into the normal march of the future." Thanks to his scientific training, Agilberto Xavier saw the change as one of inevitable transition quite beyond the control of the orators and demagogues, as outlined by Comte in his "imperishable pamphlet" *An Appeal to Conservatives.* This work set forth "a series of sociological predictions of scientific veracity, similar to those of astronomy save for the ability to reduce such problems to a mathematical solution."

It is evident that Positivists of this type and background agreed that Brazilian development would be directed by something other than politics, particularly politics corrupted by rhetoric. But it is also certain that some of the Brazilian Positivists themselves were orators and rhetoricians in their own way, attributing a scientific validity to abstract sociological formulas that were merely doctrinaire in nature.

Despite the ideas of such Gallicized Positivists as Agilberto Xavier, however, Positivism never became so deadly an enemy of oratory that it rejected eloquence entirely. Such Positivist republicans as José Isidoro, Martins Júnior, Alexandre José, Barbosa Lima, and Benjamin Constant were noted for their eloquence, and this eloquence was not always free from rhetoric and verbalism. But none equalled Ruy Barbosa in vigor and oratorical floridness. This tremendous figure, who began as a somewhat anti-clerical spiritualist and ended a virtual Catholic, was a middle-class industrialist in his political thinking and thereby inimical to the Positivists, who in those days advocated the incorporation of the proletariat into Brazilian society. For this reason, during the period of the provisional government, he was constantly in conflict with Positivists such as Benjamin Constant and Demetrio Ribeiro, who at the time wished to introduce quite extensive social reforms, perhaps prematurely, in a Brazil heavily burdened by the spirit of the past. It was Ruy Barbosa, with his bourgeois liberalism, who defeated these Positivist ventures, as he also defeated Joaquim Nabuco, whose policy during the monarchy had been frankly social but without Positivist orthodoxies. Until 1919, Ruy Barbosa continued to disparage the social and labor issues agitated by the Positivists and by Nabuco. By this attitude he made many supporters, particularly among younger men and those of his own age group who, seduced by his oratory and persuaded by his rhetoric, remained indifferent to the fact that such discourses only barely touched on the social problems created by the abolition of slavery.

Demóstenes Ipiranga de Sousa Dantes (b. Pernambuco, 1876), in a most interesting testimony, confesses that, as a "feverish supporter of Pedro II," he had had a "horrible" impression of the Republic when it was first proclaimed and had considered Benjamin Constant and Ruy Barbosa "plagiarists and transplanters of a North American republican regime diametrically opposed to our customs and character," but that eventually he had become fascinated by the eloquent Ruy and his "resplendent intelligence." He saw how the "pure and eloquent Word" spread "like a hurricane," a hurricane this particular supporter of Pedro II could not resist. On the other hand, Sousa Dantes states, "I was always opposed to Positivism and considered Auguste Comte a spiteful lunatic."

"I was and still am a great admirer of a good orator," says Emiliano Ribeiro de Almeida Braga (b. Maranhão, 1873) who, as a boy, witnessed the proclamation of the Republic in his province "with much vandalism, always justified by the expression 'The Armed Forces in the name of the people.'" With his anti-military sentiments and his predisposition to admire good orators, it was only natural that Almeida Braga should become an ardent admirer of Ruy, the great civilian figure in the provisional government. He came to consider the eloquent Bahian as having a "great intelligence, such as is rarely found in this world." As a totally committed Barbosan, he was naturally unsympathetic to Auguste Comte and Benjamin Constant. "I believe that Auguste Comte, with the best of intentions, created Positivism as a religion, but I knew many a Positivist who was black as pitch! Well do I remember a certain governor of Amazonas and his gang, all Positivists . . . in their shenanigans!" And of this Amazonian governor, he continues: "When I first began to hear about Benjamin Constant, it was in Manaus, from this same governor F.B.F., who was a relative of the Positivist and who, in referring to his kinsman, always rose, removed his hat, and cited his name in full, an action which naturally was imitated by all the others in the company. This governor cultivated his relative's name, but not his virtues, and after only one year in government he was able to retire and establish a string of garden apartments in Rio de Janeiro!"

Orators of a new type began to appear and to express themselves in a less baroque manner, best described as functional and essentially substantive in nature. Such was the eloquence of David Campista, of Manuel Vilaboim, of Carlos Peixoto, of Gastão da Cunha, Epitácio Pessoa, Medeiros e Albuquerque, and Lauro Sodré. And it is worth noting that with the decline of this exaggeratedly baroque—even rococo—oratory came a corresponding decline in the taste for the Italian opera which had so vividly characterized the last quarter of the nineteenth century. W. J. Cash's remark that in the antebellum American South—a region so similar to Brazil—oratory had served as "a direct instrument of emotion, like music" [5] is also relevant here.

It would be difficult to imagine a society more in love with rococo oratory and more intoxicated by vocal music than the Brazil of the two or three decades of transition from monarchy to Republic and from slavery to free labor. It was a period in which these problems of transition were given far less attention in the form of political analysis or social science and philosophy than they got from emotional oratory and purely rhetorical tensions. The solutions brought about were merely juridical, or at best political. And quite often they were solutions proposed with the collaboration of music or drama.

Under the spell of a myriad siren voices, the harsh social realities were avoided or overlooked by government, by administration, by schools and churches in their search for solutions. With their excessive taste for music and rhetoric, shared by the vast majority of Brazilians, these supposedly responsible agencies failed to guide the

[5] Wilbur J. Cash: *The Mind of the South* (paperback, New York, 1954), p. 90.

country in the sober and objective course it so urgently needed.

There were some realists of the highest caliber in the public life of the period, both in the monarchy and the Republic, such men as Cotegipe, João Alfredo, Antônio Prado, Tavares Bastos, Couto de Magalhães, Saldanha Marinho, Prudente de Moraes, Campos Sales, Rodrigues Alves, Afonso Pena, Lauro Müller, Júlio de Castilhos, and Rosa e Silva.[6] But the number who clung to the Athenian tradition under critical conditions that demanded a new type of public servant was also considerable. The social order produced as many of one kind as the other: those who could size up the situation as it was and those who sought a merely rhetorical solution along general principles of European or Anglo-American origin. Thus for every Cotegipe there was a Lopes Trovão; for every Antônio Prado a José Mariano; for every cold, calculating, quietly effective Floriano Peixoto, a Coelho Neto all fuss and feathers, lyric and romantic in his almost messianic republicanism. It cannot be said that the period produced men too platonic and theoretical to face concrete problems objectively, for this would be unjust to men of administrative efficiency and practical knowledge like Cotegipe, on the one hand, or Rodrigues Alves on the other. Both these men showed great political sagacity and flexibility in furthering the rapid disintegration of some of the most characteristic features of the Brazilian social system; Cotegipe, as we have seen, in calling for the immediate abolition of slavery and Rodrigues Alves in his practical activity during the Republic. Both were statesmen who gave their attention to the aspects of Brazilian social structure most capable of being transformed into a new social order. In this spirit, and employing such criteria, they and others of their type such as Rosa e

[6] A mixed bag of prominent monarchists and republicans of the late nineteenth century. Cotegipe was a conservative Prime Minister from 1884 to 1888, who resigned over the abolition issue and was replaced by João Alfredo (Correia de Oliveira), under whose ministry the emancipation was proclaimed. Antônio Prado and Tavares Bastos were liberal monarchists who accepted the inevitability of the Republic. Couto de Magalhães was a leading publicist of the time, author of *O Selvagem*. Saldanha Marinho was a journalist and a founder of the first republican club and republican newspaper. Prudente de Morais, Campos Sales, Rodrigues Alves, and Afonso Pena were successive Presidents of Brazil between 1894 and 1909. Lauro Müller was a Cabinet officer in the Rodrigues Alves government and in 1912 became Foreign Minister on the death of the famous Baron do Rio Branco. Júlio de Castilhos was a powerful political leader from Rio Grande do Sul who constantly opposed the centrist tendencies of the republican government. Rosa e Silva, a one-time monarchist, was leader of the conservative republican faction in Pernambuco. (Translator.)

Silva and Aníbal Freire were men of quiet and serious action facing the orators and rhetoricians who abounded in the political field. The Cotegipes and Rodrigues Alves could when necessary make their speeches; speeches which were expressive if not eloquent, but which never descended to the level of mere oratory.

❧ [I I I] ❧

From Empire to Republic

MEN OF COTEGIPE'S STAMP were perhaps more concerned with order than with progress; those of Rodrigues Alves's mold were more attentive to the interests of progress than to the demands of order. But both types almost invariably saw the problems of the one as inextricably connected with those of the other, thus identifying themselves closely with a social and cultural viewpoint dating from pre-national times and extending back as far as the reign of Dom João VI. The announcement therefore by the Positivist-oriented Republic, proclaimed by Deodoro in 1889, to the effect that the new government would be a political order dedicated to the conciliation of these sociological values did not really represent a new science applied to the political scene (as the Positivists believed) so much as a confirmation of an established constant in Brazilian development, traceable to remote colonial times.

In seeking to examine the relationship of the Republic of 1889 to the cultural development of Brazil during the late monarchy and early Republic, I shall use the term "cultural" in its sociological context to signify a combination of values, styles, techniques, and habits, rather than in its more narrow sense in reference to the arts and sciences. And in speaking of "progress," I am using the term to indicate a relative development rather than in the messianic sense of designating an evolution moving constantly and completely toward social betterment. I take my place among those who are inclined to believe less in a complete and monolithic progress toward such betterment than in a *multiplicity* of progresses, which are sometimes neutralized when judged in the light of purely ethical, aesthetic, religious, or intellectual values—or by the purely technical and mechanical criteria of the avowed progressives. Moreover, these two ways of measuring progress, must be seen as *parallel* rather than *convergent*. Using this dual standard of analysis and comparison, we can place the Athenian assessment of customs and values on a relatively (but not absolutely) superior plane to that which governs values in Chicago or São Paulo or Johannesburg. The British historian G. M. Trevelyan correctly warns us, in an already classic statement, that: "Progress, as we of the twentieth century are better aware than our Victorian ancestors, is not always change from bad to good or from good to better. . . ."

In visiting Brazil to observe the general effects of the transformation from monarchy to Republic, the Anglo-American publicist Isaac N. Ford noted that Brazilians were prone to procrastination, a habit which he rather flippantly asserted was "formed under the influence of an enervating climate." [1] He noted the continual use by Brazilians of such expressions as "Wait a while" or "Be patient," and concluded that it was also a matter of "race instinct," beyond that of climate, that caused Brazilians to adapt themselves so slowly to the political and social changes brought about by the Republic. Since they were not a people who, in work or play, hustled to make tomorrow arrive more quickly, they were not impatient with republican institutions, nor did they appear to hope that these institutions could quickly bring about a national regeneration.

"They believe," said Ford of the Brazilians of 1890, "that they have entered upon a future of brilliant promise." That is to say, he found Brazilians already living psychologically in the future industrial development proclaimed by the decrees of the provisional government and, under the charm of this mystical faith, quite willing to reconcile themselves to the "disordered finances," the "temporary military usurpation," and the "constitutional anomalies" that characterized the first two years of republican experience.[2]

Of all the visiting foreigners who busied themselves in analyzing the first reactions of the Brazilians to the future which faced them so abruptly, perhaps none has been so exact as Ford in linking these reactions to the peculiarly Brazilian psychological, social, and cultural climate. He saw that Brazilians had no objection to the intrusion of the future upon the present just so long as the change was gradual and did not involve a complete repudiation of the past. Gradual, without eagerness and impatience, with the new President

[1] Isaac N. Ford: *Tropical America* (London, 1893), p. 72.
[2] Ibid., p. 73.

of the Republic giving himself the airs of a constitutional Emperor; with the separation of Church from State without the weakening of Catholicism as a national institution; with the employment of former members of court in important administrative posts under the Republic; with the transformation of the former provinces into states unaltered in their social, cultural, and ecological characteristics; and, finally, with experienced and titled Imperial political figures such as the Baron de Lucena, Counselor Antônio Prado, and the Viscount de Cabo Frio carrying on as before. Then there seemed to be nothing precipitate about the new order.

Nevertheless, there was a considerable change in the cultural order with the transformation of Brazil from Empire to Republic. Instead of emanating from France and England (the nations most influential during the monarchy), the new inspiration, thanks to Ruy Barbosa, came almost entirely from the United States. And it was from this shift in influence that there arose a series of consequences of signal importance to Brazilian culture. Prominent among these was the study of constitutional law and administrative law, a task which had to be performed in a language with which most Brazilian jurists were as yet little acquainted. It is true that the parliamentary system followed by the Empire had been to some degree inspired by the British example and that the English language already enjoyed prestige among Brazilian politicians and jurists of the élite. (The subtleties of English pronunciation had even been debated in parliamentary sessions.) But it is also true that the British system of government had been extensively studied by French writers well known in Brazil, and it was through them that parliamentarians of the period of Pedro II learned most about the British legal system. Now the situation was different; to understand the American government, it was necessary to read books written in English.

Already in the decade preceding the Republic, the United States had influenced Brazilian culture in various significant ways. This influence had increased with the proclamation of the Republic which, incidentally, almost exactly coincided with the first Pan-American Conference in October, 1889. In the previous chapter it was pointed out how, even in Imperial times, French ballroom dances were being replaced by those of the United States. The same thing was occurring with British influences; for example, the taste for Sir Walter Scott was being overtaken, if not surpassed, by that for James Fenimore Cooper. The Emperor himself had taken the initiative in directing attention to the United States after returning from that country much impressed by certain marvels of technical progress, some of which he immediately introduced into Brazil. I say "the Emperor himself" because nobody during this period was more cautious than he in insisting that cultural progress be consistent with the existing social order. Thus Republican or quasi-Republican caricaturists found considerable material for satire in the alleged declaration of the Emperor in Philadelphia in 1876 that he wished to see in Brazil, not cannons, but modern industrial and agricultural machinery. In its issue of January 7, 1877, the anti-clerical and anti-monarchical *O Diabo a Quatro*, published in Recife, featured an article interpreting Dom Pedro's remarks as expressing a desire to bring American civilization to Brazil in the form of machinery. Recalling impishly that the Emperor's first visit to Europe had resulted in "a veritable reform of Brazilian customs and institutions: the abolition of hand kissing," the writer found the "pretentious" declarations of Pedro II in Philadelphia to be merely an attempt "to cut a good figure with the Americans, without regard for the anvil chorus they would provoke in Brazil." [3]

The fact is that Pedro II bore himself in the United States less like a visiting head of state than a mere Ambassador of his country, anxious to see American civilization at close range and to learn from it things which could best be applied to the development of a still-backward nation. In this vein he had conferred with the New Orleans Health Commission on the problems of yellow fever, had inspected modern fire-fighting equipment in New York, and had visited the Armed Services academies in Annapolis and West Point. But in the United States, as in Europe, his curiosity for the technical marvels of modern civilization had not prevented him from seeking the acquaintance of famous poets and men of learning: Longfellow, Lowell, and Whittier in Massachusetts; Bancroft in Rhode Island, and Professor Loomis in New Haven. Earlier he had represented the only American monarchy at the Philadelphia Centennial Exposition, where Brazil had won more prizes than any other South American country (421 against 80 by Argentina and 40 by Chile).[4] These awards not only signified the greater order prevailing in Brazil than in the Spanish-American countries but also

[3] *O Diabo a Quatro* (Recife), January 7, 1877.
[4] James C. Fletcher and Daniel P. Kidder: *Brazil and the Brazilians* (4th edn., Boston, 1879), p. 592.

testified to its greater cultural progress, even in the field of industry. The Emperor's visit to the United States symbolized the eagerness with which his country was striving to accelerate a progress recognized by the Philadelphia Exposition as already far from inconsiderable when compared to other such countries.

It is natural that Dom Pedro's visit to the United States should have opened new perspectives in the cultural progress of Brazil, hitherto confined largely to European models. The same purpose was served at the time by the extended visit to Brazil of the Swiss-American intellectual Louis Agassiz, and by the residence in New York of the Brazilian-Jewish journalist José Carlos Rodrigues. During his several years in New York, Rodrigues published the journals *Novo Mundo* and *Revista Industrial*, acquiring printing and journalistic techniques which he later applied in Rio de Janeiro to the notable advantage of Brazilian culture, despite the horror of Ruy Barbosa, whose romantic tastes in journalism were outraged by the industrialized and commercial tone of Rodrigues's publication in a city still half European in its journalistic tastes.

It was to Agassiz that we owe the visit of William James, who came to study the Brazilian tropics in 1865.[5] The same purpose brought Hartt, Orville Derby, Orton, and Branner. By 1880 this field of research in its crudest but most seductive form—the Amazon—had also attracted the British Wallace, Bates, and Chandler, the French Marquoi, and the Brazilian Costa Azevedo, Soares Pinto, and Couto de Magalhães. Among these, the work of the Americans in disseminating a greater knowledge of equatorial Brazil had particular impact on Brazilians. Some of these men, such as Branner and Derby, in addition to their geological studies, examined other aspects of Brazilian culture, and Branner, through his knowledge of Portuguese, was able to write a grammar of the language of Brazil. Hartt in his study of the myths surrounding the Amazonian tortoise contributed to the development of Brazilian ethnological research.

The reports of the American naval officers Herndon, Gibbon, and Maury on their studies of the Amazon aroused the interest of the Brazilian government in those waters, and the maps made by Maury figured in the treaty with Peru resulting in regular naviga-

[5] Carleton Sprague Smith: "William James in Brazil," in *Four Papers Presented in the Institute for Brazilian Studies, Vanderbilt University* (Nashville, Tenn., 1951).

tion of the Amazon by Brazilian vessels embarking from Belém de Pará. The Maury maps, published in the *Correio Mercantil* of Rio de Janeiro, caused considerable indignation against the United States, an indignation spurred by the apparently sincere words of the Reverend James Fletcher, a fellow American, who found extra-scientific elements in Maury's cartography which he felt would cause Brazilians to suspect filibustering or imperialism behind his activity. Nevertheless, in 1867 the Amazon was opened from the Atlantic to Peru to ships of all flags, a measure extraordinarily advantageous to the Empire in its awakening in the United States of a dream of developing this vast area to a degree denied any other people of Nordic extraction. Brazil, according to Fletcher, "differs from all other tropical countries"; so that its civilization, with its already evident progress, could perhaps be extended to the Amazon. The United States could take advantage of this Brazilian capacity to carry development to the area by intensifying its efforts to make the American presence felt in the form of labor-saving machines. By 1870 there were already a number of Brazilian firms dealing in such machinery and other North American products.[6]

Since 1855, in letters to American newspapers, the Reverend James Fletcher had been extolling Brazil as being not merely "the only monarchy in America" but also the "only constitutional government" in the hemisphere, except for the United States, which was advancing into the future "in tranquility and material prosperity." In other words, one in which order and progress were combined. It was a country already devoting much attention to education, one containing flourishing learned organizations comparable to the New-York Historical Society. Mr. Fletcher wished to see developing relations between men of learning in Brazil and the United States, to see good textbooks, American style, in the hands of Brazilian schoolchildren, and American products in the Brazilian market, a market which could prove itself a great consumer of such articles.[7]

With these three ends in view, Fletcher promoted an exposition of American products in Rio de Janeiro, including photographs, maps, books, engravings, lithographs, and farm implements. This exposition can be considered a historical landmark in the development of cultural relations between Brazil and the United States and a great

[6] Fletcher and Kidder: op. cit., pp. 580, 196.
[7] Ibid., pp. 238, 239.

stimulus to the progress of American influence in that country. The event took place at the National Museum and the Emperor himself attended. Attracted particularly by the scientific exhibits, Dom Pedro II spent half an hour poring over Youmans's *Atlas of Chemistry*. He expressed interest in works dealing with the American Indians and in schoolbooks and maps. Also in machines, in farm implements, in wallpaper designed by students of the Philadelphia Art Academy, in bookbindings, and in various matters of physical science.[8] All in all, the exposition was an event in Rio de Janeiro. Without being pretentious, it awakened the curiosity of Brazilians of many professions—intellectuals, industrialists, planters, scientists, businessmen—toward a civilization which most had not previously considered capable of competing with Europe in matters of technology.

Under the influence of this exhibition and other comparable stimuli, Brazil soon came to admire the many American products arriving in the country, some of which were considered by local engineers and technicians to be superior to those of Europe. Such was the case of the Baldwin locomotive, known everywhere in Brazil as the *Balduína* and used figuratively in common speech as the symbol of a force capable of overcoming all obstacles. The Singer sewing machine also enjoyed great popularity, surpassing that of the British Excelsior manufactured by Gipping. Both the locomotive and the sewing machine, each in its own way, developed new dimensions in the cultural life of Brazil.

We should not forget that it was during the reign of Pedro II that, in addition to the establishment of regular navigation on the upper Amazon, Brazil underwent the initial period of railway construction that made the Baldwin locomotive with its inscription "Made in the U.S.A." a familiar object on the Brazilian landscape. This was also the period that saw the laying of the submarine cable to Europe, the introduction of gas for illumination, and the extensive modernization of dock facilities, of water and sewage systems, of public parks, bridges, markets, theatres, hospitals, and penitentiaries. Urban transportation also was greatly modernized, with the streetcar, the familiar Brazilian *bonde*, making its distinctive contribution to the democratization of everyday life. Many of these technical innovations that so markedly changed the Brazilian scene and Brazilian living habits were projects financed and undertaken by

[8] Ibid., p. 240.

British and French interests; but a great and increasing number of them were the result of American capital and know-how.

After the Fletcher Exposition at the National Museum, and in spite of the brief wave of patriotic indignation against the United States aroused by the Maury incident, anything American began to be regarded by progressive Brazilians as veritably charismatic in value and influence, particularly in the sense of being free from the complications of the European past. It was Ruy Barbosa who, though no economist and even less of a sociologist, did much to transplant the American political system to Brazil and who introduced a number of reforms "appropriate to our present-day civilization," which, abandoning "the framework of old-fashioned Roman formalism," moved toward "the simplification inherent in an industrial civilization," as he said in a report to General Deodoro in 1891.[9] The fact is that since the 1870's American inventions and technology had attracted the attention of the more progressive Brazilians, who saw in them the hope of freeing Brazil from the remaining elements of its feudal past as well as from certain pernicious archaisms of Latin origin.

These Latin vestiges in Brazilian cultural life had greatly surprised Agassiz on his visit there in 1865. In the Brazilian Empire, he noted at the time, "public procedures, resulting probably from old social conditions, offer certain obstacles to progress." These obstacles, he felt, were due to the fact that, during the period of discovery, "Portugal was the European nation . . . least affected by modern civilization. . . . The great transformations which had overturned Europe during the Middle Ages and at the beginning of modern times had scarcely reached Portugal. . . . Roman traditions, Roman architecture, and a degenerated form of the Latin language still were flourishing there when that nation founded its transatlantic colonies and, in all these colonies, the conditions of the metropole were never changed."[1]

It will surprise no one that the older structures of Rio de Janeiro can be compared with the architecture of ancient Rome. The very administration of the Brazilian provinces was patterned on Roman forms; in the Empire of Pedro II the Romanism of the physical architecture extended to the social structure as well. And what Bra-

[9] *Govêrno Provisório dos Estados Unidos do Brasil—Anexos ao Relatório do Ministro da Fazenda* (Rio de Janeiro, 1891), p. 20.
[1] M. and Mme Louis Agassiz: *Voyage au Brésil* (Paris, 1872), pp. 252–3.

zil needed most, as progressives like Agassiz pointed out, was not to strengthen the authority of the national government over that of the provinces, but rather to "develop the country's natural resources." Within the framework of this Roman form of government, the provinces found themselves led by "young lawyers" when what they really needed, according to Agassiz, was "practical men familiar with agriculture and industry and not mere speech makers." [2]

Thus Ruy Barbosa, although more of a speech maker than a practical man of agriculture and industry, nevertheless was a good pupil of Agassiz when he called for the abandonment of "the framework of old-fashioned Roman formalities" inherited from a Portugal more Roman than the Romans, in favor of "simplifying reforms inherent in an industrial civilization." It was such reforms which would facilitate the replacement of the monarchy by the Republic. Once pointed in the direction of industrialization, it was understandable that Brazil had turned eagerly to the economic and political patterns of the United States, had become the champion of Pan-Americanism in Washington, and had allowed itself to enter into a commercial treaty "most favorable to the United States," as Ford wrote in 1892.[3]

How did Brazilians of this period of transition react to the new presence of the United States in the political and cultural life of the country and to the injection of machinery from American factories into the recently agrarian economy based upon slave labor? The reactions were mixed. Amílcar Armando Botelho de Magalhães (b. in the province of Rio de Janeiro, 1880) tells us that he had admired the United States from childhood because of the "splendor of its liberty and its democracy," as well as for its industrial progress. Raised under the Positivist influence, the son and brother of illustrious military figures and the nephew of Benjamin Constant, it always seemed to him necessary that Brazil adopt a republican system which would bring "greater benefits to the proletariat in the form of general education, technical specialization, and artistic and cultural development, together with material support, sanitary living conditions, a scientifically regulated diet, and a system of hospitals, maternity homes, and medical clinics." These humanizing factors would be developed under an industrial system, once the country was free of the long years of backward monarchy.

[2] Ibid., p. 253.
[3] Ford: op. cit., p. 396.

On the other hand, Higino Cícero da Cunha (b. Maranhão, 1858) stated in 1940 that as a child he had no sense of the presence of the United States in Brazilian life and that this came "only after the proclamation of the Republic in the constitutional law of Ruy Barbosa, in finance, in the cinema, and in exotic dances"; while Demosthenes Iparanga de Sousa Dantes (b. Pernambuco, 1880) considers the United States as the "nation which has brought us the greatest number of evils."

José Alves de Figueiredo (b. Ceará, 1879) testifies: "When I read *A Ilusão Americana* by Edward Prado, I hated the United States, but as time went on I saw my error and came to adopt the ideas of this fiery Brazilian author." He eventually saw the United States as having, "after Switzerland, the most perfect republic in the world and one which must of necessity act as the hub of civilization in our continent."

Raimundo Dias de Freitas (b. Piauí, 1874) states: "In my adolescence I saw the United States as the enormous devourer, the dominator of the small nations of Central America and perhaps of South America as well, despite the proclamations of the celebrated Monroe Doctrine." American intervention in the Central American nations made a bad impression on him. In his childhood, the predominating foreign influence was that of France. Nevertheless, in time he came to admire the United States. And despite this French influence which, as we have seen, caused young girls to play with French dolls and seek French luxury articles, Dona Antônia Lins Vieira de Melo (b. São Paulo, 1879) confesses that since her youth she had been most impressed by "the deeds of Edison, which seemed fantastic." Such an impression was not rare among Brazilians of the era and there were some for whom, from this point of view, the United States became almost prophetic—the land of promise for mechanical marvels, the paradise of inventors. Florêncio Carlos de Abreu e Silva, native of Rio Grande do Sul, saw the United States as "the land of electricity governed by the magic wand of Edison"; while Tomás Pompeu de Sousa Brasil of Ceará, as a young man wished his country to become an amalgam of "American progress, British democracy, French culture, German discipline, and Italian artistry."

Manuel Duarte (b. 1883 in Rio Grande do Sul, where he was a companion of Getúlio Vargas) states that his youthful impression of the United States was one of "supreme grandiosity"; its industries seemed to manufacture everything used in Brazil. He was early convinced that the presidential form of government in the American style was the best for Brazil, seeing it as "the socio-political remedy for our ills" through "administrative responsibility, ample publicity for all acts of government, economy in public finances, parsimony in necessary expenses, unrestricted respect for individual and collective opinion, shelter and initial help to the poor farmer, continuous development of public education, personal and professional liberty, a legislative budget with auditing of public expenses, municipal plebiscites in executive actions, and wide participation of the people in the making of laws."

Padre Leopoldo Fernandes Pinheiro, born in Ceará of an intransigent monarchist family, grew up believing "republicanism to be a satanic form of government" and, though still too young to read, "clapped my hands when I heard that Antônio Conselheiro had destroyed a battalion of government troops" because "I thought that the victory of the fanatic of Canudos would be the easiest way of restoring the monarchy." But he still admired the United States, "a great machine run by the largest citizen body on earth."

Manuel Pereira Dinis, a *mestiço* born in Paraíba in 1887, was disappointed by the American-model Republic of 1889 and saw it as "a federalist regime which put us forty years behind . . . almost to the brink of economic and political ruin." He adds that for a part of his life he saw both the United States and England as powers which, through their industries, "strove to be absolute rulers of all other nations." Despite a brief period of republicanism as a law student in Recife, Senhor Dinis returned to the conclusion that "the republican regime with us is . . . merely a syndicate of exploiters of the public treasury to the increasing detriment of our people and our authority. . . ."

The United States to some extent had also made its presence felt in Brazil through the arrival of immigrants from the American South after their defeat in the Civil War. This was particularly true in the state of São Paulo where, according to some, the newcomers brought their racial prejudices and had some influence on Paulista planters opposing the abolition of slavery. (In one instance, an American was blamed for the assassination of an abolitionist in São Paulo on the eve of emancipation.) Nevertheless, it would be unjust to deny that these and other Americans of the late nineteenth century had brought ideas leading to cultural progress in the provinces and not only in the court. São Paulo became notable in the late nineteenth century for its reforms in educational methods, improvements which can be attributed to the presence of the Americans, although also due in part to the presence of British and German teachers, tutors, and governesses.[4]

The transition from slavery to free labor in areas where there was considerable European immigration had not come about without some previous anticipation of new industrial or farming methods and these areas suffered little change outside the political field save for a slight period of depression. This fact justifies the comment of one observer that the Republic had been a light dessert after a heavy *feijoada* served at dawn. Both North European and American influences, however, undoubtedly had an effect on the cultural rhythm of the period in government and in labor and gave another dimension to the Luso-tropical patterns of Brazil.

It is not surprising that, during the reigns of Dom João and the two Pedros, Brazilian culture, despite its deviation from the free-labor republican pattern dominating the rest of the continent, allowed itself to be infiltrated and influenced in many ways by patterns of life from other American and Western nations of quite different economic and political format. Infiltrated it was. The streetcar, to invoke a picturesque example, symbolized the transigence of this aristocratic slave-owning culture in accepting the leveling equalitarian European or North American system of mass transportation. Not the least significant feature of the streetcar—and the same could be said for the train—was that all classes in the community were now conducted to their destination at the same rate of speed.

Similarly, European immigrants in southern Brazil, in their role as poor white laborers, small farmers, mechanics, artisans, and craftsmen, effected a change in a society accustomed to associating those activities essentially with Negro slave labor. The machines imported from Europe and the United States had much the same impact, since these machines were run by men of varied ethnic and social conditions in a vivid demonstration of the ability of all classes to develop the aptitudes needed to assimilate and cope with the innovations of a technological culture.

[4] The influence of formal education on the cultural progress of Brazil during this transition period deserves more specialized study. Here it can be considered only in connection with other intellectual aspects of the same progress—journalistic, literary, medical, and technical.

It should be understood that these cultural innovations took place in Brazil without dependence upon either the political system or the established patterns of labor in the country. Some students of the situation have therefore reached the conclusion (already advanced by Oliveira Lima during the period in question) that it would have been not only possible, but also desirable, to prolong both the monarchist regime and the slave system somewhat to allow time for a better assimilation of these innovations. This had been the desire of the Emperor, as well as of such objective statesmen as Cotegipe, who like Lafayette had been accused by republicans like Maciel Pinheiro of wanting to perpetuate slavery "as a source of public income." [5]

Joaquim Nabuco, on the other hand, always separated the cause of abolitionism from that of the monarchy. Favoring the latter, he also supported the former, in either case with such courtly elegance as to gain the respect of abolitionists and republicans alike.[6] Nabuco nevertheless remained convinced for a long time that it had been an error to replace the monarchy with the Republic, and it is possible that he went to the grave with this conviction still in his secret thoughts. Though he served the Republic, he continued to consider the Empire the more authentic sociologically, not only in the sense that it was peculiar to Brazil but also because he felt it could better achieve a national culture through the combination of intellectual, aesthetic, and scientific factors already favored by the Empire. This monarchist tradition, however, was actually followed by the Republic in its most creative periods, for example, during the presidency of Rodrigues Alves in the early years of the century, when foreign policy was directed by the Baron do Rio Branco and the diplomatic corps was served by such monarchists as Nabuco himself.

It was through the efforts of these men that Brazil eventually recovered the equilibrium lost during the Canudos episode, when

[5] Maciel Pinheiro: "A Indenização," *A Província* (Recife), December 2, 1888.

[6] So much so that, while the enthusiasm of republican victory was still at its height, Martins Júnior, in the *O Norte* of November 23, 1889, expressed his feeling for the defeated monarchist in particularly honorable terms, calling him a "great thinker" with the "mind of a poet," who now ought to be "entirely convinced of everything he had been told" by the republicans. It was the "little enemies of yesterday" who should be "tormented by remorse," and not "ingenuous brothers" like Joaquim Nabuco, to whom Martins Júnior extended a "fraternal embrace," reminding him that the "distinguished and circumspect citizen Ruy Barbosa" had come over to the Republic.

the valiant resistence to the Army of the Republic on the part of Conselheiro and his *bravos* seemed to threaten the stability of republican institutions and to favor a return to a monarchy supported by an alliance of back-country farmers and members of the urban élite, an alliance supported in turn by the powerful Catholic sentiments of both groups. By now it appears that the thesis that accorded to the Canudos movement—a rustic revolution—the dignity of a monarchical Catholic resistance to the Republic has been amply demonstrated. The so-called "breviary" of Antônio Conselheiro found in Canudos does not confirm the emphatic assertion of Euclydes da Cunha that the famous mystic was a rebel against the Catholic Church and a votary of "free love." It is a pity that Euclydes, to whom Afranio Peixoto offered Conselheiro's precious manuscript, should not have felt impelled to rectify his opinion of Conselheiro on the basis of the breviary. What this document really says about matrimony does not oppose monogamy but rather civil marriage. A Church marriage is seen as being an expression of the grace of Our Lord, a "ceremony uniting its participants with the Mother Church." The Republic, says Conselheiro, is a "great evil for Brazil," because it wishes to "end religion." Republicanism is based upon a "false principle . . . even though it brings good to the country it is still evil in itself, because it is contrary to Divine Law." By Divine Law was meant that the Brazilian ought to obey "Pope, Prince, and Parent" and not the so-called "President of the Republic." For its defiance of the Divine Law, the Brazilian Republic would "fall to the ground" through the "true judgment of God." [7]

In the light of the breviary, the Canudos uprising is shown to have been extremely conservative, without the slightest rebellion against either the Church or the sacrament of marriage. On the contrary, it sought to reaffirm traditional, purely Brazilian values, some of which were eventually revived by the Republic to the extent that Rodrigues Alves, like Pedro II before him, came to be known affectionately as "Big Daddy."

Prominent in Antônio Conselheiro's conservatism was the cult of the Father, as indicated in the terms "Pope, Prince, Parent." This cult, a reaction to the excesses of the alleged anarchic and antireligious demagoguery of the Republic, coincided with the tradi-

[7] Luciano Carneiro: "Os Conselhos de Antônio Conselheiro," *O Cruzeiro* (Rio de Janeiro), December 5, 1953.

tional conservatism of the Brazilian élite, many of whom were similarly disenchanted with the Republic of 1889. In 1909 Sousa Bandeira, in his book entitled *Reformas,* stated that only a conservative Republic could save Brazil, a fact recognized "by republicans who must assume the responsibility for what they did in 1891." It was, in effect, time to "turn back" before "things become even worse." "Let us not be ashamed to confess our errors; let us now attempt to consolidate the Republic along the lines of the experience of our forefathers, the deep source of our national traditions. . . ." [8] The only thing lacking here to match the traditionalism of the "Counselor" is that, to the "national traditions," we add the "Catholic traditions" of order, authority, and hierarchy.

[8] Sousa Bandeira: *Reformas* (Rio de Janeiro, 1909), p. 16.

❧ [IV] ❧

Education and Urban Culture

Isaac Ford returned to New York from Brazil in 1891 convinced that the new Republic represented one of the two countries in tropical America where public education was making good progress. The other country was Mexico. "It is in the direction of popular education that progress unerringly lies in Mexico no less than in Brazil," [1] he wrote, with an emphasis more journalistic than sociological. The Mexico he referred to was that of Porfírio Diaz; Brazil, though republican in appearance, was still largely monarchical in its cultural system, including education. The Empire had always concerned itself almost lovingly with education, though not with that of the public at large; and within its limits of selective enrollment, the Emperor did just about everything except teach the children himself.

In 1869 Brazil had one primary school for each 541 free-born children between the ages of six and fifteen. Five years later, this figure had improved to one school for each 314.[2] By 1889 the number of primary schools, both public and private, had risen to nearly 7,500, with a total enrollment of approximately 300,000 students, as against 3,516 schools and 115,735 pupils in 1869.

The educational darling of the Emperor during most of his reign was the Imperial Academy, which bore his name, "Pedro II," and which was located in the court itself. Under his paternal vigilance,

---

[1] Isaac N. Ford: *Tropical America* (London, 1893), p. 340.

[2] These figures are taken from *Brazil in 1869*, a publication directed by the Baron of Santa Ana Nery with the collaboration of the Baron do Rio Branco, Luís Cruls, Eduardo Prado, and others. It was published in Paris in 1889.

this school offered a quality education ending with the granting of a degree of considerable distinction: the Bachelor of Letters, a designation reserved exclusively for the graduates of Pedro II. This diploma was not easy to obtain. In 1887, out of a total enrollment of 569, only 12 degrees were granted.[3] Those fortunate enough to earn the title, however, were able to enter triumphantly into any institution of higher learning; graduates of Pedro II were virtually academic princelings, holding free access to all branches of humanistic knowledge.

Carlos Luís de Vargas Dantas (b. in the province of Rio de Janeiro, 1870) gives us interesting information about the Imperial Academy, from which he was graduated with the Bachelor of Letters. He had gone there from the Portuguese Literary Lyceum, which operated from seven in the morning until eight at night in a building in the Rua da Carioca. He was no rich man's son but rather a scholarship student at the Lyceum, who had attended primary school in the interior of the province of Rio de Janeiro, where he was born (on a farm in Macacos in the Realengo area). Having been instructed at home in his alphabet "in the lap of the most sainted of mothers," Carlos Luís first entered public school in Queimados, where his family had subsequently moved, under the dedicated tutelage of one Estevão dos Santos Fasciotti. There he learned the elaborate calligraphy of the time, "what we called the twigs, curves, stem letters, advancing later to the covered letters." Other subjects were reading, beginning grammar, dictation, sentence analysis, arithmetic up to the metric system, physical geography, and religion. It is interesting to learn that the instructor "from his monthly salary of 100 *milreis* on which he had to maintain his not inconsiderable family, nevertheless managed to save out enough to grant prizes to deserving students at the end of the academic year." Each Saturday "students carried home a report card with grades for the week in attendance, lessons, and deportment. . . ." Punishments "consisted of admonishments, reductions in weekly grades, enforced periods of standing, loss of recreation periods, detention after school hours, being made to pick up small pieces of paper, and, in extreme cases, 'intimate acquaintance with the

---

[3] For reference to the Imperial Academy and its relationship to the Imperial cultural system, see the *Memória Histórica Comemorativa do 1º Centenário do Colégio de Pedro II,* written by a professor emeritus of this school, Escragnolle Dória (Rio de Janeiro, 1937).

ruler.' " As for recreation, the school was "housed in a rented building without a yard appropriate for games or physical education of any kind. Recess was thus largely limited to moving about a bit and stretching the legs after hours of immobility."

At the Portuguese Literary Lyceum, the boy increased his knowledge of Portuguese through the grammar of Coruja and started French by the Ollendorff method. His studies were so assiduously pursued that he received the highest grade in the official examinations. In a school of 400 pupils of all ages, including adults and almost all of Portuguese descent, he was the only one to receive the gold medal of the Passos Manuel Prize instituted in good Lusitanian fashion by the Count of São Salvador de Matozinhos. "It is worth pointing out," says Carlos Luís parenthetically in his testimony of 1940, "that this generous gesture by the school was made to an eleven-year-old boy of undistinguished parentage on the first occasion when the prize was offered."

Anyone coming from a farm in the interior who could still achieve such an academic triumph in the capital city had his next step already dictated for him: he would attend Pedro II. The Imperial Academy existed to educate the best intellects in the country, regardless of race, creed, or social condition. Under the vigilant eye of the Emperor, its function was to provide a Brazilian élite notable for its humanistic training, a training which would later be increased, rather than overshadowed, by studies of a university or technical nature. A degree holder from Pedro II belonged to the intellectual nobility, having gained the clearest title to such a distinction then existent in Brazil.

Carlos Luís, as a poor country boy of proved merit, received a full scholarship to Pedro II. "I am honored to confess my undying gratitude to the Brazilian government of this time, to whose generosity I owe whatever small value I may have," he states. Wanting to become an engineer, he buried himself in the study of mathematics, even to the point of having a private teacher: Luís Pedro Drago. He attended classes in the supplementary course, which in this period prepared for entrance into the Polytechnic School. With the coming of the Republic, it was not long before engineers were much in demand, not only for their services to reputable firms, but also for the prestige they gave to the so-called "supervising board" of enterprises whose existence was merely fictitious. These ghost corporations paid their "advisers" magnificently, but were generally so short-lived that engineers seduced by mere numbers seldom received more than a fleeting taste of the promised honey. But such were the fluctuations of the republican job market that the over-valued engineers soon fell from favor and Carlos Luís, after his graduation from Pedro II, decided to enter medical school and ulti-mately became a physician.

He recalls that instruction in languages had been deficient at Pedro II; English, German, and French were taught as though they were dead. For this reason, he mastered only French, then consid-ered an essential second language in Brazil. Books written in Ger-man and English were little used by teachers at the time; but Portu-guese, Latin, and French were languages an educated person needed to know well. A single incorrect syllable in Latin could prove a misfortune to a man with pretensions of culture, and an error in French pronunciation was an intellectual sin with almost equally disastrous consequences. A misplaced pronoun in parliamentary discourse could mean ostracism for a law graduate. One of the ob-stacles impeding the political rise of Estácio Coímbra was his fail-ure in a discourse to pronounce the word *élite* in the French manner.

In his days at Pedro II, Carlos Luís knew the famous Benjamin Constant, but without admiration. He was a man toward whom "the magnanimous ruler acted as a tolerant and loving father," but who "from the stronghold of his academic chair preached the ne-cessity of transforming the form of government, thereby calling for the deposition of the venerable old man to whose limitless good-ness he owed the opportunity to continue this practice with impu-nity."

Of Benjamin Constant and Pedro II, Carlos Luís gives us a detail which remained in his memory until old age, without his ever hav-ing previously divulged it: "Benjamin Constant had a son, named after him, who was a day student of the sixth year at Pedro II. One day near the end of the academic year of 1889, this boy called upon me, as a seventh-year student, to sign my name at the head of a petition he was bringing from home in which students of all classes would request the new Minister of Instruction [Benjamin Con-stant, Sr.] to dispense with final examinations. Constant, Jr., was a happy-go-lucky type. I had at first taken the matter as a joke, con-vinced that his father would pay no attention to the request, but after a brief conversation I learned that the whole thing had been cooked up between the minister and his son. . . . Surprised by this information, I promised to sign, though not at the head of the list, so that my first refusal would not be misinterpreted. The petition was sent, but no action was taken. One of the leading beneficiaries of the suggestion would have been Benjamin, Jr., who had low grades in General History."

At Pedro II—which, under the Republic, was known for some time as the National Gymnasium—there was at least one professor who did not allow himself "to be intimidated by the discretionary powers of the Minister of Instruction. His name was Ramos Melo. Ramos Melo . . . calmly averaged the grades of Benjamin Constant, Jr., and failed him." Carlos Luís, in recalling this hitherto unrevealed bit of history, praises the "good lesson in manliness and civic responsibility" given by Ramos Melo, but does not fail to add that this quixoticism had brought about the professor's "compulsory retirement a few days afterward," the ministry's vengeance against a professor scrupulous in carrying out his duties.

In this and other actions, Benjamin Constant appeared to Carlos Luís to have been a public servant of somewhat less than authentic virtues and one who hardly deserved the epithets "pure" and "model" accorded him by republican sympathizers. "Protected by the Emperor," says Carlos Luís, "he did not fear to depose him." ". . . Having sworn to defend the monarchy, he did not hesitate to preach the necessity for its extinction and to conspire for the proclamation of the Republic"; a soldier, whose duty it was to maintain discipline, he used his professorial chair as a stronghold for creating republican propaganda; ". . . as a Positivist, he should have received no more than maintenance pay, but each month he took the salaries of his military rank, his professorial chair, his position in the Normal School, his directorship in the Institute which today bears his name, in which last function he also received living expenses including a house, bed and board, servants, light, etc., for himself and his family. . . . As Minister of War, he accepted his promotion at a grand demagogic manifestation in front of the Itamaraty Palace, in which Major Serzedelo Correia shouted that the public had proclaimed Deodoro Fonseca a *generalíssimo* and Benjamin a general. Without even asking the Major to present his alleged petition from the people, Benjamin Constant immediately acceded to the request, brushing aside all considerations of morality and the legal and pecuniary rights of those who preceded him in seniority. And to compensate Serzedelo for his dedication, he promoted him to colonel on the spot."

Thus in 1940 this one-time graduate of Pedro II concluded: "If I had to advise any adolescent boy on the choice of a model, the last person I would choose would be Benjamin Constant." For one Brazilian citizen, the Republic had made a bad start, at least so far as educational morality was concerned.

This morality, during the Empire, was not confined to the Imperial Academy, nor to teachers such as Ramos Melo. In 1884 Raimundo Dias de Freitas (b. in Piauí, 1874) entered the Gymnasium of Pernambuco, the Pedro II of the northeast, where he encountered an atmosphere of such austerity as to intimidate him. He had done his primary studies in Piauí, first in Jerumenha and later in Amarante. His teachers had been Dona Ludovica, a "cultivated lady" who "taught with affection and never spared herself in her duty to her pupils," and another whom he characterizes merely as "old José." In both schools "the method of instruction was the same. We were taught the letters of the alphabet, then the formation of syllables, which were recited in a singsong manner as were the arithmetic tables. One learned by rote and developed the habit of studying aloud."

Old José was a severe teacher and Raimundo, an indolent scholar interested only in play, was very much afraid of him. He may have missed in José the "goodness and affection" he had found in Dona Ludovica, particularly since his father was a widower and, in addition to being saddened by his condition, "was constantly worried about the duties of his public office."

In José's school, the principal punishment was the *palmatória*, but at times his errant schoolmates were forced to walk in the street carrying ridiculous placards or wearing the mask of an ass. The *palmatória* was forever active during the everyday lessons, as well as in tests and discussions, and the blows were given with a vengeance. In neither school was there any provision for playgrounds or recreation periods.

From the interior of the province of Piauí, Raimundo and his brother Cándido went to the province of Maranhão, where his uncle was a judge and provincial president. Here he attended his third primary school, where he records that "notebooks for the teaching of writing and arithmetic were unknown in the north": calligraphy was learned "by the tracing in ink over letters previously made by the teachers." This did not terminate his wanderings as a primary pupil; he attended a fourth school in Recife, where, under a Dona Maria Rita, he followed the same teaching methods—and the same punishments—as in previous institutions. Once, however, he received a different punishment, which revolted him. "I was put into a messy, dirty room filled with soiled clothing and containing a used chamber pot which gave off a nauseating odor. I rebelled against this and started to cry and beat on the door. This angered the teacher who, indignant, tried to quiet me by seizing me by the ears and holding me against the wall with her knee while she beat me furiously. I returned the assault when and where I could, but neither this nor the subsequent complaints of my Aunt Teresa did any good. Within a few days the teacher was calling me all kinds of names and generally enhancing my reputation as a rowdy and insupportable brat."

It was with this reputation that Raimundo entered the first year of the Gymnasium of Pernambuco. The teacher in this class was a strict and demanding man named Miranda, under whose tutelage the boy from Maranhão made progress in reading, writing, and arithmetic. His uncle, now provincial president in Pernambuco, had instructed him to study Portuguese, French, and arithmetic preparatory to a career in business, and the boy continued in this curriculum through secondary school. He had excellent teachers. His French instructor in the first year was Father Joaquim Arcoverde, a future Cardinal of Rio de Janeiro, and in the second a Dr. Sarmento. His textbooks were J. F. Halbout's French grammar, readings from Chateaubriand, and the Portuguese grammar of Dr. Abílio César Borges.

Raimundo believes that, by failing twice in his catechism lessons, he incurred the antipathy and nagging of some of his teachers, and it is clear that, despite being the nephew of the provincial president, he was punished like any other pupil when he failed to measure up to standards. In his opinion, this punishment was "barbarous" when administered by the "two centurions" in the form of powerful blows on the palm. Once, seeing his hands already bleeding from the *palmatória*, he refused to submit to further punishment; he was taken to the office of the principal, who summarily expelled him from the school. It should be noted, however, that when this happened his uncle was already dead.

At sixteen Raimundo matriculated in the Military School of

Ceará. This was done on the advice of a relative who was a lieutenant in the Brazilian Army and who believed that "the military
school is a national institution where poor boys, through their own
efforts, can rise in the world and be useful to their parents without
the help or protection of anybody." One only had to "adhere to
the inflexible line of duty appropriate to a soldier and citizen." To
adolescent Brazilians, the Army meant prestige—a distinction
which it had lacked during the Empire. Raimundo benefitted from
the "real and positive" military discipline at the Ceará institution,
and the "incorrigible" youngster finally became tractable, a fact
which possibly explains his respect in old age for this type of education and for its directors, both before and after the proclamation of
the Republic.

Of these directors of military education, none appeared greater
to young Raimundo than Benjamin Constant: "a proud, sober, and
independent figure." Raimundo had early been a supporter of the
republican regime, a preference "certainly influenced by reading
French history, which greatly interested the Brazilian youth of his
time." "Benjamin Constant was a teacher loved not only by military students, but also by young people in civilian life. His republican ideas and his studies in Positivism made him highly esteemed. It
is in large part to Benjamin Constant that we owe the extinction of
the monarchist regime in Brazil; he personally carried the fight to a
victorious conclusion in extinguishing the last pockets of resistance
to the coup of November 15."

Born in Rio Bonito in the state of Rio de Janeiro in 1890, Astrojildo Pereiro Duarte da Silva tells us that he had an early desire to
become a monk ("a monk, not a priest"). This false dawn of a
religious vocation came while he was a somewhat less than seraphic
pupil at the Colégio Anchieta in Novo Friburgo. Astrojildo entered
this aristocratic school, run by Jesuit priests, after a routine primary
education marked by the usual schoolboy pranks and time-wasting
nonsense. But since his father was prospering, he was able to enjoy
the luxury of attending a rich man's school which had the additional distinction of enlisting the son of Ruy Barbosa himself as a
member of the student body. At this very school, a short time before, Ruy had delivered a famous discourse conciliating orthodox
Catholicism, previously outraged by the introduction to his book *O
Papa e o Concílio* (*The Pope and the Council*).

The teaching methods of the aristocratic Colégio Anchieta were, naturally enough, Church-oriented, with daily masses and *Paternosters*, *Ave Marias*, and *Salve Reginas* ten times a day. Astrojildo became the best algebra pupil of his class, though his favorite reading was the *Antologia Nacional* of Laete Barreto. Though he felt himself to be a sincere Catholic at the time, he was a poor student of catechism and religion and "at the same time, along with X.Y., was author of a clandestine pornographic manuscript. Later, X.Y., repenting of his pornographic adventure, departed for Rome to study for the priesthood."

From Anchieta, Astrojildo went on to the equally famous Colégio Abílio in Niterói. Here, he recalls, there was a lay atmosphere with few physical sports. Now fifteen, he participated for the first time in literary groups and began to write amorous verse, as well as to become interested in political questions. He also became an anti-militarist and an avowed atheist. In his third year he abandoned his gymnasium course to follow one which he styles as "chaotically autodidactic." He feels that no teacher ever influenced him very greatly and records those confused tastes which characterize the self-teaching of adolescence. In literature he read Machado de Assis, Raul Pompeia, Euclydes da Cunha, João Ribeiro, and Graça Aranha; admired both Benjamin Constant and Ruy Barbosa; and preferred France to the United States. Because of the influence of Ruy Barbosa, he liked England, but held Germany in antipathy.

It is perhaps no exaggeration to say that Astrojildo Pereira lacked a systematic education such as that given at Pedro II. "The Colégio Anchieta is one of the worst memories of my adolescence and the Colégio Abílio never taught me what I wanted to learn," he confesses. Perhaps this accounts for what he terms his "intimate religious crisis," in which he passed through the successive stages of anti-clericalism, anarchistic atheism, and finally Marxism.

Amílcar Armando Botelho de Magalhães (b. in the province of Rio de Janeiro, 1880) was a nephew of Benjamin Constant and learned his first letters on the family coffee plantation from his godmother, Dona Elvira Chaves Fernandes. He already knew how to read and write when he went to live at court, where he was placed in a kindergarten—an innovation at the time—run by Dr. Meneses Vieira, one of Brazil's foremost educators in the time of Pedro II. At the age of twelve he entered the Brazilian Atheneum in São Cristóvão, a school directed by a retired Army lieutenant named

Ulisses José da Costa Cabral. "His lessons in the humanities," recalls
Amílcar Armando a half century later, "were always accompanied
by opportune patriotic pronouncements and arguments to support
the conquests of Liberty, of Democracy, and of the republican
form of government over the entire civilized world. . . . He
impressed us with his eloquence and his elegance of style." Cabral
constantly directed the attention of his pupils to passages from the
works of Samuel Smiles, principally *Character* and *Power of Will*,
as well as Colonel Carlo Corsi's *The Education of a Soldier* and
Edmundo de Amicis's *The Heart*. Punishment was moral, "a
method much more effective than corporal punishment when employed by a master of psychology such as Ulisses Cabral." The
books cited above were among the most widely read by children of
the era, largely under pressure from adults concerned by the excessive adolescent taste for works they considered frivolous: the
novels of Jules Verne and Arthur Conan Doyle's tales of the adventures of Sherlock Holmes.

The Brazilian Atheneum was co-educational: another pedigogi-
cal innovation in a period virtually Moorish in this respect. Amorous dalliance was, of course, frowned upon, and the director of the
school, perhaps under Positivist influence, taught his boys to regard
Woman as "superior to the man in sentiments, in emotions, in kind-
ness," a thesis which appeared to Amílcar Armando at the close of
his life to have been "a great error . . . it is only the exceptional
woman who deserves this sort of veneration. . . . In general, the
fair sex is devoid of character, frivolous, egotistic, concerned only
with appearances, full of unreasonable whims with which it tries to
dominate the men. Futile, and unpatriotic, its members regard
themselves as the central point of the family and consider themselves more important than the very country itself!"

Altogether it would seem that this illustrious nephew of Benjamin Constant—the latter an extreme devotee of the cult of the
Woman-Republic—had a somewhat restricted sense of the Positivist mystique of the female goddess and the identification of this
goddess with the image of the Republic. In his old age, he also came
to regard Positivism itself as "utopian," although he still thought it
contained, like the Catholic Church, much valuable knowledge and
served as the source of many useful principles. He continued to see
Auguste Comte as a philosopher who "left Nietzsche, Karl Marx,
and Spencer far behind" and the Republic as "the goal of all civilized people in their search for the ideal form of government."

He tells us that the Brazilian Atheneum was "constantly holding ceremonies to celebrate national holidays and the anniversaries of great battles in which Brazil had been involved." Of these ceremonies, the ones which impressed Amílcar Armando the most were those dedicated to the Rondon Mission, then in its heydey of heroic deeds in the backlands.

Amílcar Armando's higher education was pursued in military and civil engineering. Before matriculation in the Military School of Rio Grande do Sul, he had already had some experience as a soldier, having joined a patriotic battalion in the early days of the Republic, training under "the members of the artillery squadron which had revolted at the fortress of São João" in Rio de Janeiro. Though a soldier from a very early age, Amílcar Armando never was given to quarrels. "There were very few persons with whom I broke relations, argued, or had fist fights." He read a great deal and, as a student at military school, "outside the regular textbooks, enjoyed the poems of Gonçalves Dias, Casimiro de Abreu, Castro Alves, Guerra Junqueiro, as well as the novels of José de Alencar." As a result, perhaps, of the lessons of the director of the Brazilian Atheneum, he detested "obscene or even outspoken works," so much so, in fact, that "when a fellow student loaned me a well-known volume of this type by Bocage, I returned it to him, informing him that I had read only one sonnet ('Do not lament your condition, O Nisé . . .') and it had nauseated me. Nor, as a mature man, have I changed my tastes."

Manuel (Carneiro de Sousa) Bandeira (b. Recife, 1886), one of Brazil's greatest poets, has already noted how he did his primary schooling in Recife and later went for his secondary education to the new federal capital, where he followed the humanities course at Pedro II, then recently rechristened the National Gymnasium. Following the full course for the degree of Bachelor of Sciences and Letters, he studied such nonpreparatory materials as drawing, music, mechanics, literature, and logic. Of his teachers, some of Imperial vintage, he states: "I had great admiration and respect for Silva Ramos (Portuguese), José Veríssimo (geography), Cabrita (mathematics), Frontin (mechanics), Said Ali (German), Alexander (English), Paula Lopes (natural history), Nerval de Gouveia (physics and chemistry), João Ribeiro (history)." Some were Positivists, he recalls; others were Catholics or materialists. The teacher who influenced him most in his literary development was João Ribeiro, "with whom students used to converse after class. He

made us appreciate the superiority of Raimundo Correia over Bilac,
of Machado de Assis over Eça de Queiroz, at a time when Bilac and
Eça were idols in their respective fields of poetry and prose."

Of the National Gymnasium, Manuel Bandeira says "it had a
conventional appearance: a large patio with cloister where we
played violently during the ten minutes recess between classes."
The games were racing, hide-and-seek, leapfrog, jumping, and all
sorts of activity with gymnasium apparatus. They hazed the fresh-
men, but without resorting to cruelty. "There were never any civic
ceremonies, so far as I can remember."

In his secondary school years, Manuel Bandeira read widely outside school hours. "I devoured the *Lusiads*, the Portuguese classics,
Bocage (minus the controversial seventh volume), Filinto Elísio,
and the Brazilian romantics such as Castro Alves, Gonçalves Dias,
Bilac, and Alberto de Oliveira." At fifteen he read a great deal of
Guy de Maupassant and Anatole France, "the latter little known in
Brazil at the time." In his sixth year he received a prize of Taine's
book on La Fontaine, of which he notes "I read this book very
carefully and consider it as having had a great influence on my ideas
of poetry."

One of the most evident advantages of the Imperial system of
education in Brazil was its tendency to unify the regional cultural
centers: Rio de Janeiro, Bahia, São Paulo, Olinda, and Recife. This
encouraged high standards instead of spreading education thin and
substituting quantity for excellence. Brazilians from all parts of the
country felt obliged to send their children to these centers if they
wanted to see them well educated, whether such training was in
law, medicine, engineering, or pharmacy, in military science or in
the humanities. In these cities, Brazilian students from the most diverse provinces became acquainted and associated with one another
in their studies, their leisure hours, and their pranks. They lived
together in the famous student "republics" and carried on their traditional rivalries with the "castles" of commercial employees, the
latter being boys of poorer families who, paradoxically enough,
represented the more conservative side of the social order and
hence were associated with the medieval symbolism of the castle.
To complete the paradox, it was the sons of well-to-do parents,
students of law, medicine, and engineering, who stood for the spirit
of "progress," at times carrying their enthusiasm to virtually anarchic extremes.

Brazilians from Rio Grande do Sul or Sergipe, from Maranhão or Minas Gerais, frequently married girls from Bahia, Pernambuco, or Rio de Janeiro whom they had met during their student days. Future political leaders living together as flexible youths in the intimacy of the "republics" more than once maintained their friendships into maturity, even when the association involved differences in political affiliation. Further, in these centers boys of routine provincial background allowed themselves to be influenced by teachers of progressive ideas in politics, literature, or philosophy and returned to their homes with new tendencies and new attitudes.

One of these was Higino Cícero da Cunha, born in 1858 in São José das Cajazeiras, in the then province of Maranhão. Cunha's preparatory education was conducted in the lyceum of the provincial capital of São Luís, after which he spent several years as a store clerk in the interior. At this time, he became greatly influenced by the weekly *O Pensador* (*The Thinker*) of Manuel Bittencourt and Aluísio Azevedo, which was then engaged in journalistic warfare with the Catholic review *Civilização*. Becoming anti-clerical himself, he became "a *tabula rasa* in regard to ancestral beliefs after reading the works of the German philosopher Büchner, *Force and Matter* and *Man According to Science*." His radicalism was intensified when he went to study law in Recife, where he enlisted among "the phalanx of devotees of Tobias Barreto, in whose ranks were included Artur Orlando, Clóvis Beviláqua, Martins Júnior, Faelante de Câmara, Benedito Leite, Viveiros de Castro, and Urbano Santos." He took part in abolitionist and republican campaigns "under the leadership of José Mariano, Joaquim Nabuco, and Martins Júnior," collaborating "in various journals, especially in the *Fôlha do Norte* of Martins Júnior and Faelante da Câmara."

During his years in Recife, he "read many French and English periodicals" and "became acquainted with the works of Comte, Littré, and others." After completing his law studies, he went in a spirit of adventure to Amazonas, but eventually returned to his native province. Here he lived a life of active leadership, his Recife experience apparently having contributed to prolonging the spirit of his youth and keeping him physically as well as mentally young. (In 1940, at the age of eighty-two, he was still "organizing concerts in the governor's palace, the local theatre, and in private homes" in the city of Teresina.) In the Pernambucan capital, he had been "in constant attendance at the dramas, comedies, and opera" presented at the Santa Isabel and Apollo theatres, then in their heydey, and had danced quadrilles, lancers, waltzes, and polkas in the mansions of the fashionable quarters of Mondego, Madalena, and Ponte d'Uchoa, as well as in the residences of Santo Antônio and São José, where students were sometimes permitted to take part in the festivities. A bit uneasy in their borrowed frock coats, boys from remote provinces here had the opportunity to mingle with prim aristocratic young ladies who wore Parisian gowns and spoke French as well as any Frenchman, with viscountesses who had traveled extensively in Europe, and with baronesses who in their youth remembered having been courted by Antônio Peregrino Maciel Monteiro.

It was here in this same Recife that such provincial students and future men of the world and of letters as Araújo Jorge, Pontes de Miranda, Gilberto Amado, Aníbal Freire, Augusto dos Anjos, Francisco de Assis Chateaubriand de Melo, and José Américo da Almeida—and, in an earlier period, Graça Aranha, Epitácio Pessoa, and Sylvio Romero—increased their knowledge and polished their manners.

On the distaff side of this educational picture is the testimony of Dona Virgínia Cavalcante (b. Pernambuco, 1879). Dona Virgínia attended primary school in a public establishment in the Rua do Cotovêlo: "Here the method of instruction was to recite aloud and to memorize lessons down to the last comma. The weekly arithmetic tests, complete with *palmatória*, were the terror of the students. . . . There was also the punishment of remaining standing with one's book open for long periods of time. . . . The textbooks were the grammar of João Ribeiro, the arithmetic of Castro Nunes, the geography of Eleutério Ribeiro, and the geometry of Abílio César Borges. We copied English calligraphy."

From girlhood she amused herself by "making doll's clothes with a skill and taste that earned admiration at home" and made it unnecessary for her later to take lessons in dressmaking. Always an admirer of France, she taught herself the French language and came to read, not only magazines and fashion books, but the works of Mme de Staël, Bossuet, and Mme de Sévigné. "I did not learn a bit of English or German," she confesses. "I know that these countries were very powerful and far advanced, but they simply didn't interest me." She regrets that she did not attend the theatre as a girl, but her grandfather would not allow it. The idea of a trip to Paris "was the dream of my youth" and she also notes her preference for the romances of Jules Verne.

These very romances of Jules Verne, widely read by children and adolescents of the time, perhaps did the most to develop a Brazilian taste for inventions and an enthusiasm for technical marvels, particularly for balloons and the so-called "conquest of the air." This enthusiasm, carried into mature years, had its repercussions in the Brazilian Congress itself, where there was considerable to-do on the part of imaginative technicians to reach a Brazilian solution to the problem of aerial navigation. Two of these public figures interested in what was known as the "Brazilian secular problem" were José de Patrocínio and Augusto Severo de Albuquerque Maranhão. The latter, a congressman from Rio Grande do Norte, had since 1894 experimented unsuccessfully in Realengo with a balloon of his invention named the *"Bartolomeu de Gusmão."* A second balloon, *"Pax,"* also failed later in Paris.

This urge to solve the problem of aerial navigation was an important aspect of Brazilian culture during its years of transition from slave to free labor in its attempt to consolidate the Republic and to colonize the country through the employment of new methods. It was as though, in this absorption with such a dramatic means of transportation, the country was trying to make up for lost time after the extremely slow-moving economy of the oxcart and the Negro slave.

Aeronautics absorbed Augusto Severo from early youth, when, with his cousin José Antônio Gonçalves de Mello, he talked constantly of flying and, on Sundays, went to the country to fly kites not merely for diversion but also in an endeavor to solve the problem of aerial conquest.

The desire to achieve national unification was what absorbed Commander Luís Gomes, who believed that Recife should be the starting point of a rail line linking the Atlantic with the Pacific. And it was the commander's son Eduardo, born near the end of the nineteenth century, who would carry much of this enthusiasm for Brazilian progress into the field of actual aerial transport.

Antônio Carlos Pacheco e Silva (b. São Paulo, 1898) attended a kindergarten connected with the Normal School, whose installation, he believes, "was the work of Miss Brown and Cesário Mota, two great reformers of public instruction in São Paulo." Miss Brown was an American and her year-end ceremonies were an event, with recitations and exhibitions of manual arts. The proceedings were presided over by Dr. Thompson, director of public instruction in São Paulo at a time when names of Anglo-Saxon origin were in all parts of Brazil almost mystically associated with education in the minds of those who hoped shortly to make of Brazil another United States of America. This accounted for the vogue of so-called "American" schools, and it was in such an American school that Antônio Carlos, an elegant young Catholic boy, went to study under a dedicated Presbyterian missionary he refers to as "old Lane." Old Lane approached his teaching duties with apostolic zeal: "Tolerant but energetic, the old educator, flanked by his son Rufus and a pleiad of professors, almost all graduates of Mackenzie,[4] knew how to maintain an attitude of discipline without hindering our freedom or administering severe punishment." On clear days, classes "were given outdoors under the trees or in open sheds," an American custom very popular with the children. Textbooks, some written by members of the faculty, were furnished by the school and were almost all printed in the United States and illustrated with attractive pictures. The grammars were by Júlio Ribeiro and Eduardo Carlos Pereira, two Brazilians who turned Protestant and who, possibly in compensation for having abandoned the Mother Church, devoted themselves like Catholic priests to the preservation of the mother tongue. The arithmetic book was by another Brazilian Protestant, Trajano, and from it the students "were given daily problems which the teachers corrected with frightening rapidity." This efficiency was another American attribute which was beginning to have its effect in Brazil; the often heard pedagogical expression "Time is money" was transforming Brazilians of the middle and upper classes into champions of efficiency and speed in contrast to the "Have patience" or "It will wait until tomorrow" so traditional in Brazil. In geography, the texts were by Lacerta and Scrosoppi, but there were also practical classes in which the pupils made their own maps, "locating the rivers, mountains, and principal cities." Another American innovation was a class in manual training under a master carpenter.[5]

[4] Mackenzie College, founded in São Paulo by American Methodist missionaries, is still one of the best institutions of higher learning in Brazil. (Translator.)

[5] The American School in São Paulo was itself "excessively American" in that it was of "plain red brick like the majority of American schools and universities." In Recife, however, both the Presbyterians and the Baptists, though following American systems of instruction, founded their schools in old patriarchal houses, former residences of important families of the city. The Cesário Mota of Recife

In recreation periods, recalls Antônio Carlos, the favorite game was football, with a ball made of cloth by the pupils themselves. Other games were "*barra à cega, barra-manteiga, acusado,* broad jump, *sela,* hopscotch, *bolinhas, bilboquet, diablô,* top spinning, etc." But despite the rapid Americanization and Italianization of São Paulo, Antônio Carlos's childhood contained much that was purely Brazilian: the bonfires and balloons during São João festivals; the water bombs, confetti, and streamers during Carnival; the *capoeira* wrestling; the tops, kites, sling shots, and bean shooters, "the last two the terror of the neighbors, whose cracked windows testified to errant—and sometimes purposeful—marksmanship." It is surprising that in the case of games and toys there was an almost complete uniformity between the north and south of the country and among children of all classes, although as the upper classes developed linguistically they added European elements—French, German, or English—to the traditional Portuguese amusements, a tendency increased by the employment of European governesses. Thus they played tennis and rode velocipedes and bicycles.

German governesses were particularly in demand and often maintained relations with—and even a certain domination over—former pupils long after returning to Germany. The lives of these governesses in a Brazil which had only recently abolished slavery was no bed of roses. Often pretty, not at all old-maid type, these girls often suffered as much from the insolence and stubbornness of their charges as they did from the unaccustomed tropical sun. The frustrations attendant upon supervising spoiled and ill-mannered little boys or imperious little girls, together with the physical discomfort engendered by an overabundance of sun and rain, is indicated in the letters of some of them to Dona Feliciana de Barros, who when a young student of music and French literature had known and liked many of these Europeans adrift in the Brazilian tropics.

There was, for example, the case of Mlle Ida, who for many years had been governess to a family in the interior of the state of Pernambuco. In 1912 this German lady wrote from Engenho X [6] to her "dear Dona Sana": "In this solitude not a day passes that I don't

---

was Alfredo Alves da Silva Freyre Júnior, and his Miss Brown was a Miss Elise Reed, a cultivated and pretty woman in happy contrast to the buck-toothed horrors Brazilians generally saw as American missionaries, caricatures of the thin, angular, sexless old maid.

[6] The author is preserving the anonymity of the plantation cited. (Translator.)

suffer from *mal du pays*. I am furious with these stupid rains. . . . Now I am studying much with the girls, the best of which are M. and L., but all of whom are as unmannerly as ever; I certainly won't remain here after my contract runs out. . . . Are you practicing the piano? I am now learning the waltzes of Chopin, which are pretty but too difficult. . . . I would like to read a lot of French, English, and Portuguese, but I am always so tired and not as strong as I was at first; I don't know what makes me so listless . . ."

On the beach at Boa Viagem, Mlle Ida felt better. In her letter to "Dona Sana" on October 27, 1911, she tells of enjoying the sea bathes "sometimes twice a day" and of the "nightly music in a neighbor's house." Here she met one of Dona Feliciana's nephews, who, in her romantic eyes, was "very, very intelligent" and possessed of "much talent." Seeing him drawing and even painting, she gave him some lessons in water colors. "Dona Sana" should speak to his father and encourage him to send the boy to study in Germany.

In 1913 it was an English governess, Miss Ella Ireson, who wrote to Dona Feliciana in virtually the same tone; she was much obliged to the Brazilian lady for having made her acquainted with several English families in Pernambuco, in addition to persons native to the territory. Her indebtedness was "great and deep"; she no longer felt herself a stranger in a strange land, under a brutal tropical sun.

This sense of isolation in truth must have been terrible for the German and English governesses who came to Brazil around the turn of the century, unfamiliar as they were with the country, the tropical climate, or even with the New World as a whole. Still, these things did not prevent some of them from making good marriages.[7]

The greater part of the cultural movement of the time, it seems, stemmed from Rio de Janeiro, Recife, and São Paulo. Conservative São Luís de Maranhão, despite an ephemeral revolutionary movement impelled by Aluísio de Azevedo,[8] was already in decline; and Pôrto Alegre, a future leader in regional and national culture, had not as yet begun its rise to importance. But there was also Bahia,

[7] The same thing often happened with theatre artists who, like the singer Cerutti, left their companies to marry and settle in Brazil. Sometimes they helped their husbands financially by teaching singing, piano, mandolin, violin, or harp to well-to-do young ladies, of whom there were many who performed on those instruments, their fingers heavy with rings and their arms covered in bracelets.

[8] Aluísio de Azevedo is a well-known novelist. His principal works are *A Casa de Pensão* (*The Boardinghouse*) and *O Cortiço* (*The Tenement*). (Translator.)

which during this period had as its most eloquent revolutionary spirit the great Ruy Barbosa. A towering national figure, Ruy never ceased to be a Bahian in his habits and particularly in his propensity, very typical of his region, to adopt a conservative approach even when advocating the most wildly liberal ideas. Thus it took him until 1919 to discern the importance of the "social question," an issue agitated half a century earlier by the Positivists of Rio, São Paulo, and Rio Grande do Sul, as well as by his old law school colleague Joaquim Nabuco.

Nobody was more Bahian than Ruy in his liking for oratory or for the eloquent and often purely rhetorical expression of ideas and sentiments. And nobody was more conservative in his regard for the purity of the language; a language which he felt should shield itself against the increasing flood of Africanisms, Indianisms, Teutonisms, Italianisms, Gallicisms, and modernisms to remain even more Portuguese than the Portuguese of the mother country. These two tendencies in Ruy—conservatism and a passion for the language—seem to have been more typical of Bahia than of any other part of the country. In the light of this, it seems paradoxical that the city had no high school comparable to Pedro II, the Pernambucan Gymnasium, or the Mariana Seminary, and no law school on the level of those of Recife or São Paulo. Rather, it gained its academic fame through its School of Medicine, in which the scientific study of this subject was often subordinated to the study of classical literature, oratory, rhetoric, elegance and purity in speaking and writing, to debate over questions more grammatical than physiological, and to dissecting problems closer to the pathology of literary style than human anatomy.

Three foreigners and one Brazilian from Maranhão in the last years of the monarchy had the temerity to intrude upon this Bahian tradition of cultivating the classical and liberal arts behind a facade of medical studies. These were the Englishman Patterson, the German Wucherer, the Portuguese Silva Lima, and the Brazilian Raimundo Nina Rodrigues.

Before considering the contribution of these four scientists to the cultural progress of Bahia, I should point out that the culture they revolutionized in its intellectual habits was already considerably commercial and (unlike that of Pernambuco, Rio de Janeiro, or São Paulo, which were suffering from the evils of monoculture) enjoyed a great variety of products, as noted by the Austrian Maurício Lamberg in a study written during the early years of the

Republic.[9] Beside sugar, the state of Bahia in the late nineteenth century produced cacao, cotton, tobacco, coffee, hides, wood, ornamental feathers, rare birds, and fruits; it also worked mines of diamonds and other minerals. Its population was about 1.8 million, more than half of which was black or *mestiço*. Its cuisine was nationally famous for its delicacies, and its capital contained two theatres, one for opera and one for operetta and drama. There was a public park and two hotels of some importance. Its religious art was notable for the baroque splendor of its 120 churches, and for its many monasteries in which more than 100 monks from south Germany and Belgium were numbered among the members. The Austrian visitor also noted with interest the brightly colored shawls and immaculately white turbans of the market women, whose stands on the street corners or in the churchyards offered a surprising and lovely variety of native fruits, particularly the enormous navel oranges for which the city was world famous. In the tobacco shops he saw the local cigars and rolls of native leaf equally famous in Europe.[1]

But from the cultural point of view, no local art or product, whatever its European fame, aroused the pride of the true Bahian more than its Academy (not "Faculty" or "School," but "Academy") of Medicine. In its vast amphitheatres Lamberg learned that "professors of great knowledge and ability" gave lessons to "happy and lively" young men from the whole range of Brazilian provinces.

In short, says Lamberg in a celebrated passage, Bahia was the intellectual inferior of no other province and had given the nation "some of its most eminent statesmen." Intelligence was certainly not lacking among Brazilians, continued this astute observer. What was lacking—and here he must have been thinking of the Bahian doctors he had met during his visit—was "profound seriousness, firmness, patience, and constancy, and also the scientific passion to learn everything about a chosen field." [2]

[9] Maurício Lamberg: *O Brasil* (Rio de Janeiro, 1896), pp. 198, 201.
[1] A German merchant named Mann, who during the reign of Pedro II was in Brazil arranging for the export of Brazilian tropical products to Germany, could not resist the charm of another tropical product: a lovely "Bahian" miss with romantic black eyes and possibly some Indian blood. He married her, and the result of the union was one of the great German novelists of all times: Thomas Mann.
[2] Lamberg: op. cit., pp. 201, 203, 293–4.

The Medical School in Rio de Janeiro seemed to him better organized than that of Bahia, with students "drawn from all parts of the Republic and differing little from their counterparts in the most civilized European countries." The same could have been said for the students (many of them of mixed blood) of the schools of medicine in Bahia, the law schools of Recife and São Paulo, and the Polytechnic Institutes of São Paulo and Rio de Janeiro, as well as of the seminarists of Mariana, Itu, and Olinda. All were well cultivated in the humanities and excellently prepared for higher education. The greatest deficiencies of the Brazilian university system of the time, in comparison to those of Europe and the United States, lay in the methods of teaching and in the resources available for applied study. Rarely did foreign scientists find Brazilian schools well equipped with—or even aware of—certain teaching materials. Lamberg noted that the Polytechnic School of Rio de Janeiro had had a German chemistry professor "highly regarded by his pupils," so much so that after his death "his innumerable Brazilian admirers had his bust in marble placed in the ceremonial hall of that school." But this was an exception: "rarely does one find such an attitude toward the illustrious foreigners living here." [3] The prevailing attitude in this matter was generally one of sufficiency: why have foreign teachers when there are so many brilliant Brazilians? Brazilians so eloquent, so elegant in speech and so correct in the art of writing? It is true that Brazil—or Bahia, to be precise—had produced a jurist of such high quality as Teixeira de Freitas, a doctor such as Tôrres Homem, and an engineer like Rebouças. But men of this caliber were not sufficiently numerous to justify the luxury of downgrading the science of European-born professors.

Perhaps São Paulo was an exception in this respect, since it was superior to Rio de Janeiro in energy and the practicality of its teaching. Lamberg attributed this "to the fact that they have a better appreciation of the German language and German culture." In São Paulo he met "many Germans in charge of practical scientific establishments which, for this reason, give excellent service. This would be impossible in Rio, where they do not look favorably upon the employment of Germans in public services, even in secondary positions. Many Paulista families have German teachers or tutors, and others, of greater means, send their sons to Germany when they are still very small. Here they receive an excellent edu-

[3] Ibid., pp. 295, 324.

cation and eventually return as well-trained men." This was written, of course, before American educational methods had pushed the European system aside in São Paulo and elsewhere.

In Recife too, Lamberg had noted this "great veneration for German science," and "the desire to impart it to others" on the part of the best students of Tobias Barreto, who had gained renown "in the scientific world of Europe, thanks to his encyclopedic knowledge and his many published works." [4] He was "particularly known in Germany, whose culture interests him greatly and whose men of science hold him in high regard," says Lamberg, with a certain exaggeration as to the European impact of Barreto's works. Pernambuco—and Pará as well—seemed to him to be trying to make up for lost time in the study of the arts and sciences, with the sciences "in better condition than the arts" in this process of recovery. "The progressive spirit of the times" was perhaps more notable in Recife than in any other city of the north. Beside the School of Law, there was an Institute of Archeology, History, and Geography that contained "many . . . truly learned men" but which so far "has produced nothing of universal importance." The same was true of the School of Medicine, although one of its members, Joaquim de Aquino Fonseca, as early as the first half of the nineteenth century had been trained in medicine at the University of Paris and had been effectively interested in problems of urbanization and public hygiene.

The reason for the lack of scientific works "of universal importance" in both north and south Brazil seemed to Lamberg (who overlooked completely such men as José Bonifácio, Teixeira de Freitas, or João Vieira) to be attributable not to "lack of intelligence and good intentions," but rather "to the nature of inhabitants of the tropics, who lack the capacity of learned men in colder climates to devote their entire existence to the examination of a single scientific problem, even when such a course means the sacrifice of many of the comforts of life." [5] Tobias Barreto was to him an exception to this rule. Unfortunately, Lamberg lacked knowledge of many Brazilian works far more systematic than those of Barreto.[6] Among these I would include Morais, author of the first dictionary of Brazilian Portuguese, written largely in Pernambuco; the legal

[4] Ibid., pp. 12, 325.
[5] Ibid., p. 12.
[6] The American economist Roger Babson, whose *The Future of South America* was published in Boston in 1915, showed the same deficiency.

studies of the Bahian Teixeira de Freitas; the historical studies of
João Lisboa of Maranhão. Then there were those in botany by Ar-
ruda Câmara and Joaquim José de Serpa, the latter for some time
director of the Botanical Laboratory at Olinda—the first Brazilian
effort to make a systematic study of tropical plants useful in medicine, a field which his preceptors at the Bahia Academy of Medicine
had completely neglected.

The Reverend Mr. Fletcher, writing of the Rio de Janeiro Medical School during the reign of Pedro II, noted that there were several doctors trained in Europe on its faculty. The school had an
association with the Misericórdia Hospital, a "vast field for medical
observation." He had virtually the same to say of the school in
Bahia, stating that many of its professors, both foreign and Brazilian, were "men of talent and learning," so that their courses were
probably equal to those given by good professors "in any medical
school on the Continent." [7] He was perhaps referring to such men
as Patterson, Wucherer, or Silva Lima, whose work in Bahia, if not
contrary to academic conventions, was at least on the borderline of
established practice. It is hard to know, however, whether another
of his observations should be taken seriously or ironically: that the
library contained "large and costly volumes on anatomy in the
Russian language." These books had recently arrived from St.
Petersburg and were of excellent appearance—an appearance they
would probably preserve for a long time, unless violated by tropical
insects.

As for student observations on the hospitals of the time, we have
no information at all. Whatever study of this type existed seems to
have been insignificant. In his *Memória Histórica da Faculdade de
Medicina da Bahia Relativa ao Ano de 1891* (published in 1893) the
candid Luís Anselmo da Fonseca notes that the teaching in that
school was hampered by a number of "lamentable tendencies":
"verbosity," "theatricality," and a taste for "rhetorical emphasis"
and the "refinements of classical grammar." Oscar Freire, in an article entitled "Evolução da Medicina no Brasil" published in the
newspaper *Estado de São Paulo* of September 7, 1922, complains of
much "book learning" to the sacrifice of "practical studies."

Kidder in 1839 had written that the library of the Law School of
São Paulo, then installed in a former Franciscan convent, was defi-

[7] James C. Fletcher and Daniel P. Kidder: *Brazil and the Brazilians* (4th edn.,
Boston, 1879), pp. 180, 490.

cient in both scientific and literary works and overloaded with books of a theological nature.[8] The courses were also antiquated and followed the model of those of Coimbra. In both 1855 and 1878, however, Fletcher found that these courses had been modernized and followed the pattern of those in the United States. In São Paulo and also in Recife, he observed, future statesmen were being prepared under conditions of juridico-humanistic instruction superior to those existing in Spanish America.[9] He might also have observed that in the Academy of Medicine in Bahia, thanks to the broadly humanistic approach to medical instruction (despite the "fine laboratory" noted there by Lamberg), students also developed talents for parliamentary careers, though with evident sacrifice of the practical aspects of their medical training. Not a few medical graduates during the Second Empire became rivals of former law students in the political field, some even achieving notable stature as political orators. A good example here is Manuel Vitorino, almost another Ruy Barbosa in eloquence. Others brought to their political activities an objective approach to social problems, particularly those related to hygiene, in which field they often surpassed the achievements of graduates of law, engineering, and theological institutions.[1]

It was the doctors of Rio de Janeiro and Recife who showed themselves as most active in the study of these problems of hygiene, not only through published works but also in the realms of social activity. In examining the doctoral and postdoctoral theses of some of these men, one finds a preponderance in these cities of works on social problems, though it is true that studies of nutrition or racial problems, or of the practice of burial beneath the floors of churches, were to be found in Bahia as well. The latter, however, are characterized not so much by their zeal as by their careful attention to linguistic elegance and other purely academic virtues.

When Professor Agassiz made his criticism of Brazilian medical training, he did not limit himself to the Academy of Medicine in Bahia. Throughout the country, he felt, the program lacked the scientific preparation indispensable to preparing good medical practitioners: "Not enough importance is accorded by schools of medi-

[8] Ibid., p. 371.
[9] Ibid., p. 372.
[1] Among the publications of Manuel Vitorino his "Higiene das Escolas," published in the *Gazeta Médica da Bahia*, XXI, No. 7, is particularly important.

cine to zoology, comparative anatomy, botany, physics, or chemistry. Teaching is accomplished through books instead of through actual practice." In this, he was touching on the sensitive nerve of the situation; the slave economy of Imperial Brazil made applied instruction difficult in all fields—in engineering and agronomy, as well as medicine. As Professor Agassiz observed: "In short, so long as prejudice against manual labor exists in Brazil, applied instruction will be badly done; so long as students of nature feel that it is not appropriate for a gentleman to carry his specimens or his geologist's hammer or to make his own preparations, they will never be more than amateurs in the subject. They can learn admirably the facts discovered by others, but they will never do any original research on their own." [2]

The truth is that, to Agassiz, the Brazil of Pedro II was deficient in intellectual progress, particularly in the sense of needing a greater attention to experimental science, a greater use of the laboratories, and a greater amount of manual work on the part of both professors and students in Brazilian schools of higher education. So marked was this lack of intellectual progress that it affected the entire life of the country, showing a lack of substantial achievement in all fields. However, in a patriarchal slavocracy such progress is enormously difficult to attain. The dilemma of Brazil, to put Agassiz's reactions into modern sociological terms, lay in the incompatibility in Brazilian life between the substance and the forms, and in the tendency of Brazilians to conclude that "intellectual progress" could be achieved in the same way that independence was gained from Portugal: less through hard work than mere volition. In his words: "As a desire, so to speak, that gives birth to a step forward toward something that is not as yet a fact." [3]

This "step forward" in modern experimental science could have been made in places like the Recife law school or the Polytechnic Institute of São Paulo more easily than in intellectual centers like Bahia which remained imprisoned by the traditional social order. The most conservative of all cities, Bahia maintained an almost oriental zeal, similar to that long preserved in Coimbra, for the purely decorative aspects of learning. What was really lacking in nineteenth-century Brazil was the desire to achieve—not by means of individuals, but institutions acting concertedly—some evidence of

[2] M. and Mme Louis Agassiz: *Voyage au Brésil* (Paris, 1872), p. 249.
[3] Ibid., p. 247.

this "step forward" in the form of the ascendancy of experimental methods over those purely mnemonic or rhetorical, evidence of the desire to live in the modern Western world instead of trying to remain in the splendid days of an archaic humanism devoid of scientific interest or methods of research.

Thus Bahia had reached the end of the nineteenth century with an Academy of Medicine more notable, all in all, for its old-fashioned "academic" manner than for its modern spirit of medicine. Behind the times in every way, it reacted to the foreign professors and the Brazilian from Maranhão who attempted to reform it from top to bottom as though they were traitors to an almost sacred Bahian tradition. For this reason, the efforts of these outsiders must be considered most praiseworthy in developing intellectual progress in the face of clerical and academic atrophy. Similar attempts were made by Tobias in Recife, Pereira Barreto in São Paulo, and Aluísio Azevedo in Maranhão. But even more than in Rio de Janeiro, or São Paulo or Recife, in Bahia it required a spirit of virtually heroic proportions to fly in the face of an intellectual order that was geared to prevailing social, economic, and religious elements, constituting a society dedicated to a type of "order" which meant only rigidity, routine, and the prevalence of the mystique of tradition over the charisma of innovation. More than any other province in the nation (although Maranhão was a close second), Bahia represented a resistance to cultural progressivism of all types in its quiet affirmation, through a sometimes healthy inertia, of purely Luso-Brazilian values in the face of bizarre innovations and daring foreign "isms." Positivism, for example, never found a notable champion in Bahia; the Teutonism of Tobias Barreto would have been impossible in that city; the very abolitionism of Joaquim Nabuco, advocated as it was in terms more sociological than oratorical, would have been out of its element in the province of Nabuco de Araújo.[4] Because all these ideas were presented to

[4] José Thomaz Nabuco de Araújo, one of the most distinguished statesmen of the Empire, for a time represented the province of Bahia in the Imperial Senate. He also served as Minister of Justice in the 1850's. A pioneer of the abolitionist movement, Nabuco de Araújo was author of the Law of the Free Womb enacted in September, 1871, which provided that all children of slave mothers could be freed by their owners (in exchange for an indemnity from the government) at age eight or would be automatically free at twenty-one. His biography, written by his even more famous son, Joaquim Nabuco, is one of the best documents on the Empire of Pedro II—*Um Estadista do Império: Nabuco de Araújo, Sua Vida, Suas Opiniões, Sua Epoca* (3 vols., Paris, 1900). (Translator.)

their Brazilian audience in a language that was something less than pure Portuguese, they would have failed to win the Bahian public. But the ideas themselves would also have failed to attract; Bahian tastes, nourished on traditional Luso-Bahian delicacies, would have rejected the intellectual rare beef and sausage of British or German origin.

One of the last provincial presidents of Bahia stated that "the area could never be properly developed economically so long as there were no geographical, topographical, agricultural, and transportation survey maps," an omission which a careful contemporary student of Bahian culture, Durval Vieira de Aguiar, attributed to the Bahian indifference to progress in a province "so vast and so unhappy, so sadly unprogressive amidst its natural God-given weath; so poor in its industry, commerce, and agriculture despite its size, its riches, and its fertility . . ." [5]

This was so, in his opinion, because the Bahian forgot his province in favor of the court, "where all of our resources, both material and intellectual, converge and where, if it were possible, our pure atmosphere itself would migrate in exchange for the pestilent climate which prevails there in certain seasons." He need only have added that this "pure atmosphere" in Bahia was a gift of nature, and not the result of any systematic effort on the part of its doctors to extend their practice to others than the rich or to establish hospitals or develop programs of public health and sanitation based on ecological studies. He could also have mentioned that, with few exceptions, priests were content to say mass and to marry and baptize the rich; only the most learned engaged in sermons of extensive eloquence on the religious festival days so numerous in Bahia. Bahian citizens were indignant when they learned that priests of foreign extraction were preaching to the poor in what one critic of the period called "mutilated, almost unintelligible language": a presumptuousness intolerable to Bahian ears. It was equally irritating to those sensitive ears to hear foreign physicians speak of illnesses and fevers in somewhat less than the elegant Portuguese expected of members of the profession, and particularly of graduates of the local Academy of Medicine, whose language was almost as sacerdotal as that of the priests. Or, for that matter, to hear about social ills or cultural backwardness from a Joaquim Nabuco or a Tobias

[5] Durval Vieira de Aguiar: *Descrições Práticas da Província da Bahia* (Bahia, 1888), pp. 5–6.

Barreto, or a Pereira Barreto, none of whom was scrupulous in the mother tongue. (Nabuco was Gallicized and Anglicized; Tobias, Teutonized; and Pereira Barreto corrupted by a long stay in Europe, from which he had returned a Positivist.)

"When one mentions the provinces in which the abolitionist movement had its greatest impact, one has to include Pernambuco, Rio Grande do Sul, Goiás, and later São Paulo and Pará," wrote the Bahian physician Anselmo da Fonseca in the twilight of the Empire; "when, on the contrary, you wish to indicate those in which slavery has its greatest support, you have to cite Maranhão, Rio de Janeiro, Minas, Espirito Santo." [6] And Bahia? According to this unorthodox Bahian physician, Bahia had to be considered "ultraslave-conscious" in its attitudes. It was a province in which public sentiment always bowed before the "nobility," that is to say, the patriarchs of the big houses of the interior and the town houses of the capital, those whose "privileges are respected" and whose interests were considered more sacred than the general welfare. Bahia was attached to this economic and social caste as though the word of the privileged was its own voice, eloquent, sacerdotal, devoted to the mystique of order and nearly always suspicious of progress. It is true that some celebrated Bahians of the nineteenth century had freed themselves from the bonds of this mystique: Teixeira de Freitas, Nabuco de Araújo, the first Rio Branco,[7] Luís Gama, Castro Alves, Ruy Barbosa. But these acted under the stimulus of other elements, in conjunction with other Brazilian environments, in which their peculiar Bahian tendencies could be combined with other factors, particularly dynamic, to produce results. There were, for example, some magnificent combinations of contrasting aspects of Bahia and São Paulo, seen in the scientific reformers of the turn of the century—Manuel Vitorino, Teodoro Sampaio, Juliano Moreira, Oscar Freire, Afrânio Peixoto—most of whom operated outside the state of Bahia and probably none of whom would

[6] Anselmo da Fonseca: *A Escravidão, o Clero, e o Abolicionismo* (Bahia, 1887), pp. 134, 172.

[7] Freyre is referring to the Viscount of Rio Branco, a distinguished statesman of the middle years of the Empire and Prime Minister at the time of the enactment of the Law of the Free Womb. Known as the "Rio Branco Law," this decree was actually drawn up by Nabuco de Araújo. The Viscount of Rio Branco was the father of the Baron do Rio Branco, Brazil's most celebrated Foreign Minister. The other Bahians mentioned in this paragraph were writers generally associated with liberal movements. Castro Alves, of course, is internationally famous as the great poet of the anti-slavery cause. (Translator.)

have considered himself a reformer by Bahian standards. The case of Nina Rodrigues is, of course, truly impressive. But Nina was fleeing from a society as static as that of Bahia and even less exposed than Bahia to the reforming winds blowing from the court; he saw his position as newcomer as an advantage. The prevailing disapproval of outlanders quickened his audacity; his consciousness of being an immigrant placed him in the same situation as that of Patterson, Wucherer, and Silva Lima, and raised him to a level of daring he never would have attained in his native province. This spirit also must have motivated the outsiders Patterson, Wucherer, and Silva Lima in founding their school of tropical medicine. Would that this school had specialized in the diseases of a near sociological nature predominant in Bahia! This would have been truly revolutionary and would have reached to the heart of the Imperial social order: particularly of that of the province characterized by Agassiz as most typical of Brazil.

"No other city so visibly represents the physiognomy or manifests so saliently the caliber of the nation to which it belongs," he wrote. To which the physician Anselmo da Fonseca, with his progressive prejudices, added: "We are not unaware of the fact that the causes by which we explain the backwardness of Bahia have also operated throughout the rest of the country. What we are stressing is that here in Bahia these causes have had a more profound, more accentuated, and more intense effect." [8] To this fanatical disciple of absolute progress, it seemed that Bahia, like Spain, "should destroy that useless past" represented by "slavery, the priesthood, and the nobility." Bahia, says Fonseca, adored the past, it "loved the status quo and detested all movement forward." It was a province in which "to be considered a man of good judgment, a person ought to avoid public affairs and affect ignorance and a certain disdain for the affairs of the province and of the nation." [9]

Topics to be avoided by "men of good judgment" in Bahia were not only those related to slavery but also those of education and public health, added Anselmo da Fonseca.[1] In short, the average Bahian was "essentially reactionary" and whoever did not conform to "the maintenance of stability" was considered a "vain theorist." Thus the backwardness of Bahia was manifested everywhere: "in

[8] Fonseca: op. cit., p. 173.
[9] Ibid., pp. 173–4.
[1] Ibid., p. 174.

customs, in buildings, in street-cleaning, in public hygiene, in finance, and in education." [2] As a physician, Fonseca was particularly concerned about public hygiene, an area in which Bahia, despite its "pure atmosphere," was at the time notable for its lack of interest, particularly in the indifference of government and inhabitants alike to the sanitary measures necessary to meet the increase in urban population, measures already taken in many other tropical cities, including Rio de Janeiro.

In 1875 a graduate in physical sciences, mathematics, and civil engineering named Luís Rafael Vieira Souto invaded a field hitherto considered that of the doctors when he wrote his *O Melhoramento da Cidade do Rio de Janeiro* (*The Improvement of the City of Rio de Janeiro*). What he says of Rio perhaps applies even more directly to Salvador da Bahia: "The interests of humanity, of decorum, of national pride, and of national progress urgently demand that living conditions in the city of Rio de Janeiro be improved," for "in saying 'city,' we are also saying 'civilization.'" [3] It was high time for the city or the state to intervene in matters of domestic hygiene as well, a responsibility which, in Imperial times, rested traditionally with the head of the family. It was time, as Vieira Souto pointed out in another book, for the city to codify the rules concerning the height of a building in relation to the width of the street; the specifications recommended by the Court Planning Commission in this respect seemed to him exaggerated.[4] If in 1875 the downtown area of the nation's capital was still a "maze of crooked streets, badly ventilated and without drainage facilities against the rainfall"; if the "houses are crowded beyond reason, without light, ventilation, and other conditions necessary to health, and utterly lacking in architecture or alignments"; if the waterfronts call for wharves, the swamps for filling, the markets for better locations, and the squares for trees and pavement, just imagine what it must have been like in Salvador da Bahia, a city far more indifferent than Rio de Janeiro to problems of public health and to the type of progress manifested in improvements in lighting, paving, ventilation, tree planting, sanitation, and building alignment. The state or the city should also exercise some control in the matter

[2] Ibid., p. 176.

[3] Luís Rafael Vieira Souto: *O Melhoramento da Cidade do Rio de Janeiro* (Rio de Janeiro, 1875), p. 6. (Hereafter referred to as *O Melhoramento*.)

[4] Luís Rafael Vieira Souto: *O Melhoramento da Cidade do Rio de Janeiro: Refutação da Resposta à Crítica dos Trabalhos da Respectiva Comissão* (Rio de Janeiro, 1876), p. 132.

of domestic architecture, so that throughout the country cities would develop in harmony with tropical conditions. This was particularly important in sanitation, where it was not enough to imitate the progress of European cities in employing modern urban techniques in medicine and engineering technology. On the contrary, for moderate progressives such as Vieira Souto, it was time, even in 1876, "to cease the pernicious practice of molding our construction along foreign lines, without the slightest attention to the climate, wealth, or customs of the country."[5] Vieira Souto accused the architects and officials of the court of using artificial stone and marble slabs, despite the fact that the country possessed the "finest granites." Nor was this all; in Rio there were buildings servilely copied from models furnished by architectural handbooks and reviews.[6] All of this caused him to hope that there would be an eventual "adoption of a more rational, more Brazilian type of architecture instead of the system followed by some imitative builders who carry their scruples of 'fidelity' to the point of including false fireplaces in their buildings, certainly the extreme of all nonsense in a city as hot as ours."[7]

"And what shall we say," the critic continues, "of that well-known form of *châlet*, so appropriate to the suburbs but so absurd for erection in a business street, as some are presently doing?"[8] The vogue for this type of imported construction, even in business streets, was not confined to Rio de Janeiro; it was also rampant in Recife, a city which in other respects had benefitted more from private initiative in following European techniques of construction and hygiene than either Bahia or Rio de Janeiro. This was due to the presence in Pernambuco of a technical mission led by the engineer L. L. Vauthier and by both previous and subsequent contacts with other French technicians who had the good sense to adapt European methods to fit the peculiar tropical situation in Brazil. Thus, for a period, there existed in this part of the Empire a healthy conciliation between the past and the future represented by those European innovations in urban architecture, sanitation, illumination, paving, and street alignment.

These technical infiltrations also had much to do with the great

---

[5] Ibid., p. 121.

[6] In this matter the more conservative cities such as Salvador, Ouro Prêto, and São Cristóvão (Sergipe), were far more faithful to these considerations of climate and local taste than were the more progressive centers.

[7] Viera Souto: op. cit., p. 121.

[8] Ibid.

influx of foreign terms into the Portuguese language. As one Brazilian engineer wrote, in defense of the use of neologisms by himself and his colleagues: "In the matter of technical terms, it is well known that the Portuguese dictionaries are as incomplete as one could possibly imagine. Whoever looks for a technical term in one of our dictionaries either will not find it or will find it incorrectly defined. . . . In this respect our language is still in its infancy." The same critic goes on to say that these conditions would become even more backward if the professionals themselves failed to take the initiative in resolving the problem of linguistic deficiency, using, if necessary, the homely terms invented by common laborers. A case in point would be the word *embasamento* (foundation), a corruption of the more classical *envasamento* (base of a column) used by some Imperial architects and altered by workers who traditionally had trouble with the *b-v* distinction. Such corruptions were hideous to conservative Bahians or learned citizens of Maranhão, who traditionally kept their distance from members of the working class. But they became tolerable in Rio de Janeiro, São Paulo, and Pernambuco, largely because of the presence in those cities of the master technicians, who had to employ such terms in order to be understood at all. Workers—Portuguese and *mestiços* in the north and often Italian, German, or Swiss in the south—employed terms like *embasamento, sulipa* (railroad tie or "sleeper"), *breque* (brake), *balduína* (locomotive), and perhaps *encrenca* (difficulty, from German *Kränke* (?)) as though they were current Portuguese and, by means of popular sovereignty—or proletarian preponderance—managed to incorporate these expressions into the vernacular.

This sort of assimilation also took place, naturally enough, in other circles less adherent to Lusitanian tradition. The assimilation of these foreign technical terms has occupied the attention of Professor Aurélio Buarque de Holanda, an expert well qualified to evaluate the phenomenon in terms of the cultural and technical progress of Brazilian society. A number of assimilations are listed below, along with others introduced not by technicians or laborers but by wealthy voyagers, traveling salesmen, *modistes*, writers on world affairs, sports chroniclers, or publicists in the fields of law and finance. Most of the following terms, used in either their original English or French form or slightly altered to conform with Brazilian pronunciation, are still current in present-day Brazilian Portuguese:

Madame (or *madama*), *five-o'clock tea*, *jóquei* (jockey), *turfe*, *spleen*, *snob*, *causeur*, *wagon* (or *vagão*), *dogue* (dog), *toilette*, *bife* (beefsteak), *menu*, *restaurante*, *funding*, *impeachment*, *tílburi*, *cabriolé*, *landô* (landau), *cupê* (*coupé*), *deck*, *smart*, *ragu* (*ragoût*), *élan*, *warrantagem* (warranty), *casse-tête*, *lorgnon*, *charrette*, *raquete*, *pince-nez*, *étagère*, *etiquêta*, *clube*, *clichê*, *peignoir*, *repórter*, *tête-à-tête*, *bonde* (streetcar, from the bond issue floated to construct the trolley lines in Rio de Janeiro), *bulevar*, *water-closet*, *vaudeville*, *enveloppe*, *élite*, *comitê* (committee), *clown*, *bureau*, *iole* (Yawl), *iate* (yacht), *faisandé*, *trust*, *maple*, *bufete*, *box*, *rosbife*, *toast*, *tênis*, *pule* (*poulet*), *linchamento* (lynching), *coterie*, *high-life*, *sabotagem*, *hotel*, *macadame*, *bombom*, *festival*, *batiste*, *atelier*, *meeting*, *echarpe*, *bouquet*, *abajur* (*abat-jour*), *soirée*, *marionette*, *garçon*, *récamier*, *surmenage*, *grogue* (grog), *chalé*, *vitrine*, *turista*, *chaise-longue*, *breque*, *mise-en-scène*, *valet*, *vieux rose*, *marrom*, *budget*, *lider*, *groom*, *cache-nez*, *gare*, *pastel*, *detalhe* (*détail*), *apache*, *escalope*, *puré*, *gaffe*, *canard*, *placard*, *entourage*, *dreadnought*, *scout*, *destroyer*, *tender*, *boycott*, *boulanger*, *conhaque* (cognac), *Noel*, *pônei* (pony), *lorde*, *blague*, *suite*, *omelette*, *bluff*, *true*, *trottoir*, *detective*, *maquette*, *mayonnaise*, *institutrice*, *dossier*, *mitaine*, *manteau*, *beige*, *gris perle*, *diseuse*, *passe-partout*, *marquise*, *guichet*, *forfait*, *film*, *gaucherie*, *matinée*, *guidon*, *croquis*, *mignon*, *gigolot*, *demi-monde*, *crochê* (crochet), *crèche*, *debutar* (to make a début), *nuance*, *cocotte*, *champanha* (champagne), *gendarme*, *hors d'oeuvre*, *bijoux*, *joujou*, *fin-de-siècle*, *frappé*, *flaneur*, *robe de chambre*, *tableau*, *tailleur*, *plastron*, *rôtisserie*, *rendezvous*, *lanche* (lunch), *bibelot*, *écran*, *plateau*, *demarche*, *complot*, *raté*, *caften*, *micarême*, *match*, *goal*, *troupe*, *tournée*, *équipe*, *crayon*, *vernissage*, *aplomb*, *bijuteria* (*bijouterie*), *boudoir*, *carnet*, *interview*, and many others.

The word *boss* seems to have been used for the first time in Brazil in 1912 by the then reporter Assis Chateaubriand.[9] *Footing* seems to be a Brazilian invention, *smoking* an adoption from the French use of the term. There isn't a single one of these "barbarisms" without its sociological importance in interpreting the period.

And this is so despite all the protests of purists and grammarians who in their last strongholds—in Bahia and Maranhão, as well as elsewhere—never ceased to exercise vigilance against what seemed to them a peril to the national language, an expression of a cultural order they wished to keep pure, undefiled by such unnecessary

---

[9] The late Assis Chateaubriand was one of Brazil's most influential publishers and owner of a national chain of newspapers known as *Diários Associados*. (Translator.)

neologisms and barbarisms. Why say *menu* when there is the vernacular *cardápio*? Why *abat-jour* for *quebra-luz*? Why *pince-nez* when you could say *nasóculos*? A significant work in this respect is *Neologismos Indispensáveis e Barbarismos Dispensáveis* (*Indispensable Neologisms and Dispensable Barbarisms*) by the master lexicographer Castro Lopes, published in its second edition in Rio de Janeiro in 1909, "the first edition having been quickly sold out." "It is unfortunately a well-known fact that there is a decline in good studies in our country," says Lopes in his introduction. "Nevertheless, we cheat ourselves with our false methods of studying the humanities and make students believe that this indispensable literary knowledge is generally administered." It is a pity: one studies the fundamentals "merely in order to obtain admission, often through illegitimate means, to courses in higher education and to obtain, without having the necessary talent, the degree of doctor. . . . In the age of steam, electricity, and aviation" it is no longer possible to run; one must fly. And as a linguist, Castro Lopes registers an obvious change in the Brazilian social climate: "We are in a hurry; nobody wants to go slowly. . . ."

One necessity recognized by Lopes in the face of accelerated technical progress was that of creating new words. But these should be created within the framework of classic Portuguese and not by adopting exotic terms. It gave him great pleasure to announce in the second edition of his book that some of his suggested neologisms had "already been adopted by the press and by people in general." The press, he felt, could continue to be an influence in this matter, and he called upon the "worthy directors of our journals" to take part in creating the good neologisms required by Brazilian progress, and, at the same time, to help in "eliminating foreign blemishes" from the Portuguese language.[1]

In general what was happening was that, so far as language was concerned, anarchy was being confused with progress; under the pressure of new necessities, some sort of order must be introduced into this progress. "Progress is confused with perversion," Castro Lopes believed. In relation to language, true progress is made by "creating terms presently lacking in Portuguese by translating the foreign expression."[2] He was in no way "antagonistic to interna-

[1] Castro Lopes: *Neologismos Indispensáveis e Barbarismos Dispensáveis* (2nd edn., Rio de Janeiro, 1909), p. xii.
[2] Ibid., p. xiv.

tionalism," but rather concerned merely to preserve "literary order" in the language of Brazil in line with the effective authority of philologists, grammarians, and masters of literary style. These authorities "should be respected by the insurgent public"; otherwise "only anarchy will prevail." After all, if "popular usage" will permit anything in the way of usage and spelling, what use are the dictionaries and the rules of orthography? In Brazil, however, one sees very little respect for philological or literary authority, complains Castro Lopes. There are countries where the arts and sciences form "a serious branch of public administration," but what Minister in Brazil who "still has some pretense to letters" is able to free himself from "political intrigue long enough to consider such bagatelles"?

Castro Lopes confesses in the introduction to his significant book that during the Empire he had already proposed compiling an "Orthographic Code for the Brazilian Empire" and that this proposal, which would not have been excessively expensive, had been presented to the government by a distinguished man of letters, but nothing came of it and the proposal had not even been returned to the sender. This, in a country "where many of the ministers have the honor to be literary masters . . ." but where the only things that count seem to be "appearances and theatrical tricks." [3] Nevertheless, the disenchanted philologist, faithful to his mission, attempted to exert his influence through the press and his book. Unable to count upon the help even of friendly ministers, he no longer expected anything from governments, present or future, monarchist or republican, even though he realized that the only road to the conquest of official circles lay in "becoming a political pamphleteer and selling oneself through one's writings." [4]

To Castro Lopes, one of the most irritating of Gallicisms used constantly by the daily press was the word *réclame* (in the sense of advertisement), which Morais unfortunately had included in his dictionary under the Portuguese from *reclamo*. *Réclame* in French has, among other meanings, that of "an announcement in which something is praised or built up; *une réclame* is therefore a *favorable* announcement." Instead, Castro Lopes suggested the neologism *preconício* (Lat. *precon*, voice of the preacher and *nuncio*, news, announcement). Such a word "has a learned basis and a legit-

[3] Ibid., p. xxxix.
[4] Ibid., p. xl.

imate derivation." Unfortunately, the suggestion was not received
sympathetically by the "worthy directors of the press." It may well
have been that this lack of enthusiasm on the part of the prsss, some
of whose leading figures were men of considerable prestige and
learning, lay not so much in the love of the Gallic neologism as in
the pedantry of the suggested substitute. In fairness to the great
newspapers of the period, it must be admitted that their use of language rarely fell short of correctness and at times attained a certain
elegance in their editorials and literary, political, and scientific articles. Some of these journals, directed by such men as Machado de
Assis, even employed language of ostentatious pedantry.

Before considering this aspect of a journalism which at the time
played so active a part, for better or worse, in the development of
the country's culture, let us look at those nonliterary sections of the
daily press which so characteristically represent the ethos of a national character: the advertisements, notices, complaints, and want
ads, some of which, according to the splendid custom of the day,
even appeared in verse form. If the inclusion of this sort of material
in a study that professes concern with "cultural progress" is questioned, the explanation is that such material reveals the presence and
participation in Brazilian life of a level of society which, through
increasing literacy and an effective press, was taking a greater part
than its ancestors had in shaping the cultural patterns of its country.
True, many of these announcements and want ads were inserted by
illiterates through the offices of a third party. Such professional
scribes, known as *testas de ferro* (ironheads), existed at the time
and were employed not only by illiterates, but also by persons who
wished to avoid having to answer for the accuracy or effect of their
own words in print.

The influence of the illiterate, however, was the stronger, and
the classified material appearing in Brazilian newspapers of the period is interesting for its lively and spontaneous suggestion of
everyday spoken Portuguese, in contrast to the more erudite, academic, even artificial tone of the editorials. In psychosociological
terms, the former could be called Dionysiac and the latter would
represent the Apollonian element. An expert study of this material
is much needed; such a study would probably show that in language and substance these announcements and advertisements were
far more genuinely Brazilian than the more erudite sections of the
newspapers and equivalent almost to folklore in their freshness,

rough-and-ready language, humor, and their often rude methods of wit, satire, or caricature, as well as in their often immoderate criticism or approbation of contemporary and traditional social values.

The more picturesque announcements are to be found in the newspapers of the first half of the nineteenth century. For example, the following from the *Diário de Pernambuco* of June 28, 1838:

> Whoever, either as a joke or in earnest, picked up a sunbonnet on Monday, the 25th inst. in the cell of Father José in São Francisco monastery, should return the article to the same locality if he doesn't want to see his name published.

> The person advertising for a volume of Pope may direct himself to the Rua das Flores, last house, beside the shop with the large door, where he will find such a volume with translation at the side.

> Senhor C.F.Y. must reclaim the articles he pawned within the space of three days or these articles will be sold in payment of principal and interest, the last three payments of which have not been made.

> Foreigner, experienced farm overseer, wanted; bachelor or married man without family preferred.

> For sale: One repeating watch, excellent timekeeper, one finch, and one Imperial canary.

> Escaped, one black named Antônio, of Congo stock, about 25, with the following characteristics: no fat, thin legs, small feet, short face, scars on his neck, bald crown, lively eyes, accustomed to going with free Negress named Paula and he also calls himself free when he goes about selling cloth, is known to many under the nickname of Peddlar or Wart . . .

Similar announcements may be found in any newspaper of the period.

The spontaneity of this humor and the picturesque language did not disappear during the period of transition from slavery to free labor. Rather, they continued into the Republican period until after the First World War and served to implant a sense of proletarianism among workers long removed from the patterns of slavery. In fact, during the transition period such material increased in volume and, in abolitionist papers in particular, gained in picturesqueness, sometimes to the point of becoming downright abusive in its treatment of respectable, even venerated persons and institutions. In February, 1882 an abolitionist paper called *Club 33* published an extended attack on persons who continued to speculate on the slave market. Names were named freely, as, for example, that of a certain

"Baron of ———, whose title was chosen at random from the name of a Hebrew city and for whom Hell, if there is such a place, is waiting with wide-open doors. . . ." [5] Nevertheless, this trafficker in slaves eventually turned abolitionist, "perhaps in order to rise more easily to the heights of provincial political office and to prove once and for all that he had succeeded in fooling both God and the Devil." In the same article, we learn that "Lieutenant-Colonel . . . Cavalcanti d'Albuquerque is still in healthy activity, thanks to the milk from his own cows (*vacas*). It is said that most of the stock (*crias*) he possesses is of his own breeding, giving him the double distinction of being both lord and father! If it weren't that we wish to avoid offense to the poor slaves, we would call him 'Boss Stud-horse' (*Pai d'Aguas*)." [6]

Equally interesting for their revelation of the social life of the late Empire are the news reports and articles in abolitionist papers dealing with relations between slaves and masters. The following notice, for example, appeared in the *Cidade do Recife* for October 1, 1888. "The slaves freed today, grateful to those who have worked so hard to free them from the yoke of servitude, are adopting the names of Dantas, Prado, etc., in contrast to their tendency, before Emancipation, to take the names of their masters even when those masters were their cruelest tormentors. A short time ago the parties to a marriage in Piedade, Minas Gerais, were Casimiro Vincente Dias Ferraz Clap and Severiana José do Patrocínio Nabuco de Araújo Prado." At times master and slave relationships were made the source of sardonic humor, as in the *O Binóculo* for January 18, 1883, which contains the following dialogue between a Father Gama (perhaps Friar Miguel do Sacramento Lopes Gama, about whom many jokes were circulated) and a "certain baron of our acquaintance":

"So you made your fortune in hides?" and the Baron: "That's right, but there were people inside them."

There were also many items in the want ads, personal columns, or notices which testified lyrically to purely private events: "Hail! Hail! Hail! With my heart full of joy, I send affectionate compli-

[5] Although the polemicists apparently named names, the author is more discreet and veils the identity of the victims of this abolitionist blast. (Translator.)

[6] Much of the point of this canard is lost in translation. The Portuguese word *vacas* could be translated both as "cows" and "wenches," and *crias* (calves or any young animals) is also applied to foundlings and illegitimate children. *Pai d'Aguas* is an insulting term equal in force to "son of a bitch." (Translator.)

ments to my beloved cousin A.P.C.B. on her birthday and hope that there will be many more days like this one." Sometimes the message was more serious: "We request the presence of the student A.F.N. in the patio of Building No. 8 to deal with a matter which he had best not try to forget. (signed) The Victims." And there were the numerous complaints of tradesmen, particularly tailors and hatters, against those students who had neglected to pay for the elegant dress coats and resplendent high hats which were their badge of office.

In the same *O Binóculo* there was a humorous section entitled "Binoculated Advertisements," which reproduced advertisements from various journals of the period, along with often spicy editorial comments. Many dealt with relations between master and servants; one, in the issue of January 12, 1895, under the heading "Maidservant Wanted" was virtually Fescennine in its audacity. The original notice read: "Wanted, a maidservant to take charge of birds . . .", to which *O Binóculo* added:

> I have a lovely little bird (*pássaro*)
> Of bright tomato-red
> Which, being very coy,
> Needs a place to hide its head.

A second announcement read: "Wet nurse needed; must furnish character references . . .", to which *O Binóculo* responded lyrically:

> I also need a nice young girl,
> A girl as fine as silk;
> She needn't be a wet nurse,
> But she must know how to milk.[7]

It was as though, once the emancipation euphoria had passed and the barons and the slaveholders had been sufficiently roasted in the press, a certain dissatisfaction with the new order of labor grew up, a dissatisfaction which frequently found its outlet in the want ads and paid notices of the newspapers. Reflecting their disdain for the women who advertised their domestic services, some householders felt it necessary to remind prospective applicants that, as free employees, they would still be expected to assume the same sexual

---

[7] The *double-entendre* of the Portuguese words for "bird" and "milk" needs no explanation. (Translator.)

subservience as in the old days of slavery. Thus, in the home, the emancipation was not accomplished as immediately as the lyrical enthusiasm of the abolitionists led one to believe it would be. A significant passage in *O Binóculo* for January 14, 1888, stated that, in the face of municipal regulations requiring "the registration of nurses and other private servants, some inconvenience has been caused by the ill will of servants who through ignorance refuse to obey this law, alleging it to be a new form of slavery."

But the *O Binóculo* also ran an editorial acknowledging the incapacity of former slaves to adjust satisfactorily to the role of free domestic servants: "It is proved that the slave is an element incompatible with our social structure. In the face of the great law of social evolution and even in consideration of capital or mercantile values, the slave is an impossible element, nonsustaining and indisputably absurd . . . reduced for so long a period to a condition of servility, he now deserves merely to be classed as useless."

The dissatisfaction was intensified during the early years of free labor, and calls for good cooks, maids, and nurses multiplied in the pages of the newspapers. But even before abolition, there had been calls in the classified sections for free servants who would live with their employers. In the *Diário de Notícias* of Bahia for July 19, 1884, for example, was an advertisement for "a cook who will live in" and another for a "nursemaid to take care of children," who must be of "adult age," have "good background," and be willing to "live in."

It is in the *Jornal do Commercio* of Rio de Janeiro—a newspaper which at the time contained more advertising than any journal in the world with the exception of *The Times* of London (and the *New York Herald*)[8]—that the development of these tensions in hiring domestic help are seen most clearly. From 1890 on into the new century, there was a great wave of demand for foreigners, sometimes designated specifically as German, Portuguese, Spanish, or Japanese. In the issue of September 3, 1909, we read: "Wanted —a maid of all work for a family without children, foreigner preferred, apply Rua do Resende, No. 180"; "Wanted—a good German cook for refined family, good pay, apply Rua Cosme Velho, No. 113 . . ."

[8] Fletcher and Kidder state in 1879 that the *Jornal do Commercio* "has the honor of having the greatest number of advertisements of any journal in the world, except the London *Times* and the *New York Herald*," op. cit., p. 253.

Nor was there any lack of foreigners to fill these positions. The same issue carries many applications for "Situations Wanted": "Portuguese wet nurse with three months' milk, married, good references; apply Rua General Polidoro, No. 177, Apartment No. 1"; "Portuguese wet nurse, five months' milk, healthy and affectionate, will submit to examination; Rua da Gamboa, No. 117, upstairs"; "Portuguese wet nurse, seven months' milk, reference from Dr. Moncorvo, apply Rua Marechal Floriano Peixoto, No. 191 (new numbering), upstairs"; "Spanish girl wishes employment as dry nurse, recently born child preferred, apply Rua do Santo Cristo, No. 112"; "Available, with one month's milk, Portuguese, Rua Macedo Sobrinho, No. 21, second door, Largo dos Leões"; "Portuguese girl seeks employment to wash and iron for a reliable family; Rua de S. Cristóvão, No. 36, apt. 14"; "Portuguese maid-of-all-work; Rua dos Inválidos, No. 145, apt. No. 12"; "Recently arrived Portuguese girl available as cleaning woman, live out, Rua da Imperatriz, No. 120"; "Perfect laundress, Portuguese, foreign family preferred; Avenida Ipiranga, No. 6, Laranjeiras"; "Japanese chef, cook, and baker, Rua São Clemente, No. 216"; "Good Chinese cook and baker, Rua do Lavradio, No. 53"; "Italian cook, knows French and Brazilian cuisine, *pastas*, and desserts; Rua da Lapa, No. 12, bakeshop"; "Good Portuguese landscape and vegetable gardener, good-conduct card, Largo da Misericórdia, No. 15."

These "Situations Wanted" advertisements inserted by Portuguese and other foreigners appeared in far greater number than the rare: "Negress for light work for couple or to take charge of a child, Rua da Misericórdia, No. 75"; or "Colored boy wants situation as cook, references, Travessa de S. Francisco de Paula, No. 6, 2nd floor"; or "Colored cook to live in, small family preferred, Rua Miguel de Paiva, No. 13, Catumbi"; or, finally, "Colored maid, speaks some French, boardinghouse experience, apply Rua das Palmeiras, No. 75."

In the middle of the nineteenth century, the proportion was inverted and advertisements for foreigners figured rarely in notices of this type: "Need servant, free or slave, to wash and iron for small family . . ."; "Will sell a pretty slave girl, strong, does laundry, sewing, cooking; Rua das Trincheiras, No. 29"; "In the Rua Estreita do Rosário, No. 25, first floor, Negro girl of 20 for sale, pretty figure, does ironing, cooking, and scrubbing, and another of 35 with the same abilities"; or "For sale, a mulatto boy of 22, good tailor and coachman; Negro of the same age and a middle-aged Negress who cooks very well and sews, of very good conduct; and another Negress of 22 who cooks very well; Rua do Livramento, No. 4"; or, finally, "Two pretty mulatto girls for sale, aged 16 and 20, skilled," and "two pretty mulatto children, 11 and 12 . . ."

In the period immediately before that covered in this book—the heyday of slavery and agrarian economy—the Europeans most sought after in the classified columns were those who understood the duties of sugar-mill overseer in the north or plantation in the south. When foreigners also began to be employed in domestic service in the more elegant middle-class homes, this acted as a repudiation of the recently liberated Negro who came from the country mansions to seek employment in the cities.

One interesting detail in these advertisements for domestic service is the appearance of the word *senhora* applied to foreigners seeking employment as laundresses, nursemaids, cooks, or serving maids, thus using a term of dignity hitherto inconceivable to Brazilians in association with domestic labor. The dissatisfaction of these same Brazilians with the new type of free Negro servant seems also to have increased the rush to hire white foreigners, even when it was necessary to pay these new servants wages which, for the period, were very high indeed. Well-to-do families in Rio de Janeiro or in the provincial capitals considered it most elegant to make a show of servants who were not only white, but often blond as well —perhaps German—and who would be addressed as *senhora*. One of these German *senhoras*, after several years of service in the home of one of the wealthy families of Recife, married a hardworking Swiss of equally modest origins, a ship's chandler in Salvador and later in Recife, who became a millionaire during the industrialization of the north in the early Republic. At the same time, the descendants of the family of merchant princes she had served as a young girl went downward in the economic scale in a complete reversal of social status. Such reversals were frequent in the period and came not so much from the change in government as from the revolution in working conditions; many of the foreign *senhoras* who had started as servants thus became leaders in society, often acquiring the jewels of some impoverished family through the medium of the pawnshop.

If it is true that some of the upheaval in fortune and social status during this period was due to the sudden change from slave to free labor, it is equally exact to say that in many cases fortunes were reversed by the financial policies of the new Republic. Criticism of these policies was not lacking in the press: "In the Federal Capital, speculation on the stock market, promotion fever, and the seeking of lucrative concessions that enrich the holder and impoverish the Treasury have been the center around which the entire Republic has been revolving," complained the publication of the Republican Club of Boa Vista, Recife, on April 7, 1891. For such Republicans, the government was following an erroneous course; it was "false progress" to favor "a half-dozen bankers" on the one hand, while "inundating the country with depreciated currency" on the other. What could be the outcome save the enrichment of the few at the expense of the many? The nation had lost its sense of values: ". . . individuals whose dreams in Imperial times never exceeded that of becoming secretary to a minor bureaucrat" were now being appointed to "posts beyond their abilities." In government offices, in the courts, and in the universities the game of politics "is compromising the very institutions of which the country expected the most," by the appointment of the "dullest mediocrities" and the "most incompetent and pretentious politicians" to high official positions or to professorships in law.

Authorities of the new regime were apparently not slow to answer this criticism in the press with "beatings and personal reprisals," for the *Jornal Pequeno* (Recife) of April 7, 1891, complained: "What progress can be made if the government answers its critics in the press with blows and personal attacks?" and then proceeded to attack violently some of its Republican co-religionairies, whom it considered perverted, and to accuse "Sr. Lucena" of "continuing the discreditable work begun by Ruy Barbosa," classing both Lucena and Ruy as persons "whose incapacity is equalled only by their infatuation."

Personal reprisals were certainly not lacking. The *Gazeta de Notícias* (Rio de Janeiro) of February, 1888 published a letter by José de Carapebus in reply to a previous letter published under the epigraph "Fidalgo de Lama" (Baron Muck) challenging the author of the first to "declare his name so that I may give him a proper answer whenever I meet him." Violent language was always to be found in the Brazilian press, but never was it so vehement as in the squabbles which took place among the Republicans themselves. On December 11, 1889, the Recife *Lancêta* stated that the attack against José Mariano appearing in another Recife paper had been the work of "mercenaries . . . capable of taking refuge in anonymity and thereby escaping the horsewhipping they deserve." The editor of the paper in question "ought to be sufficiently scrupulous to refuse to publish such stuff, for the press is not a gutter for the putrid waters of defamation and calumny." But it was the same *Lancêta* which on May 31, 1890, could attack Ruy Barbosa, then Treasury Minister, aggressively and maliciously for an official pronouncement considered unfavorable to local business. The minister, it stated, "should learn how to treat an honest group," which "lived by its own efforts" and was not accustomed to "the parasitism of official administration." "There is no bigger bully among ministers than Ruy Barbosa," the journal continued, in terms only silghtly less aggressive than the insinuation of "parasitism."

But such language in Recife was nothing unusual. Martins Júnior, a native son, was accused of effeminacy, along with an insinuation of pederasty. When a lawyer friend of Martins's attempted to sue the defamer, the latter demanded a medical examination to prove or disprove the truth of his statement. It was in this amosphere that the first Barbosa Lima forced a flippant journalist literally to eat the words he had written about a member of the family of that irascible politician; the offending article was reduced to a ball of paper and swallowed by its unhappy author.

In the case of married politicans, insinuations were made about their wives' fidelity, but the most frequent accusation was that of improbity, and nobody was a more frequent target of such abuse than Ruy Barbosa.[9] There were times, however, when these attacks were turned back on the attacker. Ruy Barbosa had been a journalist and had lived in the atmosphere of anti-government journalism since birth. Perhaps it was this background which inspired his occasionally violent language. On May 15, 1869, in a paper called *A Ordem—Periódico político, imparcial e noticioso (Order —A Political, Impartial, and Newsworthy Journal)* published in Santos, he went to such extremes in his criticism of the Empire as to call the provincial president "the notorious jackass of Itaúna, the most accomplished pimp for São Cristóvão [the residence of Pedro II], and the most shameless president the stinking court has ever

[9] An equally frequent accusation was that the Bahian statesman was the son or grandson of a slave woman, though with the acceptance of Nilo Peçanha and General Glycério, both of Negro blood, such insinuations soon lost their force.

sent to contaminate this province." On another occasion, he quoted articles from the *Rio-Grandense* in which the southern newspaper attempted to defend the Duke of Caxías under the heading "Delenda Caxías." [1] Taking advantage of the slip in Latin gender, Ruy announced that "the *Rio-Grandense* has discovered that Caxías is a woman! . . . I don't wonder that Brazil has a female general and senator, because Rome also had a female Pope who enjoyed great success in the Vatican. Perhaps this explains the rapid rise of certain officers close to the General." When he published these insults against a man of Caxías's stature he was an impressionable youth of twenty, but it is no wonder that he later became so effective in his attacks against government officials. It was equally predictable that, once Treasury Minister of the provisional government, this journalist, who had nearly always been numbered among the opposition, should have become the target of attacks similar to those he himself had perpetrated as a youth against court ministers, provincial presidents, senators, and counselors, against the Duke of Caxías, Bishop Dom Vital, and even the Emperor himself. Some of the attacks on Ruy almost stigmatized their victim for life, and it was only in old age, through his triumph at the world court in The Hague and his distinguished civil campaign, that he was able to clear himself of the stain of dishonesty occasioned by press attacks in the early days of the Republic.

Literature in the period up to 1900 was not unconnected with the quasi-literary activities of the press, nor did the press ignore literature. The purely journalistic function of the press was, of course, carried on at a much more vigorous rate than the production of books and, all in all, had a greater impact upon the reading public. But in its quasi-literary aspects, the press acted as an intermediary between journalism and literature. Rare were the authors who did not make their presence felt through articles in the newspapers and magazines, who did not extend beyond their purely literary creativity to take an interest in national life, to participate in politics, or to take a hand in influencing public opinion on the problems of the day. Such participation was neither purely journalistic nor purely literary, and the best journalists themselves—Quintino

---

[1] The Duke of Caxías, Brazilian commander in chief during the Paraguayan War, is probably the greatest Brazilian hero of the nineteenth century. A character of irreproachable nobility, Caxías after the war also attained distinction as a conservative statesman. (Translator.)

Bocayuva, Carlos de Laet, Medeiros e Albuquerque, Ruy Barbosa (during his great days on the *Diário de Notícias*), Alcindo Guanabara, young Félix Pacheco, the first Júlio Mesquita, Nestor Rangel Pestana, Tobias Monteiro, and João do Rio—all had something that distinguished them from everyday journalists, not only in their superior knowledge and talent but also in their written style, which fell somewhere between common journalism and creative art. Raul Pompéia, for example, was sensitive, artistic, and literary in his role of man of letters, but he was also a talented journalist and man of action. Indeed, among journalistic leaders, pure newspapermen were rare. One such was José Carlos Rodrigues who, upon returning from New York where for years he had published the *Novo Mundo*, directed the *Jornal do Commercio* from 1890 to 1915 as a journalist pure and simple. (Only at the end of his life did he become interested in historical research, but he never considered himself a literary man.) Another was Edmundo Bittencourt, whose only interest was to influence present opinion incisively and vigorously, in a newspaper always in more or less violent opposition to the government.[2]

Even during an earlier period the political and literary press had played an important role in the cultural development of the country. Since the beginning of the Empire, thanks to the freedom of publication, there had been "intensive press activity throughout the country, in which literature and politics were mixed together in the manner so typical of the period."[3] This mixture established a bond between writers and the Brazilian public and proved as favorable to belles-lettres as to the more occasional types of writing, particularly in helping to break down the rigid divisions between the two styles, as well as those of a racial or sexual nature. Nevertheless, this political and literary fusion, useful as it was in the development of a country still sub-European in its culture, also had its unfavorable aspects. There is no doubt that it "developed the type of writer known as 'publicist': a mixture of journalist, politician, and man of letters capable of flitting from one subject to another without identifying himself clearly with any . . .", giving rise to "the ascendancy of the dilettante over the professional writer, with grave consequences upon the quality of both the literature of imagination

[2] Another such figure was Ferreira de Araújo. (Translator.)

[3] Afrânio Coutinho, *et al.: A Literatura no Brasil* (Rio de Janeiro, 1955), I, No. 2, 579.

and that of ideas." [4] In any case, it was through journalism, "whether literary or political, whether in the news columns or through translations" that "the rarefied incipient Brazilian cultural atmosphere maintained its spiritual contact with the great foreign centers."

By the turn of the century, the prestige and influence of journalism had surpassed the earlier supremacy of the pulpit and was challenging that of the tribunal. It was at this time, thanks to the development of a considerable reading public, that the position of the writer attained a new dignity and independence. This had already been anticipated to some extent by the popularity of the romances of Macedo and Alencar, but it was the French publisher Batiste Louis Garnier who really brought about a new relationship between writer and public. Brazilians had always had some sense of literary values, gained through sermons, lectures, theatres, and political oratory. At home, within the pattern of patriarchal domesticity, they had heard substantial books read aloud, *Don Quixote*, for example, or the Negro slave women's tales of Trancoso or other legendary figures. They had even done some reading on levels commensurate with their education, intelligence, or economic situation. But the true phase of literary appreciation came at the end of the monarchy with the appearance of the Garnier publications.

The first French-style paperbacks to be published were the standard Brazilian authors of the day: Álvares de Azevedo, Gonçalves de Magalhães, Pôrto Alegre, Macedo, Alencar, Bernardo Guimarães, Manuel de Almeida, Pereira da Silva, Canon Fernandes Pinheiro, Joaquim Norberto de Sousa, Melo Morais Pai; then came the newer writers whose youth brought new values to the Brazilian scene: Escragnolle Taunay, Luís Guimarães, Tavares Bastos, Augusto Teixeira de Freitas, Joaquim Maria Serra, Pimenta Bueno, the Viscount of Uruguay, Bittencourt Sampaio, Cândido Mendes de Almeida; then, later, Machado de Assis, Melo Morais, Jr., Sylvio Romero, Aluísio Azevedo, Joaquim Nabuco, Alberto de Oliveira, Medeiros e Albuquerque, Nestor Vitor, Afonso Celso, Olavo Bilac, Clóvis Bevilaqua, Domício da Gama, Graça Aranha, Júlia Lopes de Almeida, José Veríssimo, Antônio Sales, Laudelino Freire, João do Rio (Paulo Barreto), and many others: all issued by Garnier.

Thus Ernesto Senna was not exaggerating when he wrote (in his

[4] Ibid., p. 579.

book on the former commerce of Rio de Janeiro) that "the service of Garnier to Brazilian literature was highly significant, despite his stinginess in regard to fees. He published a great many national authors, and the number of titles by these writers surpassed 665, not counting the numerous translations also made by Brazilians." [5] One of these translations was Southey's *History of Brazil*, a work of fundamental interest to Brazilians, in the Portuguese of Luís de Castro. And in fairness to Garnier it must be pointed out that, though tight-fisted with his authors, "there was nobody like him in his enthusiasm and good will in undertaking the risky business of publishing national authors," especially authors of such weight as Cândido Mendes, with his *Código Filipino* and his codification of arrests in the old Court of Relations (Tribunal da Relação), or A. J. Ribas, with many juridical titles, or, for that matter, the Holy Bible, translated by Antônio Pereira de Figueiredo, in an edition illustrated with 30 steel engravings and printed in Paris by Blot.

Garnier also introduced Brazil to the 7-point and 12-point long formats made popular in France by Calmann-Lévy, and established the magazines *Revista Popular* and *Jornal das Famílias*. His press dates from the 1870's, when, with modern machines imported from Europe, he published the so-called *Universal Library* in octavo and the *Pocket Library* in duodecimo with Portuguese translations of the works of Musset, Droz, Gautier, Sardou, and Jules Verne.[6] These publications earned him 30 *contos*. Priding himself on his knowledge of the Brazilian market, Garnier once said to a regular customer who had advised him to reduce the price on a book which wasn't going well: "That won't work; there are some books which, no matter what their price or critical acclaim, won't sell more than 300 or 400 copies; whereas with the popular ones it is easy to sell 600 to 800 the first year. . . ." [7]

Everything seems to indicate that Garnier was fortunate enough to begin his publishing activities just when improving economic circumstances were creating a demand throughout the country for private libraries of favorite authors, both national and European. Even so, it is to the credit of "Jew" Garnier, as he was sometimes

[5] Ernesto Senna: *O Velho Comércio do Rio de Janeiro* (Rio de Janeiro–Paris, n.d.), p. 29.

[6] Ibid., p. 12.

[7] Ibid., p. 22. See also Olavo Bilac: *Crítica e Fantasia* (Lisbon, 1904), who states that at the turn of the century editions ran to between 2,000 and 2,500 copies.

called, that (despite a nature more prudent than daring) he had the good sense to publish a writer of the quality of Machado de Assis, who was certainly no truckler to popular tastes. That this "daring" may have been simply good business sense, however, is suggested by the fact that the first work of Machado published by Garnier sold 800 copies the first year, a good sale for the time and equal to the record of the works of the sure-fire Jules Verne.

On the other hand, Garnier was not above exploiting the intellectuals of his day. Lopes Trovão, for example, was used merely for editorial duties, particularly the monotonous task of proofreading manuscripts. Nobly republican in his ideas and a bit of a dandy in his dress—which included top hat and monocle like any British lord —Lopes Trovão had been forced to make his living by giving Portuguese lessons to the children of the rich and by translating labels and promotional material for European patent medicines. Other intellectuals of the caliber of Salvador de Mendonça were paid between 250 and 280 *milreis* for the translation of an entire work by Verne or Montepin.

However strong his business sense, it was still to be expected that, in a country governed by an Emperor who was devoted to books and friendly to authors, Batista Luís Garnier should have been decorated with the Order of the Rose. He died a Commander of the Brazilian Empire for "services rendered to Brazilian letters," [8] a service which ranged from the publication of works of the most practical utility to those of literary stature which, if not overintellectual, at least had a positive effect on the development of Brazilian culture. [9]

Among the authors of nearly 700 Brazilian works published by old Garnier in the last decades of the nineteenth century, most would have been pleased to consider themselves professional authors on the strength either of their style or their highly literary subject matter. Unfortunately, save for Machado de Assis, and a handful of works by Taunay, Joaquim Nabuco, Aluísio Azevedo, Olavo Bilac, Alberto de Oliveira, João Ribeiro, or João do Rio, very few of these 700 works became classics. The last-named, writ-

[8] Senna: op. cit., p. 25.

[9] Garnier's publications ranged from the Holy Bible to the *Cornucópia dos Salões* and the *Manual de Dança*. Far be it from me to deny the literary quality of a book merely because it deals with the dance—or with law or medicine, for that matter. The habit does not make the monk, nor the subject matter the literary value of a book.

ing audaciously in the 1890's on subjects ostensibly outside literary,
in fact came closer to producing true literature than many of his
more conventional colleagues who dealt with noble themes in a pure
style closely imitative of that of bygone masters. At the time, however, João do Rio was nearly destroyed by accusations of Gallicism, of not following the style of the masters, and of dealing with
ephemeral rather than noble subject matter. He was a revolutionary
for his time, although both Joaquim Nabuco and Aluísio Azevedo
before him had shown a tendency to rebel against Lusitanian purism and to adopt daring new French and English expressions in
their writing. The same rebellion was taking place in Portugal
with Eça de Queiroz, whose impact upon Brazil at the time was
almost that of a new saint; Brazilians even pardoned his humorous
barbs against themselves in general and the Emperor in particular.[1]
The Portuguese skill in caricature revealed by Rafael Bordalo in
connection with the social criticism of Eça de Queiroz or Ramalho
Ortigão had its counterpart in Brazil in the work of Ângelo Agostini, Fleiuss, Crispin Amaral de Vera Cruz, and, in the first decade

---

[1] It is true, however, that in 1872, half a century after independence, there were
anti-Portuguese movements in Pará and Pernambuco which were, to a point,
anti-Eça. It is also true that, because of the passion of this debate on the part
of certain inferior writers, Eça de Queiroz came to think of the province of
Pernambuco as "barbarous." In reality, it was at the time the most intellectual and advanced of all parts of the Empire in the matter of social reform.
Indeed, such subjects as the relative intelligence of men and women could be
debated in the state legislature by the jurist Tobias Barreto and the physician
Malaquias Gonçalves; a debate provoked, incidentally, by a petition for government aid on the part of a parent who wanted to send his adolescent daughter to
study medicine in the United States.

These provincial conflicts of opinion over Eça de Queiroz had further repercussions when Eça visited Brazil in 1887. He was received in Pernambuco by progressive Lusophiles such as Joaquim Nabuco, but as a study by the Brazilian writer
Paulo Cavalcanti reveals, the visit caused anti-Lusitanian outbursts in Pernambuco,
particularly in the city of Goiana.

Eça de Queiroz everywhere continued to enjoy a popularity equal to that of
Alencar and Bilac and acted in a way as a unifying force in the country's in-
tellectual aristocracy. Similar cults had existed previously in Brazilian history.
From colonial times Brazilians from various regions had united around Santo
Antônio de Lisboa, São João, São Pedro, São José, Sant'Ana, the Virgin Mary,
or the Infant Jesus; in a secular sense, similar cults were formed around such
charismatic figures as the Emperor, the Duke of Caxías, General Osório, the
Baron do Rio Branco, Ruy Barbosa, Santos Dumont, Joaquim Nabuco, Castro
Alves, Gonçalves Dias, José de Alencar, and Princess Isabel. I believe it was a
similar tendency to cultism that attracted the aristocracy and middle class of the
period to certain literary "saints," both national and foreign.

of the twentieth century, João Carlos and the caricaturists of the magazine *O Malho*.

None of the caricaturists of the 1890's, however, attained the stature of the now almost forgotten Emílio Cardoso Ayres, a name hard to disassociate from the receptions at the home of the much-Europeanized Madame Santos Lôbo (known more familiarly as Dona Laurinda). It was in her home that Emílio Cardoso Ayres found an ideal vantage point for his observations of the social and literary élite of the First Republic. Educated in France, he was able to observe these figures with a continental sophistication and to present them in caricatures of great psychological and sociological value. It is a pity that Emílio did not find a writer-collaborator in Brazil for his presentation of a polite society half European in its tastes but very Brazilian in many of its attitudes.[2]

Evidence collected between 1938 and 1950 from Brazilians over fifty years of age from all parts of the country and of varying economic conditions indicates a marked similarity of reading preferences during the late Empire and early Republic. José de Alencar was the favorite national author, with Eça de Queiroz the most-read Portuguese, and Dumas and Jules Verne, followed closely by Zola and Anatole France, among the French. The favorite poets were Castro Alves and Gonçalves Dias among the established figures, Olavo Bilac from the younger generation, and Guerra Junqueiro from the Portuguese.[3]

In a period marked by the advanced disintegration of the old patriarchal family system, with its code of relations between men and women, between old and young, and between owner and slave, there now began to develop a new Brazilian society marked by a

---

[2] The credit for some of Emílio Cardoso Ayres's work should go to Dona Laurinda, who entertained so many of his subjects, both domestic and foreign, in her elegant home in Santa Teresa, which abounded in European comforts and yet was so characteristic of tropical Brazil. Dona Laurinda, or Madame Santos Lôbo, if you will, furnished a genuinely Brazilian meeting place of the most distinguished sort for literary figures, pundits, politicians, diplomats, and artists, both local and foreign, of the day. Similar *salons* existed in other parts of the country, too, with ladies as their organizers.

[3] Seventy-two of these depositions are listed in the Brazilian edition of this work, but have been omitted here because of their similarity. Of the considerable number of authors named as favorites, only two were American: Mark Twain and Longfellow, each mentioned twice. One person deplored the lack of English-language authors on his list and blamed it on the inadequate teaching of that language in the schools. (Translator.)

confusing admixture of sentimental fondness for the past and enthusiasm for a future considered by the young as of almost unlim-
ited potential. This enthusiasm was reflected in the great vogue,
especially among the young, for Jules Verne, with his fantasies involving the possible development of technical inventions already in
the discussion or drawing-board stages. As a publisher, Garnier
well understood the intensity of this public interest, and in publishing translations of Verne he was perhaps responsible in part for the
number of Brazilians who turned to studies of the increase of man's
power over time and space, studies which had great practical application in a country as vast as Brazil. Most of this research had to do
with ballooning, in which José do Patrocínio, August Severo, and
Santos Dumont were the principal pioneers. It is no surprise to find
that Santos Dumont, the most famous of the three, confesses in his
memoirs to having been influenced by reading Jules Verne.[4]

Equally notable was the vogue for the romances of Alencar. The
appeal of these works is attributable partly to nostalgia for a past
unencumbered by the risks and possible evils of a progress too drastic in its ideas and reforms; but it is even more clearly attributable
to the desire to exalt the virtue and sincerity of traditional Brazilian ways of life. To this was added an overtone of conscious pro-
Americanism, in the larger sense (an enthusiasm which even extended
to the American Indian). Alencar thus to some extent acted
as an opposing influence to Jules Verne. The same effect can be
attributed to the poetry of Gonçalves Dias, Fagundes Varela, and
Casimiro de Abreu; to the romances of Walter Scott, Dumas, Alexandre Herculano, Almeida Garrett, or Camilo Castelo Branco; to
the serials of França Júnior; to the chronicles of Melo Morais; to the
pioneer studies in folklore of Celso de Magalhães; and finally to the
notable apologies for the Empire written by Eduardo Prado,
Afonso Arinos, Carlos de Laet, the Viscount de Taunay, and
Afonso Celso. On the other hand, the much-read poetry of Castro
Alves, Tobias Barreto, and Guerra Junqueiro bore a message of
mystical, almost messianic, progressivism, as did the romances of
Aluísio de Azevedo, the popular *Uncle Tom's Cabin* (translated
from the English), the discourses and essays of Ruy Barbosa, and
those of Joaquim Nabuco, along with extracts from Sylvio

---

[4] Henrique Dumont Villares: *Quem Deu Asas ao Homem. Alberto Santos Dumont. Sua Vida e Sua Glória* (São Paulo, 1953), p. 43. See also Alberto Santos
Dumont: *Dans l'Air* (Paris, 1904).

Romero, Martins Júnior, Euclydes da Cunha, Graça Aranha, Inglês de Sousa, Medeiros e Albuquerque, and Araripe Júnior.

A third category, neither nostalgic nor progressive but rather uniting these extremes with a spice of sometimes exaggerated skepticism, was to be found in the stories, novels, and essays of Machado de Assis, in Joaquim Nabuco's *Minha Formação* and *Um Estadista do Império*, in the critical studies of José Veríssimo, and, naturally, in the much-read and much-imitated novels of Eça de Queiroz. In fact, one can attribute the contemporary predilection for English court dress among elegant Brazilian males to the influence of Eça's character Fradique, who also seems to have started the fad for the monocle and spats. a case of Anglomania induced not by direct contact, but by the worship of a literary character.

It has already been shown that Brazilians during these years had a great love for the lyric theatre, but it must be emphasized that this did not preclude a taste for dramas and comedies. Such works, however, were usually translated from the French; the purely native creations of the time did little to enhance the status of Brazilian literature, and only the work of the humorist Artur Azevedo is remembered with interest by survivors of the period. But not even Azevedo, whose principal writing lay outside the theatre, could produce a dramatic work which even came close to approximating the stature attained by Machado de Assis, Raul Pompéia, and Euclydes da Cunha in fiction and the essay; by Carlos Gomes and Alberto Nepomuceno in music; or by Joaquim Nabuco and Ruy Barbosa in an eloquence which meets the challenge of moving the reader even when reduced to the medium of cold print.[5]

The memorable figures of the theatre at the time were the actors and actresses, most of whom were Portuguese and, during the second decade of the Republic, French. The latter, particularly the actresses, caused considerable repercussions in both theatrical and literary circles. There were a few Italians as well, and there was Isadora Duncan, whose dramatic dances captivated such young Brazilian writers as João do Rio, Gilberto Amado, and Oswald de Andrade.[6]

[5] Other much-praised orators of the time, such as Silveira Martins, Júlio de Castilhos, Coelho Lisboa, Lopes Trovão, and Martins Júnior, do not meet this test. No sacred orator, noted for his literary talents, existed to match Frei Francisco de Mont'Alverne in an earlier period; nor was there any João Caetano to grace the theatre.

[6] In *The Big Money*, John dos Passos states that Isadora "picked up a Brazilian

The dramatic success of some of these artists often extended into a social success as well. One researcher into the Imperial archives in Petrópolis[7] discovered that the "great success of the actress Lucília Simões in *O Anjo da Meia-Noite* had resulted in her christening in 1880 of a Petrópolis emporium named after the play." This advertised itself as "the only establishment selling . . . toys, perfumes, office materials, wax, snuff, sunbonnets, ready-made clothing, wicker baskets, silks, linens, cottons, thread, ladies' and children's hats, fancy-dress articles, etc., at reasonable prices." Many Brazilian products made of native materials took their names from characters in the romances of José de Alencar. Others celebrated the novel *A Moreninha;* and many were the children born in the period who were named after fictional heroes and heroines, Machado de Assis's Helena being particularly popular.

What impression did this literature have on the foreigners of the period? In concluding this chapter, let us look at the little material left by illustrious foreigners who visited Brazil at the time.[8]

"In literature, the Brazilians already can point to many excellent works, particularly in lyric poetry and in the novel," wrote Maurício Lamberg in 1896, in one of the best books on Brazil in the late nineteenth century. "In the first place, one must cite the late poet Castro Alves, and in second, José de Alencar, also deceased, many of whose books have been translated into English. Recently another author has become well known through a romance [sic] as distinctive as any that has appeared in any language in Europe. This romance is called *Inocência* and its author is the Brazilian Viscount de Tonnay [sic], descendant of a noble French family whose members, some learned men and others most distinguished artists, emigrated to Brazil at the beginning of this century." According to Lamberg: "Brazilian literature moves nimbly and sometimes elegantly on the high levels of jest and fantasy."

The examples he gives of outstanding Brazilian authors include

---

poet" on this trip. Gossip identifies this "poet" as a handsome young *gaúcho* law student, later to become a famous statesman: Osvaldo Aranha. But Dos Passos, in a conversation with the author, was unable to substantiate this rumor and confessed himself unaware of the details of the story.

[7] Guilherme Auler, in an article in the *Tribuna de Petrópolis* and especially in oral information to the author.

[8] One of these, Guglielmo Ferrero, was so enchanted by Graça Aranha's *Canaã* that he wrote the preface to the English translation of that novel, which was so typical of its period.

the two Azevedos—Artur, author of "little dramas and comedies," and Aluísio, writer of naturalistic fiction—Valentim Magalhães, Coelho Neto, and Sylvio Romero—the last-named "pupil of the most illustrious and talented man in Brazil, the law professor Tobias Barreto." He makes no mention of Machado de Assis or Ruy Barbosa, but lists several journalists who seemed to have intellectual value and national influence. He also names many men of learning, particularly in historical research, but states that "a classic work in this field has not as yet appeared," which evidently shows his lack of interest in the works of that illustrious Brazilian of German origin, Varnhagen, Viscount of Pôrto Seguro. Among the journalists Lamberg includes intellectuals who were authors in other fields: Joaquim Nabuco is named along with Afonso Celso Júnior; Carlos de Laet is characterized as "a convinced monarchist" writing in "noble and well-chosen language . . . like a diamond," while his opposite number, José do Patrocínio, is described as "a colored man . . . always impassioned," but "ingenious" and appearing to express himself "through a burst of blinding fireworks." He praises Ferreira de Araújo, Pederneiras, Quintino Bocayuva. He considers that José Carlos Rodrigues must be "a man of weight," judging partly from the many enemies he has, "a fact which according to the German proverb bespeaks superior qualities," and partly from his being director of the *Jornal do Commercio*, which "can align itself among the first newspapers of the world." [9]

In his 1879 edition of *Brazil and the Brazilians*, the Reverend James C. Fletcher had already suggested that Brazilian literature, produced in part by *mestiços*, was the best in the Portuguese language. "The only recent Portuguese writer who excels those of Brazil," he had written, with some exaggeration, "was the late Alexandre Herculano of Lisbon. As a prose writer, the late Tôrres Homem, a Brazilian statesman tinged with as much African blood as coursed in the veins of Alexandre Dumas, was by the admission of literary men at Rio their first prose writer." [1] Fletcher did not fail to point out that Brazil had also shown its superiority in producing a man of science of the stature of José Bonifácio de Andrada, a stature never attained by any Portuguese in that field. In fact, the Portuguese had borrowed Bonifácio from Brazil for service in the University of Coímbra.

[9] Fletcher and Kidder: op. cit., p. 601.
[1] Ibid., pp. 602–3.

Other Brazilian writers who seemed to Fletcher to be worth attention were: Ottaviano for the elegance of his prose; Alencar for his good taste, broad vision, and his introduction of the American Indian; the Viscount of Pôrto Seguro and Pereira da Silva for their abundant historical studies; and those "well-known literati of Rio de Janeiro," Pôrto Alegre, Macedo, Norberto, and Machado de Assis. But it was particularly in poetry that Brazil had the advantage over Portugal, with Magalhães, Gonçalves Dias, Azevedo, Junqueira Freire, Castro Alves, and Varela. It should also be noted, says Fletcher, that in recent years Dom Pedro II, through his interest in British and American poets, had exerted a considerable influence in encouraging young Brazilians to study these writers. As a result, there were already "excellent translations" of Longfellow and Whittier by Dom Pedro himself, by the Baron of Japurá, by Pedro Luís, and by "Bittencourt S. Paio [sic]." To Fletcher, there was no reason for the prevailing foreign prejudice against the Portuguese language as a means of literary expression. On the contrary, the classics of that language deserved study and esteem on the part of Europeans and Americans, particularly since, among modern writings, they came closest to Latin and thereby retained certain advantages over their sister neo-Latin tongues. The Portuguese language, Fletcher felt, preserved the gravity of Latin, to which it had added the sweetness and flexibility of Italian without the disadvantage of the harsh guttural sounds of Spanish. With this language, combined with the necessary genius and concentration of force, it was quite possible that the Brazilians would one day create a literature that would attract the respect and admiration of the entire world. Despite the ignorance on the part of the *literati* of Europe and the United States of the language of Portugal and Brazil, it was a living language in all parts of the world where the Portuguese had founded colonies: not only in Brazil, but also in the islands of the Atlantic, in India, from Guinea to the Cape of Good Hope, and from the Cape of Good Hope to the China Sea, extending to the islands of the Malay Archipelago. "How interesting it would be," exclaimed the enthusiastic Fletcher, "to see the light and the truth irradiate from Brazil (through the Portuguese language) to every one of those distant regions!"

Before this great event could take place, however, there would have to be considerable changes in the moral and religious conditions of the Brazilian Empire. The "light and the truth" to Fletcher meant evangelical Christianity; if Brazil was to progress, it would need to submit its Roman Christianity to Anglo-Saxon modifications, which he somewhat ingenuously identified with the "true" apostolic Christianity that existed before the rise of the political power of the Church of Rome. It did not occur to him that this modification, radically instilled, would have caused Brazil to lose the very Latin or Roman virtues found in its literature and its general culture. It was these qualities which were essential to the preservation of the Portuguese language and its literary classics in tropical America, in a situation involving new values, new social conditions (order—or disorder) and new physical and racial influences, such as those of the American Indian reflected in the works of Alencar and Gonçalves Dias, or in much of the music.

At the end of this period of cultural transition, another Anglo-Saxon studied the literary scene in Brazil and reached the conclusion that of all the various literary expressions in the New World, this was furthest from being a branch of European culture, "because this country has so largely developed a series of writers who take native Brazilian life for their theme." So wrote the British cultural geographer L. E. Elliott in his *Brazil, Today and Tomorrow* (1917).[2] And he added, "I know no other South American country where literature is so emancipated, not from French style so much as from European subject matter." As for the writers he felt to have left significant "records of Brazilian life," he names Taunay, Gonçalves Dias, Alencar, Coelho Neto, Aluísio Azevedo, Macedo, Olavo Bilac, João do Rio, Euclydes da Cunha, Xavier Marques, Rodolfo Teófilo, Lindolfo Rocha, Afrânio Peixoto, Júlia Lopes da Almeida, José Veríssimo, Ruy Barbosa, Alberto de Oliveira, and, most important of all, Machado de Assis.

It is important to point out that these "records of Brazilian life" cited by Elliott had a considerable social impact, in addition to their merely historical or picturesque qualities, and that many cultivated Brazilians were dedicated to manifesting their freedom from Europeanism in thought and behavior. Such manifestations are given epic expression in the vigorous pages of Euclydes da Cunha's *Os Sertões* (*Rebellion in the Backlands*), and in many of the works of Sylvio Romero, Simões Lopes Neto, and Lima Barreto—though not in those of many others who remained part-European in their ap-

[2] L. E. Elliott: *Brazil, Today and Tomorrow* (New York, 1917), pp. 97–8.

proach even when, as in the cases of Coelho Neto and B. Lopes, they were *mestiço* in appearance. This second group, inwardly, considered themselves, perhaps too literally, as the "Hellenes," or "Aryans" or "Latins" of the New World. The fact that the period was ennobled by the presence of various illustrious philologists, some of them intransigent purists, can perhaps be linked with this identification with a Hellenic, Aryan, or Latin heritage. Certainly such identification was an advantage to those who wished to protect the language and other aspects of intellectual behavior from what they felt to be the crude adulterations of nativists, nationalists, or *caboclistas*. It was also an advantage, unfortunately, to others who were merely simplistic, or to ignorant youngsters who, without the talent to compensate for their lack of knowledge, placed improvisation above sheer intellectual effort. The excesses of this improvisation were deplored by Europeans who visited the country during the period.

Nevertheless, the purism of the classicists in general and of the anthropologists and the social scientists in particular, was often exaggerated to the point of being ridiculous. Some of the first group often lost themselves in burning contention over linguistic problems of Byzantine proportions; others persisted in maintaining European attitudes toward problems of the mixture of races or of the African factor in the ethnic composition of Brazilian society. The work of Ruy Barbosa himself in connection with the revision of the civil code was affected by these excesses, as were the studies of Nina Rodrigues on the African Negro in Brazil. It would be many years before such studies would achieve a salutary equilibrium between the forces of classicism, Europeanism, and Aryanism on the one hand and of nationalism on the other. It would be some time before Brazilians would have the courage to recognize—if not as values, at least as aspects in their culture—those elements originating from the Indian or brought from Africa. The pioneers who did recognize the presence and importance of such elements were Sylvio Romero and João Ribeiro at the end of the nineteenth century and J. B. de Lacerda and Roquette-Pinto at the beginning of the twentieth, although earlier studies by Gonçalves Dias and Couto de Magalhães are not to be scorned and some of José Bonifácio's ideas anticipate those of Roquette-Pinto.

The period covered here came to a close with Ruy Barbosa supporting the Aryan myth by proclaiming that Brazilians were the descendants not of Guarinis but of Latins, and with a young *mestiço* from the state of Rio de Janeiro, Oliveira Viana, preparing to embark on a notable series of sociological and historical tracts to support the Aryan thesis and combat the nativist tendencies of other young intellectuals such as Gilberto Amado. The chief attention of foreign observers was attracted more by these eloquent and brilliant defenses of a thesis than by the ethnic situation itself or by the aspects of that situation presented in works by more realistic and objective writers. Such works would include those of Sylvio Romero, *O Mulato* by Aluísio Azevedo, *Pesca na Amazônia* (*Fishing in the Amazon*) by José Veríssimo, the Amazon stories of Inglês da Sousa, and the studies of Alberto Tôrres, J. B. de Lacerda, and Roquette-Pinto. The geographer Elliott, in *Brazil, Today and Tomorrow*, went for his information to literary and semi-sociological works of this nature, which he considered more authentically Brazilian. He devoted entire pages to a résumé of the ideas of Sylvio Romero on the contribution of the African Negro, in contrast to the American Indian, to Brazilian culture. Theodore Roosevelt had the same ideas as Elliott on this subject, and even Bryce admitted their importance in the development of Brazilian civilization. This included the development of a literature worthy of European attention in which Negroid men like Tobias Barreto and Machado de Assis and coal-black Negroes like Cruz e Sousa played a brilliant part. Bryce, referring to the Brazil he knew at the turn of the century, wrote that he had found among Brazilians a far greater affection for their national literary traditions than in the corresponding countries of Spanish America.[3]

Brazilians were notable, according to Bryce, for their "quick susceptibility to ideas, like the French and the Russians." Despite this, "they have not to this time made any great contribution to science, neither in the field of physical research, nor in economics, philology, or history." However, the young Brazilian Republic contained "admirable orators, clever and subtle lawyers, and astute politicians"; also administrators whose talents were "demonstrated through triumphs such as the extinction of yellow fever in Rio and Santos." In addition, the love of what he calls "polite letters" was common among persons of the upper class. "Skill in writing good verse is by no means rare, the Brazilians retaining in their language

[3] James Bryce: *South America, Observations and Impressions* (New York, 1913), p. 418.

qualities established by Camoens in his *Lusiads*, a poem which, in his opinion, continues to contribute much toward the maintenance of good taste and literary talent among the Luso-Americans." [4]

In reply is Bryce's statement to the effect that Brazil had made no contribution to economics, philology, or history, it could be argued that Brazilian economists had just enriched economic science with the technique of "valorization," that Antônio de Morais had just completed his *Dicionário*, and that in historical research Varnhagen had already produced his *História do Brasil*, Sylvio Romero his *História da Literatura Brasileira*, and Martins Júnior his *História do Direito Nacional*. In historical literature, two works of great authority had been published in Rio de Janeiro with Oliveira Lima's *Dom João VI no Brasil*, much praised by British critics, and Joaquim Nabuco's *Um Estadista do Império*. These books compare with the best in their field published in Europe or the United States at the end of the nineteenth century, the works of James Bryce himself included. If in Brazil, as in other parts of America, Bryce could note that "men of undoubted talent" were "often beguiled by phrases, and seem to prefer words to facts" [5] (a reference perhaps to Ruy Barbosa, who since his days at The Hague had often been referred to rather unjustly by European diplomats and journalists as "Dr. Verbosa"), the truth is that there were many Brazilian intellectuals who could have impressed him with their acute objectivity and their anti-rhetorical style: João Ribeiro, José Veríssimo, Capistrano de Abreu, Tristão de Araripe, Carlos de Laet, Inglês da Sousa, Medeiros e Albuquerque, João do Rio, Mário de Alencar, along with Joaquim Nabuco, Oliveira Lima, and Sylvio Romero, as well as authors like Cármen Dolóres and Júlia Lopes de Almeida whose feminine sensibility did not in any way dull their critical spirit.

Among other foreign observers, García Merou, in his *El Brasil Intelectual*, gave particular attention to the literary scene, with special emphasis on the *mestiço* Tobias Barreto. Henri Turot dedicated the best pages of his *En Amérique Latine* to Brazil and did not hesitate to scandalize Latin Americans of other areas by saying: "Brazil is considered to be the only Latin-American country possessing a literature," which he attributed to the fact that "in an organized society, enjoying complete freedom of speech, literature

4 Ibid., p. 416.
5 Ibid., p. 417.

can expand and flourish at will. . . ." [6] Nor was this developing literature entirely neglected by Brazilian society; Turot noted that, in more than one Brazilian city, monuments to artists, poets, and orators existed alongside those dedicated to military and political figures. To M. Turot, poetry and oratory seemed to be the particular Brazilian forte in the early days of the twentieth century.

In his *Al Brasile*, Alfonso Lomonaco was impressed by the fact that in Brazil there seemed to be more poets than prose writers worthy of European attention. However, this did not prevent him from anticipating the recognition of Machado de Assis, whom he referred to as "the greatest Brazilian writer of the present day, a poet of the romantic school, a delicate novelist and short-story writer, and possessed of the most polished style of any to be found at present in that country." [7]

To Georges Clemenceau, who visited the country in the early twentieth century, Brazilians of the élite were "passionately intellectual idealists," capable of producing works of great culture along with many "ungrateful studies" of a practical sort. The country could look forward to "a great literature," so far only in its initial stage.[8] And in his observation that in Brazil material progress was being accompanied by similar advances in literature, music, and science, Clemenceau had been preceded by Eugène de Robiano, who had visited the country in late Imperial times and whose book *Dix-huit Mois dans l'Amérique du Sud* had appeared in Paris in 1892. In contrast to the backwardness that Robiano found in painting and sculpture, he was able to cite the excellence in music, supported by the Emperor, as well as in letters and science.[9]

All in all, then, this literature, although it had not produced great repercussions in the more advanced intellectual circles of Europe and the United States, had not failed to reach those circles, if in some cases very slowly through the medium of translations. Some of these translations were received with interest, if not with the same enthusiasm previously accorded the Russian novels or the works (in Europe) of Mark Twain, Walt Whitman, or even Rubén Darío. French and English editions of Taunay's *Inocência*, of Graça Aranha's *Canaã* (*Canaan*), and of some of the short sto-

[6] Henri Turot: *En Amérique Latine* (Paris, 1908), p. 208.

[7] Alfonso Lomonaco: *Al Brasile* (Milan, 1889), p. 343.

[8] Georges Clemenceau: *Notes de Voyage dans l'Amérique du Sud* (Paris, 1911), p. 216.

[9] Eugène de Robiano: *Dix-huit Mois dans l'Amérique du Sud* (Paris, 1892).

ries of Machado attracted attention, as did later English and French versions of the novels of Aluísio and of Euclydes's *Os Sertões*. Novels by Alencar had already been translated, of course, and Richard Burton had rendered several of Gonçalves Dias's poems into English, but this had taken place at an earlier period.

Some writers of the time, with a certain literary coquetry, wrote and lectured in French: Joaquim Nabuco and the Viscount de Taunay were among these, as was Oliveira Lima, perhaps the first Brazilian literary man to give lectures in the Sorbonne. Ruy Barbosa, at the beginning of the twentieth century, also indulged in the luxury of receiving the much-admired Anatole France with an address in French at the Brazilian Academy of Letters, though neither this discourse nor Anatole France's reply made any deep impression. Equally without lasting impression were the literary lectures given at American universities, in English, by Joaquim Nabuco. Still, there was the statement by as responsible an intellectual as Henri Turot in 1908 that Brazil was the only Latin-American country to have a true literature. Perhaps the principal difficulty in trying to capture the interest of European or American readers lay in the tendency of Brazilian writers to imitate European models in theme, methods, and style. Foreigners, seeing nothing new in Brazilian writing—even that of Machado—preferred to enjoy well-known delights in literature of purely European origin.

Os Sertões was probably the first Brazilian book to give Europeans a picture of rural tropical Brazil incorporating (along with virtues that exceed its many defects) a true spirit of the people and the setting which could be understood by Europeans as essentially different, bearing the mark of a culture and a destiny apart from European patterns. The same effect was produced, without the emphasis or the oratory of Euclydes, by some of the characters portrayed by Machado de Assis. Escaping the commonplace through the subtlety of their portraiture, these characters, created by the "British mulatto" as Machado was called, emerge as the Brazilian counterparts of the gentlemen and ladies of Victorian England. Pedro II himself noted this similarity, which is not surprising in a monarch who has been described as a tropical Queen Victoria in beard and black trousers.

Because of this similarity, it is understandable that Europeans and North Americans should have exhibited little interest in the best Brazilian author of the time. Interest did grow moderately, but only in the United States, after it was discovered that this "Englishman" was not an aristocrat of the Empire but a plebeian of mixed racial stock, who, by his own efforts and intelligence, had managed to assimilate the most sophisticated literary and artistic values of Europe and to use them to supplement his keen insights into men and society. The more informed view of Machado's background added to his stature as a writer, particularly among Negroes, where he is appreciated now perhaps not so much for his social analysis of the bourgeois society of the Brazilian Empire as for his status as an Afro-American. Though this sort of appreciation does not affect an author's literary merits, it is hardly the sort of tribute Machado or any of his contemporaries would have foreseen or even wanted.

❦ [V] ❦

Political and Racial Problems

THE FIFTEENTH OF NOVEMBER in Brazil was only a slight tremor compared to the earthquake of the thirteenth of May, which shook Brazilian economic and social traditions to their foundations and caused profound changes in the organization of Brazilian society. Some superficial observers have attributed these changes to the establishment of the almost innocent Republic. But the fact is that, as hitherto noted, the new form of government from its inception made every effort to continue the monarchic principle of order and paternalistic authority within the framework of a democratic social structure characterized by a fluidity among races, classes, cultures, and regional populations. At times, in fact, the interpenetration between these antagonistic elements had to be controlled with considerable political force.

"It would be vain to expect a constitution modelled on that of the United States to operate smoothly in Brazil," noted Bryce; for, being a child of its own past, its behavior would necessarily be conditioned by that past. Thus, in no part of the world of 1910 was it more imperative to develop what Bryce called a "constructive statemanship." [1] This would necessitate the presence of leaders capable of constructing, creating, and recombining—instead of merely copying from other nations—in the manner of the best statesmen of the Empire, who understood that the monarchical-parliamentary system of Brazil was not a direct descendant of the British model but rather only a poor and distant relative of the European system. As a result, these statesmen had been obliged to

[1] James Bryce: *South America, Observations and Impressions* (New York, 1913), pp. 418, 419.

adapt constantly to non-European situations, situations physically and to a certain extent socially American and tropical, situations archaically feudal or patriarchal on the one hand and advanced and modern—sometimes more modern than their British counterpart—on the other. Such situations, needless to say, were not related so much to the general level of culture as to ecological factors, elements known in modern sociological terminology as "tropisms": situations predominantly neo-Latin in their cultural substance, but combined with subcultures of *mestiço,* Indian, or Negro pattern.

In the face of these situations, new to a monarchical-parliamentary form of government, the Empire had functioned as a sort of Imperial Republic, favoring almost a symbiosis between patriarchal liberalism and authoritarian democracy. The Emperor, through his famous "moderating power" (a more sociological and political than juridical description and one which still awaits competent analysis and interpretation) regulated the power of the patriarchs, some of whom were almost republican in the sense of being aristocrats of the Big House.[2] In turn, he had also been regulated by them, not for his excesses of monarchic authority so much as for his modern liberalism, which at times also approached republicanism. Never in the New World had there been such an interesting, and often paradoxical, political struggle between two opposites, divided more sociologically then politically, with the patriarchs of each faction lining up according to regional interests but seldom diverging very greatly on purely national issues, and with the Emperor in the middle trying to soften the shocks. These shocks, further more, were not limited to those between the different factions of aristocrats; there was also the opposition of classes: of aristocrats against bourgeois, against the working class, and against the slave, the last often being protected from the excesses of the masters by the Crown itself, whose own attitudes were a confusing combination of liberalism and superpaternalism.

Thus the political ballet danced in Brazil was one distinguished for its constant movement: its advances and retreats, its temporizing and compromises, its paternalism of the Crown on the one hand and of the plantation on the other. Politically, this dual paternalism became a mere shadow of its former self, the second type disappear-

---

[2] The Big House (*Casa-Grande*) is the home of the large rural landholder and serves as the principal symbol of Brazilian plantation economy during slavery days. Cf. Gilberto Freyre: *The Masters and the Slaves* (*Casa-Grande & Senzala*), the first volume in this series. (Translator.)

ing with abolition and the first with the coming of the Republic. Sociologically, however, both types survived the coming of the Republic, and the President was thus forced to assume in some respects the role played by the Emperor during the monarchy. The Army also came to play its paternalistic role in rising above party strife to act as pacifier of Brazilians divided by factionalism or subnational antagonisms. And the spirit of paternalism survived too in the so-called "colonels" of the interior, whose leadership preserved a considerable part of the heritage of the former Imperial barony, and some of whom were virtually feudal in their patriarchy, though aristocratic-republican in their disdain of Imperial power.

This attitude was often passed on by these men to their university-bred sons and sons-in-law who, like their elders, were disdainful of Imperial power for its limiting effect on the Big House and the intellectual élite. Theoretically extremely romantic in their liberalism, but in practice not always attentive to the public good, these sons of patriarchs formed a solid front with other university graduates, priests, and military figures from ethnic and sociocultural groups considerably less adjusted to the patriarchal society of the Empire, which they regarded as an archaic force in the New World quite incapable of making up for time lost by the Brazilian people, in comparison to the United States or Argentina, in the march of progress.

Nevertheless, after the first two or three years of the Republic had passed without fulfilling the messianic promise of the fifteenth of November, some of these disenchanted intellectuals turned to a vehement defense of the former Empire and Emperor. One of these intellectuals was Alfredo de Paiva, a native of Minas Gerais, who published a pamphlet entitled *Questões Políticas e Sociais* in the city of Juiz de Fora in 1891.

"Where, then, are the statesmen of this Republic?" he asked. And proceeded: "Pedro II, who was accused of exercising personal power, used to say to his ministers: 'You know that I was never an obstacle to any reform desired by the nation.'" According to Paiva, Pedro II had lived up to these words and had accepted the wanted reforms. What had happened was that "in São Paulo, in Recife, the self-styled élite," imbued with "demagogic literature," was persuaded that the Brazilian monarchy was a useless, morbid, and even rotten archaism.[3]

[3] Alfredo de Paiva: *Questões Políticas e Sociais* (Juiz de Fora, 1891), pp. 19, 48.

Statements like this one marked the beginning of the so-called "repentence" which has been studied in a perceptive essay by Luís Martins of São Paulo. Martins deals principally with the members of the paternal and intellectual aristocracy, men generally of the white race (or with only a slight touch of Indian blood) who were considered, however remote the comparison, as noble as the European aristocrat. As we have seen, the Negro or *mestiço* elements in the population, the former slaves and present servant class, had never been seduced by the Republic and accepted it merely on tolerance, conforming with its new ways but never really losing their almost mystical veneration for Princess Isabel, the Redemptress.

On the other hand, the anonymous author of another pamphlet entitled *Um Estadista da República (Joaquim Murtinho)*, published in Buenos Aires in 1897, pointed out that during the monarchy, political offices had "born successors," thus favoring certain families, naturally of the white race or nearly so; and that these, in the exercise of their offices, formed what was virtually a caste system, "an august temple rarely penetrated by the profane without the dispensation of special grace."

This apologist of the Republic exaggerated, however, in stating that the new government would act as a democratizing force to allow Brazilians to enter the academies and hold important political offices without consideration of race or social origin. There is not a single foreign observer of life during the Empire—and foreign observers are the most reliable in this case, being free from prejudices and special interests—who has failed to point out that the democratic practices of the Empire helped persons of humble descent to the best schools and even to political office.

In the 1879 edition of *Brazil and the Brazilians*, the Reverend James C. Fletcher pointed out a fact perhaps scandalous to Americans: that, according to the Imperial Constitution, considerations of race or color could not be either directly or indirectly the basis for civil rights. Thus, once he was free, the black or brown individual could attain through his own talent and energies positions which he would not be permitted to gain in the United States, whatever his abilities and virtues. Consequently, the American clergyman had encountered some of the most intelligent men one could possibly know, men educated in Paris or in Coimbra, who were "of African descent . . . whose ancestors were slaves." [4] In the Brazil of this

---

[4] James C. Fletcher and Daniel P. Kidder: *Brazil and the Brazilians* (4th edn., Boston, 1879), p. 133.

period, "if a man has freedom, money, and merit, no matter how black may be his skin, no place in society is refused him. . . . In the colleges, the medical, law, and theological schools, there is no distinction of color." There was a certain prejudice in favor of the purely white, Fletcher noted, but this was "by no means strong." Earlier in his book, Fletcher insists on the fact that in Brazil there were opportunities for the advancement of the Negro or the mulatto entirely lacking in the highly Christian country of his (Fletcher's) birth: "when freedom is once obtained, it may be said that no social hindrances, as in the United States, can keep down a man of merit." He attributes this condition to the fact that Brazil is a Latin nation and the Latins, in contrast to the Anglo-Saxons, tend to set "merit before color."

Another Anglo-Saxon, the Englishman Frank Bennett, after living in Brazil for four decades published his *Forty Years in Brazil* in Lodon in 1914. He pointed out that, during the reign of Pedro II, several Brazilians of African origin had received decorations and titles.[5] The condition of "people of color" was much different from that in the United States. To illustrate this, Bennett cites two striking incidents: that of the Viscount of Jequitinhonha, a nobleman of the Brazilian Empire who was refused a hotel room in the United States; and that of a recent medical school graduate of African origin who, at a court ball, was asked by the Emperor himself to dance with the Imperial Princess. In addition, Bennett observes, the Baron of Cotegipe, great leader of the conservatives during the Empire, was a man of color and yet so respected at home and abroad that during his regime as president of the Council "the rate of Exchange was nearly always higher than under the administration of any other political leader." Since Bennett writes "Exchange" with a capital letter (as though it were a goddess obedient only to her priests, whose almost supernatural powers were exercised in that Mecca of international finance that was London), we can sense the importance that this long-time Brazilian resident placed on the moral influence of an individual over the fluctuations of the money market. And in Brazil men capable of inspiring such confidence in foreigners could be mulattos like Cotegipe, to whom the government would entrust its destinies as though such men were dyed-in-the-wool Europeans trained in the most conservative London School of Economics.

5 Frank Bennett: *Forty Years in Brazil* (London, 1914), p. 61.

In his book *Vida Parlamentar*,[6] Antônio Pereira Rebouças points out that the Portuguese monarchy had always distinguished native-born Brazilians from native-born Portuguese without consideration of race or color. Joaquim Nabuco, in his *O Dever dos Monarquistas —Carta ao Almirante Jaceguay*,[7] cites Rebouças in pointing out the traditional identification of the *mestiço* and the Negro with the Empire and stating that it was royalty itself which had acted "as much as anyone could to diminish the idea of racial superiority" on the part of the whites. Attacking the idea of the continuation of the monarchy, Jaceguay had stated: "By a phenomenon which I am not sure will some day be scientifically explained, the dominant sentiment of the mixed races of America is one of equality. How can one reconcile this sentiment with that of affection for the monarchy, which is a government of privilege par excellence?"

In answer to this last argument, the future Brazilian Ambassador to the United States had cited the whole tradition of dynastic sentiment held by his *mestiço* compatriots and noted by Rebouças, himself a man of color. Beside which, continued Nabuco, "nowhere is the sentiment of racial inequality so strong as in a tyical republic —the United States." While in that nation the Negroes form "an inferior caste," in monarchical Europe "one finds the Negro every-where, living in the best hotels, travelling in first-class carriages, seated as an equal on the benches of the greatest schools of arts and sciences," without noticing "the slightest signs of prejudice . . . on the part of the press or in literature. . . ." It was not Nabuco, but in fact the Reverend John Snyder, who wrote this last sentence in the *Forum* for October, 1889. But it was Nabuco who asked if, in the United States, "it would by chance be possible for a mulatto, whatever his genius, to attain the almost regal position enjoyed by an Alexandre Dumas in Paris"? The same question could be asked with equal vigor of the position held in the Brazilian Empire by Cotegipe, or Jequitinhonha, or Rebouças, or Tôrres Homem, or for that occupied in the national literature by Machado de Assis or Gonçalves Dias.

There is no doubt that the fifteenth of November, following after the thirteenth of May, came to mean to Brazilians—and espe-cially to colored Brazilians, who had until then been somewhat in-

[6] Antônio Pereira Rebouças: *Vida Parlamentar*, I, 524.
[7] Joaquim Nabuco: *O Dever dos Monarquistas—Carta ao Almirante Jaceguay*, p. 7.

different to their relations with their white superiors—the feeling of being "as good as anyone." Bennett described how, at the proclamation of the Republic, a sort of mystical confidence developed, especially among the young, in the marvelous transformation that was going to take place as the result of a simple change in the political regime. "Strange notions of equality" sprang up; enthusiastic republicans began to talk not in terms of being merely "as good as anyone" but actually a little better. But the abolition of titles did not seem to end the "curious notions of equality" on the part of certain republicans who, in Bennett's eyes, seemed covetous of the title of "doctor." This, in Brazil, could be used by anyone who had completed his undergraduate course in any institution of higher learning: law, medicine, engineering, or whatever. It was "not uncommon for a lawyer to be styled doctor when he has only taken his bachelor's degree," said Bennett. And it was not long before Captain-Doctors, Major-Doctors, and Colonel-Doctors began to make their appearance, an extravagance roundly satirized by Eça de Queiroz in his "Última Carta de Fradique Mendes." But Eça's satire was to no avail; in this exaggerated scramble for military-academic titles, not even five Eças, using all the powers of satire at their command, could have succeeded in making the slightest impression. The Positivists themselves, who should have been the first to set an example of virtuous renunciation of titles of all kinds, were as bad as the rest in their use of such honorifics: Captain Dr. Alexandre José Barbosa Lima, for example. "Great is the power of these two letters [Dr.] before one's name in a country that has done away with titles of feudalism," noted Bennett.[8]

Moreover, it is important to stress that the prestige acquired by the Army during the Paraguayan War and increased during the proclamation of the Republic gave military titles even greater prestige than academic ones in the eyes of the great mass of Brazilians. This explains why Floriano had declared that the investing of Ruy Barbosa with the title of Brigadier-General on May 25, 1890, was the "greatest honor the nation could confer on her benefactors." The initiative in this case had been taken by Deodoro; according to Ruy himself, in a letter to *La Prensa* of Buenos Aires published in November, 1890, the granting of such honors had been "an anomaly." In a "solemn ceremony," with all the military forces gathered on "the immense field of São Cristóvão," Deodoro, "moved by

8 Bennett: op. cit., pp. 119, 131.

emotions which were manifested by the pallor of his countenance and the trembling of his voice," declared "amidst the most profound silence of the crowd that in recognition of the extraordinary services his ministers had extended in the organization of the Republic, he was investing them forthwith with the title of Brigadier-General." According to Ruy, his "recoil" from assuming "the weight of a distinction so incongruous" to the nature of his work, his character, his ideas, and his past history was "almost impossible to express in words." Unaccustomed to decking himself with the trophies of battles he had never fought, he stated he would accept this title from no one, such honors being incomprehensible in "a person so essentially civilian as myself, whose life, in every way, has been a radical negation of the arts of war." It was in this same excessive spirit of civilian squeamishness that Ruy in 1909 repudiated the candidacy of Hermes da Fonseca, calling it "militaristic," and instigating against the honest Fonseca one of the most unjust campaigns ever undertaken in Brazil against a public servant. Hermes da Fonseca was caricatured as a glorified drill sergeant deserving only the contempt of cultivated and clearheaded civilians. The law school graduates, from whose ranks most of the republican politicians were drawn, were particularly vehement and grouped themselves into an aristocracy if not of birth, at least of education, in maintaining their aloofness from other Brazilians less academically favored.

In short, in this glorification of titles, the Brazilian "doctors" soon became legion, as did the "colonels," a tendency which appeared to one French observer as "very Latin." According to Father Joseph Burnichon, there were proportionately more titles sported in republican Brazil than in any of the old monarchies of Europe. When he visited Salvador in 1908, he noted that, among the sixteen new members of the Municipal Council, five were "colonels" and nine more "doctors." [9]

In *The Masters and the Slaves* I attempted to show that since Imperial times academic titles in Brazil had been the means of social advancement which particularly favored youths of humble or mixed racial origin. They were in effect patents of sociological "whiteness," which turned their possessor into the equal of Caucasians of noble origin. In fact, when such degrees were linked to a career in political science, law, medicine, divinity, or engineering,

[9] Joseph Burnichon: *Le Brésil d'Aujourd'hui* (Paris, 1910), pp. 249–50. See also p. 17.

they often accorded a social prestige even superior to that of an aristocratic title.

This process of upgrading men of modest origins or ethnic inferiority through the use of academic titles increased with the advent of the Republic, not only via civilian institutions of higher learning, but also via the military and naval academies. With the Armed Forces playing a more active political part in the affairs of the nation, a military career offered a greater opportunity than ever for the social and political ascension of *mestiços* and humble whites. And with the founding of the Republic, the prestige of the military was greatly augmented through its adoption of the role of nonpartisan moderator in the nation's affairs. Not that the position of the political "doctors" had in any way diminished; it was simply that that of the military had gained added importance. This political prestige of the Armed Forces (which, as we have seen, had been on the rise since the Paraguayan War) did not, however, develop any sudden martial spirit or liking for military activity in the Brazilian people. Such feelings are not and never have been characteristic of our society. In his *Le Brésil d'Aujourd'hui*, Father Burnichon tells of having witnessed a naval parade in Rio de Janeiro in 1908. The sailors, "many of them dark-skinned and a considerable number of them authentic Negroes," were resplendent in newly laundered uniforms the immaculate whiteness of which contrasted dramatically with their dark skin. The officials, who were nearly all whites in this period, were "svelte, neat, irreproachable in appearance." But everything seemed "a bit too pretty, perhaps" to be really martial. The banner carried at the head of the line by a marine infantryman seemed bizarre and incomprehensible, "a sort of Chinese hat or staff of plenty suspended with all sorts of decorative objects: yellow horses' tails, glass jewels, and goodness knows what else." [1] The typical Luso-Brazilian love of the baroque blended with something of the oriental and expanded into a sort of military rococo.

The impression of a group more elegant than martial would certainly have been deepened in Burnichon's mind if he had heard the marchers singing their military songs and patriotic anthems. The period was rich in such songs, the "Hymn to the Republic" being particularly popular. None of these, however, was notably martial in character and still less so in performance, to judge by my own

[1] Ibid., pp. 318, 319.

early memories of military bands in the cathedral square or on parade through the downtown streets.

Admittedly, these military parades were accompanied by wildly dancing children, high-spirited roughhousing, and even a little knife-play on the part of rivals in the *capoeira*. But this increasing enthusiasm aroused in the people by martial display was less due to feelings of raw militarism than to an overflow of abundant patriotic lyricism, a substitute, perhaps, for former feelings toward the Princess Isabel, now transformed into a feminine symbol in the form of an image of an Indian maiden representing Brazil. Or by the idea of the Republic itself, regarded with filial tenderness as a sort of protective goddess who, on rare occasions, might herself be in need of protection. But when these moments of need occurred, as in the Paraguayan War, the many Brazilians who enthusiastically came to her defense did so more in the spirit of the warrior than the professional soldier. No wonder, then, that in the performance of military music the spirit registered was more lyrical than martial, and that the singers assumed the aspect of warriors in repose singing love songs, not just to some mere girl called Maria but to a more exalted Maria—the Nation, the Republic, the mystical, venerated Super-Mother of us all. The words of one patriotic song:

> We are faithful soldiers of the motherland we love
> and which loves us also.

are a typical lyric example of this spirit of reciprocal devotion, a sort of Mariolatry transformed from the Catholic Church to the altar of the Nation.

This explains Father Burnichon's comment "hardly military" as he watched the parade file through the streets of Rio de Janeiro in 1908. "Oh, I know very well that such ideals vary with the time and with the climate," he wrote, perhaps remembering the plumes, velvet, and lace of the gentlemen of the court of Louis XIV.

It should be noted, nevertheless, that the young Republic, however civilian its government, was taking great pains to strengthen the prestige of its Armed Forces and to help assure the cause of peace both at home and in the Americas. The National Congress voted for compulsory military service, and in England superdreadnoughts were being constructed for the Navy of the still-young Republic. There was no desire anywhere to incur the same error as had Pedro II in remaining indifferent to the aspirations and necessities of the military. Nor, after the time of President Prudente de Morais, to run the risk of being once again embarrassed in some remote backland by the defiance of another Antônio Conselheiro and his bullyboys. Such incidents not only destroyed the efficiency of the Army and the good name of its leaders, but also raised the rebels, in the eyes of foreigners, to the level of heroic warriors.

Warriors they were, capable of great and desperate deeds in areas which were, by their nature, the most deeply nationalistic of all, areas no European or American would ever pretend could be conquered by military means. And these back-country fighters who surprised foreigners by their inconquerable spirit were not the only ones to rally to the defense of a nation in peril; there were also the *mestiços* and descendants of Africans along the coast, the fishermen and sugar-cane cutters who formed the Black Guard to defend the Empire against the republican "agitators" and "demagogues" in the last days of Pedro II. With the triumph of the Republic, this Black Guard came to be treated casually or contemptuously by official historians (as we have seen). But the truth was that, in their anti-republican efforts, they were expressing their passionate devotion to a cause and manifesting their gratitude to the government which had given them their freedom.

One of the principal weapons used by these freedmen in their cause was the art of *capoeira*. Through their expertness in this art, many free Negroes in Imperial times became professional body-guards, a group which in the cities formed "a real power, contracted by political figures for personal protection, whose services were especially useful during elections."[2] In 1873, Police Chief Ludgero Gonçalves da Silva declared these *capoeiras* "a disgrace to the capital of the Empire"; they were "inordinately bold," they "promoted disorder," and often "committed assault and murder in cold blood, sometimes merely for amusement." This "disgrace to the capital," however, stemmed not so much from the *capoeiras* themselves as from those "political influences" who employed them for electoral purposes. When they were used, also by "political influences," in defense of the throne against republican agitators, their actions (often prompted by feelings of gratitude toward the government which had been acting in their favor since the passage of the Law of the Free Womb) were interpreted by some analysts as a patriotic service worthy of respect.

[2] Elísio de Araújo: *Estudo Histórico sôbre a Polícia da Capital Federal* (Rio de Janeiro, 1898), p. 113.

The Republic is generally praised for having succeeded, through its energetic police chief Sampaio Ferraz, in crushing the *capoeira* in Rio de Janeiro. The truth is that the republican police seem to have acted against this group—all of whom were Negroes or mulattos— with a rigor which seemed to stem less from impulses of police order than of republican revenge against the group who had supported the Empire through activity in the Black Guard. Not all of those punished were malefactors; many were maladjusted adolescents and young men regarded as the source of future trouble, a problem which later came to be called that of the "middle force," because of their enduring monarchism in a Republic whose status was still weak and insecure.

The punitive attitude of the police toward this anti-republican element was probably a mistake from the national point of view. Another error might have been the failure of the police to employ the *capoeira*, then in its fullest flowering, as a weapon in their own arsenal for the preservation of order. The Armed Forces also could have used the technique, both in suppressing disorders and as an exercise in physical conditioning, an adjunct to the imitations of Swedish and Japanese exercises already employed at the time. The Japanese were said to have triumphed over the Russians in 1905 largely through their greater agility and flexibility. Small but vigorous, virtually acrobats, they held an advantage over their larger, more stolid blond opponents. The Brazilian Army, composed mainly of *mestiços* and plebians, could have developed the same virtues as the Japanese by adopting the *capoeira* and would at the same time have developed a technique that was ecologically nationalistic.

Instead of looking immediately to the problems of repairing the Imperial neglect of the Armed Forces, the Republic appears to have taken account of this national deficiency only after the disasters suffered by the line troops in the so-called "Federalist Campaign" in the south, and later in Canudos. In 1900, a tenacious monarchist, Andrade Figueira, spoke strongly in favor of better organization of the Armed Forces, particularly after "the resistance of the Canudos hillbillies, armed more with fanaticism than weapons of combat," had impressively turned back "no fewer than four military expeditions," thereby indicating, on the one hand, "the efficacy of popular resistance against unjustifiable military domination," and, on the other, the need for the Brazilian nation, now a Republic, to "guarantee the independence and integrity of its territory against foreign aggression." [3] Brazil was "surrounded by young and uneasy nations, all dominated by the spirit of expansionism natural to youth and by the type of government which we too now unhappily possess." Beyond this, with the country "agitated with the revolutionary spirit of which the fifteenth of November was the highest expression, moved by feelings that were in the best interests of peace and public order," the need for a "seriously organized armed force" —not only to act as a bulwark against outside forces but also to maintain domestic "order in the face of anarchy"—could not be underrated. To this the former Imperial counselor could have added that the threats to domestic order after ten years of the new regime no longer came from the *capoeiras* or the loyal devotees of the Princess Isabel. Rather, they came from the white republicans of Rio Grande do Sul in their differences with their white republican brethren in the federal capital, or from other new republican leaders, now officially "white and as good as anybody," against their co-religionaires in other parts of the country.

Officially white, now that they had become prestigious leaders of the Republic, were such *mestiços* as Francisco Glycércio, who held the honorary title of General, and Nilo Peçanha, who eventually became President of the Republic; and although some other new leaders, such as Campos Sales, muttered about their not being entirely Caucasian, their position among their incontestibly white brethren was assured through the force of their political triumphs. Nevertheless, power in the new Republic continued to be held generally by pure whites, just as it had been in the Empire. A glance at the photographs of members of the republican Constitutional Assembly in 1891 reveals no new social levels represented among public figures, though an occasional Negroid set of features was visible in either period. Gradually, with some difficulty, nonwhites began to ascend in the political scale, but the process of selection was rigorous and there was always a certain discrimination against persons whose appearance, whether in skin color or facial characteristics, was conspicuously African. As some republican patriots of the time pointed out—Senator Antônio Massa among them—it was vitally necessary that Argentinians did not come to regard the new Republic as a large-scale counterpart of Haiti or Nicaragua. Thus, it was only gradually that persons with Negroid features began to

[3] Andrade Figueira: *A Década Republicana—Cousas da República* (Rio de Janeiro, 1901), VII, 294–5.

rise to positions of importance in the Army, the courts, the clergy, the law, in journalism, or in Parliament. And it is possible that, had there been a third Imperial reign, this rate of ascent would have been about the same as under the Republic.

During the presidency of the Paulista Manuel Ferraz de Campos Sales (1898–1902), however, there was much discussion of white supremacy. And when, as President of the Republic, he made a naval trip to Argentina with the accompanying vessels manned by pure-white crews, many accused the illustrious republican leader of open "hatred" not only toward the African race but also toward the Indian and its derivatives. This "ignominious selection of crews," as it was termed by a monarchic critic, was incomprehensible in the republican government of a "nation populated by a generalized mixture of races whose members have always affirmed their patriotism and moral and intellectual aptitudes in the discharge of the highest duties of the state in the Senate and the Chamber of Deputies, in the government councils, in diplomacy, in the Church, and in the arts and sciences. . . . For the first time we may begin to suspect or condemn the regime which has declared itself to be based on the spirit of equality." This mixture of races is so general in Brazil, this critic goes on, that "it is difficult to find a single family or a single individual free from the characteristic odor of these mingled races diffused through the heat of the tropical climate." [4]

Perhaps there was a certain *arrivismo* on the part of these men who suddenly became leaders after the proclamation of the Republic that led them to attempt to appear ethnically as acceptable to foreigners as their Imperial counterparts had been. This desire probably led to a careful selection of entourage, such as that of which Campos Sales was accused, in official trips to foreign countries. If Princess Isabel had chosen to be protected by a "Black Guard," the new princes preferred to travel with a "white guard" in order to give an ethnically aristocratic tone to the new regime.

Another form of apparent *arrivismo* on the part of republican leaders (as we have seen) was the urge to make themselves known by their academic and/or military titles. This search for status, prompted by insecurity, naturally led to a good deal of display of recently acquired status symbols. The tendency was satirized by former Imperial Counselor Domingos de Andrade Figueira, an intransigent monarchist critic, particularly of what he called "the ri-

[4] Ibid., pp. 245–6.

diculous itch for military honors" during the first years of the Republic. According to Figueira, "even well-bred persons did not escape the urge to throw their civilian attire into the ragbag and disguise themselves with caps and uniforms which fit properly only on the professional soldier." A typical example of this tendency was the astute politician Francisco Glycério, whose assumption of an honorary military title and military insignia betrayed his desire to appear to the populace as much a prince of the Republic as any professional general smothered in gold braid.

If it is thought that military figures who, since the Paraguayan campaign, had "inclined toward a republican solution for Brazil," were moved by the urge to gain status in the new government by posing as academic graduates, this idea, according to Andrade Figueira, was erroneous: there never had been any monopoly of government posts on the part of the college-bred civilian. There was only the "inevitable" influence in a new country of "citizens trained in the law and in social and political science." In fact, many military figures had been called by the Empire to occupy "the highest offices, such as those of provincial president, minister, state counselor, deputy, and senators." It was also true that the old regime had provided four military schools "where students were clothed, fed, educated, and otherwise trained from preparatory courses until graduation at the cost of the state and with the soldier paid for his services, with additional half-pay benefits going to his family. . . ." [5] This arrangement perhaps accounts for the considerable number of young people of modest origin, often of mixed racial stock, who instead of studying law or medicine or engineering chose to follow a military career and at the same time to attempt in their studies to master not so much the arts of war as a knowledge comparable to that of their counterparts in more purely academic institutions. With the acquisition of such knowledge it was natural that some military graduates should consider themselves half-degree holders in law, or political science, or engineering, and therefore as qualified as their civilian compatriots to participate in the political life of the country. Since the Emperor had never accorded the military the attention they deserved, it is natural that these half-academic soldiers should incline in considerable numbers toward republicanism. Some, like Benjamin Constant, wanted to establish the new regime through Positivism; others looked to a di-

[5] Ibid., VI, 226–7, 228.

rect, nonpartisan intervention by the Army in national affairs, Deodoro in the provisional government, for example, and also, to some extent, Floriano.

With the government in its early days led by military figures such as the *Generalíssimo*, some of the academic republicans felt themselves incomplete in not being half-military, particularly when so many of the new military leaders were at least half-academic; hence the "itch for military honors" found so ridiculous by Andrade Figueira. This quest was particularly absurd because during the Empire, according to Figueira, legislators had exercised the nonpartisan function aspired to by the republican military. At one time, some 90 members of the legislature had endorsed "the incompatibility of the electoral and the parliamentary functions, with the latter demanding the suicide of special interests." Such special interests could be the business of others; but it was the business of those with an academic degree to devote themselves to the most prestigious activity of all: the parliamentary. And Andrade Figueira, in 1901, could state that the lawyers, successors to the Imperial legislators, had never to his knowledge voted for anything that could be considered specially beneficial to the interests of their own class.[6]

This sublime ingenuousness on Figueira's part overlooks the fact that when a lawyer-parliamentarian casts his vote, he is considering not his profession but rather the economic and other special interests of the group who elected him to office. For this reason, it would seem that the military, stemming largely from more modest social and economic levels than most of the academically trained, would better represent the national interest than the lawyers, many of whom were the sons or sons-in-law of powerful planters or businessmen. Although it is fair to admit, with Figueira, that in the Brazilian Empire there were many law school graduates "who were never able to accumulate the profits of their profession," we do not have to agree with him in concluding that everything favored these same graduates because they formed "a class educated at the expense of their families and not at the expense of the state" which "contains the flower, the cream of Brazilian society, persons, who, through their talents and their power to inspire confidence in their fellow citizens, have become the most famous and most solidly respected figures not only in local and national political life, where they have always acted with the highest prudence and patriotism,

[6] Ibid., p. 230.

but also in journalism, in literature, and in various branches of administration, of government, and of political economy, . . .", so much so that "to list their names would be to write the general history of Brazil and of every one of its ex-provinces." [7]

Certainly this is an exaggeration on the part of the former Imperial counselor and author of *A Década Republicana—Cousas da República*. During the Second Empire there were many good administrators, government men, and legislators who through their training in military science, medicine, divinity, engineering, commerce, or agriculture tendered notable services to the nation in public office. One thinks of such names as Mauá, Viscount Rio Branco, Morais Âncora, Rebouças, Taunay, Caxías, Francisco and Sebastião do Rêgo Barros, Buarque de Macedo, Father Pinto de Campos, Antônio Peregrino Maciel Monteiro, Aquino Fonseca, Rodolfo Galvão, Manuel Vitorino. Many of these men were also educated at their own or their family's expense. Some, like Maciel Monteiro, the Rêgo Barros, and Aquino Fonseca, pursued their higher education in Europe in universities of far higher caliber than those of their native country, just as had José Bonifácio de Andrada. Others, such as Irineu Evangelista de Sousa, were educated through their own hard efforts and still were able to become part of the "cream" or "flower" of society through their virtue and talents, both professional and civic. As we have seen, it was quite possible during the Second Empire for Brazilians of modest social and ethnic origin to receive instruction in military schools at state expense and to be trained not only in purely military matters, but also sufficiently in law, medicine, engineering, and theology to give them a certain aptitude for the exercise of public office, a fact the social significance of which has still not been given its proper attention.

Thus there developed a rivalry between the academics and the graduates of military schools in the matter of planning the national reorganization after the proclamation of the Republic. Positivism, formerly the virtual monopoly of the lawyers, now became—to an extent which still needs to be examined—the ideological instrument of conquest for the politically ambitious military. In addition, these men had the advantage of professional disinterest, since their military service had removed them from considerations of profit or class interest to a degree rarely attained by persons of academic training.

It was through Positivism that Benjamin Constant Botelho de

[7] Ibid., p. 230.

Magalhães, a man of humble birth, became the principal figure in the provisional government which organized the Republic. Accused by his adversaries of being an Imperial scholarship student and protégé of Pedro II; of having been trained more in philosophy and social and political science than in military practice; as a teacher in the military school, of having produced at public expense hundreds of little Benjamin Constants; and of having used his military status as a means of political conquest, Constant became the symbol of the whole movement on the part of young men of modest origin to enter public office in rivalry to their more well-to-do compatriots of orthodox academic education. The opportunity for military education at state expense, together with the prestige enjoyed by military figures in the minds of adolescent Brazilians in the period following the Paraguayan War, encouraged many a humble young Brazilian to seek to become a combination of Osório and Vasconcelos: captain and doctor, soldier and intellectual. This does not mean that the military schools did not enroll some students of more aristocratic origins, attracted by the prospect of a military career as such, or that the academic institutions did not begin to attract an increasing number of students from the lower levels of society. Examples of this latter group would be Nilo and Alcebíades Peçanha, law graduates of the University of Recife; or Rebouças, trained in engineering; or Juliano Morcira in medicine; or Silvério Pimenta in theology. All were "doctors" (according to the Brazilian fashion of granting this title to persons with bachelor's degrees), all were learned, all aristocrats in the eyes of unlettered plebians who looked up to them with the devotion usually reserved for the image of a saint. The only thing lacking to attain the highest prestige was for these "doctors" to obtain a military rank or for their military counterparts to annex the designation of "doctor." Serzedelo Correia was an example of the former, as were Alexandre José Barbosa Lima and that principal model and inspiration for all, Benjamin Constant.

It is easy to see why a person like Benjamin Constant would run into direct conflict with that archetype of the Brazilian "doctor" (though strictly speaking, the holder of a mere bachelor's degree) Ruy Barbosa, elevated by that purest of military figures, *Generalíssimo* Deodoro, to the post of Prime Minister of the provisional government. It is equally understandable that this doctor par excellence should have entered into still more painful conflict with the arch-military successor to Deodoro, Floriano Peixoto. And that in 1909 he should have unfurled the banner of civilian anti-militarism in his presidential campaign against the military candidacy of Marshal Hermes Rodrigues da Fonseca, reorganizer of the Armed Forces along the patriotic lines suggested by the arch-academic Andrade Figueira. It is also clear that Ruy would be the principal obstacle to the adherents of Positivism, a doctrine espoused less by civilians than by military figures dedicated to the study of the country's political and social problems. Thus Ruy, the law school graduate and scion of a bourgeois family who could afford to educate him in the universities of Recife and São Paulo, became the most vigorous opponent of the attempt to infiltrate the Republic with Comtian principles. And he fought particularly against the "incorporation of the proletariat" in the new Brazilian society which, according to the Positivists, should become even more democratic than it had been under the Empire.

In this respect it is noteworthy that, during the monarchy, before the Positivist doctrine had become a well-defined program of social reform in Brazilian politics, such ideas were defended with objectivity and great clarity by another statesman whose family was not bourgeois, but aristocratic: Joaquim Nabuco. Unlike Ruy Barbosa, Joaquim as a young man (and a young man whose handsome mien and bursting health contrasted sharply with the pallid, weazened appearance of the illustrious Barbosa) forsook the viewpoint naturally associated with the interests of an aristocratic, slaveholding class and drew up the beginnings of a program of social reform which extended far beyond mere abolitionism to envisage the development of a laboring class similar to that later developed in Great Britain. This program, however, did not prevent him from entering into conflict with the Positivist in their attempt to imbue the Republic with Comtian social reforms especially favorable to the working class.

Thus certain clearly defined questions, which reached beyond the mere transformation from a slave to a free economy, preoccupied the Positivists as they also preoccupied those who agreed with Joaquim Nabuco and Sylvio Romero. But it is curious to discover that such questions were avoided by Ruy Barbosa until 1919, avoided so assiduously as to give the impression that he was wilfully attempting to deny their existence. In this respect his attitude resembled that of Tobias Barreto toward the Negro or the slave, problems always minimized by this vigorous revolutionary intellectual in order to avoid associating his own ethnic condition with that of the enslaved race. Barreto's strong preference for German culture was undoubtedly a form of compensatory vengeance on the part of a Negroid Brazilian against his white countrymen who, being neo-Latin or neo-Mediterranean, fell short of the perfect Nordic Aryanism with which his own spirit, culture, and intellect —if not his origin—were so deeply identified. Saturated with German philosophy, literature, and jurisprudence, he could never become an abolitionist in the neo-Latin Joaquim Nabuco's style, much less that of Luís Gamas or José de Patrocínio, those rhetorical and sentimental mulattos whose elevation of the Brazilian race represented to Barreto the denial of intellectuality in its noblest (i.e., Germanic) form in favor of such lesser qualities as strength, sensitivity, and sentiment.

As a matter of fact, no Negroid intellectual of the period, with the perhaps unique exception of Antônio Pereira Rebouças, openly championed abolition. Tito Lívio, for example, distinguished himself by a socio-anthropological defense of women which could be interpreted as a subtle defense of the Negro, whose race is seen by some sociologists as matriarchal or otherwise woman-directed. And Anselmo da Fonseca, in a work entitled *A Escravidão, o Clero, e o Abolicionismo (Slavery, Abolition, and the Clergy)*, confined himself to criticizing those Negroes who betrayed the cause of their race rather than identifying himself as a paladin of that cause. In the course of this book Anselmo da Fonseca suggested that it was in his opinion an error to seek the origins of Brazilian social, economic, and political evils in the "physiology of the Brazilian race," when the "lessons of history" show that "people whom we today admire, when they were in a more primitive stage, were even less advanced socially than we are at present." But nowhere does he call for racial liberation with anything like the clear insistence of Joaquim Nabuco in his work *O Abolicionismo*. Perhaps, as Fonseca seems to imply in the preface to his study, this discretion is exercised so that no one will suspect that, as a Negro, he is harboring "some private resentment, or some pain or disaffection for a personal offense or injustice received from others." [8]

It is interesting, nevertheless, to note that Anselmo da Fonseca has dedicated some of the best pages of this work to examining the

---

[8] Anselmo da Fonseca: *A Escravidão, o Clero, e o Abolicionismo* (Bahia, 1887), p. 82.

fact that the "principal adversaries of the slaves" are often to be found among Negroes and mulattos. This phenomenon had also been noted previously by Ruy Barbosa, who, like Victor Hugo, had explained the situation by stating that such Negroes, hating their African blood, persecuted others of their race in order not to appear African. As a concrete example, Fonseca states: "In 1884 nearly thirty persons presented their candidacy for posts as general deputies to the Bahian state legislature. Among them there was only one colored man, Counselor Domingos Carlos da Silva, ex-professor of the School of Medicine of that province. He was the only one who in a written public document had the courage to ask for votes in support of slavery. And, together with Sr. Pedro Moniz, who represented the sugar mills of Santo Amaro, and Srs. Lacerda Werneck and Coelho Rodrigues, he voted against the abolition of flogging." Domingos Carlos da Silva was one of those who at the time served as a counterforce to men like Joaquim Nabuco and several of the Positivists, men who deserted their own race and class in order to work for a social reorganization of Brazil which would eventually erase all arbitrary ethnic standards of special privileges. Silva does not appear to have been just another vulgar politician; rather, he was a responsible conservative who wished to prevent an over-rapid change which, while benefiting the slaves, might nevertheless endanger the general agricultural economy and, in so doing, place the entire nation in peril. His identification with the national interest and with agriculture—which was the bulwark of the national economy and, to his mind, of the entire social structure as well—was made in spite of his color and his recent African origin. If this prevailing economic pattern were to be too suddenly disturbed, he felt, not only the planters, but the nation as a whole, would find itself "without resources for cultivation" and "given over to the horde of outlaws" the freedmen would inevitably become. Everyone would suffer, he insisted, including (perhaps thinking of the Joaquim Nabucos and the José Marianos) "the prodigal sons and insensitive ones who live off the sacrifices of the nation without remembering that the money they dissipate always comes directly from the land." [9]

It does not seem to us that, because of his color, Counselor Silva should have been deprived of his right to be a conservative identified with the agricultural interests or to repudiate the demagoguery

[9] Ibid., pp. 143, 146, 149–50.

of some reformers who were willing to risk an overnight transformation from slavery to free labor. By the same token, neither should the Joaquim Nabucos have been deprived of their right to be revolutionaries simply because they were white. The pro-slavery thesis was defended "in a publication directed solely by Silva and entitled *União da Lavoura.*" Although in fact printed in the Bahian capital, it was published with the dateline Caitité, October 15, 1884, in order to accentuate the agrarian flavor and bring out the local color. It was not possible for me to see this publication except in the transcription of Anselmo da Fonseca, but even so it seemed to be one of the most interesting documents in Brazilian history for its presentation of the conservative viewpoint and for the evidence it gives of the interpenetration of ethnic elements on all sides of questions which by their nature apparently called for clear-cut ethnic alignments. But paradoxical or no, it does not seem fair that Anselmo da Fonseca should find the conservative, pro-slavery position of Domingos Carlos da Silva "ridiculous." Rather, it seems that Silva's attitude was that of a Brazilian, taken up in the interests of Brazil, and not that of the descendant of a race who decides all questions along lines of purely ethnic or biological interest.

Given the conditions analyzed above, we should not be too amazed or shocked to learn of the case reported by Anselmo da Fonseca of a certain colored man who in 1887 cancelled his subscription to the *Diário da Bahia* "because that newspaper, as was its policy, refused to publish the notice of an escaped slave." This subscriber, according to Anselmo, was "known as one of the most intolerant slavocrats in Bahia." [1] Perhaps this was just one more case of an individual reacting as a Brazilian of conservative tastes and way of life rather than as the representative of a political party or ethnic group.

In referring to the overseers on the plantations, Fonseca calculated that certainly "two-thirds of the persons who descend to the performance of these ignoble duties in this province—and probably in the country at large—are Negroes or mulattos," [2] and thereby "betrayers of their own brothers." This attitude, be it said, is essentially non-Brazilian in that it considers men of color as a separate class with specified duties in the Brazilian community. Such a bio-

[1] Ibid., pp. 148–9.
[2] Ibid., pp. 150–1.

logically ethnocentric attitude, if it had been general, would have
resulted in a Brazilian society as segregated as that of the Jew in the
ghetto or the Negro in the United States and South Africa. It was
fortunate for ethnic democracy in Brazil that, before abolition, men
of color often acted as overseers, gang bosses, or dispensers of punishment, just as it was fortunate that there were colored slavocrats
like Domingos Carlos da Silva and aristocratic white abolitionists
like Joaquim Nabuco and José Mariano. It was equally fortuitous
that *mestiços* of aristocratic tastes, such as Glycério or Nilo and
Alcebíades Peçanha, would lend their weight to the significant
movement of effecting racial integration and social advancement
through a military affiliation.

The social dissatisfaction behind this military participation was
far more profound than it appeared. Numerous Brazilians of modest
background and often mixed racial stock, craving social advancement and political participation, used the military schools as virtually the only means of ascent.[3]

On the lower level, the technical and vocational school, developed during Imperial times, also served as a means of racial and
social integration. In voicing the need for such instruction, no one
was more insistent than Joaquim Nabuco and no one more objective in pointing out the error of associating the exercise of the mechanical arts ethnically with the Negro or mulatto and socially
with the slave. To Anselmo da Fonseca, it had become axiomatic in
Bahia that the only fitting occupation for the free Brazilian was in
the liberal arts; and it is evident that this dogma extended to the rest
of the country, being challenged only in those few areas containing
colonies of Swiss or German immigrants. These colonies of new
Brazilians were noted for their accomplishments in small farming
and in the various crafts. Within a few years of arrival, the colonists
had mastered the art of tropical cultivation and had learned to use
tropical woods in carpentry and cabinetmaking. The German arti-

[3] One reason for the failure of the gown to establish a clear ascendancy over
the uniform—as it had clearly done in Portugal with the graduates of Coimbra—
was the very fact that the traditional student garb (frock coak, stovepipe hat,
high laced shoes, and gold-headed cane) was much too expensive for students of
limited means, even when daily living expenses were reduced to a minimum by
living Bohemian fashion in one of the austere, comfortless student "republics."
For military students, the uniform furnished by the state acted as a satisfactory distinguishing mark of their class. This is partly why the military school, since the
Empire, has acted so strongly as a democratizing force in Brazilian society.

sans of Recife and Petrópolis were particularly famous, and the furniture turned out in Pernambuco by Spieler in the second half of the nineteenth century rivalled that of the Bérangers, father and son, in the first half of the period. Both the French and German masters passed on their art to future generations through the employment of Brazilian apprentices. These northern Europeans, by the exercise and teaching of their arts, helped to give a new sense of dignity to manual labor. But it was the vocational schools, through their free courses open to all, which gave a more systematic training in this field and acted as the greatest source of master carpenters, cabinetmakers, and other artisans in the Brazilian economy. Such schools were not as likely as the private masters to keep trade secrets to themselves in the traditional medieval fashion. In addition, they afforded a more favorable ambience for the development of a proletarian or class consciousness, a development Joaquim Nabuco sought so assiduously to implant in the workingman of his native Recife. Although there had been occasional vague signs of such a consciousness since colonial times, there was, until the middle of the nineteenth century, very little acceptance on the part of the poor, whether white or *mestiço*, of the necessity of labor. Durval Vieira de Aguiar, in his *Descrições Práticas da Província da Bahia*, tells us that until the end of the Empire there were groups of persons in that city so lazy that their only activities were "to watch the coming and going of ships in the harbor, to trap birds, and to talk big." Nevertheless, he did not feel he had the right to criticize this shiftlessness, since he considered it "a natural consequence of the lack of industries, agriculture, or natural resources sufficient to offer a decent living in this blessed region." By lack of agriculture, he meant the deficiency of small and medium-sized farms devoted to the cultivation of diversified crops, which he felt should replace "the sugar plantation, now defunct in spite of all the concessions, tax exemptions, and capital subsidies offered the depleted lands until they are by now virtually mortgaged out of their economic existence." Even in the capital, a city considered at the middle of the century to be "the nation's second in agriculture and commerce and enjoying direct communication, through its ships and its submarine cable, with all the capitals of the world," the principal problem was "unemployment in the face of the continual increase of the working class," a problem not helped by the fact that food was easy to obtain, thus limiting begging to the ill and the decrepit. Nevertheless, it was time to control this growing populace through education and productive labor.[4]

From another observer of the period, also a Bahian, we learn that in the "second capital" of the Empire the carpenters, street pavers, cobblers, boatmen, blacksmiths, hairdressers, and gardeners were "nearly all slaves placed by their masters in posts of gainful employment." Even after the middle of the nineteenth century, it was still rare to see carts bearing commodities, so numerous were the slaves available for these services. Burdens of average weight were carried on the head; those of greater volume were moved by the "pole and rope" method, where two or three men, walking Indian file, supported a long pole on each shoulder, with the burden resting in a rope cradle slung between the parallel shafts. Wealthy persons continued to employ the sedan chair as a means of transport, again with slaves acting as the beasts of burden. And since the city lacked running water, illuminating gas, and sewers, slaves were used for a much longer period than in Rio de Janeiro and Recife as water carriers, torch bearers, and disposers of garbage and excrement on the city's beaches. These practices persisted despite the reforms inaugurated in 1850 by a provincial president of superior vision, Francisco Gonçalves Martins, later to become Viscount of São Lourenço. Obviously, it was not possible for Martins to abolish all these colonial forms of labor overnight, but his administration dealt a decisive blow to such archaic practices. This reform attitude, which caused deep repercussions, enabled the Cardoso Brothers, for example, to take advantage of an existent but hitherto unenforced law to "organize a barge service with free labor . . . the first instance in Bahia of the replacement of slave labor by free workers."[5]

The importance of this development to the freedmen themselves is indicated by their later practice of annually commemorating the event with all the pomp so characteristic of Bahian celebrations. Such replacements of slave with free workers were repeated on a large scale in other occupations, including that of the carrying of burdens, despite the difficulties of overcoming the shame felt by a freeman at having to do the work so closely associated with slavery. It was thus not until twenty years after the first step had been taken that this latter reform became effective, significantly during the

[4] Durval Vieira de Aguiar: *Descrições Práticas da Província da Bahia* (Bahia, 1888), pp. 287, 316.

[5] Ibid., pp. 183–4, 188, 195.

second regime of Francisco Gonçalves Martins as provincial president. At this time a transport organization of free carriers known as the Companhia União e Indústria was formed and advertised itself in the *Diário da Bahia* of December 8, 1870, as being prepared "to offer occupation and legitimate wages to many unemployed Brazilians seeking manual activity." [6] Many veterans of the Paraguayan War became members of the Companhia União e Indústria. It is curious, however, that shortly after the formation of this pioneer organization of free workers, a movement on the part of some members developed to bar Africans and restrict membership exclusively to "Brazilians," [7] a manifestation of gross nativism which did not escape censure on the part of the better newspapers of the city.

What was most needed by these early labor associations was, of course, education. Martins, both as political leader and private citizen, made every effort to develop vocational instruction for the poorer classes of Bahia. This type of instruction emphasized the need for employing whites as well as Negroes in tasks previously performed exclusively by slaves and even for encouraging the immigration of Europeans to augment the labor force. Many Brazilians of the period began to consider the expense of this type of program necessary to speed up the trend of replacing slave with free workers as a result of the passage of the Law of Free Womb, and they looked to the Imperial government to put the ideas outlined by the Viscount of São Lourenço (who died in 1872) into general practice throughout the nation. Such a program would include the training of poor Brazilian children for useful occupations, and the rescuing, through government and private sources, of "thousands of abandoned children from the depths of misery," who would be trained to become "healthy and intelligent workers." [8] Vocational training in specially established schools seemed to be the most effective means of developing these hitherto neglected human resources.

It was to fill this need that the vocational schools began to appear in the principal cities of the Empire, as well as in Amazonas, where the Providência Institute, founded by Dom Antônio Macedo Costa, gave Christian training to Indians to help them in their assimilation into Brazilian civilization. The Positivists also took a hand in this

[6] *Diário da Bahia*, December 8, 1870.
[7] Vieira de Aguiar: op. cit., p. 209.
[8] *Anais do Senado do Império* (Rio de Janeiro, 1869).

latter activity, and through the efforts of military figures such as
Cândido Mariano da Silva Rondon, director of the Indian Protective Service, soon rivalled the Church in their missionary activity in
the region, though not in a way that would hinder or limit the
effectiveness of the Catholics at all.

Among the notable figures of the decade of the 1890's, none was
more representative of the spirit of healthy Brazilianism and the
best Positivist virtues than Rondon. His work in attempting to integrate the Amazon region—its lands, its waters, and especially its
Indian population—into the complex of Brazilian society corresponded to that of Euclydes da Cunha in the backlands of the
northeast. The efforts of these two men are reflected romantically
but vigorously in some of the most distinguished works of Brazilian
literature; those of Euclydes himself, together with those of Euclydes's disciple Alberto Rangel and some of those written by Inglês
da Sousa and José Veríssimo. In science, there was also the memorable work *Rondônia* by Roquette-Pinto, written at the end of the
period. Roquette-Pinto, in some senses a disciple of Rondon's, in-
terprets the life and culture of the Indian with an intensity and a
blend of analysis and synthesis that surpasses all previous works in
this field, including the admirable study by Couto de Magalhães
entitled *O Selvagem*. Another outstanding book, this time a literary
work published in Rio Grande do Sul, was Coelho Neto's *O Negrinho do Pastoreio* (*The Little Negro of the Pasturelands*), a tale,
seen through the eyes of a child, of the victimizing and martyrdom
of virtuous primitive folk at the hands of their civilized oppressors.
And in Bahia Nina Rodrigues, though somewhat prejudiced by
Aryanism, produced his notable studies of the social problems of
the Brazilian Negro in passing from slavery to emancipation and
from monarchy to Republic. Unfortunately, nobody in the period
undertook a large-scale study of the changes undergone at this time
in normal labor conditions, a question merely sketched briefly in
Joaquim Nabuco's *O Abolicionismo*.

Pires de Almeida, in a work published in French in 1889 under
the title *L'Instruction Publique au Brésil*, stated that "in Brazil the
number of those who are able to live without working has been
considerably reduced over the past twenty years and is getting
smaller every day. . . . The most precious, most indispensable
qualification for obtaining work is education. Without this, a man
is worth only the sum total of his manual strength and skill plus

whatever innate spiritual qualities he may possess. . . .", while the educated man, "no matter what his conditions of birth, may climb the ladder and become worthy through his energy, his morality, and his intelligence." [9]

This reflects the official, if somewhat platonic, attitude of the Empire to education in general and to the virtues of vocational training in particular, for bettering the lot of the freeman of modest circumstances. Such instruction became an ever-increasing necessity after the passage of the Law of the Free Womb. The days of the slave were numbered. It was now necessary to replace this sort of labor with the free worker and to furnish the instruction through which any man, regardless of color, could by his intelligence and determination rise, like a Rebouças or a Tôrres Homem, to a position of greatness in the Empire.

As early as 1858 the School of Arts and Trades had been established in Rio de Janeiro in one of the rooms of the consistory of the Church of the Blessed Sacrament. In its thirty years of activity, as observed by Pires de Almeida, it had extended notable service to the capital city and had been the model for the eventual founding of similar establishments in Salvador and Recife. According to Pires de Almeida, this type of instruction was of great social value in preparing useful citizens and, at the same time, in "closing the doors to ideas of revolution and change of government . . ." [1]

In 1878 the School of Arts and Trades in Rio de Janeiro had 1,049 students, of whom 359 were between ten and fifteen years of age; 405 from sixteen to twenty; 170 from twenty-one to twenty-five; 70 from twenty-six to thirty; 32 from thirty-two to thirty-five; 9 from thirty-six to forty; and 4 over forty. The Brazilians numbered 814, the Portuguese 177, the French 14, the English 4, the Italians 17, the Spanish 10; there were also 2 Germans, 1 Austrian, 1 Chilean, 2 Orientals, 2 Argentinians, and 5 Paraguayans. The school boasted a physics laboratory, a chemistry laboratory, and a library. By 1880 the number of students had increased to 1,341.[2] In 1883 the city of Niterói, across the bay, also had its School of Arts and Trades, directed by Salesians, with workshops for printing, bookbinding, tailoring, and even musical instruction.

[9] Pires de Almeida: *L'Instruction Publique au Brésil* (Rio de Janeiro, 1889), p. 530.
[1] Ibid., p. 685.
[2] Ibid., p. 697.

At the university level, there were already several institutions of a technical nature serving young Brazilians during the Empire: the Polytechnic School of Rio de Janeiro, that of Minas Gerais in Ouro Prêto, the Institute for the Deaf and Dumb in Rio de Janeiro; the Academy of Fine Arts, also in Rio de Janeiro; the Pharmaceutical Institute; various normal schools; a school of horticulture in Santa Cruz; the medical schools of Rio de Janeiro and of Bahia, with their additional courses in pharmacy; the Providência Institute founded in Amazonas by Bishop Dom Antônio Macedo Costa and devoted to the education of Indians, with classes in reading and writing and with various shops for vocational training; several courses in elementary military science for Army and Navy cadets, in addition to those devoted to the formation of officers. From these establishments issued an ever-increasing stream of trained personnel capable of replacing older workers and craftsmen, including slaves, and of instituting new methods in fields of activity hitherto hampered by the persistence of traditional and outmoded practices.

The development of these arts, begun in the Empire, took on additional importance in the Republic, particularly during the administration of Nilo Peçanha who, as Vice-President, succeeded to the presidency after the death of Afonso Pena in 1909. Once the period of consolidation was past, the Republic, in the spirit of Positivist progressivism, devoted itself to projects of engineering, sanitation, and hygiene calling for a vast number of trained technicians. These technicians thus began to assume a considerable social and political importance, and some of them came to enjoy a status in state or national politics equal to that of the academics and the sociologically minded military during the early days of the Republic. This was the case with engineers such as Pereira Passos and Paulo de Frontin, with physicians such as Joaquim Murtinho and Afrânio Peixoto, with pharmacists such as Graciliano Martins in Pernambuco and Lindolfo Color, also renowned in the field of letters, in Rio Grande do Sul. And it should not be forgotten that this period, which marked the beginning of a proletarian consciousness in Brazilian life, was also a period in which representatives of the working classes began to appear in the state and national legislatures. Ordinarily, such men were *mestiços*, but at least one, Jerônimo José Teles Júnior, was a white of Nordic origin. In his diary (written in Recife during the late Empire and early Republic and still existing in manuscript), Teles confessed himself disillusioned with his companions in the struggle for recognition of the artisan and laboring class, a group he felt was still too close to slavery to begin behaving like the free workers of Europe.[3]

In the 1890's the Austrian Lamberg also observed that, while the workers of the new Republic were generally honest, they were often of poor quality. Many of them already had their organizations, however without manifesting any great desire thereby "to alter radically the bases of Brazilian society." Because Brazilians as yet did not understand the nature of communism, anarchism, or social democracy, there had been "no popular uprisings, no dynamitings, or general massacres." Nor had there been any apparent struggle between capital and labor, perhaps because there had so far been no development of large industries. Most of the workers "live apart from political contention, often to the detriment of a good cause." It did not seem to Lamberg or to other foreign observers that the workers suffered any systematic oppression from either government or the rich. The Brazilian workers, says Lamberg, "are good people, easygoing, and not at all prone to heroics," although in certain instances they have "given ample proof of their courage and their love of country." [4]

One detail ought to be pointed out here: since the late 1880's the Santos and São Paulo Railroad Co., under the direction of Mr. C. C. Andrews, had quietly and without pressure of any kind introduced the "British weekend," along with facilities for recreation and instruction aimed at improving the lot of railway personnel. "I had never before seen anything of the sort [in Brazil]," confessed Mr. Andrews.[5] It is true that in contrast with this progressive policy, there were still slaves ill treated by their masters, who were mostly *nouveaux riches* eager for great profits, and that even after abolition practices that amounted virtually to slave labor continued to exist on the rubber plantations of the Amazon. At no other time in its history did Brazil live under such contradictory social conditions as during this painful period of transition from slavery to free labor, a subject that will receive further treatment in a later chapter.

One factor favorable to the development of Brazilian ethnic and social unity was the spread of slave labor toward the south during

---

[3] From the diary of Jerônimo José Teles Júnior, in the possession of his family and partially copied by the author.

[4] Maurício Lamberg: *O Brasil*, pp. 69–71.

[5] C. C. Andrews: *Brazil, Its Condition and Prospects* (New York, 1887), p. 145.

the last decades of the Empire. The greater part of this movement concentrated in the state of São Paulo, with its increasingly prosperous coffee plantations and its large admixture of Italians, seldom reluctant to form sexual unions with dark-skinned women. A considerable part of the Negro population in the São Paulo area was thus absorbed in the formation of a handsome and healthy new ethnic group: the Afro-Italian. This development was noted with approval by a Portuguese visitor, Sousa Pinto, who in 1905 in his book *Terra Moça (Youthful Land)* wrote that "here in São Paulo, more than in Rio, one receives the impression of racial penetration," with the Italian element predominating. The state capital seemed to him "an Italian city," while the state, with a population of 3 million, contained approximately 1 million Italians from all parts of Italy from Lombardy to Palermo. The Portuguese were outnumbered not only by this group but also by the Poles, and yet problems of racial and cultural conflict were being resolved by "strange associations and unexpected marriages," from which there emerged "new types of the most diverse origins," including one with pale complexion, blue eyes, and blond hair attributable to the union of northern Italians with Negroes. Another type seemed to be the crossing of *caboclos* with Italians. Both groups were considered by Sousa Pinto to be "truly exceptional and gracious." [6] The Brazilianization of Europeans and Africans could thus be clearly observed, despite the feeling prevalent in São Paulo at the beginning of the twentieth century that it was the Luso-Brazilian who was becoming Italianized. Shop signs were a constant mixture of Italian and Portuguese, and Italians worked as streetcar conductors, carters, servants, shoeshine boys, businessmen, industrialists, journalists, restaurateurs, and haberdashers. In the bookstores, the vogue for Eça de Queiroz was threatened by that for D'Annunzio or Ferrero. The Italian shoeshine boy became a Brazilian—not merely a Paulista—institution, along with the Italian tenor, the Italian tragedian, and the Italian cuisine. D'Annunzio, Ferrero, and Ferri were for a time among the most widely read foreign authors, not only in São Paulo but also in Rio de Janeiro, Pôrto Alegre, Recife, and Manaus. And these cities were further marked by the influence—usually bad—of Italian architects, one of whom was Januzzi of Rio de Janeiro. From north to south, finally, many were the children born at the turn of

6 Manoel de Sousa Pinto: *Terra Moça. Impressões Brasileiras* (Oporto, 1905), p. 336.

the century who received from their romantic or anti-clerical parents the resounding name of Garibaldi.

The Italian presence in Brazil was also accentuated during this period by an immigration which surpassed that of any other nation and which gave considerable support to the Latin-Catholic-European element in Brazilian society, an element somewhat challenged, in Rio Grande do Sul, Santa Catarina, São Paulo, and Espirito Santo, by the growing influx of Germans. This ethnic-cultural reinforcement came at a time when the average Brazilian was feeling a certain disenchantment with his Hispano-Catholic, or, more specifically his Luso-Catholic origins in the face of what he considered evidence of the absolute superiority of the Germanic-Protestant groups in matters of technology. This simplistic notion, which was held in other countries too—even in France—caused writers of the time to call for a strengthening of the Latin-Catholic structure of Brazil. One of these, A. D'Atri, in a book on Quintino Bocayuva published in Paris in 1901, called attention to what he designated the Pan-Germanic peril to Latin Brazil. Another work on this subject was *A Necessidade de um Equilíbrio Americano ante a Política de Expansão dos Estados Unidos* (*The Necessity of an American Equilibrium in the Face of United States Expansion Policy*) by Luciano Pereira da Silva, which appeared in Recife in 1905. A further movement contributing to the same end of rehabilitating Latin-Catholic values was the spiritual reaction in intellectual circles headed by the philosopher R. Farias Brito. This hit particularly at the Teutonism of Tobias Barreto who, as we have seen, had been fascinated by the scientific spirit of the German philosophy of the late nineteenth century. A sociological paradox of this attempt to restore Latin-Catholic values was that the movement was strongly supported by German monks and friars who had replaced churchmen of national origin in the Franciscan and Benedictine monasteries of Brazil. This brought about a revolt by Masons and other anticlericals against the influence of the "foreign monk" which, paradoxically enough, shaped up as a revolt against German Catholicism in Brazil instead of merely against the "decadent" Latin nations.

❧ [VI] ❧

Miscegenation

I HAVE SUGGESTED that the Republic of 1889 brought about considerable progress in ethnic democratization, not so much in creating new opportunities as in extending those social and political opportunities which already existed to persons of color who had made themselves worthy of advancement through education, economic position, or through military service on behalf of the new regime. The *caboclo* or Brazilian with some trace—no matter how faint—of Indian blood, enjoyed under Floriano a renewed phase of romantic prestige, in which patriotic fervor was added to his already widely proclaimed virtues as the aboriginal and only authentic Brazilian. It was a prestige similar to that which had followed the proclamation of independence, when even Brazilians of purely European descent (whose only claim to a darkened skin was that caused by the tropical sun) chose to call themselves *caboclos* in order to be considered pure Brazilians, heart and soul. Some of them even went so far as to change their Portuguese family names to Tupi or Guarani designations. Others contented themselves by pretending that they couldn't eat meat or fish without the accompanying element of *mandioca* in the form of mush (*pirão*) or dry meal (*farofa*). And still others, in conversation with foreigners, spoke ostentatiously of Indian forebears, to whom they gave all the credit for resisting the French or Dutch invaders in colonial times, thereby negating any glory which might have accrued to their own white Portuguese ancestors. One such Indiophile, a Paulista of pure-white ancestry, told the American Consul C. C. Andrews that in these colonial wars "the Tupay Indians did the fighting" and that by the nineteenth century the blood of these valiant fighters had become "mixed more or less with the Brazilians." [1]

Even more interesting is Silva Jardim's account of the Paulista Sampaio Ferraz, his colleague in the Information Office of the Republic and later chief of police in the federal capital. An ardent republican, Sampaio Ferraz was "tall, heavy, strong, elegant, athletic, and heavily bronzed by the sun. In conversation, he always referred to himself as a *caboclo*, particularly when he wished to give the impression of being a man of decision capable of making any sacrifice for his ideals. It was through him that we spontaneously formed a serious discussion group known as the Caboclo Club. Under the presidency of the arch-*caboclo* Xavier da Silveira, there were Padre João Manuel, Aníbal [?], Júlio [Prestes], Teixeira de Sousa, myself, and two or three others." These *caboclos* met "around a table laden with regional culinary delicacies, particularly the *feijoada*." Essentially republican, the group—which included some Negroid persons—believed that Nordics such as Dona Isabel and the Count d'Eu, for reasons the French would today call ethno-psychological, were deliberately preventing the *caboclo* element in the country (including those of Negroid origin) from gaining the power their majority force deserved. This in spite of the fact that the cohorts of the "Nordic" Prince and Princess included such distinguished *caboclos* as João Alfredo and such high-caliber Negroids as Cotegipe.

Beyond the avid *caboclismo* shown by the admirers of the undeniably Indianoid Floriano Peixoto, there was a significant romanticizing of the Indian in the sciences, as exemplified by Roquette-Pinto, the distinguished anthropologist whose *Rondônia*, a study of Indian tribes of the Brazilian Serra do Norte in the central Amazon region, is the best expression of this attitude. For Roquette, the increased respect given the *caboclo* extended to *mestiços* in general, even those with a sprinkling of African blood, as seems to have been the case with Roquette himself. And it is not insignificant that the first South American cardinal should have come from the north of Brazil, a handsome eugenic type who mixed the blood of an Indian princess with that of two of the oldest families of Italy and Spain. In the noble Roman profile of Joaquim Arcoverde de Albuquerque Cavalcanti, there is more than a trace of the features of the American Indian chief.

Among the Brazilians of his time, Roquette-Pinto was one of the

[1] C. C. Andrews: *Brazil, Its Condition and Prospects* (New York, 1887), p. 148.

most attractive examples of the eugenic man in the service of his country. He took his place among a group, some of them *mestiços*, which in the early decades of the Republic amply compensated for the loss of titled Brazilian aristocracy at the head of the intellectual, diplomatic, or political affairs of the nation. With the passing, for the time being, of such Imperial patrician types as the Viscount of Ouro Prêto, Joaquim Nabuco, Silveira Martins, Ferreira Viana, the Viscount de Taunay, the Baron de Sabóia, Nabuco de Gouveia, or Saldanha da Gama, it was imperative that the Republic find replacements from men of equal stature, even though of modest origins.[2] The first of this group to make a good impression on foreigners were men like Deodoro, who turned republican only under pressure of circumstances. Another group to make an excellent first impression included those whose republicanism had been of long standing but whose manners and bearing bore the unmistakable stamp of Imperial good breeding: Quintino Bocayuva, for example, Rodrigo Otávio, Assis Brasil, Júlio de Castilhos, and Coelho Lisboa. To these were added a group of former monarchists who, having given distinguished service under the old regime, were not hesitant to put the national interest above personal political preference in becoming reconciled to the Republic: Antônio Prado, the Baron de Lucena, the Baron de Jaceguay, and the Baron Ramiz Galvão; followed in later times by the Counselor Rosa e Silva, the Baron do Rio Branco, and the engineer Pereira Passos.

In the second decade of the Republic, similarly illustrious figures emerged in Sampaio Ferraz, Osvaldo Cruz, Miguel Calmon, Epitácio Pessoa, Pinheiro Machado, Estácio Coímbra, Germano Hasslocher, Herculano de Freitas, Gastão da Cunha, Augusto Severo, José Marcelino, Rivadávia Correia, Fausto Cardoso, Silvério Gurgel, Otávio Mangabeira, Graça Aranha, James Darcy, Washington Luís, and Flores da Cunha. All these were men who graced an élite of intelligent, attractive figures that did much to compensate in the

---

[2] In this list of representative monarchists, two figures need further comment. Silveira Martins was an especially powerful political force in Rio Grande do Sul and, like so many of the strong men from that area, a bitter opponent of the centrist principle in government. He was a particular enemy of Deodoro da Fonseca, and it is said that the deciding factor in winning Deodoro to the republican cause in 1889 was the possibility that, if the monarchy was not overthrown, Silveira Martins would become the next Prime Minister. Admiral Saldanha da Gama was a confirmed and unrepentant monarchist who led the famous naval rebellion during the Floriano Peixoto administration. (Translator.)

eyes of foreigners for the mongreloid and socially awkward republicans. The latter, in high places, could have given the false impression that the monarchical leaders had been replaced by an anti-élite deficient in any of the best qualities of the Brazilian character. It is the historian's duty to include among such mongrel types men like Ruy Barbosa, Barbosa Lima, Augusto de Lima, Santos Dumont, Severino Vieira, Alcindo Guanabara, Olavo Bilac, and Euclydes da Cunha—all people of superior intelligence, but conspicuously puny, malformed, ugly, and often unhealthy in appearance. It is possible that it was the preponderance of such types that caused the Argentines of the early twentieth century to speak of Brazilians in general as *macaquitos* (little monkeys), a designation which could hardly be applied to Rio Branco, Nabuco, or Cardinal Arcoverde, for example.

And it is thus that caricaturists of the period depict those important but ugly and pallid men, hybrids apparently deficient in vigor. Frequently the political malice of the artists caused them to depict their victims as *mestiços* with African blood: those whose hair was bushy and somewhat rebellious became in these cartoons as kinky-headed as the typical bucko ruffian. Thick lips were turned into Bantu labial monstrosities. Noses not quite classically aquiline became broad and Africanized. In compensation, in the portraits of the period, the retoucher's art was taxed to the utmost to transform the least Caucasian features into perfectly Aryan ones and to provide rosy complexions for those of sickly pallor or whose pigmentation was suspiciously suggestive of the tar brush.

From Imperial times, the Brazilian had been portrayed in the European theatre either as a brilliantined parvenu who sported scandalous waistcoats and too much jewelry, or else as an upstart *mestiço* whose apparently Negroid features had earned him the name of *Baron du Chocolat*. But such unfavorable impressions began to disappear when these same Europeans came to know a Penedo, a Bom Retiro, a Baron do Rio Branco, an Estrêla, Joaquim Nabuco, Eduardo Prado, or such martial yet indisputably elegant naval officers as Saldanha da Gama or Jaceguay. Or, for that matter, certain Brazilians of color—some almost pure Negroes—with the princely bearing and noble airs of Juliano Moreira, Teodoro Sampaio, or of any of the Rebouças. William James, while in Brazil on a scientific expedition to the Amazon, was deeply impressed by the manners and conversation of "gentlemen" of color whom he met in the rural areas of the north. There was a considerable number of such "gentlemen" among Brazilians of color at the time, just as, among *mestiços* who became viscounts or counselors, there were some who were less polished in their speech and manners. One of the latter, according to an English observer well versed in the gossip of the period, was Jequitinhonha. In the United States on a special diplomatic mission his *arriviste* arrogance was given such a dressing down by racially conscious Americans that he became considerably more modest and soft-spoken ever after.

The Baron do Rio Branco, as a result of his long residence in Europe, was well aware of the importance of foreign representation and, while Foreign Minister of the Brazilian Republic, took great pains to see that the young nation was well represented in the Old World by diplomats who were tall, well groomed, and personally attractive. In this attempt to place the emerging Brazilian "race" in the best possible light, he allowed himself to be carried to Aryanist extremes in demanding that those representing Brazil abroad, in addition to being well born and well educated, should also be Caucasian (or nearly Caucasian) in appearance. And this was not all; they should be married to wives who were, if not always beautiful, at least as elegant as possible in dress and bearing, white or near-white in appearance, and reasonably fluent in French or English.[3] One of the Baron's most persistent ideas was that the Portuguese, to whom Brazil owed so much, had ceased to be an admirable people and, like certain South Americans, were beginning to verge on the ridiculous. And it was one of his strongest wishes to free Brazil from this ridicule, so that progress under the Republic (which, if he had had his choice, would never have replaced the Empire) would be realized not only socially and ethically but also in matters of an aesthetic nature; in deportment and appearance, particularly of those who were involved in the sacred mission of representing their country in Europe. The very names of Brazilian diplomats greatly concerned the Baron, fearful lest they should sound stupid or even scandalous to foreigners—just as those of unfortunately named diplomats assigned to Brazil had evoked strong ridicule. For example,

---

[3] The attentiveness of Rio Branco to these ethnic and aesthetic details was confirmed by my late friend Pedro Paranhos Ferreira, nephew to Rio Branco. Born in 1875, Paranhos Ferreira was brought up by Rio Branco as one of his own sons and in later years shared his confidences, so far as diplomatic discretion would permit.

Querica; or Buceta; or Porras; or Ku. It is said that Rio Branco succeeded in preventing the acceptance of an Italian diplomat named Puto and a Central American named Porras y Porras.[4]

Did this Aryanism of Rio Branco's correspond to the general attitude of cultivated Brazilians of the period? For a considerable number, it seems that it did. Others, however, despite being white or nearly white, did not hesitate to go to extremes in expressing their belief in ethnic democracy, even to the point of admitting indeterminate or mixed racial types to European diplomatic posts. Had it not been Ruy Barbosa, thin, wilted, and monstrously ugly, before whom Europe had paid tribute at The Hague? Had not an equally ugly little Brazilian been even more applauded for his triumphant flight over Paris? And had not the Germans expressed their excellent impressions of the Brazilian Negro physician Juliano Moreira? Thus some Brazilians began to consider that the country need not feel ashamed of its persons of color to the point of denying cultivated individuals the right to exercise important offices, to mix in the best society, or to marry into patrician white families. Among these more liberal few was the scientist J. B. de Lacerda, sometime director of the National Museum, who became the champion of a racial mixture commensurate with the ethnic-social situation in Brazil. At the Universal Congress of Races, held in London in 1911, his presentation of these ideas had considerable repercussions in Europe, repercussions even greater, in fact, than those caused by Ruy Barbosa's brilliant speech to the same effect at The Hague Peace Conference in 1907. Others advocating similar ideas were João Ribeiro and José Veríssimo, although the latter it must be recognized, had a touch of both Indian and African blood in his veins. As for Sylvio Romero, who was frequently an ardent champion of racial mixture, he showed a certain ambiguity, although on the whole his attitude seemed to favor the Brazilian tendency to reach a racial common denominator. Let us now examine this question of racial mixture through the testimony of a number of survivors of the period.[5]

Born in 1882 in Rio de Janeiro but brought up in Rio Grande do Sul, Florêncio Carlos de Abreu e Silva states: "My attitude toward

[4] These names are all obscenities, mostly anatomical, in Portuguese. (Translator.)

[5] The following declarations represent somewhat less than half those given in the original Brazilian edition. Much duplication of ideas has been omitted, but no significant observation has been passed over, and every effort has been made to preserve the proportions of opinion found in the Brazilian text. (Translator.)

Negroes and mulattos has always been one of tolerance and good will. My father's secretary in the São Paulo government had been a mulatto of talent. Another gifted mulatto, secretary to the Rio Grande government, was a frequent guest in our home, where he was received with every consideration. . . . The racial question never concerned me at the time, because it had been settled by the Portuguese, contrary to what has happened in the United States, where the Negro problem is both serious and insoluble." Only in later years did Florêncio de Abreu begin to worry about the situation, and he finally arrived at the conclusion that, in order not to upset the ethnic order in Brazil, the government ought to prevent "further immigration of Asian and African elements."

Heitor Modesto d'Almeida (b. Minas Gerais, 1881) as a child "reacted with great sympathy to the abolition of slavery." In his home the slaves were considered "a part of the family," and many of them "after being freed, remained in the house for the rest of their lives." Modesto confesses, however, that he has always preferred Negroes to mulattos and considers the latter "the natural enemy of the white man."

Antenor Nascentes (b. Rio de Janeiro, 1886) testifies: "Being a mulatto, my feelings toward mulattos and Negroes has to be one of solidarity, because since childhood I have suffered the social inferiority of the colored man in my country. These persons are the victims of an odious prejudice that lacks the courage to be displayed openly. Nevertheless, if you wish to cite a great poet, it is Gonçalves Dias, a *mestiço*, who comes to mind; a great prose writer, another *mestiço*: Machado de Assis . . ."

"I have always been against the union of Negroes and mulattos with whites," says José Rodrigues Monteiro (b. Ceará, 1887). He states further that he would be "greatly displeased" if one of his children or his brothers or sisters married a person of darker skin.

Manuel Duarte (b. Rio Grande do Sul, 1883) shows rather more delicacy in his treatment of this sensitive subject, but feels that it is "undeniable" that there existed and continues to exist "a frank distinction between persons of color and the so-called whites of European origin, thus creating a perennial social inequality and an automatic separation of the races by voluntary choice." Everything is moving, however, toward the "minimizing of racial barriers," which should be considered "a sensible and constructive tendency for the nation's future." As for the marriage of a member of his family with a person of darker skin, he feels that the old proverb "Marry equal, marry well" would apply best, thus indicating little disposition to take a personal part in the "minimizing of racial barriers." Recognizing in the Baron do Rio Branco "the ideal symbol of our public men of the time, who both summed up his period and built for the future," a man with the "appearance of an athletic Apollo," this witness seems to admit also to an adherence to Rio Branco's Aryan policy of selection of diplomatic representatives.

Armando Silveyra (b. Rio Grande do Sul, 1887) remarks upon the relationships between white and colored peoples in the extreme south: "More than a century ago, Europe sent people here—Germans, Italians, Poles—who were utterly against any sort of mixed marriage. However, the environment effected a slow change upon many of them." He speaks of a lady of his acquaintance, a granddaughter of Germans, who had become a typical Brazilian lady except for the color of her hair, with all the "elegance and somewhat sensual abandon characteristic of our women," along with the "customs, language, and quirks of the region." Nevertheless, upon the outbreak of the First World War she confessed that she still felt basically German in the matter.

Dona Isabel Henriqueta de Sousa e Oliveira (b. Bahia, 1853, but brought up in the Imperial capital) confessed that she had always been against abolition. Considering the Negro "an inferior race," she felt that any racial mixture, "legal or illegal," between blacks and whites merited only condemnation.

An opposite point of view is registered by João Barreto de Meneses, son of Tobias Barreto (b. Pernambuco, 1872): "I always felt most sympathetic toward the Negroes and mulattos of my area and, for that matter, of all parts of the country. I do not know why I am so fond of the Pernambucan mulatto (and especially the *Mulatta*), who, if they lack the artificial magic of the Bahian, nevertheless show a natural aptitude, in their laughter and their facial expressions, for making their presence felt without adopting the bizarre raiment of the land of *vatapá*.[6] Our racial problem, both historical and social, must be understood as part of our destiny and our aims. Our society did not make the mulatto; he entered through the door of history. He is part of all of us. The Brazilian, though priding himself on his Aryan purity, is always a mulatto in spirit. My

[6] Bahia is famous for its *vatapá*, a highly tasty fish delicacy, probably of African origin. (Translator.)

father still lives in our conception of Law, and Machado lives in our conception of Form; no more incisive or eloquent proof is needed." [7] As for the marriage of a member of his family with a person of darker skin, Barreto de Meneses states that he would accept the situation "without the slightest reluctance or regret. . . . It would be attractive both physically and psychologically, particularly the former. It is a fatal law which governs human beings. Who wants it otherwise? Who is going to change it? Neither I nor society in general. I am not, because I have in my veins a portion of the blood of that race through whose martyrdom we have built our economic affluence. Society is not, because all of it, despite its occasional blue eyes and golden hair, also shares the blood of the generous and suffering Negroes of Brazil."

For Durval Guimarães Espínola, a Bahian of rural origin (b. 1883), the abolition was a good thing, particularly since the Princess Isabel "had intended to indemnify the landholders, who suffered a considerable loss at the time." But in 1942 he lamented that the race had shown itself to be "degenerate." For this reason, he says: "I strongly favor the whites and do not like to see marriage between the races, common as this is among us, and I equally condemn the mixing of racial characteristics which results therefrom."

Plínio Barreto (b. São Paulo, 1882) writes: "I have never looked down on Negroes and mulattos. As a child, I never ceased to admire the physical superiority of some of them. I have no particular opinion on the abolition, because I was a child when it was proclaimed. As for the racial problem in Brazil, I cannot bring myself to admit that such a problem exists; it seems to me that there is a room and a climate in our country for the intimate mingling of all races." As for the marriage problem: "It is difficult to decide how I would react to the marriage of a son, daughter, brother, or sister to a colored person. I don't have any racial prejudices. I don't consider the black man inferior to the white man. I think, however, that I would experience some difficulty in introducing a member of my family to a colored person, unless that person were somehow outstanding in his intelligence and culture. But if the case were one of love, this hesitation would disappear."

The Pernambucan Adolfo Faustino Pôrto (b. Olinda, 1887), after declaring himself free from racial prejudice, goes on to say:

[7] Barreto de Meneses is here referring to the fact that both his father and Machado de Assis were mulattos. (Translator.)

"My response [to your specific question on racial preferences] will probably appear shockingly contradictory to my previously expressed opinions on Negroes. In expressing the graduations of my preferences in skin pigmentation, I must establish that such preferences seem to me to be based on physiological and aesthetic considerations. On this basis, the white comes first, followed by the Indian, then the mulatto, and, finally, the Negro. I have never been fond of black as a color; it is not a synthesis, as white is. I associate black with mourning, darkness, smoke, perhaps due to childhood influences and the reading of the 'stories of Trancoso' which contained a number of old Negroes of perverse and horrid aspect. And, to be perfectly truthful, I would not look with favor upon the marriage of son or daughter, or brother or sister to a black-skinned person."

Pedro de Coutto (b. Rio de Janciro, 1872) confesses: "I am of Portuguese descent on both sides, but I am convinced that I am of mixed blood because the Portuguese are the most racially heterogeneous of all European peoples. The Negro has had a valuable place in that mixture; so have the Italians, the Spanish, and the French. Thus our Negroes and mulattos may rest assured that Beguine[8] at the hands of the Portuguese has no reason for existing, its being the case that it is impossible to 'purify the race' as people say." And, "since I have no racial prejudices whatsoever . . . I would not look for a blond wife—French, German, or Swiss—but would instead marry a worthy *mestiça*."

Júlio de Mesquita (b. São Paulo, 1892) goes into the question of relations between blacks and whites at length from a sociological standpoint and concludes: "One can state categorically that 'Western values' are more and more becoming the most strongly determining factors in facing the problems which confront us. Among these values, one would have to include both ethnic and aesthetic considerations. In other words, there is a constantly increasing desire to see Brazil, through racial intermarriage, approach more and more closely the pure white type. The aesthetic canons which have always inspired our country are those which have governed the other so-called Western nations. Even the most superficial observation will affirm that we are withdrawing further and further from African values. There is no other way to account for the desperate effort made by mulattos to appear white and, at all cost, to disguise

[8] A Catholic lay sisterhood dating from the twelfth century. (Translator.)

whenever possible all characteristics of their race. For example, consider the mania of the Negroes for using all sorts of mechanical means to straighten their kinky hair. Another example would be the terrible discriminations made by the middle group against those of clear and unmistakable negritude. Such a group, being neither white nor frankly black, remains in a constant state of shock against the extremes on either side." And he adds: "For all these reasons, it is obvious that I would never willingly accept the marriage of any member of my family with anyone who was clearly a person of color. This I say, because I cannot agree to bringing people into a world where they would be unfortunate, and in Brazil it is the Negro and the mulatto who are increasingly, in every way, among the unfortunates."

From Dona Elisa Vilhena Ferreira (b. Minas Gerais, 1864) comes the following testimony: "The slaves on my father's plantation were treated like human beings. No corporal punishment was ever inflicted, and after abolition they continued to live with us for the rest of their lives, never failing to bless us in their evening prayers." But as to the concrete aspects of the question, she states: "Frankly, I would not be pleased by an unequal marriage in my family. This is a purely personal opinion. Formerly, society was more demanding and parents stricter in this respect. Unequal marriages were frowned upon and those who made them, or who were not married in church, were not well accepted."

Guaracy Silveira, a Paulista (b. 1893) who designates himself as "a descendant of the Bandeirante Carlos Pedro da Silveira, discoverer of the Cataguases mines," confesses that: "If I were black, I would seek marriage with a colored girl a bit lighter than myself, in order to make it possible for my children to enjoy better conditions of life. As a white, however, I would not consider it wise to marry a girl with Negro blood, even though I feel no repugnance toward such persons. If I did, my children would never forgive me for bringing them into a world where they would suffer humiliation because of race. By the same token, I would be unhappy at such a marriage by one of my sons or daughters, because of the ridicule that they would have to bear and the danger of unhappiness they would risk, as well as because of the responsibility they would bear to their children. I am referring, however, to cases where differences in color are very pronounced. When there is very little difference, I would have no objection, because the children would not be affected in a country where not infrequently members of the most illustrious families can trace their origin to the slave quarters."

Roberto Christiana Naegeli, a Brazilian of European ancestry, born in Rio de Janeiro in 1881 and educated in Switzerland, states: "I can remember that during my childhood in Switzerland persons to whom I was introduced would often exclaim with surprise and no great delicacy: 'White Brazilians?', all of which would cause my mother to become very angry." As for miscegenation, he gives the opinion that "the system of intermarriage adopted by Brazil for the solution of the racial question is having splendid results. I have been watching this phenomenon since my return to Brazil in 1901. Almost all workers on the docks of Recife, Bahia, and Rio used to be pure Negroes. Often in Rio I would see tattooed Africans and hear them conversing in African tongues. Such pure Negroes are now seldom encountered. The white population has risen from 40 per cent to about 65 per cent, and the remaining 35 per cent, to my eyes, seem to be at least 50 per cent lighter than they were in 1901. I predict that in another 75 years the question of color will have disappeared completely in Brazil. Nevertheless, I would not look favorably upon a marriage of one of my family to a person of color."

Erasto Gaertner, born in Paraná of German-Brazilian parentage in 1900, brings out a different aspect of the question in saying: "The fact of having been born and raised in the south, where the black population was at a minimum, caused all of us to take an off-hand and completely tolerant attitude to the question of our melting-pot tendencies. Being few in number, blacks and mulattos were quickly absorbed by the white population, whose numbers were rapidly increasing through the rush of immigration. The problem is not so simple in other parts of Brazil, in Rio de Janeiro or in the north, where the proportion of blacks is heavy and the potential for Negro multiplication noticeably increased. This potential is much more significant when one notes the comparative decline in the white birth rate through the use of contraceptives, a decline which becomes increasingly accentuated in direct proportion to the standard of living. In the more advanced areas, where the rapid growth of industrialization brings about marked economic disruption, birth control increasingly becomes a factor in limiting population. Among the blacks, however, this factor is not so clearly discernible, whether because of lack of education or because of the irregularity and irresponsibility of sexual unions. One indication of this latter is the enormous number of abandoned black children to be found in our orphanages. In one such institution in São Salvador, I saw that nearly 80 per cent were Negroes and mulattos. What results, then, is a growing Negro population as compared to an almost stationary white group, in contrast to the previous and longtime tendency to the contrary. To alleviate this tendency, only one solution seems practical: the energetic intensification of European immigration. This heroic effort would work toward a solution not only of the demographic situation but also of a vast majority of other national problems. European immigration has always been the means through which North America has made its stupendous progress. . . . As for miscegenation, I do not feel that it will lead to the absorption of the black race. It is my impression that such means were most resorted to in colonial and Imperial times, thanks to the special conditions engendered by slavery. Since then, except for those unions made by newly arrived Portuguese immigrants, and by sexual extravagances of a possibly anomalous sort, I feel that the tendency has been clearly and definitely toward a separation of the races." As for the personal question, he confesses: "I have no marriageable sisters and my two daughters are already wed. If they had chosen colored husbands, I should have considered them mad. If I could not prevent such a marriage, I would be most profoundly displeased, not because I am racially prejudiced, but simply because present realities make me fearful for the tranquility and happiness of a white person obliged to face for the rest of his life the results which such a strange and unusual union would necessarily produce."

Still more intransigent is the testimony of José Magalhães Carneiro (b. Sergipe, 1880), a graduate of medical school in 1901, after having studied humanities in Rio de Janeiro "under Sylvio Romero, whose pupil I was for eleven years." Living with Sylvio, who was a relative, this Sergipean nevertheless took a position strongly against the interpenetration of races sometimes defended (and sometimes not) by the contradictory author of the *História da Literatura Brasileira*.

"I always thought," says Magalhães Carneiro, "that the abolition of slavery, instead of helping the slaves, probably did them a harm that was never intended by the abolitionists. With freedom, the Negroes found themselves utterly unprepared, obliged to fight for their subsistence. All that remained for them was the recollection of the good they had done in our behalf, which we have repaid by the annihilation, to which, despite our good intentions, we have condemned them." As for the marriage question, Magalhães states that he would react "in the worst possible humor," and that he considers the mixing of races "an irremediable misfortune. Along with the blood conflict, there is a corresponding disequilibrium in the metabolism of the three elements [white, black, mulatto]. Whoever has seen a really creative mulatto? Nobody will make me admit that Tobias Barreto and others of his ilk were any geniuses. . . ."

Of a quite different tone is the statement of Antônio Pires da Fonseca (b. Maranhão, 1870): "I was always favorable [toward abolition] because I could never agree with a law which allowed for the enslavement of one's fellow man," but "the loss to the landholders should have been indemnified, in order to avoid an economic collapse." Since in Brazil "the problem is not principally one of race, because all Brazilians are racially mixed," more attention should be paid to the eugenic aspects of the situation, "a health program to prevent luetic and venereal diseases, along with the consequent defects which could only result in the degeneracy of the race." He suggests a program of sterilization [of the unfit] and of intensive hospital treatment for syphilis. In this way eugenic order could be imposed on the presently chaotic process of miscegenation, for the union of white with black will continue "to militate against the improvement of the breed, because it incorporates the psychological and biological contingencies of an inferior race" and thus demands the preventive measures he suggests. With these measures, however, there will be the assurance of the development of a eugenic "dark Brazilian type, characterized by a transparent skin, delicate features, and fine, silky hair" in contrast to the "flat nose, obtuse-angled features, receding chin, and dry kinky hair indicative of recent Negro origin. . . ."

The Cearense physician Alberto de Paula Rodrigues (b. 1882) declares: "I have always had great sympathy for Negroes and *mestiços*. . . . It happens that I never knew slaves, because they were freed in Ceará in 1883, but I did know many old former slave women who remained with their white families and were affectionately addressed by the children of those families as 'Mother': 'Mother Maria,' 'Mother Domingas,' etc. From them I heard strange stories of werewolves and water-sprites and spirits from the other world, and, on rare occasions, of the bad treatment they had received as slaves. . . . I don't know if the United States is following a better course than we are, because there they have outstanding Negroes who have distinguished themselves in sports or in intellectual pursuits. The degeneration of certain mixed bloods in Brazil, however, seems to arise more through such endemic rural tendencies as alcoholism and malnutrition than from ethnic factors. The problem of Brazilian development is still in an embryonic state and must be resolved with our own elements, particularly since the wave of immigration is bringing us persons from imperialist nations or adherents of world revolution with purely subversive ties."

Amílcar Armando Botelho de Magalhães (b. 1880 in the interior of the state of Rio de Janeiro) states that he has been an abolitionist from a tender age. "I feel that it is a sign of backwardness to pretend to find supremacies among races whose development has been simultaneous and along parallel lines. But without having the slightest prejudice, I can recognize the inferiority of the Negro, who is superior only in a degree of emotionality. All the white elements and all the aborigines, on the other hand, given equal conditions of space and time, have made greater achievement in the progress of their civilization." As for Brazil: "I believe that there is no real racial problem in Brazil as such and that the natural tendencies of individual selection, according to biological and sociological principles, will result in an amalgam and in an increasing stability. What is needed is to facilitate racial interbreeding and to avoid, through adequate measures, the perpetuation of basic types, Indian or Negro, as separate entities apart from the whites. But this fusion is possible only on the lower levels of these races, among the workers, the peasants, the persons of least education." As for the personal question: "I would repudiate and do everything possible to prevent miscegenation within my own family. I have already done so in one specific instance. Such things are highly prejudicial."

An equally Positivist opinion is expressed by Alfredo Severo dos Santos Pereira (b. Ceará, 1878). The growing miscegenation in Brazil, he states, was encouraged by the thirteenth of May and the fifteenth of November and indicates ethnic and biosocial progress, because the ideal racial type would be one which would result from a mixture of the three fundamental types. "This mixed breed would with us become not a subrace, as the followers of Gobineau, Nietzsche, and others would assert, but rather a superrace." This was what the great José Bonifácio meant when he said: "Brazil will be a great nation only when you can look at any Brazilian without being able to distinguish the race from which he sprang." And this is what is happening. Having abandoned racial unity and having had diversification, we are now "approaching a new unity, with all differences extinguished." We cannot, of course, neglect the fact that miscegenation in Brazil is the result of "the degradation of the Negro through slavery (Joaquim Nabuco, Gilberto Freyre)." For this reason, he confesses himself honestly to be a "victim of those prejudices which still exist" and says that he could not "view with complete pleasure the marriage of a member of my family to a colored person; but neither would I try to prevent such a union if it were the result of spontaneous and mutual feelings. . . . In future times, such prejudices as mine will certainly disappear." And recalling Comte: "Augusto Comte, in his eighth letter to Dr. Audiffret, after having pointed out that the division between white and black is analogous to the division between the sexes, concludes: 'The white race has dominated through that great part of human development which required spirit and character. It won't be this way in the final stage, where sentiment will become more and more the prevailing quality. When all the nations of the human family attain a normal level, the Negro, like the female sex, will attain an importance and will exercise an influence which we cannot even imagine today.' "

Alfredo Bartolomeu da Rosa Borges (b. Pernambuco, 1864), after registering his standing as abolitionist, republican, and follower of Martins Júnior, confesses to having been always dominated by "white instincts" of an absolute nature. "I have arrogant racial prejudices. It would be most contradictory for me to permit a member of my family to marry a colored person." And Dona Virgínia Cavalcante, another Pernambucan (b. 1879), after affirming her assurance that abolitionists such as the Princess Isabel are "enjoying their Divine reward in heaven," states unequivocally that "in the case of marriage with persons of color, I am in complete disagreement. White with white, mulatto with mulatto, black with black."

After calling abolition "a purifying crusade," the Cearense José Alves de Figueiredo (b. 1879) expresses his confidence in the eventual assimilation of the Negro by the whites, an assimilation which will result in a "strong race" and which will occur through contact with "great waves of immigrants." He "would receive the marriage

of one of his children to a Negro or a mulatto with great reluctance," believing that such assimilation should take place on other
social levels than his.

João d'Albuquerque Maranhão (b. Rio Grande do Norte, 1883)
seems to concur. For him the "poor *mestiço* population" of Brazil,
and especially in the north, has shown itself since abolition to be
"undernourished, sickly, lazy, and stupid . . ." in contrast to the
Italo-Brazilians, who continue to develop "in a superior way, knowing how to read, write, live, and eat, and moreover who have been
educated along economic lines." Thus we should encourage more
and more of the European immigration which has aided other parts
of Brazil in the "formation of a strong, healthy, and intelligent
race." Considering himself a blue-blooded Luso-American, Maranhão states that he would never allow anyone in his family to marry
a person of African blood.

José Maria Moreira Guimarães (b. Sergipe, 1864) was trained
for a military career at Praia Vermelha, where he "had the good
fortune" to have Benjamin Constant as one of his teachers. Admitting to having been an abolitionist since his youth and favoring the
Republic "from the political standpoint," he adds: "Logically, I
would receive the marriage of a member of my family to a colored
person without any prejudice whatsoever, so long as the individual
concerned was a good person."

Maria Teodora dos Santos, a poor white (b. Pernambuco, 1878),
states that she was married at sixteen to a man given to drinking.
She says that she does not feel that blacks are the equal of whites,
but rather that "they were born to serve the white people." If her
daughter married a Negro, she "would regret it, unless he happened
to be of good character and took good care of her."

Eduardo Jacobina (b. Rio de Janeiro, 1869) feels that "the immense moral qualities of the Portuguese degenerated in Brazil in
consequence of miscegenation and promiscuity among the Negroes
and the Guaranis. These two races are anatomically inferior, as nobody with any judgment will deny. They are not merely immoral;
they are amoral. They lack initiative and self-esteem and have no
desire for progress or comfort. They know nothing and have no
comprehension of the values of education. They have their prejudices and their vanities and nothing more. This explains why this
country is swarming with 'geniuses' and why every day we wallow
more deeply in the mud. It also explains why *mestiço* assassins,

cowards, and traitors are appointed to represent this country abroad! . . . Manipulated by secret organizations, the *mestiço* masses have submerged, if not completely destroyed, our élite." In the light of these sentiments, it is understandable that this witness would be averse to the marriage of a near relative to a person of color.

Raimundo Dias de Freitas (b. Piauí, 1874) laments the colonization of Brazil by the Portuguese. It was they who exaggerated the need for the importation of African slaves, thus causing "the superabundance of Negroes in the former population of Brazil . . ." This mistake was made because of a "lack of vision" in Portugal. "Everything there is small, from its territory to the cultural outlook of its people." He recognizes, however, that "through their civic and moral virtues," which predominate over any possible racial inferiority, "the Brazilian Negroes and mulattos are the lever which gives the necessary impulse and brings about industrial progress in our factories, our mills, and all other places where hard labor is necessary to the country's welfare. In instances of great danger in the defense of our beloved Brazil, it has been the Negroes and mulattos who have been the first to sacrifice themselves for their country. . . . They have also distinguished themselves in intellectual and cultural activities and in various branches of science, helping Brazil to gain good standing in the cultural circles of the world." However, "for reasons of natural selection and racial purity, I would condemn the marriage of anyone in my family to a colored person."

Artur Roberto Coelho de Sousa, born in Paraíba in 1889 and for many years resident in New York, says that he first learned to know "real racial prejudice—against the Negro and the Jew—in the United States," where he went as a young man to study mechanical engineering. It is true, however, that "even in Brazil I had noted among the people certain indications of racial prejudice; for example, in an old street song: 'Nigger, if you want to sing with me, wash your mouth with soap,' or in various popular expressions: 'Nigger standing is a tree stump; Nigger lying down is a pig,' or, needling a mulatto: 'When the billy goat doesn't jump, he yells.' [9] But I always regarded these things as being said in jest; it never occurred to me at the time that they were subtle manifestations of our

[9] Comparison of the Negro to a goat is common in Brazil simply because the goats there are black. (Translator.)

own prejudices." As for the marriage question: "I would oppose it on simple aesthetic—and perhaps economic—grounds. In a predominantly white civilization with strong racial prejudices such as that of the United States [where Coelho de Sousa had married an American woman and raised his children], the matter would be completely out of the question. This is not color prejudice on my part; it is an attitude far more practical than racial."

Quite different is the attitude of Dona Henriqueta Galeno (b. Ceará, c. 1890). "I would not make the slightest objection to the marriage of any member of my family to a person of color. I have no racial prejudices: a *mestiço* of talent and culture, in my opinion, is worth far more than an ignorant, loud-mouth white man."

The Pernambucan José Maria da Silva Freyre (or Freire) (b. 1887) states that he has been more happy in his "friendship with a Negro woman" than with his marriage to a white girl. In this he followed his uncle Manuel da Rocha Wanderley, who was "blond, white-skinned, and blue-eyed as a foreigner, and to whom a white woman was no woman at all." His preference for Negro women became total, and the only reason he didn't marry one was that he feared "offending his family and being ill regarded by society." He also tells us that as a young man he had a German friend who felt the same way, considering the black girl "the queen of all womanhood."

❧ [V I I] ❧

Agricultural and

Commercial Development

T HE PERIOD OF BRAZILIAN HISTORY considered here is that from
the 1870's, with their Law of the Free Womb and Republican
Manifesto, to the end of the First World War, marked by the close
of the administration of Venceslau Brás and the beginning of that of
Epitácio Pessoa. The presidency of Venceslau Brás ended a period
of economic and social patterns which stemmed from the early
years of the reign of Pedro II. This was an era of relative stability in
the cultural norms and general way of life in Brazil, a stability
interrupted by only a few years of political and economic indecision contingent upon the change from monarchy to Republic. Because of this relative equilibrium over a long period, the monarchy
was able to project itself into the early Republic by the continued
presence in the government of counselors, barons, viscounts, commanders, and other Imperial dignitaries, who served along with the
republican college graduates and military men, many of whom had
themselves started their own careers under the monarchy.[1] The
move from monarchy to Republic was clearly not one from night
to day. In its effect upon society and institutions, the change was
gradual, and any chronological delimitations represent only the
most artificial boundaries. The real changes which took place were

[1] At the time of the fall of the Empire, the Brazilian nobility consisted of 7
marquises and 1 widowed marquise, 10 counts and 10 widowed countesses, 20
viscounts and 18 widowed viscountesses, 27 barons and 11 widowed baronesses,
34 honorary viscounts and 6 widows, 280 baronets and 55 widows. From the
Almanaque Brasileiro Garnier, published under the direction of João Ribeiro (Rio
de Janeiro, 1908), p. 151.

neither chronological nor logical, but psychological and sociological.

In an interesting study, *Brazilian Exchange—The Study of an Inconvertible Currency*, published in English in Buenos Aires in 1896, J. P. Wileman pointed out what he terms a *degringolade*, or weakening, in Brazilian finance after the proclamation of the Republic, a softening he attributes in large part to European lack of confidence in the new regime. This lack of confidence stemmed largely from the failure of the leaders of the new government, in particular Ruy Barbosa, to attain some sort of objectivity in their messianic new policy of "broad horizons." Ruy, who in this study is accused of "exuberant fancy," was nevertheless aware in 1890 that the financial situation encountered by the Republic was not so much the result of a daring republican policy as attributable to the economic effect of abolition. As Wileman himself recognized, the immediate consequence of abolition was "the increased cost of production," along with "the reduction of nominal profits [in paper money] caused by the rise of exchange." As a result, there was a virtual "epidemic," beginning as early as 1888, which attacked all classes and created "an unprecedented expansion of credit that only fed still more the adventurous spirits." [2] This speculative mania, or *encilhamento* as it was called at the time, turned contagious and assumed epidemic proportions under the provisional government. In Wileman's opinion this morbid development would not have taken place had not the governments—late Imperial as well as early Republican—encouraged it through "imprudent and unreflected measures."

Wileman's words confirm the thesis presented here: that the Republic at its birth was already infiltrated by the monarchy. Its anti-monarchism was merely superficial; in great part it was essentially a continuing agent of the former regime. If the fifteenth of November had never taken place, the economic situation created by abolition would have plagued the monarchy also, and the same measures would have been taken. What was needed under the circumstances was an entirely new approach to national economic problems, and such an approach was not forthcoming under the Republic.

Wileman advised the new leaders of Brazil to be more assiduous in the matter of statistics. The absence of such data was an anomaly

---

[2] J. P. Wileman: *Brazilian Exchange: The Study of an Inconvertible Currency* (Buenos Aires, 1896), p. 256.

and an evil in a country as important and progressive as Brazil. Had it not been for the annual summaries of the *Jornal do Commercio*, with their excellent statistics, he probably could not have written his book. But these figures indicated that national progress in Brazil was perhaps being "too dearly bought." [3]

Naturally, it was not possible to have progress, with its railways, steamships, telegraph, and immigration, without spending a great deal of money. But was Brazilian life any less pleasant before the coming of the railway and the steamship? Wileman asks this rhetorically. For him it was dubious sense to fill the country in the name of progress with a foreign and heterogeneous population which would produce wealth but which would be difficult to assimilate. Progress, of course, is a good thing, even an excellent thing, says the economist-moralist, but only when it does not degenerate into mere "money grubbing." If the moral and intellectual development of a country does not parallel its material growth, its customs, manners, and morality will suffer and the national character deteriorate. [4] What economists and financial experts like Wileman feared at the time was that Brazil, with its national character already fixed by its past, would give itself over to a mystique of future progress that would sacrifice that past and that national character for purely material ends. In order to prevent this, it was necessary to establish an orderly development which would ensure the preservation of values and would encourage, along with material growth, a corresponding development of intellectual and moral awareness.

Wileman's point of view was reflected to a certain extent in the attitudes of two Finance Ministers from Central Brazil, Joaquim Murtinho and Leopoldo de Bulhões. And also to some extent in David Campista, who was scandalized by the expenditures of Rio Branco (who, as Foreign Minister, installed luxurious bathrooms and other purely material items in the palace which housed his department and acted as the "reception room" of Brazil). The problem also concerned such serious Brazilian students of economics and finance as Sousa Carvalho in *A Crise da Praça* (*The Market Crisis*) (1875) and Amaro Cavalcanti in *Resenha Financeira do Ex-Império do Brasil* (*A Financial Report on the Former Brazilian Empire*) (1889).

Concern over material progress was one of the liveliest topics of

[3] Ibid., pp. vi, 179.
[4] Ibid., p. 180.

the period covered here. In his book *Os Republicanos Paulistas e a Abolição,* José Maria dos Santos notes that "the close of the Paraguayan War and the proclamation of the Law of the Free Womb were coincident with the inauguration of the first docks in the port of Rio de Janeiro and the granting of concessions for the construction of railways throughout the provinces. From this time on there was a notable development of interest in matters of material progress. . . . From the visual standpoint, this interest was especially noticeable in the disappearance of old-fashioned buildings with overhanging roofs in favor of the smooth facade and in the laying of paving blocks in the streets and public squares." [5]

Although I would question the use of the expression "especially noticeable" in this respect, I agree with the estimated point at which Brazil began to take an interest in matters of material progress. It must be remembered, however, that this country was never one to move at a uniform social, cultural, or psychological rate throughout its vast extent and that there were always some places more advanced, and others more retarded, than the average. This difference in rhythm was at times so varied that it would seem almost impossible to reconcile the progressivism of Ceará or Rio Grande do Sul with the ultra-conservatism of the state of Rio de Janeiro, of Bahia, of a large portion of Minas Gerais, or, for that matter, of even that part of São Paulo which had relied on a slave-labor force for the coffee plantations. Before abolition and the proclamation of the Republic, these elements had made up an economic bloc so full of antagonisms and contradictions that it is a tribute to the traditional wisdom and skill of the statesmen of the time that they were able somehow to maintain some sort of equilibrium, a skill which failed only under the Ouro Prêto government, characterized by an almost Germanic intransigence in political controversy.

The case of São Paulo in this situation was unique: that of a province agitated by both extremes. Only in the first half of the nineteenth century had it developed the opulence and vigor which had been experienced since colonial times in Bahia, Pernambuco, Maranhão, and Rio de Janeiro. It became a region of Big Houses and slave quarters, of masters and slaves, quite in contrast to its colonial life. Formerly, the way of life had been sober and almost ascetic, balanced by a diversified economy, with an agrarian land-

[5] José Maria dos Santos: *Os Republicanos Paulistas e a Abolição* (São Paulo, 1942), p. 81.

scape marked by modest homes and small-scale cultivation. Ethnically, São Paulo had been more similar to Paraguay, with its heavy Spanish-Guarani element and consequent rampant miscegenation.

However, in changing from a sugar to a coffee economy, São Paulo imported slaves from the north and joined them with the typical Paulista elements of Hispano-Indian origin. In addition to slaves, the nineteenth-century neo-aristocracy imported college-trained men, the younger sons of sugar planters hit by the decline in the Brazilian sugar market. These young men came to São Paulo to make their fortune, married into established Paulista families, and assimilated into the culture of the province. Some of them were dark-skinned; many of them became leaders, men like Albuquerque Lins of Alagoas, who became a state governor, or Manuel Vilaboim, a Bahian who became a prominent lawyer and federal deputy during the second and third decades of the Republic.

This assimilation and absorption brought a corresponding transmigration of sociological patterns from the slave areas to the coffee plantations of neo-aristocratic São Paulo: the transmigration of a whole complex of forms, values, and social rituals expressive of an aristocratic way of life. The architectonic pattern of the Big House and the slave quarters was incorporated, as well as the master's manner of living with slaves, followers, and poor tenants long since followed in older regions of Brazil. In addition, the relationships between the master's wife and her servants, between the children and their black mammys and their Negro companions, the patriarchal fathers and their sons, were adopted from Pernambuco or Bahia or Rio de Janeiro or Maranhão. One difference, however, in the coffee area was the presence of German governesses and European *institutrices*. And a further element was that of the former slaveholders from the United States who moved to São Paulo after the defeat of the Confederacy in the American Civil War. But in the main the pattern was transported in its entirety from north to south.

With the exhaustion of the gold mines, São Paulo had found itself "in a position of inferiority compared to most of the other provinces." Its recovery was made through the cultivation of coffee, with the aid of an excellent system of highways (much superior to the simple dirt roads of Minas Gerais) which facilitated the economic growth of the province and helped it attain the highest state of development of any area during this period. The sums advanced by the provincial government between 1860 and 1870 for the construction of rail lines were quickly repaid; by 1874, the roads were virtually debt-free so far as the state was concerned, thanks to the increase in exports of coffee and cotton. In 1870 and 1871, 96 transatlantic and 151 coastal ships had entered the port of Santos; in 1872 and 1873, the number rose to 475 and 678 respectively. No other Brazilian port saw anything like this increase. It marked the economic hegemony of São Paulo over the other provinces of the Empire; the triumph of coffee over sugar.[6]

In his *Brazil: A Study of Economic Types*,[7] J. F. Normano points out that the first decade of the Republic had been marked by the establishment of São Paulo as the economic center of gravity of the country. During this decade not only had São Paulo's coffee become the country's leading agricultural product, but the state's industries, thanks to the influence of Mauá, had also begun to produce materials which, by the dual avoidance of shipping costs and protective tariffs, began to be competitive with foreign imports. For Normano the great growth period of Brazilian industry extended from 1885 to 1914. A report published in 1891 by the Treasury Department of the provisional government rather arbitrarily sets this beginning date to coincide with the establishment of the Republic.

Felisbelo Freire in his *História Constitucional da República*[8] seems to put the matter in exact historical terms by showing that a government report of 1864 (*Relatório da Crise do Mês de Setembro de 1864*) gave the number of industrial firms in the country as 124, whereas in 1881, during an industrial exposition sponsored by the court, the country could boast of 46 cotton textile mills: 1 in Pernambuco, 12 in Bahia, 7 in Rio de Janeiro province, 9 in São Paulo, 9 in Minas Gerais, 10 elsewhere. The textile industry was about

---

[6] See Sérgio Milliet: *O Roteiro do Café* (São Paulo, 1938); Robert Simonson: "Aspectos da História Económica do Café," reprinted from *Revista do Arquivo*, LXV (São Paulo, 1940); and Alfred Ellis, Jr.: *O Café e a Paulistânia* (São Paulo, 1951). Also see the half-forgotten *L'Exportation Caféière au Brésil* (Gand, 1889) of Hubert van de Putte and Ladislas d'Almeida; Eugênio Lefèvre: *Il Caffè* (São Paulo, 1904); Louis Couty: *Étude de Biologie Industrielle sur le Café* (Rio de Janeiro, 1883); Francisco Peixoto de Lacerda Werneck: *Memórias sôbre a Fundação e Custeio de Uma Fazenda na Província do Rio de Janeiro* (4th edn., Rio de Janeiro, 1878); and especially J. R. de Araujo Filho: "O Café, Riqueza Paulista," *Boletim Paulista de Geographia*, No. 23 (July 1956). Also the studies of Afonso de E. Taunay, Pierre Monbeig, and Aroldo de Azevedo.

[7] (Chapel Hill, N.C., 1935), p. 98.

[8] (Rio de Janeiro, 1894), II, 342.

evenly divided between north and south, although the south had the edge in the actual number of mills. Felisbelo Freire is therefore not far off in suggesting that this period marked the beginning of the shift of capital funds from agriculture to industry, a shift that was accelerated a few years later when abolition changed the country's labor patterns from a slave to a salaried economy. The shift was also seen in government aid, the first landmark in this respect being the decree of December 18, 1892, merging the old Bank of Brazil with the Bank of the Republic to form a new organization keyed to the ascendancy of capitalism over agriculture. But this decree was not the only victory for industry; it was accompanied (and in a few cases even preceded) by official acts exempting industrial machinery and related apparatus from taxes, guaranteeing interest on industrial investments, nationalizing coastal navigation, and establishing bonuses in aid to individual industries. And in 1891 there was a so-called "Stock Exchange coup" which was considered by some to be "an excessive and illegitimate defense of capitalistic interests on the part of the government."

Freire points out that it was the loans from the provisional government which enabled some of these states to prosper. But in the case of a state like São Paulo, these loans not only supported an agriculture which had become the most important in the nation, but also aided an industrial economy which already enjoyed conditions for development far superior to those prevailing elsewhere: a population capable of consuming local manufactures; a phenomenal distribution system instituted through the coffee economy but easily adaptable to industry; the absence of competition from neighboring states; and a corresponding absence of small coastal cities to compete with Santos as the regional port and railhead for the area. There is also no question that in those decisive days São Paulo possessed a group of leaders more flexible, more energetic, and more aware of the problems of a salaried labor economy then were their counterparts in the north. Perhaps it was their wider association with Europeans newly arrived from capitalist and industrialized countries which accounted for these qualities. Another factor is that the military leaders who were responsible for the transformation of the Empire into a Republic, though men of far greater public spirit than the Paulista industrialists, were nevertheless lacking in the practical political wisdom necessary to contain the exaggerated state consciousness of men like Francisco Glycério, whose parochialism became a perversion of the spirit of federalism instituted by the Republic. What these military leaders should have done was transform this dynamic state consciousness into a sense of national unity, even intervening in the economic life of the nation. In this way they could have used its power, not merely to strengthen regions already prosperous, but also to aid in the recovery of the north, victim of the decline of the sugar economy and, because of its tropical climate, less attractive to European immigrants.[9]

In any case, the pre-eminence of São Paulo in the national economy was assured. Thus we have the paradox of a state which at the end of the Imperial regime was marked by the greatest rate of increase in both slave and European immigrant population, which was developing on its coffee plantations all the patterns of life and culture that characterized the north, and which could nevertheless through the influence of immigration make a relatively easy and definitive transition to an economy based upon free labor.

It is not surprising, in the face of these conditions, that São Paulo should have been the site of the sometimes violent abolitionist activity of the *mestiço* Luís Gama, an activity which would have been inconceivable in Bahia. Nor is it surprising that the same province should have promoted the republican movement, which had dawned without great consequence in Pernambuco, Minas Gerais, and Rio Grande do Sul: a movement envisaging the solidarity of a Brazil without slavery with a democratic and republican America. In his study *O Precursor do Abolicionismo no Brasil*, Sud Menucci points out that it was Luís Gama who, in a letter of 1870 to his son Benedito, first used the expression "the United States of Brazil."[1] This is evidence that the Anglo-American example of republicanism, of so-called "democracy," had begun to seduce Brazilians some thirty years before the appearance in the same province of Eduardo Prado's vigorous anti-republican tract, classic of its kind, *A Ilusão Americana*.

It is curious that the republican and abolitionist movements

[9] One of the things the government should have done was to redivide the provinces of the north into new states and territories along lines more commensurate with their economic and ecological nature and more favorable to interregional economic and cultural balance. During the early days of the Republic there was apparently no individual or group of any prestige who understood the importance to the economy of this interregional adjustment. Instead of passively copying the federalism of the United States, Brazil should have evolved a system—experimental if not definitive—based upon existing conditions. Had it done so, the economy would not have suffered from the excesses of state-minded republicanism.

[1] Sud Menucci: *O Precursor do Abolicionismo no Brasil* (São Paulo, 1938), p. 92.

which appeared simultaneously in São Paulo during the last days of the Empire should finally have been reconciled, despite their many basic points of difference. This reconciliation was encouraged, not by Luís Gama, whose radicalism led him to oppose the coalition, but rather by another *mestiço* of talent, Francisco Glycério.

The thirteenth of May had been the most important factor in preparing the ground for this union. In São Paulo, as in other predominantly agrarian provinces, republicans had been few and generally regarded as merely romantic young men. The main element consisted of a solid aristocracy—planters, sugar-mill owners, country squires—for whom abolition had created a new economic order which no longer bore any relationship to the political system represented by the Empire. For this reason, many of these barons, usually very able men, regained respectability by joining with the disenchanted in support of the Republic. Since 1884 Glycério, whose political subtlety suggests a trace of the Bahian in his makeup, had been attempting to convince his co-religionaries that the objective of the republicans was "to found the Republic—a political fact; not to free the slaves—a social fact." [2] Privately we may be sure he realized that as a common denominator of what he called "political" and "social" facts, there existed the unifying fact of the economic situation.

In an analysis of the ensuing confusion in Brazil—when the Imperial government was attempting to fraternize with the common man through an abolition supported even by the conservatives and when, in the face of the same abolition, the rural aristocracy was leaning toward republicanism—José Maria dos Santos would write (recalling the Brazil he had known as a dark-skinned adolescent) that the monarchy had played a compensating role, placing itself "on the side of the people, against the slaveholding interests." Remembering the republican-minded deputies who represented São Paulo in the Imperial Parliament, he states: "They were nothing more than legitimate and confirmed representatives of the agrarian interests, despite all their efforts to convince the public of their devotion to the name and theories of the party under whose banner they had been elected." [3]

Prudente de Morais disagreed with this interpretation, much to the disapproval of Glycério, who saw the pro-slavery elements threatened by the approach of the Paulista republicans to the

2 Ibid., p. 152.
3 Santos: op. cit., p. 222.

"royal program of servile reform." Glycério's attitude, republican but not abolitionist, was echoed in the same province by such monarchical conservatives as Antônio Prado, an emancipationist who turned "liberal" and "republican" in order to "attack openly the provincial vice-president, who according to him and his fellow conservatives was placing himself outside the laws of the country in his local application of liberation measures." [4]

Actually, these "conservatives," when examined closely, proved to be the true progressives in their desire to take advantage of local conditions—climate, soil, geographical position—to establish a coffee economy based on the free labor eventually supplied by the Italian immigration. It was by following this line that São Paulo, unlike most of the other provinces of Brazil, could effect a rapid transition from slave to free labor; but in so doing it neglected to consider that other parts of the country equally dependent on agriculture but less able to abolish slavery were also part of the national picture. In the face of the resulting economic dislocation, Silveira Martins's remark to the effect that he did not belong to a group that loved the Negro more than it loved Brazil was not mere rhetoric.

In São Paulo militant republican *mestiços* like the clearsighted Glycério strove to conciliate the original Paulista republicans—students and clerks—with the rural interests alarmed by the abolitionist line followed by the Imperial government. In turn, conservatives such as Prado worked for the conciliation of these interests with abolition by encouraging the immigration of Italian field workers to São Paulo.

This then was the complex but advantageous position enjoyed by São Paulo during the transition from Empire to Republic: an excellent aristocracy of old Hispano-Amerindian stock, enriched by a gracious way of life imported from the north and northeast, joining with a powerful democratic element in its readiness to develop the industrial potential of the state.

Articles published in the *Correio Paulistano* of 1887 under the inspiration, if not the actual authority, of Antônio Prado, justified "the increase in fugitive slaves through the fact that they have before their eyes, in the recent Italian immigration, the suggestion of the value of paid labor." [5] There were others, however, who, like José Maria dos Santos, attributed the depression in the north merely

[4] Ibid., p. 245.
[5] Ibid., p. 316.

to the fall in the prices of cotton and sugar, disputing the fact that, before the proclamation of abolition, great numbers of slaves had already moved to the provinces of the south, and especially to São Paulo. Nevertheless, if the emancipation laws were the same for the entire nation, the fact is that the means and methods of replacing slave with free workers differed greatly in the various provinces. It was not the mere substitution of Italian for Negro labor in São Paulo; it was the example of the quality of labor exhibited by free workers which communicated itself to the Negroes, to the subsequent advantage of the regional economy. Such replacement and such examples were lacking in the north and northeast, largely because the electoral interests had favored the south at the expense of the north and because southern climatic conditions favored the settlement of white immigrants. Finally, it was also because the monocultural sugar economy of the north had created conditions of labor that were virtually feudal and consequently inimical to Europeans.

Durval Vieira de Aguiar, in his study of Bahia at the end of the Imperial era, recalls that in 1872 a colonizing service was established at Comandutuba by contract between the governor general and two citizens: Counselor Policarpo Lopes de Leão and the future Baron de Muniz. This enterprise was no less a failure than that of a German colony earlier attempted in Pernambuco. The Bahian lands were clearly "of superior quality" and the climate "truly European," but the unfavorable location of the colony, far from the sea and uncomfortably close to the interior badlands, marked it for failure as clearly as a similar type of location had doomed the Pernambucan colony of Catucá. The colony was actually started on cleared lands, but insufficient selectivity was exercised in obtaining settlers. The colonists were a heterogeneous mixture of Austrians, Germans, and Poles contracted in Antwerp at so much per head; most of them were completely ignorant of farming and were even less prepared for tropical living conditions. The result was that they did nothing, earned nothing, and quickly contracted all the local ailments: chiggers, lice, gangrene, dysentery, malaria, and all varieties of tropical fevers. Even if the Europeans had developed the tropical custom of taking a daily bath and examining their feet (there were native women available who were skilled in the extraction of chiggers), the pests would probably still have devastated their hands and faces as well as their extremities. As it was, the colony folded up miserably, with the colonists fleeing from the death and disease of the interior to gain their living by begging on the streets of the capital city. The Imperial government finally repatriated a large number.[6]

A second European colony to fail in Bahia was that founded in 1882 in the tropical undergrowth of Caravelas. This time the colonists were Spaniards, who should have been more equipped to adapt themselves to the tropics. But months passed and the settlers still had not managed to clear even the smallest plot of land for planting.[7] And here too the chiggers regarded the Europeans as a banquet sent from the gods. Liver ailments, malaria, and yellow fever set in. The Brazilianization of these Europeans, in short, proved to be a most macabre experience.

All this occurred because feudal landholders did not want free white workers in the vicinity of their properties, particularly since the cultivation and extraction of sugar is a species of agriculture much more difficult for Europeans to learn than coffee cultivation. The only lands these proprietors would grant to colonists were those far from their *fazendas,* where there was still virgin forest to be cleared. And they were not interested in encouraging the development of small farming since this enjoyed practically no government protection.

Nevertheless, there were those who felt that "with one-twentieth of the support it affords the aristocratic cultivation of sugar, the government could support the municipalities of the north in the development of small farming by sending handcarts, cotton gins, corn huskers, and portable manioc flour mills to farmers, who could repay the cost of this equipment out of crop incomes on a long-term basis." And Vieira de Aguiar goes on to say that such support "would not only develop our agricultural potential but would also afford our unprotected small farmers a greater opportunity for well-being, a process which could eventually be furthered by the subdivision of lands. The entire plan is easily within possibility; all that is needed is to pass the necessary laws." Nor should the foreign immigrant be overlooked—"the indispensable adjunct to our future aggrandizement." How can we expect Europeans to come over "to do slave labor in the sugar mills? Such a supposition would be absurd." The real European colonizer would come to Brazil, "not to work for the landlord, but to have his own farm, where he would

[6] Durval Vieira de Aguiar: *Descrições Práticas da Província da Bahia* (Bahia, 1888), p. 272.

[7] Ibid., pp. 290–1.

raise whatever crop he wished and for which he was adapted," [8] Vieira de Aguiar says flatly, thinking mainly of conditions in Bahia. But it was São Paulo, with its quite different ecological situation and its large-scale coffee economy, which won out. Though a monoculture under the aegis of a landlord, coffee offered advantageous opportunities to the immigrant, at least in the initial stages. There was no slave labor, and there were opportunities to follow other pursuits, though always within the framework of the coffee economy. This contrasted strongly with what happened in the sugar industry and what did not take long to develop on the rubber plantations, where there was a stubborn adherence to the strictly tropical system that had existed since colonial times.

Echoing the warning of the German writer Ernst Samhaber in his *Sudamérica, Biografía de un Continente*, it is important to remember that the simultaneous, complementary development of temperate and tropical agriculture which brought quick prosperity to the United States was not possible in Brazil, where there was a nearly uniform climate which demanded an exclusively tropical economy. Thus Brazil came into competition with other tropical countries. In Ceylon, coffee planting, which had been prospering since the early days of the nineteenth century, was virtually wiped out in 1880 by a devastating blight. This happened at a time when the cotton and sugar industries of northern Brazil had declined to about 60 per cent of their former value. The situation thus favored the sale of slaves to the coffee plantations of the south, despite the vain efforts of some state governments to prevent an acute labor shortage by impeding such sales. The movement of slaves to the south had been, in effect, "a powerful lever in their liberation, and at the same time the means by which the flourishing south could most effectively weaken its ancient and hardhearted northern competitor," says Samhaber.[9]

It is curious that Ceylon, in losing its coffee supremacy to Brazil, should at the same time have robbed the north of its dominant position in rubber, thus intensifying the lack of balance between north and south Brazil to an almost tragic degree. Nevertheless, the assurance of economic supremacy to São Paulo was beneficial to the country as a whole, in that it gave leadership to old and respected families. Such families, while not necessarily the wealthiest in the

[8] Ibid., pp. 317, 318.
[9] Ernst Samhaber: *Sudamérica, Biografía de un Continente* (Buenos Aires, 1940), p. 650.

country, were still able to win the confidence of Brazilians and thus to act as a block to the development of that *caudilhismo* so common in Spanish-American countries which could very easily have arisen, destroying all the nation's best social and economic traditions.

The Republic led most Brazilians, fearing military dictatorship, to find refuge in the social and economic status quo represented by local leaders. These local leaders were for the most part manifestations of what Ernst Samhaber calls "the flood tide of the great families," a term which indicates his acceptance of the thesis that the formation of Brazilian society had been patriarchal in nature. Under the influence of this patriarchal impulse, Brazilians could accept those Paulistas who, as "local leaders" and members of old families, seemed to offer some guarantee of national security. Among these were Prudente, Campos Sales, and Rodrigues Alves. Interested in maintaining the supremacy of their state, these men subordinated their political to their economic impulses and refrained from interfering greatly with the internal political life of other states.

In the neighboring state of Minas Gerais, economic diversification had been developing since the failure of the mining economy in the early days after independence. The gold rush which developed in colonial times had originally caused agriculture to play only an ancillary role in the early economy of the area; but once the disastrous mining fever had abated, the Mineiros were wise enough to seek economic recovery through a diversified agrarian program which included the cultivation of sugar, coffee, and corn.

In answer to questions about life on a typically progressive Mineiro *fazenda* of the period covered here, Cássio Barbosa de Resende (b. 1879), in a long testimony written in 1937, tells us of his recollections of the small (250 acres) but well-organized and profitable plantation of his father, Counselor Francisco de Paula Ferreira de Resende. The Big House was an ample, imposing two-story affair, equipped with such modern conveniences as running water and electric heaters even in slavery times. The principal crop was coffee, but there were also subsistence crops which fed the family and its slaves. There were mills for sugar and corn, and a water-powered installation for the sifting and pulverizing of coffee beans. Transportation of crops was still effected by oxcart.

After the proclamation of abolition in 1888, the slaves offered their services for the current coffee harvest, but once this was in they left one by one until the only ones remaining were "my father's old Negro page; a young mulatto girl who had two small children and who soon left to marry a Negro on a neighboring plantation; and my old wet nurse, of whom I was very fond, together with her son and two daughters. . . ." In 1889 Counselor Resende went to the immigration office in Juiz de Fora to hire "four Italian families to work on the plantation, but they stayed for only a short time, and by 1891 the *fazenda* was completely abandoned. My father, being ill, had no more energy to try to find workers and it was his four youngest sons, now graduated from secondary school, who gathered the last two coffee harvests, with the help of the old Negro and my nurse's son, who was of about my age. . . . For two years we did all the work of the *fazenda* until one day, to our surprise, my father was invited to become a judge of the Supreme Court. His first impulse was to refuse the offer, but thanks to the importuning of my mother, who could not reconcile herself to the fact that her sons were doing manual work to the detriment of their further education, he finally accepted, and in 1892 the whole family moved to Rio de Janeiro." In retrospect he states that this disruption of his family was not an isolated case, but rather one which affected a considerable number of similar plantation owners, not all of whom had the good luck to be offered a magistracy in the government. Abolition, he says, "in the way it was carried out, constituted an assault on private property and showed the lack of foresight of our government leaders in not preparing the country to support such a powerful blow to the agrarian economy. It was probably the preponderant cause of the great economic crisis through which the country passed during the early days of the new regime."

From Cássio Barbosa's testimony, we see that it was not always easy to substitute Italian for slave labor, even on small coffee plantations in an agreeable climate. What then of the large plantations in areas with a climate less favorable to Europeans than that of southern Brazil?

"Nobody liked the Republic because of the disorganization it had caused in rural life," says Dona Antônia Lins Vieira de Melo (b. São Paulo, 1879, but brought up in Paraíba). "Certainly in Engenho Novo [the family home] the slaves for the most part remained with their families after the thirteenth of May; only those of ill will decided to leave."

But gradually the most intransigent monarchists among the landholders began to shift the blame for the agricultural upheaval from abolition to the Republic. They were headed in their opinion by such enemies to national order as Ruy Barbosa, with his heretical book *O Papa e o Concílio*, and Benjamin Constant, with his equally heretical doctrine of Positivism. Because of the labor policies of these and other republican statesmen, the new regime was considered inimical to the national economy, especially in those parts of the country where progress had been less marked and where the profits of agriculture depended upon the use of slave labor.

In the light of such conditions, the decline of many of the patriarchal families of the northeast from their former splendor to a most dismal mediocrity is very explicable. It is also clear why many of these families disintegrated, with the more capable members migrating to the south or seeking adventure and possible economic salvation in the strange territories of the extreme north. A few, like the Pernambucan João Alfredo Correia de Oliveira, remained at home and encountered their fortune by becoming sons-in-law in baronial sugar families—a fate escaped almost miraculously by Joaquim Nabuco. But for the most part the collapse of the sugar aristocracy made migration not only attractive but also a virtual necessity. Thus some of the best intelligence of the area, college men with degrees in law, medicine, engineering, and military science, left their homes to become magistrates, bureaucrats, and professional men in the south, marrying into southern families and often becoming the sons-in-law of wealthy cattle ranchers or coffee barons.

As we have seen, this migration of young aristocrats to the south was matched by a similar migration of emancipated slaves, thus strengthening the south at the expense of the north and greatly affecting the national unity. Furthermore, the exodus of these northerners had additional economic consequences of a biological nature, through the loss of men whose families from colonial times, through their aptitude in agriculture, had formed the regional élite, an élite strengthened rather than weakened by the endogamous customs of the colonial era.

Other more adventurous young northerners were attracted by the romance of the Amazon, a region which also had its attractions for young Brazilians from provinces as far distant as Rio Grande do Sul. The attraction, of course, was the rise of rubber, a rise which coincided with the debacle in sugar and which caused the new product to rival coffee as the prestige element in the national economy. Thus the same sort of influx of young aristocrats took place in the Amazon as had earlier occurred in the south, with the result that the agrarian aristocratic patterns of the north and northeast began to be repeated in still another corner of the nation.[1]

One young Brazilian lured by the Amazon was Artur Roberto Coelho de Sousa (b. Paraíba, 1889). Coelho tells us that, after the death of his father, a descendant of an old sugar-planting family of Sapé, he had felt the call of adventure. "For a northeasterner, the Amazon at the time had the force of a powerful magnet," he recalls. "Thousands had answered the call of the 'green Sphinx' and had been mired in the jungle; the few who returned, however disillusioned, nevertheless brought enough money to justify the legend that the streets of Manaus were paved with gold. . . . When I announced my plans to go there, several young men from my town of Itabaina stated that they would go with me. Most of them were better off than I and didn't really have to go as I did out of economic necessity. Result: on the arranged day of departure, I left alone! I had a third-class passage on the Lloyd steamer Maranhão. (What a tub! How filthy it was! But what could you expect when you paid only 65 *milreis* for a two-week passage?) On disembarking in Manaus, even before finding a place to sleep, I went to the office of the *Jornal do Commercio* to apply for a job as a printer. I was lucky, and by the time I joined the companions from my voyage at lunch, I already had a job! And as a press employee, a position considered very high by my stevedore companions!" It was while in Manaus that Artur Coelho felt that he gradually "ceased to be a boy and became a man."

After two years the newspaper bought "the first linotype machines imported into Brazil, except for those in Rio de Janeiro and São Paulo. Once again Amazonas, thanks to the boom in rubber, was able to put all the other states in the shadow." Manaus at the time already had been the first city after Rio and São Paulo to have

[1] The prestige and renown formerly held by sugar and cotton had as yet not favored the cattle ranchers and *maté* growers of the extreme south, where Brazilians of Portuguese origin (some with traces of other European stock) formed a so-called "lard aristocracy" or meat barony, with customs and a way of life similar to those of the oldest blue-bloods of the Empire. Some of these southern aristocrats, such as the Carneiro Monteiros, the Morais Âncoras, and the Fonseca Galvãos, had been northerners who, charmed by the legendary beauty of the southern women, had remained in the area after the Paraguayan War. In this way, aristocratic northern patterns found their way into the extreme south, just as they did in São Paulo.

an electric street railway, paved streets, and electrified port facilities. Its opera house was "the most famous and beautiful theatre in all America," a perhaps ingenuous opinion, but one echoed by many sophisticated persons who went to Manaus at the time. The Bahian Joaquim Pereira Teixeira (b. 1870)—a close friend of José Joaquim Seabra, an Amazonian who in the 1890's became positively oriental in his wealth and living habits—recalled in his old age that the Manaus Opera House was a triumph of Italian art in the midst of the jungle. It was a theatre where people attended in formal dress: the men in white tie, the few respectable ladies *décolletées* and resplendent in jewels, the less respectable ones grossly exaggerated in both departments. Among the new rich, says Pereira Teixeira, there were men who lit their cigars with 100-*milreis* notes, whose patio fountains spouted champagne instead of water, and who imported by British steamship not one but several French girls, not only for the secret pleasures of an oriental pasha, but also for display en masse before the envious eyes of less fortunate adventurers.

Artur Coelho was not one of these luxurious plutocrats; even if he had had the wealth, his puritanical Protestant upbringing would have deterred him. And as a Puritan, with some trace of the Yankee success drive, he prided himself on the fact that as an adolescent he became one of the first Brazilian linotypists to operate the keyboard of a Mergenthaler press, an experience which gave him the same voluptuous pleasure a music-lover would have in playing Bach or Mozart on a grand piano. The sound of machinery itself was music to his ears, so that in Manaus he worked as he played, enjoying every moment of it, priding himself on his luck in being part of this wonderful exciting hubbub, the dream come true of a boy from the Paraíban interior. Manaus, to be sure, was paying plenty of money so that Artur could have all these wonders within his grasp, so that he could eat *pâté*, go to the theatre, and keep in touch with Europe through the steamers which came to the electrified port to deposit their French girls and French wines, their Italian paintings and *objets d'art*, their British biscuits and fashionable clothing, in exchange for cargoes of rubber.[2] But it was paying him well also; his wages were from 3,000 to 4,000 *milreis* per month, a fabulous sum

[2] Unfortunately, one of those outgoing cargoes contained surreptitiously smuggled seedlings of rubber trees which, planted in Asian colonies by the astute British, ended once and for all the economic splendor of Amazonas.

for a northeastern farm boy, vastly superior to that paid at the time to an old and distinguished federal judge in his home state.

Encouraged by his success in the Amazon, Artur, under the influence of his Protestant training, soon sought to conquer another world: the United States. Manaus had given him the opportunity and the leisure to invent certain improvements in the Merganthaler press which he tried, without success, to sell in New York. This adventure ended with his obtaining a modest but respectable job as translator of movie subtitles, but without diminishing his ardor to patent some new invention. He believed the machine to be "the only really new element in the so-called Western civilization" and saw in it the way to bring the world to a peaceful collectivism without shedding the blood of a Marxist revolution. "The machine is a true manifestation of human intelligence; we must dedicate ourselves to its mission of redemption through human effort." Mixing his youthful religious training with the new mystique of the Machine learned in Manaus, he asks in 1940: "What were the first inventions, what were any inventions or discoveries, if not revelations of a great truth? . . . Every machine has a mission of redemption: to enable man to produce at a maximum with a minimum of effort . . . a socializing mission which will be carried out through the machine." This evangelical mission must have had its origin in "an aching muscle. . . . Physical force produces pain. . . ." Words he must have heard from old Negroes, perhaps former slaves of the small Coelho sugar plantation at Melancia in the interior of Paraíba, words that sprang from the pain of dreary labor of planting cane and extracting sugar with archaic horse-powered—or slave powered—machinery.

The Amazon experience of João d'Albuquerque Maranhão, another native of the agrarian northeast, where he was born in 1883, differed somewhat from that of Artur Coelho. João recalls that when he was a pupil at the Colégio Pestalozzi in Recife there was a terrible outbreak of bubonic plague that claimed hundreds of victims. The schools were closed. Doctors died, infected through contact with the afflicted. A pest house was set up on the island of Pina. It was at this time that João, whose brother Afonso was a judge in Manaus, left for the Amazon. The idea was for him to continue his college preparatory study in Manaus while acting as clerk in the police department. The police chief at that time was Estevão de Sá Cavalcanti de Albuquerque, a Pernambucan politician who had fled from his native state "in order not to be assassinated by the government of Alexandre José Barbosa Lima." [3] During an election campaign when Estevão de Sá was running for mayor of Recife, one of his supporters, José Maria de Albuquerque Melo, had been murdered by a police officer of the same Barbosa, and Estevão, feeling that his turn would be next, had departed for Amazonas.

Once in Amazonas, João d'Albuquerque Maranhão marveled at the technical superiority of the region in comparison to that of his native Pernambuco. "The people of Amazonas traveled a great deal in Europe during the first decade of the present century," he recalls. "It was the height of the rubber boom and we were virtually the only source of this material for the world market. This fact was reflected in the oriental luxury displayed by the rubber barons in their vacation trips to the European beaches and in their custom of sending their children to the most fashionable schools of London and Paris. I married an Amazonas girl who had been educated in Lisbon and who had uncles and cousins resident in Paris. In Manaus, we subscribed to French magazines and heard operas sung by artists of the Paris Opera."

The first decade of the present century in Manaus was, if anything, even more splendid than that of the 1890's and contrasted violently with the tropical landscape which formed a setting for this artificial capital city—as artificial as a set of solid gold teeth on a bushman still prepared to eat raw snake, if not human flesh itself. João d'Albuquerque remembers having applauded D'Angeville, Armel, and Ricordeau of the Comédie Française, as well as Ângela Pinto, Lucinda Simões, Dolores Rentini, Chabi Pinheiro, Cristiano de Sousa, and the maestro Nicolino Milano. In 1899 the Amazonas Theatre had presented Giovanni Emanuel, an Italian tragedian famous for his performances of Shakespeare.

On a less imposing scale, the economic vitality of Manaus and of the Amazon region was manifested by elegant shops like the Bijou

[3] Alexandre José Barbosa Lima at the time was a young politician whose newly acquired powers had somewhat gone to his head. In spite of his violence, however, he turned out to be an efficient and progressive administrator. Liberal in many of his ideas, he nevertheless believed, possibly under the influence of Comte, that one should not employ democratic processes in the solution of technical questions. Accordingly, he was the first republican governor to resume the tradition of such Pernambucan monarchists as the Baron da Boa Vista and the Baron de Lucena in employing foreign technicians to develop the material and cultural progress of the state.

Confectionary, which rivalled that of Pascoal in Rio de Janeiro, and the Café Itatiaia, owned by another Pernambucan named Fausto Pôrto, son of a well-known abolitionist, Dona Leonor Pôrto. Like Estêvão de Sá, Pôrto had also come to Amazonas to escape the violence of Alexandre Barbosa Lima. It seems that his mother, Dona Leonor, had claimed the body of José Maria de Albuquerque after the assassination. As a result, young Pôrto had felt his popularity with the local government to be limited and had left to seek his fortune in Manaus, an ideal spot for a youth of liberal tendencies, particularly since the chief of police there shared similar political views.

All in all, Manaus represented a reaction to the routine nature of the rest of Brazil, a reaction made easy by its geographical and cultural distance from Rio de Janeiro and by its huge influx of foreign adventurers, particularly French, Spanish, and American. The area had also attracted Brazilians impatient with the economic and cultural inertia of their own areas and anxious for adventure in a region which promised quick profits. These men, if not exactly Bohemians, were nonconformists of somewhat less than conventional views, a band of fallen angels in rebellion against the moral, social, and economic inertia of Brazil. They were men like Carlos Dias Fernandes, who had been guilty of pecadillos against the Treasury; or Euclydes da Cunha, Alberto Rangel, João Barreto de Meneses, Efigênio Sales, Gonçalves Maia, Quintino Cunha, Aníbal Teófilo, to name only a few of the most renowned. Not all of these had mongrel backgrounds like that of Euclydes da Cunha; some came from excellent families, as in the case of Carlos Dias Fernandes, a member of one of the most civilized, Europeanized, aristocratic families in the country. One of the sons of the Baron de Contendas was also attracted to the Amazon, where he made a mixed marriage and brought up a *mestiço* family. Augusto Galvão preferred Amazonas as the place to make a career in law, Gaspar Guimarães became a federal judge there. All these were men of aristocratic bearing and origin.

Many of the new arrivals lived in "republics" as though they were still students. Manaus did not possess a hotel or boardinghouse to equal the grandeur of its theatre, a fact which throws some light on the nature of the Amazonian idea of progress, or, for that matter, of that of some of the other Brazilian cities which prided themselves on their modernity. (Rio, Belém, and São Paulo also possessed theatres which rivalled that of Manaus in the sumptuousness of their facades and the golden luxury of their appointments, but none could boast of a hotel of any quality.) At any rate, in Manaus, the bachelors, such as Euclydes da Cunha, Firmo Dutra, and Alberto Rangel, lived in "republics"; the married men sought private houses, none of which was noted for comfort or luxury.

"In Manaus there was never a luxury hotel, largely because this was not a city of transients," writes João d'Albuquerque Maranhão, somewhat apologetically. But the apology would have been more in order had other supposedly modern Brazilian cities been able to boast of such accommodations to go along with their pompous theatres, government palaces, and railway stations, their advanced docks and port facilities, and their handsome boulevards.

It appears that in Brazil, unlike the United States and Argentina, the hotel did not develop as a species of cathedral, a symbol of the new cult of progress. In this country the private residence continued to act as a hostelry for travelers who came with the recommendations of mutual friends or members of the family. Also, there were boardinghouses, comfortable if not modern, which were run more or less as patriarchal establishments offering elegant guest facilities. For a long time, one of the best boardinghouses in Recife was run by the Baroness de Landy, and the so-called "International Hotel" was a similar enterprise in the even more aristocratic home of a German baroness in the Madalena quarter. In a book entitled *Equatorial America (Descriptive of a Visit to St. Thomas, Martinique, Barbados and the Principal Capitals of South America)*, the American Maturin M. Ballou tells of the hospitality afforded by the latter, with its beautiful fruit trees surrounding the house, and gardens enlivened by lively and amusing monkeys and a number of caged parrots. Excellent French meals were served outdoors in surroundings rich with tropical flowers. The servants were well trained and came from the region. The house itself had once been the home of a wealthy landholder who after abolition had been forced to sell it for a fifth of its cost. In becoming a hotel, it had somehow preserved its original atmosphere of patriarchal nobility.[4]

It was with the agreeable impression left by this aristocratic Recife boardinghouse that Mr. Ballou came to Rio de Janeiro, and it was there that he reached a rueful conclusion. In 1890 the Brazilian capital had more than half a million inhabitants and boasted

[4] Maturin M. Ballou: *Equatorial America* (New York, 1892), pp. 132–3.

many of the characteristics of a first-class American city, with one notable exception: there was no good hotel. "There is not a really good and comfortable public house in all Brazil," he wrote. The best he could find was Whytes, in Tijuca, which was more boardinghouse than hotel.

The fact is that Rio de Janeiro, like other important Brazilian cities, was actually an immature urban expression of a predominantly rural economy, and its imposing public buildings and private houses testified to the fact that even in cities the society was essentially patriarchal in nature. As late as 1890, many of the commercial establishments maintained rooms on their upper floors for the convenience of important customers coming in from the interior. These firms also followed the patriarchal custom of providing rooms in the rear of the upper floors for their employees and of serving them ample daily lunches presided over by the head of the firm. Mr. Ballou noted in Rio that this Luso-Brazilian custom of housing employees on the premises had spread to British and French establishments as well,[5] but the practice of the communal lunch for proprietors, clerks, and out-of-town customers seems to have been confined to Brazilian firms.

Another source of hospitality at the time was the monastery, where visitors and even students could often obtain room and board. Some of the monasteries of Rio de Janeiro had ceased to be religious establishment and had been turned into public libraries, schools, military barracks, and even customshouses. The transference from a religious to an economic or political function seemingly did not affect the dignified appearance of these buildings or their basic comfort. Adapted to the tropical climate, they were of ample, even monumental, proportions and flexible in their interior construction. No wonder many eminent Brazilians—Counselor Ferreira Viana, for one—preferred them as places for rest and study, and that they could be adapted so easily to these varied purposes.

In the last decades of the Empire the hotels, though not modern in architecture or appointments, began to function as gathering places for business and professional men, serving lunches which were often very luxurious. Richly decorated—in a style that was soon adopted in many private homes—these hotels acted as clubs where members of the commercial or political élite could transact

[5] Ibid., p. 169.

business or discuss books, the theatre, music, political affairs, or
women over a bowl of delicious soup or a dish of exotically fla-
vored ice cream, *pitanga*, *cajú*, *cajá*, from Francioni's, the "largest
importer of ice in Brazil." It was to Francioni too that Brazil owes
another combination of European civilization and tropical climate:
the outdoor ice-cream parlor. This innovation was first seen at the
Hotel do Norte during the early days of the reign of Pedro II,
and the novelty soon spread to all parts of the country.[6] In the most
tropical cities, such as Manaus and Belém, these outdoor cafés, with
their enormous shady trees and their exotic ices and fruit drinks,
became famous. There, at a certain hour, one could always encounter the important men of the region in deep discussion over the
price of rubber—or of French girls—perhaps with a bottle of Ten-
nent's beer or Dewar's whiskey to accompany their refreshments.
Half-Anglicized in their taste for whiskey and imported foods from
Percy Vaughan's, "specialist in canned goods and fine beverages,"
these northern potentates still dressed in a local style impossible to
carry off in the south, with Panama hats, white rubber-soled shoes,
and immaculate Indian-made jackets. The outdoor cafés of Rio de
Janeiro, presented a very different picture. There the business
moguls and politicians affected an almost priestly dignity in their
black Prince Alberts and high toppers. After 1875 their favorite
haunt was the Hotel Globo, successor in some ways to the establishment of Francioni. Celebrated for its cuisine and banquet hall,
the Globo served mouth-watering meals that were a privilege to
enjoy. During the market speculation fever of the 1890's, this aristocratic hotel was the scene of "Sardanapalan banquets," washed
down "with costly wines and Champagne Clicquot." Along with
the Brazilians these were important European industrialists and
businessmen, to whom perhaps we can trace the popularity of ver-
mouth, whiskey, the cocktail, the gin fizz, the pick-me-up, and the
sherry cobbler, elegant imports which took their place alongside
the traditional port and champagne for snob appeal.[7] There was
also the draft beer, which appealed less to the princes of power then
to the Bohemian coterie of journalists and literary men, as well as to
clerks, students, or foreigners whose daring in defying the fashion
and dressing in tropical white extended to an equally daring preference for cold light beer. Attempting to attract these foreigners, the

[6] Ernesto Senna: *O Velho Comércio do Rio de Janeiro* (Rio de Janeiro–Paris,
n.d.), pp. 99, 100.
[7] Ibid., pp. 108, 109.

Hotel Globo ran its advertisements in French: "*Ce magnifique res-taurant offre aux étrangers arrivant à Rio, toutes les commodités pour Lunch, Dîners, etc.*" including "*cabinets particuliers pour familles, splendide buvette au rez-de-chaussée, boissons glacées*" (private booths for families, a splendid bar serving cold drinks on the ground floor).[8] One of the novelties of the period was the Prana Sparklet Siphon, which yielded charged water said to be equal in therapeutic value to that of Vichy, Carlsbad, or Seltz. The concession for this supposed marvel was held in Rio de Janeiro by Louis Hermanny & Co., and it is no exaggeration that the vogue for mineral waters in fact contributed to the decline among the middle classes of such diseases as dysentery and typhoid fever.

The rococo interior decorations of these fashionable hotels, par-ticularly the huge mirrors, were soon imitated in the homes of the newly rich. Rather bewildered as to what to do with their recently acquired affluence, these latter-day aristocrats engaged foreign dec-orators and through them attempted to acquire all the trappings of culture and gracious living as swiftly as they had acquired their fortunes. One such was the Count of Leopoldina; another was Del-miro Gouveia, who rose almost overnight from suburban station agent to great industrialist, and who celebrated his rise by installing a marble bathroom of Imperial grandeur in his old house in the outskirts of Recife and lyrically christening the modernized resi-dence with his wife's name: Villa Anunciada. Other obscure Brazil-ians became suddenly powerful when appointed by Floriano Peixoto to important offices in the new Republic. Still others were invested with instant culture, as was the case with several relatives of the Baron de Lucena, *éminence grise* of the *Generalíssimo*. These worthies, to the surprise of everyone including themselves, were made masters of science and given university appointments which they had never contemplated in their wildest dreams.

Under the Republic, then, the rococo style was not confined to mere decoration; it became a psychological state and a way of life which characterized the new era. For most Brazilians, accustomed to the economy of the old regime, this new opulence seemed little short of scandalous. Almost until the end of the Empire, the na-tional economic policy had been one of orthodox moderation in areas outside agriculture, with little speculation and an almost total absence of grandiose commercial or industrial schemes. With aboli-

8 *Almanaque da Gazeta de Notícias para 1887* (Rio de Janeiro, 1887), p. 128.

tion, however, this slow pace, to the horror of conservatives, was radically altered in a surge of industrial development that gained the favor of even so highly placed an official as the Viscount de Ouro Prêto, the last Imperial Prime Minister.[9] The sudden boom was deceptive, however, despite the strength of the national currency and the vastly increased volume of trade between May, 1888 and November, 1889 which apparently refuted the theory that abolition would upset the entire Brazilian economy and not merely the agrarian interests. It was not long before this appearance of strength degenerated into a fever of speculation—the *Encilhamento*—the likes of which Brazil had never before experienced. And it was from this unhealthy situation that the new élite arose— the urban bankers, industrialists, and businessmen who gathered to sip champagne in the salons of the Hotel Globo and to glory in their newly acquired ascendancy over an older order they referred to disdainfully as the "slavocracy."

Thus the Globo can be seen almost as a symbol of the new order: grandiose in appearance without being a really good hotel; shabby bedrooms and inadequate bath facilities, but salons of the greatest possible luxury where the new magnates could satisfy their narcissism by examining themselves in full-length mirrors (framed patriotically by gilded motifs representing pineapples and other national fruits) while sipping their *apéritifs* of gin or champagne.

Certainly the Hotel Globo attracted persons of all shades of political and economic opinion. It was there that João Alfredo, a political conservative but radical abolitionist, told a banquet audience that "the Conservative Party must, can, and is willing to settle the slavery question." And it was there that the Baron de Cotegipe, a slaveholder of the old order who never would have shared João Alfredo's sentiments, used to go when the occasion promised an encounter with one of the elegant French ladies or fashionable *cocottes* for which he had a notorious weakness. And it is quite possible that on such occasions he found himself dining near such avid republicans as Francisco Glycério, Quintino Bocayuva, or Aristedes Lobo who, spurning the traditional conspiratorial tavern, used to meet at the Globo during the last days of the Empire to discuss preparations for the coming new order.[1] Other frequenters of the Globo at this time were José Bonifácio the Younger, Martim

---

[9] See *A Década Republicana* (Rio de Janeiro, 1899–1901).

[1] Prominent republican figures of the period. (Translator.)

Francisco, José Mariano (the same José Mariano who in his native province could often be seen eating *sarapatel* at some sidewalk lunch counter with persons of dubious occupation, some of whom were his bodyguards), and, occasionally, the Baron de Tôrres Homem, who continued the traditions of Pedro II and the days of Francioni by always having ice cream for dessert.[2]

After the coming of the Republic, the Globo also attracted another former aristocrat who distinguished himself in the service of the Republic: José Maria da Silva Paranhos, Baron do Rio Branco. His companions would sometimes be South American diplomats like Fernando Guachalla or Cláudio Pinilla, sometimes native figures like Euclydes or Gastão da Cunha, or Assis Brasil. It was an ideal restaurant for this statesman, who in his old age seems to have replaced his youthful passion for women with the sensual passions of the table. Another distinguished figure of the Brazilian foreign service who found the Globo an ideal spot for encounters with colleagues and national leaders was Salvador de Mendonça, one-time Ambassador to the United States, where he concluded an economic pact with his host country widely criticized by Brazilian republicans as being detrimental to their country's interests.

The Globo also was suited to foreign businessmen, and it is not unlikely that its private dining rooms were a frequent setting for intimate dinners of French roast beef, *feijoada Brasileira*, or *peixada à baiana*. But these glorious days, enhanced by the excesses of the *Encilhamento*, were doomed to oblivion after the turn of the century. When the vertiginous boom of the nineties had expended itself, the hotel sank into decadence, its elegant salon shabby, its paintings blackened with mold, its famous mirrors covered with leprous spots, in whose dulled and lusterless surfaces survivors of the great days "could see reflected the passage of their glory."[3]

The Globo had its successors: the Hotel dos Estrangeiros, the Internacional, the Avenida; the ground floor of the last housed the famous Brahma Restaurant, to which the Baron do Rio Branco transferred his allegiance during the final days of his *gloutonnerie*. The Brahma also attracted the Cearense historian and ethnologist Capistrano de Abreu, noted for his almost Germanic devotion to draft beer. It replaced the Globo as the rendezvous of the great in all walks of life, particularly in the fields of commerce and industry

2 Senna: op. cit., pp. 108, 118.
3 Senna: op. cit., p. 122.

which by now were enjoying the prestige and sharing the powers formerly the prerogatives of the landholders, the professionals, and the military.

"The best hotel in those days was the Estrangeiros," says Antenor Nascentes (b. Rio de Janeiro, 1886), an opinion shared by several other witnesses, although the Avenida also had its supporters. In São Paulo, the principal hostelries mentioned were the Grande and the Hotel d'Oeste, while in Pôrto Alegre it was the Brasil, considered by one enthusiast equal to the Estrangeiros of Rio de Janeiro, although its supremacy in the southern capital was challenged in 1908 by the opening of the Grande.

To return to the Amazon, another early adventurer was João Barreto de Meneses (b. Pernambuco, 1872), who also went to the area as a young man after a period of service in the Army, during which he served in the "Revolution" of September, 1893, and in Canudos. Though cited for bravery and slated for promotion to officer's rank, he decided that there was something incongruous in a man of his "ardent liberal temperament" wearing a uniform which, "however glamorous, nevertheless denotes the idea of force, always the enemy of ideas." As a result, he resigned and "sought other fields to conquer." And for a Brazilian of his type, what field more seductive than the Amazon territory? There he could start a business or industry and eventually return to his native state to live like a nabob. Unfortuntely, he never succeeded in advancing beyond the position of department head in the office of the Secretary of State, after having begun as a modest police clerk. Despite the abundant opportunities in Manaus for all sorts of initiative and speculative daring, the "ardent liberal temperament" of Tobias Barreto's son somehow never managed to adapt to the dreary and utterly nonliberal life of a police department bureaucrat. Probably this was the result of his independent attitude which, he says, he received as a birthright from his famous father.

His exuberant temperament found an outlet, however, in his participation in the so-called "Acre Revolution." João Barreto de Meneses served in the "assault on the fortress of Pôrto Alonso, held by the Bolivians, who still exercised control over the territory." This assault was "before the time of the influential action of Placido de Castro" and resulted in "the expenditure of several thousand cartridges, the use of one cannon and one machine gun, and the loss of a few companions. Obliged to retreat, we nevertheless learned later that, in addition to inflicting material damage, we had also killed a company commander and wounded a high-ranking officer. Among my unforgettable companions in this expedition were my fellow Pernambucans Trajano Chacon and Samuel Rios, as well as Efigênio Sales, who later became a federal deputy and governor of Amazonas."

We know from the geographer Elliott that the Acre Territory was thickly sown with rubber trees. It was in tropical lands such as these of the Amazon Basin that the *Hevea negra* could produce the strongest rubber, in contrast to the product of the "white" variety, which was weak, and the red, which coagulated badly. Elliott says it was the seedling of the white variety which Wickham had smuggled out of the Tapajós in 1876 for development in the Orient. Inferior in quality to the black rubber of Amazonas, this oriental rubber was nevertheless developed so systematically by the British as to reduce the superior Brazilian variety to economic insignificance.[4]

The hero—or, from the Brazilian viewpoint, villain—of this economic rape was Henry Alexander Wickham. Wickham was a sort of precursor of Lawrence of Arabia, an agent for the development of British interests in tropical areas. His first visit to the Amazon was as a scientist interested in the tropical forest, and especially in the rubber tree, which he saw growing in great abundance along the Amazon, the Orinoco, and the Rio Negro. The result of this first difficult expedition was his *Rough Notes of a Journey Through the Wilderness*, published in London in 1872.

In 1876, Wickham returned to Brazil. This time, he went up the Tapajós from Santarém and in the course of his expedition collected some 70,000 seeds of *Hevea brasiliensis*, which he transported in a multitude of boxes to Kew Gardens in London. There the seeds were successfully germinated in greenhouses and the resulting sprouts transported with loving care to Ceylon, Java, Burma, and Singapore. Two thousand were planted in Ceylon alone, and by 1881 they had begun to flourish. It was a signal victory of scientific technique over the nonchalance which characterized Brazilian practices in exploiting its vast riches in latex; practices that were without method, without planning, carried on merely as an insensitive and insane adventure.[5]

Elliott states that when the first news of Wickham's triumph in

[4] L. E. Elliott: *Brazil, Today and Tomorrow* (New York, 1917), p. 194.
[5] The whole adventure is treated in an excellent study by C. E. Akers: *The Rubber Industry in Brazil and the Orient* (London, 1914).

Ceylon reached Brazil, nobody would believe that the Amazonian rubber industry could be duplicated in the Orient. Nevertheless, legislation was effected, and in a law of almost Byzantine complications, the exportation of rubber seeds was prohibited, along with the exportation of the ouricuri nuts used in smoking the latex. Too late. British astuteness had dealt a death blow to the Amazon economy.[6]

By the turn of the century, the effect of the Anglo-Oriental competition began to be felt. The 4 tons of crude rubber produced by the East in 1900 became 145 in 1905; 8,000 in 1910; 28,000 in 1912; 71,000 in 1914; nearly 107,000 in 1915; and about 150,000 in 1916. All this from a systematically ordered plantation of 1,350,000 acres scattered throughout Ceylon, Malaysia, India, Borneo, and the Dutch East Indies.[7]

Even so, until 1910 there was great reluctance on the part of large buyers to replace black Amazon rubber with the new plantation product of the East. They were accustomed to working with the Brazilian product and, besides, it was considerably superior in quality. Apparently only the excessive cost of Amazon rubber, together with the larger margin of profit insisted on by its producers, forced manufacturers to turn to the plantation variety. An increasing variety of products—from tires to the most delicate articles of medical prophylaxis—were using rubber as a basic element, but instead of being beneficial to Brazil, this increasing industrial use favored lower-priced British and Dutch competition. Brazilians could take some satisfaction, of course, in the fact that on the New York market "fine hard Pará" was selling at 75 cents a pound while oriental rubber brought only 65 cents. But this tribute to quality was of little value in the face of the greater quantities and smaller markup of the Eastern merchants.

[6] Elliott: op. cit., p. 189. Also see Akers: op. cit.

[7] See *Documentos Parlamentares, Política Econômica. Valorização do Café (1896–1906)* (Rio de Janeiro, 1915), particularly the parliamentary report of the representative from Rio Grande do Norte, Elói de Sousa. This report was later published under the title *A Crise da Borracha (The Rubber Crisis)* (Rio de Janeiro, 1913). See also J. C. Macedo Soares: *A Borracha—Estudo Econômico e Estatístico* (Paris, 1927); C. E. Akers: *Relatório sôbre o Vale do Amazonas* (Rio de Janeiro, 1913); *Rubber Production in the Amazon Valley* (Publication No. 23, United States Department of Commerce, Washington, D.C., 1925); José Jobim: *História das Indústrias no Brasil* (Rio de Janeiro, 1940); Artur E. M. Tôrres: *Expansão Econômica do Brasil* (Rio de Janeiro, 1935); Durval Bastos de Meneses: *À Margem da Borracha* (Rio de Janeiro, 1943); and Willard Price: *The Amazing Amazon* (New York, 1950).

The story is lucidly told from a Brazilian point of view by Elói de Sousa in his *A Crise da Borracha* (*The Rubber Crisis*), published in Rio de Janeiro in 1913. For Elliott "there is perhaps no better presentation of the subject" than that of the then federal deputy from Rio Grande do Norte. Elliott agreed with the Brazilian parliamentarian in considering the Amazon rubber industry an "economic paradox" which created millions in wealth without employing even the smallest portion of this affluence to achieve systematic improvements in the region itself. Not even in establishing a good hotel, he adds ruefully.

Nevertheless, it was during this period that construction was begun on the Madeira-Mamoré railroad, a project which in its early stages cost many lives. Also at this time attempts at urban improvements were being made in Manaus and Belém, those of the latter, under the leadership of Mayor Antônio Lemos, being particularly important. Both the construction of the railroad and the improvements carried out in northern cities had their effect on the Brazilian scene as a whole. Osvaldo Cruz, called to the Amazon during the construction of the railroad, produced a notable report establishing the need for general prophylaxia against hookworm, dysentery, beriberi, and the tropical pneumonia brought about by sudden changes in temperature. In addition to his recommendations for the control of these standard tropical diseases, he also advocated an agricultural program which would give the region the fresh vegetables needed to form a balanced and healthful diet. With all the opulent growth of *Hevea brasiliensis*, the region passed through the entire rubber boom without ever attempting to grow the food products necessary to human health. In 1915, Pará, Amazonas, and Acre were still importing beans, rice, sugar, dried beef, salt cod, animals for slaughter, and canned goods in such quantities and at such fantastically high prices that one would have thought the region utterly barren and totally incapable of producing for its own needs.

At the same time it became apparent that the exploitation of rubber was being realized in some places only through the often cruel oppression of the native population. It is shameful to have to note, in all objectivity, that during this period when so many men of "ardent liberal temperament" were seduced by the romance of the Amazon, not one showed the daring to penetrate the tropical forest and observe the drama of the rubber plantations in all its minutiae as Euclydes da Cunha had done in the case of the Brazilian backlands.

Such an observer could have presented a most interesting documentation of the exploitation of native labor on the part of profit-hungry whites and given a definitive account of the terrible struggle to construct the Madeira-Mamoré railroad. But except for Euclydes himself, or Firmo Dutra, Albert Rangel, or a few writers of the days before the rubber boom such as Inglês de Sousa (*O Missionário*) or José Veríssimo (*A Pesca na Amazônia*), none among those migrant Brazilians had the literary talent to write even a pamphlet or a brief journalistic account of the sufferings of the native population.

To awaken European sensibilities to this situation (which was common to the entire Amazon Basin and was not exclusively Brazilian), it was necessary for a romantic Irishman, Her Britannic Majesty's Consul in Rio de Janeiro, to produce a vigorous report in English, a report which, while vehement, was also well documented after careful research in the area. His name was Roger Casement, and he revealed himself as one of those rare Europeans who could summon up the courage to denounce the cruelties perpetrated by a so-called "civilized" society against those generally designated as "savages." His book on the situation in Brazil and Peru takes its place alongside *Os Sertões* of Euclydes or *Canaã* of Graça Aranha as a critical account of a major ethno-cultural conflict. True, the work was that of a European diplomat in the service of his country and not of an Indo-Latin writer closer to the subject and having more freedom of expression; but it was the first of its kind.[8]

It is a pity that Euclydes da Cunha had not anticipated Sir Roger by writing an Amazonian equivalent of *Os Sertões*, thereby registering some species of Brazilian concern for the drama—one might even say tragedy—which was being played out in the region.

Despite the temporary prestige it afforded the Brazilian economy, the rubber boom did not begin to be as important, either economically or culturally, as those in sugar and coffee. Nevertheless, it served for a time to awaken national awareness of the extreme north and to bring about a vogue of Amazonisms of all kinds. Visitors to the region brought back a taste for such delicacies as duck with *tucupi* sauce, turtle soup, Brazil nuts, *açai, guaraná, copuaçu,*

[8] Unfortunately Casement soon afterward became a notorious traitor to the government he was serving on this occasion. Convicted of an act of espionage in favor of the German Empire, he was condemned to death and executed by the British government.

puxuri, ground-cherry roots; for a huge variety of aromatic, medicinal, aphrodisiac, prophylactic, or decorative plants; and for exotic woods from Pará, for Indian hammocks, and Panama hats (which Brazilians call *chapéus de Chile* or Chilean hats). The Panama hat became extremely popular at the time with Brazilians anxious to add a native touch to their European elegance; it made a happy combination with the English frock coat, the high-laced American shoes, and the Doucet silk ties currently sported by the fashionable male. Pinheiro Machado, a *gaúcho* as famous for his elegance as for his image as virile and romantic leader, made the white Panama almost liturgically *de rigueur* for use on horseback, and no landholder or public figure would have been without one. They also made the most appreciated gifts, and the best ones were so light and fine they could be placed in a tissue-paper envelope. Women from the north were brought to various parts of the country to teach the fine art of weaving this delicate headwear, but their efforts were in vain: the fabrication of a Panama hat proved to be a profoundly ecological process, unteachable to those outside the tradition.

White English-type jackets from Pará also became fashionable at the time and were sold in all parts of the country, as were the famous Brazil nuts (*castanhas de Pará*), canned sweetmeats made of tropical fruits, and even tame snakes for household use as rat catchers. At the same time there was a boom in northern medicinal herbs, and the newspapers would be filled with advertisements such as these from the Rio de Janeiro *Tayupira* of 1909: "Brazilian vegetable tonic, a pure vegetable product for syphilis and skin diseases. Contains the active ingredients of the most precious purifying plants to be found in the majesty and abundance of Brazilian floriculture." These plants bore such exotic names as *azogue-dos-pobres, velame-do-campo, sucupira, manacá*, and *junca*. The manufacturer of this magic elixir was Silva Araújo & Co., who had to compete with such foreign products, also advertised in the *Tayupira*, as "Pilules Cronier, L'Iodure de Fer et de Quinine," or "Dr. Churchill's Lime Phosphate Syrup for tuberculosis, anemia, neurasthenia, rickets, cough, bronchitis, and general weakness," to "Quina-Laroche, for stomach diseases, fever, lack of strength." [9] Of the Amazonian *guaraná*, Luís Pereira Barreto states: "Metchnikoff

[9] *Almanaque Brasileiro Garnier* (Rio de Janeiro, 1909). See also *Relatório do Delegado Engenheiro João Alberto Massô sôbre o Guaraná e Suas Propriedades* (Rio de Janeiro, 1912), p. 10.

knew *guaraná* only as a useful remedy for infant diarrhea." Had the Russian scientist, celebrated for his studies of old age, known of the full properties of the plant he would have recommended it instead of yogurt as a means of preserving and prolonging life. "If you are wise, you'll follow my advice and adopt the Indian method," concludes Barreto.

All in all, then, a vast number of Bahians and northeasterners left home to seek their fortunes in other parts of the country, some marrying into the white aristocracy, others taking wives of African or Indian blood, and nearly all managing to improve their economic condition through success in business or the professions. Some learned from their contact with foreigners. João d'Albuquerque Maranhão (whose youthful Amazon adventure has already been described) recalls his later days in Rio Grande do Sul, where "I had the opportunity to see the superior effectiveness in commerce and industry of Brazilians of German or Italian origin. They knew how to read, write, live and eat properly, and many of them had training in economics." This was in sharp contrast to what he had seen in the north, particularly on one trip to the territory of Acre near the Peruvian border: "It was almost a desert, although there were signs of incipient life in Sena Madureira, a town founded by Siqueira de Meneses and already possessing mail, telegraph, and streetcar services, as well as newspapers, clubs, and a theatre." He spent three years on the border, where he had been sent by Pandiá Calógeras to set up a customs agency at the mouth of the Santa Rosa River. "I managed to put up with the desert . . . Euclydes da Cunha had also been here when he headed a commission to determine the boundaries between Peru and Brazil resulting in the treaty of November, 1903. It was as a result of this that he wrote his famous *À Margem da História*. . . ." The treaty added "territory more extensive than that of any one of the states of Ceará, Rio Grande do Norte, Paraíba, Pernambuco, Alagoas, Sergipe, Espirito Santo, Rio de Janeiro, or Santa Catarina," and produced an annual income "greater than that of any one of half the states of the Union." It was during his stay in this newly acquired territory that João d'Albuquerque Maranhão made contract with the semicivilized tribes of Colina and Tucarina, members of whom "visited me to obtain articles of domestic use in return for *xerimbabos*, a species of tamed jungle animal. These Indians were peaceful by nature and would come often to gather turtle eggs from the shores of the Purus River." But apparently neither they nor the civilized whites of the extreme north had the "training in economics" which caused the Germans and Italians of the south to play such a dynamic role in the modernization of the national economy.

To return to the more progressive south of João d'Albuquerque Maranhão's post-Amazon days, the year 1915 marked a signal victory for one of Rio Grande do Sul's most traditional industries, an industry which far preceded the wave of German and Italian immigration and had existed, in fact, as long as Brazil was Brazil. This was, of course, the raising of beef cattle. From the earliest times, Brazilians had considered dried beef a staple of their everyday diet and an indispensable ingredient to the national dish, the *feijoada*. But it still seemed fantastic to most Brazilians when in 1915 the French government ordered large quantities of this commodity for their armies engaged in the First World War. The order came only one year after the Brazilian meat-packing industry began to adopt modern practices with the installation in São Paulo of the country's first meat refrigeration plant. From this time on, Brazilian meat products, both dried and frozen, began to assume importance in the European market, and there were some who saw in this development a possible compensation for the disaster which had overtaken *Hevea brasiliensis*. In 1916, the encouraging total of 29,000 tons of frozen meat was exported, with an equally encouraging rise in the sale of dried beef from the south and northeast. To make the picture still happier, the industry was created, not by foreign capital, but entirely by Brazilian initiative, as in the case of the Companhia Frigorífico e Pastoril de São Paulo, presided over by a genuine Paulista of Indian blood, Antônio da Silva Prado. In November, 1914 this company, as an experiment, shipped the first ton of frozen beef from Brazil to England. The attempt was a success and was followed by a second shipment of 4,360 tons, a third of over 2,000 to Italy, and a fourth of about the same size to the United States. Encouraged by this Brazilian success, the Chicago firm of Sulzberger, in conjunction with the Brazilian Farquhar group, installed a new refrigerating plant in Osasco, a suburb of São Paulo.[1]

At the same time, Brazilian experiments with Pará grass established a better type of forage for tropical beef cattle. In this case it was not Texan or Argentinian experience which was called in, but rather a Brazilian continuation of the Portuguese method of learn-

[1] Elliott: op. cit., pp. 209–10, 211.

ing from the tropical population how best to adapt to local conditions. It was in this same spirit that similar experiments were made in cattle breeding, particularly in the crossing of the Indian Nellore breed with local stock to create a mixed type, in the form of the zebu, highly adaptable to tropical Brazil. These experiments, which were particularly successful in Minas Gerais and had much to do with making the Mineiro Triangle one of the most important regions in the Brazilian economy, were also very significant in encouraging a regional approach to Brazilian economic problems. Though it was possible to import European breeds of cattle—Devon, Hereford, Flamengo, Durham, Jersey—for Paraná and Rio Grande do Sul, it was beginning to be understood that for the warmer parts of the country a stronger type of animal was needed, one which could resist not only the intensely tropical climate, but also the insect pests and diseases peculiar to such regions. For this reason Brazilians, disregarding the warnings of American experts, developed the *caracu* breed and proved, in the words of one English writer, that specifically Brazilian problems in cattle raising were "not to be solved by applying [the] experience of Texas or Argentina." [2]

Another routine aspect of the cattle industry during this period was the exportation of hides to the United States. This activity made a fortune for the young Delmiro Gouveia, who later carried his industrial daring, as we shall see, into a vast project of regional rehabilitation by harnessing the energy created by the cataracts of Paula Afonso.

At this time, Brazil also began to gain prestige in foreign cotton markets, although the products of the northeast, such as the Mocó of Ceará and Paraíba and the Seridó of Rio Grande do Norte, still lacked the standardization necessary for effective competition with cotton from other nations. Brazilian textiles were also developing and formed an outlet for the cotton produced in Pernambuco and Paraíba.

Still another developing industry was that of *maté* (Paraguay tea), thanks to the energetic efforts made throughout the country by one of the sons of Silva Jardim. So great was the increase in Brazilian consumption of this product that the powerful Companhia Maté Laranjeira of Mato Grosso was forced to discontinue

[2] J. O. P. Bland: *Men, Manners, and Morals in South America* (London, 1920), p. 85.

its exports to Argentina in order to supply the demands of the local market.

The production of cocoa, tobacco, corn, rice, and beans was not attended by the political, social, or cultural changes noted in the rubber, sugar, cotton, coffee, or beef cattle industries. Nevertheless these products, hard hit economically by the abolition of slavery, had to struggle for their economic existence under the new order. The sugar industry, on the other hand, was able to some degree to compensate for the loss of its foreign markets by developing the manufacture of sweet foods for national consumption. This development will be studied in greater detail in the next chapter. Here it is only necessary to emphasize that with the Republic the economic life of certain regions of Brazil continued to impinge strongly upon the fortunes—or misfortunes—of the sugar market, just as it had from the earliest days of the Empire, although the political influences exerted by this industry were somewhat lessened. Nevertheless, in the early days of the Republic, it was still necessary to maintain a political equilibrium between the coffee and sugar interests, an activity in which Captain-Doctor Alexandre José Barbosa Lima, governor of the state of Pernambuco, was particularly assiduous. Barbosa Lima, following the previous example of the Baron de Lucena, undertook to restore the prestige of sugar by an extensive modernization of the industry. The attempt was only partly successful, however, and the region never managed to regain even half its former eminence, when most of the political leaders of the early Empire had come from the cane fields of the north. The new order came from the south; by the last decades of the Empire, it was coffee that was king.

In 1870, on the eve of abolition, Brazil had exported 3 million sacks of coffee; by the end of the century, despite the shift from slave to free labor, this figure had risen to 10 million. It must be noted, however, that the change from Negro to free Italian labor could be effected only through the intervention of the state, which instituted an Agricultural Protective System (*Patronato Agrícola*, in Portuguese; note the preservation of the Imperial paternalistic principle in this designation) to guard the new laborers from the greed of their employers. This was perhaps the first instance under the Republic of the direct intervention on the part of a state in economic affairs of national importance. Through the Patronato Agrícola, the state attempted to end the *laissez faire* of the first disordered years of the Republic, when landholders were retaining all the vices, and none of the virtues, of the old paternalistic slave system.

State intervention was also a factor in the so-called "Valorization Plan," an attempt to systematize the resources of the nation, especially in the production of coffee. This plan was vehemently debated in all quarters, but was imitated in several other countries and, all in all, constituted one of Brazil's most notable contributions to world economic progress, having particularly distinguished itself, in the eyes of one foreign observer (Elliott), through "the merit of boldness." [3] By the terms of the Taubaté Agreement, Brazilian coffee producers were prohibited from selling their product for less than the fixed price and from exporting beans of any grade below 7. They were required to promote foreign sales by advertising abroad, to collect a surtax on every bag exported, and to limit production on their plantations. The surtax would remain in the hands of the federal government, where it would be used to amortize the cost of establishing the Emission and Conversion Bank, which handled the financial aspects of the plan. [4]

The full economic weight of this plan, one almost fantastically adventurous for its time, fell at first on the shoulders of the state of São Paulo, although later the federal government also took up its share of the burden. Abroad, financial support was obtained, not from French or Anglo-Saxon interests, which were too conservative to approve of state intervention in matters of this kind, but rather from the Germans who, through the Brasilianische Bank für Deutschland, furnished a preliminary loan of £1 million to the undertaking. It was only after obtaining the German funds that such firms as J. Henry Schroeder & Co. of London and, later, the National City Bank of New York were willing to subscribe the aditional £3 million necessary for acquiring and warehousing coffee under the terms of the plan. In 1907 the Brazilian federal government gave further support by buying up coffee of inferior grades and by obtaining from Rothschild of London an additional loan of £2 million for the redemption of coffee consigned to commissioners. This sum was later duplicated to enable the state of

[3] Elliott: op. cit., p. 71.

[4] See *Documentos Parlamentares, Política Econômica* . . . See also Francisco Ferreira Ramos: *La Question de la Valorisation du Café au Brésil* (Anvers, 1907); Amaro Cavalcanti: *A Vida Econômica e Financeira do Brasil* (Rio de Janeiro, 1915); and Afonso Costa: *Questões Econômicas* (Rio de Janeiro, 1918).

São Paulo to lease the Sorocabana Railway from the syndicate directed by the American promoter Percival Farquhar.[5]

It is necessary to emphasize that the coffee industry, which reached its peak of international importance during this period, was a completely Brazilian development, as had been the cultivation of sugar, cotton, *maté*, beef cattle, and—to a certain point—rubber. I stress this not out of simple patriotism, but rather the necessity to emphasize the capacity of the Brazilian for economic activities— agrarian, industrial, and commercial—both intra- and extra-political and despite the traditional mystique of the *fidalgo* (the belief that, in addition to landholding, the only occupations worthy of a gentleman of quality were those of judge, military officer, college professor, doctor, lawyer, or civil servant). Even after the formation of the Brazilian Warrant Company, predecessor of the São Paulo Pure Coffee Company, with headquarters in London and branches in Santos and Rio de Janeiro, a considerable majority of coffee exporters continued to be Brazilians. As Elliott put it: "Coffee is not one of the businesses which the South American leaves for the foreigner."[6] (The same could have been said of sugar.) And since coffee at this period constituted almost half the country's total export, it is easy to understand that the industry in all its phases—commercial as well as agricultural and industrial—attained considerable social prestige and that its promotion in other countries became an act of patriotism.

It was not only in promotion of coffee or rubber or *maté* that Brazil was making great publicity efforts at this time; there was also a good deal of propaganda of a patriotic nature being disseminated in Europe and the United States. The Baron do Rio Branco proved to be a master in the creation of the mystique of the Brazilian "genius," "culture," or "civilization," a mystique which was given

[5] Farquhar is an interesting figure who from the beginning of the twentieth century was deeply implicated in the economic progress of Brazil. Born in the United States of a respectable religious family, he became an ardent champion of Brazil, foreseeing a magnificent future for the country which grew to be more his own than the land of his birth. Other American enthusiasts from late Imperial times were the geologists John Casper Branner and Orville Derby. The latter, who became a naturalized Brazilian citizen, was a friend and collaborator of Euclydes da Cunha and worked on several volumes of Brazilian history and geography. After a life of great intellectual and economic value to Brazil, Derby committed suicide as the result of a scandal (caused by the ill-considered, perhaps merely jesting remarks of his superior officer, the powerful and illustrious but foul-mouthed Minister of Agriculture, José Bezerra).

[6] Elliott: op. cit., p. 179.

further credence by the impact of Ruy Barbosa at The Hague
Peace Conference in 1907. Or one could cite the country's attempt
to share in the great popularity attained in France by Alberto Santos
Dumont. And during the presidency of Rodrigues Alves, probably
under the guiding hand of Foreign Minister Rio Branco, there was
considerable *réclame* over the achievements of Osvaldo Cruz in the
fight against yellow fever, of Mayor Pereira Passos in the modernizing and beautification of the nation's capital, of Field Marshal
Hermes da Fonseca in the reorganization of the Army, and of Admiral Alexandrino de Alencar in the improvement of the Navy and
particularly the acquisition of the famous dreadnought *Minas
Gerais.*[7]

In this campaign for prestige the Negro was considered a "blot
on the national civilization," and was a source of great shame to
Aryanists and racial purists of the time. It was felt in these quarters
that only through great waves of white European immigrants could
Brazil develop a modern economy and a modern civilization and
culture. In addition to invigorating the economic life of the country, these immigrants would hopefully also discharge a eugenic mission, that of "Aryanizing" the country through the absorption of
the Negro, producing lighter-skinned children whose appearance
and features would carry some distinguishable resemblance to their
German, Italian, Spanish, or Portuguese parent. In this way the official propaganda would be sustained, propaganda which in Europe
presented Brazil as a "great Latin nation" or as a "new European
civilization," complete with photographs of white—or apparently
white—citizens, European-style avenues, neoclassical theatres, and
elegant Norman town houses.

The greatest hopes were placed in the Italians. Of all the new
immigrants, they were the most wanted, the most imitated, and received the highest praise. They were not rude like the Germans,
nor were they the country bumpkins who furnished so much material for Portuguese, Galician, or Spanish jokes. They were intelligent, adaptable, friendly, likable, and they worked very hard. They
were not clannish, but rather mixed happily with Brazilians at religious festivals and during Carnaval. They quickly learned to sing
Brazilian songs along with their traditional operatic tunes. They
were of great value to the economy, to the material progress of the

---

[7] It was aboard this same dreadnought in 1910 that a Negro seaman, João Cândido, led a revolt against the ships officers and, involuntarily, did much to counteract previously favorable impressions of the Brazilian Navy.

country, and to the transition from slave to free labor, and at the same time helpful in the "Aryanization" of the population, for they were not lacking in a taste for darker-skinned women. And since, in the eyes of most Brazilians, it was not possible for the country to achieve greatness without this "Aryanization," the role of the Italians in Brazilian society began to assume almost messianic proportions. According to the patriots, if Negroes continued to preponderate in the working class, it would appear as though slavery still existed; if Portuguese and Galicians alone were brought over, the cultural and intelligence level would not be improved. The Germans would not quickly bring about this desired "Aryanization" because of their tendency to live apart from the Brazilians. Reaction to the Japanese was mixed, but in any case their part was at the time insignificant; it was not until the 1920's that this group began to come to Brazil in any great numbers.

When, in a lecture delivered in Buenos Aires toward the end of this period, Ruy Barbosa declared that Brazilians were descendants of Latins and not of Guaranis, he was simply trying to get the Argentines to look upon his countrymen as neo-Europeans. He was no doubt exaggerating but he revealed a state of wishful thinking common to many Brazilians of the time. Having performed the apparent miracle of replacing slave labor without disrupting the economic order, the Italians would also reinforce the Latin element of the culture. From 1820 through 1914, 1,361,266 Italians had come to Brazil; by the end of 1915, that figure exceeded 2 million, forming a group which surpassed all other European nationalities for the period, not only in numbers but also in cultural and economic value to Brazil.

These other groups—apart from the Galicians and Spanish, who were difficult to consider as foreigners—were the Russians and Poles in Paraná, more Russians in Nova Odessa in the state of São Paulo, Austrians, Turks, Syrians, Lebanese, Jews, French, English, Swiss, Swedes, Japanese, and Germans throughout the south. The most important of these were the Germans, who began coming to Rio Grande do Sul as early as 1826. In 1847, others settled in Espírito Santo, and after 1849 there was a continuous and vigorous influx of Germans to Santa Catarina. After 1852 German immigration also extended to Minas Gerais.

It is no exaggeration to say that, before the settlement of Germans in southern Brazil, this area had been a poor relation within the essentially tropical Brazilian economy. Elliott points out that "the South attracted few Brazilians," possibly because of the preference for the tropics which seems always to have characterized the Spanish and Portuguese colonists and explorers. But he does recognize that it was the Bandeirantes who prevented these less tropical lands of southern Brazil from falling into the hands of the Spanish settlers of the Río de la Plata and who brought Portuguese cattle to the region and encouraged Azorean settlers to live in strategic economic and military points throughout the area.[8]

There is no denying that these European immigrants contributed greatly to the development of the south, particularly in such towns as Blumenau (Santa Catarina), Teófilo Otoni and Visconde de Baependi (Minas Gerais), and Vergueiro (São Paulo). The last is associated with the system of sharecropping used on the coffee plantations, a system praised by J. L. Moré in his *Le Brésil* (1852) but sharply criticized by other students of the subject. A similar system was later attempted by a group of French Fourierists in Santa Catarina, but the only socialist colony in the nineteenth century was one founded at the end of the period near Curitiba by a group of Russians and Germans who acted as though they had arrived from the moon, taking no account whatever of the climate, or of the political, social, or cultural aspects of Brazil. They insisted on cultivating the subtropical fields of Paraná as though they were steppes and, living under a communist system, kept the local police busy settling their intercommunal disputes. Most of the group eventually returned to Europe; those who remained adapted themselves to local conditions and became useful citizens, devoting themselves to transportation and to the cultivation of grains and *maté*.

Almost as unprepared for Brazilian conditions were the southern Americans who left their country after the victory of the Union Army in the Civil War. Arriving in 1867, some settled in Santa Bárbara and later in Vila Americana in São Paulo, while others went to the Amazon, where the more adaptable ones effectively "went native." A few attempted to settle in Pernambuco but failed completely. Apparently expecting to encounter ideal conditions for the continuation of their former lives as gentlemen farmers, these former slave owners, according to Elliott, "were less fitted to make a living from the soil than the Negroes they left behind."[9] Ruined by the war, they were not able to acquire slaves and the only crop

[8] Elliott: op. cit., p. 59.
[9] Ibid., p. 64.

they knew—cotton—could not be raised in Brazil by American methods.

More successful were the Japanese, who later established themselves in lands near those where the Americans had failed and devoted their efforts to the cultivation of rice. Accustomed to this sort of climate, adaptable, and hard-working, less rigid than the Anglo-Saxons and other northern races in their attitude toward the land and people in their new homes, the Japanese became happy and prosperous farmers, though without the complete flexibility and almost total success of the Italians.

The economic success of those who, along with the Germans, went into agriculture was also greatly favored by the reform movement against the *latifúndio* in the form of so-called "territorial taxes." These taxes, considered "repugnant" by the large landholders, favored the owners of the small farms, native Brazilian as well as European immigrant. Considerable reform sentiment was generated on behalf of these helpless victims of the land barons. Indeed, by the end of the period the land barons no longer dominated the affairs of the nation, which were now beginning to be directed from key areas within the coffee plantations of the south.

❧ [V I I I] ❧

The Growth of Industry

I N H I S B O O K *Le Brésil d'Aujourd'hui*, Father Joseph Burnichon reached several interesting conclusions about the tropics based on his observations during his visit to Brazil. It is an incontestable fact, he says, that tropical lands exercise a powerful charm; men have always been attracted to places "where the orange trees bloom." Human migrations have never been made from hot or temperate regions to cold areas; the direction has always been from cold to warm or temperate.

But not everything in the tropics is conducive to the good of mankind. Perhaps the struggle against the rigors of a cold climate is necessary to man's preserving his physical and moral energy. When Father Burnichon, newly arrived from France, declared in Bahia that he found the climate bearable, he was told: "You have just come from Europe and still have a reserve of energy. Wait a couple of years and then let us see how you feel about our indolence." [1]

Certainly the climate of the tropics arouses little inclination for hard labor. The rhythm of life which prevailed in Brazil was one that favored easy living, difficult to reconcile with the type of existence found in France or England or, especially, in the United States. Nevertheless, this reconciliation was beginning to take place. Elihu Root, who visited Bahia shortly before Burnichon, praised the Bahian way of life, and Burnichon himself, after spending several months in this city, not only came to understand the Brazilian placidity but also to ask himself if Americans did not suffer from the equally exaggerated reciprocal defect of too much excitement.

In any case, during the course of the nineteenth century, a grad-

[1] Joseph Burnichon: *Le Brésil d'Aujourd'hui* (Paris, 1910), p. 13.

ual harmonization of these extremes came about with the arrival of a growing number of European immigrants, who planned to make their living not as nonworking slaveowners, but rather as artisans, skilled workers, machinists, and industrialists, and who, initially at least, had to dirty their lily-white hands in establishing new techniques of production and transportation. This trend, of course, was accelerated during the last decades of the century and after the proclamation of the Republic.

It is true that the process was less marked in Bahia than in São Paulo, but it did take place there—as also in Rio Grande do Sul, Rio de Janeiro, Pernambuco, Minas Gerais, and Pará. Industries were founded in all these provinces—including Bahia—housed in factories using modern techniques of production. Some of these establishments were the result of European initiative, others were of Brazilian origin; but in either case the result was to speed up the tempo of life, if not to the pitch of Europe or the United States, at least to the point of creating an intermediate rhythm that could be called the Brazilian tempo. It was this new "third tempo" which Ramalho Ortigão seems to have had in mind as the "x factor" which he said separated the most enlightened element throughout much of Brazil from the monarchical system of government under an Emperor whose archaic liberalism stemmed from the time of Voltaire—an Emperor who lacked the "enterprise and daring" to undertake "big things" through "progressive rehabilitation projects" such as "sanitation systems in the coastal cities or the rebuilding of the city of Rio de Janeiro." It was not a "Time is money" mentality which Ortigão was striving to implant; it was merely a less routine and more innovative course of existence; a renunciation of the cigar smoked slowly in the hammock, to the accompaniment of popular music played on the guitar, without the consequent adoption of Yankee extremes of "hurry-hurry." [2]

A good Brazilian Emperor, by the very fact of representing in America a nobler past than that indicated by the unstable republican governments of the continent, was in a unique position to correct any tendency on the part of Brazilians to fall into the "Time is money" attitude which characterized the United States, reducing everything to money at the expense of human values. And Dom Pedro II—let there be no doubt about it—*did* oppose too rapid a change from slavery to free labor. At first he also opposed what he

[2] Ramalho Ortigão: "O Quadro Social da Revolução Brasileira," *Revista de Portugal* (Oporto), II, 99.

considered to be the excessive American materialism of Mauá's daring plans for industrial development. On the other hand, he had been opposed since his early youth to the archaic feudalism of the slavocracy. His failure as a political leader lay in his inability to develop the "third tempo" in Brazilian life, falling somewhere between the medieval agrarianism of the plantations and the European-American industrialism which utopian-minded individuals wished to transplant bodily to Brazil in complete disregard of Brazilian geography and Luso-Spanish traditions.

Did the Republic attempt to rectify this Imperial failure to establish a "third tempo"? There are those who feel that it did not, for the provisional government immediately declared itself in terms of the narrowest type of progressivism: the identification of national growth with the development of industry. Some students of the period believe that a broader base should have been adopted and that the programs of the early Republic should also have included plans for a systematic valorization of agriculture and stock raising as well. I take the view expressed by the Baron d'Anthouard, French minister to the early Republic, in his book *Le Progrès Brésilien*. In the face of the exaggerated protection afforded Brazilian industries, Anthouard asked: "Would it not have been less costly and more profitable to have given agriculture the supports that have been granted to manufacturing?" [3] His argument ran that agriculture furnished two-thirds of the country's exports, while production was shackled with a "secular routine" of periodic crises that placed the economy in no position to withstand the competition of better-equipped nations. Support to industry is necessary, of course, but shouldn't the country try to colonize and develop its agricultural lands? Protection to industry would only bring a rush of workers to the cities to complicate the already numerous urban problems with an additional conflict between capital and labor. Good sense would seem to indicate that, in a country as predominantly agricultural as Brazil, the most urgent need was to develop the agrarian economy which already existed before trying to create an artificial one through manufacturing. Aid to industry should be limited and selective, following a "rational" protective policy that ran no danger of becoming an arbitrarily directed economy.[4]

[3] Baron d'Anthouard: *Le Progrès Brésilien* (Paris, 1911), pp. 149–50.
[4] Such arbitrary direction was not unknown to Brazil in 1908. We have al-

In 1908, *O Brasil*, the official publication of the Industrial Center of Rio de Janeiro, gave the number of manufacturing establishments in the country as approximately 3,000. The most important manufacturing states were the Federal District, with 35,000 industrial workers; São Paulo, with 24,000; Rio Grande do Sul, with 16,000; Rio de Janeiro, with 14,000; and Pernambuco, with 12,000. The principal industry was textiles. Minas Gerais was still of considerable importance in mining, and there was an as yet small-scale salt mining industry, located principally in the region of Rio Grande do Norte. Other manufactures mentioned were furniture, beverages, cigars, cigarettes, tobacco, mosaic tiles, soap, matches, ceramics, canned foods, and wagons.[5]

At the Rio Exposition of 1908, Brazil attempted to demonstrate its progress by a display of the best products of its young industries. People came from all parts of the country to visit this exposition, some arriving via the Lloyd Brasileiro steamers considered *chic* at the time, others coming from the south or the interior by train. The hotels were filled with visitors anxious to see not only the exhibition pavilions, but also the work that was being done to modernize the nation's capital: the widening of streets and boulevards; the destruction of the dilapidated old buildings used as grubby stands by the sidewalk vendors, and of houses without running water; the construction of new buildings, the most elegant being in "Moorish" style, marvels of *art nouveau*. And everything so brightly lighted that every night seemed a festival. Thus Rio was "civilizing" itself, as one of its journalists put it. No more yellow fever, no more street stands, no Negro women selling things on the elegant new mosaic sidewalks. It was a city which seemed to be making every effort to show how different republican Brazil had become from the Brazil of Pedro II. And with a different tempo of progress. It was a difference for the better, nearly everyone agreed, though there was the occasional protest from an old diehard. Even crime was changing; no longer merely the common rustic disorder perpetrated by lout-

---

ready seen an example of state intervention in the Patronato Agrícola created in São Paulo for the adjustment of relationships between planters and immigrant workers and for the promotion of Brazilian coffee in the foreign market. Such intervention in fact fitted the traditional Luso-Spanish colonial policy of state aid to weaker economies and populations.

[5] *O Brasil* (publication of the Industrial Center of Rio de Janeiro, Rio de Janeiro, 1908), III, Appendix 13.

ish Negroes, it was becoming European in pattern and being practiced by sophisticated Italians. The greatest contributors to the renewed Latin quality of Brazilian culture, the Italians also became notorious for robberies and legendary murders. During a visit to Brazil in 1890, Maturin M. Ballou noted "the objectionable character of the Italian emigrants, who come hither as well as to our own States," and found the Italian concierges, dock workers, and boatmen of Rio to be "a lawless, vagabond element of the community, giving the police force a great deal of trouble." [6]

This is undoubtedly Anglo-Saxon exaggeration, but the fact remains that the police were forced to respond to the wave of industrial urbanization by becoming more astute and considerably less easygoing than in the days before abolition. They were dealing with a more subtle type of criminal: white-skinned, flashy types with rings on their fingers and gold buttons in their shirt cuffs. Italians, French, Jews; contrabandists, pimps, swindlers. Compared to such men the "*capoeiras*" who plagued Sampaio Ferraz were reduced to the stature of disorderly overgrown children, mulattos who sadistically carved up Portuguese bellies out of pure adolescent jealousy of the adult rich. They did not steal their victims' pocketbooks or take the diamond rings from their fingers or gold cuff links from their sleeves. They didn't intend to kill them; they simply knifed them for the pleasure of knifing. But with the growth of industrialism came a corresponding growth in violence in the cities. The police were forced to become much more scientific in their methods of combatting robberies and assassinations, some of which, like those of Carleto and Rocca, fascinated the entire country and passed into folklore.

It is certain that the exaggerated protection of national industries contributed greatly to the growing traffic in contraband. Contraband in linens, silks, watches. Some articles were brought in in the hollowed wooden images of saints, others between the breasts or under the corsets of elegantly dressed women, the latter method greatly aided by the fashion for large bosoms and narrow waists. Many a forbidden article went through Brazilian customs beneath the protuberances of female anatomy or the folds of ample attire.

But it was neither these developments in crime which attracted the attention of the visitors to the Rio Exposition of 1908, nor the city's abundant natural beauties. The thousands of postcards sent at

[6] Maturin M. Ballou: *Equatorial America* (New York, 1892), p. 162.

this time to all parts of Brazil showed not so much the splendors of Corcovado or the Tijuca Forest or the palm trees of the Botanical Gardens—scenes beloved by foreigners but less interesting to Brazilians—as pictures of the Monroe Palace, Central Avenue, or the Avenida Hotel. And on these cards (which at the time were carefully pasted into handsomely bound albums and placed alongside the stamp collection and family photographs) came the sender's enthusiastic comments on the urban progress of the nation's capital. On the docks, the shipyards, the cinemas, the wonders of the exposition, and the new Brazilian mineral waters served, along with the customary beer and soft drinks, on the café terraces of the Hotel Avenida. On the electric streetcars, the electric lights, the elevators, the automobiles, the new fire engines, with their extension ladders which made the firemen seem like circus acrobats and enabled them to fight fires in the tall new buildings, in the factories, and in the shops, where new Brazilian products abounded alongside the more familiar imported articles. On the sweet shops, the dresses worn by pretty women, and the elegant—but, to the simple provincial, scandalous—male attire, complete with monocle and spats. Seen from a distance, the wearers of these last items appeared to be Englishmen, but any Englishman would have been horrified by the excessive rings and jewelry, the brilliantined hair, and the perfumed handkerchiefs and finger tips.[7] A closer examination of some of these "Englishmen," however, might have revealed the thick-skinned provincial who, on arrival in Rio de Janeiro, adopted superelegant attire and acquired a few *petites maîtresses* or *grandes cocottes* to advertise his prosperity. Some of these new arrivals sought still further distinction by insisting on spelling their names in a foreign manner—"Cavalcanti" with the *ti* or Wanderley as Van der Ley—and at least one designated himself "Prince," a title which, by hook or crook, he had managed to obtain from the Vatican.

These Vatican titles, incidentally, were granted quite frequently during the period and a number of illustrious Brazilians were named Counts of the Holy See. Brazilian receptivity to such titles (to some

[7] J. O. P. Bland: *Men, Manners, and Morals in South America* (London, 1920). Of the abuse of perfumes by the Brazilian male of the period, Bland wrote: "The Brazilians' penchant for scents amounts to a passion: upon their coming aboard, all the perfumes of Arabia contended for mastery in the social hall and even in the smoking-room the fragrance of Havana and bird's-eye was smothered by patchouli, verbena, and fleur d'amour. . . . The race's sense of smell seems to have gone on a perpetual 'jag' that nothing but the strongest excitement can satisfy" (pp. 36–7).

extent substitutes for the lost Imperial nobility) seems to have been great, despite the French observer A. D'Atri's remark that Brazilians regarded such things as a joke. We have already seen how much the new leaders (such as Francisco Glycério and Ruy Barbosa as General of the Army and Imperial Counselor respectively) enjoyed their newly granted titles. With the coming of industrialization, it is interesting to note a similar acceptance of such foreign titles as "Count" or "Commander," the new order's way of demonstrating status in the face of the barons and viscounts surviving from the old days.

Some of the exposition visitors wrote their families and friends that, while walking on the Avenue, they had passed "the Baron" en route to the Brahma Restaurant; or that they had seen Ruy Barbosa, small, ugly, wearing *pince-nez* and gray frock coat, descending from his Victoria to visit the bookstore or his favorite cinema. Or Lopes Travão, with his monocle; Pinheiro Machado, with his Panama hat, his proud and masculine air, and his small, almost girlish feet; or Estácio Coimbra, pale, handsome, romantic, wearing the inevitable gloves. Or Sister Paula, with her severe black gown and white cowl, collecting alms from the rich for the poor who were flocking to the city and whose numbers were rising as alarmingly as were those of the French *cocottes*, the mulatto prostitutes, and the homosexuals who could be found every evening in the Praça Tiradentes.

Veterans of the federal capital warned their newly arrived friends of the confidence men, the fake promoters, the society thieves. There was a certain "Dr. Antônio," black sheep of an important Rio Grande do Sul family, who was said to be a perfect gentleman in appearance but a terror in the art of robbing the ingenuous in fashionable hotels. Provincial young girls were likewise warned of mellifluous Don Juans, of whom the capital held an abundance. And the old folks, with their outdated clothes and archaic hairdos, were equally cautioned against the ridicule of students, particularly students of engineering and medicine. Conservative dressers were advised to get rid of their provincial styles in suits, dresses, hats, shoes, false teeth, jewelry, and hairdos and replace them with the newest things to be found in the stores and *modiste* shops of Rio. Rare was the backlander who did not return from his adventure in the capital without his tailor-made suit, his hat from Watson's, his silk tie bought on Central Avenue, his gloves, and his spats, the last two items carefully preserved in bureau drawers as souvenirs of the visit, since to wear them at home would only incur the ridicule of street urchins.

In *Le Brésil au XXᵉ Siècle*, Pierre Denis treats some of the aspects of the Brazilian scene of the early century from the standpoint of the economic geographer. The policy of tariff protectionism, he found, had many flaws and was almost always contrary to the national interest. There was a high duty on woolen goods, for example, without the country's having its own woolen mills or having adopted a systematic program of wool growing. There was the manufacture of umbrellas, where the handle, frame, and triangular materials had to be imported, leaving the "manufacturer" only the task of assembling the component parts. The same unnecessary importation occurred with wallpaper. Or matches. Brazil, the country of vast virgin forests, was importing laminated matchwood from Norway.[8]

In short, it was an industrial economy almost carnivalesque in nature and a dream of progress more fictitious than real. The Exposition of 1908 seemed almost pretentiously self-deceptive, and those from Amazonas and Paraná who came to visit it on the proudly nationalistic ships of Lloyd Brasileiro must have felt the cruel injustice of a protection which meant nothing for nonmanufacturing regions like their own except a rise in their already precariously high cost of living. As the Baron d'Anthouard noted, the state of Amazonas, not having its own manufacturers, was paying "a veritable tribute" to the manufacturing states, "so that they may keep their market."[9] It is curious that a Frenchman had to point out this interregional maladjustment so reminiscent of conditions between colonies and mother country.

No wonder, then, that at the time of the exposition the state of Amazonas petitioned the national Congress, complaining of the abuses of metropolitan industrialism. This petition gave ample evidence of the economic imperialism practiced by Rio de Janeiro and perhaps also São Paulo[1] at the expense of their helpless sister

[8] Pierre Denis: *Le Brésil au XXᵉ Siècle* (Paris, 1909), p. 88.

[9] Anthouard· op. cit., p. 148.

[1] And to a lesser degree by Minas Gerais, Rio Grande do Sul, and Pernambuco because of the prevailing import duties: 562 per cent on rice, 383 per cent on white potatoes, 122 per cent on onions, 161 per cent on beans, 117 per cent on butter, and 50 per cent on tinned meats and coarse cloth. See the *Anais da Câmara dos Deputados* (*Annals of the Chamber of Deputies*) (Rio de Janeiro, 1908). For

states, an imperalism which reminded these states of the old practices of the Imperial court. Rising living costs brought about by the industrial mystique had the paradoxical effect in nonmanufacturing areas of acting as a recessive force against progress that constituted a grave economic, social, and political danger for the country as a whole. This was a situation in short which caused the best European immigrants to avoid Brazil in favor of Argentina and Uruguay, republics which had undertaken a healthy program of agrarian development, with a balanced production of agricultural, meat, and dairy products and a group of related industries to process these commodities. As a result, life in these countries was cheap and easy in contrast to Brazil, where similarly favorable agro-pastoral opportunities had never been properly developed.

Even though Brazil, during the period covered here, did not have the concentrated industrial areas found in the United States, and even though its disbursed manufacturing was carried on largely in what Pierre Denis called "minuscule factories in even the small villages," the result was still disruptive to interregional unity. In later times, beyond the scope of this book, this disruption was intensified with the development of the megalopolitan industrial complex of São Paulo and the then Federal District.

One area that benefited from the continual development of Rio de Janeiro into a modern city was that of Minas Gerais. Not only did its mines furnish raw materials for manufacturing; its agriculture, which had never been neglected, also supplied the city with food. Pierre Denis had suggested that Rio de Janeiro, situated as it was on the seacoast and bordered by tropical forests, could easily "surround itself with a belt of orchards and truck gardens, like most of the other great cities of the world." [2] But with the growth of its population and with its increasing attention to manufacturing, Rio had to constitute Minas Gerais as its "green belt." The city lived on products from beyond the Serra do Mar; each day long trains arrived from Minas Gerais loaded with milk, meat, and fresh vegetables. Feeding the nation's capital became a lucrative business for the Mineiros, and their butter, cheese, mineral waters, and pork products became famous throughout the land.

In 1909, Denis had foreseen the development of a truly national

---

the last years of this period see Pedro Cavalcanti: *A Presidência Venceslau Brás (1914–1918)* (Rio de Janeiro, 1918) and Isaltino Costa: *A Indústria Têxtil Brasileira e os Mercados Sul-Americanos* (São Paulo, 1920).

[2] Denis: op. cit., p. 161.

economy, with a balance of industry and agriculture and a greater coordination of markets and production among the various states. For example, ranchers in Rio Grande do Sul imported salt for their stock from Cádiz when this need could be filled by developing the salt industry of Rio Grande do Norte and Ceará. Resinous woods could be obtained from Paraná instead of from Norway. Wheat flour from Argentina could be replaced by that produced in southern Brazil.[3] A later writer, Isaltino Costa, in 1920 went beyond Denis to suggest the expansion of the Brazilian textile industry to cover export of cotton fabrics to other South American markets.

Denis also foresaw the emergence of São Paulo as "a great commercial and industrial center." Its prosperity had already given it the strength to resist the "coffee crisis," and its development, though disorderly, was vital and progressive enough to realize the industrial potential and at the same time withstand crises of an agrarian nature.[4] Not only did this growth represent a combination of agriculture and industry; it also represented a new combination of peoples, as we have seen, with large numbers of Europeans attracted to the area because of its excellent climate and economic opportunities.

Leaving aside the chronological limitations of this study for a moment, the progress shown by São Paulo in its urban and industrial growth to the present day has been due largely to its immense efforts to assimilate these foreigners into the preponderantly Spanish culture of Brazil. This was done through the city and suburban schools, a procedure that was impossible in rural areas; hence the much slower assimilation of those foreigners who settled in Rio Grande do Sul, Santa Catarina, and Espírito Santo. In the latter regions, the settlers could enjoy the luxury of an isolation denied to those in urban industrial centers. The Italians who came to the coffee plantations on the eve of abolition rarely remained there as field hands; after a period of farm labor, they were attracted by the commercial and industrial opportunities of the provincial capital. Under the Republic, this migration intensified. Once in the city, the Italians had to compete with native Brazilians. They had to speak the Portuguese language, know the geography and history of Brazil, and acquire technical and scientific knowledge through reading books in the vernacular. And they did so.

The Republic well understood its own role in this delicate pro-

[3] Ibid., p. 104.
[4] Ibid., p. 146.

cess of assimilation, at least in the two largest cities. It was less active
in Rio Grande do Sul and Santa Catarina, where Italians, Germans,
and Poles were allowed to continue as ethnic minority groups so
long as they voted en bloc for government candidates in elections.
Because of the large number of foreign pupils in the schools of the
Federal District, superintendents of education from the outset of
the Republic directed their teachers to make their pupils understand that the idea of "country" referred not to the land of one's
birth but rather to the land of adoption. Furthermore, the school-
master must insist that Brazil was "of all the countries in the world,
the most beautiful, the noblest, and the most worthy of our love."
Vanity made official. It was from such patriotic exercises that books
like Afonso Celso's *Por que Me Ufano do Meu País* (*Why I Am
Proud of My Country*) or Virgílio Oliveira's *A Pátria Brasileira*
(*The Brazilian Nation*) emerged. Nor was it long before Olavo
Bilac was creating patriotic propaganda for the country and its military service by giving talks in schools and barracks and, along with
other intellectuals, by writing articles inspired or commissioned by
the Baron do Rio Branco in favor of Brazilian foreign policy. There
are those who allege that the Baron, using a special fund placed at
his disposal, brought eminent Europeans such as Ferrero, Ferri,
Anatole France, and Paul Adam to Brazil for exactly the same purpose.[5]

Denis found that the schools of São Paulo were not doing as
good a job as those of the Federal District in assimilating the newly
arrived immigrants. The Paulistas appeared to be satisfied to allow
this assimilation to take place through business activity and through
participation in the "intense life" of the city. Contact with "a people full of energy and ambition" was sufficient to absorb the adults,
says the French observer. "Economic prosperity has given São
Paulo a power of absorption superior to that of all the other Brazilian provinces."[6] This power applied not only to foreigners but also
to Brazilians who arrived from other states or provinces and
quickly became even more Paulista than the Paulistas in developing
a spirit of initiative and business enterprise. And such enterprise
brought about good results, socially and economically, for such
transplanted Brazilians as Saldanha Marinho, of Pernambuco; or

[5] In his intelligent use of this fund he anticipated the modern political practice
of spending large sums on propaganda and information.
[6] Denis: op. cit., p. 153.

Artur Neiva, of Bahia; or Albuquerque Lins, of Alagoas; or Washington Luís, from the state of Rio de Janeiro. There were also those who failed, both natives and immigrants, many foreigners in particular being too steeped in their native traditions to adapt to the unscrupulous methods of quick success, methods which would have been considered shameful in their countries of origin.

Not all the new arrivals were attracted by the mystique of the "red lands"; some of them came directly to the cities, drawn by the prospect of rapid—even magical—prosperity. Many of these started as bootblacks, scissor-grinders, street peddlers. But wherever they began their Brazilian experience, whether on the streets of São Paulo or on the coffee plantations of the interior, they quickly learned the Portuguese language, employing it by preference in direct proportion to their ascension up the economic ladder. Their own Italian was generally a dialect and so clearly betrayed their humble provincial origins that they made every effort to learn Portuguese in order to keep their background from becoming apparent to Brazilians and, especially, to new arrivals from the old country. Some of those who came directly to the city became political journalists, willingly turning out polemical articles and political handouts so unscrupulous that no native journalist could be found to handle the assignments. The brilliant Portuguese João Laje was perhaps the most famous of these political journalists, but there were Italians as well, writers capable of extraordinary violence in their adopted language, which they learned to write in masterful fashion. Some of these moved to other states where, as complete strangers, they were under obligation to no one and could with impunity accept orders to attack or praise any political dignitary the higher-ups chose to give their attention to at the moment.

The industrial progress of the country also encouraged mobility in fields other than those of communication, particularly among unattached males, and this tendency not infrequently resulted in the formation of a double moral standard. Young men who were timid under the surveillance of their families suddenly became completely uninhibited in their new homes. In this respect, however, the Germans of Rio Grande do Sul and Santa Catarina seemed superior to other immigrants of non-Lusitanian origin; perhaps their strongly moral upbringing and their preference for agrarian pursuits protected them from the "get-rich-quick" fervor of the urbanized Italians.

This last statement does not mean that the spirit of industrial progress had not reached the German colonists of the south. It had. "From São Leopoldo to Hamburger Berg the smell of hides followed us," wrote Denis.[7] These hides were not of local origin, but rather from the slaughterhouses of Bagé and Pelotas to the south. Originally this product had been exported, but the Germans had developed it into the basis for a local industry, thanks to their native skills, and were now shipping their leather articles to all parts of Brazil. A good example of the effect of protectionism, one could say, but it also had its disadvantages. Drawn into the mystique of industrial progress, the Germans of Rio Grande began to desert agriculture.[8] As early as 1899, President Campos Sales, with these developments in mind, had warned Brazilians of the dangers of the "completely artificial industries" which had begun to appear in the new Republic.

On the other hand, the drift toward industry on the part of the Germans held in advantage which might have outweighed the previous objection: it integrated them more rapidly into Brazilian culture. It brought them into greater contact with the Portuguese language and caused them to think along national rather than parochial lines. "The German fortress in Rio Grande do Sul will soon surrender to economic progress," wrote Denis. "Already there are great breaches in the walls."[9] And these remarks could equally have applied, for the same reasons, to the German strongholds in Santa Catarina.

Nothing could be more correct than Denis's generalizations to the effect that the protectionist policy, intended to protect the nation, was in reality protecting a class or a region. But one must still admit the advantages of this policy for Brazil as a whole, because the protection of so-called "national industries" after the coming of the Republic encouraged the development of new enterprises. These new enterprises made use of hitherto neglected raw materials and at the same time created jobs for those young men who, wishing to be considered sociologically white, shunned agricultural

[7] Ibid., p. 317.

[8] For the progress of German Brazilians in Rio Grande do Sul, Santa Catarina, and other parts of Brazil, see the collaborative work directed by Alfredo Funke: *O Brasil e a Alemanha (1822–1922)* (Berlin, 1923), especially the chapters "A Civilização Brasileira e o Elemento Alemão no Brasil" (Alfredo Funke) and "A Cooperação do Trabalho Alemão na Indústria Brasileira" (Mark Neven du Mont).

[9] Denis: op. cit., p. 329.

tasks as appropriate only for Negroes or slaves. Such industrial developments also served to promote better communication with regions which had formerly led an isolated agrarian existence and, in developing this communication, also promoted the growth of transportation facilities.

What was unfortunately totally lacking, however, was a master plan for national development in which agriculture would not be subordinated to manufacturing, or the country to the city, or the native worker to the foreigner, as was the case in the Patronato Agrícola of São Paulo, which offered no corresponding support to the ex-slave or the migratory worker from Ceará or the northeast. The freedman, fleeing the rural areas, wandered through the cities in a state of morbid anxiety, the anxiety of an ex-slave who also wished to become an ex-Negro. And an ex-Negro with opportunities equal to those of the Italian, the European, or the white man in general under the paternal benevolence of the Republic as represented in the Patronato, the Immigration Service, or the Ministry of Agriculture. Some of these former slaves became nostalgic for the monarchy and Princess Isabel; it is quite possible that such maladjusted ex-slaves were among those who joined the rebellious whites and *caboclos* under Antônio Conselheiro in their uprising against the republican Army—an aspect of that struggle between soldiers and backlanders which seems to have escaped the notice of the engineer-sociologist Euclydes da Cunha.

It has already been suggested that, along with the mystique of industrial progress, the position of urban engineer began to acquire considerable status. As early as 1875, Luís Rafael Vieira Souto had written in his *O Melhoramento da Cidade do Rio de Janeiro* (*The Improvement of the City of Rio de Janeiro*) that "this great city is a center of intelligence," whose "agglomerate population," with its "division of labor," would facilitate the "growth of production" and the development "of all sorts of industries." It was these engineers who began to evolve a sociology that could not fail to help Brazil. Without becoming politicians, they became public figures. The most enlightened among them wished to do through construction what José de Alencar and his followers had done in literature: to develop a style that would represent not merely the individual but rather "the people; that is to say, the nation as a whole." For Vieira Souto this style was precisely what was lacking in the urban architecture of the Empire, that victim of the "pernicious practice of modeling our construction along foreign lines, without paying the slightest attention to the country's climate, resources, or traditions." This was the result, as he saw it, of leaving the designing of buildings in the hands of "any construction boss or simple worker" who liked to feel himself "a qualified engineer or architect." Perhaps this last statement was a bit unjust; more than one construction boss at the time showed himself superior to most engineers in such matters as regional appropriateness and traditional style of design.[1]

Given this call to architectural nationalism, it might have been expected that, with the coming of industrialism, such cities as Rio de Janeiro, São Paulo, and Recife would begin to show an architecture similar to that of Barcelona of the same period; that is to say, a combination of Spanish tradition and industrial necessity. This, however, never occurred. The best urban residences of the time were those which continued the basic colonial Portuguese design and merely added a modern touch here and there. And as for the railway stations, slaughterhouses, commercial and public buildings, mills, factories, machine shops, industrial schools, cemeteries, and bridges, nothing built at this time revealed the slightest inclination on the part of the architect to rise to the level of José de Alencar or Gonçalves Dias or any other nationalist writer in his attempt to develop an architectural style that would express the new Brazil. Even the great Amazonas Theatre—with its fusion of European styles with American-Indian motifs glorifying Carlos Gomes and José de Alencar—was hardly more than superficially Brazilian, a combination of Italian spirit with Brazilian decoration.

It is true that there were those who since 1872 had wished to use the lands adjacent to the ditch that ran behind the country house of the Viscount de Mauá for the construction of "a vast edifice designed to serve as a permanent exhibit of machines and apparatus used in manufacturing, and especially in agriculture, the latter being the principal source of our national wealth." It would not have to be a monumental structure: merely a "large building, well lighted from all sides," illuminating the "machinery in movement." [2] We are not told, however, what sort of architectural style Pereira Passos and his collaborators wished to adopt for such a ca-

---

[1] Luís Rafael Vieira Souto: *O Melhoramento* (see fn. 3, p. 132), pp. 6, 71.
[2] Francisco Pereira Passos, *et al.*: *1⁰ Relatório da Comissão de Melhoramentos da Cidade do Rio de Janeiro* (Rio de Janeiro, 1876), p. 12.

thedral in honor of Brazilian industrial progress. We only know that this model building would have no place on its facade for Portuguese colored tiles. Such materials, according to Passos, absorbed the sun's rays and made the interior unbearably hot. Nor would there be "windows of multicolored, badly combined stained glass"; such anachronisms, "besides being harmful, are also an eyesore."

Thus Pereira Passos, future rebuilder of Rio de Janeiro, revealed himself in 1875 as a terrible enemy of the colorful street stands which hindered the city from assuming the appearance of a modern industrial European center, and which were "cluttering the few public squares that we have." [3] It is quite possible that these stands were of no value, and one can readily admit that in the traditional Portuguese *sobrado* there was little that could be adapted to an industrial civilization. But there is no evidence that either Passos or any of his collaborators, in their desire to achieve this adaptation, ever designed a project or uttered the slightest suggestion leading to the creation of an architecture expressing the Brazilian way of life. Or that they ever approached, as Vieira Souto did, the criterion later defined by Professor Lewis Mumford in his *Sticks and Stones* by which a building designed to take care only of the physical comforts of its future occupants—to the exclusion of biological, psychological, and sociological considerations—is seen as the product of "a limited conception of science." [4] From this point of view, it is a pity that none of the great Brazilian engineers of the period were influenced in their science of Man, Home, and City by a somewhat less scientific, more human Positivism graced with an additional touch of creative genius. It was Professor Mumford who had to point out that the machine age in the United States had produced an architecture adapted merely to housing machines and dynamos at the expense of the human values without which material existence is incomplete. [5] Incomplete, arid, and melancholy. Throughout the whole long process of industrialization, in fact, there was a lack of scientific consideration of the worth of human beings to complement the worth of things. Much attention was given to natural and animal products; hides, woods, stones, drugs, resins, plants, minerals, water resources: all came to assume an entirely new value,

---

3 Ibid., p. 28.
4 Lewis Mumford: *Sticks and Stones—A Study of American Architecture and Civilization* (New York, 1924), p. 179.
5 Ibid., p. 188.

and their exploitation gave Brazilians a new sense of the specific material possibilities inherent in natural and animal resources, a sense of value quite different from that which obtained during the days of a purely pastoral or agrarian economy. Nevertheless, in this new perspective there was a lack of the industrial sense of things, of any instinct for the quickened tempo of life or efficient use of time and space that would have made it possible for Brazil to become another United States. Probably this was the result of having developed from an aristocratic-democratic monarchy with a different social structure to that of the United States. Different, but still compatible.

"Under Dom Pedro Brazil was free from despotism and at the same time from disorder," observed Ballou in 1892. In comparing the Brazilian situation with the United States, on the one hand, and with the Spanish-American republics on the other, he characterized the latter as being subject to "an alternation of revolution and military despotism." In comparison with Chile, Brazil, by virtue of its Lusitanian and monarchical background, seemed much superior "in intelligence and civilization." Ballou singled out several aspects of Brazilian progress, praising the country's railways, its streetcar systems, the great shipyards of Rio de Janeiro, the public and commercial buildings. At the same time, he remarked on the "picnic mode of life which has conformed to climatic influence. . . . Everything is very quiet, there is no hurry. It all seems to a stranger to be the very poetry of life. . . ." Still, in Pará, where he made his first contact with the Brazilian people, he noted "an excellent port of great capacity" where large ships were loading and unloading the products of the tropics, particularly rubber.[6] Thus a land of easygoing tempo could still make itself respected economically, socially, and politically.

For those Brazilians who were uneasy at the thought of being the only monarchy in the New World, there were grave doubts as to whether their country really was superior to its neighbors. To them the Empire seemed archaic and routine, the very negation of progress, particularly in the field of industry. As we have seen, there were Brazilians who, in childhood, had read Jules Verne and had become incurably enamored of machines and inventions, and of French, British, and Yankee gadgetry which accelerated the rhythm of progress—gadgetry which would give them far more

[6] Ballou: op. cit., pp. 103, 96, 206, 207.

mastery over the vast expanses of Brazilian territory than they could ever hope to gain under the leadership of a Voltairean Emperor whose sole gadget was an ever-present umbrella.

The triumph of Santos Dumont in Paris did much to soothe the spirits of these early readers of Jules Verne and to satisfy their appetite for magic carpets to whisk people from Amazonas to Rio Grande do Sul or from Rio de Janeiro to Mato Grosso. Perhaps this triumph would mean a new life for Brazil, a life faster even than that of Europe, faster than that of other Americans, including the Yankees.

Nobody was ever more of a hero to his people than Alberto Santos Dumont, a pioneer in heavier than air navigation who made a much-publicized biplane flight in Paris in 1906. Through him, the Brazilian had his revenge on those petulant foreigners who disdainfully dubbed Brazil the land where people were told to "have patience," to "wait until tomorrow," or even the "day after tomorrow." Santos Dumont became suddenly a symbol in Brazilian eyes of a nation capable, by its own efforts and inventions, of raising itself to a level of progressivism where the impact of its technical advances would be felt throughout the world. Thus, almost by a miracle and completely to his surprise, the young Mineiro acquired a charisma that made him the most glorious figure of his period.

The myth of Santos Dumont soon became part of an even greater myth: that of Brazilian progress through science. This second myth assumed its greatest legendary and heroic symbolism during the last decades of the period. Brazil needed a Santos Dumont to awaken its faith in a messianic future, and the little aviator responded to this need in the most splendid manner imaginable, passing rapidly in the eyes of the public from individual to symbol, and from symbol to myth.[7]

It is quite possible that Brazilians exaggerated their glorification of Santos Dumont; but the significance of their feelings lies in the fact that Dumont became a symbol of Brazil's ability to conquer space and time, elements which hitherto had been the greatest enemies in its struggle to gain prestige in the eyes of the world, in its attempt to appear modern, even *dernier cri*, and at the same time to

[7] The original Brazilian text includes the depositions of 65 representative contemporaries of Santos Dumont as to the aviator's impact on the Brazilian public, particularly Brazilian youth. Since all these merely support the conclusion already offered by the author, they have been omitted in the interest of brevity. (Translator.)

be master of the vast territories within its boundaries. He was a symbol also of Brazilian capacity for technical, mechanical, and industrial progress in spite of physical appearance. As we have seen, some famous Brazilians of the time (the Baron do Rio Branco, Saldanha da Gama, Joaquim Nabuco, or Santos Dumont's aeronautical rival Augusto Severo) were strong and handsome in physical aspect. But the majority of Brazilians were not, and to these small, thin, and pallid individuals, the figure of Santos Dumont corresponded more to the Brazilian of the "Amarelinho" myth, the little man capable of performing great deeds of valor against blond, pink-cheeked giants, the Brazilian David against the Nordic Goliath.

The "Amarelinho" story acted as the Brazilians' compensation for the climate, tropical conditions, improper food, malaria, and often inadequate clothing which gave so many of them the appearance of convalescents or chronic invalids, but still did not hinder them from performing great deeds of physical endurance in the Amazon or at Canudos. Santos Dumont represented the idealization, par excellence, of the little man of yellowed countenance, the Cearense, the type which during the early Republic many felt to have been responsible for retaining Brazil's dominion over the Amazon in the face of the United States. This was the type which spread most rapidly throughout Brazil; not, like so many other northeasterners, as a lawyer or judge or politician, nor even as a soldier, but rather as a man with a talent for creating and developing wealth through commerce and industry. So much so that Dumont became a figure inseparable from Brazilian economic progress, particularly in the field of trade. He stood in contrast to most Brazilians of the north or from Bahia or Rio de Janeiro, people whose talents and inclinations lay more in arts and letters, who were desirous of triumphing through genius or simple inspiration, rather than through patient and incessant effort. There were exceptions, of course, such as the engineer and industrialist Meneses in Pernambuco; or Delmiro Gouveia, another Pernambucan, a self-made man who in harnessing the energy of the falls of Paulo Afonso exhibited a daring unmatched by that of any Paulista or Cearense. Or Luís Tarquinho, the complete negation of the slow, soft Bahian. Or Osvaldo Cruz, Pereira Passos, the Baron do Rio Branco, Roquette-Pinto—all negations of the legend that the atmosphere of Rio de Janeiro was as hostile to creative technical or industrial effort as that of the north. This legend was believed by the economist Roger W. Babson, who took quite seriously the words of a certain Brazilian Jeremias, who told him: "There is something about the climate here in the tropics which takes out the ginger in all of us. Did you ever hear of a great inventor, artist, writer, or any other man of real note who did his work in the tropics?" [8] A statement typical of the attitude of many Brazilians of the period, and responsible for many a rich man's son being sent to cooler, more stimulating countries to complete his education.

Nor were rich children sent only from São Paulo for their higher studies; they also went from Rio de Janeiro or Pernambuco or Bahia, and they often went to England, as well as to Paris and Switzerland. St. Joseph's, a boarding school near London run by a certain Brother Hyacinth, attracted a considerable number of Brazilian boys. One was a Pernambucan named Emílio Cardoso Ayres (the famous caricaturist), born in Recife at the end of the nineteenth century and brought up by his mother with an indulgence which allowed him to satisfy every whim. His father, who at times protested against this permissiveness, was an elegant bourgeois, owner of a pink châlet complete with French garden and British tennis court, and proprietor of one of the richest sugar warehouses in Recife. Emílio could not contribute personally to the questionnaire on which this study is based, for he committed suicide in France in 1916; but from letters preserved by his family we can gain a good impression of his English schooling. In a letter directed to "Mama" and dated October 21, 1904, Emílio writes: "We have been at school for several days now. I am very well pleased and nothing is lacking. My room is very good and contains everything I need. Papa was here today to see if we were well established. He gave me three postal cards from you, which gave me great pleasure. The food is good and very plentiful. We have breakfast at eight, with bread, butter, and milk. Lunch is at midday, with soup, two main courses, and dessert. Later we have tea and supper, which are also very good. . . . The class is good and we hope to show some progress shortly. . . . I began to study piano today and tomorrow my painting instructor will come. At present I am studying only English, and when I understand it well I will be transferred to a class where I can take all the other subjects. The director is very good . . . and the other padres are agreeable; I hope they stay that way. . . . Every day we go to mass in the chapel, which is very

[8] Roger W. Babson: *The Future of South America* (Boston, 1915), p. 293.

pretty." He asks his mother to give a hug to his aunts and cousins and also to Mademoiselle, the French family governess. (Mademoiselle, as we have seen, was almost a member of the family among these rich Gallicized bourgeois who would no more think of entrusting their pink-faced children to the care of a Negro *babá* than of allowing them to spoil their pale complexions by exposure to the vicious rays of the tropical sun.)

In another letter, dated May 7, 1905, Emílio told his mother that, although homesick for Pernambuco and dosing himself with medicines (he was always a sickly boy), he was still enjoying football, cricket, and tennis. At the time, such games were played only by the elegant bourgeoisie of Rio de Janeiro, São Paulo, or Pernambuco, made popular through the influence of resident English families, as well as through that of Brazilian children who, like Emílio, were receiving their education in the British Isles.

Along with his interest in sports, which he enjoyed more as spectator than participant, Emílio also liked to paint water colors, play the piano, and collect postcards. The collection of postcards became a craze of the period. There were cards showing aspects of the new Rio de Janeiro or the new Manaus or the new Belém or the new São Paulo. And there were cards with colored pictures of lovers, of pretty women, of golden-haired children, of European peasant girls. In the Thieves' Market in Lisbon today such postcards from early twentieth-century Brazil, sent by recent arrivals in Rio de Janeiro or Belém or Manaus to relatives back in Portugal, can still be found. These colored pictures showed a Brazil whose progress contrasted sharply with the routine life of the Portuguese villages of the time; their messages were enthusiastic in praise of Brazilian urban and industrial developments, messages which certainly aroused the envy of the placid, agrarian friends and relatives to whom they were addressed. And it is quite likely that similar cards went from São Paulo or Rio Grande do Sul to equally envious relatives back in Italy.

Such postcards constituted one of the liveliest expressions of Brazilian sociability at the beginning of the twentieth century. People preserved them with great affection, not only for the pictures, but also for the messages. One received from Switzerland in 1907 by Dona Maria (Iaiá) Cavalcanti de Albuquerque, of Pernambuco, showed a colored figure of St. Joseph holding a book and contained the message, written by a traveling Bahian lady friend: "May this messenger plunge into seas of happiness the one who today plucks one more lily from the garden of her precious existence." Typical language of the period, found not only in postcards but also in diaries and public utterances.

There were also colored cards advertising commercial products, such as that for Roche's Syrup, portraying the happy life of an Indian family, the man lying in his hammock and the wife seated on the ground with a pet pigeon. Or that for Manon's Purgative, which symbolized its virtues in the form of an automobile, while "other purgatives" were portrayed as lumbering oxcarts. Or of Noel Syrup, which showed a Santa Claus distributing his product to a group of happy children.

Incidentally, it was at about this time that the figure of Santa Claus began to displace that of the Christ Child in the more progressive bourgeois circles of Brazil. To such parents, the Child, the manger, the little household chapels, and Christmas Eve *pastores* all seemed ridiculously archaic.

In 1911 relatives of Iaiá Cavalcanti de Albuquerque wrote her in São Paulo, where she was living, to tell her of the progress being made in her native Recife, and sending pictures of the Central Station, the new port facilities, Independence Square, and Republic Square (formerly the Square of the Princesses). Not all these relatives were enthusiastic over this sort of progress; nor, as members of an old noble family, were they sympathetic toward the "other people" who were becoming more and more a part of that society. In 1912 Dona Iaiá received a card from a Recife relative stating that "our country is full of illiteracy, political shenanigans, Negroes and mulattos and is definitely going to the dogs." Progress in Recife is "comical, I can assure you. In the square before the City Hall they have made more flower beds and have taken away more of the fences. And do you know what the mayor plans to do with these flower beds? In the middle of one of them in front of the Treasury and the Public Library, at the end of the Buarque de Macedo Bridge, as a monument to the foreigners who have just disembarked in this Venice of America, he has built (this is wonderful!) a *pissoir!* It must be seen to be believed. . . ." And later: "What shameful people with their heads full of tapioca, mush, black beans, and sawdust!"

At the same time another relative wrote asking "Dinda Iaiá" if, immersed in the São Paulo fog, she ever missed the "northern delicacies." She must have felt such longings, despite the tendency in Rio de Janeiro and São Paulo to ridicule anything smacking of the provinces.[9] In these modern cities, it was considered inelegant to like regional foods, whether "northern delicacies" or Mineiro mashed beans, Rio Grande barbecue, or even the *cuscuz* of São Paulo. Anything from Rio de Janeiro, on the other hand, was held in high esteem and in sophisticated circles throughout the country turkey Carioca became the supreme concession to the national cuisine, replacing *feijoada, caruru, vatapá,* and other dishes repugnant to French tastes—dishes which, above all, were much too African and plebian in origin to continue as part of the national culinary tradition.

One dish of Amerindian origin which did not lose caste was the rich chicken soup known as *canja,* Pedro II's favorite dish and one highly praised by Theodore Roosevelt during his expedition to the Brazilian backlands in 1913. According to Marshal Rondon (the military engineer who devoted his life to the betterment of living conditions for the Brazilian Indian and for whom the territory of Rondônia in western Brazil is named) with whom Roosevelt made the journey: "This dish was a veritable revelation to our new acquaintance. He was never tired of praising it or seeing it as part of the menu of every single meal. He vowed that he would make it known in the United States. Whenever we were in a place where we could buy chickens, we fixed a *canja* for Mr. Roosevelt's lunch and dinner. When we were deeper into the interior, navigating the waters of the River of Doubt, we shot wild *jacu* and *jacutingas,* which were as good as chicken for this purpose." [1] It is unfortunate that *canja de jacu,* a Brazilian dish of the first order, never became known in the cities, not even in Belém. But the cities were studiously avoiding such rusticisms, to their own loss. The same could be said of the rustic use of medicinal herbs, which never received the benefits of industrial development.

The first Roosevelt did not restrict his admiration for tropical

[9] The fondness for caricaturing rustic characters is exemplified in the carved figure of the mythical Mineiro Manuel Tibúrcio de Anunciação, created by the young humorist Mario Brant; or in the typical vulgar comedian of the burlesque show.

[1] *Missão Rondon. Apontamentos sôbre os Trabalhos Realizados pela Comissão de Linhas Telegráficas Estratégicas de Mato Grosso ao Amazonas sob a Direção de Coronel de Engenharia Cândido Mariano da Silva Rondon de 1909 a 1915* (Rio de Janeiro, 1916), pp. 436-7.

dishes simply to *canja*. "The illustrious guest found our beans excellent and often requested that a large pot of them be prepared for his friends and for members of the party." In addition to food, Roosevelt (whose enthusiasm for Brazil suggests that of Lawrence of Arabia later for the Orient) praised the *caboclos* he saw in the backlands struggling for existence against the most rigorous natural hazards. "A country which can produce such sons as these," he stated, "is bound to go far." [2] That Theodore Roosevelt could say this of a people with a touch of African blood must certainly have disconcerted the Brazilian Aryanists, horrified as they were by the number of Negroes and mulattos that were filling the country. They must also have deplored his praise of foods of equally non-European origin, foods which would never be served in the fine houses of the time.

When Emílio Cardoso Ayres returned to his native land in 1910, after finishing prep school in England and studying painting under French masters in Paris, what disturbed him was the lack of depth, as he saw it, of the artistic life of the country, "an artistic life so limited that one could say it scarcely exists," as he wrote his mother from Rio de Janeiro on August 29. It was an artistic milieu dominated in painting and sculpture by such figures as Bernardelli, Eduardo de Sá, Amodeo, Parreiras. The School of Fine Arts seemed to him "a miserable place in the eyes of anyone who comes from where I have been." And this could be said without implying that everything abroad had been so perfect as to preclude his receiving a good impression of his own country.

The modernization and metropolitan progress of the city did not discourage him, as at least one of his letters shows, but he was saddened by the poverty and sterility of the artists in a country whose charm lay precisely in the fact that it *was* so different from Europe. It was a pity that Emílio did not also go to Bahia, or to Pará, or to the interior on one of Rondon's expeditions. They might have supplied the vitality essential to his sickly nature. A handsome lad, always very elegant in his double-breasted coats made by Brandão, he suffered, like Ruy Barbosa, from very bad eyesight, as well as from other less evident ailments. His disenchantment with Brazil probably explains why he subsequently became a caricaturist—perhaps the best of all Brazilian caricaturists and certainly the best, most acute, and most complex of his time. During his later life in

[2] Ibid., pp. 437, 438.

Africa,[3] he became a painter, particularly of portraits. It is significant that in Brazil, whose spirit of industrial and commercial progress he associated unfavorably with his father, the only portrait he ever painted was that of Dona Emílio, his mother.

If Santos Dumont was the superhero of the "Amarelinhos," Emílio Cardoso Ayres seems to have been the supermartyr of a myth. His suicide in a provincial French hotel is significant in its sociological implications: the inability of this small man, ailing from birth, to accept what his sharp caricaturist's eye saw as being his almost scandalous physical deterioration, in contrast to the vigorous, athletic, rosy-cheeked youths he had seen in Sweden skating, skiing, romping in the snow. The example of Santos Dumont was no consolation to him. Instead, it was a different part of Brazilian folklore that defeated him: the myth of the pale little weakling who turned himself, not into a hero but into a werewolf, a werewolf fated to roam the docks and stews of Europe, to the scandal of his friends and family and that Brazil which the Baron do Rio Branco was trying to make respectable in the sight of Americans and Europeans. Emílio Cardoso Ayres did not wish to become a negative "Amarelinho." His suicide was that of a wilted Narcissus, as well as of an artist falsely convinced of his failure. Had he been another Santos Dumont in spirit, he would have compensated for the physical inroads of time by turning to those maternal aspects of his native land represented by his mother, the mistress of the Gaipió plantation, rather than to those of his father, the rich sugar warehouseman anxious for his son to take over the business and make his mark in the booming economic life of the new Brazil.

[3] In 1914 Emílio wrote from Toguer, a small native village in Tunisia: "This is a beautiful place, hidden in an oasis of 400,000 palm trees, an Arab town full of interesting types," in contrast to Algiers, which had "nothing of interest along native lines, because the French have spoiled everything with their modern buildings and have done away with everything that is Arab. There is only one native quarter left and this is interesting only because of the types one sees there."

❧ [I X] ❧

The Religious Order

I N 1879 THE CHAMBER OF DEPUTIES was discussing the problem of
the relationship between the Church and higher education in
Brazil. One of the speakers, at a certain point during a long discussion, was moved to exclaim: "I am not an enemy of the Catholic
Church, gentlemen. But it is enough for this Church to have encouraged the development of the arts, to have played the part it has
played in history, to be the Church of the great majority of Brazilians and of our race. I am not against any of these things. And when
Catholicism becomes part of the soul of everyone, I respect it: it is a
religion of conscience. . . . But what I do oppose is this political
Catholicism, this Catholicism which allies itself with all absolute
governments." [1]

The speaker was a deputy from the province of Pernambuco:
Joaquim Nabuco. Joaquim Aurélio Barreto Nabuco de Araújo was
born in a Recife *sobrado* and brought up in the Big House of an
aristocratic sugar plantation, Maçangana, property of his godmother Dona Ana Rosa; the plantation where he learned to repeat
his *Paternoster* in the chapel of São Mateus. What he was opposing
was the Brazilian tendency to create more free Catholic colleges,
similar to those of Belgium, colleges which he feared would become
bastions of orthodoxy in opposition to science. And without science there could be no true Brazilian progress. "Scientifically speaking," he said, "the people who know Brazil least are the Brazilians
themselves . . . the domain of nature, so prodigiously open before
our very eyes, has never been developed through our own

[1] Joaquim Nabuco: *Discursos Parlamentares* (Rio de Janeiro, 1949), p. 106.

285

efforts. . . ." This was his goal: "national progress, scientific freedom." [2]

Brazil was then just at the beginning of a period when Progress
was the god and Science the goddess of the intellectual élite, so
much so that it was considering, with Martins Júnior, the replacement of lyric poetry with "scientific poetry" and, with others, of
substituting the traditional faith with "scientific religion." "Scientific politics," "scientific dictatorship," "scientific critcism" were
yet further expressions current in a Brazil already republican in
some aspects of its life. Thus it was that men like the young Joaquim Nabuco could not conceive of religion except in a scientific
context.

This was the way another ardent apologist for "national progress," Ruy Barbosa, also felt about matters of religion. In the Imperial alliance of Church and State, he, along with other young public
figures of intellectual bent, perceived the principal obstacle to both
science and progress in Brazil.

On September 30, 1879, Nabuco returned to the subject, this
time with a proposal in favor of the secularization of cemeteries. He
was not defending Protestantism or Judaism, he explained; both had
shown themselves quite able to handle the problem of burying their
dead. "The English race could not have populated the world, could
not have created great colonies which testified to the future destiny
of Britain to rule the world, without having everywhere, in some
form or other, found the means to bury its dead according to the
dictates of its religion, its customs, and the sentiments which obtained in the Mother Country." The Anglo-Saxon Protestants
would not have become established in such cities as Rio de Janeiro
"if they had not been able to live according to their religion in matters of both life and death." The same could be said for the Jews,
who for religious reasons preferred to inter their dead in separate
cemeteries. There were others, however, who in Brazil continued
after death to be subjected to what Nabuco called "religious perse-
cution" in the form of the temporal jurisdiction exercised over the
cemeteries by the Catholic Church. Stating again his conviction
that the present religio-political order was contrary to progress,
Nabuco told the Chamber of Deputies: "One of the duties of the
statesman, of the man who really interests himself in his country's
progress, is to succeed in resolving all the antagonisms standing in

[2] Ibid., p. 110.

the way of the achievement of such an end, so that the sentiments which cause citizens to love their country are constantly multiplying, so that the ideas on which all are in agreement become more and more numerous." [3]

Nabuco was also touching here on a problem developed further in a later speech (that of July 16, 1880) on the subject of religious freedom in relationship to civil marriage, to the organization of the family, and to immigration. He could not conceive of a free and progressive country in which "all of the immense power involved in the authority to authorize or prohibit marriage" was in the hands of the clergy, and in which "all the questions relative to the constitution of the family" depended upon the judgment of the ecclesiastical courts. Nor could he understand how such a country could continue to educate ministers and priests for one specified religion only. "Yesterday I voted against the appropriation for the seminaries" largely because in such seminaries children are led to become priests through the glib persuasions of their teachers, who educate them "in a special atmosphere of mysticism, isolated from all ambitions and patriotic aspiration. . . ." [4] The Church, therefore, ought to do this sort of education at its own expense.

In these three speeches Joaquim Nabuco expressed the leading objections on the part of some Brazilians to the union of Church and State. These Brazilians were for the most part young men who, with the abolition of slavery, were looking ahead to the day when free labor would replace it and were aware of the necessity of according the non-Catholic immigrant the same civil rights as those enjoyed by members of the traditional faith. It was a necessity which, once generally accepted, would profoundly alter the existing religious order, obliging the Church to give in on the questions of civil marriage and the secularization of cemeteries. Such concessions, brought about by pressures from the state in frequent conflict with the Papal Nuncio in Rio de Janeiro, would finally bring about a complete separation of Church and State, as in fact it did with the coming of the Republic. And in so smooth a manner that Catholicism did not resent this apparent lack of respect for the country's long religious tradition. On the contrary, because of the way in which the Empire, through some of its Masonic statesmen (one of them the Viscount do Rio Branco), had acted against the

[3] Ibid., pp. 197, 199, 202.
[4] Ibid., pp. 251, 252.

Church in the celebrated affair of the bishops, many Brazilian Catholics, including some particularly conscious of their religious responsibilities, were already predisposed to accept this separation.

Prince Dom Luís d'Orléans-Bragança, the most illustrious grandson of Pedro II and sometime pretender to his throne, recognized this in his perceptive analysis of the collapse of the Brazilian monarchy published in Paris in 1912 under the title *Sous la Croix du Sud* (*Under the Southern Cross*). He recalls that the affair of the bishops was the result of "too close a union between Church and State," a union which had "numerous inconveniences," including a lack of tact on both sides.[5] When the prelates insisted on prohibiting the entrance of Masons into religious organizations, the Imperial government "took the side of the Freemasons." As a result, the two bishops most active in the anti-Masonic cause, Dom Frei Vital, Bishop of Olinda, and Dom Antônio Macedo Costa, Bishop of Pará, proclaimed an interdict against the churches and chapels of the orders that refused to obey the anti-Masonic decree, a decree supported by Papal bulls. The government, in its turn, responded through the courts, and the bishops were condemned to spend four years in prison at hard labor. Through an Imperial act of clemency, the hard labor requirement was dispensed with, but the condemned men actually spent more than a year in prison before being released in 1875 under a decree of amnesty following the fall of the Rio Branco Cabinet.[6]

It was because of this "deplorable conflict"—as Prince Dom Luís calls it—that the Brazilian high clergy lost interest in the monarchy and came to regard the fifteenth of November as "a desirable liberation." [7] This also explains the publication of a pastoral letter on March 19, 1890, in which the Brazilian episcopacy expressed its rejoicing over the end of the "regal oppression" under which it had

[5] Luís d'Orléans-Bragança: *Sous la Croix du Sud* (Paris, 1912), p. 15.

[6] Dom Vital was a churchman whose influence was prolonged into the early Republic, reflected not only in the newspapers but also in many popular manifestations which turned the bishop into a charismatic figure and the object of almost saintly devotion. Some of these tributes were less ecclesiastical, however. One tobacco firm produced a cigarette named in his honor bearing the masculine, black-bearded portrait of the bishop as its trademark. For some time it was a favorite brand with Catholics, whereas the anti-clericals smoked José Marianos or Joaquim Nabucos. Brazilian newspapers of the time also contained advertisements for lotions and brilliantines which asserted that these brands were favored by Dom Vital in the care of his beard.

[7] Orléans-Bragança: op. cit., p. 16.

been living and looked forward, under the decree of separation enacted by the provisional government, to a degree of liberty never obtained by the Church under the monarchy.

Father Joseph Burnichon devotes an entire chapter of his *Le Brésil d'Aujourd'hui* to this affair, pointing out that under the Empire priests had become government functionaries, paid by the state like any other employee, and consequently drawn spiritually into the atmosphere of monarchic bureaucracy. No good had come of the "large proportion of priests" in the first Imperial Assembly, particulrly since some, if not all, of these clerical deputies were among the progressives who in 1828 favored legislation making way for the eventual suppression of religious orders in Brazil. This was the beginning of the long-drawn-out death agony of these orders, during which old and illustrious convents were degraded by being turned into barracks, public offices, libraries, provincial legislative assemblies, and asylums. An entire religious order was being disrupted under the pretext of bringing Brazil into the rhythm of Anglo-Saxon Protestant progress, an action which such men as Feijó and Abreu e Lima initially and later such others as the young Joaquim Nabuco and the young Ruy Barbosa—of the memorable preface to *O Papa e o Concílio*—maintained was not merely a progressive act but Progress itself. Absolute, unique, all-inclusive Progress in which Brazilian religion, repudiating the Hispano-Latin Catholicism which was causing it to fall behind Anglo-Saxons and Protestants, should without delay adjust to the present, divorce itself from the tutelage of Rome, and preserve merely a personal Catholicism, a Catholicism of individual conscience and sentiment and no more. Such was the advice of Joaquim Nabuco. These radical young men completely failed to see the value of Catholicism as a preserver of the family, by that cult linked to the patriarchal system in which the priests became a softened version of the Patriarch, the fashionable churches such as Nossa Senhora da Glória in Rio de Janeiro served as the locales for trysts and social gatherings, and aristocratic young ladies donated their long, silken hair to cover images of the saints and the Virgin, making these images virtually members of the family. Foreign Protestants naturally looked upon this poetic association with the patron saints as a simple evidence of superstitious popery, but it is difficult to excuse the Nabucos, Ruys, and Silveira Martins, who were brought up in the tradition, for their pedantic repudiation of the values embodied in these ritual relationships that were so vital a part of the religious order and so closely linked to the traditions of the family.

It is possible that some of these traditions were a survival of the Indian liturgy of the pagodas, absorbed by Catholicism through contact with the tropical Orient. Ewbank was convinced of this by the custom of votive offerings to the saints made in Brazilian churches and also by the Carnival, which he had seen in Rio de Janeiro during the early reign of Pedro II. But it has always been the custom of the Church to tolerate these practices whenever they are useful to the Catholic cause and in no way compromise the essential orthodoxy of the faith.

It must be noted that Protestants like Kidder and Fletcher found it merely picturesque that Brazilians of the nineteenth century should make gifts and vows to Our Lady in the form of varicolored ribbons, flowers, or precious stones, and of clothing for people of all ages—the latter the gift of mothers whose vows were made under the affliction of a sick child in the family.[8] In fact, this aesthetic of vows and offerings was merely an extension of the patriarchal era in which the very choice of clothing, houses, and furniture, instead of being made at personal whim, followed a religious order and system that governed virtually the entire existence of the individual. We need only note the influence this system has had on the academic dress, and particularly the academic rings, of the different schools and disciplines, in which colors, insignia, and jewels differ entirely from the system established in Europe during the Middle Ages. In Brazil, for example, the ruby stands for Law, the emerald for Medicine, the sapphire for Engineering. Nobody has been able to explain this aberration, but the Portuguese social historian João Lúcio d'Azevedo conjectures that it could indicate some remote oriental influence; the same sort of influence which probably affected the Church in its contact, both direct and indirect, with India and China.

So, too, the fireworks, to this day are inseparable from public celebration of saints' days, as well as from other celebrations in honor of important persons or events. On such days the firecracker, the set piece, and colored fires played an important role in the vigorous enthusiasm commemorating various saints, kings, princes, and also Brazilian victories which would aggrandize the country in foreign

---

[8] James C. Fletcher and Daniel P. Kidder: *Brazil and the Brazilians* (4th edn., Boston, 1879), p. 98.

eyes. For many of the ordinary people, even these secular demonstrations had a religious flavor; such victories could not have been gained, they would say, without the help and protection of God and the saints.

The oriental art of pyrotechnics in Brazil reached a peak of artistry perhaps unequalled in any other country in the hemisphere. Widely traveled foreign observers, on seeing the great fireworks displays held during Imperial days on Glória Hill in Rio de Janeiro, have stated that such artistry was matched only in China.[9] This skill had been developed through the long association of this undeniably pagan art with the festivals of the Catholic Church, particularly those in honor of Santo Antônio, São João, and São Pedro, when all Brazil—city, town, and village; farm, plantation, and ranch—became one scintillating display of fireworks. Every public square had its elaborate and dazzling set piece, every home its bonfire, and every child his cap pistol, pinwheels, and firecrackers. Then there were the celebrations of regional saints, or of the particular saints of the neighborhood, the street, or even the individual farm or plantation, celebrations which to this very day divide Brazilians into a complex of private cults and produce the additional spice of vigorous rivalries, with each group trying to outdo the other in its devotions to this or that Sainted Lady: the followers of Our Lady of Guadalupe disdaining the followers of Santa Ifigênia, both Negresses; those of Our Lady of Carmo lauding their patroness over those of Our Lady of Penha, both white, but one blond and the other brunette.

But these rivalries always paled beside the massive solidarity of Brazilians of all colors, races, climates, and regions behind the figures of São João, Santo Antônio, and São Pedro. In naming children, for example, the name Benedito (a black saint) is given only to Negroes or descendants of Negroes or to white boys whose pious Catholic mother, desperate to see her child survive, offers to humble both herself and her child by giving him a Negro name. The same could be said of such names as Ifigênia, or Maria do Rosário among the girls. But João, Antônio, and Pedro (along with José, Francisco, and Manuel) are names given to boys of all races, classes, and regions, as are Maria, Ana, and Teresa for girls.

It is interesting to note that, among the founders of the Brazilian Republic, there was Manuel Deodoro da Fonseca, whose name

9 Ibid., p. 99.

(generally under the form of Deodoro rather than Manuel) was given to many a Brazilian born in 1889. And there were many Ruys, Benjamins, and Florianos after the fifteenth of November, marking a new civic tendency in nomenclature in a country where the tradition had been to give the names of saints, classical figures, authors and literary characters such as Milton or Lamartine, heroes of the Paraguayan War, men of science and invention such as Newton, Franklin, Edison, or—in an affirmation of nativism—of American Indians. Nor was there any shortage of Catholic names among the orthodox: Vital, in honor of the bishop who became disillusioned with the royalism of the Empire, or Pío (Pius), or Leão (Leo), or Luís Gonzaga, or Francisco de Assis, or Vicente de Paulo. There were also numerous Marias de Lourdes in honor of the new Catholic devotee, or Marias de Nazareth, or Marias de Aparecida, or Maria Isabels—the last in honor of the Princess considered by many, and especially by Negroes, as a great Catholic and redemptress of the Negro race. There were many Teresas, for the Empress Teresa Cristina, "mother of Brazilians," as well as Franciscas and Januárias after the royal princesses. And despite the opposition to Jesuitism both within and outside the Church, there continued to be admirers who gave their children the name of Inácio Loyola.

One who certainly was no admirer and whose younger years were marked by strong anti-clerical feelings was Ruy Barbosa, author of a proposal in 1890 to separate Church and State. Passed into law and incorporated into the Constitution one year later, this proposal continued the interdiction of the Company of Jesus and prohibited the foundation of convents and monasteries. Another, as we have already seen, was Joaquim Nabuco, who twenty-five years earlier had anticipated Ruy in his advocacy of a Catholicism of "conscience and sentiment." A Catholicism almost devoid of ritual, without processions in the streets or novenas to the saints; without festivals, or chaplets or cults of the Virgin in the home. A Catholicism which would become Anglo-Saxonized, Protestantized, copied from the Methodism of England and the Quakers of the United States as, in other walks of life, Brazilians had copied these countries' laws or customs or sports (at a time, strangely enough, when these countries, through the Oxford Movement and the growing Romanism of the Episcopal Church, were going through the most Latinizing process in their religious history). Actually, it was Nabuco's or Ruy Barbosa's kind of exhortation which led a considerable number of the Brazilian élite to become indifferent to the Church, with the result that, even during the Empire, the priesthood attracted a substantially smaller number of candidates. And with the Republic, there were many who added anti-clerical sentiments to their republicanism.

The clergy in due time rebelled against the provisions in the Constitution of the Republic which excluded the Company of Jesus and the foundation of monastic institutions. And they rebelled with such vigor that even Ruy Barbosa had to give way before the traditional Catholicism represented with unequalled authority by Dom Antônio Macedo Costa, Bishop of Bahia. The bishop demanded the right of all Brazilians to worship God and practice the Christian religion according to the traditions of the country, traditions he implied, if not declaring in so many words, were Latin, Roman, and Spanish. As a Brazilian Catholic, he was consequently directly opposed to the un-Brazilian and un-Catholic proposal which would be the first step in separating Church and State.

As a result of this vigorous protest on the part of the Brazilian episcopacy, the separation law which was finally enacted in 1890, in the words of Father Joseph Burnichon, "could hardly have been more benevolent and amicable." And the good French Jesuit, writing in 1908, could not forego the temptation to add the ironic commentary: ". . . the author of the law punished himself later by entrusting the Jesuits with the education of his son." [1] We shall see later that Joaquim Nabuco ended up as a practicing Catholic and completed his reintegration with Brazilian religion when one of his sons entered the priesthood.

The decline in the calling to the priesthood, nevertheless, was one of the gravest problems of the period. With the gradual breakup of the patriarchal system in family, economic, and political life, the priest was faced with an entirely different situation. Formerly the religious activity of the country had been more under the control of the patriarch than of the bishop, with the clergyman filling the comfortable role of uncle-priest, more a member of the family than an individual priest at the service of the Church. As this pleasant and easy relationship disappeared, many young Brazilians who would formerly have tamely entered the priesthood in accordance with the fondest wishes of a pious mother or the stern orders of an

[1] Joseph Burnichon: *Le Brésil d'Aujourd'hui* (Paris, 1910), pp. 192, 193.

imperious father found their interests turning to other professions. And the former patriarchs themselves were less anxious to have their sons enter a calling whose duties, now become exclusively clerical or monastic, would be of considerably less advantage to the institution of the family. In an oral testimony, one illustrious Brazilian who at the end of the past century decided to enter the priesthood confesses that his experience was vastly different from that of his uncle, a classical type of uncle-priest. For the younger man, the association was not one of private chaplain to a family whose interests were tribal and, by extension, national, but rather to the Church, whose prestige now surpassed that of any individual patriarch and whose laws demanded a religious devotion and a fidelity to duty far greater than anything which had existed in previous generations. In the face of these demands, together with the simultaneous decline in the prestige of the family, there was a decline in the number of young men entering the seminaries. By 1907 Brazil could claim only 1 priest for every 15,000 Catholics, whereas the United States—a Protestant country—had a ratio of 1 to 867.[2]

This decline in numbers, however, seems to have brought about a not inconsiderable strengthening of the intellectual and moral qualities of the Brazilian clergy. Under the patriarchal regime, far too many agreed to enter the priesthood simply for the social prestige then attached to an ecclesiastical career, with the result that the Brazilian clergy became notorious for its "immorality." "There is no class of men in the whole Empire whose lives and practices are so corrupt as those of the priesthood," says Fletcher and Kidder in the 1879 edition of *Brazil and the Brazilians*.[3]

Certainly the duties of a priest were not particularly onerous, in Fletcher's opinion. At a time when almost everyone suffered from wearing clothes "exceedingly inconvenient in a warm climate . . . under a hot sun that makes everyone else swelter, the padre, with his uncovered tonsured head, with his thin gowns and airy laces, seems prepared for a tropical clime." His religious activity consisted largely in saying mass in the cool of the early morning, bringing the Host to the dying, and accompanying funerals, almost invariably in a car or wagon. He also baptized, performed marriages, and heard confessions. Church holidays, both solemn and festive, were no longer so numerous as in former times and by 1878 were confined

2 Ibid., p. 198.
3 Fletcher and Kidder: op. cit., p. 141.

generally to Easter, Palm Sunday, Allelujah, with its Judas, and the festivals of São Jorge, São João, Santo Antônio, and São Pedro, with their fireworks, their horse racing (a British import), and their "auctions." [4] In some places, to the scandal of Protestant foreigners, images of the Holy Spirit could be bought in gold, silver, or some other silver-like metal: each with its respective price. Priests were often professors, or poets, or journalists; others were politicians, members of the Chamber of Deputies or the Senate. Thus even the average padre, according to Fletcher, was most eloquent *"in ore rotundo Lusitaniam"* and in the pulpit.

Anglo-Saxon visitors like Ewbank, Kidder, and Fletcher, whose close attention to Brazilian religious life during the late Empire convinced them that the Brazilians were victims of popery, were further astonished to see advertisements for prayers to be used against illness and pestilence appearing in the Rio de Janeiro newspapers alongside similar displays pushing the sale of drugs and remedies: "Prayers to bless the home against the present epidemic, ornamented with religious emblems. Price 80 *reis*, Rua dos Latoeiros, No. 59." Or "Sainted Words, Religion's weapon against the terrors of cholera, which will be calmed by Divine Justice, as was the case in the royal monastery of Santa Clara in Coimbra in 1480. Sold in the Rua da Quitanda, No. 174. Price, 320 *reis*." [5] Fletcher also noted that many Brazilians relied as well on a scapular worn Arab-fashion around the neck to protect them from the plague.

For this same reason there were frequent processions of penitents during the Second Empire, with men dressed in rags and fine ladies going barefoot. Though such processions disappeared in the capital cities with the coming of the Republic, they continued to exist in the interior during the early decades of the century and, indeed, in some places are still to be seen to this day, particularly in sanctuaries such as those of Lapa, Aparecida, Santo Amaro de Serinharém, or São Severino dos Ramos, and occasionally in urban centers as well, for example at Nosso Senhor de Bonfim in Bahia or Nazareth in Santa Maria de Belém. The puritan in the Reverend Mr. Fletcher caused him to be repelled by "the grand annual festival of Nazareth"; to him such things were not religious edification but merely excuses for dancing, fireworks, and games of chance. [6] And another

4 Ibid., pp. 144–5, 147–8.
5 Ibid., pp. 158–9.
6 Ibid., p. 562.

Protestant clergyman, the Englishman Walsh, stated that the Brazilians were rivalled only by the Turks in the vast quantities of gun-
powder they managed to explode on these festive occasions.

All these observers noted, as might be expected, that Brazilian
Catholics had considerably less respect for the Sabbath than did the
Anglo-Saxon Protestants. In this the Brazilians, of course, were not
exceptional; the same attitude could have been found among the
French and Italians. There were military parades on Sundays, and
the theatres and opera houses were even more crowded than on
weekdays. This was also the day for lively percussive music in the
parks and public squares, played from those oriental-style band-
stands found in every Brazilian small town during the early century.

The Church, for its part, was generally indifferent at the time to
the significance of the Sabbath, both as an occasion of strict religious observance and as a period of rest for the workingman, including the store employees of capitals such as Rio de Janeiro, Salvador,
Recife, São Paulo, and Belém. In 1878, while all the foreign commercial establishments closed their doors on Sundays, many domestic retail stores remained open, at least during the morning hours.
Sunday was also the favorite day for auctions, a Brazilian custom
which continues to this day despite a law prohibiting it passed in
1852. But those who were most scandalized by this treatment of
Sunday as just another working day overlooked the number of
saints' days during the year which closed the stores and gave their
employees enough holidays almost to compensate for the Sunday
rest and recreation denied them by their employers.

In this connection it is interesting to note the listing of saints'
days found in the *Teologia Moral* of Father Manuel do Monte
Rodrigues d'Araújo, professor of religion at the Olinda seminary
and later Ninth Bishop of Rio de Janeiro and Count de Irajá. Here
it is shown that Brazil under Dom Pedro II celebrated not only
those specific days decreed by Urban VIII in 1642, but also added,
as the decree permitted, the local celebration of the patron saint of
the province, the city, and the neighborhood. Such days were divided into days of rest, of which there were from 20 to 25, and
some 10 to 15 days of dispensation, when working was allowed but
attendance at mass was obligatory. This will perhaps indicate the
greater importance attached to saints' days than to Sundays and
suggest the paralyzing effect such celebrations tended to exert on

commerce, industry, and farming at the time. It was therefore in the economic interest of the country that the Church permitted Sunday labor, just as the businessmen, together with the plantation owners and industrialists, tacitly accepted their obligation to observe the splendid religious festivals with which the Catholic Church maintained the religious order of the country without feeling itself obliged to take up a strict position on the keeping of the Sabbath.

There were those who noted that on Sundays, in cities throughout the Empire, "many shops are kept open and some kinds of outdoor labor carried on. Billiard rooms and other places of amusement are more frequented than on workdays." [7] In fact, it was only on Sunday afternoons that workers and shop clerks were able to enjoy a holiday. One clerk at the end of the nineteenth century states that on two Sundays a month he had to remain in the store all day, acting as a guard while the others took their afternoon off. Only the clerks whose establishments closed on Sundays could have the whole day free from billiards, for lounging in the public square, or for the theatre.

At the theatre one of their great favorites at the time was Ester de Carvalho, whose fans among the clerks sported a white carnation as a sign of their almost idolatrous worship of this artist. The university students, who favored the Spaniard Pepa Ruiz, indicated their preference by a red carnation.[8] Unlike the clerks, they also carried canes. Each group had its own particular patron saint as well and kept to itself in the religious processions. It was not long before the military cadets formed a third group, with their particular favorites among actresses and saints and their own fraternal or social organizations. And the same thing happened with the young proletarians, except that, not having the money to attend the theatre, they chose their favorite performers from among the *pastôras* of the folk plays.

In conjunction with the patriarchal order, the Church through its various organizations also took on the responsibility for treating illness and for assisting the aged and the needy; the importance of its contribution in these fields cannot be exaggerated. Some of these organizations were Masonic in nature, but despite the violence within the Church over the question of Masonry, no one was in-

---

[7] C. C. Andrews: *Brazil, Its Condition and Prospects* (New York, 1887), p. 52.
[8] Múcio da Paixão: *Cenográfias* (Rio de Janeiro, 1905).

clined to fault the order for its works of benevolence. Enormous sums were spent on these works, which were the essential objective of the order, and the organization of such services was so highly perfected that no commentator on the religious life of the period has failed to recognize the positive contribution of Masonic activities to the Christian civilization of Brazil.

Émile Allain says that the Santa Casa de Misericórdia of Rio de Janeiro was a "magnificent establishment of the first order," able to accommodate 1,200 patients; the wards and consulting rooms, supervised by the Sisters of São Vicente de Paulo, also served as a clinic for the Medical School.[9] Here in 1884 free treatment was given in dentistry, electrotherapy, ophthalmology, gynecology. Medicines were furnished without charge, and there was a division for homeopathic remedies. The poor could obtain the services of this clinic through a simple certificate signed by a responsible authority, and foreigners would be extended the same privileges on the request of their respective consuls. Seamen of all nationalities were entitled to free treatment, not only in this hospital but also in any other institution of the Misericórdia, such as that of Pernambuco, Bahia, or Santos. Nowhere in this association was there any discrimination of patients on grounds of race, color, or creed. Other hospitals in Rio de Janeiro at the time included that of Nossa Senhora da Saúde, in Gambôa, for treatment of contagious diseases; Nossa Senhora do Socorro, in São Cristóvão; São João Batista, in Botafogo; Cascadura, for tuberculosis; Pedro II, for mental disorders; a home for abandoned infants; and an orphanage.

The administration of the Misericórdia had from early times been in the hands of men who were "good" in a double sense of the word: in terms both of public benevolence and nobility of family, men whose devotion to charitable deeds was alike an expression of Christian devotion and *noblesse oblige*. José Clemente Pereira was one who particularly distinguished himself in the administration of the Misericórdia, which he turned into a sort of superministry dedicated to the protection of the sick, the orphaned, the poor, and the unfortunate in a society where the paternalism of the old order was disappearing. We know that the initiative for erecting a marble statue to this man came from Pedro II himself, a deserved honor to one who knew so well how to put his Christianity into practice and whose post in the Misericórdia was raised by his own work into one

[9] Émile Allain: *Rio de Janeiro, Quelques Données sur la Capitale et sur l'Administration du Brésil* (2nd edn., Rio de Janeiro, 1886), pp. 232–8.

of the most honorable offices a man could hold in the Imperial capital. Indeed, this is attested to by the category of his successors: the Viscount do Paraná; the Marquês de Abrantes; Counselor Zacharias de Góis e Vasconcellos, who was director until his death in 1877 and was often caricatured dressed as a friar—or nun!; the Viscount de Jaguari; or the Baron de Cotegipe, another figure much caricatured, though more for his taste for elegant French girls than his layman's piety. Nevertheless, this man of the world was an excellent administrator from 1882 to his death in 1889, and it was during his administration that the Pasteur Institute was created within the Misericórdia system.

Under Cotegipe's successor, the Viscount de Cruzeiro, the Misericórdia system was separated from the Church; the Viscount resigned in protest. Under Counselor Paulino José Soares de Sousa (1890–1901) the juridical situation of the institution was finally worked out to conform with the new policy of separation of Church and State and the various Misericórdias were given a tax-exempt status.[1]

It should be noted that the Misericórdias and other religious orders were at this time receiving sizable bequests from Brazilian and foreign businessmen who had made their fortunes in Brazil. In this connection Allain wrote that "the love that these orders engender in a great number of their members is remarkable; it is very rarely that they are not included, sometimes very substantially, in the legacies left by members who have been favored by fortune. This practice is particularly frequent in the Portuguese colony."[2] It was through such legacies that the institutions were able to expand and improve their services. The practice of bestowing gifts or legacies to the orders became one of the most characteristic expressions of the religious life of the time, so much so that any rich Catholic not given to religious or charitable works was seen in a very bad light. The gesture also had its overtones of status; a rich man gained prestige as a member or benefactor of one of the orders able to display its regalias and insignias. Those of the Misericórdia were long sleeveless garments and black staves with gold trimmings used by members at funerals, processions, and other solemnities. Members of the governing board were distinguished from the ordinary members by a cross of purple velvet on the left breast; the Pur-

---

[1] Ataulfo Nápoles de Paiva: *Assistência Pública e Privada no Rio de Janeiro— História e Estatística* (Rio de Janeiro, 1922), p. 287.

[2] Allain: op. cit., p. 240.

veyor, or head of the order, by a jacket lined with purple silk, a cap of gold cloth, and a staff bearing the arms of the Misericórdia, the five wounds on a cross circled by a crown of thorns.

Another prestigious order of the time in Rio de Janeiro was the Candallária. During the late Empire it took charge of the Imperial Hospital for Lepers founded in the eighteenth century by the Count da Cunha. This was a public institution, in contrast to many of the nineteenth-century religious hospitals, which restricted their excellent medical and surgical services (and their cemeteries) exclusively to members of the order. Such were the Third Orders of San Francisco and of Carmo in Rio de Janeiro and other cities; the latter became famous in the capital for the burial of its members in a private church constructed for the exclusive use of the Third Order, which formerly had conducted its services in the Convent of the Carmelites.[3] Bodies of deceased brethren were interred in separate graves under the interior of the temple, but this practice was later discontinued because of excessive "olfactory discomfort" and "danger to health," though the principle of burial in a private church remained unchanged. Subterranean burial was merely replaced by a gallery of vaults, a system which was generally practiced in Brazil until interior burials were prohibited in 1850. This prohibition encountered some resistance from Catholics, such as those of the Third Order of Carmo, who had become accustomed to consider the churches as their private cemeteries. But in 1857 the order resigned itself to urban progress and acquired a portion of the public cemetery of São Francisco Xavier for the exclusive use of its deceased members. Other important orders throughout the country generally followed similar practices.

During the last half of the nineteenth century, special charity funds were instituted for indigent members, as in the case of the Order of the Blessed Sacrament of São José Parish in Rio de Janeiro. One was that of Nossa Senhora da Piedade, founded in 1855 at the Church of Santa Cruz dos Militares in Rio de Janeiro largely through the efforts of the Baroness de Taquari. According to its somewhat poetic declaration of purpose, this fund was intended "to perpetuate the art of clemency through which the Divine Providence, through the intervention of the Blessed Virgin, our Lady of Piety, brought an end to the scourge of cholera morbus which assailed the people of Brazil, and to commemorate the act of humility

[3] Ibid., pp. 234, 254.

and Christian charity on the part of many ladies of the Church of Santa Cruz dos Militares, who set an example by begging alms for those afflicted by the plague." One of the activities of this fund on behalf of church members was to assist spinsters, widows, and wives whose husbands were "unable to provide support for the family, though those who have fallen into indigency, as certified by a commission of the Order, will be judged closely for their moral probity." [4]

During this period the Spiritists, with their benevolent associations, also began to play a notable part in Brazilian religious life. Many of these associations were similar in nature to those of the Catholics, one of the first being the Confucian Group, founded in 1873 but dissolved two years later. A second, the God, Christ, and Charity Society for Spiritual Studies, was founded in 1876, out of which was born a third: the Society for Spiritist Brotherhood, which was given to abolitionist activities. In 1882 the Federation of Brazilian Spiritists was organized; one of its founders was a future marshal of the Army, Francisco Raimundo Ewerton Quadros. This federation included an assistance fund for the needy and also established a "school for mediums." In 1912 a Spiritist Hospital was founded in Rio de Janeiro for "persons afflicted by mental alienation" who wished to submit themselves to treatment "by the fluid currents organized by the upper astral regions." [5]

It was also during this period that evangelism became a characteristic part of Brazilian religious life through meeting houses organized for members of the various evangelical sects. Most of the persons belonging to these sects were Brazilians of humble origin, though there were also enthusiasts of cultivated background, such as Júlio Ribeiro, who for a time was a great advocate of Tolstoyan Christianity. In 1893 the members of one of these congregations founded the Brazilian Y.M.C.A., which in Rio de Janeiro gave considerable impetus to the teaching of physical education. [6] In 1887 another Protestant group in the capital had organized to establish a hospital for Protestants and for the unfortunate, regardless of creed. In 1912 this institution, the Evangelist Hospital, began a course for the training of nurses, an American innovation in a country where nurses had customarily been Sisters of Charity. It was

[4] Paiva: op. cit., pp. 235, 236.
[5] Ibid., pp. 243, 245.
[6] Ibid., p. 103.

not long before the American mission school, the Colégio Americano, was established in Rio de Janeiro, followed by similarly sponsored and named institutions in Recife, Salvador, São Paulo, and
Minas Gerais. These "American" schools gained some prestige at
the time through the Pan-American Conference, which took place
in Rio de Janeiro in 1906 under the presidency of Joaquim Nabuco,
first Ambassador of Brazil to the United States. The spirit of Pan-
Americanism held a particular charisma at the time. The figure of
Uncle Sam, which appeared very frequently in Brazilian magazines,
symbolized a new material and moral force in the world, a symbolism which also reflected on these schools that called themselves
"American" and whose patron was Joaquim Nabuco—despite the
fact that Nabuco at this period was no longer an anti-clericist and
had returned to the most correct practice of Catholic ritual.

Older than the Spiritists and the Protestants among the minority
groups were the Jews and the Moslems, but these did not make
their presence particularly felt in the religious life of the nation.
During the last decades of the Empire, a considerable number of
Negro Moslems were brought to Brazil as slaves, and their brown
and black descendants, once having attained their freedom, made
their money in commerce or technical trades and returned to Africa. In *Brazil and the Brazilians*, Fletcher and Kidder describe how
a travelling group of English Quakers in Rio de Janeiro was sought
out by a group of Mina Negroes. "They had earned money by
hard labor and had purchased their freedom and were now desirous
of returning to their native land." But, having saved their passage
money, they wished to learn from the English Protestants whether
or not the African coast was really free of slavers. The Quakers
could hardly believe that these people really had money, but they
were shown "a copy of the charter under which sixty of their
number had [already] sailed, and which showed that they had paid
four thousand dollars passage money." [7] The sixty had arrived
safely on the coast of Benim the year before. Soon after their interview with the Minas, the Quakers Candler and Burgess received the
thanks of these Negroes on "a paper beautifully written in Arabic
by one of their chiefs, who is a Mohammedan."

What is particularly interesting about the Negroes who returned
to Africa is that, whether Moslem or animist, they continued to live
like Brazilians in Africa, remaining apart from the native Africans

[7] Fletcher and Kidder: op. cit., p. 136.

and to a large extent retaining the Catholic religious practices they had learned in Brazil. About the only significant change in their worship was that the devotees of Nosso Senhor do Bonfim, once in Africa, changed the sex of their patron to Nossa Senhora do Bonfim. This altered survival of Brazilian culture in Africa probably occurred for reasons that call for psychological, as well as sociological, analysis.[8] The change might have been effected to efface the memory of the patriarchal power of the white man and to replace it with the glorification of the mother, or of Woman in general, so characteristic of Brazilian Catholicism in the late nineteenth century. Christian purists have accused Brazilian Catholics of Mariolatry. In its highest form, it was this sort of Mariolatry which probably motivated Dom Vital Maria de Oliveira himself when he took the side of the Mother Church against the paternal Imperial government.

Father Joseph Burnichon, on attending a Day of Kings festival in Bahia, was impressed by the cult of the Infant Jesus so prevalent there, particularly among the colored people. Most of the devotees were women dressed in white, who were divided into various groups, each with its separate symbol: the Sun, the Earth, the Dawn, the Lamb, the Buzzard, the Butterfly.[9] Each group was preceded by its own band and sang its own Christmas songs in honor of the Infant Jesus and the Mother. The central figures of the cult were, of course, Christian, but the rites were largely African in nature. Even more African was the cult of Iemanjá, where the maternal central figure was a fusion of Our Lady with the African goddess of the waters.

The combination of African and Christian elements in the religious life of Brazilian Negroes interested several students of Brazilian life during the period. One was the Bahian physician Nina Rodrigues, whose essay "L'Animisme Fétichiste des Nègres de Bahia" appeared in French in Bahia at the end of the century. The infiltration of the African voodoo element not only intrigued foreigners but also absorbed—and often scandalized—Brazilian Catholics, who saw it as both a problem in pathology which defied the doctors and a disturbing liturgical question for the Church authorities. Fa-

[8] This is emphasized in the second edition of my *Problemas Brasileiros de Antropologia* (Rio de Janeiro, 1943), written with the collaboration of the French scholar Pierre Verger.

[9] Burnichon: op. cit., p. 72.

ther Burnichon, an erudite and orthodox Jesuit, naturally took the latter view; while Nina Rodrigues saw the diabolic possession of the rites as a form of hysteria.[1] Both theologians and medical men had equal cause for alarm, which was compounded by the fact (shown by the systematic studies of Nina Rodrigues) that in Bahia, along with the Negroes, many whites in moments of affliction sought neither physician nor priest, but rather the witch doctor and the *orixá*. The number of these whites was "incalculable," said Nina Rodrigues, because "nearly the entire population, with the exception of a few individuals of superior enlightenment," allowed itself to be drawn to voodooism. It is curious that Nina himself, while still a young men, died in Paris at the beginning of the twentieth century of a mysterious disease which baffled the European physicians. More than one Bahian stated darkly that Nina had died a victim of an evil spell brought upon him for his scientific meddling in matters which his African friends had often warned him to shun.

The Brazilian situation did not seem as alarming to Father Burnichon as it did to orthodox Brazilians; he probably recalled that even in French provinces like Brittany there were simple folk who still mixed pagan elements with their Catholic faith. In Bahia, "for the most part, they have a naïve but sincere respect for sacred things." This respect was seen in the custom of giving the sign of the Cross when passing a church, and also in the habit on the part of both whites and Negroes of donning ceremonial surplices and robes during processions. It was shown too in the warmth with which men and women at Christmas or after midnight mass kissed the image of the Infant Jesus, and in the veneration accorded the well-dressed images of the Virgin and the saints. As for the cult of image worship, Father Burnichon noted, as had Ewbank during the early reign of Pedro II, that Brazilians "spend hours in contemplating them and in giving them their homage and their prayers." [2]

This image worship was carried to extremes in Bahia in the cult of Nosso Senhor do Bonfim, as it had been during Imperial times in Rio by the cult of St. George (always depicted riding a white horse). These were the most popular cults of the period—for saints had their transitory vogues in Brazil and rarely achieved the permanent veneration of Santo Antônio in Lisbon. Others were Nossa Senhora Aparecida in São Paulo, Nazareth in Pará, and São Se-

[1] Ibid., p. 78.
[2] Ibid., pp. 78–9.

verino dos Ramos in Pernambuco. Vows and obligations to these saints were not limited to giving thanks for past benefactions to oneself or members of the family, but extended also to domestic animals, farm equipment, boats, wagons, and other means of transportation. I believe that such vows on behalf of technical and economic objects during the late nineteenth century were the first example of the interpenetration of religious and economic elements in the development of Brazil in general, and rural Brazil in particular.

Vows to the saints were also made for political ends, but such ends were frequently served by recourse to witchcraft, with the evocation of charms and *"despachos"* (packages containing charmed objects sent to or left on the doorstep of the intended victim). Well-known public figures have been known to participate in these activities, invoking the aid of voodoo priests and sorcerers in their political battles, either for their own success or for the defeat (even death) of a political adversary. Gossip has it that the attempt to kill Governor Barbosa Lima of Pernambuco with a poisoned dish at a political banquet, an act involving the governor's political adversary José Mariano, was made only after the original plan to have him done away with by witchcraft had been abandoned. The poison had been prepared by white medical friends of Mariano's and had been placed in a dish of fried meat by a Negro cook, perhaps indicating a lack of faith in the efficacy of magic on the part of the scientific-minded physicians. Nevertheless, it was science which failed, because the governor did not die; perhaps an evil charm would have done a better job after all. According to good authority, the cook, who narrowly escaped being a murderer, on his deathbed years later begged the pardon of Barbosa Lima for his criminal act and died a devout Catholic.

In Bahia Father Burnichon, in the church of Bonfim, observed an ex-voto placed there by the governor himself in gratitude to Our Lord for having escaped an assassination attempt at the hands of one of his most dangerous political adversaries. "Dr. Marcelino de Sousa was struck by the assassin's bullet," reads the text of the offering, "but Our Lord of Bonfim made the ruffian's hand tremble and the wound was not fatal." [3]

At about the same point early in the century, Paulo Barreto, collecting material for what is perhaps the best piece of sociological reporting to date, his *As Religiões no Rio* (*The Religions of Rio,*

[3] Ibid., p. 81.

written under the pseudonym João do Rio), tells of having heard
old Negro conjurers "speak of being on most intimate terms with
the most important persons in recent history—with the former Emperor, whose portrait they had, with Cotegipe, with the Baron de
Mamanguape, as well as with the Presidents of the Republic." This
distinguished author tells us that he lived for months amid Negro
practitioners of witchcraft, "whose way of life people pretended
not to know about" but "whose ministrations they sought when
tormented by a personal sorrow or a secret ambition." Such conjurers, who flocked to Rio at the time, were scattered throughout
the city, from the docks to the Santa Cruz Highway, and performed their craft with a degenerated admixture of Mohammedan-
ism or Catholicism. Their "eminent friends" did not hesitate to
listen to them, and the conjurers became wealthy at the expense of
their well-heeled clients.[4] They formed "a sort of Masonic order,"
of which the chief officer was one Ojó, of the Rua dos Andradas.
But within this general defensive alliance there were many dissen-
sions, particularly between members of the rival African and Brazilian traditions in witchcraft.

We can assume that these divided traditions also had their political significance during the first years of the Republic, some being
on the side of Floriano and others on that of the rebellious military.
João do Rio learned of a white political conspiracy which employed Negro conjurers for "nothing more or less than the murder
of a former President of the Republic." And he adds: "At first I
thought this impossible, but my informants simply cited the names
of those publicly implicated in conspiracies. . . ." According to his
Negro informants, it would have been sufficient for the President
to have been seen at a palace window in order to ensure his death
within two months. When asked how this was to happen, the informants said that it was difficult to explain but that it had something to do with "prayers and large-scale slaughtering" which had
taken place in the fields, an ox being employed to represent the
important person who was intended to die.[5]

This author also tells us that some of these houses of witchcraft
were connected with houses of another category and that in 1906 he
had seen "ladies of high position descending furtively from hired
carriages as in the cheap romances, their faces hidden by heavy

[4] João do Rio (Paulo Barreto): *As Religiões no Rio* (Rio de Janeiro, 1906), pp.
9, 26–7.

[5] Ibid., p. 30.

veils, running quickly into these houses. . . ." Furthermore, he was able to follow a certain sorceress to various houses in "Bota-fogo and Tijucá, where, during the winter, there are receptions and conversations at five in the afternoon just as in Paris or in the palaces of Italy." Once he was shown the portrait of a young lady whom he had considered respectable. "But why?" he asked his informant. "She wishes to marry this man," responded the sorcerer, showing the portrait of a well-known lawyer.[6]

In questioning Martiniano do Bonfim in Bahia and a "Father Adam" in Recife, I was given information on the secret relationship between well-known whites and conjurers which corroborated the material presented by João do Rio as a result of his earlier investigations in the capital. During this period, more than one elegant white client who read Renan and quoted Le Bon, Spencer, and Comte had solicited the aid of Martiniano or Adam in resolving some political or amorous difficulty.

Could it be that the Catholic saints, after the separation of Church and State, had refused any longer to attend to afflictions, desires, and promises of this sort? There were some requests, of course, which they never had honored: those requiring the mysterious death of a chief of state, for example. But vows or requests related to marriages, political success, professional triumphs, success in examinations, and cures for diseases or vices—to judge by the grateful testimonies of beneficiaries, some of which appeared discreetly in the classified advertising pages of the newspapers—were clearly being attended to efficiently. It appears, then, that the large clientele of well-known persons who resorted to witch doctoring represented a mystical element that sought out the African "saints" for matters they considered unworthy of attention by the Catholic contingent: political or erotic desires, business deals of a dubious nature, and the like. In going to the conjurers, such whites were involuntarily paying some sort of homage in reverse to the saints and priests of the Church, however unsaintly they continued to be in certain aspects of their lives.

The truth is that there were a number of Church figures during the period who were looked upon almost as saints, not only for their piety but also for their services to the poor. Such a person was Sister Paula in Rio de Janeiro, and there were also the monks who made missionary journeys into the interior to combat Protestantism, to marry and baptize persons in remote areas that lacked the

[6] Ibid., pp. 33, 34.

regular services of the clergy, and to warn the folk against the se-
ductions of self-styled "prophets" like Antônio Conselheiro, José
Maria, Padre Cícero, or the notorious Jacobina, the last-named operating among the rustic Germans of the south and spreading a fanaticism equal to that of the former Anabaptists of Central Europe.

The Capuchins were perhaps the most notable of these missionary workers for ethical and religious order, but the Franciscans also
did much to bring the Church to the humble folk of both the cities
and the rural areas, adopting a type of sermon that was at once
populist and missionary in nature. It was this type of activity that
afforded the greatest resistance to the Protestants, the Spiritists, and
the African sects in their infiltration of every level of Brazilian society. Such non-Catholic infiltration, encouraged by the lack of
priests, was particularly easy among the descendants of slaves who,
having lost the religious services of the patriarchal system, were left
without priests of their own. Many of these former slaves fell easily
under the spell of witch doctors, some of whom were not the most
scrupulous of individuals. Finding themselves suddenly free, these
former slaves also felt the anguish of a loss of protection and direction, far from adjusted to a liberty suddenly thrust upon them by
romantic abolitionists who failed to realize that the gift of freedom
could amount to a mere gesture and constitute a real danger to the
beneficiaries when not accompanied by some modicum of religious
and social assistance. It was only natural, then, that the recipients of
this false liberty should seek support and consolation in the African
sects and at the hands of witch doctors. And what happened at
these hands was also to be expected: the supplicants were all too
often exploited and deceived by the unscrupulous conjurers. Once
having been taken in, however, many began to experience a nostalgia for the religion they had known on the plantations, with its
festivals, processions, and rosaries, as well as for the protection
against the abuses of their masters they had felt through membership in the cult of the Blessed Virgin.

For these reasons, the Capuchins enjoyed great success in recon-
verting these people. Frei Pazza, an Italian Capuchin, told João do
Rio in 1905 that every Friday he worked from four in the morning
until four in the afternoon at "exorcising" penitents and that in the
year 1905 he had reconverted more than 300 of the "possessed." [7]
Satan was now threatening Brazil more than ever, he stated, and it

7 Ibid., p. 177.

was necessary to defeat him by uprooting his influence through individual exorcism, performed often in private so that the Devil, speaking through the mouth of the possessed, could not tell things which would injure others. In these ceremonies the priest, in purple vestments, would read the act of exorcism from the ritual, making the sign of the Cross on the head, belly, chest, and heart of the penitent, and, in the name of Jesus Christ, calling a powerful curse upon the "spirit-minion of Satan." Most of these cases of possession, said Frei Pazza, were to be found "principally in the unwashed lower classes." This to some extent confirms the progressive mystique of Osvaldo Cruz, who stated that the Devil loved squalor. However new this discovery may have been for the scientists, it had long been part of the knowledge of the Church and the Capuchins, well acquainted with persons who, under a spell, would bend double, or become clairvoyant, or speak in tongues. Frei Pazza tells of one young girl who spat on the Cross and said evil things of other persons. Worse still was the case of a woman of Rio, one Cabocla, who claimed to command 250 spirits and whose presence caused strange rumblings, the falling of furniture, and the breaking of glass.[8] Frei Pazza never did succeed in exorcising this one; she claimed to have been born with the spirits and did not want to lose them. Perhaps understandable resistance on the part of a primitive native to a foreign monk—one of the many Italians, Belgians, and Germans who were the principal agents of victory over the Positivism, Spiritism, and vague mysticism resurgent in the Empire during the last years of the Voltairean Pedro II.[9]

[8] Ibid., pp. 181–2.

[9] In the original edition a series of individual responses to questions on religious matters follows: 106 persons are quoted, almost all of whom claim Catholicism to a certain degree, though some are critical of Catholic practices and many admit respect for or even adherence to Positivist thought at one time or another during their lives. (Translator.)

❦ [X] ❦

Catholicism and Progress

T HE DECADE OF THE 1870's was for many reasons a decisive one in Brazilian development. From the economic standpoint, it was the decade of the Law of the Free Womb (1871), which marked the beginning of a national revolution in the field of labor. Politically, it was the period of the Republican Manifesto, which for complex ecological as well as political reasons marked the emergence of the São Paulo–Minas Gerais–Rio Grande do Sul region as the leading force in the nation's political life. Considered as a point in cultural and intellectual history, it was the great age of Positivism in the south and Teutonic and Spencerian thought in the north, all of which had an adverse effect on orthodox Catholicism, as well as on jurisprudence and belles-lettres and on the general aesthetic values of the more sophisticated.

And it is from the 1870's that we must date the volcanic presence of Dom Vital, Bishop of Olinda, in the Catholic life of the Empire: a conservative revolutionary whose relatively brief ascendancy marked the beginning of a new tempo in the religious life of Brazil, in which a series of changes in the established routine began to have both quantitative and qualitative effects on the behavior of the clergy and on Brazilians in general. These changes can be said to have constituted a phase of Catholic progress, a relative progress to be sure, but progress toward developing a closer approximation between the conduct and events of daily life and the religious and ethical ideals of the Mother Church in particular and Western Christianity in general.

It is for this conduct and these events that the past is of interest to this study: the social, sexual, cultural, and, so far as possible, intimate past of the Brazilian people. Critics of the two previous volumes in this series have accused them of sacrificing the finer aspects of Brazilian civilization to a study of the crudest aspects of the nation's life. In other words, of having emphasized the most genuinely Brazilian elements instead of the surface veneer, the facade, the pretensions. Like certain exaggerations dating from colonial times—that on the part of the Jesuits of granting degrees of Bachelor or Master of Arts to boys who had scarcely had more than a secondary education, for example—these "finer aspects" merely serve to impress outsiders or to favor the pretensions of Brazilians who prefer to live outside the national reality.

Dom Frei Vital was no man to content himself with appearances. What he most vigorously strove for was to establish an authentic Catholic life in Brazil, where a clergy of more or less bureaucratic priests, some linked more closely to Masonic orders than to the Church and others figuratively equipped with a bourgeois parasol instead of a shepherd's staff, allowed the greater part of the population to exist without benefit of religious instruction, exposed to anti-Catholic infiltrations of every sort. A population which knew only how to make the sign of the Cross, to repeat the *Paternoster* or *Ave Maria*, to kneel before the Host, to go to mass on Sundays, and to have its children baptized. A population with a smattering of religion, of course, but not enough to characterize itself as truly Catholic.

Knowing that the religious vitality of a people depends largely on the corresponding vitality of its clergy, the Bishop of Olinda turned his principal attention to the development of such a condition. Many priests rebelled against him: priests with concubines, priests more politician than padre, Masonic priests, Jacobin priests, uncle-priests more at the service of the landlords and their slaves than the bishops of their Church. With a fearlessness seldom before seen within the Church, Dom Vital threw his forces against these wayward priests as though it were they, and not the Protestants or the African witch doctors, who were the corruptors of the purity of the Faith, as though it were they who formed the principal obstacle to the development of Catholicism as a guiding force in Brazilian thought and behavior. And the paradox of this courageous intervention on the part of Dom Vital was that foreign priests soon began to replace nationals in a concentrated crusade to bring Brazilian values more closely into line with those of the Catholic Church. This replacement, while not always agreeable to Brazilians of the period, was necessary to the revitalization of the Church. Many of the Brazilian priests were good men and devoted pastors, but there simply weren't enough dedicated native churchmen to fill the country's needs.[1]

Although the presence of the Capuchins in Brazil preceded the founding of the Republic, it was only after 1889 that, thanks to the efforts of Dom Vital over a decade earlier, the way was opened for the repopulation of the convents and monasteries with foreign churchmen: Benedictines, Carmelites, Franciscans, Capuchins from Italy, France, Germany, and Belgium. These newcomers, Father Burnichon recalls, were charged with the duty of "restoring the rules to the houses of the respective orders." This was not easily done, says the French Jesuit, for whom "this chapter of monastic history was not lacking in either the tragic or the grotesque"; there were just too many native priests with double lives who "did not want to have their comfortable existence disturbed."[2] There were lively moments in Rio de Janeiro when the last Brazilian monks— old and very few in numbers—were replaced by foreigners. The occasion was made the excuse for nationalistic demands agitated among the humble folk, perhaps through the activities of politically influential Masons who felt their cause threatened by the continuers of the policies of Dom Vital. They were in fact correct in their assumptions; it is from the time of the Bishop of Olinda that we can date the decline of Masonic influence in the life of Brazil.

About the time that foreign monks were systematically being placed in the hitherto almost abandoned monasteries, there was a corresponding installation—or reinstallation—of various active and militant Catholic orders. Some, such as the French Marists, the Trappists, the Redemptorists, the Jesuits, the Lazarists, and the Do-

---

[1] Some of the less dedicated, admittedly, were not really bad men, but they were too often remiss in their priestly functions, particularly their inattention to the vows of chastity. True, in establishing an irregular family, these Brazilian priests were at least not effeminate, whereas the foreign priests, who were almost never guilty of starting a family, were judged by some to be far more inclined than the Brazilians to other irregularities of behavior equally compromising to the priestly office and dignity of the Church. Numerous uncomplimentary stories to this effect were in circulation during Imperial times, particularly about the Italians, but perhaps such accounts can be traced to the Jacobinism of some Catholics of the period.

[2] Joseph Burnichon: *Le Brésil d'Aujourd'hui* (Paris, 1910), p. 201.

minicans, were merely returning to Brazilian territory; others came in for the first time and established themselves in old patriarchal residences and suburban farms of the interior. Many of these were monks and nuns who had been expelled from France and Portugal.

After having visited many of these establishments, particularly the schools maintained by the French sisters of the orders of Zion, of the Sacred Heart, of Ursula, of the Blessed Sacrament, of St. Vincent de Paulo, or of St. Joseph de Chambéry, along with those of the Belgian Order of the Christian Dames, Father Burnichon concluded that "the religious life of Brazil has made undeniable progress over the past twenty years." [3] The regrettable part of this progress, as he saw it, was that Brazil apparently continued to be a *"pays de mission,"* whereas it should have recruited most of its religious workers from the ranks of its own population. It was this scarcity of Brazilians in the religious orders which facilitated Masonic or nationalist campaigns in the newspapers and magazines against foreign churchmen, campaigns which provoked the greatest Catholic journalist of his time, Carlos de Laet, to write his famous apology entitled *O Frade Estrangeiro (The Foreign Monk)*.

It is evident that Catholic schools gained a new vigor with the presence of academically trained foreign priests and nuns in the country after the founding of the Republic. The geographer Elliott in 1916 found many of the older schools conducted by the Benedictines, the Jesuits, and the sisters of the Sacred Heart to be "splendid" in quality.[4] Nor can it be said that these foreign teachers in any way tended to lower the prestige of the language; most of them spoke and wrote impeccable Portuguese, and the Marists in particular contributed greatly to the preparation of textbooks in the national idiom. The German Jesuits in Rio Grande do Sul distinguished themselves by scientific studies of the local flora written in excellent Portuguese, and the lectures and sermons of the German Franciscans were also frequently notable for the correctness of their grammar and style.

Naturally, not all were so successful in gaining command of the language, so that pulpit lapses in pronunciation and grammar sometimes became the material for ridicule. It was probably this linguistic problem that Armando Silveyra had in mind when he spoke of the lack of adjustment between the foreign clergymen and his con-

[3] Ibid., p. 202.
[4] L. E. Elliott: *Brazil, Today and Tomorrow* (New York, 1917), p. 116.

gregation in Rio Grande do Sul, although some of the difficulty could easily have been psychological and cultural as well. "Being generally cultured men," says Silveyra, these foreigners who "expressed themselves so badly that the congregation at times could not help smiling must have encountered psychological difficulties which were even greater than those encountered with the language." Those constant smiles on the faces of the congregation did not establish the atmosphere of respect which ought to exist between pastor and flock, particularly in the light of the "differences in temperament and education" existing between them.

Nevertheless, it was imperative that these foreign churchmen be imported to fill the gap caused by the reluctance of Brazilians to enter the Church after the rigorous reform measures of Dom Vital and his successors on the conduct of the clergy. It was not long, however, before the foreign-born priests were also being supplemented by second-generation Germans, Italians, and Poles, many of them recruited by the Marists for duties in parochial schools throughout the country. In the north, with monastic discipline much more austere than formerly, children of some of the best families began to be attracted to the Church. The Republic and the separation of Church and State had given a new impulse to Catholicism and the field of religious education began to produce a new Brazilian élite, membership in which proved attractive even to sons of such one-time anti-clericals as Ruy Barbosa. Particularly associated with this new élite were the Jesuits of the Colégio Anchieta in Nova Friburgo, those of São Luís in Itu and São Leopoldo in Rio Grande do Sul, and, somewhat later, those of Antônio Vieira in Salvador and Nóbrega in Recife.

"When my mother died," writes Heitor Modesto d'Almeida (b. Minas Gerais, 1881), "I was enrolled in the Colégio Anchieta in Nova Friburgo. It was then operating in the old building known as the Château. Discipline was severe; neatness and order imperative. The teachers were all padres who knew how to teach; I came out with a solid preparation in the humanities. I remember when the news arrived of Roentgen's discovery of the X-ray. The day before, Father Prosperi had given a lesson on cathodic rays; he seemed to have had a premonition of the discovery."

At Anchieta there were no classes on Sundays, and only those in Italian and German on Thursday. German could be elected instead of English in the upper division. The school had a good library, and the works of Chateaubriand and Jules Verne were much read. Heitor Modesto also states that Leo Taxil's *Assassinatos Maçônicos* (*Masonic Assassinations*) was much in demand, a demand undoubtedly stimulated by the suggestion of the good padres.

Another new aspect of educational life at the beginning of the century was the emphasis given to physical education, an emphasis which began with the Protestant schools in many cities of the Republic. At Anchieta the students played football; not the customary soccer, but "a less violent form of rugby." They also played batball, "*quadrado*," and "*guerra*." [5]

"We were allowed out once a month, provided we were accompanied by parents or their authorized representative," continues Heitor Modesto. "We left after mass and had to return before nightfall. I used to spend such holidays at the old Hotel Engert. . . . Old Engert was still alive then and set an excellent table, with turkey and fresh butter in abundance. I valued the butter very highly, because at school we had butter for our bread only on the first Thursday of every month, on which days we went on a picnic and our lunch was brought to us in a dump cart."

As to the religious life of the students: "There was a congregation of the Sons of Maria and of the Heart of Jesus, with a blue or red ribbon worn at mass. Confession was obligatory only once a year, during Holy Week." These were times, as we have seen, when few Brazilians were called to the priesthood. "During the four years I was there, only one student, Militão de Castro e Sousa, declared for a religious life. But even he, after serving his noviate, failed to confirm his vocation."

There was a student band and orchestra under Italian teachers—first Maestrini and, later, Corali Ungo. Using only what he had learned at Anchieta, Alberto Teixeira da Costa "was able to compose an opera produced at the Municipal" in Rio de Janeiro, as well as to

[5] *Quadrado* (square) is a game in which four players are stationed on four bases forming a square, with a fifth player in the center. As the players on the bases exchange positions, the fifth man tries to reach one left temporarily empty. If he succeeds he becomes a baseman, and the player caught off base takes his place in the center.

Guerra (war) is a game in which players divide themselves into two teams, each with a flag. The object is to plant the flag at a certain point in the opponent's "territory." Players are "killed" if held motionless for a specified time. The resulting mayhem can be imagined if you envisage a football game in which there are two balls and both teams are simultaneously on the offensive and defensive. (Translator.)

compose such songs as *"Canto da Saudade"* and *"Serenata,"* pieces often performed by his niece Bidu Sayão.[6]

The annual prize for the best student in each class was a medal stamped with the features of Pope Leo XIII. During his entire four years, Modesto informs us, there was no scandal of any kind at the school. Supervision was constant; the students were always under the eye of one or another of the padres. There were "no cases of pederasty as such, but there were some of those amorous friendships characteristic of all boarding schools." [7]

It was these religious educators—Jesuits, Benedictines, Salesians, and Marists—who accepted the Protestant challenge of curriculum reform and improvement, and did much to improve methods of primary and secondary instruction in Brazil, including such items as supervised sports and recreation. These activities had been introduced in the Anglo-American schools of the time, possibly with the tacit intention of competing with Catholic educators in influencing the youth of Brazil. Competition furnished by the American schools in turn stimulated the Catholics to greater efforts to develop a predominantly Latin culture in tropical America. The constants of such a national and regional culture, subjected to technical and ethical innovations from the outside, could not avoid becoming both socially and psychologically disturbed, but generally these novelties were altered or modified by local conditions and were more easily assimilated into the national culture. Such an alteration could be found in the Brazilian style of soccer football, which, from the rather Apollonian importation, became Dionysiac, with something of the *maxixe*, the *samba*, and the *capoeira* in its transformed nature. And the folk songs and evangelical hymns introduced by Anglo-Saxon teachers and missionaries were subjected to the same sort of transformation. Sung in Portuguese by ordinary Brazilians, these hymns lost their four-square tempo and changed into lively *dobrados* or langorous *modinhas* of an exoticism in evi-

[6] Teixeira da Costa's songs are well known to Brazilians and frequently figure on programs by native singers, but unfortunately have had very little promotion outside Brazil. Bidu Sayão, on the other hand, is a Brazilian opera and concert singer whose distinguished career flourished largely in the United States, where for nearly two decades she was a valued member of the Metropolitan Opera. (Translator.)

[7] It is true that one J.S.M., who as president of the Sons of Maria of Anchieta had distinguished himself for his extreme piety, had after graduation become involved in a sexual scandal, but this in no way reflected on the moral and religious instruction students received from their Jesuit preceptors in Nova Friburgo.

dent contradiction to the spirit of the originals. This sort of inter-penetration deserves careful and detailed study. The first steps in such a study were made by Professor Émile G. Leonard in his *L'Il-luminisme dans un Protestantisme de Constitution Récente* (1953). Although this book does not assess the most intimate consequences of this interpenetration, it does point out for the first time such matters as the influence of Protestantism on the *cucurus*—the popu-lar song contests between two singers accompanied by guitar—where the Bible began to compete with Brazilian history as a source of textual material. The young Brazilian sociologist Renato Campos has also begun to investigate this matter in studying the song con-tests in the sugar-cane areas of the north, where the decline of the patriarchal system favored the development of Protestantism among the rural peoples.

This development was preceded by a similar Protestant impact on the Brazilian élite through the influence of the Anglo-Saxon schools on the children of the rich, even during Imperial times. Ed-uardo Jacobina (b. in the court, 1879) was one of those so influ-enced. For several years he studied in a Rio de Janeiro academy significantly entitled "Progresso" and directed by Miss Eleanor Leslie, an American born in Philadelphia, but of Scottish descent. Miss Leslie was "an extraordinary woman: beautiful, tall, well-groomed, cultivated, and very learned . . ." She became a great friend of Eduardo's parents, and when Eduardo was still a small child she had said, half jokingly, "I would like to direct this boy's education from the very first lessons."

In a statement written in 1938, Eduardo stated: "This is just what happened. In January, 1886, already having learned from my father to read, write, and do simple arithmetic, I entered the Colégio Progresso, from which I graduated in 1892." His diploma was a statement from the Philadelphia pedagogue: "Colégio Pro-gresso. This certifies that Sr. Eduardo Jacobina completed his liter-ary course at my school, where he attended the primary, second-ary, and upper courses, and demonstrated considerable ability in all his subjects, particularly in the Natural Sciences, Physics, and Chemistry, as was more than adequately proved in his final exami-nations."

It was a school where there were no punishments—an innovation on the Brazilian scene. "Bad marks and good marks were sent to the parents in the form of monthly report cards. In serious cases, pupils were made to stay after school for a short period, and boarding students sometimes lost their weekend privileges. (I was a day student.) The moral atmosphere was very pure. Miss Leslie, later Mrs. L. Hentz, did everything 'for righteousness' sake' and created in us a horror of everything low and vile. And in moments of great nervous stress, it was merely necessary for this haughty Junoesque director to make her appearance and ask in Olympian tones: 'Girls! What is the matter, girls?' (the school was principally for girls) to bring about the re-establishment of order." [8]

Education in an Anglo-Saxon environment had perhaps created in Eduardo Jacobina—and others of the beautiful Miss Leslie's pupils as well—a certain sense of being a member of a minority, even part of a Protestant rebellion. This was useful to a point, but it also made it difficult in future years for these pupils to conform to the traditional values and standards of a predominantly Catholic society. From his Anglo-Saxon teachers, Eduardo seems to have acquired a predisposition to ethnocentricism more Aryan than Latin, and at an advanced age, with the image of the beautiful Miss Leslie still clearly before him, had come to believe in a Jewish plot, "with ample means of propaganda," to confuse and confound "the sense of Race." He was not about to be influenced by such propaganda, certain as he was that "the great, the immense moral qualities of the Portuguese would degenerate in the Brazilian as a result of the mixing of races. . . ." Both the Negroes and the Guaranis lacked "initiative, self-respect, love of progress, and comfort"; Anglo-Saxon qualities par excellence.

Of the young Brazilians educated in Anglo-Saxon schools, many must have entered manhood bearing a secret image of one of their beautiful, serene, Olympian teachers and cherishing a desire to see

[8] But despite the "Olympian serenity" of Miss Leslie, a true Apollonian, Eduardo grew up to be a man of Dionysiac Latinity who in his day perceived valor almost exclusively in his relative Ruy Barbosa. Thus he wrote rather irritably in 1938 of the Baron do Rio Branco: "He was a great man on a small scale. Within restricted limits, he performed an estimable service. But what people he had around him! . . ." Eduardo also considered Santos Dumont insignificant alongside the Wright Brothers and found Pedro II guilty of "moral failings very serious in a sovereign," besides being "intellectually mediocre, with an education based purely on memory"—a mortal sin from the viewpoint of Anglo-Saxon educators of the time. And he states that Benjamin Constant's celebrated course in Infinitesimal Calculus at the Military School was "shameful" and that his students, many of them now teachers themselves, were ridiculous clowns who aroused only laughter in persons with any real knowledge of mathematics.

other such lovely creatures as the mothers of innumerable pink-cheeked, fair-skinned blond Brazilian babies. And not a few of them married Europeans or Americans of just this type. Even near-Negroes espoused white Europeans, and after marriage many of them tried to renounce their Brazilian traits, to the point of attempting to acquire their wives' accents in speaking Portuguese.

Catholic schools tried to counteract this new fascination with Anglo-Saxon Protestant values by adapting some aspects of this culture to a Catholic sense of education, deportment, and even of art. One of the most interesting instances of this adaptation was the vigor with which the Salesians, who were for the most part Italians, developed football teams which frequently defeated representatives of the so-called "American schools" at their own game.

One of the Catholic schools which at the time contributed greatly to the progress of the Church in Brazil was that of the Monastery of São Bento in Rio de Janeiro. Cássio Barbosa de Resende (b. Minas Gerais, 1879) recalls that he and his brother Gaspar for some time attended the free courses given here by the Benedictines. Not all the teachers were priests; the mathematics teacher, for example, was an engineer "already very old, almost entirely bald, with a pointed beard, and heavy drooping mustaches which obscured his complete absence of teeth. He wore a long black coat buttoned to the neck and an equally black high hat, as was the fashion of the period. His name was Alfredo Coelho Barreto and he was the father of Paulo Barreto [João do Rio]." "Coelho Barreto didn't spend much time teaching," recalls Cássio Barbosa de Resende, preferring to "entertain the students with other matters," including Positivism, of which, strangely enough for a teacher in a purely Brazilian Benedictine school, he was a supporter. He was a picturesque character who ordinarily called his students "turkeys." [9] His classic expression in reproving a pupil of extreme ignorance was "*Vá beber mijo!* (Go take a drink of piss!)" At other times, "without saying a word, he would with his hands trace the outline of a shoeblack's box or a donkey cart and the student would very well know what he meant."

According to Cássio, the teacher for universal history, one Magalhães Castro, "knew nothing of his subject." He always taught "with the book open before him, and in order to make use of it, he pretended to cough and clear his throat throughout the lesson.

[9] Birds associated in the Brazilian mind with extreme stupidity. (Translator.)

These interruptions, during which he covered his mouth with his handkerchief, gave him time to lower his head enough to read what was written in the book."

The Latin teacher was quite a different sort. His name was Canon Loreto, a tall, dark, stone-faced individual who also acted as assistant principal. "He dressed neatly and elegantly and walked very deliberately. His classes terrified the students because of his nasty habit of making sarcastic remarks at student errors." Some of these observations were so impious one could hardly think of the speaker as a priest. One "poor, skinny, ragged boy named Abelardo, an impoverished student from Mato Grosso, was one day called upon to recite. He stood before the priest unable to repeat a word of the lesson. Canon Loreto exploded at him, 'Shameless runt! You're so scrawny you look like an ear of corn grown out of a rock.' Humiliated before everyone, the poor boy could only burst into tears. . . ." Such teaching procedures naturally did little to help Catholic educational prestige in its competition with Anglo-Saxon methods, even though all Protestant teachers were not the equal of Miss Leslie or Mr. Lane of São Paulo or Mr. Muirhead of Pernambuco.

Canon Loreto was the author of a Latin grammar that "the students were required to buy and memorize in daily excerpts of 15 to 25 lines," a procedure hardly acceptable to the Anglo-Saxon idea of teaching the student to understand, analyze, and interpret his material. At lesson time, "the student stood before the padre's desk, recited the lesson from memory while the teacher followed with the book. After completing this textbook, the author stated that the student was ready to translate any Latin text, and he was set to work on the writings of Tacitus." Canon Loreto's grammar was sold at the office of the Catholic-monarchist paper *Apóstolo*, of which Cássio believed Loreto to be the editor. This paper was one whose offices were wrecked "during the political riots common at the time, one of which ended with the assassination of Gentil de Castro in consequence of the failure of the Canudos expedition under Col. Moreira César." [1] It is possible that the scrawny Abe-

[1] In an anti-monarchist uprising touched off by the failure of the Moreira César expedition against the peasant rebels at Canudos, Gentil de Castro, a prominent monarchist and a close friend of the Viscount de Ouro Prêto, was murdered by a mob in the station of the Rio-Petópolis railroad on March 7, 1897. The Viscount de Ouro Prêto and one of his sons, who were with Gentil de Castro at the time, narrowly escaped with their lives. (Translator.)

lard (Abelardo de Sousa) took part in the assault on the offices of the *Apóstolo*, but that is another story.

To return to Cássio Barbosa de Resende, he says that "once a week we had a general review, and the student who performed the punishments blistered the palms of the ignorant with blows of the *palmatória*." Cássio had already known this "degrading instrument" at the Ateneu Leopoldinense in Minas Gerais, but he was disagreeably surprised to find it also in operation in Rio de Janeiro in a Benedictine monastery school.

During Cássio's time, Canon Loreto died of a ruptured hernia. Abelardo de Sousa "could not contain the joy this occurrence occasioned in him. He felt revenged for all the humiliations he had suffered in the past and expressed his desire that the padre be buried with the entire Sugar Loaf on his grave." [2] A few days after the death of Loreto, another canon took over the class. His name was Serejo, and he was "the antithesis of Padre Loreto: good, patient, paternal . . ." He also followed different methods of teaching Latin, indicating that even among the older churchmen of the time there were some who did not believe in teaching by rote and who, like the Protestants, insisted on the student's understanding rather than merely memorizing the material studied.

One curious fact noted by Cássio Barbosa de Resende was that, in none of the schools in which he studied "was there any attention paid to the civic education of the students." In none was there any understanding between parent and teacher in their common cause of instructing the child, and the result was that there was often friction between the two. On one occasion, the assistant principal in one of Cássio's schools, "having given one pupil a light blow with a ruler, brought about a scene of mayhem which caused a scandal because of the social and political prominence of one of the contenders." The assistant principal's name was Napoleão Reis; the father of the castigated student, who lost no time in appearing at the school, was none other than the Viscount de Ouro Prêto. There were a few words exchanged between parent and teacher; then the enraged Viscount raised his umbrella and delivered "a powerful blow on Napoleão Reis's forehead, causing a slight wound." Immediately, the two adversaries were locked in deadly struggle, to the scandal of the students. Perhaps it would have been even more

[2] Sugar Loaf (*Pão de Açucar*) is of course the picturesque and much-photographed rock at the entrance of Rio de Janeiro harbor. (Translator.)

scandalous if Reis had been a padre; a fight between a frocked clergyman and a tailcoated statesman would really have been something.

Cássio Barbosa de Resende could have remarked on another deficiency in the schools of the time: nowhere in the secondary school
curriculum was there any place for the manual arts, these things
being left entirely to vocational schools and to shop apprentice-
ships. Here it was the Catholics who filled this gap; the Salesian
schools founded throughout the country in the late nineteenth century eventually began to introduce technical courses into the secondary curriculum, giving instruction along modern lines in many
of the manual arts. One such school was Santa Rosa of Niterói,
which Father Joseph Burnichon found to be admirably progressive,
with "the most modern machinery." Nor were these institutions
limited to the capital, he observes. "There are to my knowledge a
dozen such establishments in Brazil, of which five are in the state of
São Paulo alone. . . ." [3] In offering this technical instruction, the
Catholics showed themselves well aware of the importance of the
new directions and developments in the Brazilian scene, particularly
in such subareas as São Paulo.

It should be emphasized that the French influence on Brazilian
religious education was not confined to elegant schools for society
girls in Rio de Janeiro and the provinces. Many institutions for the
poor had French churchmen in their service. There were several
such schools for orphans and underprivileged children of both
sexes, where the boys were taught trades and the girls given instruction in embroidery and dressmaking. In his *Visions du Brésil*,
Father L. A. Gaffre noted that "benevolent institutions of all sorts
are found all over Brazil and testify to the Catholic vitality of the
nation." Moreover, several rural schools were run by the French,
including that of Tremembé, founded in 1903 by French Trappists, where large areas of overgrown land were transformed into
rice fields. When Father Gaffre visited them in 1911, the Trappists
had 300 Brazilian workers in their service at Tremembé. All were
paid weekly without fail, in contrast to the irregular payments customary on most plantations of the region. By paying regularly, the
Trappists saved their employees from the hands of loan sharks who
were in the habit of fattening on the prevailing system of irregular
compensation. And by offering good wages they virtually caused a

[3] Burnichon: op. cit., p. 219.

revolution in employer-employee relationships in rural São Paulo, a revolution which must figure in the story of Catholic contributions to progress in early twentieth-century Brazil. Because even the relatively good wages they paid could not be as high as they should be without turning the plantation owners against the Church, the Trappists made up for this deficiency by taking a paternal interest in their workers through "a perpetual distribution of goods, clothing, drugs, and medical assistance to large or indigent families." [4] They also built houses for these families, houses which, while simple and rustic, were nevertheless superior hygienically to the old-style barracks and offered each family the opportunity of having its own garden. The approximately 300 families benefiting from the program were of all kinds: *caboclos, mestiços*, Italians, former slaves, all typical of the abandonment descending upon the rural population after abolition. Victims of all sorts of exploitation, these people under the intelligent care of the French Trappists became a small island of hope in the midst of rural misery.

One of the worst systems of exploitation, the Trappists found, was that of sales on credit, a system which was nothing more than the means of enabling a few individuals to become absolute masters over whole families of creditors. Thus a large part of the rural population of Brazil lived in semi-slavery, bound to the tyranny of the storekeeper, who was often an associate of the large landowner. This was the system the Trappists of Tremembé sought quietly (the rules of their order forbade verbal exuberance) to combat. Discreetly and silently, they gave protection and social assistance to hundreds of rural workers and their families, much to the honor of their order and to the credit of Catholic progress in Brazil. It is a pity that this system was not adopted and expanded by the Republic instead of being limited merely to one subarea of São Paulo.

In a country where people liked to say that there was not as yet any "social question," Father Gaffre noted the contradiction between the wages of rural workers and the price of foodstuffs, a condition he considered to be the cause of "a state of physical misery [among workers] unworthy of a great country striving for progress as is Brazil. . . ." The young Republic was thus drifting toward socialism, which was less far off than one might think. To this European, awakened to the "social question" by the warnings of Leo XIII, the Brazilian peasants seemed "more like dust than

[4] L. A. Gaffre: *Visions du Brésil* (Paris, 1912), pp. 7, 125, 293.

human beings; without ethnic cohesion, without traditions, without community of interests, there is nothing to bring them together." [5] If any common ground could be found in this mixture of elements, the first demagogue to come along would mold this amorphous proletariat into a violently rebellious force. With the country careless as to the fate of its rural population, such insurrection did not seem far distant; to Father Gaffre in 1911, Brazil appeared to be on the brink of a devastating social crisis.

The French padre could not understand why the Brazilian government did not intervene in the relations between landowners and rural workers to protect the latter against exploitation and slavery through debt. "In certain countries," he wrote, "the government establishes a legal limit on the price of necessities: bread, salt, sugar, etc. In Brazilian rural areas the field of price control should be greatly extended. If this were done, the rapacity of the storekeepers, who sell what they will at the price they want to receive, would be somewhat restrained." [6]

What repercussions did these words of Father Gaffre's have in the Brazil of 1911? What repercussions were caused by the work of the Trappists of Tremembé? Virtually none. There was no clear or serious commentary by any influential journalist, old or young. There was no Ruy Barbosa. No Graça Aranha. No Sylvio Romero. No Gilberto Amado. In a Brazil which was falling under the spell of elegantly skeptical prose writers like Anatole France, pedantically sententious sociologists like Gustave Le Bon, or merely mellifluous poets like Edmond Rostand, there was little room for Catholic commentators whose words were rude and whose ideas uncomfortably honest. These Frenchmen, ahead of their time in their observations on the Brazilian worker from the Catholic—and profoundly Christian—point of view, tried in vain to communicate their ideas to Brazilian Catholics (and Brazilians in general). Similarly, in a less Anatolian and more authentic France, the Bragança Prince Dom Luís, heir to the throne of Pedro II, had anticipated the Brazilian republicans in voicing his ideas for the rehabilitation of the worker degraded by slavery and cut loose through abolition. But neither the visiting Frenchmen nor the Gallicized Brazilian could make any impression on a Brazilian public contaminated by skepticism and bourgeois smugness.

[5] Ibid., p. 298.
[6] Ibid., p. 300.

It is true that when the abbé Dom Chautard had come to Brazil in the turn of the century to found the Trappist monastery of Maristela, he had been well received by the Republican authorities. The President himself had said: "I should like to see not one, but twenty Trappist establishments in Brazil." [7] But this does not mean that words became deeds capable of elevating the French Catholic initiative in this work which, economically or technically, to say nothing of the social objectives, so deserved encouragement. Visiting the Trappists in 1908, Father Joseph Burnichon stated that the Tremembé group was "giving a magnificent lesson . . . without subsidy or favors of any kind." This impression was confirmed by the American agronomist Bradford, who had been contracted by the state of São Paulo to help develop the cultivation of rice.[8] Bradford stated that the Trappists were doing well-organized pioneer work in raising that crop, so vital to the Brazilian diet. The important factor, however, was that, in achieving this success in tropical agriculture, the European churchmen were also succeeding in the Christian task of bettering the lot of native and immigrant rural workers of all ethnic groups. Considering it impossible to separate the fortunes of one group from those of another, the Trappists gave equal attention to all, thereby avoiding the error of believing that the mere presence of a few Germans or Italians amid the mixed Brazilian population would by some sort of sociological magic elevate the *caboclo*. The truth is that without the extension of religious assistance to the immigrants and material, as well as religious, aid to the natives, the immigrants, instead of regenerating others, would have fallen into degradation. And indeed, this is what happened in some instances, according to the testimony of such reliable observers as Fletcher.[9]

[7] Ibid., p. 276.

[8] Burnichon: op. cit., p. 281.

[9] In their classic book on Brazil, Fletcher and Kidder made an intelligent commentary on the degradation which occurred among the German immigrants even during the days of slavery. In Petrópolis, they report, the Germans "brought with them few arts and but little education. It seems difficult in a tropical climate to prevent the morals and industry of emigrants from deteriorating and this is particularly to be observed in slave countries. The degraded colonist, while setting himself above the African, engrafts the vices of the latter upon the European stock, and thus sinks to a lower grade than the Negro. The German in Brazil has the want of a sound moral people surrounding him, to sustain and elevate him: therefore it is no marvel if he sinks lower and lower in the scale of civilization. Much, however, is being done for the Germans of Petrópolis. The clergyman, as the

Along with the Trappist experiment in Tremembé, the efforts of the industrialist Carlos Alberto de Meneses in the newly developed industrial areas of Pernambuco and Bahia should be mentioned. In 1904, through the initiative of the Christian Federation of Workers of Pernambuco, a petition was presented to the Chamber of Deputies expounding the necessity and advantages of organized labor and requesting a law enabling such organization. "The petition was signed by the Federation of Workers, representing seven affiliated organizations, and by fifteen other labor organizations representing some 6,000 workers in the states of Pernambuco, Alagoas, Sergipe, Bahia, Paraíba, and Rio Grande do Norte," says the economist Tadeu Rocha. "In the following year, the Bahian deputy Joaquim Inácio Tosta, who had been connected with the Social-Labor movement since 1900, with the collaboration of the engineer Carlos Alberto de Meneses, reintroduced the ideas of the petition in the federal legislature in a bill which eventually became Law No. 1635 of January 5, 1907." [1]

Professor Tadeu Rocha states that this law "was based upon Catholic social doctrine and on the experience of an industrialist of good will—Carlos Alberto de Meneses—and would have been destined to be the instrument for collaboration between management and workers had not the individualism of Brazilian society and the political and economic liberalism of the country relegated it to a most unjust disdain. . . . At the time political considerations held the ascendancy over economic and social realities. . . ." [2]

Between 1891 and 1904 Carlos Alberto de Meneses had developed considerable social action based upon Catholic principles and Christian feelings. As general manager of an industry in Pernambuco, he had made his company include "various principles of social Christianity" in its statutes. Nor was he quixotically alone in this action: he worked in collaboration with Antônio Muniz Machado, Pierre Collier, and with the future federal deputy Luís Corréia de Brito. He instituted a program of social services for his workers at the Goiana Mills and the Camaragibe Factory. More-

pastor of the church and superintendent of the schools, takes a deep interest in the welfare of his countrymen both spiritually and intellectually" (p. 301).

[1] Tadeu Rocha: "Partiu de Pernambuco o Movimento Sindicalista" (The Syndicalist Movement Has Left Pernambuco), *Diário de Pernambuco*, January 6, 1957.

[2] Ibid.

over, it is to his pious interest in the "social question" that we owe the first Catholic cooperatives in Brazil. Again in the words of Professor Tadeu Rocha: "With the spirit of cooperation as a basic principle, Carlos Alberto brought about the first cooperatives in Brazilian territory. There being no laws to govern this sort of organization, these cooperatives had to be organized as corporations offering a dividend of 8 per cent plus a bonus of 10 per cent on the total purchases of each member. On January 1, 1895, the Camaragibe co-op opened with a stock of foodstuffs, fabrics, baked goods, and meat. In May, 1896, a similar operation was begun for the employees of the Goiana Mills, with a grocery and dry goods line. . . . Crowning this work of nine years of social education, Carlos Alberto de Meneses reorganized the social program of the Camaragibe Factory into a large Worker's Corporation, which was inaugurated on July 1, 1900. The organization took the then possible and most advisable form of a mixed syndicate of management, office staff, and factory workers from the highest executive to the most humble laborer. All were required to belong to the corporation, so that the most ignorant and most backward were still benefited and their future and that of their families guaranteed. . . . The example of the Camaragibe Factory was soon imitated by the Paulista Company, which set up a similar workers' co-op on May 1, 1902, through the initiative of the institution's director, Custódio José da Silva Pessoa, who prided himself on having risen from the ranks of the textile workers and being therefore well acquainted with the needs and aspirations of his former working companions. The Goiana Mills, after overcoming a multitude of obstacles, also started its co-op on September 3, 1903. It was not easy for Carlos Alberto de Meneses, even with the help of Luís Corréia de Brito, to bring about this integration of employees, working as he was with a very ignorant rural proletariat barely emerged from slavery and still imbued with all the vices of that institution." [3]

But this was not the end of the Catholic engineer's activity. It was through his initiative that the Federation of Christian Workers was established. "At the First Catholic Congress in this state, held in Recife in June, 1902, under his presidency, he declared the immediate necessity for the founding of an organization to act as a center for direction, doctrine, study, inspiration, and strength" and petitioned that "the Catholic Congress support this idea and con-

[3] Ibid.

stitute a commission immediately to found such a center. . . . In 1903 this pioneering action was taken through the first Groups for Social Studies in Brazil." [4]

Pernambuco seems to have been the part of Brazil most predisposed to initiative of this kind, for it was in the former Imperial province that Louis Vauthier propagated the Fourierism which apparently in large part inspired the "Christian Socialism" of Antônio Pedro de Figueiredo.[5] Following Figueiredo, another disciple of Vauthier, the French engineer Milet, became interested in the social problems of the agrarian north. Milet, who had married a Brazilian woman and become completely assimilated, was able to study these problems from a practical and Brazilian, rather than a visionary and European point of view, and to pass on his ideas and interests to the young Joaquim Nabuco. If the coming of the Republic in 1889 had not interrupted his career, always more social than political, Nabuco might have developed into a social Catholic—or even a syndicalist Catholic; for, as we have seen, he eventually became even more deeply reconciled to the Church than Ruy Barbosa, and in the last years of the Empire had given somewhat British-oriented lectures on the "social question" which made him a precursor of the country's labor movement.

Brazilian Catholicism in this period had a number of apologists who produced articles of genuine literary value. Some were written by Joaquim Nabuco near the end of his life; there were also those which Eduardo Prado dedicated significantly to Father Anchieta, and those of Carlos de Laet in defense of the foreign monk. In the pulpit Father Júlio Maria distinguished himself for his persuasive and unrhetorical eloquence. His sober and polished sermons, some of which were courageously polemical in criticizing certain priests of his day, reduced the customary style of pompous oratory (in imitation or caricature of Mont'Alverne but often indulged in by Ruy Barbosa) to a matter for ridicule.

But most sermons of the day took little account of the social problems of the country. Some priests, to be sure, were active in politics and one of them, Monsignor Olímpio de Campos, had been assassinated in Sergipe over some political triviality. Another priest had been an effective governor of Paraíba, still another a federal deputy from São Paulo. But most were silent on social issues.

[4] Ibid.

[5] See my *Um Engenheiro Francês no Brasil* (Rio de Janeiro, 1960) for further commentary on this matter.

Of the four priests born between 1880 and 1882 who have kindly furnished testimony in the preparation of this book, not one indicates having had any concern with the social problems of the period. "I have nothing to say on this," writes Father Florentine Barbosa, canon of the metropolitan center of Paraíba. The same response was elicited from another Paraíban, Canon Matias Freire, despite the fact that, grandson of Imperial barons, he had often been politically militant during his career. Father Leopoldo Fernandes Pinheiro, from Ceará, states that he was "enthusiastic for social and political reform in Brazil and for the ideas of Alberto Tôrres," but platonic in that enthusiasm. And Father Manuel Higino da Silveira, vicar of Livramento, states that he had always considered the social problems of his country "in the light of the Christianity and religion under whose aegis Brazil came into being."

The first Brazilian cardinal, Dom Joaquim Arcoverde de Albuquerque Cavalcanti—the first cardinal in Latin America—seemed also not to have become disturbed by these problems. Perhaps he found Father Gaffre's fears of insurrection excessive and even a bit comical. Descendant of rural gentry from the backlands, Arcoverde nevertheless had not lived in the interior himself and had had no contact with the agrarian misery which followed abolition. He was essentially a priest occupied with religious rather than social problems. He had acted as chairman of the Catholic committee which in Rio de Janeiro had sponsored the lectures of Father Gaffre in response to those of the socialist Ferri and the anti-clerical Clemenceau, but he seems to have considered those lectures only in their apologetic aspects. To the French speaker's occasional discreet references to the Brazilian labor situation he was virtually indifferent.

Catholic socialism like that of Father Gaffre, which brought many Brazilian Catholics together in a spirit of solidarity, actually preceded the purely humanitarian or "scientific" socialism of the non-Catholics and the anti-clericals. "Scientific" socialism had begun to appear in the early twentieth century, although with less impact than had been exercised by anti-clericals of the romantic, eloquent type of Coelho Lisboa of Paraíba. It was this type of anti-clerical who had chiefly supported the radically anti-Jesuit policy of Nilo Peçanha when members of that order, expelled from Portugal after the coming of the Republic of 1910, sought refuge in Brazil as the most natural shelter from the persecutions of Portuguese anti-Catholics like Afonso Costa. Peçanha eventually relented in his anti-Jesuitism and Brazil consequently benefited from the presence of such learned and virtuous Portuguese Jesuits as Luís Gonzaga Cabral. Men of this caliber, speaking the common language of Brazil and Portugal, were able to offer a great service to the youth, and to the cause of Catholic progress in general, in their adopted country. This was true despite the fact that other newcomers, embittered by the violence of their expulsion from Portugal, comported themselves in Brazil with an almost morbid intolerance toward any views differing from their own.

In 1891 the American Maturin M. Ballou, visiting Brazil, was interested by the fact that, in separating Church and State, the Republic had effected a pacific transformation without disturbing churches and convents, without turning any Church property into public offices, and without in any way degrading their architecture and their art. Mr. Ballou visited some of the 77 churches of Rio de Janeiro, and like a good Yankee Protestant hastened to criticize the lack of ventilation which turned all Catholic churches in Brazil and southern Europe into an olfactory torment. Coming from a country where congregations were segregated even within the same Protestant sect, Ballou must have been markedly uncomfortable in churches heavy with the accumulated odors of centuries of worship by persons of all colors and from all walks of life. Perhaps he would have liked some good Yankee architect to visit Brazil and cut broad windows in the old churches in order to give them the proper ventilation.[6]

Mr. Ballou found the cathedral in Rio de Janeiro under repair, full of scaffolding and dust. Nevertheless, he thought the building "very striking in its architectural effect." [7] The scaffolding and repairs perhaps indicated the beginning of a new and debatable phase of Catholic "progress" in Brazil: the excessive modernization and embellishment of traditional church and convent architecture. Following this course of "progress," such architecture often lost all trace of its historical and artistic qualities. Baroque became Gothic; antique images were replaced by commercial statues made in Italy. This was the sort of "progress" which replaced antique ceramic tiles with painted imitation marble, which sold the old carved jacaranda of sacristy and convent for woods ephemerally in vogue at the time.

[6] Maturin M. Ballou: *Equatorial America* (New York, 1892), p. 166.
[7] Ibid., p. 167.

With the separation of Church and State the government subsidies for the preservation of works of religious art in the churches and convents came to an end.[8] At the same time the clergy, now largely of foreign origin, were more in command in their establishments than during Imperial times, when religious emblems and the Imperial crown were displayed jointly on the pediments of most church buildings. And since many of these foreign priests and monks lacked any sense of the national significance of this architecture and religious art, the result was what might have been expected: they showed not the slightest hesitation in decharacterizing, destroying, and "modernizing" it. Thus began an era of decline in the Brazilian Church tradition of ecclesiastical art and architecture. Or perhaps I should say that this decline, rather than beginning, was accentuated, for the tendency was already beginning to appear at the end of the Empire with the erection of such edifices as the church of Nossa Senhora da Penha in Recife. The work of Italian Capuchins, this building is grandiose, admittedly, but in it there is no trace whatever of the religious past or the artistic traditions of Brazil.

In 1891 Mr. Ballou noted that several of the churches of Bahia were "in a very dilapidated condition" and probably would not be restored or repaired.[9] The fact is that this deterioration of churches of artistic interest was general throughout Brazil during the period, thanks to the attitude of many churchmen that the Church was not an antiquarian society to spend its money and waste its time in trying to preserve or protect old buildings from the ravages of the tropical climate. Brazilian bishops should be young and dynamic, they felt. They should build new churches, new chapels, new schools. It was thus that illustrious and progressive bishops like Dom Luís de Brito and Dom Adauto de Miranda Henriques must have thought as, like fearless businessmen, they ordered the demolition or alteration of venerable buildings in the interest of financial benefits to the episcopal economy. Precarious benefits, perhaps. Through them Brazil at the turn of the century lost forever some of the best monuments of its past, works which since colonial times had ennobled its landscape and afforded a sense of dignity and his-

---

[8] See Manuel Barbosa: *A Igreja no Brasil* (Rio de Janeiro, 1945) and the biographical essay of Francisco Lima: *D. Adauto-Subsídios Biográficos* (Paraíba, 1956), I.

[9] Ballou: op. cit., p. 145.

torical continuity to its development as a Catholic culture and a nation. Luckily, a number of old churches and characteristically Brazilian religious works of art escaped this degradation.

In poetry, belles-lettres, and music during this period, the mark of Catholic inspiration is clearly visible. With the possible exception of members of the school designated by Sylvio Romero "decadent and symbolistic"—writers such as Alphonsus de Guimaraens, Augusto de Lima, and Auta de Sousa—most of this literature achieved an integration of the Catholic spirit with that of the American tropics. In prose, the work of Afonso Arinos in Minas Gerais and Simões Lopes Neto in Rio Grande do Sul formed a Catholic-oriented apology for Brazilian rural values. In Neto's *O Negrinho do Pastoreio* (*The Little Negro of the Pasturelands*) we have a work of permanent literary merit, marked with a suggestion of the religious sentiment that, in the Brazilian tropics, distinguished the relationships of whites with Negroes. With some generosity perhaps, Sylvio Romero in his *Evolução da Literatura Brasileira* (*Evolution of Brazilian Literature*) also lists several religious orators of this period as being of literary importance: Father Patrício Moniz and Dom Antônio de Macedo Costa, whom he associates with the Bahian school of the nineteenth century; Dom Luís Raimundo da Silva Brito; Father Júlio Maria; Canon Francisco de Paula Rodrigues; and Monsignor Manuel Vicente.[1] All these men possessed an eloquence which must have contributed to Catholic progress, but it was one that in fact did not make for literature (except possibly in the case of Júlio Maria) and did not serve to bring about a permanent union of the new phase of Catholic thought with that of the developing Brazilian culture. In this pre-republican period Catholicism had divested itself of many of the defects of the patriarchal age; but it had not yet acquired the sense of responsibility of a religion which in 1889 ceased to be official without losing any of its ability to imbue Brazilian culture in general, among all races and nationalities from north to south, with the ideals and values of Latin Catholicism.

Paul Adam, in a visit to Brazil, found confirmation for the idea already current in Europe that "despite princes and politics [the Catholic Church] is still mother of the people." In Europe there was much talk of socialism and some were even seeing communism as a modern solution to social maladjustment. Paul Adam verified

[1] Sylvio Romero: *Evolução da Literatura Brasileira* (Campanha, 1905), p. 78.

that in Brazil the deeds which most resisted the tropics and the
passage of time were those performed by Catholic churchmen
through a sense of collective action that was no more nor less than
socialism or communism in its best sense. It was, after all, "the only
durable attempt at communism and socialism which had really been
tried and has really succeeded." Among these religious men there
was "nothing of individual luxury. . . . But for the order, for the
union of these agricultural workers, these masons, these illumina-
tors of manuscripts, these gardeners it represented a magnificent
luxury indeed." [2] Thus spoke a Frenchman in the face of a Brazilian Catholic progress which was clear to every visiting European,
evidence of a solid Catholic constancy merged with all that was
most authentic and solid in Brazilian civilization. This phenomenon
had been noted by Clemenceau, by Ferrero, by Lamberg, by Elliott, by Bryce. It may be that it had its throwbacks to European
patterns; but it represented a complex of progress in the face of a
tropical situation violently non-European in many of its aspects, a
progress difficult to deny or underestimate when seen by any visitor not rigidly predisposed to find in Brazil a mere copy or passive
imitation of French or British social patterns.

Thus had Father Gaffre given his Christian indulgence to the ir
regularities of certain wayward priests of the interior, considering
such irregularities less important than the victories already earned
by the Church in the face of the harsh realities of the environment
and of the equally barbarous state of indecision existing between
the jungle and the city. The man of the interior was still a man
dominated by the jungle: "In the Brazilian spirit, I have often perceived feelings and tendencies which betray the extraordinary force
of dissimilar growths; growths which have their origin in many
sources and which enrich the physical substratum as the vines and
various growths embellish the trunks and limbs of the great vegetation of the jungles." [3] In bestowing order on this confusion of influences, Brazilian Catholicism seemed to Father Gaffre to have
made "remarkable progress." Not that everything was exemplary,
but the European Catholic could not fully understand the situation
of the priest of the interior, condemned to live in tropical heat
"among rudimentary creatures whose mentality is scarcely superior
to that of the aborigines." Given these conditions, it was not sur-

[2] Paul Adam: *Les Visages du Brésil* (Paris, 1914), pp. 188–9.
[3] Gaffre: op. cit., p. 343.

prising that there were occasional transgressions. Priests were "fallible heroes" in the struggle against the violent aggressions of the Masons and anti-clericals of the period.[4]

Despite these aggressions, the balance sheet for the period must show more success than failures, must add up to Catholic progress and a corresponding decline—notable since the imprisonment of the bishops—in the political power of the Masons and anti-clericals.

[4] Ibid., p. 115.

✿ [X I] ✿

The Republic Twenty Years After

NOTHING MORE CLEARLY EXPRESSES the relativity of time than the ease with which the future dissolves into the past, leaving a present with no significance. The Republic of 1889 was to a certain point a Toynbecan response to the challenge of the future: the democratic, American future which some Brazilians of the late nineteenth century sincerely believed was being impeded by the existence of an Imperial and slavocratic society.

This response had begun to take form in the 1870's with the Republican Manifesto and the Law of the Free Womb. It became a well-defined reality in 1889. But by 1910 this messianic future had already begun to merge into the past—even into aspects of the remote past—to become part of a continuity without which analysists and critics a generation later would have found the utopian suggestions of the fifteenth of November for the solution of the country's problems completely irrelevant. And without which such political sociologists as Alberto Tôrres and his school, Euclydes da Cunha, Sylvio Romero, José Veríssimo, Oliveira Lima, and Professor Gilberto Amado, followed later by Vicente Licínio Cardoso, Oliveira Viana, Alceu Amoroso Lima, Professor Delgado de Carvalho, and Professor Pontes de Miranda, would have been wrong in their opinion that the first two decades of the twentieth century were part of the same Revolution envisaged by Benjamin Constant, Silva Jardim, Martins Júnior, Quintino Bocayuva, or Prudente de Morais. In addition, Brazilians like Afonso Celso Júnior and Manuel de Oliveira Lima, who had been republicans in their youth, after the end of the nineteenth century became so sympathetic to the monarchy and nostalgic for its virtues that some in turn began to be considered dangerous to the republican regime by others more mystically faithful to the Republic of their adolescent dreams, men like José Gomes Pinheiro Machado.

Pinheiro Machado, according to his friend Estácio Coímbra, used to pronounce the word *Re-pú-bli-ca* enunciating each syllable as though he were repeating a sacred or magic formula.[1] For him it was loaded with suggestions of the past—a past he had himself experienced—to which were joined all sorts of suggestions for the future. But principally for the future, for Pinheiro refused to come to terms with the monarchical past of Brazil. On his lips, *República* preserved its youthful sound, even when the speaker himself had become an elderly romantic dreaming of the future of Brazil as though of an adored daughter.[2]

"The Brazilians like to say that theirs is a young country," wrote Pierre Denis when he visited Brazil in the early twentieth century. "In fact, they have the greatest hopes for their country and believe that the present is loaded with promise." But this same Brazil, said Denis, was not young in the sense of having had no past. It was the Brazilian past (he might even have said the past of the Brazilian Republic) which so vividly impressed him, even after having visited other American countries, such as Argentina and the United States. "One feels less expatriated in Brazil," he wrote. "There one does not have the feelings of fear or surprise which strike one in Argentina or the United States, with their nebulous society without roots and without hierarchy, oriented exclusively toward the love of individual independence and directed by the desire of making a fortune." Brazilian patriotism encompassed more memories than that of Argentina or the United States.[3] In 1918, at the end of the so-called "Era of Venceslau" with its marked upsurge in industrialism, Brazilian republicanism contained memories along with hopes

---

[1] When he visited Brazil, Paul Adam recorded this impression of Pinheiro Machado: "Pinheiro Machado is the present political leader in Brazil . . . his reign over the entire country is absolute." *Les Visages du Brésil* (Paris, 1914), pp. 219–20.

[2] Afonso Celso Júnior was the son of the last Imperial Prime Minister, the Viscount of Ouro Prêto. Manuel de Oliveira Lima was a distinguished historian of international renown. Estácio Coímbra was a Pernambucan politician who was majority leader of the Chamber of Deputies in 1918, Minister of Agriculture, Vice-President of the Republic under President Arthur Bernades, and from 1926 to 1930 governor of the state of Pernambuco. (Translator.)

[3] Pierre Denis: *Le Brésil au XXᵉ Siècle* (Paris, 1909), pp. 5, 6.

for a future capable of correcting the errors of the past thirty years of republican experience. Since 1910 the Republic had ceased to be merely the present and had developed a past, a past susceptible to retrospective analysis, to evaluation, to interpretation.

It is certain that the republican experience from the outset had been moderated by the strong influence of the monarchy, despite the desires of republican purists like Pinheiro Machado or Quintino Bocayuva. The first such influence (as already outlined) was that of the Baron de Lucena, who became the political adviser of *Generalíssimo* Deodoro da Fonseca, founder of the Republic of 1889. Another was that of José Maria da Silva Paranhos, the Baron do Rio Branco, whose authority, according to Georges Clemenceau, was "sovereign" in the foreign policy of early twentieth-century Brazil.[4] The Baron's influence was not limited to foreign policy: he was also a force in domestic affairs, striving constantly for the maintenance and even the strengthening of those monarchical traditions which so distinguished Brazil from the rest of Latin America. Clemenceau was well aware that the Baron, though sympathetic to France, wished to import German military instructors into the Brazilian Republic in the hope that the Republic would surpass the Empire in the efficiency of its Armed Forces. "A person very close to him has confided to me that he feels that German instruction would be best for the inculcation of ideas of military duty," wrote Clemenceau, and could not fail to agree: "Too many acts of insubordination—some of them very serious—have emphasized the urgency of this sort of teaching." But the "absolutist ideas of Wilhelm II on the subject of military duty" seemed to Clemenceau incompatible with the spirit and habits of Brazilian democracy, hardly a society whose troops could be indoctrinated with discipline and what a Mineiro politician of the time, João Pinheiro, called "an alarming sense of order."[5] Perhaps one could say that Clemenceau agreed with the second Rio Branco to the extent that the Brazilian Army could profit by Prussian organization without attempting to force the attendant military ideology on an unreceptive Brazilian democracy.

When he was Foreign Minister, Rio Branco (although the son of

---

[4] Georges Clemenceau: *Notes de Voyage dans l'Amérique du Sud* (Paris, 1911), p. 212. See also Ernest Hambloch: *British Consul* (London, 1938). Former British Consul in Rio de Janeiro, Hambloch is also the author of *His Majesty the President* (London, 1935).

[5] Clemenceau: op. cit., pp. 212, 213.

a former Masonic Grand Master of the Brazilian Orient) did not hesitate to receive Catholic priests like Father Gaffre with the greatest cordiality, even when such visitors on leaving Brazil often expressed opinions strongly contrary to the radical republicanism of Clemenceau or the skeptical or atheistic socialism of Enrico Ferri and Anatole France. Certainly, Rio Branco remained loyal to the Brazilian Republic through three presidencies, without ceasing to dedicate himself to the preservation of the maximum number of positive values—organization, order, discipline—from the past, those of Catholicism included.

Invited to lunch with the Masonic statesman at his home, Father Gaffre gained the impression of having visited a man sympathetic to the Church. In Rio Branco's study, famous for its disorder, the desk piled so high with papers and books that its owner would constantly lose his *pince-nez* amid the rubble, Gaffre was pleased to find a beautiful and carefully treated image of Christ, whom the supposedly heretical statesman introduced as "the real master of the house." And in the bedroom he found not only another image of Christ, but also one of the Virgin and another of Santo Antônio de Pádua, all of which led him to observe: "I wish that many of our great men of conservative reputation, several of whom I have met, could give their visitors the impression of moral and religious enlightenment that I carried away from this home." [6]

Father Gaffre, in noting that French Lazarists were replacing the few Brazilians of this order, stated that the newcomers "had restored the most exact discipline on the ruins left by the native members." [7] It was this sort of "exact discipline" that the Baron was seeking for the Armed Forces, and as Foreign Minister he was not content merely to reorganize and tighten up the diplomatic services, but was using almost Jesuitical methods to recruit bright young men. Nor did he neglect the problem of educating the wives of these diplomats, so that they would be as attractive and well informed as possible. He encouraged with the greatest sympathy the development of schools run by French nuns for the education of young ladies. According to traditional Itamaraty gossip, which was supported by the testimony of persons who knew him well, the Baron was overcome with terror when forced to invite illustrious Brazilians with badly trained wives to diplomatic gatherings. He

[6] L. A. Gaffre: *Visions du Brésil* (Paris, 1912), p. 131.
[7] Ibid., p. 107.

must have felt this same embarrassment at the spectacle of the frayed Brazilian military, and we have already seen that he experienced the same feelings toward racially mixed or Negroid representatives of his country in Europe or the United States.

The truth is that, like his two great contemporaries Joaquim Nabuco and Ruy Barbosa, the Baron do Rio Branco belonged to a group of Brazilians who, paradoxically enough, were at one and the same time conservative and revolutionary. And all three statesmen could reconcile these extremes so that none was divided against himself; each could use the full range of his qualities in rendering notable service to his country.

Visiting Ruy Barbosa, with whom he also enjoyed a cordial luncheon, Father Gaffre was well aware that he was in the company of an old adversary of the Church who, in many celebrated pages, had spoken "against the Church—or to be more exact, against certain representatives of the Church, the Jesuits in particular." But more recent events had dissolved these earlier "skirmishes" in smoke; Ruy had since revealed a "great breadth of sentiments" which made it impossible to consider him anti-clerical, much less anti-Catholic. Besides which, Father Gaffre noted, Brazilians were never as rigid as Frenchmen toward persons of different ideas or creeds; in this new Republic it was impossible to imagine rifts between adversaries like those in France at the time.[8]

It is true that during the time of Floriano, with the so-called "consolidation" of the Republic, there was some intransigence, with political hatreds of an almost Spanish-American crudity. But this tension lasted only for a short time, too short to constitute an era. Hatreds were soon dissipated in the amiable Brazilian tradition of overlooking the occasional peccadillo—an election or two marked by bloodshed, or the odd sedition—in the spirit of easygoing intranational cordiality. Once recovered from the initial shock, the Republic from 1889 to the end of the Venceslau Brás presidency suffered no disturbance of that spirit of cordiality, except for the occasional outburst sparked off not so much by political hatred as by lack of adjustment between regions or cultural tensions arising out of the differing rates of development in widely separated parts of the country.

One could say that the Republic represented the eagerness of a considerable group of Brazilians to overcome social and cultural

[8] Ibid., pp. 212, 213.

problems more rapidly than the rather leisurely methods of Imperial political administration would permit. An example was reflected in the so-called "João Cândido" naval revolt, an event
which for a few days in 1910 shook Rio de Janeiro and alarmed the
politicians. Competent observers such as Bryce and Father Gaffre
saw this uprising as the result of social maladjustment. Gaffre cited
the current methods of naval recruitment as the cause of this "brutal uprising." [9] The rebels were mere boys, almost all Negroes or
mulattos, who looked to naval service merely as a means of existence. The descendants of slaves, no longer under the patriarchal
care of the landholders, they had grown up in a republican Brazil
where social distances between ethnic groups were growing ever
greater, and had been abandoned by a government whose paternalistic affections after 1889 turned rather toward the wave of immigrants arriving from Europe.

Once these boys were taken into the naval services, however, the
Republic gave them nothing in the way of civic instruction or religious training. Preoccupied with modernizing everything from industries to railroads, it had no time for descendants of slaves. For
them there was only the lash. Even in the days of slavery, the lash
had been only a part of the story, along with instruction, religious
assistance, medical aid, and the like. Nobody with good sense
would argue that the Navy should have abolished flogging overnight in 1889 just to prove that the republican regime was better
than that of the Empire. But since the Republic had come to place
such importance on the development of its Navy and the necessity
of recruiting more men for the service, the sensible thing would
have been to remember the origins of the mystical cry "To the
Sea!" [1] and, along with its zeal for acquiring the latest technical
materials and machinery from England and Scotland, to have paid
at least minimal attention to the human aspects. It was this human
rehabilitation that was lacking, not only in the Navy, but also
among some of the most progressive politicians of the early twentieth century, in their eagerness to make up for the time lost to progress through the slow administrative methods of the Empire. Because this subject is vital to an understanding of the period, I shall
develop it more fully at this point.

9 Ibid., p. 34.
1 *"Rumo ao Mar!* (To the Sea!)" is the traditional cry of the Portuguese sailors
dating from the age of exploration. (Translator.)

No observation is more exact than that of Father Gaffre in evaluating the progressive zeal of the young Republic. This zeal, the padre felt, characterized the abolitionist, the republican, and the industrialist alike and inspired a mystique common to all; the mystique of progress, and as rapid a progress as possible. "In my humble opinion," wrote Gaffre in his excellent *Visions du Brésil*, "in this country which so readily expresses its ardent yen for progress and its intense wish to bring itself to the level of the great civilized nations, the great mistake has been its desire to burn its bridges." [2] Like Bryce, Father Gaffre found this type of precipitous progress dangerously uncontrolled; it was useless for Brazil to invite comparison with the older nations of Europe merely through the acquisition of superdreadnoughts, when the social condition of the greater part of its population hardly coincided with this level of material or technical improvement. And a false improvement at that; an acquired benefit, labelled "Made in England" or "Made in the U.S.A." or even "Made in Germany." The perfection of *things*: of cities, docks, industries, railroads, passenger and cargo ships, as well as of warships, but never the perfection of human beings.

But it cannot be denied that, in this disorganized material progress, people were also obliquely benefited on more than one occasion. It was during this period that the Lloyd Brasileiro, with its cargo service, and the railroads, with their lines of communication to the interior, brought about a development that made previous efforts in the field of transportation seem regressive and even decadent. At this time, too, the automobile, imported from Europe and later from the United States, began to pass from a novelty to a regular means of transportation. All these systems acted as a constant challenge to business, industry, and government to meet the problems of distance and, in so doing, to bring about often beneficial changes in the social and cultural order.

Elliott noted in 1916 that automobiles, limited for some time to use by the rich in the principal cities, were now becoming more numerous in the agricultural areas. From this he surmised that there would be improvements in the highways of the interior, always more of a problem in Brazil than in temperate countries. "The climate of half the country opposes itself to road permanence with all the force of the tropics," wrote Elliott. [3] Admittedly, in certain re-

[2] Gaffre: op. cit., p. 34.
[3] L. E. Elliott: *Brazil, Today and Tomorrow* (New York, 1917), p. 128.

gional areas, roads had already been cut: by the carts of the Russian
or Polish immigrants in Paraná, for example, or by the oxcarts of
the agrarian north, or even by the Army under a commission
headed by that energetic spirit Cândido Mariano da Silva Rondon
in his geological and geographical studies in the interior and in his
great work among the Indians.

As for railroad construction, Brazil in 1916 already had small factories capable of making the necessary materials, including sleeping
and dining cars from excellent native woods. This was particularly
true of the railroads most necessary to westward expansion, the
North-Western of Brazil. This company, with a British name and
Belgian management, was operated on a guaranteed profit agreement with the republican government, through the aid of a loan
floated in Paris in 1909. The construction of the railway was carried out under the direction of a distinguished Brazilian engineer,
Firmo Dutra, friend of Euclydes da Cunha and, like him, imbued
with the mystique of Brazil and of the engineer. Called "an able
Brazilian engineer" by Elliott, Dutra preferred to do his work in
the more primitive regions where he had spent the greater part of
his youth. Under his direction the company not only laid tracks,
but also lined the right of way with the fruits of social engineering:
coffee groves, pasturelands, and new towns.[4]

Moreover, Firmo Dutra was not the sole engineer of the time to
reveal abilities comparable or superior to those of British and Americans like Hammond, Fox, and Derby in organizing and directing
the technical aspects of railways or of port, sanitary, or geological
services. There were also Ceciliano Mamede Ferreira, Lauro
Müller, Paulo de Frontin, Pereira Passos, Pandiá Calógeras, and
Saturnino de Brito. The last-named, whose career as engineer and
public administrator deserves a special study, set the example,
which was scrupulously followed by the sanitary engineers under
his direction, of remaining completely apolitical and impeccably
honest in the discharge of his official duties. Like Rondon, he was a
Positivist. He was also a major instigator in the successful campaigns waged by the Republic against infectious diseases in Recife,
Santos, and other principal cities, where he installed modern systems of water supply and sewage disposal.

The Republic, all things considered, made a considerably better
showing than had the Empire in matters of sanitation and modernization of port facilities. "When I came to Rio in 1887," wrote Hei-

4 Ibid., p. 136.

tor Modesto in 1940, "the city was periodically devastated by smallpox and yellow fever. In the center of the downtown area, where the coffee businesses were located, the toll was great, notably in the Saude and Gamboa sections. There was no isolation of the victims; the patient was treated at home. It was said that yellow fever hit the foreigners in particular and smallpox struck the Negroes. Our physician was Dr. Miguel Couto who had just started his clinic in a two-story house in Prainha. He had a number of cases of smallpox and yellow fever, but he never lost a patient."

The fear of epidemics was constant. People spoke darkly of "black vomit" and "sandpaper skin." Upon learning that his mother was stricken with smallpox, Heitor Modesto recalls having prayed to the image of the Virgin hanging in his room: "Dear Lady, give me smallpox too so that I can be near my mother!" Luckily, his mother recovered "with very few pockmarks." Many other Brazilians of the time were not so fortunate and went through life with their faces horribly pitted by the disease. Once-pretty girls became ugly women; others lost their hair, that precious insignia of beauty and nobility. The Miguel Coutos alone could not conquer smallpox, typhoid, or yellow fever; it was necessary for sanitary engineers, public health officers, and hygienists to take over the job which for so many years the Empire had left in the hands of clinics and pharmacies helpless in the face of the contaminated water, poor drainage, and improper diet which prevailed.

"Many years later, toward the end of his life, I heard Dr. Miguel Couto speak of former residents of my childhood home," writes Heitor Modesto. "He remembered even their nicknames. When I praised this feat of memory, he explained: 'I could never forget. . . . It was a great day for me when I was called to attend a patient at the Casa Barão de Ipanema. In these early days of the clinic, such visits gave me considerable prestige.' "

The Casa Barão de Ipanema was a wholesale coffee company, a large three-story building located in the midst of a complex of other such establishments in downtown Rio de Janeiro. At this time, as in the sugar commissaries of the north, the proprietor's family, together with visiting clients, lived in the office building itself. Heitor Modesto's father was office manager of the company, and the family lived on the third floor of the company building at Rua Municipal, No. 5.

Transient visitors to the coffee commissaries were usually rural landholders who often arrived with their entire entourage, includ-

ing nursemaids and attendants. When there was illness among them
it raised a major problem with urban physicians, unused as they
were to treating country ailments. It was by treating these aristocratic families and their servants that men like Miguel Couto or
Francisco de Castro became familiar with rural diseases. The average city dweller at the time also began to develop the same famili-
arity, and as a result became fearful of the countryman with his
exotic illnesses. On one occasion Dr. Miguel Couto was summoned
to treat Heitor Modesto's visiting Uncle Oscar. When the symptoms of his illness were listed, the physician declared that it sounded
like a case of yellow fever. On overhearing this declaration, the
patient came into the living room from the sickroom in which he
had been lying, "staggering and weak, dressed in a nightshirt, his
eyes popping, muttering 'But I'm all right, I'm all right.'" He
feared the city-bred yellow fever much more than smallpox or
cholera, which were diseases well known on the plantations.

The new water and sewage systems installed by the court in 1880
undoubtedly did much to improve hygienic conditions in Rio de
Janeiro. By 1887 there were 33,713 houses in the city, with 29,261
toilets and 37,080 water connections. But the city flats, particularly
on the ground floor, continued to be "the worst possible dwellings
in the downtown area," not only because of the "inconveniences
caused by bad materials and small rooms, but also by the scarcity of
light, air, and sunshine" (such inconveniences were less acute on
the upper floors, of course, particularly in the bedrooms with eastern exposure). Some of the coffee commissaries were of this type
and were thus most susceptible to the development of typhoid,
diphtheria, and tuberculosis. Most city hotel and rooming house accommodations were even worse; one hygienist called them "me-
phitic stews"[5] in which syphilis, alcohol, and gambling attacked
the moral and physical fiber of visitors from the country who, having no better place, were forced to seek shelter in such dens.

To these could be added the so-called *freges*, fly-trap lunch
counters and food stands which, like other commercial establishments, were subject to no sanitary inspection whatsoever during
the Empire.[6] Compared to the fervent sanitary measures undertaken by the Republic virtually from its inauguration, those of the
Empire merited the severest criticism. Under the Republic, there

[5] Antônio Martins de Azevedo Pimentel: *Subsídios para o Estudo da Higiene do
Rio de Janeiro* (Rio de Janeiro, 1890), pp. 179, 180, 189.
[6] Ibid., p. 345.

was constant prosecution of irresponsibles who out of sheer greed committed abuses against public health. In Pernambuco the Barbosa Lima government was outstanding in controlling these abuses; in Rio de Janeiro it was the hygienist Rodolfo Galvão during the late nineteenth century and, after 1900, Osvaldo Cruz, whose public health measures became world famous. In this sense, the Republic seems to have heeded the appeal of the great Portuguese journalist Ramalho Ortigão who, having visited Brazil at the end of the reign of Pedro II, roundly denounced the government for its lack of attention to problems of urban hygiene and scored this indifference as one of the greatest defects of the Imperial regime.

In the 1909 volume of the *Almanaque Brasileiro*, published in Rio de Janeiro by Garnier under the direction of João Ribeiro, an intelligent analysis of the last Brazilian Emperor appeared, written from the vantage point of twenty years later. The conclusion reached by this judicious summary was that the old monarch had lost his throne as a result of not knowing how to bring his reign into line with the realities of the Brazilian situation. This study in many ways anticipated the evaluation of the Republic as opposed to the Second Empire made in 1922 by Joaquim Viana in a short but suggestive essay "Por que Caiu o Império" (Why the Empire Fell) in *À Margem da História da República* (*Notes on the History of the Republic*), a collective work published in Rio de Janeiro. Viana defends the thesis that Dom Pedro II was "neither an authoritarian nor a rigorously constitutional monarch." Rather, he wished only to live in peace—a bureaucratic peace—at a time when Brazil needed a ruler who could preside as constitutional leader able to organize, to undertake, to direct, and even to summon up the courage to make enemies.[7] He needed the courage the Republic was able to produce in Floriano, in Prudente, in Rodrigues Alves; the courage the Paulistas evinced in their plan for the valorization of coffee in the face of the contrary ideas of all the British and American economists; the courage manifested by energetic public administrators such as the engineer Pereira Passos, the public health director Osvaldo Cruz, Governor Barbosa Lima, state ministers like the Baron do Rio Branco, Joaquim Murtinho, and Hermes da Fonseca, who reorganized the Army, or Alexandrino de Alencar, who to a certain extent did the same for the Navy.

The second Emperor never took the slightest interest in the

[7] Joaquim Viana: "Por que Caiu o Império," *Almanaque Brasileiro Garnier* (Rio de Janeiro, 1909), p. 270.

Armed Forces. An anti-militarist, he distrusted the Army to such an extent, says Viana, that "at a certain point he had the whim of replacing it with a national guard, in the manner of the do-nothing King Louis-Philippe." A freethinker, "he did not know how to communicate with the Church," thereby failing to use the clergy in a way that would be advantageous to the monarchical government. "He always nourished a secret spite against the padres, because of his bitter recollections of his early education at the hands of a churchman," says Viana. He did not believe in the "theorists'" capacity for action and neglected always "to speak directly to the people, to appeal to their imagination, to their patriotic sentiments in words which would leave an everlasting impression on the popular spirit . . . which would provoke popular enthusiasm, define a course of action, create an indestructible affection even in the face of major errors." As a result he found himself "one fine day without anyone on his side," particularly because of his Anglomania— his attempt to turn his reign into an imitation of British liberalism and parliamentarianism—to say nothing of his attempt to imitate the psychic aspects of the Victorian era: the cult of myths, rites, and ceremonies with which the Queen imparted almost religious prestige to her presence on the throne. And not being a man of action, he showed himself incapable of resisting "demagogic ideologies" and "inept utopias." When there was need for political decision, he escaped into the study of astronomy, natural history, philology, the geology of Agassiz, the cosmography of Liais, or the archeology of Lund (though not the social sciences). Or he would behave like "the most exemplary of administrative division heads" by examining his ministers, pencil in hand and bureaucratic spectacles on his nose, as though they were his secretaries, which was, in truth, what he had made of them. His political demise, therefore, was, in Viana's opinion, that of "a retired government employee." [8]

Any one of the subsequent Brazilian Presidents during the period of this study, with the possible exception of Afonso Pena and Hermes da Fonseca, was more authoritarian and even more monarchical than Pedro II in the exercise of his official functions. And the results are seen in such developments as the rapid rehabilitation of Rio de Janeiro, the conquering of yellow fever, the penetration of the interior by the Rondon commission, the peaceful solution of old boundary questions with neighboring republics, the reorganization

[8] Ibid., pp. 271, 272.

of the Army, the re-equipping of the Navy, the enlargement of the railway network, the modernization of principal ports, the installation of sanitary services in the large cities, and the development of new industries, such as meat packing, necessary to the stimulation of the Brazilian economy.

With the Republic, Brazil began to be recognized by educated Europeans as a new civilization in the tropics where people of northern climates could not only live comfortably but also enjoy economic advantages. In 1909 *Le Figaro* ran an article by P. Bernier in which Rio de Janeiro was characterized as a city comparable "to the most salubrious places of Europe," and which would be even healthier when the authorities there succeeded in conquering tuberculosis in the same energetic manner in which they had vanquished yellow fever.[9] Foreigners could now become very active in the Brazilian capital, said *Le Figaro*, "in exploiting the country's inexhaustible sources of wealth without the slightest danger to life or physical health." This condition was partly due to French science, the magazine pointed out; the Instituto Manguinhos was a sort of branch of the Pasteur. But it was also due to the action of the Rodrigues Alves government, which was able to place a man of the stature of Osvaldo Cruz in the direction of this establishment. No bureaucratic hack, no mere time-server, Osvaldo Cruz was a man in white, in the midst of battle, in the service of his country.[1] The article also pointed out the great energy with which the state of Minas Gerais was replacing its former capital with an entirely new city: Belo Horizonte.

Guglielmo Ferrero, the Italian classicist and social historian who visited Brazil during this period of change, had the impression that it was the newly arrived Europeans who were the real revolutionaries of Brazilian society. Or perhaps the Brazilians were the conservatives and classicists in the order, with the immigrants supplying the creative and innovatory romantic disorder. Ferrero wrote these impressions in connection with his comments on *Canaã* (*Canaan*), the sociological novel in which Graça Aranha attempted to define the conflict between the old and the newly emerging Brazil.[2]

The fact was that after abolition and the proclamation of the

[9] *Almanaque Brasileiro Garnier*, p. 170.

[1] Ibid., p. 170.

[2] In the preface to the English-language edition of *Canaã* which appeared in New York in 1916.

Republic, Brazil was revolutionized from the inside out. The basic classic forms remained: but the motives and style of living became romantic. This romanticism affected not only the literature, but also the politics and jurisprudence of the time. It was a romanticism, however, that did not go to Spanish-American extremes. In literature, in politics, in the artistic and social life there was always a touch of classic restraint to moderate the romantic excesses, to prevent Hispanic extravagances, or to tone down the furors of Garibaldi-type revolutionaries. Even in the south, the temper of the Brazilian *gaúcho*, with his taste for violence, was somewhat balanced by the sober, responsible, feet-on-the-ground orderliness of the Azorean immigrant. But anyone looking backward from 1918 to the period of the Republican Manifesto and the Law of the Free Womb would realize that, while the basic national norms had not changed, the whole tone of life proclaimed a different age.

Though long since dead, José Bonifácio continued to be the principal guide to Brazilian development. The Positivists, champions of movements they mystically, almost religiously, considered progressive, recognized in Bonifácio the greatest master of political and sociological thought produced by Portuguese America. In the twentieth century he was still the figure most capable of inspiring Brazilian desire for progress, including democratic progress, which somehow became conciliated with the Luso-American tradition of political authority and social protection. The principles remained; only the forms showed signs of change. Charity, which in colonial times followed a system whereby the rich took care of the poor, was replaced by a complex of Misericórdias, Third Orders, and monastic Brotherhoods which carried out the same function. Political authority, with its tradition of "personal power" or "moderating power," managed to embrace the American concept of republicanism without destroying the traditional force of the personal leader. At times this personality cultism was exaggerated, although, unlike similar political phenomena in Spanish America, always kept within at least the appearance of legality. Leaders were often referred to by descriptive nicknames: Floriano Peixoto became "the Iron Marshal"; Rodrigues Alves "Big Daddy" (*Papai Grande*); Borges de Medeiros, authoritarian Positivist governor of Rio Grande do Sul, "the Grasslands Pope"; the equally authoritarian Barbosa Lima of Pernambuco "Barbosa the Fury" (*Barbosa Fera*); the Baron do Rio Branco was known simply as "the Baron"; Pinheiro Machado as "the Chief"; Rosa e Silva as "the Counselor." To some extent, this giving of nicknames harks back to the custom of Imperial titles, as the sentiments behind them can similarly be traced to a more frankly patriarchal period in the nation's history. The principal difference between this survival of patriarchism in Brazil and the *candilhismo* of Spanish-American countries is that the former custom stems from the existence of a titled aristocracy which was entirely lacking in the Hispanic republics.

This difference did not escape the sharp eye of Clemenceau in his comparison of the Republic of 1889 with its older Latin-American sisters. "In São Paulo or Rio de Janeiro," he wrote, "political figures to whom I have talked can measure up to any standards in their culture and their penchant for methodical action. There was an aristocracy around the Emperor whose vestiges are being employed by the new democratic order. . . . It will suffice to mention the case, rare among Latin countries, of a leader who is universally obeyed. I do not doubt that Mr. Pinheiro Machado possesses all the qualities of a leader of men, but I am less astonished to find these qualities than I am to note the forbearance with which he is able to discipline so many politicians of Latin mentality." [3]

It was difficult for Clemenceau, in his violently anti-clerical, democratic-republican radicalism, to understand how a country which had become republicanized without losing its Imperial aristocratic traditions could permit an ethnic democracy in the Armed Forces—a situation which had also struck more orthodox Europeans, such as Bryce, Burnichon, or Gaffre, as being almost scandalous. On inspecting troops come to Rio de Janeiro for a parade, Clemenceau could not repress his European prejudices: "The young officers gave an excellent impression and the barracks installations left nothing to be desired. But there are really many colored men in the ranks." [4]

In São Paulo, Clemenceau visited a detachment of military police being trained by a group of French officers and discovered how it was possible to turn humble folk, many of them of non-European blood, into a well-disciplined military body. He reported that one of the French officers stated: "My men are docile, but at the same time they are alert and always good-humored." And it was not difficult for Clemenceau to see how such men, generally regarded as

[3] Clemenceau: op. cit., p. 218.
[4] Ibid., p. 220.

impulsive, could attain these qualities: along with the "pecuniary advantages" of their situation, they enjoyed installations that were both comfortable and hygienic, superior in fact to those afforded the soldiers of France. The social factors of good pay, good food, and good lodgings in this case, as in so many others, managed to outweigh the supposed ethnic disadvantages.

Presumably the same thing would have occurred with colored Brazilian workers, had they been given similar "pecuniary advantages," along with hygienic comforts and good working conditions, by the Republic of 1889. Clemenceau stated that in Brazil in 1910 "laws for the social protection of industrial and agricultural workers were nonexistent." [5] Not that political leaders were unconcerned with the matter, he adds somewhat apologetically, but rather because "the amorphous nature of decentralized administrations" did not seem to permit the application of such laws.

Clemenceau's apology seems a somewhat vague explanation of a grave deficiency on the part of these political leaders, who were so efficient and even authoritarian in such matters as the valorization of national resources and yet so hesitant, even blind to the crying need for protection on the part of the working class. In 1919 anyone looking back over the past fifty years would have concluded that in the matter of concern for the workingman—or the slave— the superiority would rest indisputably with the Imperial government.

During the Republic the strange silence of Ruy Barbosa on this matter cannot be overlooked. This eloquent statesman, as vigorous as Joaquim Nabuco in promoting the cause of the slaves, suddenly became silent once those slaves were made freedmen in theory. He overlooked the fact that, during the early Republic, they and their descendants often continued to exist in a state of virtual bondage which could only be called cruel.

Clemenceau was able to give credit, however, to the private interests which did not wait for the government to take action in the matter of benefits to labor. In the outlying districts of Rio de Janeiro, Bangu, for example, Clemenceau found industrialists making an attempt to establish better working conditions. "The workers of Bangu," he wrote, "spread throughout the area and living in cottages in which none of the hygienic facilities are lacking, give a pleasing appearance of physical and moral health." There was even

[5] Ibid., p. 234.

a substitute for the patriarchal Big House transferred to an industrial and suburban setting in the form of "a large community house for gatherings of all sorts, complete with a theatre where the workers can enjoy the pleasures of music and drama." [6]

Unfortunately, there were all too few industrialists during this period who gave corresponding treatment to their workers, a class which Manuel Bernárdez felt was capable of "any industrial undertaking." [7] For the most part people were abandoned both by their employers and the Church, as we have seen, and ripe for the proselytizing of evangelical Protestants, with their sentimental compensations to fill empty lives and to give them hope in their new, if insipid, existence as free men. Some were seduced by other doctrines: the anarchist or Marxist mystiques brought from Europe by Spaniards, Italians, or an occasional German. Such doctrines, however, were less effective with the former slaves and their descendants than with whites who found themselves in a similar psychological—if not cultural—situation. For the most part these were middle-class adolescents in Catholic schools who suddenly found themselves victims, not of a lack of Catholic charity as in the case of the ex-slaves, but rather of a loss of Catholic faith itself. The faith of their childhood; the faith of their parents and grandparents.

Such was the experience of Astrojildo Pereira (b. state of Rio de Janeiro, 1890), who was, it may be remembered, a pupil at the Colégio Anchieta and later at the Colégio Abílio in Niterói. At first intending to become a priest or monk, he became disillusioned with the Church and fell under the influence of the most anti-Catholic writers: Kropotkin, Grave, Faure, Malatesta, Hamon. His dissatisfaction with the prevailing order was further increased by the defeat of Ruy Barbosa in 1909, the execution of Ferrer in Spain, and the revolt of João Cândido. To the young ex-Catholic, Ruy had become "a god"; but in time his faith in this god was also dispersed and other divinities were needed. He found one such in Bakunin, whom he read in his entirety. At first he was against Marx, "without having read him"; but after the Russian Revolution in 1919, through the influence of Lenin, he "became directly acquainted with the work of Marx" and was converted. Earlier, in 1911, he perhaps prepared the way for this conversion by a trip to

[6] Ibid., p. 234.
[7] Manuel Bernárdez: *El Brasil, Su Vida, Su Trabajo, Su Futuro* (Buenos Aires, 1908), p. 184.

Europe, intending to work and study in Paris. He had "a third-class ticket and very little money," a fact which possibly increased his disenchantment with the bourgeoisie. His friend Max Vasconcelos was awaiting him in Genoa and together they went to Paris via Berne. Always without money, he finally had to be sent back home at the expense of generous countrymen. "We were repatriated by the Associação da Colônia Brasileira, which bought our passages and gave each of us 50 francs pocket money. We spent the money on books. General impression: disenchantment . . . but a delicious sort of disenchantment." Such is the confession of a middle-class Catholic boy who became anti-bourgeois and anti-Catholic largely because of the lack of professional training for restless and talented youngsters of his period.

In Paris Astrojildo Pereira could have encountered a rich Brazilian of about his own age who had lived most of his life in France: the caricaturist Emílio Cardoso Ayres. Emílio was also disillusioned with Brazil (as already mentioned), not because he had lost his faith in religion or in the superficial civil reform of Ruy Barbosa, but rather because he was a so-called "artist" in rebellion against the philistinism of the middle class, a rebellion which led him to an anti-militarism and a pacifism almost anarchistic or socialistic in its intensity. His anguish was increased by his effeminacy and his almost infantile physique, though without becoming complicated by the overt, if elegant, pederasty which marked the lives of two other Brazilian artists: João do Rio and Virgílio Maurício, the latter also for some time a student in Paris. It is difficult to say which of his many sufferings led Emílio to commit suicide in a hotel in southern France on his return from a trip to North Africa which, without being too far from Paris, had for him become a substitute for his own Brazil.

We have seen that Emílio Cardoso Ayres worked out some of his pique against Brazil through his caricatures of the elegant society of Rio de Janeiro. But he was not the only caricaturist of his day, nor were Rio society figures the only victims. Political figures from the Emperor on down were portrayed, sometimes with considerable malice, by Ângelo Agostini, Bordalo Pinheiro, Crispim de Amaral, Vera Cruz, and other talented journalistic artists. One frequently portrayed political leader seldom presented unfavorably was the Baron do Rio Branco. This can be attributed partly to the ability of the popular minister to maintain a nonpartisan political position; but it could also be due to his unsurpassed friendliness toward newspaper men and his generous protection of men of letters outside the journalistic field.

One of his protégés was Aluísio de Azevedo, who without the merited and intelligent favor of the Baron might have remained a caricaturist—and a bitter one at that—for the rest of his life. Talented from childhood but equally uneasy in both imperial and republican Brazil, Azevedo was recruited by Rio Branco for the consular service, where he served effectively for many years. Unable to live happily or comfortably in republican Brazil, he was willing to serve his country abroad, though he was never completely at ease in any of his posts and seems constantly to have yearned for the days of his youth in Maranhão. He hated England, became sick of Argentina, and even found his days in Japan and Naples rather insipid. From Naples on December 22, 1909, he wrote his friend Guimarães that the Christmas season was always a dreary one for him; he had passed so many of these holidays "in strange lands among indifferent faces." Once, in Cardiff, he had spent Christmas by giving a party for the poor children of the neighborhood. His guests "enjoyed themselves so in dancing, frolicking, and playing little dramas around the tree filled with presents" that the Consul, "smoking quietly by himself" in his study, was carried by their shouts and laughter back to his "childhood in Maranhão, with its *bumba-meu-boi*, its Nativity scenes, its folk plays and songs of the Three Magi, its midnight mass followed by the ceremonial capon soup" and fell into such a state of sadness that ever since the mere mention of Christmas caused him as great suffering as did the recollections of his native land.

Such recollections, however, did not prevent Azevedo from becoming concerned about his next consular assignment, and he prayed God that it would not be in Venezuela or Paraguay. He had already written to Pessegueiro, secretary to the Baron, and would write him again, but he was too well acquainted with "the Baron's pre-emptory manner and his secretary's scruples" to expect direct results. In a previous letter to Guimarães, written on July 11, 1902, he had stated that "the condition of the intelligence is to suffer and dislike. The pleasure of any intelligent man is fictitious and incomplete, and always takes its toll in nervous energy. Because of this the vices were invented—alcohol, gambling, women." A bitter philosopher, whose life was turned useful only through the interest of the Baron.

On December 22, 1906, Azevedo wrote from Cardiff to his best friend, referring to "the blessed Rio Branco, in whose hands the consular corps has been transformed from a constant stream of botherations to a steady career with excellent prospects." His transfer from Cardiff to Naples had given him new life; he "was positively dying" in Wales. "It is not so much the cold which bothers me as the dampness, that dampness which you can feel and hear draining the heat from our bodies, destroying our moral fiber, sucking the life out of us and dragging us into a rot of tedium; this dampness which would never leave us, I believe, even if we jumped into the fire, and which is with us everywhere—in the desk, in the bread we eat, the cigarette we smoke, the sheet we draw over us, the slippers we wear, and the thoughts we pass through our minds. . . ." In Naples this man of the tropics hoped to resuscitate himself, to rescue himself from the "exhaustion of exhaustion, the intemperance and brutalities of England," from the "land of male and female thieves" where one was irrevocably contaminated by "that obscene drunkards' gibberish which is the English language." In Naples he would have "at least a little sun to remind me of my country." And, bitterly, "humanity is worthless," and Cardiff "a small cross section of all the faults of this world."

Nevertheless, on learning in 1903 that he had been transferred from Salto to Europe, Azevedo had written Guimarães: "How grateful I am! Once I am in Europe everything will change for me. I confess to you that I did not complain more about Salto and did not kick out with more vehemence against this den of cattle rustlers and Rio Grande politicians only because I did not wish to appear cranky. . . ." Had it not been for his consular career, with its frequent changes of post and constant making of new contacts, Azevedo, I repeat, would probably have been a dissolute Rio journalist, an inveterate member of the opposition, against God and the world, probably even against the "blessed Rio Branco." Journalist, caricaturist, polemicist, he would have made another Edmundo Bittencourt, with something also of Lima Barreto. All this alongside the romantic vision of life, though a vision dampened for him by a series of frustrations perhaps more adolescent than mature. An early rebel against traditions and environment, he later felt only nostalgia for his youth and for the sunshine of his mother country. But it was too late. His desire to see the world—the Orient, Europe —had taken possession of half his being, never allowing him to reintegrate himself happily in the Brazilian scene. Perhaps, of all the

Western world, it was only Paris which softened the nostalgia he felt for the Maranhão of his childhood, a nostalgia which he kept to himself and revealed only in the fascinating unpublished letters (now in my possession) he wrote to his close friend and fellow Marinhense Francisco Guimarães.

Guimarães was a typical good, fine-grained, rose-complexioned Marinhense who became almost a perfect Parisian, like so many Europeans who, given money and opportunity, were able to expatriate themselves in the French capital and live like Frenchmen of the *haut monde*. In the early days of the Republic some achieved such expatriation by dipping into the public funds; and there were others, such as the priest Severino de Resende, who left their clerical trappings behind to live a Bohemian existence in Paris. Others again, for love of Paris, abandoned their families in Brazil or repudiated the monarchy in the dream of obtaining a republican sinecure in the City of Light.

Those who returned after several months—or even years—of residence brought with them girls as blond as the French dolls of childhood, whom they installed in discreet châlets in picturesque locations; and they also bore a supply of books (some of which were predictably erotic), prophylactics, Doucet engravings, wines and mineral waters, hats, silk shirts, and pharmaceutical remedies. Some had studied medicine in Paris, and continued to do so in Brazil by means of French books written by French teachers. Others, merely rich, had lived like *boulevardiers*, visiting the theatres, museums, and lecture halls, and developing their taste buds in fancy restaurants. Some had spent a good part of their time being treated for one or another ailment, having their teeth filled by French dentists, or merely collecting a supply of the French medicines so popular at the time.

French was not only read but spoken by cultivated Brazilians of the period, among whom an error in pronunciation or grammar could mean instant social or intellectual disgrace. It was also widely written and written well, to the point that Émile Faguet thought "Joaquim Nabuco" (author of *Pensées Détachées* written in involuntary but significant opposition to *Os Sertões*) was the pseudonym of some resident European diplomat, so excellent was his French and so European his viewpoint and his manner of thinking. And Faguet's diagnostic could have been extended, in a sense, to many other books of the period which, while written in Portuguese, were nevertheless psychologically French. This generalization could apply to several of the works of Machado de Assis, despite the Brazilian material on which they are based and the sensitivity to the tropical environment that is their inspiration.

Against this somewhat excessive taste for European imports—literary, sociological, philosophical, as well as pharmaceutical—was the movement on the part of nativists to develop indigenous materials, a movement which anticipated the daring of the technical revolution or the agricultural revival which came with the valorization of coffee. These nativist movements ranged from the literary, which began with the novels of José de Alencar in the first half of the nineteenth century, to the vogue for *guaraná* and *maté* which developed at the beginning of the twentieth. Although such nativism was more accentuated in pharmacology than literature, there was considerable interest in nativist writing, particularly centering around Recife. Here a school of writers existed who, even in Imperial times, opposed the excessive Gallicism in Brazilian letters, arts, and sciences. At first adhering to Germanic norms in its desire to purge the French influences, this school eventually developed into an expression of Brazilian nationalism. It was a nationalism colored with a feeling for the tropics which to the Francophiles seemed to connote bad taste, incontinent or inelegant language, primitivism in feeling and thinking, and general incapacity for *nuance* in the finer sense of the word—the very qualities which they found in abundance in such works as Euclydes da Cunha's *Os Sertões*.

When, in 1917, the geographer Elliott stated that the world owed much to Brazil in the fields of horticulture and medicine, there were already many physicians in the Republic who, having lived in or visited the Amazon, were using the drugs of that region almost exclusively in their practice. Among such drugs were *ipecacuanha* (the source of ipecac), *copaíba* (*copaíba balsam*), or *jaborandi*, the last considered by the famous Rabutau the equal of quinine for the treatment of fevers.[8] As early as 1865, in his *Dicionário de Medicina*, the physician T. J. H. Langaard, one of the many European physicians attracted to Brazil for the study of tropical diseases, had pointed out the virtues of national drugs. *Guaraná*, another product of the Amazon, also had its widest acceptance in France, where it was sold as a pleasant-tasting tonic; in the Brazil of 1917 it was regarded merely as a soft drink. Elliott states that a list

8 Elliott: op. cit., p. 313.

of Amazonian medicinal materials would fill several pages of his book and limits himself to the mention of the internationally famed *quássia* (used as a fever remedy), *jalapa* (a purgative), a diuretic called *lágrima-de-Nossa-Senhora* (Our Lady's tear), São Caetano melon (antacid), *cipó-caboclo* (an astringent), *cambará* (much used in the making of cough remedies), *batata-de-purga* and *purga-do-pastor* (both febrifuges), *laranjeira-do-mato*, *pau-Paraíba*, and *pau-Pereira* (tonics), oil of Andiroba (used for soap as well as for illumination), *sapucainha* (a nut used for rheumatism in Minas Gerais, Rio de Janeiro, and Espírito Santo), and *pau-precioso* (a sedative).

Thus, approximately thirty years after the proclamation of a Republic that, in the minds of many of its supporters, was to integrate the nation with the American political system, Brazil began to show some awareness of integrating itself also with its own natural surroundings to form an indigenous tropical culture. The national consciousness shown in such matters as medicine, pharmacology, hygiene, and food began to manifest itself more and more in other aspects of everyday life. Brazil began to find its own answer to elegant Europeanized tastes for soft drinks and mineral waters in such products as *guaraná* and the mineral waters of Caxambu and Salutáris. The period also marked the establishment in Caxambu, Lambari, Cambuquira, São Lourenço, and Araxá of hotels roughly imitative of those of the great European spas. Rich and elegant Brazilians flocked to these watering places; diplomats, politicians, well-to-do priests sought the cure for obesity, for intestinal disorders, and for their liver ailments, the last being the particular villain in the diagnostics of most Brazilian physicians of the period. With the coming of the First World War, when Carlsbad and Vichy were no longer available, Brazilians turned to national resources in cures and remedies, thereby raising both the resort hotels and the drug manufacturers to the level of major industries. In particular, the advertising of drug products developed, and blurbs of all kinds appeared everywhere—in the newspapers, on the walls of buildings, on streetcars. Sometimes these advertisements were in verse form, often by well-known poets. Distinguished physicians wrote newspaper and magazine articles in support of national pharmacology, an activity which scandalized foreigners. Accompanying these articles were photographs of the authors, generally robed and often very imposing in their professional garb. Other advertisements went still further, using illustrious public figures as apologists for products their manufacturers "wished to recommend to the respectable public." For example, Reuter's Soap ran copy in the *Revista da Semana* for September 3, 1906, in which three respected political figures of the time, Afonso Pena, Francisco Sales, and Ruy Barbosa, were shown beside a bathtub and a bar of soap, with the legend: "The one who uses the most Reuter's Soap is the one who will get the most votes." But these early copywriters can perhaps be pardoned for their excesses in the light of the good they brought to the public, even when their services were employed by commercial interests. Another typical advertisement appeared in the same magazine for November 26, 1905. It shows two Brazilians, one wearing a heavy suit and top hat and labelled "The Past"; the other in a straw hat and light clothing, labelled "The Future." The top hat says to his companion: "No, my dear fellow; I am a respectable man. I cannot go without my top hat . . ." To which the straw hat responds: "You are no more respectable than I am. You are Prejudice and I am Progress. You walk down the street as the last echo of Routine; I do so in the spirit of the outing and in accordance with the season, which calls for light and happy clothing . . ." And one can cite other examples: the spread for Caxambu Water in the *Revista* of September 10, 1905, showing Afonso Pena grasping a bottle of the product, with the legend: "The Favorite of Favorites!" Or that of November 5, 1905, containing a truly frightful blurb presenting a caricature of a fictitious "Judge Cardoso de Castro" thanking President Rodrigues Alves for his appointment to the federal magistracy. "I thank Your Excellency for my appointment to the Supreme Court," he says, to which the President of the Republic—the much-caricatured "Big Daddy"—replies: "Don't thank me: be assured that I nominated you only because you wear those magnificent Condor shoes bought at Silva's at 86 Rua da Uruguaiana; the brand which not only lasts longer but also brings luck to the wearer." To the Frenchman Alfred Marc, Rio de Janeiro matched New York in the furor of its commercial advertising. In the first volume of his *Le Brésil*, published in Paris in 1890, he states: "The walls on the buildings here are covered with bills, samples, and enormous figures in cardboard or metal." [9] Money was wasted on gas lamps to light these displays at night. And the bills also filled all the available space in that most Brazilian of institutions, the streetcar.

[9] Alfred Mare: *Le Brésil* (Paris, 1890).

The drug industry enriched the Daudts and the Oliveiras, with their Saúde de Mulher (Female Health) and Bromil, as well as the manufacturers of Elixir de Nogueira, Elixir Sanativo, and Regulador Gesteira. In 1916 Elliott considered it possible for Brazil to replace imported drugs with products of its own manufacture and even to export some of them, along with their mineral waters: ". . . were her resources better investigated and quantities developed, she could greatly increase her position as a supplier of medicines to international markets." [1] And in one item, that of typhoid serum, Brazil did achieve international renown. This serum was the specialty of Dr. Vital Brasil, of the Butantan Institute of São Paulo, an institution Roy Nash has called "the world's headquarters for information and serums against snake bite." [2]

Almost comparable fame was won by the Instituto Osvaldo Cruz of Rio de Janeiro, a research center which enlisted the services of such illustrious figures as Carlos Chagas, Adolfo Lutz, Sousa Araújo, Olímpio da Fonseca, Osmino Pena, J. P. Fontanelle, Cardoso Fonte, the Osório de Almeida brothers, Artur Neiva, Belisário Pena. Another notable medical man of the period, Miguel Pereira, sounded the alarm as to the deplorable sanitary conditions of the cities, conditions which Belisário Pena spent the major part of his life trying to remedy and which occupied much of the literary output of the writer Monteiro Lobato. The Bahians Pirajá da Silva, Juliano Moreira, and Oscar Freire, all of whom achieved European renown for their medical research, must also be noted here.

In institutes like the Manguinhos or Osvaldo Cruz, in the medical schools of Bahia and Rio de Janeiro, and in the public health service, doctors joined with some of the more audacious planters and industrialists to help the Republic recover from the inertia of Pedro II. They were determined to demonstrate that it was possible to establish a modern agrarian and industrial system in the tropics with technical processes equal to those employed in the more temperate countries.

In his book *The Conquest of Brazil* published in 1926, Roy Nash remarked that since the American triumph in opening the Panama Canal, it had been understood that it was possible for the white man to live and work in the tropics. Nash cited several intelligent observations made by Herbert J. Spinden in his article "Civilization in the Wet Tropics" (which appeared in the February, 1923, issue of

[1] Elliott: op. cit., p. 315.
[2] Roy Nash: *The Conquest of Brazil* (New York, 1926), p. 347.

World's Work), one being a denial of the long-held supposition
that only excessively cold, foggy climates were capable of producing civilized human beings. A similar conclusion was drawn in 1921
in Volume 3 of the *Tropical Diseases Bulletin* in an article entitled
"Report of Subcommittee of the Permanent Occupation of Tropical Australia by a Healthy Indigenous White Race," the subcommittee in question being a group of British researchers who spent
considerable time in Australia studying this troublesome ecological
and anthropological problem.[3] In Brazil there was until 1918 no
sociologist or anthropologist qualified to pronounce on this subject,
but since the beginning of the century there had been many medical studies of anthropological or sociological importance by such
men as Roquette-Pinto and Afrânio Peixoto, along with essays of
considerable intuition—often supplemented by direct contact with
the Brazilian interior or the Amazon—by such men as Eduardo
Prado, Inglês de Sousa, Sylvio Romero, José Veríssimo, Alberto
Tôrres, Euclydes da Cunha, Gustavo Barroso, Alberto Rangel, and
Professor Gilberto Amado. These writers served to alleviate two of
the deepest resentments of cultivated Brazilians: that of being inhabitants of an almost entirely tropical country and that of either
being *mestiço* or having a predominantly *mestiço* population as
compatriots. Such resentments made Brazilians feel inferior to the
Argentines, who were for the most part white, and provoked
among the most extreme a hatred for the Portuguese, the European
settlers who had made the capital error of mixing with the native
tropical peoples instead of maintaining a Caucasian purity.

Roy Nash claimed, with some humor and considerable truth,
that the principal tropical disease is in fact ignorance![4] He could
have added that the ignorance of Brazilians about themselves and
about other tropical *mestiço* societies had developed into almost a
prevailing psychosis in the cultural life of the nation, only slightly
alleviated during this period by the work of the writers already
mentioned; by other authorities such as Couto de Magalhães, Celso
de Magalhães, Nina Rodrigues, Teodoro Sampaio, Oliveira Lima,
or the Viscount de Taunay; by researchers in the medical schools
of Bahia and Rio de Janeiro or the Manguinhos and Butantan Institutes; by naturalists and ethnologists of the Goeldi Museum of

[3] "Report of Subcommittee of the Permanent Occupation of Tropical Australia
by a Healthy Indigenous White Race," *Tropical Diseases Bulletin*, No. 3, 1921.
[4] Nash: op. cit., p. 352.

Belém (which for a time became an international center in the field of tropical studies); by other naturalists and ethnologists connected with the National or Paulista Museums; as well as by foreign researchers such as Dombre, Hartt, Derby, Branner, and Von den Steinen. Finally, the agricultural research which the Republic initiated in its early existence after many years of shilly-shallying on the part of the Empire must not be overlooked.

Continuing Roy Nash's thesis, ignorance of the mineral resources of Brazil was particularly striking. Research in minerology, initiated during the Empire, was continued only casually by the Republic, so casually, in fact, that neither geologists nor the Brazilian government was aware that the country contained deposits of thorium, a most precious material found at the time only in Norway. Brazilian thorium was discovered accidentally by a British subject named John Gordon, who was wandering aimlessly on the sands of Bahia awaiting the departure of the steamer carrying him back to England. Noting the peculiar density of the sand and the tenacity with which it clung to his shoes, he gathered up a handful and put it in his pocket. On having it analyzed in England, he learned that it contained thorium. Mr. Gordon was suddenly rich; romantically rich. The incident furnishes one more example of Brazilian carelessness, the same story which had previously been told for the resources of sugar, coffee, cotton, rubber, and cocoa. It was left to a realistic Englishman to discover the thorium, just as it was left to an American geologist named White to point out early in the century that Brazil contained oil deposits sufficient for "all the requirements of the Republic." If nothing was done about this announcement, it was because the government showed not the slightest interest in the matter.[5]

In the field of stock raising the experience was somewhat happier. One of the big problems of the industry, that of finding sufficient pastureland, was alleviated by the development of Pará grass. In addition, it was discovered that the zebu type of cattle was the best adapted to tropical conditions. Such successes obtained by practical cattlemen could not fail to give a certain feeling of nationalistic triumph.

Brazilian nationalism was also reflected in literature and in certain of the arts, a movement which had its origins in the Empire but fastened upon the proclamation of the Republic as a form of apol-

[5] Percy F. Martin: *Through Five Republics* (London, 1905), pp. 220, 221.

ogy for its further development. In a collection of magazine articles published in Rio de Janeiro in 1896 under the title *Literatura Brasileira, Movimento de 1893, o Crepúsculo dos Povos*, the critic Tristão de Alencar Araripe offered an almost sociological study of the literature of the revolutionary period, a period which seemed to him to represent a resurgence of nativism in the national literature, together with a greater sense of communication between the centers and the provinces. He pointed out that the *Revista Brasileira* had been largely instrumental in improving these communications; it was this magazine which had made the "cultivated spirits" of Rio de Janeiro aware of the fact that "in 1880 there had been notable literary activity in Pará, thanks to a writer now very well known in the press of the state of Rio, but at that time an obscure and unknown figure, despite his already having shown his worth with his *Estudos Amazônicos* and other critical works worthy of being ranked alongside those of the most audacious Brazilian thinkers." [6] Araripe was referring to José Veríssimo and implying that the magazine directed by this erudite provincial Brazilian should be recognized as an essential intellectual link between the Amazon and the capital of the young Republic.

In 1893 this same capital had experienced bombardment by rebel battleships, but a bombardment that had really not had much effect on the average Carioca. The young people, in particular, were convinced that this mutiny in the Armed Forces was little more than "an accident." Which did not mean, according to Araripe, that the republican movement in Brazil had been "unfriendly toward the increase in literary expression." Quite the contrary: "There is more than one evidence of the fact that a change in institutions, the adoption of new political customs, the breaking down of ideas, and the agitations of the spirit all bring about an intense [literary] atmosphere, one of the most visible symptoms of which is the rebirth of nativism." This nativism had been seen recently in the appearance of books "purely republican in nature." One was *Festas Nacionais (National Holidays)* by Rodrigo Otávio, with a preface by the novelist Raul Pompéia, who was also an essayist and something of a political thinker. Pompéia felt that, with the Republic, it was time for Brazil to renounce its thralldom to "the great sensory centers of

[6] T. A. Araripe Júnior: *Literatura Brasileira, Movimento de 1893, o Crepúsculo dos Povos* (Rio de Janeiro, 1896), p. 3. Also see the same author's *Função Normal do Terror nas Sociedades Cultas* (Rio de Janeiro, 1891).

our organism of interests" which Pompéia felt to have been in London or Lisbon. This subordination had existed throughout the Second Empire as a result of "the mortal regime of financial deficits" and also the campaigns in the press, which continued into the Republic, "against the measures, the resources, and the energetic precautions which have been the economic and financial salvation of other nations." It was against the intervention of economic forces into Brazilian politics that Pompéia cried out in his preface; against the power which dominated the journalistic field and penetrated "deeply into the formation of public policy," and which had shown itself to be a "formidable force," backed by "the greater part of private wealth." [7]

Both Pompéia and Araripe were irritated by the "cosmopolitanism" which at the time ran concurrently with "nativism" and, to Pompéia at least, attempted to make the latter appear ridiculous. Such cosmopolitanism, characteristic of the work of Eça de Queiroz, was to be found especially in such Brazilian writers as Ramalho Ortigão, principal author of *As Farpas* (*The Barbs*) and one of the most perspicacious analysts of the Revolution of 1889. To Araripe, "Those eluders of their country responsible for the egoistic vogue of Cosmopolis" (that is, Ramalho and even Eça) were writers "whose mental attitudes would be inoffensive if they did not try to influence the youth, dazzling them with stylistic tricks . . ." and convincing them that to be "nativist" was to be "stupid." [8]

Araripe was sincerely convinced that the Revolution of 1889 differed from other events which had shaken Brazil under the guise of revolution and which had really been only the repercussions of European movements. The events of November 15 brought about a "movement that was exclusively national"; it had sprung up as "the flowering of an entire past, a past which had been quietly repressed." [9] Thus we could expect that the new order would be accompanied by an equally nationalistic literature. Either this, or it would become bastardized into a "colorless cosmopolitanism, the only possible result of a servile copying of decadent Latin literary movements."

In retrospect, however, it does not appear that either Brazilian

---

[7] Araripe Júnior: *Literatura Brasileira* . . . , pp. 7, 13, 14.
[8] Ibid., p. 17.
[9] Ibid., p. 40.

literature in particular or Brazilian culture in general became markedly republicanized after 1889 to the point of constituting patterns different from those of the monarchy or any more definitive of the national character. There had already been traces of nationalism in the works of Alencar, Gonçalves Dias, Manuel de Almeida; in the music of Carlos Gomes; in Bahian or Paraense cooking or in Pernambucan confectionary; in the *modinhas* sung by the young ladies and the *mulatas* of the Second Empire; in the manner of Teixeira de Freitas in reaching judicial decisions in consideration of New World, rather than European, social conditions; in the *capoeira* practiced by Carioca and Bahian riffraff and repressed by the Republic as a shameful art; in the *sambas* and *maracatus* which republican propagandists also attempted to prohibit in Pernambuco in the 1870's on the pretext that such folkloric dances shamed the nation's state of civilization.

The strongly Brazilian work of Sylvio Romero, so important during the period covered by this study, was begun before the proclamation of the Republic and contained nothing which could be called republican influence. Nor did the fifteenth of November have any measurable effect on the linguistic studies of João Ribeiro or the folkloric studies of Celso de Magalhães in Recife, or on the sociological studies made (again in Recife) by Joaquim Nabuco, in which Brazil was considered as a culture different in many respects from that of Europe.

For this reason a speech made by Olavo Bilac, at a dinner given in his honor in Rio de Janeiro in 1907, is relevant here. "What you, as Brazilians, are honoring and rewarding on this occasion," said Bilac, "is the hard, fruitful, courageous work of the literary generation to which I belong and the part this generation has played, through its labors, in the civilization of Brazil." Bilac was referring to the coming-of-age of the literary man, another valorization comparable to the valorization of coffee. Writing had begun to attain professional standing: "We are forcing the doors of the newspapers and are overcoming the fears and ineptitudes of their editors. . . ." In the Empire, even around 1870, "there were no men of letters in Brazil, but rather statesmen, legislators, professors, diplomats, society figures, or rich men who, from time to time, made a brief excursion into literary fields—some of them with a certain reluctant annoyance, some emasculating themselves, disguising themselves, hiding themselves, hugging the walls, afraid of the murmurs of serious persons, as though they were entering forbidden territories, centers of frivolity or of dubious diversions." [1]

Not that with the coming of the Republic any Brazilian began to live exclusively on the profits from his writing; not even Machado de Assis could achieve this rapid and complete valorization of his literary art. But it was true that the figure of the man of letters began to exist without having to disguise his literary occupation. On the contrary; he could boast of it. For the Baron do Rio Branco (as we have seen) to be a man of letters was a recommendation, if not always for the diplomatic corps, at least for the consular service, in which Aluísio Azevedo and Mateus de Albuquerque held positions. At the same time, missions or tasks of relative importance were being given to Joaquim Nabuco, Graça Aranha, Oliveira Lima, Euclydes da Cunha, Domicio da Gama, and Araújo Jorge. Hélio Lôbo, still young but already showing literary tendencies, was a further figure recruited by the Baron for service in the Itamaraty.

Another activity which acquired prestige in Brazil during the last years of the monarchy and the early days of the Republic was that of industry. The Prados of São Paulo, while not relinquishing their position as a landholding family, sent many of their members into industry. And in Rio Grande do Sul the so-called "lard aristocracy" gained social prestige through its connection with the dried beef industry, just as the sugar refiners of the north and the state of Rio de Janeiro combined the activities of raising and processing their product. The textile industry also showed great development, with the mills almost always under Brazilian direction, though some of these directors had learned much from England.

Luís Tarqüínio, an industrialist whom the historian Pedro Calmon dubbed the "Bahian Mauá," learned from his association with the British in the firm of Bruderer & Co. to consider commercial and industrial activity as honorable as any other form of making a living. By the age of forty, he had become rich, but, thanks to his British training, without letting himself become soft in his wealth "as usually occurred with the majority of Portuguese businessmen and the sons of sugar planters in the area of the Recôncavo." [2] Thus he had not invested in securities and real estate in

---

[1] *Almanaque Brasileiro Garnier* (Rio de Janeiro, 1909), p. 100.

[2] Péricles Madureira de Pinho: *Luís Tarqüínio, Pioneiro da Justiça Social no Brasil* (Bahia, n.d.), p. 46.

order to live "the carefree life of a peaceful bourgeois," but had instead turned to industrial pioneering. In 1891 he founded the Companhia Empório Industrial do Norte, giving his personal attention not only to the financial and technical aspects of the business, but also to the development of a modern pattern of employer-employee relationships. It was in the choice of machinery, writes Péricles Madureira de Pinho, that "the experience of Luís Tarqüínio best asserted itself. . . . His repeated trips to the great textile centers of Europe made it unnecessary for him to accept the offer of 'complete factories' so often made by European manufacturers of the time to budding Brazilian industrialists." Rather, "he chose the best from the entire field . . . from England he brought machinery from the famous manufacturing firm of Felber Jucker & Co.; other equipment came from Germany and Belgium, and he took advantage of the burgeoning American industry to complete the set-up and form what in the opinion of experts constituted a well-integrated whole." In the opinion of one European visitor during the late nineteenth century, whoever visited Luís Tarqüínio's Empório could "confide in the future of Brazil." [3]

The efforts of Brazilian industrialists, some of them really grandiose, became a source of national pride. The work of Antônio Prado or Jorge Street in São Paulo, for example, or Carlos Alberto de Meneses in Pernambuco, or Delmiro Gouveia in Alagoas, as well as Luís Tarqüínio in Bahia. In Rio Grande do Sul, Assis Brasil combined an elegant, if somewhat ordinary, political philosophy with considerable specialized competence in industrial agriculture, in addition to a financial and technical knowledge unsurpassed by any foreigner in his field. No matter how much one may lament certain aspects of Republican protectionism toward industry, no matter how false and pernicious it may have been in its effect on the national economy, it must be recognized that the efforts of such industrialists had many laudable aspects beyond those of a purely economic nature. Through industry, former slaves and their descendants were offered a means of livelihood. From a vagabond existence they were able to emerge as useful citizens integrated into the regular employment, cultural, and recreational patterns of Brazilian society. Thus, the contribution of industry at the time had its social value, particularly in the establishments of the men mentioned above, or of others like Hermann Lundgren in Pernambuco, the

[3] Ibid., pp. 79–80.

Mascarenhas family in Minas Gerais, or the Bangu Mills in Rio de Janeiro.

The democratization effected by industry was to be found equally in sports and dress, both of which veered at the time toward British rather than French patterns. There was the vogue for football, formerly the game of British residents and upper-class white Brazilians, and for sports in general as a means of physical culture. In dress too styles appropriate to British India began to be accepted in tropical Brazil: pajamas replaced nightshirts, undershorts ousted the prevailing "long johns," garters were abandoned, suspenders gave way to belts, and top hats and derbies, earlier obligatory among persons of importance, lost their place to headgear of felt or straw. Bow ties gave way to four-in-hands, and the starched cuffs which often served as note pads for such inveterate jotters as Euclydes da Cunha were abandoned in favor of the soft variety. Ladies substituted drawers or knickers for their many underskirts, and children adopted drawers or bloomers for household wear instead of going naked as formerly. At this time rubber-soled shoes began to be worn for sports and low shoes took over from the high-buttoned variety.

Joaquim Amaral Jansen de Faria (b. Rio de Janeiro, 1883) remembers that when he reached adulthood in republican Brazil, customs of dress were still French, anti-sportswear, and suitable only for cold climates. "Modes were Parisian for men as well as for women, although the woolens came largely from England and the linen from Portugal. . . . Shirts had starched fronts, false cuffs, and collars of frightening altitude. Vests were screamingly colorful, ties were of the bow or Ascot variety, black and tightly knotted. The canes were slender and the hats hard and of the derby variety . . . though the soft and straw varieties had begun to appear." In Rio Grande do Sul, Sebastião de Oliveira (b. Cruz Alta, 1878) found himself obliged, as an early twentieth-century businessman, to wear a derby. He wore long drawers in the winter, but in the warmer season he adventurously adopted undershorts. He preferred button shoes and carried a cane, which, as a young man, he also used as a weapon. He tells us that he never approved of jewels in men's wear. Deodoro (Machado) de Mendonça (b. Pará, 1889) writes: "I always followed the styles of my time without exaggerating. Thus I wore narrow trousers, top hats, long drawers with drawstrings to hold them up, and diamond rings which today

I detest. I also carried a heavy cane of snakewood or a light one of rush."

Emiliano Ribeiro de Almeida Braga (b. Maranhão, 1873) speaks of his boyhood sports and toys: "The toys I most enjoyed were the paper kites which in Maranhão were made with great taste and proficiency, using an entirely distinctive technique. Everybody took part in this sport: physicians, law graduates, priests, attorneys, judges—all the best people of Maranhão. I made a name for myself in this sport and was known as the 'king of the kite flyers.' When I was in Maranhão on a visit a year ago, old friends still addressed me by this title. I also used to enjoy spinning tops and playing *borroca*, a game using cashew nuts. Later I rode horseback, rowed, swam, and hunted with dogs. I continued to enjoy these sports until I was fifty-five."

Roberto Christiana Naegeli (b. Rio de Janeiro, 1881) says: "shortly after my return from school in Switzerland, Brazilians began to play football. My brother and I immediately took part in this sport, which we had played in Europe. This game, which has captured the whole world, has in my opinion been a great benefit to our country. It has taught the Brazilian to submit himself voluntarily to discipline through the love of the game and in the interest of his team. A great part of the male population on all social levels like to talk football, and it is interesting to note how much they know about all phases of the game and how well everyone, rich and poor, young and old, can criticize the players and the referees. It is true that sometimes these discussions turn into fights, but this doesn't really matter. The game diverts and interests the youth and keeps them out of trouble. Formerly, young people of the lower classes used to hang around taverns for want of anything better to do, talking big and getting into fights in which weapons were often employed. In my opinion, football has been largely responsible for changing all this."

Erasto Gaertner (b. Paraná, 1900) was the son of German and Brazilian parents and grandson of a Lutheran pastor. He studied in a German school in Curitiba and his first games had been German, though Brazilian diversions soon took over. "I spent five years in the German school," he states, "and came out with good grades. By the end of the first year I had mastered the language and could get along well with my schoolmates, most of whom were from homes where German was spoken as a matter of course. The boys, however, preferred to speak Portuguese, possibly because they had a very strong accent in that language which they wished to overcome. It was an easy way to improve, and it surprised me how those boys who spoke badly were teased by others whose Portuguese was a bit better. Since I was weak in German, I was always in trouble trying to understand the teacher, but in the recess hours I felt superior because I was often called on to settle linguistic arguments among my fellows. I was also at ease in the Portuguese class of Professor Artur Loyola, where I was able to read correctly, take reasonably good dictation, and in general follow the lessons completely. . . .

"In my time games were played in school, in the streets, or at home. At school we played hide-and-seek, cops-and-robbers, horse-and-rider, high jump, and marbles. By the time I went on to the Colégio de Júlio Teodorico and the Ginásio Paranaense, football had begun to be popular in our town."

The street games were even more Brazilian than those of the school. "In the autumn kite flying was the favorite sport. In the June festivals of Santo Antônio, São João, and São Pedro, we sent up balloons and lit the traditional bonfires. At Carnival, we dressed up, played tricks on one another, threw flour and water, had children's parties, and generally worked off our enthusiasms."

Beyond the ordinary games, "there were a number of gangs whose rivalries at times became a sort of open warfare. In our street we had the Rua 13 de Maio gang in rivalry with the Rua Saldanha Marinho gang in the next block. In addition to a few objectives better not mentioned, these small armies were organized to rob orchards, steal food and soft drinks from the groceries, as well as to inflict damage to windows, street lamps, and other property largely for the purpose of picking a fight. These fights occasionally rose to full-scale gang warfare, sometimes employing individual combat with blows and kicks and at other times developing into mass battle with stones and slingshots. The rivalry between our gang and that of the Rua Saldanha Marinho was very sharp and resulted from differences in social level. Their side was composed largely of boys from modest homes; many were colored, and most had to start at an early age to help their parents by selling papers. We were very narrow in our opinion of our rivals, stating that they were a lot of good-for-nothing wise guys, a low-life crowd who hated us out of envy and spite. They were a bunch of troublemakers, whereas we were little heroes thrown at a tender age into the harsh struggle for existence." As "children of good family," we "always fought like brave warriors. At the time we didn't have the sense to recognize the worth of our enemies, many of whom were pursuing—and still pursue—a worthy course of activity.

"Among my childhood companions, some of whom have become scholars and colleagues, the favorite diversions were hunting with slingshots and bows and arrows, fishing, swimming in the public pool or in the Belém and Ivo rivers, and making trips to the neighboring quarters of Bigorrilho and Santa Felicidade. These trips, which took considerable time, were usually made by playing hookey. We were the terror of our parents, not only because of our skipping school, but also because of the dangerous games we played and the serious accidents in which they often resulted."

Other Brazilian influences also were exerted to help Erasto in his de-Germanization. "My reading outside school consisted of *Tico-Tico* [a comic book] and the various almanacs popular at the time. I also read the Carochinha stories[4] and later Nick Carter, Sherlock Holmes, and Buffalo Bill, all of which were very popular among youngsters. Pirate stories and Robinson Crusoe were passed from hand to hand, and those who couldn't get books could find consolation in hearing these stories told. My first hero was Robinson Crusoe, with his enchanting adventures, but afterward I went for the detectives and their battle against crime."

This was the period when the sport of swimming moved from the rivers to the seaside. It also marked the beginning of elegant bathing costumes: the men in striped shirts and trousers reaching almost to the ankles, the girls and women in severely dark, voluminous flannels which covered them from neck to ankle. These costumes contrasted strongly with those of the days of river bathing, where girls and women, undressing in straw bathhouses set in the water, sometimes ventured beyond the limits of these houses and were glimpsed swimming nude by the sharp eyes of adolescent boys. Antônio José da Costa Ribeiro (b. Pernambuco, 1868) recalls that in his childhood there was a summer festival period for children, with swimming in the river, parties, folk plays, dances, and plays given on the riverbanks in the fashionable quarters of Monteiro, Caxangá, and Apipucos. In his words: "In my childhood,

---

[4] A collection of children's tales about a cockroach who marries a mouse. (Translator.)

most families lived in the city during the 'winter' [the rainy season] and spent the summer months from October to February on holiday in the country. My parents met, courted, and were married in a country place called Poço da Panela and never forgot this little town. The year before his death my father passed the summer holiday in an old house in the Largo do Monteiro. Here I can remember many parties with swimming in the Capabaribe, where I learned to swim, often crossing the river at flood tide. There were the little bathhouses, where I often saw the girls bathing nude, as I had earlier in Caxangá, where my grandparents spent one summer. My recollections of childhood and adolescence are principally of these parties at Poço and Monteiro, of what I saw and heard before being able to participate in fact. There was much society life in Monteiro. In the upper town there was a club which gave dances on Saturdays, and in the Monteiro square there was a theatre in which not only amateurs but also the traveling companies which visited Recife gave performances. The festivals at the chapel of São Pantaleão were elaborate and crowded. I also remember Poço da Panela very well, its picturesque life and its parties, where you could hear the beautiful voices of the ladies and in the corridors and patio of the church you could see so many pretty girls. . . . And I remember the fun I had riding atop the carriages, in the so-called 'gallery' as on the Parisian buses. Then there was one particular festival at Chacon, on the banks of the river, with the house full of friends and lively funmaking. There was a little stage on which the daughters of one of my father's friends performed to music by the Lisboa Brothers. Everything went well until the last day, when gatecrashers broke in and frightened the performers with their shouts. In addition to Monteiro and Poço, there was also Apipucos, where the Burle and Dubeaux families lived and there were many lively young people. There were good relations with the British colony in Apipucos and a great deal of social activity . . . swimming during the day and dancing at night."

Swimming and dancing were not the only favorite amusements of young people of the period; they also took an almost sportive interest in the revues at the theatre. Antônio José da Costa Ribeiro tells us that the boys divided into cheering sections for the various lady singers and that the competitions not infrequently plunged the galleries into a general brawl, with torn clothes and broken heads. "I remember one benefit when there was much excitement," he tells us. "Fausto Cardoso, a talented boy who met a tragic end in politics, became so enthusiastic he threw his hat, his jacket, and finally his seat onto the stage in token of his appreciation of the artist."

Returning to the subject of dress, Alberto de Paula Rodrigues (b. Ceará, 1882) says that in his youth it was obligatory for men of some stature to wear a black tailcoat, tall hat, and starched collar. As a family physician, "I never entered a home without this funereal and unhygienic garb. However, there were some who, during the hottest part of the year, changed to white duck trousers, though retaining the tailcoat and high hat. . . . The sack suit was considered vulgar, to be worn only by clerks and teen-agers. When Manuel Vitorino, an illustrious physician and professor of medicine in Bahia, arrived in Rio from Europe wearing a sack suit and colored shirt, he brought severe criticism on himself. When he tried to establish a practice in Rio de Janeiro he failed and died shortly afterward poor and forgotten."

It is to the credit of the physicians, however, that through the initiative of the Medical Club and Dr. Graça Couto, they began a campaign against "the ridiculous and inappropriate dress" of their colleagues in favor of the simple jacket without vest worn by the ordinary man. Perhaps this brought them down to the level of the clerks, but in fact the clerks were becoming industrialist and beginning to exceed the doctors in social prestige. At any rate, the professionals—doctors, engineers, lawyers—began dressing like industrialists, abandoning priestly garb and imitating the tropical Englishman. There was also a decline in the use of perfumes and jewelry so characteristic of male elegance in the nineteenth century, and a similar decline in the equally luxurious display of facial hair.

But if Brazil passed from Empire to Republic with its men excessive in their display of rings, jewels, good teeth, and glittering *pince-nez*, wearing perfume in their hair and beard and on their hands, it is not surprising that this scandalous orientalism in dress was even more extreme among the women. Rarely did the wife of a rich Brazilian of the period, even for ordinary shopping, leave her home unless dripping with jewels and doused with perfume from head to foot.

Dona Antônia Lins Vieira de Melo (b. São Paulo, 1879), who grew up on a sugar plantation in the northeast, reports that all her clothes for social wear were acquired in Paris—"bought to order by Recife dressmakers." There were hats and shoes from the same city, together with underclothes "of the finest delicacy and good taste." As for jewels, she preferred large diamond rings, brooches studded with the same stone, and a gold necklace with medallion or jeweled crucifix. "I was particularly fond of diamonds," says Dona Antônia, "but other stones such as rubies or emeralds were also used at the time. The mountings for these jewels were varied, but one noted a preference for religious symbols, the Cross being particularly in vogue. At times we were obliged to wear rings of white metal which were given us by friends and servants (*'compadres'* and *'comadres'*) at the festival of Santa Luzia. These gifts could not be refused." There were some who stopped wearing precious jewels in favor of rings of lesser value "simply because the latter had been blessed by the priest and had much more value to a good Catholic."

As for sports, Dona Antônia states that the sports of the mid-twentieth century were not current in her time. Her own favorite was riding. "I spent much time on horseback riding from one plantation to another in visits to friends and relatives. We had good horses in our stables; my father always insisted on having the best. . . . Their harness was mounted with silver, and the saddle was of the first quality. Such objects were not bought in the market but sent on order; my father spared no expense in these matters. People at the time preferred to travel on horseback. When the whole family had to travel and there were many children, an oxcart was used under the supervision of the older members of the family, but even so, the head of the group and most of the adults rode horseback. My love of horses has always been very great."

In addition to horseback riding, some of the other activities of the period at the watering places were the carriage ride and the croquet game, as well as flirting and dancing the waltz or the *pas de quatre*, the last for some reason known in Brazil as *footing*. These were the diversions of the rich, of course. For young ladies of more modest means, sports were less in favor, although some ventured to ride a bicycle or play tennis.

By the end of the presidency of Venceslau Brás many changes had taken place in the daily life of the country. The Republic had pretty well recovered from its earlier anti-clericalism, although there was still here and there a trace of Jacobinism. (There was even the dramatic case of a federal deputy who entered the religious life after a mystical experience in the legislative chamber itself.) Other things had passed also: the frock coat had disappeared except on the occasional individual; the same could be said for the top hat and the horse and carriage. The future had faded into the past; the Republic had blended with the monarchy, forming a single history: a Brazilian history. More than one republican who remembered the romantic days of the Manifesto of São Paulo reached the end of that presidency seeing the rosy future they had envisaged now become one with the colonial, the Portuguese, and the Imperial periods of the national experience, while new futures were being quickly transformed into the present.

Not that the Republic did not have the significance of a new experience for Brazil. It *was* a new experience, but a somewhat less fervent one than its most ardent supporters had looked for, less than the expectations of a Silva Jardim or a Saldanha Marinho or even a Prudente de Moraes, a Martins Júnior, or a Coelho Lisboa. Contrary to their expectations, the Church had increased in prestige. The intense republican vogue for caricaturing Pedro II as "Pedro Banana" had faded, and the butt of this satire had virtually attained the stature of a national saint, a saint whom every Brazilian increasingly regarded as his own patron figure. Benjamin Constant and his Positivism had become passé; by 1918 the doctrine held little appeal for intellectuals, the military, or the average man, and was almost without spokesmen in the political arena. The commanding voices of the period were no longer those of intellectuals like Benjamin or even Ruy Barbosa; rather, they were those of the pragmatic down-to-earth Mineiros and Paulistas who knew the political game and were enormously effective in their efforts. Pinheiro Machado, perhaps the last of the republican romantics, was silent; the socialist ideas which had begun to arrive from Europe held no appeal; Ruy Barbosa did not interest the young and, despite his erudition and vast talents, had begun to look almost like a mental defective alongside the practical energies of the pragmatists from Minas Gerais and São Paulo.

Since the early years of the century, these pragmatic politicians had given a new and disconcerting example of the techniques of state socialism, as seen in the valorization of coffee, "that operation of state socialism which is succeeding in spite of the opinions of the economists," as Georges Clemenceau put it.[5] This Brazilian innovation in socialism was perhaps the most important national accom-

5 Clemenceau: op. cit., p. 250.

plishment during the period, followed by the publication of *Os Sertões*, the integration of Acre into the territory of the Republic, the victory of Osvaldo Cruz against yellow fever, and the pioneer flight of Santos Dumont. Such things revealed a Brazil hitherto unsuspected by Europeans, a Brazil capable of effecting a concrete realization of the motto of 1890: "Order and Progress." Progress moderated, when necessary, by the exigencies of Order, the Brazilian economic and social order, with emphasis on the adjectives *economic* and *social* within the general concept of the national motto, but with even more specific emphasis on that all-important adjective: Brazilian.

❦ [X I I] ❦

The Challenge of the Tropics

THE MONARCHY, as a national system of government responsible for the health of its population, never directly and frankly accepted the challenge to Brazilian civilization posed by the country's damp, tropical climate. It remained for the Republic to take up the task the Empire had always tried to avoid, that of accepting the special problems of life in the tropics for what they were, rather than as an imaginary extension of a predominantly European civilization.[1]

Even after 1889, government health programs were not clearly nationalistic. Various aspects of such programs were hybrid and even contradictory: European methods of prevention and cure were adapted to a Brazilian context. Sometimes there was a confusion of methods, with a clash between the European and the Brazilian; sometimes the native elements were unable to tolerate the imported treatment and had to fall back on native methods which baffled and disturbed physicians of European orientation. The less orthodox, however, had since Imperial times been attempting to free Brazil from European drugs in favor of various native remedies shown to be as effective as imported ones—perhaps even more so in the case of illnesses peculiar to the Brazilian tropics. For this reason the question of indigenous medicine is by no means an unimportant sociological aspect of the period.

[1] This generalization does not imply that nobody was interested in questions of medicine and hygiene before the coming of the Republic; such interest existed even before Brazil became an independent nation. But, as Professor Nestor Duarte points out, it was an interest pursued by private persons and not by the government.

For parasitic infections, doctors of the period employed materials they referred to as "antizymotic." In the treatment of contusions they used iodoform solutions, bichloride of mercury, and boric acid. Hospitals of the time always reeked terribly of iodoform. For syphilis, the orthodox used mercury and potassium iodide. Malaria was treated with quinine. Rabies, anthrax, and smallpox were prevented by vaccination. Injections were still rare at the time, but at the beginning of the century this European technique was beginning to be used against syphilis, with the eventual use of the German-developed 606 and 914.

For anemia, scrofula, cachexia, or rheumatism, doctors prescribed iron, arsenic, aconite, phosphorous, various oils, quinine, linseed, and wines. European wines like Malaga or medicinal brews like quinoga were given to the anemic and to convalescents, the manufacturers making a special effort to advertise the effectiveness of such products against the diseases of the tropics.

Prescriptions frequently had as their base tincture of aconite, nux vomica, calomel, jalap, rosewater, belladonna, castor oil, orange-flower syrup, and jaborandi pepper. Household remedies including sabugo cactus, chicken hawk, watercress, and citron. There were also unguents of various sorts, burned in braziers to disinfect the sickroom. For this purpose rosemary was often used (it was also used as a cough medicine). Garlic was employed in poultices, and soldiers hesitant to enter combat often introduced this substance into the anus to produce fever and go on sick call.[2] Another remedy used as a septicide by such physicians as Mestre Sousa Lima of Bahia was *ararobe*, the so-called "Bahia powder." [3]

Among the familiar household remedies of the time was rue, used by midwives during labor to increase the contractile power of the uterus, and also during menstruation. For toothache it was common practice to use cloves. Caroba was frequently used in therapeutic baths. Caiapó was the purgative most used by mothers for their children and one which received considerable medical attention, including a doctoral thesis by J. M. de Castro and a study by Professor Gubler in Paris. At this time Brazil was also making an effort to

[2] Urias A. da Silveira: *Terapêutica Brasileira* (Rio de Janeiro, 1889), II, 148. See also the chapters on "Flora" and "Climate and Diseases" in J. C. Oakenfull: *Brazil* (Paris, 1909).

[3] Silveira: op. cit., II, 181. See also the chapter on "Le Malattie del Brasile" (The Diseases of Brazil) in Alfonso Lomonaco: *Al Brasile* (Milan, 1889).

replace poplar with *imbauva* or trumpet tree as the material for therapeutic charcoal, since poplar had to be imported, while *imbauva* existed locally in abundance and was even available for export.[4] The same could be said of another raw material—rubber —which was used in Europe to make probes, nipples, pessaries, elastic stockings, dental plates, and belts and supports of all kinds. It was also used for prophylactics against veneral diseases.

The most familiar medicinal tea of the period was made from orange leaves and used for toothache, headache, and head colds, and also served as a sedative and soporific. *Maracujá* juice was used too for this purpose. Beriberi was treated with baths made from *pitanga* leaves, and a lemonade made from tamarind was employed as a laxative. Ipecac, castor oil, and tincture of aconite, according to physicians of the time, made up "the basic medicines for the majority of farmers and their wives in Brazil," the first having a wide variety of uses, being employed against indigestion, gastric disturbances, biliousness, malarial fevers, typhoid, yellow fever, diarrhea, bronchitis, hemoptysis, and poisonings.[5] *Ipecacuanha*, the source material of ipecac, was exported almost exclusively to England, whence Brazil received it back in medicinal form "at exorbitant price, subject to a high rate of exchange." According to Urias A. da Silveira, a railroad line from Rio to Mato Grosso, the source area of *ipecacuanha*, would end this financial aberration and permit local distribution of ipecac at low prices. Was this a matter of British exploitation? Far from it; merely Brazilian neglect. A neglect which extended to other articles manufactured in Europe from Brazilian raw materials, articles which, with a little effort, could have been systematically manufactured or produced on Brazilian soil.

Since the vogue for bleeding as a remedy still survived, various sorts of clysters were in use: purgatives, sedatives, diuretics, caustics, febrifuges, stimulants, emollients. Some were mechanical and employed syringes made of rubber, leather, metal, or glass. Others were dietary (for digestive ailments) and involved broths, toast, or meat accompanied with white wine.

Purgatives were used to excess, as were remedies for worms, which in some families were administered at regular periods to all members of the family, black and white, master and servants, as a part of the annual routine of existence. The damp night air was greatly feared, as were the so-called "miasmas" of swampy areas.

4 Silveira: op. cit., II, 307–9.
5 Ibid., II, 594.

During this period the country was overrun from north to south by illustrated advertisements for patent medicines which became as important as rice, beans, dried beef, and chicken soup in the national diet, and which, like those foods, became unifying elements in the national culture. Some of these familiar products were Scott's Emulsion, Elixir de Nogueira, A Saúde de Mulher (Female Health), Bromil, Reuter's Soap. The prescription, that orthodox and almost priestly formula, began to be replaced by these manufactured articles, and the prestige of the pharmacist, once equal almost to that of the physician, began to decline as he became more and more the seller of industrialized drugs. There was even a decline in the so-called "medical handwriting," that secret scrawl which formed a sort of Masonic bond between the one who prescribed and the one who mysteriously prepared the remedies.

The period also marked the beginning of control over diseases which until the twentieth century had taken a great toll of the Brazilian population: smallpox, yellow fever, cholera morbus, bubonic plague, tuberculosis. This control was achieved largely through better hygiene, both public and private, in the interior as well as in the capital cities. Distinguished physicians began to warn Brazilians against the danger of seeking cures for serious diseases only in the pharmacies, when the proper defense against most diseases, childhood and adult, lay principally in the observation of proper hygiene. Family doctors, who enjoyed almost clerical prestige during the period, made an effort to advise sedentary persons, particularly elderly citizens and city dwellers in general, to get more exercise in the open air: walking, swimming, and gymnastic exercises.[6] This advice was emphasized in the case of children of consumptive parents, lympatics, or those affected by rickets, scrofula, or obesity. According to Urias, every Brazilian man, woman, and child should exercise "at least three hours a day in direct exposure to the sun."[7] He particularly recommended "rhythmic walking" and the single and double trapeze.

Hydrotherapy was also given important emphasis, and became

---

[6] For information on the family doctor during the period, see Chapter XXIII of Otávio de Freitas: *Medicina e Costumes do Recife Antigo* (Recife, 1943). Freitas states that the family doctor was a combination of "midwife, pediatrician, surgeon, oculist, and even geriatrist" and that in him "the patient found an intelligent counselor and friend."

[7] Silveira: op. cit., I, 598. See also Antônio Martins de Azevedo Pimentel: *Subsídios para o Estudo da Higiene do Rio de Janeiro* (Rio de Janeiro, 1890).

very much in vogue. River swimming was replaced by sea bathing,
which was prescribed by many physicians for digestive disorders
and malaise in general. The best time of day for these baths was
between five and seven in the morning. Persons suffering from
weakness should follow their swim with a glass of port or liqueur.
The drinking of mineral waters at the spas of Lambari, Campanha,
Baependi, Caldas, and above all Caxambu was also popular, and
Brazil began to compete with the so-called "hydrological riches" of
France, Germany, Portugal, and Italy. If in 1889 there were still
only an insignificant number of visitors to these spas, mostly in the
state of Minas Gerais, the fact is that as early as 1871 an Imperial
commission had studied the waters of Caxambu and Lambari and
had concluded that they were in no way inferior to the waters currently being imported from abroad.[8] The effect of these local
waters in the treatment of ailments had also been studied before
1889, and they had been pronounced useful in stimulating the appetite and aiding the digestion. In some cases, people using these
waters had developed such appetites that it became necessary to
"advise prudence and moderation" in their consumption.[9]

Three-quarters of the first visitors to Caxambu were sufferers
from dyspepsia, but not a few of the others according to medical
testimony of the period were troubled with liver diseases, including
some in the third state of syphilis. Sufferers from other common
tropical ailments such as colonic catarrh, amenorrhea, leucorrhea,
gall bladder trouble, enlargement of the prostate, kidney stone,
scrofula, anemia, malarial malaises, hemorrhoids, female cloroa-
nemia, and inflammation of the womb also sought solace in the
water cure, along with shower baths, exercises in the open air, and
the introduction of rare meat, eggs, and fine white wine into the
diet.

Not only members of the master class were sent to the spas of
Minas; servants were also ordered there for treatment. "A slave
from a plantation in Coração do Rio Verde [Minas] consulted us,"
says one physician of the period. "We prescribed water with high
iron content, along with Bravais, an iron preparation. It was a liver
obstruction case, with the whole panoply of symptoms. The cure

---

[8] Silveira: op. cit., II, 60. For references to food hygiene see Azevedo Pimentel:
op. cit., Chapter IV. Also see Miltão Bivar: *Flora Brasileira, Plantas Medicinais*
(Recife, 1931).

[9] Silveira: op. cit., II, 68.

was rapid." [1] Many doctors of the turn of the century also believed that, in curing lymphatic or scrofulous cases through the use of mineral water, they were preventing the "almost inevitable consequence of these diseases," namely, tuberculosis. Tuberculosis during this period continued to be "the despair of entire families," many of which were annually "driven to tears and desperation" by the infection of one of their members. The waters of Araxá were considered particularly effective in the treatment of "incipient tuberculosis." Those of Poços were prescribed for chronic bronchitis.

Needless to say, the hydrotherapy above was not a form of magic; the regimen of a watering place also played a highly important part in the cure. Sufferers from plethora, gout, kidney stone, or hemorrhoids, for example, had to omit or restrict the red meat in their diet. The lymphatic, or anemic, on the other hand, were put on a rich diet: red meats, eggs, milk. Exercise—riding, walking, gymnastics—was also part of the cure. Ladies were made to put aside their corsets; men had to wear suspenders—never belts. Everyone had to dress warmly, with flannel shirts and wool stockings. Moderation in all pleasures was the rule, and principally in smoking, drinking, and gambling.

"There are patients," wrote Urias in 1889, "who spend their time playing cards in a confined space reeking with cigarette and cigar smoke; others indulge in vigorous dancing soon after meals and not infrequently bring on pulmonary or cerebral congestions, or neuralgias, in the case of ladies who are suffering from diseases of the uterus. Even loud conversation and prolonged reading are undesirable." [2]

Castor oil was "the prevailing laxative in Brazil: 20 to 60 grams." It was considered a safe and sure remedy without the irritation or subsequent constipation that so frequently accompanied doses of salts. Repulsive to the taste, it was often taken in capsules or in coffee, chicken or beef broth, liquors, or in preparations of garlic or cloves. It was also given to women just before or during labor and was prized by mothers for its virtues in combatting worms. It was used by persons of all classes in all parts of the country and thus formed one more element in promoting the national unity, a factor whose importance should not be underestimated.

[1] Ibid., p. 83. For the human and social conditions of convalescence and rest cure in this period see Oakenfull: op. cit., Chapter XIX.
[2] Silveira: op. cit., II, 109.

If Brazil confronted the challenge of the tropics chiefly with methods of public hygiene, it would still be unfair to discount the contribution of medicines and drugs (both imported and native) toward that purpose. Nor should the efforts of individuals be overlooked, with their drive for personal hygiene, domestic cleanliness, and the proper use of home remedies, all of which received considerable development during this period.

Sometimes the Indianism reflected in the vogue for the novels of Alencar extended to a corresponding enthusiasm for Indian foods and remedies. Filipe Neri Colaço, in a book on domestic hygiene published in 1883, pointed out that in the matter of diet, Brazilians should remember that, "like the Arabs and Indians, we live in the tropics," and should therefore be moderate in the use of "fat, oily, or heavily sweetened" foods and wines.[3] In their place he recommended tapioca roots, manioc flour, arrowroot, yams, breadfruit, and bananas, all indigenous and nourishing foods. Nor did he reject the employment of certain indigenous drugs and native remedies.

In the principal cities of Brazil various medical specialists began to appear: dentists, surgeons, obstetricians, oculists. The "American dentist" became an institution in Rio de Janeiro, São Paulo, Recife, and other progressive centers. Even an Englishman like Dr. Rawlinson of Recife styled himself an "American dentist," though in fact he was more Brazilian than American or British in his propensity to play the numbers game instead of devoting himself to his profession. Nevertheless, not a few Brazilians studied odontology in the United States and returned as full-fledged "American dentists."

Most Brazilians of the time, even those in the cities, cleaned their teeth with wood or cigarette ashes or with nightshade, after which they gargled with boric acid. It was not until the toothpaste Odol appeared, with accompanying advertising and professional recommendations, that the middle class began to abandon crude traditional dental materials.

Boric acid was also used widely as an eye bath, but it too was replaced by manufactured articles such as Colírio Moura Brasil. Moura Brasil, an oculist, was perhaps the most celebrated medical man of his time. Other important doctors of the period were Tôrres Homem and the Baron de Petrópolis, among the elder generation, and Silva Lima, Miguel Couto, Francisco de Castro, Silva Araújo, Antônio Austregésilo, Osvaldo Cruz, and Miguel Pereira among

[3] Filipe Neri Colaço: *O Conselheiro da Família Brasileira* (Rio de Janeiro, 1883).

the younger men. There was also Vital Brasil, founder of an institution that soon became world-famous: the Butantan, although previous work with snake-bite poisoning had been done by João Batista de Lacerda, director of the National Museum, "who discovered the antidotic action of potassium permanganate on snake bite and won a state prize of 30 *contos* therewith." [4] Urias also believed in the efficacy of a certain buttonweed in combatting snake bite in any stage of the infection, whether administered orally, rectally, or by injection.

At this time, much was made of the virtues of *maté*, which was considered superior to East Indian teas from every point of view, particularly for consumption for tropical countries. Even Great Britain came to recommend the use of *maté* for the troops in its tropical colonies, a directive which resulted in considerable benefit to Brazilian finances.[5] Other refreshing drinks lauded as healthful and appropriate to tropical living were *guaraná*, praised particularly by the sage Luís Pereira Barreto; *açaí*; and *caju*, for which the physician Cosmé de Sá Pereira was the principal advocate.

During this period medical hygienists became more critical of an over-European manner and style of dress on the part of middle-class Brazilians. Such overdressing was the cause of much ill-health, they declared, although they continued to recommend flannel clothing for those who suffered from chest or abdominal disorders. Furthermore, in the winter, particularly at night, no aged person should be indoors without his silk or wool stocking cap. Felt hats were to be used outdoors. From the age of twelve, suspenders rather than constricting belts should be worn by men, while women should use elastic girdles in preference to rigid corsets. The feet should always be kept warm: "head cool, waist free, feet warm."

In this transitional era, certain aspects of medicine indicated the sharp contrast between the old and the new. Leeches and bleedings were still employed, yet electrotherapy had been used generally since about 1879, at least in the cities. One of the pioneer electrotherapists was Tomás de Carvalho, whose treatment included electric baths as well as dry application.

Another contrast was seen in the rapid growth of public hygiene. In 1929, in a publication celebrating the one hundredth anniversary

[4] Silveira: op. cit., II, 675.
[5] Charles W. Domville-Fife: *The United States of Brazil* (London, 1910), p. 215.

of the National Academy of Medicine, Alfredo Nascimento pointed out the "velocity" with which Brazil had raised itself to the status of a modern civilized nation in its program of medicine and hygiene. He cited the developments in sanitation, in ambulance and emergency services, in laboratories and polyclinics, and in institutes to combat typhoid and smallpox, and particularly singled out the administration of President Rodrigues Alves as a period of especially intense progress.[6] Credit for a great deal of this program, of course, goes to the Republic; but since Imperial times, private individuals also had played their part in helping to bring Brazilians into greater harmony with their tropical living conditions. Thus visiting foreigners like Lamberg could advise Europeans in Brazil that, in the case of yellow fever or other tropical diseases, they would be wise to consult a Brazilian physician in preference to a European.

In domestic hygiene, the period was still complicated by a very close relationship between man and beast, a relationship which encouraged the presence of all sorts of insect and animal pests. There were many mosquitoes, chiggers, ants, and flies both within and around the houses and in the yards and gardens. The cattle had ticks; sheep, horses, dogs, cats, and caged birds were full of fleas; the yards were overrun with bats, buzzards, spiders, lizards, toads, and beetles, and the houses full of cockroaches. Other domestic animals, pigeons, ducks, chickens, and turkeys, attracted rats, with the consequent danger of bubonic plague, and domestic nonpoisonous snakes were often used in conjunction with cats to keep down the rodent population. Intensive warfare was waged against mosquitoes; thanks to Osvaldo Crux, who was known as "Dr. Mosquito-Killer" (*Dr. Mata-Mosquito*), great strides were made in controlling carriers of yellow fever.

"No matter how clean the houses are, they are never free from cockroaches," wrote Lamberg at the end of the nineteenth century. "These pests are especially numerous in old and dirty houses, but you can also see them in the attics of the rich." They chewed everything except metals; nothing was spared: clothing, leather, books, or papers, inflicting damage that often reached serious proportions. Lamberg noted that they even "ate the pomades in the

---

[6] Alfredo Nascimento: *O Centenário da Academia Nacional de Medicina. Primórdios e Evolução da Medicina no Brasil* (Origins and Development of Medicine in Brazil) (Rio de Janeiro, 1929), pp. 217–19. See also Leonídio Ribeiro: *A Medicina no Brasil* (Rio de Janeiro, 1940).

hair of sleeping people." [7] Many pomades and salves were in use at the time, both for the care of the hair and beard and for the treatment of skin eruptions and abrasions; and there were often lice in the hair, not only of women of the poorer classes, but also of the well-to-do.

Against these multiple pests various defenses were employed. Pyrethrum was used against fleas in middle-class homes, but on the plantations a solution made from *paracari* (Brazilian mint) was placed in various parts of the house. Flypaper kept down the fly population, and arsenic was used against termites. The policing of gardens and yards was still considered the best method of mosquito control, a procedure to which many added a smudge of cumin. As for the rats, it was not sufficient to consign them to the tender mercies of cats tastefully named Mimi or Fanny, or even Noble (Fidalgo), Pasha, or Duke; they were also poisoned with a mixture of lime and flour, which caused them to swell up and die.

[7] Maurício Lamberg: *O Brasil*, pp. 22–3.

❦ [X I I I] ❦

The Restoration Movement

S TRANGE AS IT MAY SEEM, the first decades of the present century in Brazil were marked by the paradox of a monarchist
restoration movement, subscribed to by very intelligent men despite the rapid urbanization and industrialization and the waves of
European immigration that had made for rapid progress since the
late years of the Empire. The crux of this movement was the "social question," an issue consistently ignored by the republicans.
Thus a situation arose in which the "innovators," that is, the republicans, were forced to take the defensive against the monarchists,
who suddenly passed from a sort of archaic Sebastianism to assume
a modern, aggressive, and even revolutionary position on the political and economic sociology of the period.[1]

Can it be that young republicans lacked any kind of receptivity
to this sort of revolution? [2] Certainly the problem of the participation of labor in the organization and direction of national life was
never brought into focus by any republican leader, and it remained
for a grandson of Pedro II, a champion of the apparently archaic
cause of monarchism, to define the situation in political and socio-

[1] Sebastianism is a cult founded upon a sixteenth-century Portuguese king who
disappeared while on a military campaign in North Africa. Followers of this cult
believe that Sebastian never died but will return to his people in a moment of
need. The same sort of legend flourished at one time in England concerning King
Arthur. (Translator.)

[2] The statements collected seem to indicate that some were at least vaguely
receptive to such a program and were willing to go along with Pinheiro Machado
or another Joaquim Nabuco in such a movement. [In the original text, the author
includes 41 depositions at this point. Since most of them are rather noncommittal,
they have been omitted from the translation. (Translator.)]

logical terms. But the truth is (as already emphasized many times) that during the first two or three decades of the Republic there was no political leader who accorded the "social question" the vigorous emphasis it was given by Joaquim Nabuco during his great days as deputy from Pernambuco in the Imperial Chamber. Lauro Sodré[3] perhaps could have been the successor to Nabuco in this respect, but he lacked not only the talent, wisdom, voice, and charisma of the author of *O Abolicionismo*, but also the necessary spirit and enlightenment. Among the political figures of established prestige, Pinheiro Machado, noted for his quiet effectiveness rather than for legislative display, was in virtually the ideal situation to become a sort of "conservative revolutionary" over the "social question." But if Pinheiro did not lack the requisite enlightenment, he did lack allies in this difficult adventure which, if successful, could have elevated the *gaúcho* leader to the stature of a true statesman. João Barreto, in his book *Estado do Rio de Janeiro: Aspectos Políticos e Econômicos* states that Pinheiro Machado "was an exceptional type of fighter. His leadership was not that of the strong man of the pampas." He was a "good disciplinarian," but he lacked ideas and had no sense of social issues on which to exercise this discipline. Instead he dreamed of the day when he could "put aside the toga" and don the "poncho of the *gaúcho*" as a sort of Brazilian equivalent of Theodore Roosevelt.[4]

It is a pity that the Pinheiro Machado who in 1910 proclaimed himself before the Senate of the Republic as being sensible of "the rights of those who work, those who slave, those of humble origin," rights which had been "forgotten in this regime of inequality," should nonetheless have lacked the intellectual vigor to turn this sensibility into political action.[5] With his prestige and his non-demagogic personality, he could have rendered this intuition into positive social legislation, which already existed in concrete form in Uruguay and Argentina, and the lack of which had so unfavorably

[3] A disciple of Benjamin Constant and moderate governor of Pará who, in 1889, tried to avoid the rebellion of his province against the newly proclaimed republican regime. (Translator.)

[4] João Barreto: *Estado do Rio de Janeiro: Aspectos Políticos e Econômicos* (Rio de Janeiro, 1913), p. 14.

[5] From a speech recorded in the *Anais do Congresso Nacional*. For a painstaking account of what happened in the same Congress in connection with the João Cândido revolt, see José Carlos de Carvalho: *O Livro da Minha Vida* (Rio de Janeiro, 1912), pp. 399–410.

impressed both Clemenceau and Father Gaffre. Brazilian labor laws
similar to those of its southern neighbors would undoubtedly have
attracted the flower of European immigration after the close of the
First World War; instead, these immigrants chose to go to Argentina and, even more, to the Uruguay of Battle y Ordoñez.

Paradoxically, it was Prince Luís de Orléans-Bragança who,
from his Parisian exile, became the pioneer of the state socialism
advocated earlier by the Positivists but reduced to insignificance
under the program of extreme economic liberalism of the provisional
government and Ruy Barbosa. João Luís Alves, Alcindo Guanabara, and, especially, Gilberto Amado (to name only three intellectuals esteemed by Pinheiro Machado for their high intelligence)
could well have forced part of this conservative social revolution to
afford effective protection to the Brazilian laboring class at a time
when the situation in Brazil was still flexible and adaptable to social
measures so recently triumphant in Europe. Such a revolution, directed by Pinheiro Machado, would clearly have been useful for
the development not only of industry but also of agriculture within
the framework of a national economy. In a recent biography of
Pinheiro Machado, Professor Costa Pôrto said that "he [Machado]
could have been a superb leader of the masses at a time when these
masses had not attained their potential strength"; and he attributed
his failure to do so to the simple fact that Pinheiro Machado preferred "to employ trickery, directing the people through a party
which was nothing more than a legal fiction." [6]

It would perhaps have been the duty of those intellectuals,
backed by the authoritarian Pinheiro, to systematize his ideas or,
better, his intuitions, giving them the logical form of a political philosophy leading to the upgrading of the working class which, in
Pinheiro's own words, had been "so forgotten" in this "regime of
inequality." That this systematization did not take place seems to
have been less the fault of Pinheiro than of the intellectuals themselves, and particualrly of the youngest and most persuasive of
them, Professor Gilberto Amado, one of the most clearheaded and
intelligent men of his generation. But not one of them concerned
himself with the subject, even under the provocation of Clemenceau's criticism. Not one offered to serve as guide to the blindness
of a perspicacious but ignorant leader. Not one was prepared to

[6] Costa Pôrto: *Pinheiro Machado e Seu Tempo—Tentativa de Interpretação* (Rio
de Janeiro, 1951), p. 224.

clarify a problem which required the enlightenment of persons versed in sociology, as well as in finance and jurisprudence, and in addition to this enlightenment the ability to act as *éminences grises* in translating such knowledge into a plan of action for the charismatic, if somewhat rude southern leader.

And so it was Prince Dom Luís, with his manifesto published in the *Diário do Congresso Nacional* on August 27, 1913, who courageously and lucidly posed the "social question" which alarmed republicans of the old guard while the Senate was busy contesting the appointment of Manuel de Oliveira Lima to the British Legation in London on the grounds that the author of *Sept Ans de République au Brésil* had turned dangerously monarchist.

This manifesto was no innocuous document. In it the Prince declared: "Without encouraging my friends to violence, much less to an always disastrous civil war, I hope that, when the moment comes, we monarchists will know how to follow the manly course necessary for the country's salvation." And he pointed out that the monarchical regimes of Europe were distinguishing themselves by their intelligent and effective protection of the working class, a program which would be pursued by the restored Empire in Brazil and which would show that Empire as capable of being more modern than the present Republic. In a sense, the manifesto of Dom Luís was reviving the words of Joaquim Nabuco, who had warned the Empire of this problem before the pronunciation of November 15 had removed him from the political scene and replaced him with preachers of other political religions.

To this bold challenge on the part of a past that threatened to resuscitate itself in the form of a more socially advanced future, the Positivist mission in Brazil responded with its Pamphlet 350, perhaps the most significant of a series containing such titles as "Love of Principles Based on Order," "Progress as an End," "To Live for Others," "To Live Enlightened." Written by R. Teixeira Mendes, Pamphlet 350 appeared in Rio de Janeiro in 1913 ("Year CXXV of the French Revolution and LIX of the Normal Era") under the title *O Império Brasileiro e a República Brasileira perante a Regeneração Social* (*The Brazilian Empire and the Brazilian Republic Confronted by the Question of Social Regeneration*). This repudiated the accusation of Prince Dom Luís that the Republic had failed to comply with the social aspects of its program through its inability to raise itself above the conflicts of special interests. On page 30 of this important document in Brazilian labor history, Teixeira Mendes writes: "The most complete fraternity has been achieved both among Brazilians and with other peoples, wherever they may be. The coming of the Republic was necessary in order to enable the free proletariat to emerge from the oppressive situation in which it found itself in Brazil. In fact, one of the first acts of the republican regime was to establish annual vacations for workers similar to those enjoyed by public functionaries. At the same time it began the dignifying movement to dissolve the differences between day laborers and other public employees. . . . One can see that this whole movement to give dignity to the proletariat was in accord with the nature of the republican regime and quite contrary to the dynastic and aristocratic prejudices of the monarchy." And, speaking directly to the manifesto of Dom Luís: "In what European monarchy is the dignity of the proletariat more respected than in the Brazilian Republic, as the Manifesto claims?" [7]

The manifesto had declared that the Republic was "a government by and for the few at the expense of the many," that the government gave "not the slightest attention" to "the well-being of the people," and that "the labor problems . . . partly resolved by the principal European monarchies" had not even been faced in Brazil. The republican government had stood by, doing nothing, while the labor situation, becoming intolerable, was threatening Brazil, "as in the neighboring Republic, with the specter of anarchistic socialism."

The criticism of Dom Luís was largely justified. The alienation of the republican government from the labor question had been pointed out, as we have seen, by such diversified observers as Clemenceau and Father Gaffre, and still another coldly objective viewpoint was given by the Englishman Charles W. Domville-Fife in his book *The United States of Brazil*. This much-traveled British observer said that in the East End of London, as well as in the poor sections of other large cities in Great Britain, Russia, Germany, Belgium, and Spain, he had witnessed "scenes of crowded, sordid poverty, which no system of government yet devised can effectually cope with or prevent." But in São Paulo these sordid conditions seemed not to prevail, and while the people were apparently happy, with room and work enough for all, "it would be an untruth so say that the labourer enjoys more freedom or security, or even as much, as he

[7] R. Teixeira Mendes: *O Império Brasileiro e a República Brasileira perante a Regeneração Social* (Rio de Janeiro, 1913), p. 30.

does under the limited Monarchy of great and greater Britain." [8] In Brazil, "money rules as in all republican countries." And in republics ruled by money the generalization of the Prince as to the monarchies' greater sensitivity to the cause of the working man seems to have been confirmed, at least for those monarchies which were at all attentive to labor: Germany more than England; Belgium, Holland, Sweden, and Norway more than republican France.

In a pamphlet entitled *Manual do Monarquista*, issued in São Paulo in 1913, Couto de Magalhães also affirmed the superiority of the monarchy over the Republic on this issue, pointing out that, because of its hereditary nature, the monarchy was not a government of parties or special interests and, not being dependent upon elections, was also free from the influence of money. Money had played an important part in republican elections; the United States and France had become "veritable markets" in this respect. It was not rare, "in republican Brazil in 1913, to see a candidate buying votes." This being the case, what was to prevent England, for instance, "from sending money here through its agents for the purpose of electing a President congenial to its financial interests in Brazil?" The monarchy, on the other hand, was the best guarantee of order and national continuity and at the same time a "modern type of government capable of favoring progress and social reform." More than any other system, it could protect the popular interest, since it was not subject to the desires of any group. The restoration of the monarchy in Brazil, insofar as native industries were concerned, would not only include "a moderate protectionism variable with the needs of the moment, but also would be a defender of the consumer." At the same time it would clearly "guarantee employment to labor," protecting and valorizing the workers in ways that had not even been attempted by a Republic too closely compromised by its obligations to regional and economic interests. These ends could "best be achieved through a monarchy"; with "power remaining stable within one family," the chief of state would not need "to court the favor of the proletariat or request the help of the rich in an election campaign." [9]

It was in the face of such concrete arguments for a monarchical restoration that Teixeira Mendes felt himself obliged to recognize that the Republic was being compromised in its "social ambitions"

[8] Charles W. Domville-Fife: *The United States of Brazil* (London, 1910), pp. 209, 225.

[9] Couto de Magalhães: *Manual do Monarquista* (São Paulo, 1913), pp. 18, 33, 60.

by "disturbances caused by the spontaneous aberrations and the fatal intellectual anarchy in modern revolutionary movements." [1] In his opinion, however, the guilt for these aberrations could not be laid to Positivism, which, since the foundation of the Church of the Positivist Apostleship by Miguel Lemos in 1881, had continually attempted to counteract "the empirical blindness of the Imperial government" with the "political solutions" proposed by the "Religion of Humanity" for resolving the problems of Brazil. Nevertheless, the Brazilian monarch, despite having engaged Benjamin Constant "as a teacher for his children and grandchildren . . . never showed himself in any way impressed by the influence of Auguste Comte." What greater error could Dom Pedro have made, thought the Positivists, than that of being indifferent to Positivism? Evidently what the Empire desired was "to maintain the Brazilian people permanently in the same state of theological and military dissolution they found themselves in at the time of Independence"; and to close Brazil to the "peaceful scientific-industrial" regime which would have led to the happiest state in human history "through the conciliation of the forces of Order and Progress." [2] This conciliation, on which Teixeira Mendes wisely insisted, still did not quite succeed in enabling him to live up to João Camilo de Oliveira Tôrres's overemphatic designation of him in *O Positivismo no Brasil* (*Positivism in Brazil*) as "the most advanced socialist in the liberal atmosphere of the Empire." This title properly belongs to Joaquim Nabuco, whose work in this respect was continued after the beginning of the twentieth century by Prince Dom Luís.

According to the Positivists, it had been the Republic which had opened Brazil to a "scientific-industrial" regime by reconciling the forces of Order and Progress. The regime had, of course, suffered some "disturbances" in making this effort, but these were largely due to the inclusion in its ranks of "political figures from the Monarchist Party and even from the ranks of the slaveholders." Such politicians knew no policy other than that of "metaphysical democracy." It was natural that their tendency had been to act in the republican government as they had acted in the monarchy, "changing only where the popular attitudes and the nature of republicanism made their former attitudes impossible." According to Teixeira Mendes, it was the presence of such figures in the new government

[1] Teixeira Mendes: op. cit., p. 33. Also see Venâncio Filho: *Augusto Comte e a República* (Rio de Janeiro, 1937).
[2] Teixeira Mendes: op. cit., pp. 32–3.

that accounted for the many "fatuous eulogies . . . of the Imperial regime, of the Imperial statesmen, and especially of the second Emperor." Nevertheless, the eminent Positivist leader recognized that it was the Republic which had encouraged the development of "industrial fanfare under the pretext of material and hygienic improvement," of "artificial immigration," and even of "the promotion of gambling habits, from high finance down to the lotteries." Furthermore, "slavocratic tendencies in relations with the proletariat" continued to characterize republican procedures on the "social question." Despite these republican errors, however, the Brazilian people were no longer shackled with "legal institutions which sharply contradicted the normal republican regime of Humanity." In Brazil, "all the roads to human regeneration" were still wide open.[3]

From a previous pamphlet—*A Propósito de Liberdade de Cultos* (*Concerning the Freedom of Cults*), published in 1888—Teixeira Mendes, in responding to the challenging manifesto of Dom Luís, transcribed an expressive note about "parliamentary judgment." And from a publication of the same year entitled *A Propósito da Agitação Republicana* he included an even more interesting note provoked by the appearance of the first pamphlet and directed to the deputy Joaquim Nabuco. In the first note, Teixeira Mendes explained that to the Positivists the republican form of government did not mean parliamentarianism or representative government or even free elections of public servants—these things had already existed in the monarchies. To the Positivists, republican government signified "a government without the slightest alliance with Church or military, which dedicates itself politically to the systematization of industrial life based on humanitarian motives through the teachings of Science." If this type of republican government were initiated in Brazil, it would have to be under a popular leader, not a parliamentary or elective system. Therefore, it would be dictatorial. The best thing would have been for the Emperor to have taken the initiative of "transforming the constitutional monarchy into a republican dictatorship." Since "the conversion of Citizen Miguel Lemos to the Religion of Humanity in 1878," this had been the political program of the Positivist forces.[4]

Confronted with the "social question," this kind of republican

---

[3] Ibid., p. 35.
[4] R. Teixeira Mendes: *A Propósito da Agitação Republicana* (Rio de Janeiro, 1888), pp. 12, 14.

dictatorship could have acted with fewer hindrances than a regime held back by constitutional and legalistic scruples, as the Republic had been since its inception. So that, by 1913, the Positivists could pride themselves on having done very little for Brazilian labor save eliminating "the contrast between the so-called 'day laborers' and those designated as 'public employees,' " a decisive action in dissolving "the odious distinctions separating the middle from the working classes" maintained during the Empire. These distinctions, attributed by the Positivists to the Empire when they were in reality more patriarchal than Imperial, "even went so far as to use corporal punishment in the military forces, punishments abolished legally by the Army in Imperial times but kept by the Navy until the proclamation of the Republic, along with the wide separation between officers and seamen." [5]

This was the somewhat abstract and rhetorical response of the Positivists to the incisive and objective manifesto of Prince Dom Luís. It is clear that in 1913 Brazilian Positivism could boast of very few solid contributions, through the Republic which was in part its creation, to the cause of the workingman. It was private individuals of Catholic orientation like the engineer Meneses in Pernambuco or of neocapitalist—if not parasocialist—persuasion like Luís Tarqüínio in Bahia who, within the realm of possibility, did most in behalf of labor. Meanwhile the government was busying itself in developing the coffee industry, in improving public hygiene in Rio de Janeiro (a cause vigorously opposed by the Positivists and the occasion for a ridiculous revolt during the regime of President Rodrigues Alves), in building up the ports, in attracting European immigrants, in rehabilitating the Indians, and, somewhat belatedly, in exploiting the country's rubber resources.

Alongside the Catholic efforts since colonial times to further the cause of Brazilians as human beings, the Positivist contribution therefore seems rather small. Even in a Republic founded largely on non-Catholic principles, it remained for Catholic laymen to make the greatest positive contribution to the "social question," a question systematically ignored by the government as well as by the priesthood and the Church.

How little those Catholic efforts were recognized by the Positivists is indicated by the latters' erection of a monument to "the defense of the Republic as personified by Floriano Peixoto," the work

[5] Teixeira Mendes: *O Império Brasileiro* . . . , p. 28.

of a Positivist sculptor Eduardo Sá. Apparently it never occurred to this sculptor, an orthodox votary of the Religion of Humanity, to show any indication in his monumental creation of the importance of the proletariat in Brazilian society. Instead, this society is presented as a Positivist conquest, the result of the aspirations of the disciples of Comte in Brazil.

These circumstances seem to indicate that the Positivist contribution to the solution of the labor problem was very small indeed. Certainly, concrete Positivist efforts in this respect were not equal to the faction's enthusiasm for the abstraction of "Universal Fraternity," and were inferior to even the rather insignificant official Catholic contribution. Neither of these groups contributed one hundredth part of the effort which could—and should—have been made in a traditionally Christian country that was becoming industrialized and modernized at a reckless pace.

It was partly as a result of having seen the conditions of people in the interior that A. Coelho Rodrigues, after experiencing fifteen years of the regime he had hailed as the "savior from the throes of misery," publicly retracted what he had written "against the monarchy and in favor of the new government" and advocated the restoration of the Empire "as a radical remedy" for the failure of the republican experiment. According to Coelho Rodrigues, the Republic had compounded the Imperial error of "unconditional emancipation of the slaves, ejected improvidently from the slave quarters into the city streets," by developing a policy almost exclusively in favor of "the political landholders" of São Paulo and the south, regions which "extracted the maximum from the union in return for the absolute minimum of benefits." Ruy Barbosa himself had "joined the chorus of Paulistas and for a time even wielded the baton." [6] If the days immediately after the fifteenth of November were marked by the rise of an ambitious military group, almost all Positivist and particularly feared by *Generalíssimo* Deodoro, this group was no less terrifying than that made up of southern "administrative lawyers" and "commercial politicians" which developed after the consolidation of the Republic. According to Coelho Rodrigues, this was a group of "ferocious individualists," who "were all furtively out to get theirs, promoting a strong southern leader for the country and at the same time trying to hinder the development

[6] A. Coelho Rodrigues: *A República na América do Sul* (Einsiedeln, 1906), pp. ix, 4, 26–7.

of the port of Tôrres and the navigation of the Araguaia." [7] On the
Araguaia question there was conflict between Ruy Barbosa and the
two Paulista ministers in the provisional government. As these two
important economic issues emerged in the early days of the new
regime, the Republic should have developed a new type of relationship between private regional and economic interests on the one
hand and the national government on the other. In this new pattern, there had been an outstanding bloc of civilian Paulistic politicians, opposed in part by military elements from other areas who
were less committed to regional and economic advantages than the
civilians. However, only some of these Paulista politicians were notable for their promotion of purely regional advantages. Others
were distinguished for their invariable integrity in considering
problems from a national rather than a local viewpoint. It was because of the first group, and in spite of the second, that the Republic in its early days seemed to be rendering São Paulo a veritable El
Dorado, with its purchase and broad-gauging of the São Paulo rail
line and the organization of merchant shipping between São Paulo
and Rio Grande do Sul. These measures benefited the economy of
São Paulo (as already outlined) not only by supporting the increasing fame of its coffee industry, but also by encouraging immigration from Europe. It is understandable that the republican politicians interested in the development of the southern economy could
not see the protection of the workingman as a major problem. Such
protection would have substantially reduced the profits that were
making millionaires of many of them. The first years of the Republic were years of greed on the part of the industrialists and businessmen, many of whom had become politicians as well. But if such
political infiltration had occurred during the Empire, it would have
provoked the immediate intervention of the Emperor.

It is only fair to point out that among the more progressive journalists and politicians of São Paulo, there were those who were as
opposed to the opportunists and the "already demoralized republicans" as they were to the monarchists who were trying unsuccessfully to rehabilitate themselves by the inauguration of "socialistic"
reforms. One such man was Brasílio Rodrigues dos Santos, who
wrote in 1900 to his friend, the monarchists Martim Francisco de
Andrada: "It is in vain that the monarchists look for the people to
return to the past; restorations can only come about through force,

[7] Ibid., pp. 29–30.

and the force which brought down the monarchy will not be the one to raise it again. The logic of the fact (in which I believe) would not prevent it, even if the monarchists wished to attempt another fifteenth of November. (And if they attempted it, I believe it would be a grand fiasco.)" On one point, however, he recognized the deficiency of the Republic, even in comparison "to some of the least liberal [countries of] Europe": in the matter of reforms "of a socialist nature." For this reason, it was his desire that Martim Francisco go along with him in a journalistic campaign for reforms which would "make for a true Republic instead of this ugly sham we have at present." Brasílio dos Santos's socialistic letter was included by Martim Francisco in Chapter VII of his *Contribuindo* (*Contributing*) published in São Paulo in 1921. In the same book there are letters received from Dom Luís de Orléans-Bragança, who for the lofty and independent Andrada was "the perfect prince." Many of these letters (written rather more objectively than that of Brasílio dos Santos) not only declare for, but even insist on the necessity for socialist reforms to enable the working-man to achieve his due dignity. "I note with great pleasure," wrote Dom Luís "that there is at least one monarchist in Brazil who gives all his attention to the problems of labor, a question of capital importance nowadays. A few days ago, I had a conversation on this subject with my cousin, the King of Belgium. He is the sovereign who has given most time to the study of these questions. It must be said that in Belgium, as in the other principal monarchies of Europe, the laws protect the worker much more than in republics such as France and the United States." And he adds, surveying the social renovation going on in Uruguay under Battle and the repercussions of this activity in Argentina: "In South America nothing has been done until now in this respect; but it is not possible that the ques tion will fail to emerge one of these days. Since nothing has been prepared, it will quickly assume gigantic proportions. Look at what is happening in Argentina." And in another letter to his Paulista friend on September 11, 1913, Dom Luís declared himself anxious for action which would bring about a third reign that would prove the monarchy more capable than the Republic of valorizing the workingman: "The atmosphere is saturated with words. Even the admirable discourses of Ruy no longer have the same impact." It was not only rhetoric which saturated the Brazilian atmosphere of those days: there was also the saturation by a progressivism which

signified only progress in terms of things, almost completely overlooking the advancement of the people who were carrying out this
progress.

This neglect of the workingman on the part of government officials put Pinheiro Machado, the strong man of Rio Grande do Sul,
in an ideal position to do something about this forgotten element of
the population and to realize in Brazil a labor program similar to
that of Battle y Ordoñez in Uruguay. It is true that Pinheiro Machado did not enjoy Battle's advantage of more than twenty years
in Paris spent in close contact with Lafitte and the French Positivists and with masters of the Sorbonne and the Collège de France.
But he could have overcome this deficiency by ordering studies of
labor laws and organizations by those same talented men of letters
who had more than once directed their efforts to examining Brazilian economic and financial problems. It is therefore hard to understand why the most talented of Pinheiro's followers, the young law
professor Gilberto Amado, preferred to accept an innocuous mission to Holland under the supervision of Lauro Müller, for the
preparation of one more report on European immigration, instead
of undertaking the far more important task of making an objective
study of Battle's labor reforms in Uruguay and their relationship to
the various forms of European state socialism. With the help of
such a study, Pinheiro could have prepared himself for a mission of
labor organization which, as senator from Rio Grande do Sul and a
national leader at the height of his prestige, he was in a unique position to carry out. Unfortunately, as we have seen, what really happened was that the problem was neglected by the Republic, and the
mass of workers, both white and descendents of slaves, were left
almost completely abandoned.[8] No real labor leader emerged in
the early Republic, and it was not until the eve of the First World
War that Prince Luís de Orléans-Bragança took his stand in favor
of the workingman. Dom Luís's attempt at a restoration of the
monarchy based on an enlightened social program lacked the context of suitable circumstances. Nevertheless, during the regime of
President Hermes da Fonseca (1910–14), there were times when
matters seemed to favor this apparently unpropitious adventure,

[8] This abandonment of a large proportion of the population caused particular
alarm among public-spirited medical men, who began to cry loudly that Brazil
was becoming a "vast hospital." It was these cries, rather than those in favor of
labor, which roused the politicians and clergy to social action.

and when Dom Luís, in the eyes of orthodox republicans, began to appear as a threat to the established order.

One such moment, which occurred before Dom Luís issued his manifesto, was the João Cândido rebellion. It is not out of line to consider this movement, which in 1910 disturbed the traditionally peaceful relationships between officers and men, as a form of proletarian insurrection. And the same could be said of a previous movement, that of naval machinists in Recife in 1909. In the earlier rebellion, the machinists attempted to align themselves with their civilian confreres already organized under the Central Association of Seamen, the Naval Firemen's Association, and the Naval Colliers' Union, all with headquarters in Rio de Janeiro and branches in the nation's principal seaports. The Pernambucan newspaper *A Pátria*, sympathetic to the cause of the workers, had clashed with the Maritime Services Company on August 28, 1909, denouncing the company as "the property of Senator Rosa e Silva and his family," who were also proprietors of the anti-proletarian newspaper *Diário de Pernambuco*. Under its editor Públio Pugo, a Brazilian of Italian origin, *A Pátria* had styled itself the "defender of the working classes," referred to the striking machinists as "proletarian seamen," and accused Marine Commandant Cunha, Captain of the Ports of Pernambuco, as aiding the capitalists by helping "smash the proletariat."

There is little doubt that the leaders of the seamen's insurrection of 1910 conducted by João Cândido had also developed their revolutionary sentiments under European influences. In one of the most interesting books of the period, *Política versus Marinha* (*Politics versus the Navy*), written by one who signs himself merely "A Naval Officer," it is claimed that João Cândido "shaped and perfected [his revolutionary sentiments] during his long stay in England." It is also possible, however, that the Recife uprising had its influence on the action of João Cândido, as well as on the dissatisfactions of firemen and colliers in other ports. Firemen, recognized by "A Naval Officer" as being the "essential spirit of modern vessels," were in great shortage: 2,200 were needed and the Navy had only 944. How had this shortage been filled, asks the author of *Política versus Marinha*? By the contracting of "heterogeneous outside elements, incompatible with naval discipline." Even foreigners were admitted into the Navy: Portuguese, Greeks, Americans, Barbadoans. The *Minas Gerais* had engaged "Englishmen who received separate rations, more plentiful and of better quality than those given our own seamen, an odious and unjust situation." [9] Racial segregation also existed among the crew of this large ship, along with the segregation between officers and men. No mention of this irritating discrimination between Englishmen and Brazilians is made in the recent work of Professor Cruz Costa entitled *O Positivismo na República* (*Positivism in the Republic*). Cruz Costa states that the reasons for the rebellion lay in "the low salaries, the excessive hours, the bad food, and, above all, the ill treatment and the floggings." [1] Teixeira Mendes, in his monograph *A Anistia e a Política Moderna, Sobretudo Republicana* (*Amnesty and Modern Politics, Particularly Republican*) adds one further motivation: "revolutionary instincts in a state of desperation." [2]

The problem was more complex, however, than the reports of the rebellion made it out to be, and the situation these reports depict was not limited to the Navy alone. The fact is that the Navy had modernized its material equipment without having prepared its personnel for the technical requirements of such equipment. The old story of the cart before the horse. And lacking this human preparation, it was necessary to follow the characteristically Brazilian procedure of improvisation, scouring the ports for instant technicians, machinists, and firemen, incorporating native thugs and foreigners with anarchist ideas into a Navy accustomed to the old styles of discipline, including that of the lash. The result was that traditional discipline was broken down by these new arrivals, a breakdown that was hastened by the moral, religious, and educational neglect suffered by the regular crews, most of which were made up of former slaves or their descendants, accustomed to the patriarchal conditions and disciplines of the slave quarters. [3]

In 1910, according to "A Naval Officer," crews on the warships were made up of 50 per cent Negroes, 30 per cent mulattos, 10 per cent *caboclos*, and 10 per cent whites or near-whites. Of the Negroes, many were "physically inept," not even knowing "how

[9] "Um Oficial da Armada" (A Naval Officer): *Política versus Marinha* (Rio de Janeiro, n.d.), pp. 77–8.

[1] Cruz Costa: *O Positivismo na República* (São Paulo, 1934), p. 197.

[2] R. Teixeira Mendes: *A Anistia e a Política Moderna, Sobretudo Republicana* (Rio de Janeiro, 1910).

[3] In his *De Aspirante a Almirante* (*From Midshipman to Admiral*) (Rio de Janeiro, 1907), IV, 48, Artur Jaceguay too said that since the Empire, seamen had been recruited largely "from the malefactors and riffraff of the large coastal cities."

properly to eat, sleep, or dress." To "A Naval Officer," they were an inferior race, "burdened by an incapacity for progress." Their wages were spent immediately on tobacco, Minas cheese, sardines, looking glasses, and almanacs; they amused themselves by playing lotto and dominoes and dancing the *samba;* and nearly all of them were the victims of a "sickly sentimentality" which often brought about love tragedies, not only between male and female, but also between adult seamen and adolescent cabin boys. Illiterate, "without the restraints of religion"—Positivists and progressive republicans would not even consider the possibility of religious services in the Armed Forces—they lived "under circumstances most propitious for the encouragement of vice and crime." They did not feel humiliated by punishment; rather, they felt the necessity of the "authority of their officers." The lash, according to "A Naval Officer," was thus "literally indispensable," so long as the current moral conditions continued on the ships of the Brazilian Navy so proudly displayed by the Republic as evidence of its military superiority in South America.[4] This lack of discipline in the ranks accounts also for the Baron do Rio Branco's desire to reorganize the Army under German officers of the most rigid variety. The Navy was equally in need of such masters, so long as their instruction was accompanied by the medical, religious, civic, and educational services necessary to integrate these seamen into the normal patterns of Brazilian society. According to Jaceguay in his notable sociological work on the organization of the Brazilian Navy, in 1895 "through lack of physical and technical training, nine-tenths of our seamen and cabin boys in the regular Navy are still in the apprentice class; in the British Navy they would still be 'boys,' in the French, '*mousses.*' "[5]

What had happened in the Navy under the Republic was exactly what had happened to the Army, to Rio de Janeiro, to the ports, and to industries: materials and techniques had been modernized without a corresponding adaptation of persons to meet the new conditions. In 1906 a bold program of naval development was initiated, but again undertaken by the erroneous "superimposition of the material problem on that of personnel" referred to by the author of *Política versus Marinha.*[6] Nor did the republican government attempt, even while the ships were being constructed in Eng-

---

[4] "Um Oficial da Armada": op. cit., pp. 86, 89.
[5] Jaceguay: op. cit., IV, 93.
[6] "Um Oficial da Armada": op. cit., p. 84.

land, to train the better elements among its present personnel "so that the new and more powerful ships might have the advantage of being manned by selected crews."

The drama of the Brazilian Navy was thus a small-scale version of the drama of Brazil at the turn of the century; the Navy, like the country at large, was lacking in what someone has called "industrial infiltration." Even the naval officers for the most part continued to be graduates of the law schools of Recife and São Paulo: academics with archaic preparation for a new industrial era. In 1910 "A Naval Officer" wrote that his colleagues were "all extremely intelligent; many were very able, and a few even erudite." Not one, however, knew how to pilot a ship.[7] These officers clearly needed further education, having existed for years in the long-dead days of the sailing ship. A British naval mission should have been called in, corresponding to the German mission desired by the Baron do Rio Branco for the rehabilitation of the Army and to the French mission which had already transformed the military police of São Paulo into the best and most efficient organization of its kind in South America. There was also need for an educational program, which, in addition to imparting the necessary practical training to officers, would raise the "moral and intellectual level" of the warrant-officer class. The need for this intermediate class was clearly of supreme urgency in all branches of the military, just as it was in agriculture, commerce, and industry. Jaceguay, at the end of the nineteenth century, had already suggested that certain fields—for example, metallurgy, mechanics, naval construction, and fishing—were good areas "for the recruiting of more or less qualified sailors for the staffing of modern naval vessels." He also suggested that some of the pre-industrial activities be considered. The "*jangadeiro* of northern Brazil" was a good example; these *caboclos*, he pointed out, had a "notable aptitude for the life of the sea."[8]

There was no serious attempt, however, to develop technicians to serve as an intermediary class between the traditional levels of "upper" and "lower." This necessary link in the class structure was needed in agriculture, trying to become modern by training agronomists with college degrees without developing foremen and overseers; it was needed in industry; it was needed in the Armed Forces.

[7] Ibid., p. 85.

[8] Artur Jaceguay: "Condições Atuais da Marinha Brasileira," *Revista Brasileira* and *Jornal do Commercio* (Rio de Janeiro, 1896).

In the Army, the situation was faithfully portrayed by Lamberg, who had noted, at the end of the nineteenth century, that the courses at the Brazilian Military Academy were "so inadequate for military practices" that "the officers graduate with a vast general education and, at the expense of practical military science in depth, gain a more or less complete erudition in many other aspects of human knowledge." For this reason, the Brazilian Army, with its "large number of generals and senior officers of great learning," had a military capacity limited "merely to bravura, to the knowledge and practice of technical exercises, to the manual of arms, and, finally, to theoretical information." Set against this uniformed élite with bachelors' or doctors' degrees were the common soldiers— "*caboclos*, Negroes, mulattos, and ruffians of all sorts: of a very low degree." [9]

The situation had changed very little by the end of the period, when General Maitrot arrived to study military problems in Brazil and other South American countries. As a result of his studies, Maitrot concluded that the Brazilian Army was lacking in moral unity, that its ranks were formed "of elements who are strangers to one another, where the chief officers are unknown and are seen by the men only in the critical hour of battle." The whole organization needed to be changed "from top to bottom" if it was to deserve the label of a modern fighting force.[1] This could not be done by sending its college-trained officers to Germany or France, because as another perceptive foreigner—Domville-Fife—observed, the great size of Brazil (and, he could have added, its tropical nature) rendered the adoption of German organization and strategy utterly impossible. It was from the Americans in Cuba, or from the British in the Transvaal and the Orient, that the Brazilians should be learning strategy, tactics, and military organization.[2] But the basic and immediate problem of the Brazilian Armed Forces was to ensure their integral unity, by developing an "intermediary class," and so preventing their officers from being an élite utterly out of contact with the ranks when both should be finding common cause in the confrontation of a specifically tropical, South American military situation.

[9] Maurício Lamberg: *O Brasil*, p. 307.
[1] Gén. Charles A. Maitrot: *La France et les Républiques Sud-Américaines* (Paris, 1920), pp. 231–2.
[2] Domville-Fife: op. cit., p. 316.

It was also the problem of newly developing industries, where growth was handicapped by the same lack of communication between executives and workers. It was the problem of an electorate that was increasing rapidly without a corresponding understanding of the political issues raised by the political élite. It was the problem of medical graduates in Bahia and Rio de Janeiro aloof from the vital practical knowledge of tropical diseases and herbal remedies possessed by many of the Negro and *caboclo* witch doctors and medicine men. It was the problem of agriculture, where attempts at modernization were being made on an abstract academic level, without establishing practical experimental schools for the training of overseers in those specifics of tropical agriculture that could not be learned from teachers imported from Germany or the United States.

Even so, the period of Brazilian history covered by this study can boast of many achievements, some of them practical, which substantiate its claim to have been an era of national progress. A somewhat disorderly progress, but progress nonetheless. Ruy Barbosa, Antônio Prado, and Antônio Conselheiro; Santos Dumont, Machado de Assis, the Baron do Rio Branco; the epic of Acre; Joaquim Nabuco, Carlos Gomes, Delmiro Gouveia. The valorization of coffee. Butantan. The Osvaldo Cruz Institute; Avenida Central; Rondon.

I include Antônio Conselheiro on this list because the incident of Canudos was also a Brazilian victory: that of organizing backlanders of the most varied origins into a group with the social discipline necessary, among other things, to establish a community and to achieve a form of progress. The famous hamlet, though for a time a thorn in the flesh of the Republic and a countermovement to its ostensible progress, can now be seen primarily as a group affirmation as sociologically significant as that of the brave soldiers who died in an attempt to subjugate them and integrate them into the national pattern of life. From that time on, the backlander of the north was reconciled to a Republic he had formerly rejected through his traditional loyalty, stretching back to colonial times, to a King and, even more strongly, a Queen.[3] Hard as it was for the more remote

[3] This fact did not escape the Frenchman Marc, who noted that the backlanders of Ceará during the drought of 1877 received government aid in the name of the Queen. He also noted that in Rio de Janeiro Princess Isabel, on proclaiming abolition, was fervently hailed by the lower classes, not as Princess or regent, but with

backlanders to see the Emperor and Empress superseded by a Republic, it is significant that even they could eventually accept the change—the replacement of the Royal Myth by a government founded on the Positivist motto: "Order and Progress."

This was a difficult change, but that it was accomplished is a fact. And it was done by means of a new abstraction which could be termed the Scientific Myth: a myth that the Positivist élite and its sympathizers somehow managed to communicate to all other groups within the Brazilian population. And so it was that the period became one dedicated, if not to the masses at least to most of the middle class; dedicated also to the glorification of "scientific government," "scientific politics," "scientific diplomacy," and even "scientific spiritism" and "scientific religion." In 1909, as he appeared smiling and happy on the streets of Rio de Janeiro, Nilo Peçanha, President of the Republic, was saluted familiarly by a man of the people with the words: "*Eita, Presidente científico!* (Hi there, scientific President!)"

shouts of "*Viva a Rainha!*"—Alfred Marc: *Le Brésil: Excursion à Travers Ses 20 Provinces* (Paris, 1890), p. 431.

Glossary,

Supplementary Reading List,

Additional Recent Books
Published in Brazil,

Index

Glossary

abiu—Fruit of the *abieiro* (*Pouteria caimito*).

açai—Fruit of the *açaizeiro*, or assai euterpe palm (*Euterpe oleracea*).

arrivismo—Social climbing by vulgar means.

bumba-meu-boi—A traditional dance and festival held especially in northern Brazil in which one dancer wears a bull's head and is tormented by other dancers while a chorus sings appropriate folk songs.

buriti—The wine mauritia or murity palm (*Mauritia vinifera*).

caboclo—Term loosely used to indicate any inhabitant of the Brazilian interior who has a trace of Indian blood. It can also apply to a pure-blooded Brazilian Indian or a half-breed (white and Indian). Sometimes it is used with mixtures of Indian and Negro, if the individual in question has Indian features and straight black hair. By extension, the term is used to apply to any backwoodsman of north, northeast, or central Brazil.

caboclismo—An object, idea, or attitude identified with the *caboclo*. A conscious cultivation or celebration of *caboclo* traits.

cajá—The yellow fruit of the *cajàzeira* or hog plum (*Spondias lutea*). Although it has a rancid smell, it is quite edible, and a refreshing drink is made from its juice.

cajú—Cashew (*Anacardium occidentale*), from which cashew nuts are obtained. Its astringent fruit also makes an excellent drink.

cambucá—Fruit of the *cambucàzeiro* or tree myrtle (*Myrcia plicatocostata*).

capoeira—Literally, a chicken coop, but in the sense usually employed in Brazil, refers to a method of fighting in which both hands and feet are employed, sometimes with knives on the feet. It probably originated from Africa and was practiced with such effectiveness by the slaves that owners feared for their own safety as well as for that of the human property in which they had invested their money. Accordingly, *capoeira* was prohibited, but it survived among the descendants of slaves in the form of a fascinating balletic movement employing all the aggressive techniques of the art in slow motion and without touching one's opponent. Visitors to the city of Bahia may still see this half dance–half combat practiced, in somewhat degenerate form, by young men employed by the Tourist Bureau. The term also refers to the rough second-growth land found in some parts of the interior of Brazil.

carnaúba—The wax of the *carnaùbeira* (*Corpernicia cerifera*) used for the manufacture of floor wax and wax candles.

caroba—Various trees of the jacaranda group.

caudilho (Spanish *caudillo*)—Military or political leader, head of a faction, generally holding power through strong-arm tactics.

caudilhismo (Spanish *caudillismo*)—The cult of the strong leader in military or political life; the characteristic actions of a *caudilho*.

côco—Various kinds of nuts or fruits from the coconut palm. Also a popular folk dance of the northeast of Brazil.

comadre—The term used between parents and godmother. It can also be used for special friendships and is frequently employed between persons of differing social classes as a means of indicating respect without having to maintain a relationship of social equality.

compadre—The masculine form of *comadre*.

cuscuz—A popular dish made of steamed rice, manioc, or corn meal; probably of African origin.

dobrado—(1) A lively musical piece, generally in march tempo; (2) a stew made of tripe.

espanholismo—Having Spanish characteristics. A predilection for Spanish culture.

farofa—A dish made of manioc meal browned with oil or butter and mixed with eggs or meat; also used for stuffing fish or fowl.

fazenda—A large plantation of any kind.

feijoada—Virtually the Brazilian national dish. Made with black beans boiled with various kinds of meat and vegetables and served with *farofa* and rice.

fruta-do-conde—Also known as *pinha*. The fruit of the sugar apple (*Annona squamosa*).

gaúcho—The cowboy of southern Brazil. The term is applied by extension to any inhabitant of the state of Rio Grande do Sul.

grumixama—Brazilian cherry. Fruit of the *Eugenia dombeyi*.

guajiru—Also *guajuru, guajeru*. Icaco cocoplum (*Chrysobalanus icaco*).

guaraná—A shrub (*P. cupana*) from which a popular soft drink is made.

jabuticaba—A round, edible, cherry-like fruit which grows directly from the trunk of the *jabuticaba* tree (*Myciaria cauliflora*).

jacu, jacutinga—A bird of the guan family. *Jacutinga* is also applied to a form of hematitic iron ore found in the state of Rio de Janeiro.

jambo—The rose apple, which is edible and exists in several varieties in Brazil, including the *jambo-rosa* and *jambo-de-caroço*.

jangada—A raft made of five logs lashed together used for fishing in the north and northeast of Brazil. The usual raft is about 20 by 7 feet and has a mast and rudder. Highly seaworthy, although almost constantly awash, the *jangada* with its crew of two or three men often remains for days on the open sea. Until recently, nearly all the fishing industry in the northeast was carried on by *jangadeiros*.

jangadeiro—The owner or crewman of a *jangada*.

latifúndio—A large country estate; usually employed in agriculture.

macaíba—Also *macajá*. A form of palm (*A. sclerocarpa*) the nuts of which yield an edible oil that is also used in soap making.

mal du pays—A "national malady": generally applied to a social attitude or political or social problem.

mandacaru—The Peru cereus (*C. peruvianus*).

mandioca—The common cassava (*Manihot esculenta*), the source of manioc flour and tapioca. A very important plant in the Brazilian economy.

manga—The fruit of the mango.

maracatu—A Brazilian carnival dance of African origin performed in the northeast, especially in Pernambuco.

maracujá—Passion flower (*Passiflor*) from the fruit of which a pleasant and refreshing drink is made.

maté—Paraguay tea (*Ilex paraguayensis*), the source of a healthful drink very popular in the south of Brazil and recently quite important as an export.

maxixe—(1) A popular dance and the music for such a dance; (2) a gherkin.

mestiço—Term applied to any individual of mixed blood.

modinha—A popular song, usually romantic in nature.

orixá—A voodoo priest.

palmatória—A narrow, flat stick formerly used on the palms of backward or recalcitrant grammar school pupils. Some of these instruments of torture had a large hole bored in the middle. Needless to say, the holes often caused blisters regarded by their possessors as a special sort of academic *stigmata*.

pas de quatre—A dance employing four paces.

peixada—A fish stew, bouillabaisse.

pitanga—Brazil cherry (*Eugenia uniflora*).

pitomba—Fruit of the *pitombeira* (*Luschnathiana*).

puxuri—Also *pixurim;* a form of nutmeg.

sabiá—A Brazilian thrush, similar in appearance to the American robin.

samba—The most famous Brazilian popular dance, probably of African origin.

sapoti—The fruit of the sapodilla (*Achras sapota*).

sarapatel—A dish made of pig's or sheep's viscera and blood.

sertão—The semi-arid backlands of Brazil.

sertanejo—Inhabitant of the *sertão*.

tucupi—A condiment made of manioc and pepper, used in the Amazon as the basis of a delicious sauce.

vinhático—A tree (*Plathymenia reticulada*) of the mimosa family.

R.W.H.

Supplementary Reading List

1. Political

ABRANCHES, DUNSHEE DE: *Atas e Atos do Govêrno Provisório*. Rio de Janeiro, 1907.

BASBAUM, LEÔNCIO: *História Sincera da República: Tentativa de Interpretação Marxista da História*. Rio de Janeiro, 1957.

BASTOS, HUMBERTO: *Ruy Barbosa, Ministro da Independência Econômica do Brasil*. Rio de Janeiro, 1949.

BOEHRER, GEORGE C. A.: *Da Monarquia à República: História de Partido Republicana do Brasil, 1870–1889*. Rio de Janeiro, 1954.

BRUNO, ERNÂNI SILVA: *História e Tradições da Cidade de São Paulo*. São Paulo, 1953.

CERQUEIRA, DIONÍSIA: *Reminiscências da Campanha do Paraguay*. Rio de Janeiro, 1941.

CUNHA, EUCLYDES DA: *Os Sertões*. Published in English as *Rebellion in the Backlands*. Chicago, 1944.

EDMONDO, LUÍS, *et al.: A República*. Rio de Janeiro, 1939.

FIGUEIREDO, LIMA: *Grandes Soldados do Brasil*. 2nd edn. Rio de Janeiro, 1942.

FONSECA, ANÍBAL FREIRE DA: *Do Poder Executivo no República Brasileira*. Rio de Janeiro, 1916.

FRANCO, AFONSO ARINOS DE MELO: *História e Teoria do Partido Político no Direito Constitucional Brasileiro*. Rio de Janeiro, 1948.

———: *Um Estadista da República*. Rio de Janeiro, 1955.

FREIRE, FELISBELO: *História Constitucional da República*. Rio de Janeiro, 1894.

LAMBERT, JACQUES: *Le Brésil, Structure Sociale et Institutions Politiques*. Paris, 1953.

LE LANNOU, MAURICE: *Le Brésil*. Paris, 1954.

LEAL, AURELINO: *História Constitucional do Brasil*. Rio de Janeiro, 1915.

LEITE, AURELIANO: *História da Civilização Paulista*. São Paulo, 1954.

LIMA, HERMES: *Tobias Barreto*. São Paulo, 1939.

LIMA, OLIVEIRA: *O Império Brasileiro*. São Paulo, 1927.

413

Lins, Ivan: *Benjamin Constant*. Rio de Janeiro, 1936.

Magalhães Júnior, R., ed.: *Dom Pedro II e a Condêssa de Barral*. São Paulo, 1956.

Melo, Custódio José de: *O Govêrno Provisório e a Revolução de 1893*. São Paulo, 1938.

Miranda, Pontes de: *À Margem do Direito*. Rio de Janeiro, 1912.

——: *A Moral do Futuro*. Rio de Janeiro, 1913.

Morais, Evaristo de: *Da Monarquia para a República*. Rio de Janeiro, 1936.

Morazé, Charles: *Les Trois Âges du Brésil*. Paris, 1954.

Nabuco, Joaquim: *O Abolicionismo*. London, 1883.

Oliveira Tôrres, João Camilo de: *A Democracia Coroada*. Rio de Janeiro, 1957.

Roure, Agenor de: *A Constituinte Republicana*. Rio de Janeiro, 1920.

Silva Rocha, Joaquim da: *História da Colonização do Brasil*. Rio de Janeiro, 1918.

Sodré, Nélson Werneck: *Panorama do Segundo Império*. São Paulo, 1939.

II. *Foreign Observers of the Period*

Adam, Paul: *Les Visages du Brésil*. Paris, 1914.

Allain, Émile: *Rio de Janeiro*. Paris and Rio de Janeiro, 1886.

Andrews, C. C.: *Brazil, Its Conditions and Prospects*. New York, 1887.

Anthouard, Baron d': *Le Progrès Brésilien*. Paris, 1911.

Babson, Roger W.: *The Future of South America*. Boston, 1915.

Ballou, Maturin M.: *Equatorial America*. Boston and New York, 1892.

Bennett, Frank: *Forty Years in Brazil*. London, 1914.

Bernardez, Manuel: *El Brasil*. Buenos Aires, 1908.

Bland, J. O. P.: *Men, Manners, and Morals in South America*. London, 1920.

Bryce, James M.: *South America: Observations and Impressions*. New York, 1913.

Burnichon, Fr. Joseph: *Le Brésil d'Aujourd'hui*. Paris, 1910.

Chagas, João: *De Bond—Alguns Aspectos da Civilização Brasileira*. Lisbon, 1897.

Clemenceau, Georges: *Notes de Voyage dans l'Amérique du Sud*. Paris, 1911.

Couty, Louis: *Étude de Biologie Industrielle sur le Café*. Rio de Janeiro, 1883.

Craig, Neville B.: *Recollections of an Ill-Fated Expedition*. Philadelphia and London, 1907.

Delebeque, J.: *À Travers l'Amérique du Sud*. Paris, 1907.

Denis, Pierre: *Le Brésil au XXᵉ Siècle*. Paris, 1917.

Elliott, L. E.: *Brazil, Today and Tomorrow*. New York, 1917.

Ford, Isaac: *Tropical America*. London, 1893.

Gaffre, L. A.: *Visions du Brésil*. Paris, 1912.

Galdois, Eugène: *En Amérique du Sud*. Paris, n.d.

Gasparin, Agenor de: *L'Amérique devant l'Europe*. Paris, 1887.

GRELLE, ÉDOUARDE DE: *Étude du Brésil*. Brussels, 1888.

HARDENBURG, W. E.: *The Putumaya: The Devil's Paradise*. London, 1912.

KIDDER, DANIEL P., and JAMES C. FLETCHER: *Brazil and the Brazilians*. Boston, 1857.

LAMBERG, MAURÍCIO: *O Brasil*. Rio de Janeiro, 1896.

LATTEUX, DR: *Au Pays de l'Or et des Diamants*. Paris, 1910.

LECLERC, MAX: *Lettres du Brésil*. Paris, 1890.

MACOLA, FERRUCCIO: *L'Europa a la Conquista dell'America Latina*. Venice, 1894.

MAITROT, GÉN.: *La France et les Républiques Sud-Américaines*. Paris, 1920.

MARE, ALFRED: *Le Brésil*. Paris, 1890.

MARTIN, PERCY A.: *Through Five Republics*. London, 1905.

MEROU, GARCÍA: *El Brasil Intelectual*. Buenos Aires, 1900.

MICHEL, ERNEST: *A Travers l'Hémisphère Sud*. Paris, 1887.

ORLÉANS-BRAGANÇA, LUÍS DE: *Sous la Croix du Sud*. Paris, 1912.

PEARSON, HENRY C.: *The Rubber Country of the Amazon*. New York, 1911.

PINTO, SILVA: *No Brasil*. Oporto, 1879.

PRADEZ, CHARLES: *Nouvelles Études sur le Brésil*. Paris, 1872.

ROOSEVELT, THEODORE: *Through the Brazilian Wilderness*. New York, 1914.

SAMPAIO, J. PEREIRA: *O Brasil Mental*. Oporto, 1898.

SMITH, HERBERT H.: *Brazil, the Amazon and the Coast*. New York, 1879.

STEINEN, KARL VON DEN: *Durch Zentral Brasilien*. Leipzig, 1886.

TUROT, HENRI: *En Amérique Latine*. Paris, 1908.

WELLS, JAMES W.: *Three Thousand Miles Through Brazil*. London, 1887.

WITHER, THOMAS P. BIGG: *Pioneering in South Brazil*. London, 1878.

III. *Economics*

ASCARELLI, TULLIO: *Apresentação do Brasil*. Rome, 1955.

BASTIDE, ROGER: *Brésil, Terre des Contrastes*. Paris, 1957.

COURTIN, RENÉ: *Le Problème de la Civilisation Économique du Brésil*. Paris, 1941.

Documentos Parlamentares: O Brasil, Suas Riquezas Naturais, Suas Indústrias. Rio de Janeiro, 1907.

FERRAND, PAUL: *L'Or à Minas Gerais*. Ouro Prêto, 1894.

LEAL, VITOR NUNES: *Coronelismo, Enxada, e Voto*. Rio de Janeiro, 1949.

MILLIET, SÉRGIO: *O Roteiro do Café*. São Paulo, 1946.

NASH, ROY: *The Conquest of Brazil*. New York, 1926.

NORMANO, J. F.: *Brazil: A Study of Economic Types*. Chapel Hill, 1935.

TAUNAY, AFONSO DE E.: *História do Café no Brasil*. Rio de Janeiro, 1943.

IV. *Social and Cultural*

AMADO, GILBERTO: *Grão de Areia*. Rio de Janeiro, 1919.

————: *Minha Formação no Recife*. Rio de Janeiro, 1955.

COSTA, JOÃO CRUZ: *A History of Ideas in Brazil*. Berkeley, 1964.

DAMASCENO, ATHOS: *Palco, Salão, e Picadeiro em Pôrto Alegre no Século XIX.* Rio de Janeiro, Pôrto Alegre and São Paulo, 1956.

DUARTE, PAULO, and J. F. DE ALMEIDA PRADO, eds.: *Alegrias e Tristezas de uma Educadora Alemã no Brasil.* São Paulo, 1956.

HARRIS, MARVIN: *Town and Country in Brazil.* New York, 1956.

MARTINS, LUÍS: *O Patriarca e o Bacharel.* São Paulo, 1953.

NEVES, EDUARDO DAS, ed.: *O Cantor de Modinhas Brasileiras.* Quaresma, 1937.

STEIN, STANLEY J.: *Vassouras, A Brazilian Coffee County, 1850–1900.* Cambridge, Mass., 1957.

WAGLEY, CHARLES: *Amazon Town, A Study of Man in the Tropics.* New York, 1953.

v. *Religion*

ABREU, CANUTO: *Adolfo Bezerra de Menezes: Notas Biográficas com Esbôço da História de Espiritismo no Brasil.* São Paulo, 1950.

CRABTREE, A. R., and A. N. DE MESQUITA: *História dos Batistas no Brasil.* São Paulo, 1940.

KENNEDY, J. L.: *Cinquenta Anos de Metodismo no Brasil.* São Paulo, 1928.

LÉONARD, ÉMILE G.: "L'Église presbytérienne au Brésil" and "O Protestantismo Brasileiro" in *Revista de História.* São Paulo, 1951.

PEREIRA, EDUARDO CARLOS: *A Maçonaria e a Igreja Cristã.* São Paulo, 1901.

REIS, ÁLVARO: *O Espiritismo.* 2 edn. Rio de Janeiro, 1916.

RIBEIRO, BOANERGES: *O Padre Protestante.* São Paulo, 1950.

RIBEIRO, LEONÍDIO, and MURILO CAMPOS: *O Espritismo no Brasil.* Rio de Janeiro, 1931.

RIO, JOÃO DO (pseud. PAULO BARRETO): *As Religiões no Rio.* Paris, 1927.

SHUPP, S. J., FR. AMBROISE: *Os Muckers.* Pôrto Alegre, n.d.

WILLEMS, EMÍLIO: *A Aculturação dos Alemães no Brasil.* São Paulo, 1946.

ZIONI, VICENTE M.: *O Problema Espírita no Brasil.* São Paulo, 1942.

vi. *Literature Which Mirrors the Period*

ANDRADE, CARLOS DRUMMOND DE: *Confisssões de Minas.* 1944.

ARANHA, GRAÇA: *Canaã.* 1902, tr. Boston, 1920.

AZEVEDO, ALUÍSIO: *O Mulato.* 1881.

BANDEIRA, MANUEL: *Evocação do Recife.*

LIMA, JORGE DE: *O Mundo do Menino Impossivel.*

MORELY, HELENA: *Minha Vida de Menina.* 1944.

POMPÉIA, RAUL: *O Ateneu.* 1888.

QUEIROZ, RAQUEL DE: *O Quinze.* 1930.

RÊGO, JOSÉ LINS DO: *Menino de Engenho.* (*Plantation Boy*, Eng. tr., New York, 1966.) 1932.

G.F.

Additional Recent Books
Published in Brazil

ABREU, JAYME: *Educação, Sociedade e Desenvolvimento.* Rio de Janeiro, 1968.

ALENCAR, EDGAR DE: *O Carnaval Carioca através da Música.* Rio de Janeiro, 1965.

ALMEIDA, RENATO: *Manual de Coleta Folclórica.* Rio de Janeiro, 1965.

AMARAL, IGNÁCIO MANOEL AZEVEDO DO: *Ensaio sôbre a Revolução Brasileira.* Rio de Janeiro, 1963.

ANDRADE, GILBERTO OSÓRIO DE: *Propósitos de Universidade.* Recife, 1965.

ANDRADE, MÁRIO DE: *Música de Feitiçaria no Brasil.* São Paulo, 1963.

AZEVEDO, AROLDO DE, et al.: *Brasil, Terra e o Homem,* I (*As Bases Físicas*). São Paulo, 1964.

AZEVEDO, FERNANDO DE: *A Cultura Brasileira: Introdução ao Estudo da Cultura no Brasil.* 4th edn., rev. and ampl. São Paulo, 1964.

AZEVEDO, THALES DE: *Cultura e Situação Racial no Brasil.* Rio de Janeiro, 1966.

BANDEIRA, MANUEL: *Guia de Ouro Prêto.* 4th edn. Rio de Janeiro, 1963.
———: *Rio de Janeiro em Prosa e Verso.* Rio de Janeiro, 1965.

BASTIDE, ROGER, and FLORESTAN FERNANDES: *Brancos e Negros em São Paulo: Ensaio Sociológico sôbre Aspectos da Formação, Manifestações Atuais e Feitos do Preconceito de Côr na Sociedade Paulistana.* 2nd edn. São Paulo, 1959.

BASTIDE, ROGER: *Sociologia do Folclore Brasileira.* São Paulo, 1959.

BASTOS, HUMBERTO: *Desenvolvimento ou Escravidão: Aspectos de Influências Externas na Formação Econômica do Brasil.* São Paulo, 1964.

BEAULIEU, GILLES, PAUL EUGÈNE CHARBONNEAU, and LUÍS ARRÔBAS MARTINS: *Educação Brasileira e Colégios de Padre.* São Paulo, 1966.

BELLO, JOSÉ MARIA: *História da República (1889–1954).* 4th edn. São Paulo, 1959.

BEZERRA, DANIEL UCHÔA CAVALCANTI: *Alagados, Mocambos e Mocambeiros.* Pref. by Gilberto Freyre. Recife, 1965.

Borba Filho, Hermilo: *Fisionamia e Espírito do Mamulengo*. (The folk theatre of the northeast.) São Paulo, 1966.

Brito, Mário da Silva: *Antecedentes da Semana de Arte Moderna*. 2nd edn. Vol. I of *História do Modernismo Brasileiro*. Rio de Janeiro, 1964.

Britto, Jomard Muniz de: *Do Modernismo à Bossa Nova*. Rio de Janeiro, 1966.

Bruno, Ernâni Silva: *Viagem ao País dos Paulistas*. Rio de Janeiro, 1966.

Bulhões, Octávio Gouveia de, et al.: *Educação para o Desenvolvimento*. Rio de Janeiro, 1966.

Callado, Antônio: *Os Industriais da Sêca e os "Galileus" de Pernambuco*. (Aspects of the fight for agrarian reform in Brazil.) Rio de Janeiro, 1960.

Calzarava, Batista Benito Gabriel, et al.: *Culturas Principais da Amazônia*. Rio de Janeiro, 1966.

Câmara Cascudo, Luís da: *Antologia do Folclore Brasileiro*. 3rd edn. São Paulo, 1965.

———: *História da Alimentação no Brasil*, I (*Cardápio Indígena, Dieta Africana, Ementa Portuguêsa*). São Paulo, 1967.

Camargo, José Francisco de: *Exodo Rural no Brasil: Formas, Causas e Consequências Econômicas Principais*. Rio de Janeiro, 1960.

Campos, Renato Carneiro de: *Ideologia dos Postas Populares do Nordeste*. Recife, 1959.

———: *Igreja, Política e Região*. Recife, 1967.

Cândido, Antônio: *Os Parceiros do Rio Bonito: Estudo sôbre o Caipira Paulista e a Transformação dos Seus Meios de Vida*. Rio de Janeiro, 1964.

Cardoso, Fernando Henrique, and Octávio Ianni: *Mobilidada Social em Florianópolis: Aspectos das Relações entre Negros e Brancos numa Comunidade do Brasil Meridional*. São Paulo, 1960.

Carvalho, Delgado de: *História Diplomática do Brasil*. São Paulo, 1959.

Carvalho, José Rodrigues de: *Aspectos de Influência Africana no Formação Social do Brasil*. João Pessoa, 1967.

Castello, José Aderaldo: *Aspectos do Romance Brasileira*. Rio de Janeiro, 1961.

Chacon, Vamireh: *História das Idéias Socialistas no Brasil*. Rio de Janeiro, 1965.

Costa, Lamartine Pereira da: *Capoeiragem: A Arte da Defesa Pessoal Brasileira*. Rio de Janeiro, 1961.

Costa Pôrto: *O Pastoreio no Formação do Nordeste*. Rio de Janeiro, 1959.

Coutinho, Afrânio: *A Literatura no Brasil*, III (*Simbolismo, Impressionismo, Modernismo*). Rio de Janeiro, 1959.

Dantas, Humberto: *Amazônia, Caminho do Futuro: Notas de Viagem*. São Paulo, 1966.

Diégues Júnior, Manuel: *Imigração, Urbanização, Industrialização: Estudo sôbre Alguns Aspectos da Contribuição Cultural do Imigrante no Brasil*. Rio de Janeiro, 1964.

———: *Regiões Culturais do Brasil*. Rio de Janeiro, 1960.

Duarte, Sérgio Guerra: *Por que Existem Analfabetos no Brasil?* Rio de Janeiro, 1963.

Estevam, Carlos: *A Questão da Cultura Popular.* Rio de Janeiro, 1963.

Façó, Rui: *Cangaceiros e Fanáticos: Gênese e Lutas.* Rio de Janeiro, 1963.

Fernandes, Florestan: *Educação e Sociedade no Brasil.* São Paulo, 1966.

———: *A Integração do Negro na Sociedade de Classes.* Rio de Janeiro, 1964.

———: *Mudanças Sociais no Brasil: Aspectos do Desenvolvimento da Sociedade Brasileira.* São Paulo, 1960.

———: *A Sociologia numa Era de Revolução Social.* São Paulo, 1963.

Fernandes, Gonçalves: *Região, Crença e Atitude: Uma Visão da Religiosidade Reativa de Pequenos e Médios Agricultores de Sub-Areas de Pernambuco.* Recife, 1963.

Foracchi, Marialies Mencarini: *O Estudante e a Transformação da Sociedade Brasileira.* São Paulo, 1965.

Franco, Afonso Arinos de Melo: *Evolução da Crise Brasileira.* São Paulo, 1965.

Freyre, Gilberto: *Fôrças Armadas e Outras Forças: Novas Considerações sôbre as Relações entre as Forças Armadas e as Demais Forças de Segurança.* Recife, 1965.

———: *Quase Política.* 2nd edn. Rio de Janeiro, 1966.

———: *Em Tôrno de Alguns Túmulos Afro-Cristãos.* Salvador, 1960.

———: *Homem, Cultura e Trópico.* Recife, 1962.

———: *Vida, Forma e Côr.* Rio de Janeiro, 1962.

———: *Um Engenheiro Francês no Brasil.* (Intimate diary of Louis Léger Vauthier; Brazilian letters of same.) Rio de Janeiro, 1960.

———. *Guia Prático, Histórico e Sentimental da Cidade do Recife.* 4th edn. Rio de Janeiro, 1968.

———: *Olinda: 2º Guia Prático, Histórico e Sentimental de Cidade Brasileira.* 3rd edn. Rio de Janeiro, 1960.

———: *A Propósito de Frades: Sugestões em Tôrno da Influência de Religiosos de São Francisco e de Outras Ordens sôbre o Desenvolvimento de Modernas Civilizações Cristãs, Especialmente das Hispânicas, nos Trópicos.* Salvador, 1959.

Furtado, Celso: *A Operação Nordeste.* Rio de Janeiro, 1959.

———: *A Pré-Revolução Brasileira.* Rio de Janeiro, 1962.

———: *Perspectivas da Economia Brasileira.* 2nd edn. Rio de Janeiro, 1960.

Goulart, José Alípio: *Brasil do Boi e do Couro.* Rio de Janeiro, 1965.

Gouveia, Aparecida Joly: *Professôres de Amanhã: Um Estudo de Escolha Ocupacional.* Rio de Janeiro, 1965.

Guimarães, Barreto: *O Sentido Nacional dos Problemas do Nordeste Brasileiro.* Rio de Janeiro, 1959.

HADDAD, JAMIL ALMANSUR: *Revolução Cubana e Revolução Brasileira.* Rio de Janeiro, 1961.

HOLANDA, SÉRGIO BUARQUE DE: *História Geral da Civilização Brasileira.* São Paulo, 1964.

————: *Visão do Paraíso, os Motivos Edênicos no Descobrimento e Colonização do Brasil.* Rio de Janeiro, 1959.

IANNI, OCTÁVIO: *Industrialização e Desenvolvimento Social no Brasil.* Rio de Janeiro, 1963.

Instituto Joaquim Nabuco de Pesquisas Sociais: *História dos Rótulos de Cigarros: A Litografia no Antigo Recife.* Pref. by Mauro Mota. Recife, 1965.

————: *Transformação Regional e Ciência Sociológica,* I (*Considerações em Tôrno de Problemas de Reforma Agrária no Brasil, em Geral, e na Zona Canavieira de Pernambuco, em Particular*). Pref. by Gilberto Freyre. Recife, 1964.

LAGENEST, H. D. BARRUEL DE: *Lenocínio e Prostituição no Brasil.* (Sociological study.) Rio de Janeiro, 1960.

LAMBERT, JACQUES: *Os Dois Brasís.* Rio de Janeiro, 1959.

LATIF, MIRAN DE BARROS: *O Homem e o Trópico.* (A Brazilian experience.) Rio de Janeiro, 1959.

————: *Uma Cidade no Trópico, São Sebastião do Rio de Janeiro.* Rio de Janeiro, 1965.

LIMA, ALCEU AMOROSO: *Quadro Sintético da Literatura Brasileira.* 2nd edn. Rio de Janeiro, 1959.

LIMA, ESTÁCIO DE: *O Mundo Estranho dos Cangaceiros.* (Bio-sociological essay.) Salvador, 1965.

LINS, MARCIONILO DE BARROS: *Aspectos da Universidade Brasileira.* Recife, 1965.

MACEDO, NERTAN: *O Clã dos Inhamuns.* (A family of warriors and herders of the headwaters of the Jaguaribe.) Fortaleza, 1965.

MACIEL, CARLOS FREDERICO DO RÊGO: *Sugestões de Economia Educacional.* Recife, 1965.

MACIEL, TELMO FREDERICO DO RÊGO: *Nível de Vida do Trabalhador Rural na Zona da Mata.* Recife, 1964.

MAGALHÃES JÚNIOR, RAIMUNDO: *Rui, o Homem e o Mito.* 2nd edn. Rio de Janeiro, 1965.

MALCHER, JOSÉ MARIA DA GAMA: *Indios, Grau de Integração na Comunidade, Grupo Linguístico, Localização.* Rio de Janeiro, 1964.

MARINHO, INEZIL PENNA: *Introdução ao Estudo da Evolução Desportiva no Brasil.* Rio de Janeiro, 1959.

MÁRIO FILHO: *O Negro no Futebol Brasileiro.* 2nd edn. Rio de Janeiro, 1964.

MARTINS, IVAN PEDRO DE: *Introdução à Economia Brasileira.* Rio de Janeiro, 1961.

MARTINS, LUCIANO: *Industrialização, Burguesia Nacional e Desenvolvimento.* (Introduction to Brazilian crisis.) Rio de Janeiro, 1968.

MELLO, ANTÔNIO DA SILVA: *A Superioridade do Homem Tropical.* Rio de Janeiro, 1965.

MELLO, JOSÉ ANTÔNIO GONÇALVES DE: *Estudos Pernambucanos: Crítica e Problemas de Algumas Fontes da História de Pernambuco.* Recife, 1960.

MIRANDA, MARIA DO CARMO TAVARES DE: *Educação no Brasil.* (Sketch of historical study.) Recife, 1966.

MOREL, EDMAR: *Revolta da Chibata.* (Sources for the history of the revolt of the fleet by the sailor João Cândido in 1910.) Rio de Janeiro, 1959.

MOTA, MAURO: *Votos e Ex-votos: Aspectos da Vida Social do Nordeste.* Recife, 1968.

NAGLE, JORGE: *Educação e Sociedade no Brasil 1920–1929.* Araraquara, 1966.

NASSER, DAVID: *A Revolução que se Perdeu a si Mesma: Diário de um Repórter.* Rio de Janeiro, 1965.

NEVES, DAVID EULÁLIO: *Cinema Nova no Brasil.* Petrópolis, 1966.

NIEMEYER, OSCAR. *Minha Experiência em Brasília.* Rio de Janeiro, 1961.

NUNES, MARIA THETIS: *Ensino Secundário e Sociedade Brasileira.* Rio de Janeiro, 1962.

OLIVEIRA, FRANKLIN DE: *Que é a Revolução Brasileira?* Rio de Janeiro, 1963.
———: *Revolução e Contra-Revolução no Brasil.* Rio de Janeiro, 1962.

OLIVEIRA, VALDEMAR DE: *O Teatro Brasileiro.* Salvador, 1959.

PESSOA DE MORAIS, JOSÉ: *Sociologia da Revolução Brasileira: Análise e Interpretação do Brasil de Hoje.* Rio de Janeiro, 1965.
———: *Tradição e Transformação do Brasil: Análise Sociológica, Antropológica e Psicanalítica.* Rio de Janeiro, 1969.

PILÔTO, ERASMO: *Situação do Desenvolvimento Brasileiro e a Educação.* Curitiba, 1959.

PINTO, ESTÊVÃO: *Etnologia Brasileira.* São Paulo, 1956.

PINTO, L. A. DA COSTA: *Sociologia e Desenvolvimento: Temas e Problemas de Nosso Tempo.* Rio de Janeiro, 1963.

PRADO JÚNIOR, CAIO: *A Revolução Brasileira.* São Paulo, 1966.

O Problema Agrário na Zona Canavieira de Pernambuco: Conferências e Debates no Simpósio Realizado por Iniciativa do INSTITUTO JOAQUIM NABUCO DE PESQUISAS SOCIAIS, em Maio de 1963. Recife, 1965.

QUEIROZ, MARIA ISAURA PEREIRA DE: *Messianismo no Brasil e no Mundo.* São Paulo, 1965.

RABELLO, SYLVIO: *Os Artesãos do Padre Cícero: Condições Sociais e Econômicas do Artesanato de Juazeiro do Norte.* Recife, 1967.

RAMOS, GUERREIRO: *Mito e Verdade da Revolução Brasileira.* Rio de Janeiro, 1963.

REIS, ARTHUR CEZAR FERREIRA: *A Amazônia e a Cobiça Internacional.* 2nd edn. Rio de Janeiro, 1965.

RIBEIRO, DARCY: *A Política Indegenista Brasileira.* Rio de Janeiro, 1962.

RIBEIRO, RENÉ, et al.: *Vitalino, Ceramista Popular do Nordeste.* Recife, 1959.

————: *Xangô*. Recife, 1965.

RODRIGUES, JOSÉ HONÓRIO: *Conciliação e Reforma no Brasil: Um Desafio Histórico-Político*. Rio de Janeiro, 1965.

SILVEIRA, PEIXOTO DA: *A Nova Capital: Por que, para onde e como Mudar a Capital Federal*. Rio de Janeiro, 1959.

SODRÉ, NÉLSON WERNECK: *História da Literatura Brasileira: Seus Fundamentos Econômicos*. 3rd edn. Rio de Janeiro, 1960.

TAVARES, AURÉLIO DE LYRA: *O Nordeste: Aspectos Políticos, Econômicos e Psicos-sociais*. Recife, 1965.

TAVORA, JUAREZ: *Organização para o Brasil*. Rio de Janeiro, 1959.

TEIXEIRA, ANÍSIO SPINOLA: *Educação é um Direito*. São Paulo, 1968.

TELLES, JOVER: *O Movimento Sindical no Brasil*. Rio de Janeiro, 1962.

TOCANTINS, LEANDRO: *Amazônia, Natureza, Homem e Tempo*. Rio de Janeiro, 1960.

TÔRRES, JOÃO CAMILO DE OLIVEIRA: *Estratificação Social no Brasil: Suas Origens Históricas e Suas Relações com a Organização do País*. São Paulo, 1965.

————: *A Formação do Federalismo no Brasil*. São Paulo, 1961.

VALENTE, WALDEMAR: *Misticismo e Região: Aspectos do Sebastianismo Nordestino*. Recife, 1963.

VIANNA, HÉLIO: *História do Brasil*. São Paulo, 1961–2.

VIANNA MOOG: *Bandeirantes e Pioneiros: Paralelo entre Duas Culturas*. 8th edn. Rio de Janeiro, 1966.

VICTOR, MÁRIO: *Cinco Anos que Abalaram o Brasil: De Jânio Quadros ao Marechal Castelo Branco*. Rio de Janeiro, 1965.

VILAÇA, MARCOS VINICIUS, and ROBERTO CAVALCANTI ALBUQUERQUE: *Coronel, Coroneis*. Rio de Janeiro, 1965.

VILAÇA, MARCOS VINICIUS: *Em Torno da Sociologia do Caminhão: Notas para um Estudo das Relações do Caminhão e do Motorista com a Paisagem e o Homem Brasileiros, em Geral, e Nordestino, em Particular*. Recife, 1961.

VILLAÇA, MARIA JOSÉ: *A Força de Trabalho no Brasil*. São Paulo, 1961.

VINHAS, MOISÉS: *Operários e Camponeses na Revolução Brasileira*. São Paulo, 1963.

WILLEMS, EMÍLIO: *Uma Vila Brasileira: Tradição e Transição*. São Paulo, 1961.

G.F.

Index

A NOTE ABOUT THE AUTHOR

GILBERTO DE MELLO FREYRE was born at Recife (Pernambuco) on March 15, 1900. He studied under private tutors and at the Colégio Americano Gilreath in his native city. In 1920 he took a Bachelor of Arts degree at Baylor University in Waco, Texas, and in 1922 an M.A. at Columbia University, where he did graduate work under Franz Boas, Franklin Henry Giddings, Carlton J. H. Hayes, and Edwin R. A. Seligman.

Freyre has been visiting professor or lecturer at many of the leading universities of Europe and America—among them Leland Stanford, Princeton, Columbia, Michigan, San Marcos (Lima), Coimbra (Portugal), King's College (London), the Sorbonne, Heidelberg, Berlin, Cologne, Hamburg, Bonn, and Indiana. Freyre was a member in 1946 of the National Assembly that drew up the present constitution of Brazil. From 1946 to 1950, he served in the Chamber of Deputies and on its Committee on Cultural and Educational Matters. In 1949 he was a delegate, with the rank of Ambassador, from Brazil to the General Assembly of the United Nations. In 1966 Freyre was the recipient of the Aspen Award for his outstanding contribution to the advancement of the humanities.

Earlier books by Gilbert Freyre published in English include *The Masters and the Slaves* (1946, 1956); *New World in the Tropics* (1959); *The Mansions and the Shanties* (1963); and *Mother and Son* (1967).

A NOTE ON THE TYPE

THE TEXT OF THIS BOOK was set on the Linotype in Janson, a recutting made direct from the type cast from matrices long thought to have been made by Anton Janson, a Dutchman who was a practicing type-founder in Leipzig during the years 1668-1687. However, it has been conclusively demonstrated that these types are actually the work of Nicholas Kis (1650-1702), a Hungarian who learned his trade most probably from the master Dutch type-founder Dirk Voskens.

The type is an excellent example of the influential and sturdy Dutch types that prevailed in England prior to the development by William Caslon (1692-1766) of his own incomparable designs, which he evolved from these Dutch faces. The Dutch in their turn had been influenced by Claude Garamond (1510-1561) in France. The general tone of the Janson, however, is darker than Garamond and has a sturdiness and substance quite different from its predecessors.

Composed and bound by
H. Wolff Book Manufacturing Co., Inc., New York.
Printed at Halliday Lithograph Corp., West Hanover, Massachusetts.
Typography by Guy Fleming. Binding design
based on a design by
W. A. Dwiggins